FOURTH EDITION

UNDERSTANDING CONTEMPORARY
LATIN
AMERICA

edited by
Richard S. Hillman
Thomas J. D'Agostino

LYNNE
RIENNER
PUBLISHERS

BOULDER
LONDON

Published in the United States of America in 2011 by
Lynne Rienner Publishers, Inc.
1800 30th Street, Boulder, Colorado 80301
www.rienner.com

and in the United Kingdom by
Lynne Rienner Publishers, Inc.
3 Henrietta Street, Covent Garden, London WC2E 8LU

Library of Congress Cataloging-in-Publication Data
Understanding contemporary Latin America / edited by Richard S.
Hillman and Thomas J. D'Agostino. — 4th ed.
    p.   cm. — (Understanding: introductions to the states and regions
of the contemporary world)
    Includes bibliographical references and index.
    ISBN 978-1-58826-791-7 (pbk. : alk. paper)
    1. Latin America. I. Hillman, Richard S., 1943– II. D'Agostino,
Thomas J.
    F1408.U43 2011
    980.04—dc23
                                                                    2011020124

British Cataloguing in Publication Data
A Cataloguing in Publication record for this book
is available from the British Library.

Printed and bound in the United States of America

       The paper used in this publication meets the requirements
∞   of the American National Standard for Permanence of
       Paper for Printed Library Materials Z39.48-1992.

    5 4 3 2 1

Contents

List of Illustrations   ix
Preface   xiii

1 Introduction *Richard S. Hillman*   1

2 Latin America: A Geographic Preface *Marie Price*   13
   Physical Setting *16*
   Human Geography of Latin America *28*

3 The Historical Context *René de la Pedraja*   41
   The Conquest *41*
   The Colonial Period *44*
   Portuguese Brazil *51*
   The Bourbon Era *53*
   Independence *55*
   Conclusion *64*

4 Latin American Politics *Thomas J. D'Agostino*   67
   The Postindependence Era *69*
   Early Modernization and Dictatorial Rule *70*
   The Modern Era *74*
   Revolutionary Change *77*
   The Rise of Bureaucratic Authoritarianism *83*
   Democratization *88*
   Conclusion *104*

5 **The Military** *Paul W. Zagorski*   111
   The Historical Legacy of Civil-Military Relations
      in Latin America   *111*
   The Emergence of the New Professionalism   *118*
   Problems in the Contemporary Era   *122*
   Conclusion   *136*

6 **The Economies of Latin America** *Scott G. McKinney*   139
   Pre-Columbian Economic Life   *139*
   The Colonial Period   *141*
   Independent Latin America   *145*
   Import-Substituting Industrialization   *150*
   The Oil Shock and the Debt Crisis   *161*
   Latin America as an Emerging Market   *168*
   Latin America in the Twenty-First Century   *172*

7 **International Relations** *Cleveland Fraser*   185
   Organizing Concepts   *189*
   Historical Legacies   *193*
   The Cold War Era   *197*
   Dependency and Debt   *200*
   The 1980s   *202*
   The Post–Cold War Era   *205*
   The Present and the Future   *210*

8 **The Environment, Population, and Urbanization**
   Jacquelyn Chase and Susan E. Place   223
   Pre-Columbian Cultures and Latin America's Environments   *224*
   Demographic and Environmental Change in
      the Colonial Era   *226*
   Independence and the Neoliberal Era   *228*
   Globalization and the Environment   *229*
   Urbanization in Latin America   *236*
   Population: Distribution, Fertility, and Mortality   *244*
   Conclusion   *247*

9 **Patterns of "Race," Ethnicity, Class, and Nationalism**
   Kevin A. Yelvington   251
   The Intersections of "Race," Ethnicity, Class,
      and Nationalism   *256*
   Defining Key Terms   *256*

Foundations of Ethnicity, Class, and Nationalism   *260*
Contemporary Patterns   *267*
Conclusion   *278*

10 Women, Work, and Politics *Susan Tiano*   285
Production, Reproduction, and the
    Gender Division of Labor   *288*
Women in Latin American History   *289*
Women in the Formal Labor Force   *295*
Women in Latin American Politics   *311*
Conclusion   *319*

11 Education and Development
Stephen Franz and Robert F. Arnove   325
Changing Notions of Development   *326*
Education and Technology   *327*
Expanding Educational Opportunities   *330*
Education and the Debt Crisis   *334*
Popular Education and Other Educational Innovations   *344*
Mass Media and Education   *348*
Education and Democracy in Latin America   *349*
Conclusion   *350*

12 Religion in Latin America *Hannah Stewart-Gambino*   355
The Colonial Role of the Catholic Church   *356*
The Role of the Catholic Church in
    Liberal-Conservative Battles   *358*
The Modern Catholic Church   *361*
The Rise of Evangelical Protestantism   *366*
Secularization   *370*
Charismatic Catholics   *372*
Major Spiritist Religions   *373*
Conclusion   *376*

13 Latin American Literature
David H. Bost and Angélica Lozano-Alonso   379
The Colonial Heritage   *379*
The Nineteenth and Twentieth Centuries   *387*
Magical Realism and the Boom   *393*
Brazil and the Circum-Caribbean   *402*
Popular Culture   *403*

14 Trends and Prospects *Richard S. Hillman*   409

List of Acronyms   423
Appendix 1: Basic Political Data   427
Appendix 2: List of Nonindependent Territories   435
The Contributors   437
Index   439
About the Book   463

Illustrations

▦ Maps

2.1	Latin America: Countries and Capitals	14
2.2	Climates and Vegetation	18
2.3	Indigenous Peoples' Migration Routes and Empires	31
3.1	Eighteenth-Century Colonial Latin America	45
3.2	Early Independence Movements	59
3.3	Later Independence Movements	60
7.1	Boundary Disputes Since Independence	186

▦ Tables

4.1	Economic Performance in Latin America	97
5.1	Participation in Peace Missions in Latin America, 2010	132
6.1	Growth in Manufacturing During the World War II Era, 1938–1945	151
6.2	Capital Flows to the Western Hemisphere, 1977–1994	162
6.3	Impacts of the Debt Crisis on Selected Economic Indicators in Latin America, 1970–1990	164
6.4	Trade Among Selected ALADI Members, 1980, 2002, and 2008	176
6.5	Rising Commodity Prices and Economic Growth in Latin America, 1990–2009	178
6.6	Inequality and Poverty in Latin America	180
8.1	Population of Mexican Border Cities, 2005 and 2010	242
10.1	Labor Force Participation Rates for Working-Age Women and Men	296

11.1 Enrollment Numbers and Percentages by Level of Education in
        Latin America, 1960 and 1970   328
11.2 Percentage of Total Public Education Expenditure by Level
        in Five Latin American Countries, 1965 and 1970   329
11.3 Latin American Repetition Ratios and Completion Rates
        in Primary Education and Enrollment Ratios in
        Secondary Education   333
11.4 Illiteracy Rates by Gender, 2010   343
12.1 Change in Number of Catholic Seminarians, 1972–2008   366

▨ Figure

10.1 Female Labor Participation Rate by Age   301

▨ Photographs

Aconcagua, Argentina   17
Machu Picchu in the Peruvian Andes   19
Deforestation in the Brazilian Amazon   25
Kukulcan temple at Chichen Itza in Mexico   42
The Plaza de Armas and Cathedral of Santo Domingo in Cuzco, Peru   49
Luiz Inácio Lula da Silva, former president of Brazil   94
Hugo Chávez, president of Venezuela   95
Evo Morales, president of Bolivia   99
Michelle Bachelet, former president of Chile   107
Naval Mechanics School in Buenos Aires, Argentina   126
A convoy of military vehicles in Ciudad Júarez, Mexico   134
Cerro Rico in Bolivia   143
Cutting sugarcane in Cuba   155
Market in Peru's Sacred Valley   167
Zapatista mural, southern Mexico   170
The Itaipu Dam   175
Miraflores Locks on the Panama Canal   195
Zapatista leader Subcomandante Marcos   206
Haiti earthquake search and rescue in 2010   224
São Paulo, Brazil, skyline   237
A shantytown in Guayaquil, Ecuador   238
Rocinha *favela* (squatter town) in Rio de Janeiro, Brazil   240
Street children in Juliaca, Peru   241
Joaquín Balaguer, 1990   252
José Francisco Peña Gómez, 1994   253

Brazilian performer Xuxa 273
Las Madres de la Plaza de Mayo 286
Textile production outside Cuzco, Peru 292
Textile factory in Brazil 306
Cristina Fernández, president of Argentina 312
A campaign to combat violence against women,
    Santo Domingo, Dominican Republic 316
School children in Ecuador 330
School children in Cuba 332
The Metropolitan Cathedral and Zócalo (main plaza), Mexico City 359
Nobel Prize winner Mario Vargas Llosa 395
Nobel Prize winner Rigoberta Menchú 398

Preface

S ince the publication of the third edition of *Understanding Contemporary Latin America* six years ago, a variety of political, economic, and social changes have had transformational effects on the region. A number of new political leaders have taken office, and attitudes toward regionalism and globalization have been altered. Natural disasters such as earthquakes, hurricanes, and mudslides, as well as financial crises, have created new challenges. Relationships have been evolving among governments, businesses, and international organizations both within Latin America and with the rest of the world. These transitions and developments are all represented in this new edition.

Each chapter of this edition has undergone extensive review and has been revised and also thoroughly updated. The book includes original analyses of current political, social, and economic developments in the region, as well as citations of the latest research. Comprehensive appendixes of basic political data and nonindependent territories also have been brought up to date. These improvements are designed to enhance *Understanding Contemporary Latin America* as the premier resource for those interested in an informed introduction to the region.

Each of the contributors is a Latin America specialist who believes that expanding academic, economic, and policy interests requires a basic introduction to this complex and significant part of the world. We are convinced that mutual understanding can dispel myths and prejudices that detract from cooperation and peaceful coexistence. In drawing from extensive scholarly research and explaining it in clear and accessible language, *Understanding Contemporary Latin America* is intended for the many "beginners" who wish to learn about the region.

Throughout history, the importance of Latin America has been recognized in strategic geopolitical and commercial terms. And recently, increased trade, as well as a new wave of regionalism, has affected hemispheric relations and development. Still, Latin American attitudes, values, and beliefs regarding the conduct of politics, business, and life in general remain misunderstood by many. Sensationalized media coverage of issues such as political corruption and instability, narcotics trafficking, and immigration problems has overshadowed attempts to promote democracy, trade, development, tourism, and regional cooperation. The long-term health of inter-American relations, however, is contingent on accurate awareness and reciprocal comprehension. In this context, *Understanding Contemporary Latin America* introduces fundamental background, issues, themes, and directions in countries throughout the region. The book is designed as a basic interdisciplinary resource for use in college and university classrooms, foreign service seminars, and corporate training programs. Its wealth of graphic and textual information, presented in a straightforward style, is intended to enhance clarity, knowledge, and appreciation of the traditions, influences, and commonalities underlying the varying cultural orientations in this vital region.

The facts alone are insufficient for a complete understanding of contemporary Latin America. Insight and empathy are required for overcoming stereotypical characterizations and cultural biases. It is precisely this mix of knowledge and appreciation that is inherent in each chapter's treatment of Latin America's complex settings and challenges. After the first chapter's brief introduction outlining the scope and themes of the book, Chapter 2 describes the rich diversity of Latin America's human and physical geography. Legacies of the colonial era that continue to influence current realities are analyzed in Chapter 3. Chapter 4 discusses how these legacies affect ongoing political institutions, including the military, which is also treated separately in Chapter 5 due to its singular importance in the region. Chapter 6 investigates the area's economic performance over time, culminating in a discussion of current problems. Some of these problems are covered further in Chapter 8, specifically those dealing with environmental degradation, population expansion, and rapid urbanization. Chapter 7 examines international relations among countries within Latin America as well as with the rest of the world. Patterns of ethnicity and class are explored in Chapter 9, the role of women in Chapter 10, and the relationship between education and development in Chapter 11. These chapters present a human face to the problems and challenges detailed in other parts of the book, as do Chapter 12 on religious beliefs and Chapter 13 on literary expression. Finally, Chapter 14 examines where the region has been and in what direction it appears to be going. Far from a definitive closure to these matters, the book is designed to be an open-ended resource for provoking greater interest and raising more questions about a vital, complex, and increasingly important region of the modern world.

* * *

We are grateful to each of the chapter authors for finding time during busy academic schedules to participate in this collaborative effort and for making our tasks as editors intellectually fulfilling. Working with this talented group of scholars has been a pleasure. Likewise, the two of us have enjoyed working closely together on many projects over the past three decades.

We appreciate the support of several organizations and programs that either directly or indirectly made this book possible. The Fulbright Scholars Program provided multiple opportunities for Richard S. Hillman to teach and conduct research in Latin America. The Institute for the Study of Democracy and Human Rights, supported by the US Information Agency (USIA) College and University Affiliation Program, allowed him to maintain professional linkages, particularly in Venezuela, and sponsor academic exchanges and conferences. Field research in Brazil and Cuba was facilitated for Hillman by the Semester at Sea Program as well as the People to People Ambassadors Program. Thomas J. D'Agostino wishes to express appreciation to the provost and dean of faculty at Hobart and William Smith Colleges for supporting his involvement in this project and to Ronald McDonald and Irving Tragen for having shared their knowledge and passion for Latin America over the years.

We would like to acknowledge John Bogdal, who created the excellent maps that appear in the book. The staff at Lynne Rienner Publishers offered helpful advice, and anonymous reviewers made sensible suggestions that enhanced the readability of the manuscript. We are indebted to our colleagues, and especially to our wives and families, for encouraging, supporting, and assisting in our work.

This book is dedicated to Sydney Hillman Mularz, who brings great joy into the world, and to Andie and Alex D'Agostino, who continually make their father proud.

—Richard S. Hillman and Thomas J. D'Agostino

1

Introduction

Richard S. Hillman

The importance of Latin America in global affairs is not always clearly understood. Contemporary concerns about such issues as international terrorism, widespread economic recession, and nuclear weaponry have tended to divert the attention of policymakers and the media to other areas of the world. Nevertheless, astute observers have not lost sight of Latin American issues as well as the widespread influence of Latin American culture and society, especially within the Western Hemisphere.

The region's nearly 600 million people account for approximately 10 percent of the world's population and Latin Americans outnumber North Americans by two to one. Moreover, as the Latino[1] population continues to grow in the United States, its impact on politics, the economy, and popular culture is becoming increasingly significant. Even US television has seen fit to include a series depicting the Latino experience.[2] Also, in a CNN documentary aired on October 21 and 22, 2009, Soledad O'Brien explores how Latinos are reshaping US communities. And historical figures from Latin America have been portrayed on film with great critical success. For example, *Frida* (2002) presents the life story of surrealist artist Frida Kahlo and in so doing successfully depicts many of the artists and political figures of postrevolutionary Mexico. In Che Guevara's *Motorcycle Diaries* (1952), adapted to film in 2001, a youthful pre–Cuban Revolution Che discovers his socialist vocation while traveling with his friend on a motorcycle through beautiful Latin American landscapes.

Latin Americans live in a geographic region that encompasses 15 percent of the world's land surface with vast differences in terrain and climate ranging from tropical rain forests, swampy lowlands, grassland plains, and deserts to mountainous highlands, island chains, and cays. Increasingly, demographic

1

concentration in urban areas, especially in large cities, has reaffirmed some cultural traditions and torn down others. European-style central cities have become surrounded by shantytowns occupied mostly by migrants displaced from rural agrarian societies. These and other demographic trends have presented a variety of difficult socioeconomic challenges.

Issues relating to the environment, economic growth and distribution, immigration, and political and developmental concerns are most appropriately understood in historical perspective. The area has an extremely interesting past in which three major ethnic groups have simultaneously clashed with each other while forming unique fusions. Much of the Latin American story is one of confrontation and accommodation among indigenous peoples* (the Aztecs, Maya, Inca, Taino or Arawak, Carib, Aymara, and Quechua), Europeans (the Spanish, Portuguese, English, French, and Dutch), and Africans (the Yoruba, Mandingo, Fulani, Hausa, and other groups). The interaction among the European conquerors, indigenous civilizations, and imported African slaves during the colonization period left a legacy that has profoundly influenced subsequent development. Later, immigrants from many nations contributed to the multiplicity of groups interacting in the region.

The conquerors, who sought adventure and wealth in the New World, transferred a peculiar system of agrarian feudalism that was derived primarily from the reconquest of the Iberian Peninsula after eight centuries of Moorish domination. The land and the native peoples were divided among the colonizers, who created a hierarchical social order in which the landed aristocracy was supported by the church and protected by the military. Significantly, *criollos* (creoles)—Europeans born in the Americas—eventually supplanted the European-born colonizers at the top of the social order. Although they were thoroughly Spanish, English, or French, for example, the creoles often had never even been to Europe. Similarly caught between two cultures were the *mestizos,* offspring of Europeans and native peoples. Later, the offspring of Africans and Europeans identified themselves more with the *haciendas,* large socially self-contained ranches, than with the homelands of their forebears.

The plantation economy and *hacienda* life produced interactions and traditions that have continued to influence Latin American society. Moreover, the region is rich in many natural resources that have contributed to the global economy. Latin America has produced large percentages of the world's supply of crops such as coffee, bananas, linseed, cocoa, sugar, and cotton. Significant percentages of the world's oil, nitrates, bauxite, tin, copper, gold, and silver, among other sources of wealth, have also been found in the region. Nevertheless,

---

*The term *Indian* has often been used to refer to the indigenous peoples of Latin America and the Caribbean because Christopher Columbus thought he had encountered "Indians" based on his misconception of where he had landed. We break with this convention in this volume and use *native peoples* or *indigenous peoples* whenever possible.

even after the colonial period ended with independence for the countries within Latin America, foreign capital predominantly exploited and foreign interests largely profited from these resources until foreign companies were partially displaced by attempts to promote national development and social equity through state planning and governmental enterprises.

The forging of new national identities and liberation from oppressive colonial structures did not result in the rapid redefinition of political and social institutions leading to stable self-governance nor did the region's economies develop self-sufficiency. On the contrary, confusion and disorder were manifested in *caudillo* rule, control of the people by military strongmen. Initially, authoritarian solutions to this anarchic and unstable situation prevailed, despite the democratic tradition of *cabildo abierto* (town meeting) and Bolívarian ideals of independence and order. To this day, the appeal of authoritarian populism in the face of destabilizing political, economic, and social problems can be traced to the way the Catholic kings consolidated Spain under unified control. These traditions are reflected in ongoing Latin American culture—in literary themes; in gender roles; in relations among ethnic groups, belief systems, and educational systems; and in political institutions and practices.

Latin American culture has been in transition. The combinations of strong legacies of the past, many of which are worthy of preservation, and modern challenges to the traditional order have been explosive at times. Although the multiple forces operating in Latin American societies are complicated and the overarching political cultural context is far from constant, ignoring these legacies and influences is just as naïve and misleading as accepting the myriad myths surrounding the area. Evolving fusions of religious beliefs, political and social forms, and even ethnic groups have yielded a whole that is truly greater than the sum of its parts.

After the end of the Cold War, the new world order that began to emerge in the last decade of the twentieth century set into motion a process of realignment among the developed and developing nations. Latin America had not been immune to the emergence of competitive regional economics and the apparent collapse of authoritarian regimes that came to characterize the new international dynamics. Termination of General Augusto Pinochet's dictatorship in Chile, the end of military rule in Brazil and Argentina, the negotiated truces that ended the wars in Central America, the restoration of an elected leader who had been ousted by a coup in Haiti, and fairly free elections in the Caribbean, Venezuela, and elsewhere seemed to indicate a trend toward democratization and the eventual amelioration of debilitating problems such as political corruption, massive poverty, monetary inflation, foreign debt, illiteracy, crime, and disease.

In the twenty-first century, however, there is evidence of a throwback to patterns that characterized Latin American instability in the past. Issues such as the ongoing Venezuelan-Colombian dispute, the 2009 Honduran coup, the potential for armed intervention in general, and the rise in civilian violence appeared to reflect previous patterns in which a praetorian military would intervene to prevent perceived progressive threats to elite interests. At the same time, the emergence of leftist governments in such countries as Venezuela, Nicaragua, Ecuador, Brazil, and Bolivia has challenged the process of international realignment.

Secretary of State Hillary Rodham Clinton's visit to Latin America in March 2010 reveals the declining ability of the United States to determine political outcomes in the region. For example, during the visit Clinton was unable to convince Brazilian president Luiz Inácio Lula da Silva (Lula) to impose sanctions on Iran. Similarly, she had little influence on leaders such as Lula, Hugo Chávez, and Felipe Calderón who had been pushing for the creation of the Community of Latin American and Caribbean States (CELAC)—a largely symbolic alternative to the Organization of American States (OAS). CELAC, comprised of Latin American nations (including Cuba and excluding Canada and the United States), is gaining popularity as a demonstration of Latin American independence.

The complex dynamics on which we must base our interpretations raise a series of questions: Fundamentally, what constitutes Latin America? Who are the Latin Americans? How are the legacies of colonialism and nationalism being transformed in contemporary Latin America? What are the prognoses for further democratization, economic and social development, stability, and amelioration of serious crises of governance? Is a hemispheric free-trade zone viable? Will regional integration help to resolve or exacerbate the problems facing Latin America? If populist regimes continue to emerge, will they solidify a regional bloc that includes neither the United States nor Canada? In short, where has this vital region been, and where is it going? The story is far from complete. Each chapter of this book focuses on a different, yet interrelated, aspect of these open-ended questions. If we are to understand Latin America, we will continue to seek answers to these questions; develop new insights, empathy, and appreciation; and raise new questions.

To be sure, responses to these questions are far more complicated than they may initially appear. For example, Latin America can be defined as a region in a variety of ways. Some definitions are based on geopolitical and strategic concerns, others on common languages and cultures. Some include only Hispanic countries, excluding the Anglo-Caribbean, the Francophone countries, and Brazil. Others include these areas as well as French Canada, part of Louisiana, southern Florida, and the southwestern United States because of their strong Latino influence and cultural connections.

Similarly, many theories have been advanced regarding the inhabitants of the Americas. The most widely accepted view holds that, originally, groups of Asians crossed the Bering Strait, migrated south, and settled in North and South America. Another suggests that these groups crossed the Pacific Ocean on rafts. Yet another maintains that human life began in South America. José Vasconcelos, a Mexican intellectual, posited in 1948 that Latin Americans had become a "cosmic race," combining the strengths of different ethnic groups that have inhabited the region. Each theory is based on a plausible interpretation of certain aspects of the available evidence, and each definition has its own logic. Thus, a comprehensive approach is required to respond adequately to what are actually complex, rather than simple, questions about the nature of the area and the people we seek to understand.

Consider one of the first encounters between a native person and a European in the early sixteenth century: Montezuma, leader of the Aztec civilization, is reported to have told Spanish explorer Hernán Cortés, "We have known for a long time, from the chronicles of our forefathers, that neither I, nor those who inhabit this country, are descendants from the aborigines of it, but from strangers who came to it from very distant parts" (Keen 1966:47). According to Cortés's account in his letters to the king of Spain, Montezuma then related an ancient story that legitimized Spanish sovereignty in the Americas. But Montezuma added a comment that would have portentous significance in subsequent history: "'Look at me,' he said, 'and see that I am flesh and bones, the same as you, and everybody, and that I am mortal, and tangible'" (Keen 1966: 48). Since the first contact between Europeans and those who had previously settled in the Western Hemisphere, Latin Americans have been trying to define themselves and their region. Who would govern this New World inhabited by the progeny of "strangers"? What kind of world would it become?

The story of Latin America's indigenous origins, conquest by European powers, struggles for independence, and ongoing search for political and economic stability is an action-filled drama, revealing protagonists whose cultural differences have brought about conflicts as well as coalitions. Contemporary Latin America's increasingly important yet, at times, neglected role in world politics makes essential a comprehensive understanding of how its history is rooted in a complex and turbulent past. Popular discussions of Latin America and inter-American affairs, however, are generally charged with high levels of passion and scanty knowledge, resulting all too often in mutual misunderstanding due to unfortunate stereotypes on both sides. For example, some North Americans argue vehemently about their need to protect themselves against violent Latin American revolutionaries who threaten political stability in their backyard, illegal immigrants who steal jobs from US workers, and narcotraffickers who poison US youth. And some Latin Americans fear the malevolent intentions of the "Colossus of the North" that has seemed to intervene continuously in their domestic affairs.[3] They exhibit a strong tendency to resent US hegemony in the Western Hemisphere and blame the violence occasioned by drug cartels on the demands of the US market. Yet, many Latin Americans seek upward mobility by emigrating to the United States, thereby causing their "love-hate" relationship to confound many observers.

During the Cold War, many US citizens excitedly propounded the merits of military incursions or covert operations in places like Grenada, the Dominican Republic, Panama, Chile, Nicaragua, and El Salvador. When asked to locate these countries on a map, name their major cities, account for their economic status, or place them in historical context, however, they were clueless. Far too many North Americans are apt to locate Cuba in Central America or Argentina in the Caribbean and to assume Brazilians speak Spanish. Moreover, public opinion on many issues in both the United States and Latin America has become profoundly divided in the post–Cold War era. The plight of Cuba is a case in point. To many observers, the US economic embargo and diplomatic isolation of Cuba have constituted a misuse of power to the extreme detriment of masses of Cubans who, as a result, must endure suffering and hardship.[4] Many others believe Cuba's development problems should be attributed solely to Fidel Castro's adoption of the socialist model. In either case, ideological dogmatism has been reinforced by insufficient understanding and vilification of US foreign policy on the one hand or of Castroism on the other. Could it be that this is not a mutually exclusive proposition and that, in fact, both sides have contributed to the dilemma?

Unfortunately, stereotypes and myths that have fostered public impressions, as well as political actions, are deeply embedded in popular culture. Frederick Pike amply documents the pervasiveness of this type of thinking, from the speeches of early statesmen, like Thomas Jefferson and Simón Bolívar, to virtually continuous references in literature, art, cinema, and the media. According to Jefferson, for example, the superior US culture would supplant the inferior Latin American culture. He held that "it is impossible not to look forward to distant times when our rapid multiplication will expand itself . . . and cover the whole northern, if not the whole southern continent, with a people speaking the same language, governed in similar forms, and by similar laws" (Pike 1992:19). Such thinking has fueled historical US imperialism as well as contemporary reactions to waves of Hispanic immigrants such as the English-only movement and militant resistance to reform of immigration policies. Ironically, Bolívar predicted the United States would "afflict Latin America in the name of liberty" (Pike 1992:18), leading Pike to conclude that "the degree to which American stereotypes of Latin Americans are reinforced by— and perhaps sometimes even originate in—Latin Americans' stereotypes of themselves [is impressive]" (Pike 1992:116).

Impressions reflected in advertising and the popular media perpetuate myths. In a free association of ideas, what are the first images that come to mind when identifying Latin Americans? If you think of drug traffickers or baseball players, you are not alone. Nor would you be unique in conjuring up the idea of the "Latin lover" or the romantic revolutionary. Regarding politics, a US traveler in Latin America reports that "the value of stability in government is something they [Latin Americans] cannot be made to understand. It is not in their power to see it, and the desire for change and revolution is in the blood" (Pike 1992:68). Similarly, *machismo* is equated with the oppression of women, the *siesta* with laziness, music and dancing with today, work and planning with *mañana* (Hillman 2003).

Many Latin Americans also hold distorted perceptions of the United States and its citizens. These views vary from the vulgar notion that all *gringos* carry guns and walk on gold-paved streets to the more sophisticated analysis of the United States as a materialistic, mercenary culture of acquisition, devoid of the higher virtues of family loyalty, honor, and personalism. In this regard, José Enrique Rodó of Uruguay wrote *Ariel* in 1900 as a glorification of Latin America's superior cultural sensitivity. His ideas influenced other Latin American critics of the United States, such as José Martí of Cuba and Rubén Darío of Nicaragua, thus contributing to an anti-*yanqui* sentiment. Hence, mutual misperceptions, stereotypes, and myths abound, making a more penetrating and realistic portrayal of the region particularly important in an era of global change. The basic problem, according to Pike, is that "Americans remain reluctant to accept the fact that their country has become a frontier for Latin Americans. For generations, after all, Americans had assumed that Latin America was their frontier. Old myths, like hoary stereotypes, die hard" (1992:364).

Recognition of the highly misleading and counterproductive nature of portrayals of Latin America as somehow more "natural" and less civilized than the developed North is essential for understanding the region. This book is an attempt to promote such recognition through exploration of basic ideas and information that will contribute to debunking various myths about contemporary Latin America. The fundamental theme of "unity in diversity" provides a comprehensive organizing concept. Using this approach, the authors of the chapters emphasize the significance of the area as a whole, along with ample references to the individual countries within the region and their history, geography, and political culture. Our examination encompasses all territory in the Western Hemisphere south of the United States. (Latinos and Latin American enclaves within North America can be understood in the context of their ties to the region.) Hence, areas within Latin America include Mexico, Central America, the Caribbean, and South America. Countries within these areas form part of Ibero-, Luso-, Indo-, Afro-, and Hispano-America. Subareas such as the Anglo-, French, and Dutch Caribbean are also included because of underlying similarities that transcend apparent differences.[5]

Great diversities of peoples, institutions, and geography in Latin America converge in common historical, social, political, and developmental patterns. Various combinations of these patterns, similar socioeconomic problems, and analogous cultural expressions permit a unified vision of Latin America. Therefore, each chapter in this volume draws examples from several countries within the various areas of Latin America, thus allowing the text as a whole to offer a balanced representation of the entire region. The authors use a variety of specific cases to illustrate their general overviews of the geographic setting, historical context, political evolution, and political issues; the role of the military;

the ways in which economic systems function; the impacts of urbanization, demographic trends, and the environment; the influences of ethnicity, class, and nationalism; the role of women; the relationship between education and development; the impact of religion and of cultural and literary expressions; and the ways international relations have contributed to new trends and prospects for the future. In sum, the book is designed as a core text that introduces students to Latin America as a diverse, yet inclusive, region facing crucial issues in the twenty-first century.

Among the major issues discussed in the text, the most prominent are those related to socioeconomic and political development, debt, immigration, narcotics trade, and inter-American affairs. These are understood in the context of a background strongly influenced by European, Amerindian, African American, and the "fused" cultures of the New World as well as by the legacies of colonialism and the predominant impact of the United States. We introduce readers to the area by providing basic definitions, outlining major issues, discussing relevant background, and illustrating these considerations in countries within the region. Thus, the text employs both thematic and case study approaches. Each chapter contains general discussions, key concepts, ongoing questions, and bibliographic resources.

Rather than attempting to bring these issues and considerations to closure, this text is designed to advance knowledge and stimulate interest and discussion. Therefore, the contents are neither all-inclusive nor deterministic. They are selective and exemplary, based on the premises that (1) common themes tie diverse countries together in a vital region, (2) misunderstanding can be overcome through awareness of other cultures, and (3) a need exists for innovation in domestic and international policymaking as well as in education. As stereotypes are based on partial truths distorted by ignorance and bias, a more adequate comprehension of contemporary Latin America requires that distortions be overcome and that the region be appreciated as a distinctive set of cultures encompassing great diversity, unique amalgamations, and increasing global importance.

While to many observers the region and people are perplexing and unfathomable and their differences profound, we, as scholars, need to keep clearly in mind Montezuma's observation that, ultimately, we are all "flesh and bones, the same as you, and everybody . . . mortal, and tangible" (Keen 1966:48). This book is designed to clarify that proposition as it applies to Latin America and Latin Americans.

* * *

Much has occurred since publication of the third edition of *Understanding Contemporary Latin America*. The process of democratization has continued to face complicated challenges, especially from leftist-oriented populists such as Hugo Chávez, Evo Morales, and Daniel Ortega (Cameron and Hershberg 2010). However, democratically elected president Manuel Zelaya's ouster in Honduras at the hands of military-backed Roberto Micheletti in 2009 confuses matters even further. Does this represent retrogression toward the "conflict society" described by Kalman Silvert in the 1960s?[6] Do the new populists and the Honduran case coalesce in their negative impact on legitimate democratic governance and peaceful change?

Also, the threat of global terrorism since the attacks of September 11, 2001, has continued to impact international relations in adverse ways, redirecting attention from developmental issues. And the global financial crisis of 2009–2010 has weakened developing economies disproportionately. Accordingly, economic recession, along with continued globalization, has been accompanied by concomitant disillusionment with both the Washington Consensus in particular and neoliberal solutions in general. Consequently, the fundamental questions formulated in previous editions and reiterated in this Introduction emerge as even more significant than ever.

While there have been challenges and transitions, there has also been durability. The elevated expectations for deeper democratization and hopes for amelioration of socioeconomic and political problems that were identified in the first, second, and third editions have been tempered by the aforementioned new developments in the twenty-first century and constrained by legacies of the past. Therefore, this fourth edition presents a vision of the region that is the product of the new events as well as continuing patterns, building on the themes presented in earlier volumes.

Previous editions of *Understanding Contemporary Latin America* contained chapter analyses that were consistent in addressing strengths and weaknesses in confronting daunting challenges. Their general tones and conclusions reflected the great potential inherent in a region embarking on difficult transitions toward peaceful conflict resolution, social and economic equity, political democracy, environmental and cultural health, and the protection of human rights. Each chapter of this volume was updated, several contain extensive revisions, and two (Chapters 6 and 12) were completely rewritten by new authors in order to take into account recent developments and challenges.

A common theme emerges in this fourth edition that is consonant with the hopefulness of previous editions, yet much less sanguine about the time frame previously projected. The complex processes of democratization and economic development have faced challenges that will continue to inhibit the full realization of free and open societies in many countries in the near future. Elections in several countries have challenged existing political solutions while raising further questions about historical tendencies and the ability to consolidate democracy in Latin America. Developmental issues, divisive partisan struggles, security concerns, environmental disasters, and ecological challenges have complicated politics in many countries.

Although the Brazilian economy has attracted large amounts of foreign investment, poverty, malnutrition, and health issues have continued to challenge Lula's populist appeal. In October 2010, Lula's former chief of staff, Dilma Rousseff, defeated José Serra, the former governor of São Paulo, to become the first female president in Brazil's history. Although Rousseff's defeat of Serra provides continuity, her potential impact on the issues facing Brazil remains unclear.

Haiti's disastrous earthquake in 2009, followed by a hurricane and subsequent outbreak of cholera in 2010, has left the country in dire straights. Similarly, in 2010 Chile experienced an earthquake that also left the country in need of disaster relief. Other environmental issues, such as erosion of coral reefs and hurricane damage in the Caribbean, melting of ice caps off the southern borders of Chile and Argentina, and devastation of the rain forest in Brazil, have exacerbated developmental problems in the region. Interestingly, US president Barack Obama's new initiatives in clean energy might have challenging implications for oil producers like Venezuela, Mexico, and Ecuador. Yet the largely partisan obstacles that President Obama must face have stultified progressive policies of change.

Instability still prevails in many areas of Latin America. The presidency of Venezuela's Chávez continues to be fraught with controversy and the country with extreme class-based political polarization (Cardozo and Hillman 2003; Ellner 2010; Hillman 2002, 2004). The conflict in Chiapas, Mexico, continues as does the civil war in Colombia. Peace negotiations between the Zapatista National Liberation Army (EZLN) and the Mexican government have faltered and violence associated with narcotics trafficking has escalated along the US-Mexican border, especially in Ciudad Juárez. Talks between the Revolutionary Armed Forces of Colombia (FARC)—also known as *la guerrilla*—and the Colombian government suffer a similar fate and are complicated further by Chávez's alleged provision of support to the FARC. Despite several major arrests of cartel kingpins, illicit trafficking of narcotics from South America through the Caribbean and Mexico into the United States, as well as the attendant violence, continues practically unabated. Antigovernment demonstrations and hunger strikes designed to free political prisoners in Cuba; Chávez's blatant repression of dissent, manipulation of judicial institutions, and closing of banks and communications media in Venezuela; and mutinies in the overcrowded jails of the Dominican Republic, Brazil, and Venezuela draw attention to serious human rights problems in the region.

Notwithstanding the potential for renewed respect for US values that has been stimulated by President Obama's message of change, as well as many Latin Americans' identification with a US leader of African American descent, the love-hate relationship between Latin America and the Colossus of the North persists. As observers throughout the world perceive the enormity of the issues plaguing the Obama administration, the less sanguine they become that

US policies of "benign neglect" will be overcome in the short term. Although the United States has been a leader in providing disaster relief to Caribbean countries devastated by earthquakes and hurricanes and providing upward mobility for multitudes of immigrants from the region, resentment and defiance continue to affect hemispheric relations.

Other issues have strong symbolic as well as substantive significance. A case in point is President Obama's campaign promise to close the detention center at the Guantánamo Bay Naval Base and restore relations with Cuba. As this book goes to print, the facility has not been shut down and the US embargo against Cuba persists despite failure to achieve its stated goals as well as strong bipartisan and international pressure to restore diplomatic and commercial relations. In fact, free trade in the hemisphere is welcomed by some as a vehicle for development and attacked by others in both the United States and Latin America as an expression of neocolonialism.

All of these considerations require renewed focus on the basic themes of this book and the new questions that they stimulate. Will countries struggling with socioeconomic development find a novel paradigm for political organization? Will the masses be integrated through populist leaders whose regimes devolve into authoritarianism? Or will the new paradigm deepen democracy?

Hence, the story of Latin American trends and developments remains far from being completed. This fourth edition of *Understanding Contemporary Latin America* continues to seek answers and raise new questions about where the region has been and where it is going. It deals with these and many other questions by focusing on their particular significance in the context of specific subjects organized by separate chapters.

We are hopeful that our efforts will contribute to increased understanding among people of different cultures who may find that they have much in common. Hence, we offer this volume in the spirit of constructive analysis that characterizes the highest aspirations of our respective academic disciplines.

▪ Notes

1. The catchall term *Latino* refers to immigrants from all parts of Latin America and their progeny.

2. The PBS series *American Family: Journey of Dreams* (2002–2004), directed by Gregory Nava (*El Norte* and *My Family/Mi Familia*), illustrates aspects of Latin American history and culture through several generations of a Mexican American family.

3. An exception to this tendency is Mendoza, Montaner, and Vargas Llosa's (1996) vehement critique of theories that blame the United States, multinational corporations, and international institutions for development problems in Latin America.

4. Increased recognition of the mutually beneficial aspects of revising US policy toward Cuba, as manifested in growing bipartisan efforts to normalize trade, was stultified by the George W. Bush administration's stringent adherence to the embargo. As of 2010, the Obama administration had made little progress in either closing the detention

facility at the Guantánamo Bay Naval Base (although Obama reversed Bush's policies on "enhanced interrogation" [torture]) or opening diplomatic and commercial relations with Cuba.

5. For a detailed examination of the Caribbean, see Hillman and D'Agostino (2009).

6. Kalman Silvert, in his trail-breaking work on Latin American politics (1967), crafts the idea of the "conflict society" characterized by intervals of violent political change that could be considered a form of "stability" (or predictability). Richard S. Hillman recalls intense discussions with Silvert, his doctoral adviser and mentor at New York University in the late 1960s, about the inevitability and consequences of military *golpes* in Latin America.

▣ Bibliography

American Family: Journey of Dreams. Directed by Gregory Nava. Performed by Edward James Olmos and Esai Morales. PBS, 2002–2004.

Cameron, Maxwell A., and Eric Hershberg, eds. *Latin America's Left Turns: Politics, Policies, and Trajectories of Change.* Boulder: Lynne Rienner, 2010.

Cardozo, Elsa, and Richard S. Hillman. "Venezuelan Foreign Policy: Petroleum, Democratization, and International Affairs." In *The Foreign Policies of Latin American States,* eds. Frank O. Mora and Jeanne A. Hey (Lanham, MD: Rowman & Littlefield, 2003), pp. 145–165.

Ellner, Steve. "Hugo Chávez's First Decade in Office: Breakthroughs and Shortcomings." *Latin American Perspectives* 37, no. 1 (2010): 77–96.

Hillman, Richard S. "Venezuela." In *The South America Handbook,* eds. Patrick Heenan and Monique Lamontagne (Chicago: Fitzroy & Dearborn, 2002), pp. 45–57.

———. "Venezuela: The Tropical Beat." In *The Spanish-Speaking South Americans: Insights into Our Hemispheric Neighbors,* ed. Skye Stephenson (Falmouth, ME: Intercultural Press, 2003), pp. 343–365.

———. "Intellectuals: An Elite Divided." In *The Unraveling of Representative Democracy in Venezuela,* eds. Jennifer McCoy and David Myers (Baltimore: Johns Hopkins University Press, 2004), pp. 115–129.

Hillman, Richard S., and Thomas J. D'Agostino. *Understanding the Contemporary Caribbean,* 2nd ed. Boulder: Lynne Rienner, 2009.

Keen, Benjamin, ed. *Americans All: The Story of Our Latin American Neighbors.* New York: Dell, 1966.

Mendoza, Plinio Apuleyo, Carlos Alberto Montaner, and Álvaro Vargas Llosa. *Manual del Perfecto Idiota Latinoamericano.* Barcelona: Plaza y Janés Editores, S.A., 1996.

Pike, Frederick B. *The United States and Latin America: Myths and Stereotypes of Civilization and Nature.* Austin: University of Texas Press, 1992.

Silvert, Kalman. *The Conflict Society: Reaction and Revolution in Latin America,* 2nd ed. Washington, DC: American Universities Field Staff, 1967.

Vasconcelos, José. *La raza cósmica,* 3rd ed. Mexico City: Espasa-calpe Mexicana, 1948.

2

Latin America: A Geographic Preface

Marie Price

The popular image of Latin America as a major world region has existed for well over a century. The boundaries of the region are relatively unproblematic, beginning at the Rio Grande (called the Río Bravo in Mexico), usually including the Caribbean, and ending at the southern tip of South America. Its shared history of Iberian colonization, more than the current economic status of individual states, provides the region's social and historical integrity. The imprint of over 300 years of Iberian rule is still evident. Roughly two-thirds of the nearly 600 million people who live in the region speak Spanish; most of the rest speak Portuguese. Catholicism is the dominant religion, although as Hannah Stewart-Gambino explains in Chapter 12, Protestant faiths have made inroads and African religious practices have long been present. Likewise, since much of Latin America lies within the tropics, its verdant forests, exotic wildlife, and balmy weather distinguish Latin America from the temperate and subarctic climates of North America. (See Map 2.1.)

Historically, the Spanish and Portuguese who settled much of the region never referred to the area as Latin America. The term was used first by French politicians in the 1860s in an effort to suggest their own "Latin" links with the Western Hemisphere. Other labels, such as Ibero-America, the Indies, and the Americas, have all been applied. Yet the term Latin America seems to be the most popular, perhaps because it is vague enough to be inclusive of different colonial histories, but specific enough to distinguish it from Anglo-America (Price and Cooper 2007). The idea of Latin America gained support during the latter half of the nineteenth century among intellectuals in the former Spanish colonies who were grappling with a way to build political and ideological unity among the new republics. They, too, stressed a distinct "Latin" identity separate from the "Anglo" North (Ardao 1980).

Map 2.1 Latin America: Countries and Capitals

Like all world regions, Latin America is diverse, and generalizations are inherently problematic. Considering the disparate levels of economic development among Latin America countries, as well as their diverse ethnic compositions, it would be easy to emphasize division over commonality. Consonant with the theme propounded by Richard S. Hillman in Chapter 1, however, the geographic perspective clearly illustrates unity in diversity. There is little dispute, for example, that the region's human geography was completely reworked with the arrival of Europeans. The number of indigenous peoples declined by as much as 90 percent during the course of the conquest, but their presence remains strong in many parts of Latin America. Large numbers of African slaves were also added to the cultural mix of Europeans and indigenous peoples through the slave trade. Today, the African presence throughout the Caribbean, Brazil, and coastal Venezuela and Colombia is quite notable. Other immigrant groups arrived—from Italy, Japan, Germany, and India—from the late nineteenth century onward, adding to the cultural complexity of the region.

In terms of physical geography, much of the area is tropical, with a mixture of grasslands and forest as well as mountains and shields (large upland areas of exposed crystalline rock). An impressive array of natural resources includes the planet's largest rain forest, the greatest river by volume, and substantial reserves of natural gas, oil, tin, and copper. Since Christopher Columbus's journey of exploration more than five centuries ago, Latin America has provided the world with many valuable commodities. The early Spanish Empire concentrated on extracting precious metals, namely silver and gold, from Mexico and the Andes. The Portuguese became prominent producers of sugar products, gold, and (later) coffee. By the late nineteenth and early twentieth centuries, natural resource exports to Europe and North America fueled the region's growing economies. Countries tended to specialize in one or two commodities: wool and wheat from Argentina, coffee and sugar from Brazil, coffee and bananas from Costa Rica, tin and silver from Bolivia, and oil from Mexico and Venezuela. Although the national economies of Latin America have diversified since the 1950s, they continue to be major producers of primary goods for North America, Europe, and East Asia.

In the first part of this chapter, I provide a sketch of the physical environment of Latin America, drawing attention to its topographical features, climates, natural resources, and environmental issues. In the second part, I discuss the basic demographic and cultural patterning of the region, developing the concept of the Columbian Exchange as a way to understand the ecological and cultural impact of the New World's encounter with the Old World. Iberian colonization, the African slave trade, and later waves of immigrants from Europe and Asia in the nineteenth and twentieth centuries produced a multiethnic and multiracial society. Current patterns of Latin American and Caribbean emigration to North America, Europe, and Japan are creating complex transnational networks that are conduits for the diffusion of Latino culture into other world regions.

Each modern state of Latin America therefore has a diverse indigenous and migrant profile that contributes to its distinct national culture. Yet in this chapter, I reveal the common experiences shared by the nations in the region.

▓ Physical Setting

The movement of tectonic plates explains much of Latin America's basic topography. As the South and North American plates slowly drifted westward, the Nazca, Cocos, and Pacific plates were subducted below them. In this contact zone, deep oceanic trenches exist along the Pacific coasts, such as the Humboldt trench along the coast of Chile and Peru, producing surprisingly cool ocean temperatures for a tropical zone. The submerged plates have folded and uplifted the mainland's surface, creating the geologically young western mountains, such as the Sierra Madre Occidental in Mexico, the highlands of Central America, and the Andes. The Andes, the most dramatic of these highland areas, run the length of the South American continent for 5,000 miles, with some thirty peaks reaching over 20,000 feet. Created by the collision of oceanic and continental plates, the Andes are a series of folded and faulted sedimentary rocks with intrusions of volcanic and crystalline rock. Consequently, many rich veins of precious metals and minerals are found there. From Colombia to Chile, the initial economic wealth of these Andean territories came from mining. Yet the movement of plates also unleashes environmental hazards such as the earthquakes in 2010 that devastated Haiti (measuring 7.0 on the Richter scale) and seriously debilitated Chile (8.8 on the Richter scale). (See Map 2.2.)

The Andes are typically divided into the northern, central, and southern components. In Colombia, the northern Andes actually split into three distinct mountain ranges before merging near the border with Ecuador. High-altitude plateaus and snow-covered peaks distinguish the central Andes of Ecuador, Peru, and Bolivia. The Andes reach their greatest width here. Between Peru and Bolivia is a treeless high plateau called the *altiplano*. Averaging 12,000 feet in elevation, it has limited grazing potential, but important mineral resources. The southern Andes are shared by Chile and Argentina. Much of this highland region was an important zone of settlement for native peoples, who exploited the diverse ecological niches of the mountains and domesticated a tremendous variety of native crops such as potatoes, hot and sweet peppers, and quinoa (Gade 1999). In Peru, the magnificent mountaintop city of Machu Picchu is an example of the remains of a pre-Columbian settlement. Today, most of the people of the Andean states still live in or at the base of the mountains. Major cities, such as Bogotá, Quito, and La Paz, are in the mountains. The Andean states of Ecuador, Peru, and Bolivia are home to the majority of native peoples in South America.

Aconcagua, located in Argentina, is the highest peak in the Americas.

The Mexican plateau is a massive upland area ringed by the Sierra Madre Mountains and tilted so that the highest elevations are in the South—about 8,000 feet near Mexico City and just 4,000 feet at Ciudad Juárez. The southern end of the plateau, known as the Mesa Central, supports Mexico's highest population density, including the cities of Mexico City, Puebla, and Guadalajara. The Mesa Central was historically Mexico's breadbasket, but water shortages due to urbanization and rapid population growth threaten the region's productivity (Ezcurra et al. 1999). Throughout the Mexican plateau are also rich seams of silver, the focus of economic activity during the country's colonial era. Today, the Mexican economy is driven more by petroleum and gas production along the Gulf Coast and less by the metals of the plateau.

The Caribbean plate contains most of Central America, the islands of the West Indies, and part of Colombia. As the Caribbean plate moves slowly to the east, it triggers volcanic activity and earthquakes in both the Central American highlands and the islands of the Caribbean. The Central American highlands are composed of a volcanic chain that stretches from Guatemala to Costa Rica, producing a handsome landscape of rolling green hills, elevated basins with lakes, and conical peaks. Hugging the Pacific Coast, the legacy of some forty volcanoes is fertile soil that yields a variety of domestic and export crops. Most of Central America's 43 million people are concentrated in this zone, either in the capital cities or the surrounding rural villages. Yet the hazards associated

Map 2.2 Climates and Vegetation

Thomas D'Agostino

Located high in the Peruvian Andes, Machu Picchu was an important pre-Columbian Inca site.

with the movement of the Caribbean plate were plainly evident on January 12, 2010, when a 7.0 earthquake leveled many of the buildings and severely damaged the infrastructure of the Haitian capital of Port-au-Prince, a metropolitan area of over 2 million people. The tragic event affected nearly 3 million and resulted in the death of over 200,000 people, making it one of the worst natural disasters in the region's history. The tragedy of the Haitian earthquake was compounded by the state's poverty and the failure of buildings to be designed to withstand earthquakes.

Another important landform of the region is the shields. These large rocky outcroppings vary in elevation from 600 to 5,000 feet and are remnants of the ancient landmass of Gondwanaland, which began breaking apart 250 million years ago. Consequently, most shields are not noted for their agricultural potential because they lack volcanic and sedimentary soils. The Guiana and Patagonia shields are lightly settled and have limited agricultural potential. In terms of natural resources and settlement, the Brazilian shield is the largest and most important shield. It covers much of Brazil but, in the southeastern portion of the country, a series of mountains protrude from the shield. In between these mountains are elevated basins with fertile soils, excellent for agriculture. This is where many Brazilians live and Brazil's largest cities, São Paulo and Rio de Janeiro, are located.

Historically, the most important areas of settlement in tropical Latin America were not along the region's major rivers, but across its upland plateaus and intermontane basins. In these areas, the combination of soils, benign climates, and sufficient rainfall produced Latin America's most productive agricultural areas and its densest settlements. Examples of four such areas are the Brazilian shield, the Mexican plateau, the Central American highlands, and the Andes.

Major River Basins

In contrast to the western highlands, humid lowlands characterize the Atlantic side of Latin America. Across these lowlands meander some of the great rivers of the world, including the Amazon, Plata, and Orinoco. The Amazon, draining some 2.4 million square miles, is the largest river in the world by volume and area and the second longest in length. The scale of this watershed is underscored by the fact that 20 percent of all freshwater discharged into the oceans comes from the Amazon. Everywhere throughout the basin, more than 60 inches of rain falls each year and many places receive more than 80 inches. This is home to the largest tropical rain forest in the world and, thus, a treasure for genetic diversity. The Plata Basin begins in the tropics and discharges its water in the midlatitudes near the city of Buenos Aires. This basin has three major rivers—the Paraná, Paraguay, and Uruguay—that drain an area from central Bolivia and southern Brazil to northern Argentina. On the Paraná River is Latin America's largest hydroelectric project, the Itaipu Dam, which produces all of Paraguay's electricity and much of the energy used by industrial southern Brazil. The other great river of the region is the Orinoco of Venezuela and Colombia. Although just one-sixth the size of the Amazon watershed, the Orinoco's discharge roughly equals that of the Mississippi River.

Within these watersheds are vast lowlands of less than 600 feet elevation. From north to south, they are the Llanos, the Amazon lowlands, the Pantanal, the Chaco, and the Pampas. With the exception of the Pampas, which is a major center of grain and livestock production, most of these lowlands are sparsely settled and offer limited agricultural potential except as grazing lands for livestock. Long thought of as static frontiers (open lands unsuitable for permanent settlement), areas such as the Chaco and the Amazon have experienced marked increase in resource extraction in the past thirty years, especially the booming soybean market. The pressure to open new lands for agribusiness and export production is transforming much of lowland South America. Likewise, since the 1970s, the Amazon has witnessed a dramatic increase in population, with over 15 million people settling in the Brazilian Amazon alone, bringing about accelerated levels of timber and mineral extraction.

The Mexican and Central American river basins cannot match the scale of the South American ones, but they are important nonetheless. Mexico's Río Bravo (called the Rio Grande in the United States) delimits the boundary between Mexico and Texas. With headwaters in the Sierra Madre Occidental, the Río Bravo and its tributaries carry the snowmelt from the mountains through arid northern Mexico. Dams have been built on some of the watershed's major tributaries to produce electricity and to supply water to cities, towns, and farms. The rise of industrialized border cities, such as Ciudad Juárez, has contributed to the degradation of this watershed. Surface water in the lower Río Bravo is scarce, and what does exist is badly polluted. The largest watershed by volume in Central America is the Grijalva-Usumicinta Basin, which flows through a sparsely populated tropical forest zone in southern Mexico and northern Guatemala. In the Mexican state of Tabasco, the Usumicinta joins the Grijalva and flows into the Bay of Campeche, accounting for nearly half of Mexico's freshwater river flow. Political interest in the basin has intensified over the years because the watershed may be critical for satisfying the water and energy demands of Mexico.

Climate and Vegetation

In tropical Latin America, the daily high temperatures are 70°F–80°F and the daily lows are 70°F–60°F (see Map 2.2). Moreover, the average monthly temperatures in localities such as Managua, Port-au-Prince, and Manaus change little. Precipitation patterns, however, do vary and create distinct wet and dry seasons. In Managua, January and February are dry months, and June through October are the wettest months. The city of Manaus on the Amazon, however, experiences the reverse. June through August are relatively dry, and the long rainy season extends from October to April. The tropical lowlands of Latin America are usually classified as tropical humid climates that are covered in either forest or savanna (grassland with few trees), depending on the amount of rainfall. The largest remaining tropical forest is in the Amazon Basin, but much of the perimeter of this forest zone has been converted into pasture or farms. In contrast, much of the tropical forest in the Caribbean and in Central America was removed long ago for agriculture and human settlement.

Important areas of Latin America are desert. The region's desert climates are found along the Pacific Coast of Peru and northern Chile, Patagonia, northern Mexico, and northeastern Brazil in an area called the Bahia or the *sertão*. Desert areas are generally those that get less than 10 inches of precipitation a year. Thus, a city such as Lima, Peru, which is clearly in the tropics, averages only 1.5 inches of rainfall per year due to the hyperaridity of the Peruvian coast. In fact, there are parts of the Atacama Desert in northern Chile that have never recorded rainfall, giving this desert the distinction of being the world's driest. Such an inhospitable climate, however, hosts a rich assortment of phosphates and copper so that resources from the Atacama buttressed the Chilean economy for much of the twentieth century.

Not all of Latin America is tropical. In the Southern Cone states, midlatitude climates with hot summers and cold winters prevail. Of course, the midlatitude temperature shifts in the Southern Hemisphere are the inverse of those in the Northern Hemisphere (cold Julys and warm Januarys). In the mountain ranges, complex climate patterns result, so that elevation becomes more critical than latitude. The *tierra templada* (temperate lands), at 3,000–6,000 feet in the tropics, have been described as having an eternal springtime climate with warm days and pleasant nights. The *tierra fría* (colder lands) of the tropics are found at 6,000–12,000 feet. These tropical highlands support agriculture such as wheat, tubers, and even maize, but the daytime highs are cool and the lows can reach freezing. These normal climate patterns and the human ecological systems they support are periodically disrupted by weather events that can dramatically impact Latin America. Three of these that deserve attention are hurricanes, El Niño, and global warming.

Several hurricanes form each season, and the worst ones can devastate communities and agriculture in the Caribbean, Central America, Mexico, and North America. (South America is out of the hurricane belt.) Beginning in July, westward-moving low-pressure disturbances form off the coast of West Africa, picking up moisture and speed as they move across the Atlantic. The air masses are usually no more than 100 miles across but, to achieve hurricane status, their winds must reach velocities of more than 74 miles per hour. Typically, half a dozen to a dozen hurricanes form each season and move through the region, causing limited damage. There are, of course, exceptions, and most longtime residents of northern Latin America have experienced the full force of at least one major storm in their lifetime.

In 1998, the torrential rains of Hurricane Mitch, one of the most deadly tropical storms in a century, resulted in the death of at least 8,000 people in Honduras, Nicaragua, and El Salvador. Mudslides and flooding ravaged structures and roads, leaving upward of one-quarter of Honduras's population without shelter. Whereas Hurricane Mitch largely bypassed the Caribbean, Hurricane Ivan pummeled the island nation of Grenada in 2004; although only a few people were killed, the island's infrastructure suffered 85 percent devastation. Barbados, Tobago, the Netherlands Antilles, Cuba, and Jamaica also suffered damage from Ivan. In total about seventy lives and some $2 billion in insurance losses were claimed. Modern tracking equipment has improved hurricane forecasting and reduced the number of fatalities. Forecasting, nevertheless, cannot reduce the economic damage done to crops, forests, and infrastructure when a powerful storm hits.

The most debated weather phenomenon in Latin America, and perhaps the world, is El Niño. El Niño (a reference to the Christ child) is a warm Pacific current that usually arrives off the coast of Ecuador and Peru in December. Every decade or so, an abnormally large current arrives that produces torrential rains, signaling the arrival of an El Niño year. The 2009–2010 El Niño was especially bad for Latin America; scores of people were killed by floods or storms attributed to El Niño–related disturbances. Devastating floods occurred in Peru and Brazil. In Peru, heavy rains and flooding in January 2010 damaged the railroad leading to the ancient Incan site of Machu Picchu, eliminating access to this popular tourist destination until the railroad was reopened months later.

The other, less talked about aspect of El Niño is drought. While the Pacific Coast of South and North America experienced record rainfall in the 1997–1998 El Niño, Colombia, Venezuela, northern Brazil, and Central America battled drought. Hundreds of brush and forest fires left their mark; the amount of smoke produced by forest fires in northern Mexico in the spring of 1998 was so great that it caused haze in the southeastern United States. Drought also brought losses, estimated in billions of dollars, to farmers and ranchers in the region. And for areas that depend on hydroelectricity, such as Colombia and Central America, drought can cause disruptions in electrical power. The indirect costs of drought, such as fire-charred hillsides vulnerable to landslides, are impossible to measure.

Finally, a growing body of evidence suggests that global warming will have immediate and long-term implications for the region. Of greatest immediate concern is how global warming will influence agricultural productivity, water availability, changes in the composition and productivity of ecosystems, and incidence of vector-borne diseases such as malaria and dengue fever.

Changes attributed to global warming are already apparent in high-elevation regions. Tropical mountain systems are projected to experience increased temperatures of 2°F–6°F (1°C–3°C) as well as lower rainfall. Research over the past fifty years has documented the dramatic retreat of Andean glaciers; some no longer exist, and others will cease to exist in the next ten to fifteen years. Many Andean villages, as well as metropolitan areas such as La Paz, get much of their water from glacial runoff. A major Bolivian glacier, Chacaltaya, has lost 80 percent of its area in the past twenty years. Thus, as average temperatures increase in the highlands and glaciers recede, there is concern about the sustainability of future drinking water supplies (IPCC 2007).

One of the long-term effects of global warming is sea level rising and increased severity of storms. This is a major concern for low-lying coastal areas and the Caribbean. The scientific consensus is that global warming could promote a sea level rise of 3 to 10 feet (1 to 3 meters) in the twenty-first century. In terms of land loss due to inundation, the Bahamas would be the most impacted country—losing over 30 percent of its land with a 10-foot sea level rise. Mainland states such as Guyana, Suriname, French Guiana, and Belize are also extremely vulnerable to sea level rise. It is estimated that 30 percent of Suriname's population and 25 percent of Guyana's would be displaced by a sea level rise of 10 feet (IPCC 2007).

Environmental Issues
Given Latin America's immense size and relatively low population density, it has not experienced the same levels of environmental degradation witnessed

in other parts of the world such as in East Asia. The worst environmental problems are found in cities, their surrounding rivers and coasts, and intensely farmed zones (Roberts and Thanos 2003). Vast areas of Latin America remain relatively untouched, supporting an incredible diversity of plant and animal life. Throughout the region, national parks offer some protection to unique communities of plants and animals. And a growing environmental movement in countries such as Costa Rica, Brazil, and Guyana has yielded popular support for environmentally friendly initiatives. It can be argued that Latin America entered the twenty-first century with a real opportunity to avoid many of the environmental missteps seen in other regions of the world.

At the same time, economic pressures brought about by global market forces are driving governments to exploit their natural resources (minerals, fossil fuels, forests, and soils) aggressively. The challenge lies in managing the region's immense natural resources and balancing the economic benefits of extraction with the ecological soundness of conservation. Of the many environmental challenges facing the region, three of the most pernicious are deforestation, degradation of arable lands, and urban environmental pollution.

Due to international interest in tropical forests, deforestation is probably the environmental issue most often associated with the region. The Amazon Basin and portions of the eastern lowlands of Central America and Mexico still maintain important stands of tropical forest. Other areas, such as the Atlantic coastal forest of Brazil and the Pacific forests of Central America, have nearly disappeared because of agricultural use, settlement, and ranching. Likewise, extensive forest clearing for sugar plantations in the Lesser Antilles nearly eliminated all of the tropical forest there more than two centuries ago. In the midlatitudes, the ecologically unique evergreen rain forest of southern Chile (the Valdivian forest) was being cleared to export wood chips to markets in East Asia (Clapp 1998). The coniferous forests of northern Mexico are also being cut down, in part because of the boom in commercial logging stimulated by the North American Free Trade Agreement (NAFTA).

In terms of biological diversity, however, the loss of tropical rain forest is the most critical. Tropical rain forests account for only 6 percent of the earth's landmass, but at least 50 percent of the world's species are found there. Moreover, the Amazon contains the largest undisturbed stretches of rain forest in the world. In the past forty years, the region's tropical forests were seen as agricultural frontiers that governments opened up in an attempt to appease landless peasants and reward political cronies. The forests fell as colonists created farms and large cattle ranches (Hecht and Cockburn 1989). Forest clearing also occurred due to the search for gold in Brazil, Venezuela, Costa Rica, and Guyana and the production of coca leaf for cocaine in Peru, Bolivia, and Colombia (Young 1996) as well as from logging concessions to Southeast and East Asian companies in Guyana, Suriname, and Brazil.

Soil erosion and fertility decline occur in all agricultural areas. Certain soil types in Latin America are particularly vulnerable to erosion, most notably

Evidence of slash and burn agriculture in the Brazilian Amazon.

the volcanic soils and the reddish oxisols found in the humid lowlands. The productivity of the volcanic highlands of Central America, for example, has declined over the decades, due to the ease with which these soils erode and the failure to apply soil conservation measures in many localities. The oxisols of the tropical lowlands, by contrast, can quickly erode into a baked claypan surface when the natural vegetative cover is removed, making permanent agriculture nearly impossible. Ironically, the consolidation of large, modern farms in the valleys tends to push subsistence farmers into marginal areas on steep slopes. On these hillside farms, gullies and landslides are a constant threat to rural livelihoods.

The reality of poverty forcing people to degrade their environment is evident in many rural places in Latin America. Nowhere is this connection more clear than in Haiti. The inhabitants of this densely settled country are largely dependent on commercial and subsistence agriculture, which has resulted in serious problems with soil erosion and declining yields. In addition, the majority of Haitians rely on charcoal (made from trees) for their cooking fuel, which places additional strain on the island's vegetation. The deterioration of the resource base is evident from the air: aerial photos reveal a sharp boundary between a denuded Haiti and a forested Dominican Republic. The difference between the two countries is explained, in part, by the lack of affordable fuel alternatives. Whereas many Dominicans can afford to buy liquid or gas cooking fuel, many Haitians cannot.

Because the vast majority of Latin Americans live in cities, it has become increasingly clear that the environmental quality of urban settings has been a focus for local activism. While Jacquelyn Chase and Susan E. Place discuss urban environmental issues at some length in Chapter 8, it is important to recognize here that many of Latin America's environmentalists worry more about ways to make urban environments cleaner rather than about the future of distant tropical forests. In Rio de Janeiro and São Paulo alone, hundreds of local environmental organizations have pushed for cleaner air, better water, and more green space (Christen et al. 1998).

Factories, coal- and gas-burning power plants, and vehicles all contribute to urban air pollution. The environmental regulations that exist are seldom enforced. The consequences are, in the worst cases, a serious threat to people and the environment. In the 1980s, the heavily polluted Brazilian industrial center of Cubatão, near São Paulo, became synonymous with environmental catastrophe. In 1984, a leaky gas pipe was ignited and as many as 200 people were incinerated in the resulting explosion and fire. While industry leaders downplayed the disaster, traumatized residents mobilized to address the issue (Dean 1995). The events in Cubatão, more than the destruction of the Amazon rain forest, are credited with invigorating the environmental movement in Brazil.

Despite serious urban environmental issues, people in Latin American cities tend to have better access to water, sewers, and electricity than their counterparts in Asia and Africa. Moreover, the density of urban settlement encourages the widespread use of mass transportation—both public and private bus and van routes make getting around most cities fairly easy. The largest cities, such as São Paulo, Mexico City, Buenos Aires, and Caracas, have subway systems. Increasingly cost-effective high-speed bus systems, as found in Curitiba and Bogotá, are gaining popularity. Yet the inevitable environmental problems that come with primate (dominant or major) cities that grew rapidly and have widespread poverty cannot be overstated. Improving sewer systems, waste disposal, and water treatment plants is expensive. Chronic air pollution has caused debilitating health effects, most notably in Santiago and Mexico City. The money to clean up cities is always in short supply, especially with problems of foreign debt, currency devaluation, and inflation. And because many urban dwellers tend to reside in unplanned squatter settlements, retroactively servicing these communities with utilities is difficult and costly.

A Bounty of Natural Resources

Historically, Latin America's abundant natural resources were its wealth. In the colonial period, silver, gold, and sugar generated fortunes for a privileged few. In the latter half of the nineteenth century, a series of export booms introduced commodities such as bananas, coffee, cacao, grains, tin, rubber, copper, wool, and petroleum to an expanding world market. One of the legacies of this export-led development was the tendency to specialize in one or two major commodities, a pattern that continued well into the 1950s. During that decade,

Costa Rica earned 90 percent of its export earnings from bananas and coffee, El Salvador earned over 90 percent from coffee and cotton, 85 percent of Chilean exports came from copper, and half of Uruguay's export earnings came from wood (Wilkie 1997). Even Brazil, the region's largest country, generated 60 percent of its export earnings from coffee in 1955. By 2000, that figure was less than 5 percent and soy products earned Brazil more foreign exchange than coffee. While Brazil continues to rank as the world's leader in coffee exports, the country's economy has experienced tremendous growth and diversification during the past decade. As a result, coffee remains a significant, though hardly dominant, export commodity.

The trend throughout Latin America since the 1960s has been to diversify and mechanize resource extraction, especially in agriculture and mining. Nowhere is this more evident than in the Plata Basin, which includes southern Brazil, Uruguay, northern Argentina, Paraguay, and eastern Bolivia. Soybeans, used for oil and animal feed, transformed these lowlands beginning in the 1980s. Brazil is now the second largest producer of soy in the world (following the United States), and Argentina is the third largest. Between 2000 and 2003, soy production nearly doubled in both countries. Added to this crop are acres of rice, cotton, and orange groves; the more traditional plantings of wheat and sugar; and livestock. Other large-scale agricultural frontiers exist along the piedmont of the Venezuelan Andes (mostly grains) and the Pacific slope of Central America (mostly cotton and tropical fruits). In northern Mexico, water supplied from dams along the Sierra Madre Occidental has turned the valleys in Sinaloa into an intensive production zone for fruits and vegetables bound for the United States. An explosion of so-called nontraditional agricultural exports is reshaping activities in rural areas—from melons and shrimp in Honduras; to flowers and ferns in Costa Rica and Colombia; and grapes, berries and plums in Chile.

In each of these cases, the agricultural sector is capital intensive and dynamic. By using machinery, high-yielding hybrids, chemical fertilizers, and pesticides, many corporate farms have become extremely productive and profitable. What these operations fail to do is employ many rural people, which is especially problematic in countries where one-third of the population depend on agriculture for their livelihood. As industrialized agriculture becomes the norm in Latin America, subsistence producers are further marginalized. The overall trend is that agricultural production is increasing, while proportionally fewer people are employed in it, and agriculture contributes less to the overall economy than it once did. In absolute terms, however, the number of people living in rural areas is about the same today as it was in 1960 (roughly 125 million). The major difference over the past 50 years is that many of these people are worse off because traditional rural support networks have broken down and small farmers have been forced onto marginal lands that are vulnerable to drought and erosion. Peasant farmers who are able to produce a surplus of corn or wheat earn little from these crops because their value is undercut by cheaper imported grains.

Mining and fossil fuels continue to shape the economies of several countries in the region. Moreover, many commodities prices—such as gold, silver, and copper—reached record levels in 2005 through 2008, boosting foreign exchange earnings. Oil-rich Venezuela, Mexico, and Ecuador are able to meet their own fuel needs and to earn vital state revenues from oil exports. Venezuela is most dependent on revenues from oil, earning up to 90 percent of its foreign exchange from crude petroleum and petroleum products; it is the fifth largest oil producer in the world. Vast oil reserves also exist in the eastern lowlands of Colombia, yet a costly and vulnerable pipeline that connects the oil fields to the coast is a regular target of guerrilla groups. Recently discovered major offshore oil reserves in Brazil will likely change this oil-importing nation to a major exporter. While the oil will be expensive to recover, the size of the find will substantially change the geography of oil production in the region.

Besides oil, Latin America's other important exports are silver, zinc, copper, iron ore, bauxite, and gold. Like agriculture, mining has become more mechanized. Even Bolivia, a country dependent on tin production, cut 70 percent of its miners from state payrolls in the 1990s without appreciable falls in production. Increasingly, Bolivian investment has been focused on its natural gas reserves in the eastern plains, although the promise of this resource has not reduced Bolivia's poverty. Similarly, the vast copper mines of northern Chile are producing record amounts of copper with fewer miners. Gold mining, in contrast, continues to use artisanal methods and larger numbers of miners. Gold rushes are occurring in remote tropical regions of Venezuela, Brazil, Colombia, Guyana, and Costa Rica. Many gold strikes are made illegally on indigenous lands or within the borders of national parks (as in Costa Rica and Guyana). However, because gold is such a valuable export commodity, the borders of protected areas are seldom enforced.

▨ Human Geography of Latin America

Today, nearly 600 million people live in Latin America. This is a striking figure when one considers that in 1950, Latin America comprised 150 million people, which equaled the population of the United States at that time. Now, Latin America's population is double that of the United States. Like the rest of the developing world, Latin America experienced dramatic population growth in the 1960s and 1970s. It outpaced the United States because infant mortality rates declined and life expectancy soared. In 1950, Brazilian life expectancy was only forty-three years; by the 1980s, it was sixty-three; and by 2009, it was seventy-three. In fact, most countries in the region have experienced a twenty- to thirty-year improvement in life expectancy between 1950 and today, which pushed up growth rates. Today, the average life expectancy for the entire region is seventy-three years, compared to seventy-eight for the United States. Four countries account for two-thirds of the region's population: Brazil, with 192 million; Mexico, 110 million; Colombia, 45 million; and Argentina, 40 million (Population Reference Bureau 2009).

During the 1980s, population growth rates suddenly began to slow and, during the 1990s, most countries reported growth rates of less than 2 percent. The region is still growing, but at a slower pace of 1.4 percent. In the 1960s, a typical Latin American woman had 6 or 7 children. By the 1980s, the average woman had 3 children and today the average is 2.3 children. A number of factors explain this, including more urban families, which tend to be smaller than rural ones; increased participation of women in the workforce; higher education levels of women; and state support of family planning and better access to birth control. Only two countries, Guatemala and Haiti, average 4 or more children per woman (Population Reference Bureau 2009).

The distribution of population away from rural areas and into cities is the other major demographic change for the region. A staggering 77 percent of Latin Americans live in cities, which is a rate comparable to Europe and North America. This makes Latin America the most urbanized region within the developing world. The cities in the region are noted for high levels of urban primacy, a condition in which a country has a primate city that is three to four times larger than any other city in the country (Gilbert 1998). Examples of primate cities are Lima, Caracas, Guatemala City, Havana, Santo Domingo, Buenos Aires, Mexico City, and Santiago. In Brazil and Ecuador, two cities dominate all others in the country in terms of size and economic importance: Guayaquil and Quito in Ecuador and São Paulo and Rio de Janeiro in Brazil are examples of dual primacy. Primacy is often viewed as a liability because too many national resources are concentrated into one urban center. In an effort to decentralize, governments have intentionally built cities far from primate cities such as Ciudad Guyana in Venezuela and Brasília in Brazil. Despite these efforts, the tendency toward primacy remains strong. In order to appreciate the magnitude of population growth and the dominance of cities, it is important to address the demographic consequences of Iberian conquest in the Americas.

Conquest and Settlement

The Iberian colonial experience imposed a political and cultural coherence on Latin America that makes it a distinguishable region today. Yet this was not an uncontested transplanting of Iberia across the Atlantic. As a result of the papal-decreed Treaty of Tordesillas in 1493, Spain received the majority of the Americas, and Portugal received a small portion of eastern South America that eventually became Brazil. Through the course of colonization, Spain shifted its attention to the mainland colonies centered on Mexico and Peru. This left the Caribbean and the Guianas vulnerable to other European powers, most notably England, France, and the Netherlands, and each of these countries established colonies.

Nevertheless, Spain was able to conquer and administer an enormous territory in less than 100 years. The prevailing strategy was one of forced assimilation, in which Iberian religion, language, and political organization were imposed on the surviving fragments of native society. In some areas, such as southern Mexico, Guatemala, Bolivia, and Peru, native cultures have shown remarkable resilience as evidenced by the survival of native languages—Maya, Quechua, Aymara, and Guaraní. Later, other European, African, and Asian peoples, arriving as both forced and voluntary migrants, were added to the region's cultural mix. Yet perhaps the single most important factor in the dominance of Iberian culture in Latin America was the demographic collapse of native populations in the first 150 years of settlement.

Native Population Decline

It is hard to grasp the enormity of human and cultural loss due to this cataclysmic encounter between Europe and the Americas. Throughout the region, archaeological sites are poignant reminders of the complexity of precontact (i.e., pre–European arrival) civilizations (Mann 2006). Dozens of stone temples found throughout Mexico and Central America attest to how Mayan and Aztec civilizations flourished in the area's tropical forests and upland plateaus. In the Andes, farmers still use stone terraces built by the Incas; earthen platforms for village sites and raised fields for agriculture are still being discovered and mapped. Ceremonial centers, such as Cuzco (the center of the great Incan Empire), and hundreds of miles of Incan roads are evidence of the complexity of Amerindian networks. The Spanish, too, were impressed by the sophistication and wealth they saw around them, especially in the incomparable Tenochtitlán where Mexico City sits today. Tenochtitlán was the political and ceremonial center of the Aztecs, which supported a complex metropolitan area with some 300,000 residents. By comparison, the largest city in Spain at the time was considerably smaller. (See Map 2.3.)

The most telling figures of the impact of Iberian expansion are demographic. It is widely believed that precontact America (the Western Hemisphere) had 54 million inhabitants; in comparison, Western Europe in 1500 had a population of 42 million. Of the 54 million people, about 50 million lived in Latin America and the Caribbean (Denevan 1992). There were two major population centers: one in central Mexico, with 14 million people, and the other in the central Andes (highland Peru and Bolivia), with nearly 12 million. Virtually all of the estimated 3 million indigenous peoples who inhabited the islands of the Caribbean were gone within fifty years of contact with Europeans. By 1650,

NORTH
AMERICA

TARASCAN

EARLY TOLTECS   AZTEC

MIXTECAN   MAYA

MEXICO
CIRCA 1500

ARAWAK

TAINO

CARIB

SOUTH
AMERICA

LAKE
TITICACA

INCA
EMPIRE
CIRCA 1492

N
W   E
S

ARAUCANIAN

Map 2.3 Indigenous Peoples' Migration Routes and Empires

after 150 years of colonization, the indigenous population was one-tenth its precontact size. The relentless elimination of 90 percent of the indigenous population was largely caused by epidemics of influenza and smallpox; however, warfare, forced labor, and starvation due to a collapse of food production systems also contributed to the death rate.

The tragedy of conquest did not end in 1650, the population low point for indigenous peoples, but continued throughout the colonial period and, to a much lesser extent, continues today. Even after the indigenous population began its slow recovery in the central Andes and central Mexico, there were small tribal bands in southern Chile (the Mapuche) and Patagonia (Araucania) that experienced the ravages of disease three centuries after Columbus landed. Even now, the isolation of some Amazonian tribes has made them vulnerable to disease.

At present, Mexico, Guatemala, Ecuador, Peru, and Bolivia have the largest indigenous populations. Not surprisingly, these are the areas that had the most dense native populations at contact. Indigenous survival also occurs in isolated settings where the workings of national and global economies are slow to penetrate. The Caribbean coast of Panama, home to the Kuna, or the Gran Sabana of Venezuela, where the Pemon live, are two examples of relatively small groups that have managed to maintain a distinct indigenous way of life despite pressures to assimilate.

The Columbian Exchange

Historian Alfred Crosby likens the contact period between Europe, Africa, and Asia (Old World) and the Americas (New World) to an immense biological swap, which he terms "the Columbian Exchange" (1972). According to Crosby, Europeans benefited greatly from this exchange, and native peoples suffered terribly from it, most notably through the introduction of disease. The human ecology of both sides of the Atlantic, however, was forever changed through the introduction of new diseases, peoples, plants, and animals. Take, for example, the introduction of Old World crops. The Spanish, naturally, brought their staples of wheat, olives, and grapes to plant in the Americas. Wheat did surprisingly well in the highland tropics and became a widely consumed grain over time. Grapes and olive trees did not fare so well; eventually, grapes were produced commercially in the temperate zones of South America. The Spanish grew to appreciate the domestication skills of native agriculturalists who had developed valuable starch crops such as corn, potatoes, and bitter manioc as well as exotic condiments such as hot peppers, tomatoes, pineapple, cacao, and avocados.

Tropical crops transferred from Asia and Africa reconfigured the economic potential of Latin America. Sugarcane became the dominant cash crop of the Caribbean and the Atlantic tropical lowlands of South America. With labor-intensive sugar production came the importation of millions of African slaves. Coffee, a later transfer from East Africa, emerged as one of the leading export crops throughout Central America, Colombia, Venezuela, and Brazil in the nineteenth century. And pasture grasses introduced from Africa enhanced the forage available to livestock.

The movement of Old World animals across the Atlantic had a profound impact on the Americas. Initially, these animals hastened indigenous decline by introducing animal-borne diseases and by producing feral offspring that consumed everything in their path. Over time, native survivors appreciated the utility of Old World animals. Draft animals were adopted, and so too was the plow, which facilitated the preparation of soil for planting. Wool became an important fiber for indigenous communities in the uplands. And slowly, pork, chicken, and eggs added protein and diversity to the staple diets of corn, potatoes, and cassava. Ironically, the horse, which was a feared and formidable weapon of the Europeans, became a tool of resistance in the hands of skilled indigenous riders who inhabited the plains of the Chaco and Patagonia. With the major exception of disease, many transfers of plants and animals ultimately benefited both sides of the Atlantic. Still, it is clear that the ecological and material basis for life in Latin America was completely reworked through this exchange process initiated by Columbus.

Repeopling the Americas

The dramatic and relatively rapid decline of native peoples simplified colonization in some ways. Spain and Portugal were able to refashion Latin America into a European likeness. And as rival European powers vied for power in the Caribbean in the mid-sixteenth century, the islands they fought over were virtually uninhabited. Yet instead of creating a tropical neo-Europe, a complex ethnic blend evolved. Beginning with the first years of contact, unions between European men and native women began the process of racial mixing that became a defining feature of the region over time. The Iberian courts officially discouraged racial mixing, but not much could be done about it. Spain became obsessed with the matter of race and of maintaining racial purity in its colonies, which had a far larger native population than the Portuguese colony of Brazil. Yet after generations of intermarriage, four broad categories resulted: *blanco* (European ancestry), *mestizo* (mixed ancestry), *indio* (Amerindian ancestry), and *negro* (African ancestry). The *blancos* are still well represented among the elites, yet the vast majority of the people are of mixed racial ancestry.

For the Caribbean islands and the Atlantic coast of South America, the scarcity of indigenous labor hastened the development of the trans-Atlantic slave trade. Beginning in the sixteenth century and lasting until the nineteenth century, at least 10 million Africans landed in the Americas and an estimated 2 million perished en route. Nearly two-thirds of all African slaves were first sent to the islands of the Caribbean and Brazil, creating a neo-Africa in the Americas (Curtin 1969). In absolute numbers, more Africans landed in Latin America than Europeans in the first three centuries after contact. Yet because Africans were brought in as slaves, their survival rates and life expectancy were much lower than those of Europeans, which undermined their overall demographic impact (Sánchez-Albornoz 1974).

When much of Latin America gained its independence in the early nineteenth century, the new leaders of the region sought to develop their territories through immigration. Firmly believing in the dictum, "to govern is to populate," many countries set up immigration offices in Europe to attract hardworking peasants to till the land and "whiten" the *mestizo* population. Argentina, Chile, Uruguay, southern Brazil, and Cuba were the most successful in attracting European immigrants from the 1870s until the Great Depression of the 1930s. During this period, some 8 million Europeans arrived (more than came during the entire colonial period), with Italians, Portuguese, Spaniards, and Germans being the most numerous. Some of this immigration was state sponsored such as the nearly 1 million laborers (including entire families) brought to the coffee estates surrounding São Paulo at the turn of the century. Other migrants came seasonally, especially the Italian peasants who left Europe in the winter for agricultural work in Argentina and were thus nicknamed "the swallows." Still others paid their own passage, intending to settle permanently and prosper in the growing commercial centers of Buenos Aires, São Paulo, Montevideo, and Santiago.

Less known are the Asian immigrants who arrived during this same period. Although considerably fewer in number, they established an important presence in the large cities of Brazil, Peru, and Paraguay as well as throughout Guyana, Suriname, and Trinidad. Beginning in the mid-nineteenth century, most of the Chinese and Japanese who settled in Latin America were contracted laborers brought in to work on the coffee estates in southern Brazil and the sugar estates and guano (waste from seafowl used as fertilizer) mines of Peru. The Japanese in Brazil are the most studied Asian immigrant group. Between 1908 and 1978, a quarter million Japanese immigrated to Brazil; today the country is home to 1.3 million people of Japanese descent. Initially, most Japanese were landless laborers, yet by the 1940s they had accumulated enough capital so that three-quarters of the migrants had their own land in the peripheral areas of São Paulo and Paraná states. Increasingly, second- and third-generation Japanese have taken professional and commercial jobs in Brazilian cities; many of them have married outside their ethnic group and are losing their fluency in Japanese. South America's economic turmoil in the past two decades resulted in many ethnic Japanese emigrating to Japan in search of better opportunities. Nearly one-quarter of a million ethnic Japanese left South America in the 1990s (mostly from Brazil and Peru) and now reside in Japan (Kent 2006).

In the Caribbean, sugar estate owners who feared labor shortages with the abolition of slavery in the nineteenth century sought indentured labor from

South and Southeast Asia. Because Guyana and Trinidad were British colonies, most of the contract labor came from India. Today, half of Guyana's population and 40 percent of Trinidad's claim South Asian ancestry. Hindu temples are found in the cities and villages, and many families speak Hindi in their homes. In Suriname, a former Dutch colony, more than one-third of the population is South Asian, and 16 percent are Javanese (from Indonesia).

Emigration and Transnational Networks

Movement within Latin America and between Latin America and North America has had a significant impact on Latino settlement patterns. Within Latin America, shifting economic and political realities have shaped immigrants' destinations. Venezuela's oil wealth, especially during the 1960s and 1970s, attracted between 1 million and 2 million Colombian immigrants, who worked as domestic or agricultural laborers. Argentina has long been a destination for Bolivian and Paraguayan laborers. And sugar plantations in the Dominican Republic have relied on Haitian labor, just as farmers in the United States have depended on Mexican laborers. Political turmoil has also sparked waves of international migrants and refugees, such as the Cuban flight from Fidel Castro in the 1960s, the Chilean exodus during General Augusto Pinochet's reign in the 1970s, and the civil war in El Salvador in the 1980s.

One of the largest migrant flows continues to be Mexicans to the United States. In 2007, 28 million people in the US claimed Mexican ancestry according to the US Census Bureau and, of those, approximately 12 million were immigrants. Mexican labor migration to the United States dates back to the late 1800s, when relatively unskilled labor was recruited to work in agriculture, mining and railroads. Today, roughly 60 percent of the Hispanic population (both foreign born and native born) in the United States claim Mexican ancestry. Mexican immigrants are most concentrated in California and Texas, but increasingly they are found throughout the United States. Although Mexicans continue to have the greatest presence among Latinos in the United States, the number of immigrants from El Salvador, Guatemala, Cuba, the Dominican Republic, Nicaragua, Colombia, Ecuador, and Brazil has steadily grown. The US Census Bureau estimates there were 48.4 million Hispanics in the United States (both foreign and native born) in 2009. Most of this population has ancestral ties with peoples from Latin America.

Today, Latin America is seen as a region of emigration rather than one of immigration. Both skilled and unskilled workers from Latin America are an important source of labor in North America, Europe, and Japan. Many of these immigrants send monthly remittances to their home countries to sustain family members. In 2007, it was estimated that immigrants sent over $65 billion to Latin America, most of which came from workers in the United States. Through remittances and technological advances that make communication faster and cheaper, immigrants maintain close contact with their home countries in ways that earlier generations could not. Scholars have labeled this ability to straddle livelihoods between two countries as "transnationalism." A cultural and an economic outcome of globalization, transnationalism highlights the social and economic links that form between home and host countries (Jackiewicz and Bosco 2008). Declining economic opportunities within Latin America have forced many individuals to emigrate in order to sustain their families. In the process, a new human geography is being created, one that extends well beyond regional boundaries.

Language

Roughly two-thirds of Latin Americans are Spanish speakers, and one-third speak Portuguese. These colonial languages were so prevalent by the nineteenth century that they were the unquestioned languages of government and instruction for the newly independent Latin American republics. In fact, until recently many countries actively discouraged, even repressed, native languages. Because Spanish and Portuguese dominate, there is a tendency to overlook the persistence of native languages. In the central Andes of Peru, Bolivia, and southern Ecuador, over 10 million people still speak Quechua and Aymará. In Paraguay and lowland Bolivia, there are 4 million Guaraní speakers; in southern Mexico and Guatemala, at least 6–8 million speak Mayan languages. Small groups of native-language speakers are found scattered throughout the sparsely settled interior of South America and the more isolated forests of Central America, but many of these languages have fewer than 10,000 speakers.

Due to the more complex colonial history of the Caribbean, other languages are spoken there. Roughly 10 million people speak French (Haiti, French Guiana, and the islands of Martinique and Guadeloupe); 6 million speak English (Jamaica, Belize, Guyana, Trinidad, and other smaller islands of the Lesser Antilles); and there are about half a million Dutch speakers (Suriname and several small islands). Yet these figures tell only part of the story. Typically, colloquial variants of the official language exist that can be difficult for a non-native speaker to understand. In some cases, completely new languages emerge; in the Dutch islands of Aruba, Bonaire, and Curaçao, *Papiamento* (a trading language that blends Dutch, Spanish, Portuguese, English, and African languages) is the *lingua franca,* with usage of Dutch declining. Similarly, *patois* (French Creole) in Haiti has constitutional status as a distinct language. In practice, French is used in higher education, government, and the courts in Haiti, but *patois* (with clear African influences) is the language of the street, the home, and oral tradition.

Religion

Like language, the Roman Catholic faith appears to have been imposed on the region without challenge. As Hannah Stewart-Gambino shows in Chapter 12, most countries report between 70 percent and 90 percent of their population as Catholic. Every major city has dozens of churches, and even the smallest hamlet maintains a graceful church on its central square. In countries like El Salvador and Uruguay, a sizable portion of the population attend Protestant evangelical churches, but the Catholic core of this region is still intact.

Yet exactly what native peoples absorbed of the Christian faith is unclear. Throughout Latin America, syncretic religions—the blending of different belief systems—enabled animist practices to be folded into Christian worship. These blends took hold and endured, in part, because the Christian saints were easy surrogates for pre-Christian gods and because the Catholic Church tolerated local variations in worship as long as the process of conversion was under way. The Mayan practice of paying tribute to spirits of the underworld seems to be replicated today in Mexico and Guatemala via the practice of building small cave shrines to favorite Catholic saints and leaving offerings of fresh flowers and fruits. One of the most celebrated religious icons in Mexico is Guadalupe, a dark-skinned virgin seen by an Indian shepherd boy. Thought to intercede on behalf of the poor, Guadalupe has become the patron saint of Mexico.

Syncretic religious practices also evolved and endured among African slaves. Millions of Brazilians practice the African-based religions of Umbanda, Macumba, and Candomblé along with Catholicism. In many parts of southern Brazil, Umbanda is as popular with people of European ancestry as with Afro-Brazilians. Typically, people become familiar with Umbanda after falling victim to a magician's spell by having some object of black magic buried outside their home. In order to regain control of their life, they need the help of a priest or priestess. In the Caribbean, Afro-religious traditions have evolved into unique forms that have clear ties to West Africa. The most widely practiced are Vodou in Haiti, Santería in Cuba, and Obeah in Jamaica.

Race and Inequality

There is much to admire about race relations in the Americas. The complex racial and ethnic mix that was created in Latin America fostered tolerance for diversity. Nevertheless, as Kevin A. Yelvington shows in Chapter 9, Amerindians and people of African ancestry are disproportionately represented among the poor of the region. More than ever, racial discrimination is a major political issue in Brazil. Reports of organized killings of street children, most of them Afro-Brazilian, make headlines. For decades, Brazil espoused its vision of a color-blind racial democracy that refused to address racism. Evidence from northeastern Brazil, where Afro-Brazilians are the majority, shows death rates approaching those of some of the world's poorest countries. Throughout Brazil, Afro-Brazilians suffer higher rates of homelessness, landlessness, illiteracy, and unemployment. The past few years have seen dramatic changes in

Brazilian society as affirmative action measures have been implemented to open opportunities for Afro-Brazilians. President Luiz Inácio Lula da Silva's government also launched a major poverty reduction program that has seen improvements in income and a reduction in income inequality.

Similarly, in areas of Latin America where indigenous cultures are strong, one also finds low socioeconomic indicators. In most countries, mapping areas where native languages are widely spoken invariably corresponds with areas of persistent poverty. In Mexico, the indigenous south lags behind the booming north and Mexico City. Prejudice is embedded in the language; to call someone an *indio* is an insult in Mexico. In Bolivia, women who dress in the native style of full pleated skirts and bowler hats are called *cholas*. This descriptive term, referring to the rural *mestizo* population, has negative connotations of backwardness and even cowardice. No one of high social standing, regardless of skin color, would ever be called a *chola* or *cholo*. But native people are mobilizing. The presidencies of Alejandro Toledo in Peru (2001–2006) and Evo Morales in Bolivia (2006–present), both of Amerindian heritage, is a hopeful sign of greater inclusion.

It is difficult to separate status divisions based on class from those based on race. From the days of conquest, being European meant an immediate elevation in status over the indigenous, African, and *mestizo* populations. Class awareness is strong. Race does not necessarily determine one's economic standing, but it certainly influences it. These class differences express themselves in the landscape. In the large cities and their handsome suburbs, country clubs and trendy shopping centers are found. High-rise luxury apartment buildings with beautiful terraces offer all the modern amenities, including maids' quarters. The elite and the middle class even show a preference for decentralized suburban living and dependence on automobiles, much like North Americans. Yet near these same residences are shantytowns where urban squatters build their own homes, create their own economy, and eke out a living.

Geography of the Possible

Latin America was the first region in the developing world to be fully colonized by Europe. In the process, perhaps 90 percent of the indigenous population died due to disease, cruelty, and forced resettlement. The slow demographic recovery of indigenous peoples and the continual arrival of Europeans and Africans resulted in an unprecedented level of racial and cultural mixing. It took nearly 400 years for the population of Latin America to reach 50 million again, its precontact level. During this long period, European culture, technology, and political systems were transplanted and modified. Indigenous peoples integrated livestock and wheat into their agricultural practices, but held true to their preference for native corn, potatoes, and cassava. In short, a syncretic process unfolded, in which many indigenous customs were preserved beneath the veneer of Iberian ones. Over time, a blending of indigenous, Iberian, and African influences gave distinction to this part of the world. The music, literature, and artistry of Latin America are widely acknowledged.

Compared with Asia or Europe, Latin America is relatively lightly populated, yet still rich in natural resources. However, as population continues to grow along with economic expectations, there is considerable concern that much of this natural endowment could be squandered for short-term gains. In the midst of a boom in natural resource extraction, popular concern for the state of the environment is mixed. Latin Americans are more likely to mobilize around issues of clean water and air in urban environments than biological diversity in remote forest settings. But the creation and maintenance of large national parks and a growing tourism and ecotourism industry are likely to garner support for conservation.

In Latin America, the trend toward modernization began in the 1950s, and the pace of change has been rapid. Unlike people in other developing areas, most Latin Americans live in cities. This shift started early and reflects a cultural bias toward urban living with roots in the colonial past. Not everyone who came to the city found employment; thus, the dynamics of the informal sector were set in place. Even though population growth rates have declined, the overall makeup of the population is young. Serious challenges lie ahead in educating and finding employment for the cohort under the age of fifteen. Those who cannot find work often consider emigrating to other parts of Latin America, North America, Europe, or elsewhere to seek better economic opportunities, contributing to the so-called brain drain that adversely impacts societies struggling to promote socioeconomic development.

Latin America is one of the world regions that North Americans are most likely to visit. The trend, of course, is to visit the northern fringe of this region. Tourism is robust along Mexico's border and coastal resorts. Unfortunately, there is a tendency to visit one area in the region and generalize for all of it. Although it is historically sound to think of Latin America as a major world region, extreme variations in the physical environment, levels of social and economic development, and the influence of indigenous society exist. Therefore, underlying the unifying factors, these differences add much to the texture and complexity of Latin America, making it one of the world's most ecologically and culturally rich regions.

▓ Bibliography

Ardao, Arturo. *Génesis de la Idea y el Nombre de América Latina*. Caracas: Centro de Estudios Latinoamericanos Rómulo Gallegos, 1980.
Christen, C., S. Herculano, K. Hochstetler, R. Prell, M. Price, and J. T. Roberts. "Latin American Environmentalism: Comparative Views." *Studies in Comparative International Development* 33, no. 2 (1998): 58–87.

Clapp, Roger Alex. "Waiting for the Forest Law: Resource-Led Development and Environmental Politics in Chile." *Latin American Research Review* 33, no. 2 (1998): 3–36.

Crosby, Alfred. *The Columbian Exchange: Biological and Cultural Consequences of 1492.* Westport: Greenwood Press, 1972.

Curtin, Philip D. *The Atlantic Slave Trade: A Census.* Madison: University of Wisconsin Press, 1969.

Dean, Warren. *With Broadax and Firebrand: The Destruction of the Brazilian Atlantic Forest.* Berkeley: University of California Press, 1995.

Denevan, William M. *The Native Population of the Americas in 1492,* 2nd ed. Madison: University of Wisconsin Press, 1992.

Ezcurra, Exequiel, Marisa Mazari-Hiriart, Irene Pisanty, and Adrián Guillermo Aguilar. *The Basin of Mexico: Critical Environmental Issues and Sustainability.* New York: United Nations University Press, 1999.

Gade, Daniel W. *Nature and Culture in the Andes.* Madison: University of Wisconsin Press, 1999.

Gilbert, Alan. *The Latin American City,* 2nd ed. New York: Monthly Review Press, 1998.

Hecht, Susanna, and Alexander Cockburn. *The Fate of the Forest: Developers, Destroyers and Defenders of the Amazon.* London: Verso Press, 1989.

IPCC (Intergovernmental Panel on Climate Change). 2007. *Climate Change 2007: Working Group II Report Impacts, Adaption and Vulnerability.* New York: United National Environmental Programme (UNEP).

Jackiewicz, Edward L., and Fernando J. Bosco. *Placing Latin America: Contemporary Themes in Human Geography.* Lanham, MD: Rowman & Littlefield, 2008.

Kent, Robert. *Latin America: Regions and People.* New York: Guilford Press, 2006.

Mann, Charles. *1491: New Revelations of the Americas Before Columbus.* New York: Vintage Books, 2006.

Population Reference Bureau. *World Population Data Sheet.* Washington, DC: Population Reference Bureau, 2009.

Price, Marie, and Catherine Cooper. "Competing Visions, Shifting Boundaries: The Construction of Latin America as a World Region." *Journal of Geography* 106 (2007): 113–122.

Roberts, J. Timmons, and Nikki Demetria Thanos. *Trouble in Paradise: Globalization and Environmental Crisis in Latin America.* New York: Routledge, 2003.

Sánchez-Albornoz, Nicolás. *The Population of Latin America: A History.* Berkeley: University of California Press, 1974.

US Census Bureau. "Table 3: Annual Estimates of the Resident Population by Sex, Race, and Hispanic Origin for the United States: April 1, 2000 to July 1, 2009," June 2010. www.census.gov.

Wilkie, Richard, ed. *Statistical Abstract of Latin America,* vol. 35. Los Angeles: University of California Press, 1997.

Young, Kenneth R. "Threats to Biological Diversity Caused by Coca/Cocaine Deforestation in Peru." *Environmental Conservation* 23, no. 1 (1996): 7–15.

3

The Historical Context

René de la Pedraja

The conquest and colonization of the Americas in the sixteenth and seventeenth centuries created the conditions for the exploitation of the vast territories described by Marie Price in Chapter 2. Beginning in the late fifteenth century, European imperialist expansion resulted in the defeat and subjugation of the native peoples of Latin America, the first non-European continental area to be Westernized. It was not until the early nineteenth century that challenges to European domination unleashed the revolutionary forces that culminated in independence. Therefore, an understanding of the enduring legacies of a colonial system that lasted for three centuries is fundamental to the illumination of developments and issues in contemporary Latin America. In this chapter, I focus on the ways in which Europe imposed itself on the New World and how independence was achieved. Recent research has shown that the native peoples were never passive victims. Despite the ultimate failures of armed resistance, they were still able to decide what elements of the new Spanish civilization to incorporate into their daily lives.

▧ The Conquest

Spanish colonization began after Christopher Columbus arrived in the Caribbean in 1492. Ineffective resistance in the islands allowed the Spaniards to exploit conquered native peoples as virtual slaves. They did so initially through the brutal system of *repartimiento* (from the verb *repartir,* "to distribute") in which native peoples were seized and enslaved. In 1503, the crown adopted the legal system of *encomienda* (from the verb *encomendar,* "to entrust") to replace the earlier system. Henceforth, the conquerors were obliged to Christianize the native peoples and treat them justly. Nevertheless, this "civilizing" role degenerated rapidly, given an economic imperative for free labor. Therefore, captured native peoples remained in a state of virtual slavery.

European diseases ravaged the indigenous populations of the Caribbean, leading to slave-hunting expeditions on the coasts of Florida, Venezuela, Central America, and the Yucatán. These expeditions also continued the avid search for mineral wealth as the small gold deposits in the Caribbean became exhausted. The discovery of pearls off the island of Cubagua in 1510 led the Spaniards to occupy the northeastern part of Venezuela and expand into the interior in search of El Dorado (the legendary city of great wealth).

Hernán Cortés set out from Cuba in 1519 to pursue reports of a rich kingdom in the highlands of central Mexico. Cortés and his small force conquered the vast Aztec Empire—whose population of 20 million was defended by at least 100,000 warriors—by forming alliances with tribes that sought to end Aztec rule and by deceiving Montezuma, the powerful Aztec leader. By 1521, central Mexico was under Spanish control.

Indian laborers then leveled the Aztec capital, Tenochtitlán, and built Mexico City on the same site, which immediately became the wealthiest and largest colonial city in Latin America. From the central location of Mexico City, Spanish expeditions fanned out in all directions to subdue any pockets of native resistance. The march into Central America brought Spanish rule to Guatemala, El Salvador, and Honduras by 1525. The Yucatán Peninsula, however,

The Kukulcan temple at Chichen Itza,
a significant Mayan site in southern Mexico.

was successfully defended by the militaristic city-states of the Maya until 1527, when Francisco de Montejo and his son began the conquest they finally completed in 1546.

Vasco Núñez de Balboa crossed Panama and became the first European to view the Pacific Ocean in 1513, and Panama City was established in 1519. From this strategic location, Spanish explorers moved into surrounding regions. The indigenous peoples of the highlands of Costa Rica had repulsed the sporadic Spanish expeditions until the 1570s, when the Spaniards were able to complete the conquest of the Pacific Coast and the highlands in Central America. Only on the Caribbean side of Central America did Spanish rule fail to take hold, not because of any major opposition but simply because the sparse indigenous population, the lack of any immediately valuable resources, and the sweltering tropical climate combined to make the region unattractive to the Spaniards.

Rumors of a rich kingdom to the south along the Pacific Ocean led Ferdinand Magellan to discover the straits at the extreme southern tip of South America in 1520. In an attempt to find what lay between that point and Panama far to the north, Francisco Pizarro took two exploring expeditions south from Panama along the Pacific Coast of Colombia in the mid-1520s. Pizarro returned to the coast of Peru in 1532 with a force of roughly 200 explorers and soon discovered the Incan Empire, the largest in the Americas. Rather than conducting a frontal attack, Pizarro entrapped the unsuspecting Incan emperor at Cajamarca in 1533. The huge Incan armies could not be assembled in time to try to stop the advancing Spaniards. Hence, the capital, Cuzco, was captured easily, and the entire Incan Empire—which had stretched from Quito, Ecuador, to Santiago, Chile—came under Spanish control. In 1535, Pizarro established the Spanish capital in Lima, which became—after Mexico City—the second most important urban center in colonial Latin America.

Expeditions fanned out from Peru in all directions in the hope of finding either precious metals or large numbers of indigenous peoples for free labor. To occupy the southernmost parts of the Incan Empire, Pizarro sent Pedro de Valdivia, who established Santiago, the capital of Chile, in 1541. South of Santiago, the Araucanians mastered European methods of warfare and successfully resisted Spanish control. But the region contained gold, and miners and settlers continued to clash with the indigenous peoples in almost continuous warfare until the late nineteenth century.

An expedition from Spain landed on the Caribbean coast of Colombia, and Gonzalo Jiménez de Quesada took this force up the Magdalena River into the highland native kingdom of the Chibchas. After defeating the Chibchas, Jiménez de Quesada established the capital at Bogotá in 1537. To the east, through a piecemeal process, Spanish colonizers gradually converged from the original pearl fisheries on the Caribbean coast of Venezuela and the trading routes on the west toward the central region in Caracas, founded in 1567. To the south in the Río de la Plata, an expedition from Spain had established Buenos Aires in 1536, but the bitter hostility of the seminomadic native peoples forced starving colonists to relocate to Asunción, Paraguay, where the friendly Guaraní developed a uniquely harmonious relationship with the settlers. Only later, in 1580, did the Spanish colonists feel strong enough to reestablish Buenos Aires as a permanent settlement.

Spanish explorers continued to push into distant areas. Although the indigenous civilizations were advanced in aspects of astronomy and mathematics, they lacked basic elements of technology—in particular, the wheel and iron. Thus, hundreds of Spaniards could easily defeat tens of thousands of their opponents using steel swords, firearms, and cannons. Also, horses terrorized native peoples, who were unfamiliar with them. Even though the conquerors were only slightly better than armed civilians, with few professional soldiers among their ranks, the Spaniards' knowledge of tactics and strategy far surpassed the indigenous peoples' sometimes rudimentary conception of warfare. And the European diseases were the most terrifying weapon of all, decimating millions. Against such odds, the desperate native resistance against the invaders should evoke as much admiration as the boldness of the Spaniards in entering unknown regions.

The plight of the native peoples gave enemies of the Spanish crown ample reason to be extremely critical of the conquest and colonization of the Americas. For example, *La Leyenda Negra* (the Black Legend) attributed only great cruelty, evil, and exploitation to the Spaniards. Ironically, the Black Legend was based in part on information from missionaries such as Bartolomé de las Casas (1474–1566), who attempted to end the abuse and enslavement of the native peoples. Later, leaders of the Latin American independence movements used the Black Legend—a mixture of fact and myth—to justify revolution against the crown. More objective interpretations of this history include references to the achievements and loftier purposes of the conquest as well as to the negative impact of this encounter between cultures.

Although formal conquests had ended by 1580, the task of incorporating frontier regions was far from over. The Spanish Empire continued to grow until it reached its greatest extension in the eighteenth century.

▓ The Colonial Period

The conquerors gave their colonies such names as New Spain and New Granada, thus affirming their desire to reproduce Spanish civilization in the New World. Map 3.1 illustrates the colonial divisions. The colonies were treated as the personal possessions of the Spanish monarchs who created structures for government, the church, and the economy that essentially transplanted their European institutions into the Western Hemisphere. Hence, social classes and cultural

Map 3.1 Eighteenth-Century Colonial Latin America

values, particularly Latin American ones, emerged gradually—often with unexpected consequences.

Spain was able to duplicate its institutions and culture fairly closely in areas with scant numbers of native peoples such as along the Río de la Plata, as well as in areas where the indigenous population rapidly disappeared such as in the islands of the Caribbean. Spanish became the sole language and Hispanic practices rapidly took root. However, in areas of dense native populations, particularly central Mexico and the Peruvian highlands, the process of transmitting Hispanic structures and customs took much longer and was seldom ever completed. Where native peoples survived the ravages of war, diseases, and exploitation, they aptly selected those Spanish objects or traits most suitable for their daily lives. Native peoples quickly adopted practical materials like iron, the wheel, and wool clothing as well as the corresponding nomenclature. They came to accept selected Spanish items, customs, and terminology as integral parts of their timeless traditions. And they readily accepted some new foods (particularly, chicken, eggs, and sugar), but steadfastly refused to accept the wheat that the Spaniards so insistently imposed on them.

The Spanish *encomienda* succeeded only because the authorities based it on existing pre-Hispanic structures. Outwardly converted to Roman Catholicism, the native peoples preserved many of their spiritist beliefs within the new Christian rituals. In spite of repeated orders to use only the Spanish language in official documents, not until the 1770s did the native peoples of Mexico finally adopt the language of the conquerors for paperwork. As native rebellions became infrequent after the sixteenth century, the Spanish crown no longer saw the native peoples as a threat to Spanish rule and tolerated their failure to adopt all the new customs and official practices. As a result, indigenous populations of Mexico and Peru found themselves with a significant degree of control over precisely how they would coalesce with the Spanish world.

The Spanish government tried to prevent the rise of any group or rival institution that might challenge royal authority. This absolutist monarchy relentlessly sought to enforce its monopoly over political power in the newly conquered territories. The first urgent task of the royal government was to remove from power those men who had carried out the conquest of the New World under the sweeping authorizations that the crown itself had granted. Asserting royal power in the Caribbean and marginal areas like Panama proved easier than on the mainland where the conquerors were well entrenched. The opposition became so violent that in Peru the Pizarro family led an insurrection against Spain. The crown's obsession with absolute power triumphed in both Peru and Mexico largely because the government did not revoke the economic privileges of the original conquerors.

Throughout the colonial period, the Spanish government remained extremely reluctant to share any political power with the wealthy upper class. An unwieldy separation arose between political power and economic wealth, making colonial government ineffective and cumbersome at best as government officials—who were generally short of funds—tried to impose official policies on the wealthy upper classes. This pattern of conflict between economic and political power has continued to plague Latin American countries in the modern era. Spain left Spanish America a legacy—not of open government and consensus building, but of secrecy and absolutism.

The highest-ranking colonial official was the Spanish viceroy appointed by the crown, who, because of the slowness of communications with Spain, enjoyed powers almost comparable to those of the king. The viceroy in Mexico City had jurisdiction over North America, and the viceroy in Lima had jurisdiction over South America. The distances were too vast for the viceroys, so in the sixteenth century, Spain appointed captains general to rule over strategic regions such as Santiago, Caracas, and Havana. The captains general, who were also *peninsulares* (Spaniards) appointed by the crown, were soldiers whose military practices necessarily reinforced the authoritarian nature of colonial institutions. The decline of Peru and the increase in foreign threats convinced Spain of the need to create two new viceroyalties in the eighteenth century, one for Buenos Aires and another for Bogotá.

The colonial government was subject to much abuse and corruption. Moreover, *peninsulares* looked down on *criollos* (creoles; Europeans born in the Americas). Special privileges, called *fueros,* were granted to *peninsulares,* clergy, the military, and government officials. Although abolished in Spain in 1820, *fueros* were continued in Latin America even beyond independence. Membership in the *cabildo* (town council) usually remained the only form of political participation available to upper-class *criollos.* In addition, the centralizing tendencies of the eighteenth century came to reduce the modest authority of the municipal bodies and aroused *criollo* resentment.

The viceroys and captains general formed the executive branch of government, yet they also possessed sweeping legislative and judicial powers. The highest courts in Spanish America were the *audiencias,* whose number fluctuated around eight and whose *oidores* (judges) were *peninsulares* appointed by the crown. In effect, the *audiencia* formed the main council of the viceroy or captain general while functioning as the highest court of appeals in Spanish America (appeals later could be taken to Spain). Although most legislation came directly from the king's councils in Spain, the *audiencia* issued local laws and decrees. The principles of Roman law used in the *audiencia* simplified the application of laws at the personal level. Roman law, however, became one more vehicle through which to reinforce absolutism and impose authoritarian principles.

One of the most problematic legacies of the colonial period was the confusion among the three branches of government. The same officials, whether viceroys or judges, often performed legislative, executive, and judicial functions. By the twentieth century, Latin America was able to define the authority of the executive branch and, to a lesser degree, that of the judiciary. The failure to develop viable, independent legislatures, however, has often undermined attempts to practice democracy and has reinforced tendencies toward authoritarianism. The ongoing political implications of this colonial legacy are discussed in greater detail by Thomas J. D'Agostino in Chapter 4.

In pursuit of a policy of divide and rule, Spain created overlapping territorial jurisdictions for viceroys, captains general, and *audiencias* and also for the parallel structure of the Catholic Church. Spain successfully prevented any high royal or church official in the New World from ever challenging the authority of the crown, but it did so at the cost of increased inefficiency. The officials were more concerned with defending their power or spying on each other than with conducting government business. After independence, the vague lines separating the colonial jurisdictions led to conflicting territorial claims and border wars. Such conflicts have continued through the years, including a long-standing border dispute between Ecuador and Peru that was not peacefully settled until 1999. Tensions between Venezuela and Colombia persist, occasionally flaring up for political reasons, as evidenced in July 2010 when Colombian president Álvaro Uribe accused Venezuelan president Hugo Chávez of providing refuge to members of opposition groups, such as the Revolutionary Armed Forces of Colombia (FARC) and the National Liberation Army (ELN). Venezuela and Guyana continue to argue over the Essequibo region, a dispute that dates back to the late nineteenth century.

Spain justified its extraordinary authority over the Catholic Church on the grounds that civil and ecclesiastical officials had to function as one to carry out the vast undertaking of the military and spiritual conquest of the New World. The Catholic Church could do nothing without the approval of the crown, and the authority extended to matters of religious belief or dogma. Whatever doctrine the Pope proclaimed in Rome was valid for the New World only if the Spanish crown approved. But even after almost all of Latin America had been converted to Roman Catholicism, the government continued to preserve its authority over the church for the more blatantly political reason of allowing no rival power base to emerge. In Chapter 12, Hannah Stewart-Gambino shows how this affected the ongoing role of the church in Latin America.

Initially, the task of converting the large native populations to Catholicism was carried out with missionary zeal. The priests learned the native languages and established missions in remote areas. The idealism of the first generations of missionaries gradually waned, however. And in any case by the 1560s, few native peoples remained to be converted. Unable to enter local politics, the clergy devoted itself to the profitable management of wealth.

The Catholic Church soon owned the largest percentage of the land in Latin America and received a vast income from the properties. The money reserves accumulated, and the church's institutions became the financial lenders of the colonial period (banks did not appear until the mid-nineteenth century).

Thomas D' Agostino

*View of the Plaza de Armas and the
Cathedral of Santo Domingo in Cuzco, Peru.*

Land was the almost universal collateral, so the failure to repay loans meant the church added foreclosed property to its already enormous holdings.

The spiritual decay of the clergy caused the Spanish government, in part out of religious conviction but also to avoid any questioning of its authority, to attempt to revitalize the Catholic Church. Supported by the Spanish government, the Jesuits (members of the Roman Catholic Society of Jesus) entered Latin America in 1572. Although the Jesuits encouraged scholarship and independent thinking in their schools, the Inquisition (a special Spanish law court designed to identify heretics and "allow" them to repent or be put to death— at times by torture) severely limited intellectual activities. The Inquisition began its Latin American operations in 1569 in Lima and Mexico City and gradually opened branches in other major cities. Although staffed by clergy, the Inquisition was a governmental body that made its most valuable contribution by detecting and punishing sexual crimes by priests and other religious personnel.

This moralizing effect on the clergy, however, came at the high price of an unending series of witch hunts against ordinary people. The inquisitors eagerly searched for any signs among the local population of unusual behavior that could fall under the broad definition of heresy or "crimes against the faith." The favorite investigative techniques of the Inquisition were anonymous accusations and torture, and its jail cells were filled with supposed criminals. Although the Inquisition executed fewer than 200 men and women, its most ruinous effect was to stifle free inquiry in the New World. Because all native peoples were considered minors and not fully responsible for their actions, they were, in principle, exempt from the Inquisition's jurisdiction. However, in Mexico, some unlucky native peoples occasionally fell victim to it. The environment of fear made dissent dangerous, and the Inquisition reinforced the tendency toward absolutism. Spain accepted the Inquisition because, as an institution independent of the bishops and viceroys, it provided one more check on the government and the church in the New World. It could be argued that the Inquisition was the forerunner of the infamous secret police and intelligence services that emerged in Latin America in the early twentieth century.

Throughout colonial Latin America, both the Catholic Church and the Spanish government constructed extensive institutional structures that were supported by the material resources of the New World. The Spanish crown not only had expected the new institutions to be self-supporting but, from the start, had also demanded a major share of the wealth coming out of the New World. To extract the largest amount of wealth from the New World in the easiest way possible, the Spaniards established a colonial economy whose two foundations were the exploitation of local labor and the mining of precious metals—activities that often occurred simultaneously. In Chapter 6, Scott G. McKinney analyzes the negative impact of the colonial economy on future Latin American development.

Throughout the colonial period, gold and silver exports paid for imports from Europe and brought additional wealth to Spain. The apparently endless waves of precious metals leaving Latin America created the image of a rich paradise. Consequently, England, France, and Holland sent trading expeditions to the Caribbean from the 1530s until the 1620s. Gradually, a pattern of trade and smuggling with Europeans became an accepted practice for the Spanish American population, which sought to avoid high Spanish taxes on imported merchandise.

The decline of the Spanish Empire in the seventeenth century gave Europeans the opportunity to establish bases in many of the deserted islands of the Spanish Caribbean, starting with the British island of Barbados in 1627 and the Dutch island of Curaçao in 1634. Seduced by tales of great wealth and aware of Spanish weakness, a British force tried to capture the entire West Indies, only to meet with dismal failure in its attack on Santo Domingo. This same expedition did capture Jamaica from Spain in 1655, and this island became the staging base for subsequent British penetration into Spanish America. France also began to occupy islands in the West Indies and by 1665 had gained control of the western part of Santo Domingo, which is now Haiti.

The islands occupied by the Dutch, French, and British served as excellent ports for an extensive smuggling trade with Spanish America but, by the second half of the seventeenth century, the non-Spanish Caribbean had turned to plantation agriculture as the main source of its wealth. Examination of parallel events in Portuguese Brazil illuminates how the plantation system spread to the Caribbean.

Portuguese Brazil

During the same period when Spain conquered the West Indies, Mexico, and Central America, Portugal had barely a presence on the Brazilian coast. Pedro Cabral, leading a Portuguese fleet to India in 1500, was blown off course and landed on the coast of Brazil, which the king of Portugal decided to claim as a resupply base. Not until 1532 did the Portuguese establish the first permanent settlement at São Vicente (near present-day Santos on the Atlantic Coast). The two key elements of the Spanish American economy—precious metals and abundant indigenous labor to exploit—appeared to be lacking in Brazil. Therefore, the Portuguese, who were driven by profit and commercial concerns even more than the Spanish, invested not in the Brazilian wilderness but rather in the lucrative spice trade between Europe and the Indian Ocean.

The reddish dyes drawn from brazilwood trees were in demand in Europe, however. This attracted the French, who poached on the forests that the Portuguese crown considered its own private reserve. To repel both the French and expansionist Spanish expeditions, the Portuguese government sent the first royal governor to San Salvador in 1549. Ultimately, the Portuguese expelled the French from Rio de Janeiro. In the early seventeenth century, the French attempted to reestablish settlements on the north coast of Brazil, only to have the Portuguese push them into what is now French Guiana.

As brazilwoods became scarce due to excessive logging, expeditions called *bandeiras* set out for the interior of Brazil in search of precious metals and slaves. Initially, the *bandeiras* (whose members were called *bandeirantes*) found no precious metals and only a small number of slaves among the widely scattered native villages. Brazil found its economic salvation not in the interior, but on the coast.

Sugarcane grew well in the hot, humid lands along the Brazilian coastline. Spanish America had neglected the agricultural potential of its tropical lowlands for the sake of mining, and prices for sugar remained high in Europe. Portugal had only to draw on its prior experience with sugarcane plantations in the Atlantic islands of the Madeiras and the Cape Verdes to introduce a proven and profitable economic model into Brazil. Essentially, to supply the European demand for tropical crops—sugar in particular—Portugal imported large numbers of slaves from Africa annually to work in the sugar plantations in Brazil. Sugar and slaves remained an inseparable link during the colonial period, and the profits from the sugar exports sustained Portuguese colonization in Brazil.

Slaves and sugar made Brazil very wealthy, and many Portuguese migrated to the new country in the hope of finding fortunes. The Portuguese merchants enjoyed a monopoly (similar to Spain's in its empire) over Brazilian trade, and the Portuguese government taxed the European imports and the sugar that passed through Portugal. The rising revenues from Brazil were important to the Portuguese government, whose commercial empire in Asia was collapsing in the early seventeenth century. Henceforth, Brazil replaced Asia as the source of most of Portugal's wealth.

The Dutch, who had attempted to take over Brazil in the mid-seventeenth century, abandoned the struggle in the face of armed local resistance. The Dutch instead introduced plantation agriculture in the Caribbean as a more profitable alternative to hostile Brazil. Other European powers followed this example. In fact, British Jamaica and French Haiti became the principal sugar producers in the world. Production outpaced European demand, however. As sugar prices dropped, the sugar mills in Brazil entered a prolonged period of depression after 1680. Planters struggled to meet their loan payments in the face of rising production costs; in particular, the higher prices of imported slaves. Brazil stagnated, and Portugal suffered loss of income and revenue because of the colony's economic problems.

By 1700, the *bandeiras* had found gold deposits in the region of Minas Gerais (general mines). Mineral exports—mainly gold and, after 1729, diamonds—became the driving force behind the Brazilian economy as sugar sank to a secondary position. Plantation owners found the task of supplying their slave force much more difficult as the slave trade shifted to providing Africans for the mines.

Immigrants flocked from Portugal and other parts of Brazil to participate in the gold rushes, and the demand for food and goods in the new mining cities provided a powerful stimulus to agriculture and commerce. To supply the meat and leather, ranches pushed farther into the interior, thereby broadening the areas under effective Portuguese colonization. The gold fields were located primarily in the southern half of Brazil. In response, the Portuguese crown shifted the capital in 1763 from Salvador in the north to Rio de Janeiro in the south.

The reliance on mineral wealth made Brazil resemble Spanish America, but with the crucial difference that without a large indigenous labor force, the Brazilians had to turn to African slaves and, to a lesser degree, *mestizos* (the offspring of Europeans and Indians) to work the gold deposits. By the eighteenth century, *mestizos* had become the largest racial element in the interior whereas *mulatos* (the offspring of blacks and Europeans) had gradually become the majority racial element in the coastal sugar regions. Because of the constant arrival of new African slaves, many *mulatos* eventually acquired their freedom. In Chapter 9, Kevin A. Yelvington analyzes patterns of ethnicity and class that were set into motion during the colonial era.

Brazil faced hardships as gold output fell after 1750. To try to save the Portuguese Empire from economic collapse, the marquis of Pombal—a virtual dictator because the king had lost all interest in ruling—undertook major initiatives from 1750 to 1777. Pombal tinkered with the bureaucratic structures of the Portuguese Empire, but the very nature of his personal rule precluded any fundamental change.

The imperial bureaucracy—although never as extensive as that of Spain—continued to suffer under the weight of corruption, inefficiency, overcentralization, and conflicting jurisdictions. To increase trade between Portugal and Brazil, Pombal attempted to improve the system of annual fleets (similar to Spain's), but without success. He abolished the annual fleets in 1765, allowing individual Portuguese vessels to sail between Brazil and Portugal at any time. Similar to the Caracas Company in Spanish America, Portuguese monopoly companies failed and were abolished by 1779.

With gold exports declining, both Brazil and Portugal attempted to grow crops and manufacture products that previously had been imported. Pombal encouraged the expansion of agricultural production to include new crops such as rice, wheat, and coffee. This combination of import substitution and the development of new crops had restored Brazil to prosperity, although it always depended on the constant inflow of slaves from Africa.

During the second half of the eighteenth century, no serious challenge to Portuguese rule in Brazil appeared. To eliminate any possible rival power base, Pombal had expelled the Jesuits and confiscated their properties in 1759. In the more religious areas of Spanish America, the expulsion of the Jesuits had undermined royal authority, but this was not the case in Brazil where planters and merchants eagerly purchased most of the Jesuit lands at bargain prices. Rather than sell the lands to peasants, the Portuguese government reinforced the overconcentration of wealth in less than 1 percent of the Brazilian population.

Brazil, which did not have a single university or printing press, appeared content to remain under Portuguese rule, and the few failed conspiracies did not disrupt the colonial peace. The first plot was that of Tiradentes (Joaquim José da Silva Xavier) in 1788–1789 but, like the others, it gathered conspirators from only the lower and middle classes. Without the support of the upper class, no challenge to Portuguese rule could have been successful. After the slaves revolted in the 1791 Haitian Revolution, no planters dared to suggest any political change for fear of provoking a similar uprising among the slaves in Brazil.

▨ The Bourbon Era

The real danger of collapse made the reforms in Spanish America considerably more extensive than those of Brazil in the eighteenth century. When the last

Spanish king of the Hapsburg dynasty died without leaving an heir, European powers fought the War of the Spanish Succession to determine which royal family would occupy the Spanish throne. Spain ultimately selected a member of the Bourbons (the royal family that also ruled France under Louis XIV), hoping to avoid French invasions. Spanish America, however, was left exposed to repeated British naval attacks during the rest of the Bourbon period (1700–1808).

Fear of British attacks gave a military urgency to reforms in Spanish America, a strategic concern less prevalent in the more economically driven reforms of Portuguese Brazil. The economic dimension was no less absent in Spanish America than in Brazil, however, because of the bankruptcy of the model based on the exploitation of Amerindian and *mestizo* labor and the export of precious metals. The Bourbon reformers thus faced the double task of creating effective defense forces for the many distant frontiers of the Spanish Empire and of finding new sources of economic wealth to support the vastly enlarged military establishment.

Before the Bourbon reformers could make any changes, they needed to establish an effective government structure to carry out their orders. New institutions and new taxes were the order of the day. Spain had ruled Spanish America with institutions largely unmodified since their creation in the early sixteenth century. The Bourbons in the eighteenth century attempted to replace the original institutions with new dynamic agencies staffed largely by *peninsulares* and with the minimum possible participation by *criollos*. The old bureaucracy proved remarkably resistant, however, and the Bourbons could often do little more than add another layer of bureaucracy to these decrepit institutions.

Beginning in 1763, the combination of newly formed royal monopolies and the presence of the new intendants disrupted the existing power relationships. The new intendants, independent of the viceroys and the captains general, aggressively began to collect taxes in 1763, thereby antagonizing both elite groups and the masses. Rather than binding Spain closer to Spanish America, the intendants further strained the imperial relationship.

The intendants, viceroys, and judges of the *audiencia* all continued to mix judicial, legislative, and executive functions. Accountable only to Spain, each was, in effect, independent and could easily display despotic excesses of power. Secrecy remained the rule; only a few privileged insiders had access to information within the bureaucracy, and officials kept the public ignorant of deliberations and of many decisions. Therefore, the Bourbon reforms reinforced authoritarianism and the expectation that policies should flow from rulers rather than the people.

Although the local elites had always embraced the principle of keeping the masses out of government, the Bourbon challenge to the elites themselves engendered a struggle to preserve their influence. At the same time, the military began to function as a separate group and to feel superior to the rest of society in many ways. Ironically, the Bourbons trained the officers and soldiers who later gained great distinction in fighting against the Spaniards during the wars of independence. The role of the military in Latin America is analyzed further by Paul W. Zagorski in Chapter 5.

By 1800, it was clear that no further reforms were possible from the Bourbons who desperately attempted to retain their eroding power over Spanish America. Because of the rigid class structure and fears of unleashing a popular uprising by the masses, the elites were reluctant to defy the established authority of Spain. When it became clear that the monarchy was endangering the established order, however, the resulting stress gave the local elites the opportunity to escape once and for all—not only from the stifling Spanish commercial system, but also from the domineering royal bureaucracy.

Independence

Early Rebellions

Although the independence period formally began in 1808, in reality earlier colonial revolts and British attacks formed the opening acts of the struggle for independence. Amerindian rebellions had been frequent in the sixteenth century and had never totally ended whereas urban riots had shaken even Mexico City at times. In the late eighteenth century, however, two revolts of a magnitude previously unknown threatened to overthrow the colonial order completely.

The first occurred in the highlands of Peru and Bolivia, where native peoples and *mestizos* rose up in November 1780 to overthrow corrupt officials and abolish the new taxes of the Bourbons. The leader of the uprising was a *mestizo* merchant who, as a descendant of the last Incan emperor, took the name Túpac Amaru II. In an attempt to rally the native masses behind him, Túpac Amaru II declared himself king, but never declared independence from Spain. This unclear position undermined his support among Spanish Americans and many *mestizos*. The fighting soon degenerated into a war of racial extermination against the white *criollos,* who joined with the Spanish forces to crush this bloody insurrection by the end of 1781.

In contrast with the huge number of casualties in Peru, the rebellion in Colombia was relatively bloodless and lacked the racial overtones that had generated so much hatred. As in Peru, the revolt in Colombia was caused by popular opposition to the tax policies of the Bourbons, but the native population was considerably smaller than that in Peru, so *mestizos* and *criollos* made up the bulk of the rebels, who called themselves *comuneros*. During mass rallies in March 1781, the townspeople chose leaders to call for repeal of the new taxes. The movement spread like wildfire, and soon a huge crowd was marching on the capital city of Bogotá.

The Spanish government kept almost all of its forces near the coast, especially in the fortress city of Cartagena, as a defense against foreign attack; thus, the military could not quell the revolt. Consequently, on June 4, 1781, the *audiencia* in Bogotá caved in and granted the demand of the *comuneros* to repeal the taxes. The crowds dispersed, and with the exception of one rebel leader, who was later captured and executed, the movement was over.

Whereas in Colombia the revolt had taught the upper class how easily Spanish rule could be overthrown, in Peru the lesson learned was that any change in government released bitter class and racial hatreds. Thus, while the upper class in Colombia remained open-minded about exploring new political alternatives if the opportunity arose, the upper class in Peru was so obsessed with its very survival that it resisted any attempt to change the political status. These contrasting attitudes in Colombia and Peru later played a major role in shaping events during South America's struggle for independence.

External Influences

By 1800, the economic significance of Latin America to much of Europe had diminished. Nevertheless, the promise of wealth and plenty persisted for the British, who maintained their designs of conquering the region's mineral wealth. The outbreak of the French Revolution in 1789 ended Spain's alliance with the French Bourbons who were overthrown, and Spain joined England in a coalition that attempted to destroy revolutionary France. Fear of French armies compelled the Spanish government—foolishly—to switch sides and to return to an alliance with France in 1796. Once again, to safeguard Spain's frontiers, the government was willing to expose Spanish America to British attacks.

British warships began to raid many coastal ports, and old plans to capture Panama and other strategic points resurfaced. A British expedition captured the ill-defended island of Trinidad near the coast of Venezuela in 1797, but failed miserably against the determined opposition of the new militias in the fortress city of San Juan, Puerto Rico. The most significant British attack came in 1806, when a British force captured Buenos Aires after royal officials—including the viceroy—fled in panic rather than face the advancing British troops. The *criollos* were shocked by the disgraceful performance of the royal officials, and the local militias decided to avenge the dishonor by secretly organizing the expulsion of the British troops, who surrendered when surprised by the unexpected *criollo* attack. A second British expedition had come too late to save the garrison, but it did attempt to recapture Buenos Aires in 1807. The assault was unsuccessful, and determined resistance by well-prepared militias persuaded the British commanders to abandon the attack.

The British continental offensive had barely dented the outer defenses of Spanish America, whose protection depended not on the inefficient institutions of a corrupt empire, but rather on the dedication and discipline of the new militia units. Military power had passed imperceptibly into the hands of the *criollos* under the Bourbons. Thus, the transfer of political power to the *criollos* who already dominated the economy could not be far away. It later came as no surprise that Buenos Aires was the first region to throw off Spanish rule permanently.

Moreover, news of events in other parts of the world filtered in, despite the attempts of the Inquisition and the Spanish government to keep subversive ideas out of the region. After 1783, US ships engaged in smuggling brought news of US independence and ideas about how to set up a constitutional republic, thereby destroying the myth that a country in the Western Hemisphere could not exist without support from Europe.

The 1789 French Revolution seemed to offer a compelling example for all of Latin America, although the upper classes quickly tempered their revolutionary enthusiasm when the slaves in the French colony of Saint-Domingue rose up and eventually established Haiti, the first black republic in the Western Hemisphere in 1804. The landholders and miners in Latin America would not rush into independence because of fear of triggering social revolts, but no lingering attachment to the old colonial order would deter them from taking advantage of a favorable opportunity to gain control over the political structures in their regions.

The decay of Spanish institutions was pervasive and reached right up to the king and the royal family, who foolishly allowed themselves to be taken prisoners by the French. Napoleon Bonaparte attempted to place his brother on the throne of Spain, but the Spanish people indignantly rejected the new French ruler and began popular uprisings on May 2, 1808. Meanwhile, throughout Spain a large number of regional *juntas,* or governing boards, appeared to rule in the name of the captive Spanish king, Ferdinand VII.

Loyalty to the crown, the last cement bonding the Spanish Empire together dissolved as competing groups attempted to fill the power vacuum left by the capture of the royal family. French armies continued their relentless advance through Spain, until only the junta in Cádiz was left to defy Napoleon. Spanish America had watched these incredible events closely and finally, in the summer of 1810, the elites in Bogotá, Caracas, Buenos Aires, and Santiago decided to overthrow the royal officials and establish governing juntas of Spanish Americans. In other places, particularly Havana and Mexico City, elites had tried to establish their own juntas, but had failed because of fear of unleashing revolts by the black slaves in Cuba or the native and *mestizo* masses in Mexico.

The Wars Against Spain

The independence of Spanish America began without bloodshed, but the struggle soon turned into bitter and constant warfare that devastated large areas for over a decade. These independence movements are illustrated on Maps 3.2 and 3.3. The juntas tried to ease the transition by not declaring independence immediately and maintaining the fiction that they too ruled in the name of the captive Ferdinand VII, but even this concession failed to calm diehard royalists who soon started revolts against the juntas.

Caracas proclaimed itself a republic in 1811, but the next year it was recaptured by royalist forces. Simón Bolívar attempted to reestablish the republic, but a brutal royalist campaign ended Venezuelan independence in 1814. In Bogotá, Buenos Aires, and Santiago, internal quarrels and even civil wars divided the *criollos* who wasted the opportunity to drive the *peninsulares* from their last strongholds in Peru, Bolivia, and Uruguay.

Meanwhile, in Mexico a different type of independence struggle had erupted. When the elite in Mexico City threw away the opportunity to establish its own junta, the initiative passed to provincial groups. Without access to the levers of power in Mexico City, the plotters in the provinces counted on a movement of Amerindian and *mestizos* to overthrow Spanish rule. On September 16, 1810, Spanish American priest Miguel Hidalgo—a key plotter— sounded the church bells to urge his parishioners to join the rebellion, which spread rapidly throughout nearby provinces. At the last moment, however, Hidalgo turned his huge forces (more a mob than an army) away from Mexico City and toward Guadalajara. The failure to capture the capital gave the Spanish government time to regroup and to regain the full support of the upper-class Mexicans who had panicked when Hidalgo's forces engaged in wholesale slaughter of all whites, whether *criollos* or *peninsulares.*

Hidalgo was soon defeated, captured, and executed, but the insurrection continued under *mestizo* priest José María Morelos. Defeated in formal battles, the Mexicans adopted guerrilla warfare against the Spanish armies whose morale began to suffer under the constant campaigning and the effects of tropical diseases. The capture and execution of Morelos in 1815 did not end the popular insurrection, and Mexican guerrillas continued to harass the increasingly exhausted Spanish troops. Meanwhile, the efforts of the royal government to collect more taxes to pay for the large counterinsurgency army only increased resentment of Spanish rule. The Spanish government appeared to have clung to power in Mexico, but its control rested on disintegrating foundations.

The defeat of Napoleon in 1814 brought Ferdinand VII back to the Spanish throne and also released large numbers of Spanish veterans for the campaign of reconquest. Spanish battalions had contributed to the defeat of Hidalgo in Mexico, but counterinsurgency campaigns did not seem very glamorous to the Spanish government, which decided instead to pursue a grand strategy against the independent countries of South America. First, an expedition sailed from Spain to the Caribbean to crush the last patriot strongholds in Venezuela and then to reoccupy Colombia. Afterward, this force would then join Spanish forces in Peru to make a final push down the Andes to press the forces in

ATLANTIC OCEAN

UNITED STATES

THE FLORIDAS
· Ceded to the United States in 1821.

TEXAS

Chihuchua

MEXICO

Havana

CUBA

HAITI
· Gained independence from France in 1804.

HIDALGO
· 1810-1811

Dolores

Mexico

CENTRAL AMERICAN FEDERATION

MORELOS
· 1812-1815

BRAZIL
· Seat of king of Portugal, 1808-1821.
· Became independent empire, 1822-1889.

MEXICO AND CENTRAL AMERICA
· Independence won in 1821.
· Central American states annexed to
  Iturbide's Mexican Empire in 1822;
  rebelled against Mexico in 1823
  and formed a loosely united
  Central American Federation.

Ciudad Bolívar

COLOMBIA

GUIANA

Quito
Guayaquil

BOLÍVAR
· Liberator of Venezuela,
  Colombia, Ecuador &
  Peru, 1812-1825.

EMPIRE OF BRAZIL

PERU

BOLÍVAR

BATTLE OF AYACUCHO
· Assured the freedom
  of Spanish America,
  Dec. 9, 1824.

Ayacucho
Pisco

SAN MARTÍN

BOLIVIA

Sucre

BOLIVIA
· Independence proclaimed 1825.

PARAGUAY
Asunción

PACIFIC OCEAN

SAN MARTÍN
· Liberator of Chile and Peru, 1817-1822.

UNITED PROVINCES

Mendoza

PARAGUAY
· Declared independence
  from Spain and Buenos
  Aires, 1810-1811.

N
W   E
S

Valparaiso
Santiago

Buenos Aires

BUENOS AIRES
· Repudiated Joseph Bonaparte
  on May 25, 1810.
· Independence of the "United
  Provinces of South America"
  declared on July 9, 1816.

URUGUAY
· Artigas, the "Father of Uruguayan
  Independence," led fight against
  Spain but was blocked by jealousy
  of Brazil and Buenos Aires, 1811.

Map 3.2 Early Independence Movements

ATLANTIC OCEAN

UNITED STATES

MEXICO

Gulf of Mexico

CUBA
- Acquired from Spain by the United States in 1898.
- Assumed independence in 1902.

PUERTO RICO
- Acquired from Spain by the United States in 1898.

HAITI

JAMAICA (1962)

BELIZE

HONDURAS

GUATEMALA

NICARAGUA

EL SALVADOR

PANAMA

COSTA RICA

DOMINICAN REPUBLIC
- After struggles with France, Spain, and Haiti, won freedom in 1844.

CENTRAL AMERICAN FEDERATION
- 1823-1838.

**GUATEMALA
HONDURAS
EL SALVADOR
NICARAGUA
COSTA RICA**
- Emerge as sovereign states 1838.

PANAMA
- Won freedom from Colombia and became a republic in 1903.

VENEZUELA

GUIANA

COLOMBIA

ECUADOR

PERU

BRAZIL

BOLIVIA

PACIFIC OCEAN

N
W E
S

CHILE

PARAGUAY

ARGENTINA

URUGUAY
- After occupation by Brazil in 1817 and the war between Argentina and Brazil, became independent in 1828.

Map 3.3 Later Independence Movements

Buenos Aires from the north, which then would be struck from the sea by a second force sailing directly from Spain. Pablo Morillo, who imagined himself to be another Cortés, led this huge Spanish expedition that first subdued Venezuelan resistance and then sailed to Colombia and landed off the coast of Cartagena in 1815. In a supreme irony, the Spaniards, who had spent entire fortunes to build this fortress city, had to lay siege to Cartagena, which surrendered only because its defenders were starving. The Colombians, who were too divided among themselves, could put up no significant resistance, and Morillo had soon reestablished Spanish rule in Bogotá and throughout Colombia. Meanwhile Spanish forces in Peru had managed on their own to reconquer Chile in 1814 so, by 1816, of all the original independent areas, only Buenos Aires remained under patriot control. Buenos Aires too expected land attacks from the Andes Mountains and a sea invasion from Spain at any moment.

Before Spain could complete the reconquest of Buenos Aires, Bolívar returned from exile to Venezuela and raised a patriot army in the plains of the Orinoco River in 1816. Morillo was forced to postpone his plans to march against Buenos Aires until he could destroy Bolívar's forces. In Venezuela, Colombia, and Chile, the *criollos* had come to hate Spanish rule. The Spanish government, rather than seeking a reconciliation, had become more inflexible than ever. Ferdinand VII and Morillo not only refused to share any power with the *criollos,* but also took economic and political reprisals against all those who had participated in the independent regimes.

Spanish control rested only on brute force. Both Bolívar in Venezuela and José de San Martín in Argentina saw the chance to end Spanish rule once and for all through brilliant military moves. Bolívar left behind some troops to distract Spanish forces in Venezuela while he marched with his main army westward across the plains into the Andes of Colombia. His flanking march came as a total surprise and, after several engagements, he decisively defeated the Spanish army in the Battle of Boyacá in August 1819.

All of Colombia fell under patriot control and, with these larger resources, Bolívar led an expedition to drive the Spaniards out of Venezuela. This more difficult task was completed only after his troops had defeated the Spaniards in the Battle of Carabobo in June 1821. Bolívar sent another force south to expel the Spaniards from Ecuador, which joined the union of Colombia and Venezuela proclaimed in 1821. Panama, the best transit point for moving troops from the Caribbean to the Pacific Coast, had also joined the new country.

The areas of South America still under Spanish control continued to shrink not only because of Bolívar's actions, but also because of a separate campaign conducted by the Argentine San Martín who adopted a new strategy to protect Argentina from an expected Spanish invasion. Previous attempts to march north directly into Peru had failed. Instead, San Martín decided to march across the Andes to surprise the Spaniards in Chile before sailing by ship to attack the lightly defended coast of Peru.

After over a year of preparing an army on the Argentine side, San Martín crossed the Andes and defeated the Spaniards in several battles, until the last one at Maipú in 1818 ended Spanish rule in Chile. He formed a navy with British sailors and ships, and his new fleet took the army to Peru and captured Lima in 1821. The Spanish troops had merely withdrawn into the interior highlands, however, and Bolívar took over the task of destroying the last Spanish forces in South America. With the resources of Colombia, Venezuela, and Ecuador at his disposal, Bolívar arrived with a considerable force. Extensive fighting ensued but finally, in December 1824, the patriot forces defeated the last Spanish army at Ayacucho. Spanish rule had completely ended throughout South America.

Mexican independence took place in a rather sudden, but almost inevitable manner. In 1820, Ferdinand VII gathered a second expedition in Cádiz to attack Buenos Aires. A mutiny, however, forced the king to hand over power to a liberal government in Spain. By then, the Spanish forces in Mexico had become thoroughly demoralized by the unceasing guerrilla war, and the Mexican population saw the coming to power of the liberal government in Spain as an excuse to stop paying the large war taxes.

The royal government in Mexico was disintegrating but, unlike the case in 1810 when the elites missed an opportunity to take power, this time Agustín de Iturbide, the *criollo* commander of the army in Mexico, was the right person to achieve independence. The rebels who had fought against Spanish rule were brought into the movement and, without firing a shot, Iturbide was able to proclaim Mexico's independence on September 28, 1821. Only the Spanish garrison in the main fortress of Veracruz refused to obey Iturbide's orders and did not accept Mexican control until 1823.

Central America, which traditionally had enjoyed close links to Mexico, was sufficiently impressed to break its ties with Spain and join the new Mexican Empire in 1821. Thus, all of mainland Spanish America—from Mexico to Argentina and including Chile, Peru, Colombia, Central America, and Venezuela—had gained permanent independence from Spain. All that remained of the Spanish Empire were the islands of Cuba and Puerto Rico in the Caribbean and the distant Philippine Islands in the extreme western Pacific. Spain retained these territories until 1898.

Brazilian Independence

Brazil, with its large slave masses toiling in the gold mines and sugar plantations, was the least likely candidate for independence. If Cuba—with the largest number of slaves in Spanish America—had remained under Spanish dominance, then fear of slave rebellions promised to keep Brazil under Portuguese rule for a long time. However, as in the case of Spanish America, actions in Europe unleashed a chain of events that finally culminated in Brazil's independence from

Portugal. Although Napoleon was unable to capture the royal family as he had done in Spain, the entire Portuguese government had to flee to Brazil in November 1807, just a few days before French armies approached Lisbon, the Portuguese capital.

British warships escorted the Portuguese royal family to Brazil until it was safely established in Rio de Janeiro, which, in effect, became the capital of the Portuguese Empire. This was the only time in history that a government in Latin America ruled over colonies; in this case, the Portuguese territories in Asia and Africa. The British wanted favors in return, and Portuguese ruler Dom João complied by opening Brazilian ports to direct trade with the British.

Dom João was so happy in Rio de Janeiro that he refused to return to Portugal, even after Napoleon had been decisively defeated in 1815. Furthermore, he formally ended Brazil's colonial status when he proclaimed the country to be a "coequal kingdom" with the same rank as Portugal.

The printing press finally came to Brazil and, for the first time, the king established institutions such as academies, universities, and the Bank of Brazil. The Brazilian elite were delighted to have its king nearby and shared enthusiastically in the prosperity and feeling of progress that existed during the 1810s.

A revolt in 1820 brought a new government to power in Portugal, which demanded that Dom João return to Lisbon. In a vain attempt to preserve the political unity of the Portuguese Empire, the king agreed. He left his son, Dom Pedro, behind and told him to declare Brazil independent if the necessity arose. When Dom João arrived in Portugal, the government was outraged to find that he had left his son behind. Lisbon not only insisted on Dom Pedro's prompt return, but also began to strip Brazil of many of the privileges Dom João had granted. Portugal was determined to reduce Brazil to colonial status, but the Brazilian elite was not about to surrender its newly gained influence.

With the full support of the Brazilian elite, on January 9, 1822, Dom Pedro refused to obey the order to return to Portugal. Events flowed forward with an air of inevitability until Brazil's independence was proclaimed on September 7, 1822. The Brazilian elite rallied behind Dom Pedro, and only some isolated Portuguese garrisons briefly resisted the proclamation of the Brazilian Empire.

Troops from poverty-stricken Portugal deserted almost as soon as they landed, making any Portuguese reconquest of Brazil pointless. In contrast to the experience of Spanish America, Brazil had achieved independence with almost no bloodshed so the country escaped both the destruction of war and the legacy of a large military establishment. Unlike Spanish America, which disintegrated into many rival nations, Brazil—under the unifying force of a traditional monarchy—remained a single country in spite of repeated regional revolts. The Brazilian monarchy inherited the existing structure of government and retained the overwhelming majority of officials in their posts, unlike the countries in Spanish America where Spain's more extensive colonial bureaucracy usually failed to survive independence. Clearly, Brazil enjoyed distinct advantages in the challenging task of creating a new government and, at the least, seemed to have escaped the worst ravages of its Spanish American neighbors.

Conclusion

The early-nineteenth-century independence of Spain's and Portugal's vast colonial territories carries great historical significance in the emergence and subsequent evolution of Latin American countries. Three centuries of dominance were followed by the elimination of two great colonial empires from the Western Hemisphere.

Although the *peninsulares* lost power to the *criollos,* independence did not result in democratic government. Native peoples, persons of African descent, and *mestizos* did not benefit; the successful slave revolt in Haiti and the native rebellion led by Hidalgo were exceptions. Liberation allowed for expanded US, British, and French trade and investment. Hence, the newly developing Latin American economies came increasingly under the control of foreign investors. *Caudillismo* (rule by military dictatorship), civil war, anarchy, and foreign intervention in the lengthy period immediately following independence and subsequent government instability reveal the perseverance of the strong colonial impact as well as modern Latin America's difficulty in developing alternative stabilizing systems.

Conquest allowed European institutions to be transplanted in the distant territories of the New World. As in most experiments in colonial governance, political, economic, and social systems were modified by indigenous cultures, thereby producing innovative patterns. In the case of the Americas, Eurocentric societies were influenced by indigenous and African traditions. Conditioned by both integrative and disintegrative forces, the resulting fusion became known as Latin America.

The absolutist and centralized political tradition Spain transferred to Latin America continues to be manifested, even during a period of supposed democratization, in a strong tendency toward authoritarianism. This tendency had been bolstered by moral and theoretical foundations provided through the church as an instrument of the state. The power of the church and the importance of land ownership continued after independence. In effect, the separation from Spain and Portugal, far from initiating a liberal social revolution, left intact the transplanted conservative triumvirate of power: the church, the military, and the *criollo* oligarchy.

Attempts to hold on to privilege and the status quo, however, produced great political instability in the absence of a unifying central authority, such as that previously provided by the crown. Rival *caudillos* and elite factions entered into open conflict. The institutions transferred through conquest and colonialism persevered, but were highly problematic in light of changes set into motion by the new political, social, and economic imperatives of independence.

In Chapter 4, Thomas J. D'Agostino discusses the ongoing effects on politics of this historical background. In this context, it is important to remember the profound impact of the conquest and colonization periods in the evolution of contemporary Latin America.

▩ Bibliography

Bethell, Leslie, ed. *Cambridge History of Latin America,* 8 vols. Cambridge: Cambridge University Press, 1985–ongoing.

Boyer, Richard, and Geoffrey Spurling. *Colonial Lives: Documents on Latin American History.* New York: Oxford University Press, 1999.

Brown, Jonathan C. *Latin America: A Social History of the Colonial Period,* 2nd ed. Orlando, FL: Harcourt, 2004.

Burkholder, Mark A., and Lyman L. Johnson. *Colonial Latin America,* 7th ed. New York: Oxford University Press, 2010.

Burns, E. Bradford. *A History of Brazil,* 3rd ed. New York: Columbia University Press, 1993.

Bushnell, David. *The Making of Modern Colombia: A Nation in Spite of Itself.* Berkeley: University of California Press, 1993.

Haring, Clarence C. *The Spanish Empire in America.* New York: Harcourt Brace, 1985.

Hillman, Richard S. *Democracy for the Privileged: Crisis and Transition in Venezuela.* Boulder: Lynne Rienner, 1994.

Keen, Benjamin, and Keith Hayes. *A History of Latin America,* 8th ed. Boston: Houghton Mifflin, 2009.

Klein, Herbert S. *Bolivia: The Evolution of a Multi-Ethnic Society,* 2nd ed. New York: Oxford University Press, 1992.

Knight, Allan. *Mexico: The Colonial Era.* New York: Cambridge University Press, 2002.

Knight, Franklin W. *The Caribbean: The Genesis of a Fragmented Nationalism,* 2nd ed. New York: Oxford University Press, 1990.

Lockhart, James. *The Nahuas After the Conquest: A Social and Cultural History of the Indians of Central Mexico, Sixteenth Through Eighteenth Centuries.* Stanford: University of California Press, 1994.

Meyer, Michael C., William L. Sherman, and Susan M. Deeds. *The Course of Mexican History,* 8th ed. New York: Oxford University Press, 2006.

Mills, Kenneth, William B. Taylor, and Sandra Lauderdale Graham. *Colonial Latin America: A Documentary History.* Wilmington, DE: Scholarly Resources, 2002.

Pérez, Louis A., Jr. *Cuba: Between Reform and Revolution,* 3rd ed. New York: Oxford University Press, 2006.

Stavig, Ward. *The World of Túpac Amaru: Conflict, Community, and Identity in Colonial Peru.* Lincoln: University of Nebraska Press, 1999.

Woodward, Ralph Lee, Jr. *Central America: A Nation Divided,* 3rd ed. New York: Oxford University Press, 2001.

4

Latin American Politics

Thomas J. D'Agostino

Contemporary Latin America continues to experience profound transformations, most recently as manifested in a distinctly leftward political drift in a number of countries and general economic malaise associated with global recession. Although the region can be distinguished from most other developing areas by virtue of its significant advances in industrialization, urbanization, education, health care, and per capita income, we should not lose sight of the enduring legacy of Latin America's colonial past, described by René de la Pedraja in Chapter 3. The values and institutions transplanted by the European powers during more than three centuries of colonial rule have been remarkably resilient. As they have been adapted to fit new realities, the region's dual political currents of traditional authoritarianism and emerging democracy have been blended and partially reconciled. The recurring clashes between the old and the new, between tradition and modernity, have done much to shape the political systems found throughout Latin America today.

As Scott G. McKinney shows in Chapter 6, the dramatic economic changes engendered through rapid modernization have had far-reaching social and political implications. The region's political history has been characterized by governments of virtually every conceivable type: monarchies, *caudillo* rule ("man on horseback"; a strong leader, often a military figure, who dominates politics through the use of force), populist regimes, oligarchic democracy, civilian and military dictatorships, revolutionary systems, Westminster-style parliamentary democracy, and bureaucratic-authoritarian states. Over the past generation, there has been a near universal movement toward democratic civilian rule, with Cuba the lone exception. Despite the protracted socioeconomic crisis of the "lost decade" of the 1980s, the transition from authoritarian rule generated great expectations among observers and mass publics alike. Support for democratic elections, civil liberties, and greater pluralism has increased, even as the region has endured turmoil stemming from the implementation of neoliberal economic reforms and the fallout of the global financial crisis in the late 2000s. Nevertheless, the prevailing optimism has given way to the realization that the task of regime consolidation is far from complete. Indeed, the challenges confronting Latin American leaders are daunting and the perception held by some observers in the mid-1990s that democracy was "on trial" (Wiarda 1995) still holds true today.

As a result, the sustainability of democracy in the region remains in question. Despite widespread support for democratic principles, mass satisfaction with the institutions of liberal democracy generally has been low (Peeler 2009). Among other things, the implementation of painful economic reforms mandated by international lenders—often by leaders who campaigned against such policies—has severely undermined support for political parties, legislatures, and elected leaders. Mounting cynicism and frustration has sparked a decided shift to the left in Latin American politics, leading to the emergence of populist leaders whose actions have eroded the quality of liberal democracy in some countries (Weyland 2010). Will the left prove any more effective than their predecessors in ameliorating endemic problems and fulfilling the heightened expectations of increasingly mobilized publics?

Just three decades ago, most Latin Americans were ruled by authoritarian military regimes. That nascent democratic systems have endured (if not flourished) amidst socioeconomic crises and political turmoil is remarkable, yet recent experiences demonstrate that democracy in Latin America, while resilient, is also fragile (Millett 2009; Peeler 2009; Pérez and Holmes 2009). What has enabled democracy to survive and what are its greatest threats today? Is the current era of democratization an indication of genuine maturation and political evolution or merely another phase in the historical alternation of democratic and authoritarian impulses? What must be done to avert yet another devolution to authoritarianism?

Clearly, some countries have made greater strides than others in the process of democratic consolidation. In an area as diverse as Latin America, the experiences of and prospects for different countries vary considerably. Latin America is a region composed of disparate states with divergent colonial heritages, constitutional and cultural traditions, institutional structures, and levels of socioeconomic modernization (see Appendix 1 and Appendix 2). However, such differences, which have contributed to the tendency in the literature to segregate analyses of subregions defined largely by cultural and linguistic criteria, must not obscure common patterns of political evolution in the region (Hillman and D'Agostino 1992). Illuminating these commonalities as they pertain to contemporary politics and addressing the aforementioned questions is the dual focus of this chapter.

▨ The Postindependence Era

The three decades following the independence of the former Spanish colonies were characterized by economic stagnation and political turmoil. The break from Spain did not entail any fundamental socioeconomic or political transformation because the wars for independence were essentially conservative movements intended to preserve the existing structure of society and to forestall radical change. Hence, the rigid two-class hierarchical structure remained in place, with the *criollos* replacing the *peninsulares*. In fact, many colonial institutions and practices endured—including authoritarian, centralized top-down rule—well into the postindependence era. Independence removed the crown, however, the only viable form of centralized political authority the area had known. Unlike Brazil (which retained the monarchy and its centralizing presence following independence in 1822) and the Caribbean region (most of which remained under European control for some time, including the Spanish colonies of Cuba and Puerto Rico), Spanish America was basically left to its own devices. In the absence of a strong, unifying central authority and given the economic devastation wrought by the wars, the nascent Latin American states were ill-prepared for independence and the arduous process of nation building.

The most problematic challenges included determining how the newly independent countries were to be governed and, subsequently, establishing order and consolidating national authority. Although virtually all of the constitutions written after independence embraced democratic principles, they also included provisions for maintaining the power and privileges of traditional corporate groups, such as the church and the military, and for ensuring the dominance of the executive branch (Wiarda 1995:53). Early efforts to promote democracy were further constrained by the absence of a democratic tradition in the region and the dearth of viable democratic institutions. The failure of these efforts underscored the difficulty of grafting a democratic political framework onto societies with deeply rooted authoritarian heritages and rigid, bifurcated social structures. At the same time, efforts to promote other forms of governance and to maintain stability at the national level were largely ineffective. Notable exceptions included Brazil, with its centralized monarchy, and Chile, where the early development of a system of oligarchical rule paved the way for a long tradition of stable constitutional government.

Few other countries, however, were able to keep in check the powerful disintegrative forces brought on by the removal of the crown. A vacuum of power and legitimacy at the national level contributed to the devolution of power to rival regional *caudillos* or competing elites. In some countries, the early independence era was marked by an intense struggle for control over national resources among rival *caudillos* and elites who alternated in power. In other cases, virtual anarchy gave rise to the emergence of powerful national *caudillos,* who came to dominate their respective countries in the initial stages of independence. Among the most notorious of these figures was Antonio López de Santa Ana of Mexico, whose leadership exacerbated political turmoil and brought the country into a conflict with the United States that resulted in Mexico's humiliating military defeat and loss of substantial territory. Similarly, through a mix of *personalismo* (the dominance of the individual in politics), strong-arm rule, and repression, Juan Manuel de Rosas came to dominate Argentine politics from 1835 to 1852. Although Rosas provided some degree of order in a deeply divided country plagued by regional disputes, his dictatorial style of rule failed to lay the groundwork for long-term stability. In fact, although often viewed as a "necessary evil" in societies characterized by disarray and fragmentation, *caudillo* rule perpetuated the institutional void by inhibiting the formation of new institutions. As Latin America embarked on the second half of the nineteenth century, the need for more permanent institutional arrangements was clear.

Although a modicum of order had been established by the mid-1800s, national politics throughout Latin America remained highly contentious. Loosely organized "political parties," typically called Conservatives and Liberals, emerged among the elite in the decades following independence. Beyond the primary distinctions that revolved around Liberal support for free trade, federalism, and the separation of church and state as compared with Conservative support for trade protectionism, centralization of authority, and the maintenance of traditional church power, little distinguished these groupings ideologically. The competition for power, however, was intense and often violent. At stake was access to resources with which to reward supporters through patronage. Although the seemingly perpetual conflict inhibited national development early on, by 1850 signs of economic growth were appearing. Spurred by the Industrial Revolution in Western Europe and North America, an influx of foreign investment, primarily British, stimulated the expansion of national industries and economic infrastructure, all of which served to integrate Latin America into the emerging global economy as an exporter of raw materials and agricultural products. As the latter part of the nineteenth century reveals, socioeconomic modernization had profound political implications.

▒ Early Modernization and Dictatorial Rule

As the international demand for primary products increased, Latin American leaders sought to establish governmental systems capable of providing the stability needed to sustain the export model of development. Howard J. Wiarda (1995:60) identifies two general patterns that emerged during the late nineteenth century. In certain countries, including Chile, Brazil, and Argentina, the conservative oligarchy consolidated an exclusionary system of rule designed to preserve its interests. The merging of the commercial elite with the traditional landed elite enhanced their ability to confront the challenge posed by the middle sectors and working classes spawned by economic modernization and, in some cases, such as Argentina, by the massive influx of European immigrants. Ultimately, the system of oligarchic rule would give way under pressures for change engendered through rapid modernization.

Elsewhere, a second pattern of rule emerged that relied on a familiar method of maintaining stability: highly centralized, personalistic *caudillo* leadership. Often referred to as "order and progress dictators," leaders such as Juan Vicente Gómez of Venezuela, Ulises Heureaux of the Dominican Republic, and Porfirio Díaz of Mexico imposed an environment of passivity and stability that attracted foreign investors eager to open Latin America to the world. These regimes benefited from the transfer of capital and technology from countries such as Britain and, increasingly, the United States. The most successful of these regimes was that of Mexico's Díaz who dominated national politics from 1876 to 1910.

The Case of Mexico

Following its protracted struggle for independence from Spain (1810–1822), Mexico endured decades of political strife and economic stagnation as disputes between rival elite groups (Conservatives and Liberals) undermined efforts to forge a national consensus. The death in 1872 of popular Liberal reformer Benito Júarez paved the way for Porfirio Díaz to seize power in 1876. Determined to modernize the country, Díaz struck a resonant chord within a society weary of chronic conflict and instability. Through his policy of *pan o palo* (bread or the stick), Díaz rewarded his supporters while harshly suppressing opponents. The federal army and the *rurales* (rural police) enforced the regime's dictates, bringing the country under the control of the central government. Attracted by the promise of order and incentives offered by the Díaz regime, investors pumped in more capital, spurring economic growth and providing the government with resources to reward its supporters or, conversely, to bolster the repressive capacity of the state.

Mexico under Díaz experienced unprecedented political stability and extraordinary industrial and infrastructural development as railroads, ports, and electrification facilities were established. The successful promotion of "order and progress," however, which had eluded Mexico since independence, came at great cost. Critics charged Díaz with compromising Mexico's sovereignty by allowing foreign control of key sectors of the economy. Indeed, development came about largely under the auspices of European and US investors, who reaped enormous profits by exploiting Mexican labor and natural resources, particularly oil. Thus, such progress was achieved mainly at the expense of the masses and served to exacerbate the inequality between, on the one hand, *campesinos* (peasants) whose land was often confiscated to boost export production and laborers whose wages were kept low to enhance profits, and, on the other, members of the domestic elite who profited from their association with foreign investors (Meyer and Sherman 1995:487–488).

Development also occurred at the expense of basic freedoms that had been established under the progressive leadership of Júarez during the era of La Reforma (the reform). Although many in Mexico initially embraced Díaz's authoritarian rule, his regime grew increasingly repressive and dictatorial. In a pattern replicated throughout the region in the early 1900s, socioeconomic development engendered pressure for political change, most notably among the emerging middle sectors. In an ironic twist (one that would plague other Latin American modernizers), the success with which Díaz was able to promote "order and progress" ultimately sowed the seeds of his regime's demise. His highly personalized, dictatorial style of rule grew increasingly untenable amid the profound changes brought on by rapid modernization.

By 1930, these changes had undermined the old oligarchic order and facilitated the rise of middle-class politics in Latin America. In some cases, such as in Argentina and Chile, this clash between the forces of tradition and modernity was resolved relatively peacefully, and the transition occurred through electoral means. In Mexico, however, Díaz's unwillingness to accommodate demands for political reform set the stage for the greatest upheaval in twentieth-century Latin America: the Mexican Revolution.

Although it began largely as an expression of middle-class disaffection with the Díaz regime, the conflict that engulfed Mexico from 1910 to 1917 evolved into a mass rebellion that claimed over 1 million lives. In the end, Mexico had experienced tumultuous change, yet continuity with the past remained.

Despite a pledge to step down at the end of his term in 1910, Díaz was again fraudulently elected. His primary opposition, Francisco Madero, challenged Díaz's *continuismo* (the practice of extending one's term in office beyond constitutional limits) under the banner of "effective suffrage and no reelection." Unable to bring about political change through constitutional means, Madero fled to the United States where in October 1910 he called on Mexicans to rebel against the dictatorship. What followed was a broad-based rebellion composed of disparate groups united in their opposition to Díaz. The defeat of federal forces at the Battle of Ciudad Júarez and Díaz's resignation on May 25, 1911, marked the end of an era but not the end of the conflict in Mexico.

Madero won the 1911 election, but divisions soon appeared within the revolutionary coalition, dooming his presidency. Although Madero's call to arms against Díaz marked the beginning of the revolution, his objectives once in power were far from revolutionary. Madero set his sights on political reform and attempted to introduce a more open, democratic system in Mexico. His reforms failed to address the primary concerns of the peasants, however, who took up arms in the name of land reform under the leadership of Emiliano Zapata. For the vast majority of Mexicans, "effective suffrage and no reelection" had little meaning (Meyer and Sherman 1995:536). The conservative elites viewed Madero with suspicion, concerned that their power and privileges might be threatened. Madero's inability to appease either the masses or the elites sparked renewed conflict, culminating with an uprising in Mexico City in February 1913, during which Madero was overthrown and subsequently executed.

The ascension of Victoriano Huerta, a supporter of Díaz who sought to reassert centralized authoritarian rule, signified the failure of Madero's experiment with democratic reform and triggered further conflict. Huerta was faced with two rebellions—the Constitutionalist rebellion in the north, led by Venustiano Carranza and supported by General Álvaro Obregón and the legendary Francisco "Pancho" Villa, and the Zapatista revolt in the south. Huerta's attempt to consolidate his control over Mexico was complicated by severe economic dislocations and strong opposition from US president Woodrow Wilson, who objected to Huerta's seizure of power (Meyer and Sherman 1995:528–529). US support for the Constitutionalist cause and the subsequent military occupation of Veracruz contributed to the demise of Huerta's regime in July 1914.

Once again, the revolutionary forces fragmented because of their divergent interests. Villa and Zapata broke with the Constitutionalists, but were ultimately subdued as Carranza was eventually able to consolidate his control. A constitutional convention, designed to institutionalize the revolution, produced the 1917 Constitution (which remains in effect today). Radical for its time, the constitution strictly limited the power of the Catholic Church, restricted foreign corporations, granted extensive rights and benefits to labor, and called for agrarian reform.

Given Mexico's history of conflict and fragmentation, the 1917 Constitution was intended to forge consensus by including provisions that would appeal to a variety of constituencies. Its proclamation, however, did not end the conflict, nor did it bring about unanimous agreement on Mexico's future. Carranza himself, although he accepted the constitution, did not agree with all of its provisions and ignored many after assuming the presidency in mid-1917. His attempt to circumvent the no-reelection stipulation by naming his successor led to his ouster in 1920.

Nonetheless, Carranza laid the groundwork for the institutionalization of a new political system that produced unprecedented stability. General Obregón, elected to succeed Carranza in 1920, did much to enhance the power of the national government despite a period of economic decline, conflicts with the United States, and continued internal strife. Turmoil continued during the presidency of General Plutarco Elías Calles, whose implementation of the anticlerical provisions of the constitution exacerbated church-state tensions. Calles, however, helped to institutionalize Mexico's revolutionary government by establishing the broad-based National Revolutionary Party (PNR) in 1929. Designed to integrate all relevant groups into the political arena, the PNR enabled the Mexican government to co-opt those who could threaten its control. Ironically, the Mexican Revolution resulted in a "modernized" version of the centralized authoritarian state that existed during both the Díaz era and the colonial past.

* * *

The demise of Díaz's order-and-progress dictatorship in the early 1900s paralleled the emergence of similar regimes in a number of Caribbean Basin countries. These regimes, however, were not established by individual *caudillo* leaders, but rather by the United States as part of a series of direct military interventions and occupations. Thus, a third pattern of rule emerged in Latin America designed to promote stability and to enhance the prospects for national development (Wiarda 1995).

As Cleveland Fraser details in Chapter 7, following the defeat of Spain in the Spanish-American War in 1898, the United States became a major force in the Caribbean region as well as a colonial power by acquiring control of Puerto Rico (among other territories) and establishing a protectorate over Cuba. Having surpassed Britain as the primary investor in the area, the United States had extensive economic interests to protect along with the long-standing security concerns articulated in the 1823 Monroe Doctrine. After the proclamation of the 1904 Roosevelt Corollary to the Monroe Doctrine, the United States embarked on a series of military interventions and occupations in such countries as Cuba, the Dominican Republic, Haiti, Nicaragua, and Panama. Ironically, whereas these interventions were designed to establish and maintain order, they ultimately sowed the seeds of future conflict.

■ The Modern Era

The inherent weaknesses of export-led development and the elite's tenuous hold on power were evident in the early 1900s. Monocultural production and overreliance on raw materials exports made Latin American economies vulnerable to market fluctuations and increasingly dependent on the importation of manufactured goods and technology. World War I and the Great Depression exacerbated the region's economic problems and further undermined the old oligarchic order, already debilitated by the Mexican Revolution and electoral defeats in Argentina and Chile.

The 1930s were a "critical juncture" in the process of Latin American development (Wiarda 1995). As governments fell throughout the region—through elections, coups, or revolts—leaders turned to a new model of economic development that stressed industrialization. The shift away from primary product exports occurred initially in the larger, more economically advanced countries of South America and in Mexico. Known as import substitution industrialization (ISI), this new development strategy was designed to stimulate domestic production of industrial and manufactured goods that had previously been imported, creating jobs and reducing external dependence.

While the pace of modernization varied considerably by country, rapid economic growth sparked profound changes in Latin America's social structure, significant improvements in living standards, and heightened popular expectations. Industrialization contributed to the expansion of the middle class and the emergence of an urban working class whose organization into labor unions and political parties marked the emergence of a new actor in the political arena. Over the next several decades, dealing with labor was one of the most pressing concerns confronting Latin American leaders.

Modernization generated substantial pressure for change in the traditional elitist political order. In confronting this pressure, Latin American political systems were flexible and innovative. Rather than disappear in the face of rapid change, traditional patterns, structures, and values were modified to reflect new conditions (Wiarda 1995:79). For example, the old landed elite gradually absorbed the nascent commercial elite, a relatively easy process given the groups' compatible interests. Accommodating the middle sectors was more problematic because of their lack of cohesion and divergent interests. In some countries such as Mexico, accommodation occurred only after violent conflict whereas, in others such as Chile, the process was relatively peaceful because the upper classes shared a common interest in uniting against the masses. In both instances, the emerging groups were assimilated by expanding the traditional power structure—composed of the oligarchy, the Catholic Church, and the military.

In contrast, there was less agreement on how to best confront the emergent urban working class. The initial reaction from those in power was to exclude labor because the strong Marxist influence in the union movement was perceived as threatening to the elites' control. This approach became less viable in countries where industrialization increased the potential power of organized labor. Simply put, it became increasingly difficult to ignore or repress workers whose awareness and expectations had risen dramatically and who were mobilized within the union movement. Ultimately, a variety of strategies were employed in addressing the labor challenge; some proved to be effective in mediating class conflicts, and others exacerbated tensions and provoked radical challenges to the existing order.

In Mexico, emerging power contenders were peacefully co-opted into a corporatist state structure under the control of a single dominant party for the better part of the twentieth century. Through the unique sectoral structure of the Institutional Revolutionary Party (PRI), labor along with the peasants and "popular sectors" were represented, albeit under the watchful eye of the state. In contrast with Mexico's "authoritarian democracy," a number of countries in the Commonwealth Caribbean managed to incorporate labor within pluralist party systems. By the early 1900s, labor organizations had proliferated in the region, and the working class gradually emerged as a political force (Knight and Palmer 1989:12). This became apparent when labor disturbances broke out in response to deteriorating socioeconomic conditions, first in Saint Kitts (1935) and culminating in Jamaica and Guyana in 1938. In the aftermath of these disturbances, a strong linkage between political parties and workers' unions was established in most British colonies, with Trinidad a notable exception. Although this link provided workers with access to the political process, it did so under elite tutelage within the existing framework of power (Edie 1991; Stone 1985).

The assimilation of labor has been a long, complicated process, even in the most stable and democratic countries in the region. For instance, serious setbacks occurred during the 1970s and 1980s in Chile and Uruguay, when elected civilian governments were ousted by the military and replaced by brutal regimes that relied on repression in an attempt to demobilize the labor movement. As these cases illustrate, labor incorporation can be reversed or constrained during periods of crisis and when rising demands go unfulfilled or are perceived as threatening.

The emergence of the labor movement elicited different responses in Argentina and Brazil, which saw the rise of populist dictators who appealed to urban workers as a means of consolidating their power. In both cases, rapid industrialization that began in the late nineteenth century produced burgeoning working classes, which became influential political actors. Both Juan Perón in Argentina (in the 1940s) and Getulio Vargas in Brazil (in the 1930s) employed traditional practices such as the creation of corporatist structures and the use of patronage through which labor would be integrated under state control. But unlike Mexico's institutional framework, the processes in Argentina and Brazil depended primarily on the charisma of individual leaders. The dearth of viable institutions in Argentina and Brazil, exacerbated by the highly centralized authoritarian regimes of Perón and Vargas, became even more problematic after the leaders left power (Perón initially in 1955 and Vargas in 1954). By inhibiting institutional growth and the development of effective, long-term mechanisms for the peaceful incorporation of labor into their countries' power structures, both leaders left legacies of instability and conflict.

The relatively lower level of industrialization and modernization in some of the smaller countries of the region precluded the formation of a sizable, highly mobilized urban working class. As a result, rather than seeking to coopt labor, regimes such as those of Fulgencio Batista in Cuba, Rafael Trujillo in the Dominican Republic, François (Papa Doc) Duvalier in Haiti, Anastasio Somoza García in Nicaragua, and Alfredo Stroessner in Paraguay found that brutally suppressing the labor movement was far more expedient. In fact, these personalist dictatorships—in which virtually absolute power and authority were concentrated in the hands of a single individual—were among the most repressive and long-lasting regimes in Latin America.

Although the use of repression marginalized the labor movement for a time, these regimes faced mounting discontent and demands for change as the pace of modernization accelerated. The response to increasingly vocal opposition, however, was frequently an even greater reliance on coercion. For example, François Duvalier formed the dreaded Tonton Macoutes, a paramilitary force that terrorized the regime's opponents, and Trujillo transformed the Dominican Republic into a virtual police state. This type of state-sponsored repression, along with the domination of personalist dictators, greatly inhibited institutional development in societies devoid of channels through which the regimes' opponents could press for change. A persistently low level of institutionalization, coupled with the regimes' unwillingness to accommodate demands for reform, diminished the likelihood of a peaceful transfer of power and set the stage for the most turbulent period in Latin American history.

Revolutionary Change

By the 1950s, industrialization had stimulated far-reaching change in Latin America. Urbanization and technological advances facilitated improvements in both the transportation and communication infrastructure. The social structure grew more complex. Latin America was no longer dominated by a rigid, two-class social hierarchy. Instead, it now exhibited a more differentiated structure with the emergence of urban-based groups—the commercial and industrial elites; the middle sectors, composed of white-collar professionals such as doctors, lawyers, teachers, and bureaucrats; and the industrial working classes— all of which had grown in numbers and political relevance. Moreover, following the collapse of the old oligarchic order around 1930, the middle sectors—despite a lack of unity and cohesion—had become the predominant force in the military officer corps, the clergy, and the government bureaucracy.

Yet the emergence of new power contenders created problems as conflict among groups with divergent interests escalated. In a number of cases, including El Salvador, societies became so polarized and disputes among groups so contentious that it was difficult for anyone to govern effectively. With political awareness and mobilization at unprecedented levels as a result of improvements in education and greater exposure to new ideas through the media, Latin America experienced a "revolution of rising expectations." National leaders' inability, because of fiscal constraints or political opposition, or unwillingness to accommodate mass demands, along with a growing disparity between the rich and the poor (as industrialization had exacerbated preexisting inequalities),

significantly increased the level of popular discontent. This mounting frustration and the realization that, in many cases, genuine change would not come
about through peaceful electoral means fueled numerous revolts and guerrilla
insurgencies. Such revolutionary potential instilled fear in the upper classes as
well as in some middle-class elements who sometimes allied in an effort to
forestall the outbreak of class conflict. In Argentina, Brazil, and Chile, among
others, this fear led to calls for the military to restore order. In other cases, disaffected members of the middle class led movements to overthrow governments
and to bring about radical change. Both Bolivia and Guatemala experienced
attempts to promote profound social and political transformation that served
as a portent of further challenges to the established order.

The 1952 Bolivian Revolution was the culmination of two decades of political and economic turmoil, dating to the Great Depression and the disastrous
Chaco War (1932–1935) that undermined the alliance between the traditional
landed elite and the emerging mining elite that dominated national politics and
the economy. In April 1952 the conservative government collapsed following
a series of revolts organized by the National Revolutionary Movement (MNR),
a multiclass party that brought together groups opposed to the existing order
including the urban working class, disenchanted sectors of the military, and elements of the middle class whose demands went unfulfilled in the context of
economic stagnation. Once in power, the MNR under the leadership of Víctor
Paz Estenssoro pursued an ambitious agenda that emphasized economic development and social justice. Among the MNR's accomplishments were the
granting of citizenship, voting, and other rights to the indigenous peoples to
facilitate their integration into national life for the first time in the country's
history; the nationalization of the nation's largest tin mines and formation of a
state mining corporation; and a program of agrarian reform. Factional strife
within the MNR impeded efforts to sustain the revolution. A coup ousting Paz
in 1964 ended Bolivia's revolutionary experiment and ushered in an extended
period of military rule.

In Guatemala, a popular revolt that toppled the dictatorship of General
Jorge Ubico in 1944 and the subsequent election of Juan José Arévalo in 1945
launched a decade of reform that engendered strong opposition from domestic
elites and, eventually, the United States. The Arévalo government introduced
land and labor reforms, coupled with political reforms aimed at encouraging
popular mobilization and the creation of trade unions, political parties, and interest groups. The commitment to socioeconomic and political change continued
under Arévalo's successor, Colonel Jacobo Arbenz Guzmán. The introduction
of the Agrarian Reform Law in 1952, designed to expropriate uncultivated
land for distribution to peasants, brought Arbenz into conflict with the United
Fruit Company (UFCO), a US-based multinational with extensive landholdings
and political influence throughout Central America. The perceived "attack" on
UFCO caused great concern in Washington, owing in part to an exaggerated

perception of communist influence in the Arbenz administration as well as close ties between UFCO executives and high-level US officials. Portraying Guatemala as a significant national security threat, the United States supported efforts to destabilize the government. This backing culminated in an "invasion" by Guatemalan exiles, sponsored by the Central Intelligence Agency (CIA), that toppled Arbenz in June 1954.

The coup marked a significant turning point in Guatemalan politics. What followed was a series of military-dominated regimes that violated civil liberties and committed human rights abuses, prevented institutional development, and further polarized a society already deeply divided by race and ethnicity. In the decades following the coup, a protracted civil war claimed the lives of over 100,000 people and displaced thousands more. This conflict pitted the government's security forces, along with right-wing paramilitary organizations and "death squads," against a left-wing guerrilla insurgency composed of numerous groups, some of which formed the Guatemalan National Revolutionary Union (URNG). For over four decades, Guatemala endured a level of violence and repression matched by few other countries in Latin America until peace accords were signed in December 1996.

The Case of Cuba

The 1959 Cuban Revolution is one of the most significant events in Latin American history. While the Bolivian and Guatemalan reform movements failed to sustain themselves, Cuba's revolutionary leadership consolidated their movement and brought about a complete social transformation.

Postindependence Cuban politics was defined by a pattern of strongman rule and military interventionism through the 1950s. Following the overthrow of Gerardo Machado in 1933, a brief reformist period under Ramón Grau San Martín was thwarted by a military revolt led by Fulgencio Batista. US ties to Cuba were strengthened under Batista who dominated Cuban politics over the next decade. Two successive democratic governments, under the watchful eye of Batista, attempted a variety of social and economic reforms, but their legitimacy was undermined by widespread corruption and endemic political violence. In March 1952, Batista launched another coup and reinstituted a system of authoritarian rule.

On the surface, Cuba during the late 1950s did not appear susceptible to revolution. Cuba was relatively modernized and had reached a level of development comparable to some of the larger countries in Latin America. Moreover, Batista cultivated close ties with the United States, which focused considerable attention on Cuban affairs, given its proximity and extensive US commercial interests. Further analysis reveals, however, that Cuba's development was badly skewed, with enormous disparities between relatively modern cities and impoverished rural areas.

Batista's harsh rule and accommodating stance toward the United States provoked strong nationalist sentiments and widespread opposition. Among those seeking to oust the dictator was the 26th of July Movement, led by Fidel Castro. Beginning in 1956, Castro and his group (numbering less than 100) waged a remarkably effective guerrilla campaign against Batista's well-equipped army of around 40,000. Unable to quell the rebellion, the regime grew more repressive. Lacking any substantial popular support and having lost US backing, Batista fled into exile on January 1, 1959.

Batista's departure left a vacuum of power that Castro and his movement, including his brother Raúl and the Argentine revolutionary Ernesto "Che" Guevara, quickly moved to fill. Initial uncertainty as to the direction the revolution would take ultimately gave way to the realization that Fidel was committed to a radical transformation of Cuban society and the assertion of Cuban sovereignty and independence from US influence.

The Castro regime established the Committees for the Defense of the Revolution (CDRs) and other organizations to mobilize popular support. Although such organizations provided the regime with a type of institutional framework, the political system was restructured around the leadership of Fidel. Arguably the most charismatic figure Latin America has ever known, Castro came to personify the revolution. His highly personalistic, centralized style of rule was consistent with Latin America's *caudillo* tradition and allowed him to consolidate his personal control over the country.

By late 1960, the country's dependent capitalist economy had been dismantled and a majority of the economy nationalized, including the property of both domestic and foreign owners. This action, coupled with the movement toward an authoritarian single-party state, prompted the exodus of thousands of upper- and middle-class Cubans. Ironically, this exodus and subsequent ones, such as the 1980 Mariel Boatlift, served as a kind of "safety valve," helping to defuse potential domestic opposition.

Castro understood the precedent set in Guatemala and recognized that revolutionary Cuba would inevitably face US opposition. The seizure of US businesses and properties and Cuba's emerging relationship with the Soviet Union ensured this. Determined to reduce US influence and to diversify economic relations, Castro entered into a trade agreement with the Soviets in February 1960. The United States implemented a partial economic embargo eight months later. With a new source of technology and a market for Cuban sugar, Castro intensified his anti-US rhetoric, and relations deteriorated rapidly.

Alarmed by the increasingly radical tone of the revolution, in April 1961 the John F. Kennedy administration approved a Guatemala-style invasion by US-trained and -equipped Cuban exiles at the Bay of Pigs. Intended to foment a counterrevolution to topple Castro regime, the poorly organized operation failed miserably. A colossal US foreign policy blunder, the Bay of Pigs represented a monumental victory for Castro and, according to many observers, pushed Cuba further into the embrace of the Soviet bloc. Indeed, in December

1961, Castro formally declared himself, and hence the revolution, Marxist-Leninist. Within months, Soviet leader Nikita Khrushchev ordered the installation of missile bases on the island, transforming Cuba into a stage for a Cold War confrontation that brought the world's superpowers to the brink of nuclear war. The October 1962 Cuban Missile Crisis was resolved when Khrushchev agreed to withdraw the Soviet missiles in exchange for a pledge from the United States that it would not invade Cuba.

Cuba became a valuable Soviet ally over the next three decades, providing access to a critical strategic location just 90 miles from the United States. Soviet efforts to assist communist movements in Angola and Ethiopia were bolstered by Castro's desire to "export revolution" and his willingness to contribute troops and other personnel. In return, the Soviet Union provided military protection and economic and technical assistance that facilitated the institutionalization of the revolution and enabled Cuba to survive the complete embargo imposed by the United States in 1962.

Critics argue that, despite Castro's rhetoric about asserting Cuba's independence from foreign domination, he merely replaced the country's dependence on the United States with dependence on the Soviet Union. Although Cuba maintained a greater degree of autonomy than most Soviet satellite states, Soviet backing contributed much to Castro's longevity in power. He enjoyed immense popularity among the Cuban masses who benefited from the socioeconomic reforms designed to address the glaring inequalities and dire poverty that characterized pre-1959 Cuban society. The "achievements of the revolution"—the guarantee of education, health care, and other social services to ensure that the basic needs of all Cubans would be met—are hailed by supporters as one of the revolution's greatest accomplishments. To be sure, Castro depended heavily on the Soviet Union to provide such benefits, but his willingness to confront the United States did much to bolster national pride and dignity as well as his stature among the Cuban population.

The course of the Cuban Revolution was influenced profoundly by the prevailing international context. For three decades, the bipolar global structure during the Cold War enabled Castro to parlay Cuba's strategic location into leverage in dealing with the Soviet Union. The situation changed dramatically, however, with the emergence of President Mikhail Gorbachev and his introduction of reforms such as glasnost (openness regarding shortcomings) and perestroika (economic and political restructuring). With Soviet rapprochement with the West, Cuba became a costly burden, and as the Soviet domestic crisis deepened its unwillingness to continue subsidizing Cuba led to a substantial reduction in assistance. Eventually, the collapse of communist regimes throughout Eastern Europe and the dissolution of the Soviet Union deprived Cuba of its primary trading partners, its source of economic and technical assistance, and its longtime benefactor. Ironically, with Castro left to fend for himself, Cuba could be considered truly "independent" for the first time since formally gaining independence a century ago.

Nearly twenty years have passed since the collapse of the Soviet Union and, defying the odds, Cuba's revolutionary government has endured. Despite his intense criticism of Gorbachev's reforms, Castro adopted a more pragmatic approach to maintaining the revolution. For over a decade the Cuban economy was "dollarized," enabling people to trade in US dollars in order to attract much-needed hard currency. Cuba has also sought out foreign investment, establishing joint ventures with foreign firms. In particular, Cuba has banked on a revitalization of the tourist industry to keep the economy and, possibly the regime itself, afloat. This approach has its drawbacks, however, as the influx of tourists has exacerbated inequalities and the sense of deprivation felt by many Cubans. This has proven especially troubling among Cuba's youth, many of whom face bleak prospects and lack the previous generation's strong emotional attachment to Castro and the revolution.

With the transition of power from Fidel Castro to his brother Raúl, formalized in February 2008, questions were once again raised about the sustainability of Cuba's revolutionary government. Although President Barack Obama had initially spoken out against US sanctions on Cuba, aside from some easing of travel restrictions for Cuban Americans the long-standing embargo remains in place. As the island's economy continues to struggle, the regime has sought to bolster its relations with other countries, including deepening ties with the Hugo Chávez regime in Venezuela and revitalizing its relationship with Russia. It seems apparent that the future of the revolution will depend on the regime's ability to revive the economy, enhance the quality of life, and provide additional opportunities for the Cuban people.

For much of the past five decades, Fidel Castro and Cuba played an active role in Latin America. The idea that Cuba was obliged to "export the revolution" led to support for guerrilla movements in a variety of Latin American (and third world) countries, including Argentina, Chile, Colombia, El Salvador, Grenada, Guatemala, Nicaragua, and Venezuela. Cuba's regional influence has diminished as the Castro regime struggles to maintain power and the Marxist alternative has largely been discredited in the post-Soviet era. However, the revolution continues to serve as inspiration to those who view dependent capitalism and US hegemony as the principal causes of Latin America's "underdevelopment."

* * *

Fidel Castro's relevance during the heyday of the Cuban Revolution is best illustrated by the response he provoked throughout the region. For example, US policy toward Latin America after 1959 was focused primarily on preventing a "second Cuba." The Alliance for Progress was designed to stimulate development in an attempt to ameliorate conditions in which communist insurgency could flourish. After the assassination of President Kennedy, US policy became more militaristic and substantial assistance was provided to Latin American militaries to bolster their capacity to crush guerrilla movements.

The US intervention in the Dominican Republic in 1965 is illustrative of this approach. When a civil war broke out between Constitutionalist forces seeking to reinstate the popularly elected president Juan Bosch who had been ousted after winning the 1962 election and Loyalist forces opposed to Bosch's reformist government, President Lyndon Johnson sent 23,000 US Marines to Santo Domingo to aid the Loyalists, with the pretense that the Dominican Republic was in danger of falling under communist control. With the defeat of the pro-Bosch forces, the post-Trujillo experiment with democracy ended. Former Trujillo protégé Joaquín Balaguer took power and ruled until 1978, establishing a highly centralized authoritarian regime, friendly to the United States. Balaguer returned to the presidency in 1986, was reelected in 1990, and won again in 1994 amid charges of fraud.

Subsequent US interventions in Chile in 1973, in Grenada in 1983, and in El Salvador and Nicaragua throughout the 1980s further reflected the US preoccupation with containing leftist movements and regimes influenced by or with ties to Cuba. Whether through the CIA (as in Chile); direct military intervention (as in Grenada); or providing technical assistance, military training and equipment, or economic aid to governments (as in El Salvador and Jamaica) or to counterrevolutionary groups (as in Nicaragua), the United States actively opposed efforts to promote radical change. A similar response came from Latin American elites who, when civilian regimes proved incapable, often turned to the military to confront the threat of Cuban-style revolution.

The Rise of Bureaucratic Authoritarianism

The Military Returns to Power

The Cuban Revolution alerted Latin American leaders and elites, as well as US policymakers, to the potential for further radical change within the region. As Latin American societies became increasingly polarized, civilian leaders were caught between powerful opposing forces: those on the left, frustrated by the slow pace of reform and demanding radical change, and those on the right, seeking to forestall change. Both sides were willing to utilize force to achieve their objectives, leading to an escalation in violence and a forceful response from national militaries. During the 1960s–1980s, many countries experienced the breakdown of democratic governments and the onset of direct military rule. Among the more notable exceptions were Colombia, Costa Rica, and Venezuela where democratically elected civilian leaders retained power.

Even in the Commonwealth Caribbean, where most nations were attaining independence and establishing their own systems of Westminster-style parliamentary democracy, governments were imperiled by or fell prey to authoritarianism. Political violence plagued Saint Lucia and Jamaica, where several hundred people were killed prior to the 1980 election, and the collapse of liberal democracy led to military rule and the formation of one-party states in Guyana and Grenada as well as in the former Dutch colony of Suriname (Stone 1985:15). An attempted coup launched by fundamentalist Muslim officers (the Jamaat-Al-Muslimeen) in Trinidad in 1990 and ongoing concerns regarding corruption and rising levels of violence underscore the significant threats to democratic governments that remain.

A variety of factors contributed to the wave of military coups that occurred throughout the region during this period. Most were precipitated by the military's perception that civilian leaders were incapable of containing rising levels of violence. Economic stagnation was also a decisive factor in some coups, with a lack of development viewed as a catalyst of leftist insurgency. Having received extensive military and academic instruction at institutions such as Brazil's Superior War College, Peru's Center for Higher Military Studies, and US training centers, many officers were confident of their ability to preserve order and promote development.

Actions taken by civilian leaders to mobilize the masses also provoked military interventions. In Brazil and Chile, leftist leaders appealed directly to the masses with promises of reform. These actions stirred fears among the upper and middle classes of a "threat from below," leading them to appeal to the military to oust João Goulart in Brazil as well as Salvador Allende in Chile who was the first popularly elected socialist in Latin American history. In addition, these coups and a number of others can be attributed to threats, real or perceived, to the corporate interests of the military. Budget cuts, meddling in internal military affairs (e.g., promotions and the determination of strategies and missions), and plans to arm popular militias were viewed as detrimental to military interests.

That many countries reverted to military rule during the 1960s–1970s should not surprise those familiar with the history of the area. The Iberian colonial powers imbued their New World possessions with a strong military tradition. Since independence, praetorianism (a form of militarism in which the armed forces consider their corporate interests to include control of the state), in most cases, has been the rule rather than the exception. The 1964 Brazilian coup, however, introduced a new form of military government that differed from previous periods. In contrast to the pattern of individual *caudillo* rule characteristic of the early postindependence era, the new "bureaucratic authoritarian" regimes were led by the military institution with the assistance of civilian technocrats, such as economists, on whose expertise the military relied (O'Donnell 1973). And unlike the more behind the scenes moderating role some militaries had previously played, intervening briefly as needed, the new regimes pursued a much more ambitious agenda.

A New Pattern

Guided by the "national security doctrine" (analyzed by Paul W. Zagorski in Chapter 5), bureaucratic authoritarian regimes deemed internal leftist subversion—rather than external aggression—the greatest security threat confronting their societies. Acting under the premise that such subversion was fueled by a lack of social, political, and economic development, military leaders adopted a greatly expanded role that entailed long-term institutional rule. They sought the wholesale restructuring of their countries' economies and particularly their political systems, which they deemed necessary to address the root causes of instability. In order to attract the foreign investors who had the capital and technology that Latin American countries needed, military rulers believed they needed to ensure order and an environment favorable to commercial interests.

The leaders of bureaucratic authoritarian regimes considered traditional politics to be a key factor contributing to the high level of instability in Latin America. They viewed civilian leaders with disdain, judging most to be inefficient, corrupt, and absorbed in self-interest. Political parties were seen as divisive, mobilizing support for narrow political agendas that polarized badly fragmented societies even further. As a result, bureaucratic authoritarian regimes curtailed political activity by banning political parties and many interest groups. As these regimes sought to demobilize society, student associations and other popular organizations were often targets of repression, and labor movements were suppressed to keep wages down, appeasing foreign investors. With the exception of Peru, where the first phase of the military *docenio* (twelve-year period in power) was led by a reformist regime, most bureaucratic authoritarian governments were acting to preserve the status quo on behalf of elite interests.

The Cases of Brazil, Argentina, and Chile

This pattern is best illustrated by events in the three most conspicuous cases of bureaucratic authoritarianism: Brazil, Argentina, and Chile. The 1964 Brazilian coup that ousted João Goulart introduced this new form of military rule to Latin America. Threatened by Goulart's proposed reforms, the elite and sectors of the middle class supported the military, content to sacrifice certain freedoms to achieve an environment of stability needed for economic growth. For a time, the military regime delivered on its pledge of order and progress. Bolstered by intensive industrialization and expanding exports, the Brazilian economy experienced unprecedented growth. Between 1968 and 1974, average annual growth exceeded 10 percent, with a rate of 14 percent in 1973. During this period, referred to as the "Brazilian Miracle," Brazil appeared to be emerging as an economic superpower.

Brazil's economic program, however, was undermined by its dependence on imported sources of energy and its response to the oil shocks of the 1970s.

When the Organization of Petroleum Exporting Countries (OPEC) sharply increased oil prices in 1973, Brazil's leaders forged ahead with plans for large-scale industrialization and infrastructural development. In order to cover soaring energy costs, Brazil borrowed from international lenders in the expectation its economy would continue its remarkable growth. The second oil shock in the late 1970s and onset of severe recession in the industrialized world had devastating repercussions for Brazil. As export markets contracted and energy costs and the national debt continued to grow, rising interest rates on Brazil's loans sharply increased the country's debt payments and brought an end to the Brazilian Miracle.

Concurrently, opposition to the military regime had mounted. The Brazilian Miracle exacerbated the already substantial gap between rich and poor as this new wealth was skewed heavily toward foreign investors and the domestic elite while the vast majority of Brazilians saw little improvement in their standard of living. Harsh treatment of the opposition, particularly the labor movement, which organized strikes and demonstrations to protest government policies, heightened tensions. Ultimately, the inability to sustain economic growth undermined the regime as spiraling inflation and massive debt eroded the support of the middle and upper classes. As opposition grew, the military allowed an *abertura* (a gradual political opening) that facilitated the transition to civilian rule through a military-supervised election in 1985.

In contrast with Brazil's experience, the Argentine military was unable to control the transition process. Argentina has experienced considerable economic and social instability and since 1930 has been subject to repeated military interventions in national politics. Much of this turmoil has revolved around the legacy of Juan Perón and the influence of *peronismo*. Following Perón's ouster in 1955 two civilian governments failed to eradicate *peronismo,* prompting the military to seize power in 1966 and establish its version of Brazil's bureaucratic authoritarian state. However, the regime's inability to demobilize supporters of *peronismo* and to quell violent conflict compelled the military to return power to civilians in 1973, a process that culminated in Perón's return to power after eighteen years of exile. With the Peronist movement deeply divided, however, even Perón was unable to stem the tide of violence and economic decline. His death in 1974 and the disastrous rule of his second wife, Isabel Perón, led the military to seize power again in 1976.

This time the military was determined to take forceful action to stabilize Argentina, embarking on a ruthless campaign of terror targeting urban guerrillas (Montoneros) and others deemed to be "subversives." Thousands were killed or "disappeared" and thousands more were illegally detained, tortured, or forced into exile during what became known as the Dirty War. Widespread domestic opposition, coupled with the regime's inability to revive the economy, led Argentina's military leaders to search for alternative ways to legitimize their rule. In 1982, seeking to divert attention from domestic problems, the military launched an invasion of the British-held Falkland (Malvinas) Islands, a small group of islands off its coast over which Argentina maintained a long-standing claim. Badly underestimating Britain's resolve to keep control of the islands, the Argentine military was dealt a humiliating defeat that led it to relinquish power in 1983, with little control over the transition.

Chile's descent into bureaucratic authoritarianism began with the election of Salvador Allende in 1970. In leading Chile down the "peaceful road to socialism," Allende's policies engendered intense opposition and further polarized the deeply divided society. As the country fell into a period of economic and social crisis, the Chilean armed forces—with the backing of the upper and middle classes and a degree of US support—overthrew Allende in 1973 in a bloody coup that cost Allende his life and led to around 5,000 additional deaths in its immediate aftermath.

This military intervention, which was completely at odds with Chile's long tradition of democratic, constitutional rule, led to the formation of a bureaucratic authoritarian regime under General Augusto Pinochet. Pinochet abolished political parties, closed the National Congress, and carried out a brutal campaign to suppress the left. With the assistance of civilian technocrats trained at the University of Chicago, the regime adopted a free-market approach, which opened the Chilean economy to foreign investment and competition. The initial results were problematic for the working classes; unemployment rose while wages and the overall standard of living fell. The national debt soared as Chile borrowed heavily to stimulate development. Ultimately, the program paid dividends and Chile enjoyed steady growth after the early 1980s.

Despite Chile's impressive economic resurgence under Pinochet, opposition to his rule mounted. The regime's dismal human rights record, including the torture and "disappearance" of union officials, student leaders, and others deemed threatening to national security drew international condemnation. Widespread protests and strikes preceded a 1988 referendum in which voters denied Pinochet another term, paving the way for a return to democratic civilian rule in 1990.

The Demise of Military Control

Military disengagement from power and the demise of bureaucratic authoritarian rule in Brazil, Argentina, and Chile can be attributed to three factors. First, the ruthlessness with which military regimes suppressed internal opposition generated substantial criticism and condemnation. Whereas international criticism at times proved troublesome, internal domestic protests—which tended to provoke even greater levels of repression—severely undermined regime support. For example, as Susan Tiano shows in Chapter 10, the Madres de la Plaza de Mayo have been influential in bringing international attention to human rights abuses in Argentina.

A second factor prompting the military's "return to the barracks" was the generally poor economic performance of their regimes. Despite intense criticism of its civilian predecessors, the Argentine military's performance was dismal. Even in Brazil, which experienced a remarkable period of growth, the economy's long-term performance was little better than that under civilian rule. Only Chile experienced much success, although critics maintain that it was the result of massive borrowing and that the social and political costs were enormous. In any case, the poor performance of the Argentine and Brazilian militaries led to their retreat from power, and even Chile's relative economic success was not enough to prolong Pinochet's tenure.

A final factor contributing to the demise of bureaucratic authoritarianism was the perceived damage poor performance did to the military's reputation. The image of most militaries was tarnished, nowhere more severely than in Argentina. Not only did the regime fail to revive the economy, but the level of repression during the Dirty War reached horrific levels. Moreover, the military thoroughly discredited itself during the Falklands debacle. In general, concerns that perpetuating its rule could spark the outbreak of civil strife or exacerbate factional disputes brought about the withdrawal of the military from power and the transition to civilian rule.

■ Democratization

Obstacles and Challenges

As military regimes across the region relinquished power in the early 1980s, the emergence of democratically elected civilian governments signaled the movement toward more open, competitive, pluralistic forms of politics in Latin America. A decade later—following the US-led overthrow of the People's Revolutionary Government in Grenada and of Panamanian dictator General Manuel Noriega, the election of Patricio Aylwin to succeed General Pinochet in Chile, and the election (and subsequent restoration to power) of Jean-Bertrand Aristide in Haiti—the Fidel Castro regime in Cuba stood as the sole remaining authoritarian dictatorship in the Americas. This transition has sparked much debate. Whereas some observers have expressed optimism concerning the sustainability of "third wave" democratic regimes throughout Latin America, others counter that the current era is merely part of an ongoing cyclical alternation between democratic and authoritarian tendencies. Further analysis reveals a decidedly mixed record, with "significant but uneven progress" achieved over the past generation (Millett 2009). Has sufficient progress been made to enable elected civilian leaders to surmount the considerable obstacles to the consolidation of democratic rule? If not, then what lies ahead?

The return to elected civilian rule was welcomed enthusiastically in societies weary of the harshness of authoritarian military rule. The opening of political systems, however, came precisely at the time national economies were experiencing great difficulties. The profound socioeconomic crisis that enveloped the region during the "lost decade" of the 1980s—the most severe since the time of the Great Depression—seriously hindered the efforts of newly elected civilian leaders to stimulate development and meet popular expectations, which had risen to unprecedented levels. In addition, the authority and integrity of some national governments were severely undermined by their inability to maintain order, to enforce laws, and to curb political violence. The perceived "failure" of the new governments raised serious questions about the sustainability of democracy within highly mobilized yet frustrated societies.

Emerging democracies, as well as some of those considered to be more established, faced a host of challenges following the transition from military rule in the 1980s and 1990s. Most countries, in one way or another, were impacted by the explosion of illicit narcotics trafficking. The drug trade has grown into a multibillion-dollar industry that generates more revenue than most legal exports and employs tens of thousands of people. Yet it fosters an environment of corruption and violence that has compromised democratic institutions and legal systems in a number of societies.

Nowhere has this been more evident than in Colombia, the epicenter of the drug trade in the Americas. The power of the Colombian drug cartels has rivaled that of the state, as evidenced by the extraordinary violence—including the 1985 massacre of Supreme Court justices and assassination of presidential candidates and government officials—that at times has virtually paralyzed the country. The government's inability to curb narcotics-related violence and crime, coupled with endemic corruption fueled by narcodollars, has severely undermined public confidence and eroded the legitimacy of its democratic system. More recently, Mexico has suffered a similar fate as rival cartels battling for supremacy have waged war on each other amidst an aggressive antidrug campaign launched by President Felipe Calderón in late 2006. Since that time nearly 30,000 people have died in a wave of violence, much of it centered along the US-Mexican border.[1] As the cases of Colombia and Mexico attest, despite the massive infusion of US aid, drug eradication and interdiction efforts have met with limited success.

Another challenge confronting some Latin American states during the era of democratization was the threat posed by guerrilla insurgencies. This threat was most pronounced in Central America, where governments in El Salvador and Guatemala faced left-wing movements and the Sandinista regime in Nicaragua battled a counterrevolutionary group, the *contras,* supported by the United States. In neither El Salvador nor Guatemala were the rebels able to seize national power. In El Salvador, the Farabundo Martí National Liberation Front (FMLN) fought to a stalemate with US-supported government forces during a twelve-year civil war that claimed some 75,000 lives. In El Salvador and Guatemala, prolonged conflict and allegations of widespread human rights violations—mainly, although not exclusively, attributed to government forces—did much to hinder national development and to polarize society. In Nicaragua, while the *contras* lacked sufficient popular support to challenge the Sandinistas for direct control, their presence did force the government to divert scarce resources away from the economy and badly needed social programs. Ongoing civil strife and the government's inability to fulfill popular expectations contributed to the Sandinistas' electoral defeat in 1990.

Colombia and Peru have also faced significant guerrilla threats. Both the Revolutionary Armed Forces of Colombia (FARC) and the National Liberation Army (ELN) have violently opposed Colombia's civilian government and have forged alliances of convenience with narcotraffickers to fund their operations. Large areas in the south have been under the de facto control of insurgent groups, compromising democratic institutions and underscoring the debility of the state. Amidst fears that Colombia was on the verge of becoming a "failed state," President Álvaro Uribe (2002–2010) launched an aggressive campaign that has weakened the FARC through the loss of key senior leaders and the demobilization of thousands of its members. Nevertheless, the insurgents and narcotraffickers remain a threat with the potential to destabilize Colombian society.

In Peru, the government of former president Alberto Fujimori achieved considerable success in reducing political violence and containing guerrilla insurgency. Throughout the 1980s, the Maoist Sendero Luminoso (Shining Path), a group committed to the radical restructuring of Peruvian society and the formation of a communist state, carried out a campaign of economic warfare and terrorism that did much to undermine the credibility of Peru's civilian leadership. However, with the strong backing of the military, Fujimori set out to crush the movement. Following the capture of its top leader, Abimael Guzmán, in September 1992, and subsequently other top leaders, Sendero's once extensive power was reduced substantially as was the threat it posed to the Peruvian state. Although the threat posed by Sendero and other rebel groups in the region has diminished considerably in the post–Cold War era, Latin American leaders continue to struggle to ameliorate the socioeconomic conditions that have sparked rebellion in the past.

As Scott G. McKinney demonstrates in Chapter 6, the precipitous economic decline experienced throughout the region during the lost decade was a difficult obstacle for democratic leaders to overcome. In part, the region's economic malaise during the 1980s was the result of ill-conceived policies pursued in the aftermath of OPEC's oil price increases in 1973 and 1979, although other factors beyond the control of Latin American governments also were present. Rather than slowing the pace of industrialization and development, many of the region's military governments pressed forward. To pay the rising costs of imported oil and to finance developmental projects, they began to borrow from abroad. Latin America's total foreign debt surpassed $400 billion during the

1980s; Brazil, followed by Mexico and Argentina, incurred the largest national debts. The level of indebtedness within some of the region's smaller countries, on a per capita basis, was also of great concern.

All sides had expected continued growth to enable the borrowers to meet debt payments. Conditions deteriorated dramatically with the onset of global recession in the early 1980s, however, as the interest rates on outstanding loans rose sharply, and declining demand for traditional Latin American exports led to drops in commodity prices and export earnings. Ironically in the early 1980s, falling oil prices created difficulties for some of the region's main oil exporters, including Venezuela, Trinidad and Tobago, and Mexico—with the latter announcing in the summer of 1982 ("the Mexico weekend") that it was unable to service its debt.

A number of other countries, including Brazil, Argentina, and Venezuela, followed Mexico's lead. To prevent countries from defaulting, the international financial community responded to the mounting crisis by renegotiating debts and extending additional loans. Countries fell further into debt, which underscored the vulnerability of Latin America's dependent economies and generated enormous pressure on the region's fledgling democratic governments.

With rising debt payments taking up a larger share of export earnings, Latin American leaders were faced with the difficult task of balancing debt payments and stimulating economic growth to provide basic services to increasingly frustrated publics. As commercial lenders grew wary of extending further credit and both international and domestic investors were unwilling to sink capital into stagnant economies plagued by high inflation, Latin American leaders eventually found they lacked funds to repay loans or to spur growth. With more capital flowing out of their countries—through debt payments and capital flight—than was coming in, many leaders were compelled, however reluctantly, to negotiate with the International Monetary Fund (IMF) to receive emergency loans. However, such assistance often proved as onerous as the debt crisis itself because it was conditioned on the structural adjustment or "austerity" programs of the neoliberal economic agenda pursued as part of the Washington Consensus.

Economic Restructuring

The decade of the 1990s, during which the Washington Consensus and the neoliberal economic model held sway, was a critical juncture in the evolution of Latin American politics. The economic restructuring pursued by many countries in response to the dictates of international lenders and investors provoked strong reactions that have dramatically reshaped the political landscape across the region.

Structural adjustment programs were designed to stabilize Latin American economies by curbing inflation though the elimination of price controls and limitations on wage increases; privatizing state-owned firms; reducing state subsidies and public-sector spending and employment; and offering incentives to attract foreign investment. Although such austerity measures were deemed critical for the long-term development of Latin American economies, many elected leaders feared that imposing them would be tantamount to political suicide. "IMF riots" were commonplace during the 1980s and 1990s, as popular protests broke out in Brazil, the Dominican Republic, Guyana, and Jamaica, among other countries. In most cases, governments were unable to implement the programs fully because of public outrage over price increases on basic goods, job losses, and sharp declines in social spending.[2] Chile, on the other hand, was the most consistent in implementing neoliberal policy from the 1970s onward, first under the Pinochet regime and subsequently under its civilian successors.

In a number of instances this outrage was intensified when strict austerity programs were imposed by leaders who campaigned against neoliberal policies. Such was the case in Venezuela when former President Carlos Andrés Pérez returned to power in 1988 and shortly thereafter announced the implementation of austerity measures. An explosion of demonstrations and rioting ensued in February 1989 in what became known as the *caracazo,* revealing the depth of popular discontent (Hillman 1994). After surviving two attempted coups in 1992, including one led by current president Hugo Chávez, Pérez was impeached the following year amidst allegations of bribery and the misappropriation of government funds. A similar scenario played out in Ecuador where Abdalá Bucaram was elected in 1996 after campaigning on an anti-neoliberal platform. Just months into his term he unexpectedly initiated a structural adjustment program, sparking massive protests and culminating in his impeachment. In both cases, the stage was set for a period of considerable social and political turmoil that underscored the fragile nature of democracy in Latin America.

While the sense of crisis that pervaded the international financial community subsided to some extent with indications of economic recovery during the 1990s, in fact there was still much cause for concern. To be sure, after much of the region experienced negative economic growth during the lost decade it was encouraging that many countries were able to achieve positive (albeit modest in most cases) growth in the 1990s. However, a number of countries remained deeply in debt and this—coupled with declining export revenues, significant capital flight, and fiscal mismanagement—contributed to deteriorating economic conditions across the region into the twenty-first century. The magnitude of the problems was best exemplified by the situation in Argentina, whose stunning default and economic collapse in 2001 sparked renewed concerns about the sustainability of fledgling democratic governments in Latin America. Argentina's plight was widely viewed as an indictment of the neoliberal policies implemented under former president Carlos Menem. Although the policies initially achieved some short-term success in curbing inflation and stimulating growth, the country's debt continued to mount, unemployment sky-rocketed, and the number of people living in poverty exceeded 50 percent.

Once viewed as a model of neoliberal reform, Argentina erupted in turmoil as popular frustration with the unfulfilled promises of such reform (sometimes referred to as "reform fatigue") fed massive protests that led to the resignation of President Fernando de la Rua as well as three short-term successors. The Central Andean region was also beset by turmoil linked to the implementation (or proposed implementation) of neoliberal policies during the same period. Dating to the mid-1990s, Bolivia, Ecuador, and Peru each saw at least one con-stitutionally elected leader forced from power before the end of his term "due to popular mobilization and resistance" as the masses reacted to policies widely perceived to be disadvantageous to their interests (Peeler 2009:198). Although in none of these instances did democracy collapse, the experiences of these countries provided insight into the challenges facing democratic leaders and the repercussions of neoliberal reform on political parties, national legisla-tures, and other democratic institutions.

The Left in Contemporary Latin America

There is significant variation among the leftist governments that prevail across Latin America today. While all have remained open to foreign trade and in-vestment and have preserved at least the basic institutions of electoral democ-racy, policy differences have led some observers to group the regimes into two categories, the "moderate left" and the "contestatory" (or "radical") left (Wey-land, Madrid, and Hunter 2010). The former includes Brazil, Chile, and Uruguay while Bolivia, Ecuador, and Venezuela are among those that belong to the lat-ter. It should be noted that today's leftist governments operate in a very differ-ent international environment and differ in significant ways from preceding leftist regimes such as those of Fidel Castro in Cuba, Allende in Chile, and the Sandinistas in Nicaragua.[3] Even the present-day contestatory cases, including the Chávez regime in Venezuela, do not compare in terms of the extent to which they have sought to transform the economic and political order in their respective societies.

The current leftist wave is a reaction to the imposition of neoliberal re-forms in the 1980s and 1990s, with moderate and contestatory regimes emerg-ing in different contexts and pursuing divergent agendas once in power. With the collapse of communism and the ascendance of the neoliberal model, a number of prominent left-wing parties in Latin America drifted to the center and moderated. In Brazil and Chile, where market reforms proved effective in stimulating growth, the Workers' Party (PT) and the Socialist Party (PS), respec-tively, were deradicalized and "accepted the basic framework of Latin America's new market model" (Weyland 2010:10). Moreover, they elected to compete for power within the confines of the existing political systems, ultimately winning contests in their respective countries. In Chile, the PS collaborated with other center-left parties to defeat a 1988 referendum that would have enabled General Pinochet to remain in power and to support the candidacy of Patricio Aylwin to succeed Pinochet in 1990. The Concertación de Partidos por la Democracia (commonly referred to as Concertación), as the coalition came to be known, won four consecutive elections and was in power until 2010. In Brazil, the PT was established in 1980 by trade unionists and other progressive elements seeking to bring an end to authoritarian rule. Former union leader Luiz Inácio "Lula" da Silva ran unsuccessfuly as the party's presidential candidate in 1989, 1994, and 1998 before winning in 2002. He served two terms and was succeeded by his protégé Dilma Rousseff who was elected in 2010.

The rise to power of the moderate left in Brazil and Chile stands in stark contrast to the emergence of contestatory regimes in Bolivia and Venezuela. While the PT in Brazil and the PS in Chile fared well following their movement to the center, this strategy proved less effective in Bolivia and Venezuela where leftist parties fell into a period of decline. At the same time, the ineffectiveness of market reforms served to further discredit established parties and their leaders, already perceived by many as corrupt, elite dominated, and unresponsive to popular demands. The decline of the center-left created an opening for more radical leftist movements that seized upon mounting popular dissatisfaction to build support. Unlike in Brazil and Chile, where the party systems had stabilized and become relatively well-institutionalized following the transition from military rule, those in Bolivia and Venezuela had suffered

Courtesy of the Brazilian Chamber of Commerce, Great Britain

Luiz Inácio Lula da Silva, former president of Brazil.

serious decay. It was within this context of economic and political turmoil that movements led by charismatic, populist leaders like Evo Morales and Hugo Chávez were able to gain power.

The decline and eventual collapse of the Venezuelan party system was particularly stunning. Widely regarded as among the most advanced democracies in the region, Venezuela boasted a "pacted" system, established among rival elites in the 1958 Pact of Punto Fijo, that was credited with maintaining stability for more than thirty years. However, the country's long-standing democracy was challenged by the 1989 *caracazo* and the subsequent attempts to overthrow the government of Carlos Andrés Pérez in 1992. Popular opposition to Pérez was so great that the leaders of the initial coup attempt (particularly Hugo Chávez) were widely supported. The demise of the Pérez government further undermined popular perceptions of democratic rule in a country where economic decline and elite domination severely eroded support for traditional parties.

The 1993 election of former president Rafael Caldera revealed the depth of the decay of the Venezuelan party system. Caldera was one of the architects of the Punto Fijo system and the founder of the Social Christian Party of Venezuela (COPEI), one of the nation's two main political parties. However, he left the party and won the presidency essentially as an independent, supported by a coalition of small parties. His victory, coupled with the poor showing of COPEI and the other main party Democratic Action (AD) and extremely high voter abstention, reflected the disdain for traditional party politics and

Wendys Olivo/VENPRES

Hugo Chávez, president of Venezuela, uses the media in his television program Aló *presidente* to *illustrate his "connection" with the general population of Venezuela.*

served as a portent of the collapse of the pacted system. The election of Chávez in 1998 marked the end of Punto Fijismo and the beginning of a new era in Venezuelan—and Latin American—politics.

As the cases of Venezuela and Bolivia illustrate, the ineffectiveness of neoliberal market policies and the debilitation of traditional party systems facilitated the emergence of contestatory regimes led by populist leaders. These leaders have established "delegative democracies" (O'Donnell 1994) whose performance in certain key areas has differed markedly from the performance of liberal pluralist democracies ruled by moderate governments in Brazil and Chile. Which version of leftist rule—contestatory or moderate—has been more effective in power? What does the current leftist wave mean for the future of Latin American politics?

One recent study provides an interesting comparison of contestatory and moderate leftist regimes, evaluating their performance in three key areas: (1) their ability to stimulate sustained economic growth while controlling inflation; (2) their effectiveness in ameliorating endemic social problems, including poverty and inequality; and (3) their ability to maintain stability while promoting democratic values and preserving democratic institutions (Weyland, Madrid, and Hunter 2010). Although significant accomplishments have been made by both regime types across the region in recent years, an impressive feat in the context of the global financial crisis, some regimes appear better equipped to sustain such progress than others.

One of the most notable differences between contestatory and moderate regimes lies in their distinctive responses to neoliberalism. Center-left governments in Brazil and Chile have accepted the basic framework of the neoliberal agenda and maintained the market-oriented economic programs inherited from their predecessors (Madrid, Hunter, and Weyland 2010:142). This was something of a surprise in the case of Brazil, where there was much speculation at the time of Lula's victory in 2002 that the new PT government would roll back market reforms introduced by the government of Fernando Henrique Cardoso. To the delight of international investors and the domestic elite—and to the consternation of many on the left—that was not the case, with Lula's government "maintaining continuity with the policies and policy orientations of his predecessor" (Kingstone and Ponce 2010:99). Such continuity reflects a "pragmatic market orientation" that had served both Lula and the Concertación governments in Chile well as they balanced steady economic growth with efforts to alleviate poverty and enhance the quality of life for the masses.[4]

A very different approach to economic development and social welfare policy has characterized the contestatory regimes in Bolivia and Venezuela. These regimes, critical of the gradualist approach of the moderate left, have sought to effect more immediate transformation of their societies. Unburdened by the constraints facing moderate governments committed to operating within existing economic and political systems, the Morales and Chávez regimes have been able to reverse a number of market reforms implemented by their predecessors and substantially increase government spending. For example, in both cases the government role in the economy has been expanded through nationalizations and the creation of state-owned firms in key sectors such as energy and natural resources. Morales and Chávez have dealt aggressively with foreign corporations in the oil and gas industries, compelling them to accept new agreements that have increased the government stake and generated billions in additional revenue that has funded social programs to benefit the poor majority. While falling short of a "full-scale transition to socialism," these various initiatives do constitute a significant departure from the neoliberal project of the preceding decades (Madrid, Hunter, and Weyland 2010:156).

In general, the current wave of leftist governments in Latin America has an impressive record of generating economic growth (see Table 4.1). Notwithstanding the slight contractions in Brazil and Chile due to the global financial crisis of 2008–2009, moderate regimes have exhibited solid, steady growth. Chile enjoyed sustained growth during the period of Concertación rule, averaging 5.4 percent from 1990 to 2007 (Madrid, Hunter, and Weyland 2010:159) while the Uruguayan economy experienced robust growth under Tabaré Vázquez (2004–2010) following three consecutive years of contraction. Although

Table 4.1 Economic Performance in Latin America (annual percentage)

	Gross Domestic Product Growth				
	2005	2006	2007	2008	2009
Bolivia	4.42	4.8	4.56	6.15	3.36
Brazil	3.03	3.97	6.16	5.1	(–0.6)[a]
Chile	5.56	4.59	4.6	3.69	(–1.53)
Ecuador	5.74	4.75	2.04	7.24	0.36
Uruguay	7.46	4.33	7.46	8.54	2.86
Venezuela	10.32	9.87	8.15	4.78	(–3.29)

	Inflation		
	2007	2008	2009
Bolivia	4.96	11.71	11.86
Brazil	3.14	4.46	5.90
Chile	2.57	7.83	7.09
Ecuador	2.87	3.32	8.83
Uruguay	6.38	8.50	9.19
Venezuela	16.97	22.46	30.90

Source: Inter-American Development Bank. "Latin American and Caribbean Macro Watch Database." http://www.iadb.org/Research/LatinMacroWatch.
Note: a. This figure is from World Bank, "GDP Growth (annual %)." http://data.worldbank.org.

these governments did increase expenditures on education, health care, and other social programs targeting poverty (achieving considerable success), limits on spending helped to keep inflation largely in check.

Contestatory regimes have also demonstrated the potential for significant growth, although some observers are less sanguine about their long-term economic prospects. Bolivia, Ecuador, and Venezuela are all heavily dependent on energy exports (oil and natural gas), which have accounted for much of their recent growth. The windfall they have experienced as prices have risen in recent years has been a double-edged sword, however. On the one hand, this has enabled the governments to quickly boost spending on measures to alleviate poverty, one of the left's core objectives. The success of these efforts has engendered widespread popular support, critical given that the populist regimes led by Morales, Chávez, and Rafael Correa in Ecuador lack the institutionalized support typically provided by political parties.

On the other hand, increased government spending has fueled inflation, especially in Venezuela where rates averaged about 30 percent in 2008–2009.[5] Rising energy prices and export revenues have also led to an even greater reliance on this sector, undermining the development of other sectors through a phenomenon called Dutch Disease, explained in greater detail by Scott G. McKinney in Chapter 6. While Brazil and Chile have effectively diversified their economies, the contestatory regimes have thus far failed to do so. Their monoexport economies remain vulnerable to market fluctuations and this raises serious questions about the sustainability of their economic success. Ironically, Chávez may be traveling down the same path his nemesis Carlos Andrés Pérez did in the 1970s when Venezuela was awash in oil revenue but failed to diversify its economy and suffered when oil prices plummeted.

Such uncertainty about the sustainability of economic growth in contestatory regimes has significant social policy repercussions. Although neither moderate nor contestatory regimes have had much success in mitigating the socioeconomic inequalities that pervade Latin American societies, they have made impressive strides in alleviating poverty through programs focused on enhancing educational opportunities, health care, and other quality of life initiatives. The success of moderate governments in Brazil and Chile in diversifying their economies will help to generate the consistent economic growth needed to sustain this progress. In seeking incremental change, these governments have implemented new social programs gradually, funding them through the formal budget process. This has not generally been the case in contestatory regimes where ad hoc social policymaking has been the norm. While this has provided for quick, short-term successes—critical to populist regimes in need of mass support—these programs are often developed and administered in an improvised manner and financed by export windfalls outside the regular budget. Consequently, when export revenues decline funding to sustain social programs may be jeopardized (Madrid, Hunter, and Weyland 2010:163).

In evaluating the performance of the moderate and contestatory left in power, perhaps the most significant distinction has to do with the quality of democracy and the potential for democratic consolidation. In some areas, contestatory regimes have outperformed their moderate counterparts. For example, governments in Bolivia and Venezuela have enjoyed higher levels of mass satisfaction, deriving in part from the infusion of oil and gas revenues into social welfare programming directed to the poor majorities. Also of note has been the effective integration of traditionally marginalized groups into the political process through opportunities to participate in community-based organizations and periodic elections and referenda. These measures have greatly enhanced the stature and populist appeal of Evo Morales and Hugo Chávez, both of whom personify the struggle of the popular classes. The election of Morales, the leader of the coca growers movement and of Aymara descent, was unprecedented in a country where the indigenous population has been marginalized since the colonial era. Similarly, the dramatic rise of Chávez has given voice to those who were all but ignored in the elite-dominated pacted system that prevailed in Venezuela. Both leaders have endeared themselves to the masses by delivering benefits, and their regimes have enjoyed strong popular support.

Ironically, while individual leaders in countries governed by the moderate left have achieved great popularity (Chile's Michelle Bachelet and Brazil's Lula left office in 2010 with approval ratings around 80 percent) and there is widespread support for democratic values and principles, mass satisfaction

Evo Morales, president of Bolivia.

with the governments in Chile and Brazil has been low. This may be attributed in part to the governments' inability to ameliorate persistent inequalities and their ineffectiveness in integrating traditionally marginalized groups into the political process.[6] In societies where voters have turned to the left to cushion the blow of neoliberal policies and to deepen democracy, heightened expectations have not been met and these shortcomings have proven frustrating.

Notwithstanding these issues, the moderate left has performed well in terms of maintaining its commitment to liberal democracy. The quality of democracy has remained high and the prospects for democratic consolidation are good in countries like Brazil, Chile, and Uruguay. In comparison to the contestatory left, the moderate left has operated within relatively stable political systems in which vibrant and well-established political parties have enhanced the quality of democracy by fostering electoral competition and more consistent and professional policymaking. In contrast to contestatory regimes, moderates have sought to preserve existing representative structures rather than overhaul them, pursuing gradual change through negotiation and compromise with the opposition. Indeed, the moderate left maintains a much greater commitment to democratic pluralism and a willingness to provide space for and tolerate opposition, as evidenced by the 2010 election of Sebastián Piñera and subsequent peaceful transfer of power after twenty years of rule by the Concertación in Chile.

While contestatory regimes have generally been successful in mobilizing considerable popular support, concerns have been raised regarding their commitment to democratic principles as well as their potential for sustainability. Unlike the moderate left, the contestatory left seeks to radically transform the existing structures of representative democracy and establish a more participatory "direct democracy." To this end, upon taking power contestatory regimes work quickly to enact constitutional changes that solidify their hold on power. Under these new provisions power is concentrated in the executive, weakening or even dissolving legislatures and other institutions of government deemed exclusionary, inefficient, and corrupt. From the perspective of leaders like Chávez, Morales, and Correa and their supporters, such measures are necessary to create systems that are responsive to the needs of the masses and are capable of implementing policies that will bring immediate relief to them.

However, others would argue that the quality of democracy in countries ruled by the contestatory left has been severely eroded by these and other actions. In marginalizing legislatures and judiciaries, regimes seek to circumvent "established institutions of consultation and deliberation," thereby undermining the system of checks and balances that is the hallmark of liberal democracy (Weyland 2010:14). The use of harassment, intimidation, media control, and other tactics to suppress those who oppose the government has deeply polarized societies and also violates basic liberal democratic principles. The dearth of viable institutions essential to a vibrant democracy is also troubling, both in terms of the impact on the quality of democracy and the potential for consolidation. Contestatory regimes emerged in countries experiencing turmoil that weakened traditional party systems, and their mobilizational approach and the dominance of charismatic, populist leaders has further marginalized political parties and stultified institutional development. While strong charismatic leadership can help to fill the institutional void in the short term, it is unclear what will happen once such leaders pass from the political scene.

Moving Beyond Personalistic Regimes

The emergence of leaders such as Chávez, Morales, and Alberto Fujimori in Peru (1990–2000), who captured the imagination of frustrated electorates with direct, populist appeals independent of traditional parties, raises serious questions about the process of democratization in Latin America. The personalization and centralization of power, ostensibly as a means of addressing endemic socioeconomic and political problems more efficiently, has marginalized democratic institutions ranging from national legislatures to political parties, electoral agencies, and civic organizations. The tradition of powerful executives is deeply ingrained in Latin American political cultures, yet strengthening Latin American democracy will require measures to curtail the powers of the executive while bolstering those of the legislature and the judiciary as autonomous branches of government. Further, democracy must be deepened to transform the narrow, elitist rule that has long characterized Latin America (Peeler 2009). This process may come about through the formation of nongovernmental organizations, including neighborhood associations and peasant groups, to give voice to popular demands. Such demands also may be channeled through political parties and party systems, widely recognized as the key to stable, democratic rule.

Party Politics and Elections

The existence of formal democratic bodies, such as political parties and competitive elections, does not alone necessarily guarantee representative government (Edie 1991:48). Parties and elections perform critical functions, however, and are essential components of democratic systems (Przeworski 1991; Mainwaring and Scully 2010). The resurgence of party politics and competitive elections during the 1980s, after sustained periods of repressive military rule throughout much of the region, engendered great optimism regarding the prospects for (re)democratization in Latin America.

However, recent trends have tempered such optimism. Apathy and cynicism have deepened among electorates frustrated by the perceived ineffectiveness of democratically elected governments. Much of this anger has been directed toward traditional parties that have been viewed by many as corrupt, elite dominated, and unable or unwilling to address popular concerns. The precipitous drop in support experienced by such parties contributed to the rise of populist leaders such as Fujimori and Chávez and the formation of "delegative democracies," in which powerful executives dominate the political process (O'Donnell 1994). Constraints on institutional development, and particularly the marginalization of national legislative bodies and political parties, have led some to question the prospects for emerging democracies in Latin America as well as those considered to be stable and well established. Indeed, Scott Mainwaring and Timothy R. Scully conclude that "without a reasonably institutionalized party system, the future of democracy is bleak, even if feckless democracies manage to stay in place" (1995:474).

Party politics in Latin America has its origin in the early postindependence era, when informal elite groups coalesced into Conservative and Liberal Parties. Other types of parties began to appear in the more socioeconomically advanced Southern Cone countries during the late 1800s and early 1900s in response to the impact of modernization. The rise of an educated, politically aware middle class that sought access to the political process led to the formation of reformist parties such as the Radical Civic Union in Argentina and the Colorado Party in Uruguay (McDonald and Ruhl 1989:6). As electorates diversified with industrialization, party systems expanded with the emergence of Marxist, nationalist-populist, and Christian Democratic organizations. In Jamaica and elsewhere in the British Caribbean, labor union activity during the 1930s, coupled with the movement toward self-government, fostered the emergence of modern party systems. The party-union bond was strong and represented "one pillar of the democratic order" in the Anglophone Caribbean at the time of independence (Domínguez 1993:17).

Logically, there has been considerable diversity among Latin American parties in terms of ideological orientations, the structure of party systems, and the relative importance of parties in their respective systems. A significant degree of ideological variation was evident in the past, ranging from Marxism to fascism, although parties have become increasingly pragmatic in the aftermath of the Cold War. Latin American party systems have ranged from vibrant multiparty systems to stable two-party arrangements to authoritarian one-party states.

Another area of divergence lies in the nature of the functions Latin American parties perform. While some may resemble those typically carried out by North American or Western European parties (recruit new members, aggregate and articulate interests, develop programs, and select candidates to compete for office), Latin American parties also serve a number of other purposes. For example, in authoritarian systems such as Cuba after 1959 and the Dominican Republic under Rafael Trujillo, parties were created as a means of mobilizing support for the regime and of maintaining social control. In the cases of Brazil during the military dictatorship (1964–1985) and Nicaragua during the Somoza dynasty, the existence of parties and elections was viewed as a method of legitimization. In many cases, parties have served as electoral vehicles for personalistic leaders. Many also function predominantly as machines through which patronage is dispensed in return for support. In this sense, party organizations have served to channel popular participation and, in the process, have facilitated the co-optation of the masses into the existing framework under elite tutelage.

Such diversity notwithstanding, there are a number of commonalities among Latin American parties that appear to transcend cultural, developmental, and regional distinctions (McDonald and Ruhl 1989). First, they tend to be elite dominated and exclusionary, with minimal opportunity for genuine popular participation in decisionmaking. A second characteristic common to many Latin American parties has been the dominance of individual leaders and the importance of personalism in politics. As noted above, parties are frequently created to serve as electoral vehicles for those aspiring to power. Such parties typically lack any significant organizational apparatus or programmatic base, and it has been common for parties to appear around election time to support a particular individual and then to disappear when that leader passes from the scene.

Finally, while party politics in Latin America enjoyed a resurgence during the 1980s, incumbent parties across the region faced a common challenge: to govern effectively and maintain popular support in the midst of a severe economic crisis. With the ascendancy of the neoliberal economic agenda, many democratically elected leaders were compelled to implement painful economic stabilization programs that often aroused virulent opposition. The inability to promote sustained, broad-based economic growth and to improve visibly the quality of life for most citizens severely discredited some parties and their leaders. In some cases, this has facilitated the rise of populist figures who have distanced themselves from traditional parties and whose rhetoric has struck a chord of resonance among deeply disaffected publics. This trend has sparked concern as to the prospects for party politics and the consolidation of truly democratic governmental systems.

Political parties are an integral part of democratic societies, so much so that Navia and Walker conclude that "representative democracy cannot exist without political parties" and "there is no stable democracy without political parties" (2010:247). Thus, the prospects for democratic consolidation in Latin American countries are inextricably tied to the effectiveness of parties and the extent to which party systems have become institutionalized (Mainwaring and Scully 2010:377–378). Of particular concern are those cases in which populist regimes have been established amidst the decay and collapse of traditional party systems. The continued marginalization of political parties and other institutions essential to democracy calls into question the long-term prospects for stability in these countries. Yet there are also concerns elsewhere in the region. Thus far, political parties and their leaders have been only partially effective in ameliorating endemic problems. As long as basic socioeconomic aspirations go unfulfilled, support for political parties will diminish further, the legitimacy of democratic governments will be called into question, and the stability of many Latin American states will remain precarious.

*   *   *

The current transition toward democratic rule in Latin America has been bolstered by an international environment in which Western-style democracy and free-market capitalism have prevailed. Domestic conditions have been less fortuitous, however, and in much of Latin America, democratic institutions and principles are not well rooted because of the lack of a long, successful democratic tradition and a corresponding "reservoir of legitimacy." Elected civilian leaders throughout the region, including Caribbean states in which democracy is perceived to be established and stable, are under great pressure because their ability to maintain support through the use of patronage and clientelist links has been constrained by stagnant economies or the imposition of economic restructuring programs (Weyland 2004). Although democratic values are spreading and, in theory, democracy is enjoying widespread support, Latin American publics are increasingly pragmatic and demand quick solutions to their problems. Clearly, the key to consolidating democracy and averting devolution to authoritarian rule is for governments to perform effectively. Democracy is very much on trial in Latin America, and the verdict will ultimately rest on the degree to which mass publics can be satisfied without unduly provoking elites.

▪ Conclusion

Underlying the cultural, economic, and political diversity of the nearly fifty states that Latin America comprises are a number of similar patterns and experiences that facilitate (and indeed demand) a comprehensive analysis of the region. In this chapter, I have highlighted these similarities and provided an overview of the politics of this vital area. Those interested in more detailed analyses of individual countries or of the themes discussed here are encouraged to begin by consulting the sources included in the bibliography.

Contemporary political systems in Latin America, whether they are in countries where the predominant language is Spanish, English, French, Dutch, Portuguese, or an indigenous variant, have been shaped by the legacies of the past, the pressures for change that accompany modernization, and the realities of the post–Cold War international system. These systems exhibit the impact of a process inherent in transitional Latin American societies, whereby traditional institutions and values derived from a protracted colonial experience endure and blend with emergent modern ones (Hillman and D'Agostino 1992).

This blending of old and new has been evident in the patterns of leadership found within the region as personalism has remained vitally important even for democratically elected civilian leaders. Blending or "hybridization" has also been apparent in party politics, where organizations that operate on the basis of patron-clientelism remain dominated by elites, serve in some cases as vehicles for personalistic leadership, and employ increasingly sophisticated campaign techniques to contest democratic elections. The durability of the authoritarian political culture alongside the emerging democratic one attests to the fact that the past weighs heavily on the present in Latin America.

The resilience, adaptability, and persistence of traditional patterns are remarkable, given the profound transformation that has occurred in recent decades. Latin American countries are increasingly urban, industrialized, and technologically advanced. As a result, their societies are more complex and diversified, and their populations are more literate, politically conscious, and politically active. Latin American leaders now recognize that political systems cannot remain static amid such change and therefore have been compelled continually to renovate the old and to devise new institutional arrangements.

Despite divergent constitutional traditions, demographic characteristics, and socioeconomic profiles, Latin American countries have converged in several important ways over the past generation (Hillman and D'Agostino 1992; Mainwaring and Scully 2010). Most have moved toward more competitive political processes and have developed more open and proficient economic systems. At the same time, countries across the region are confronted by a host of common challenges as they seek to promote socioeconomic development and democratic consolidation. Unfortunately, as Mainwaring and Scully note, another area of convergence has been toward mediocre government performance.

In order to sustain the process of democratic consolidation in Latin America some rather significant obstacles must be overcome, many of which derive from the region's past. For example, because of persistently low levels of institutionalization, many of the former Iberian colonies possess relatively weak foundations on which to establish stable, democratic political systems. A variety of factors have impeded institutional development, including the tradition of personalism, intense repression, and demobilization practiced by bureaucratic authoritarian regimes, and the emergence of populist regimes in which power has been centralized and personalized.

Even in the Commonwealth Caribbean, where strong political institutions and democratic structures were transplanted through British colonialism, the prospects for further consolidation are mixed. The Westminster model of parliamentary democracy, "Caribbeanized" to fit the regional context, has exhibited strong authoritarian features. Elitism and limited mass participation; pervasive patron clientelism; and the dominance of personalistic leaders such as Vere Bird (Antigua), Eugenia Charles (Dominica), Eric Gairy (Grenada), and Eric Williams (Trinidad) have limited democracy in practice (D'Agostino

2009). Popular confidence in democratic leaders and institutions has diminished and consolidation has been hindered by economic stagnation and deteriorating living standards. A heightened sense of alienation and frustration pervades the region, particularly among the poor and the younger generation, contributing to rising levels of violence and emigration that threaten economic and political stability.

Elected civilian leaders throughout Latin America will have to deal with national military institutions that traditionally have played an active political role, essentially comprising a "fourth branch" of government. Democratic consolidation will require greater civilian control over the military, not an easy task given this reality. Although few military leaders in the region are eager to return to power, the constitutional mandate to preserve order and stability and a long praetorian tradition raise the possibility of some form of military intervention if civilian leaders prove incapable of keeping the peace. Indeed, the June 2009 coup in which Honduran president Manuel Zelaya was removed from power reminds us that Latin American militaries are significant political actors.

Finally, democratically elected governments will continue to be challenged to perform more effectively. This implies not only promoting sustained economic growth, but also distributing benefits more equitably. Latin American societies have long been characterized by deep inequities and neoliberal policies served to exacerbate the gap between the haves and have nots. Despite impressive growth in the region in the mid-2000s, over 200 million people continued to live below the poverty line and neither governments on the right or left (moderate or contestatory) have achieved much success in reducing inequities (Navia and Walker 2010:261). To that end, democracy must be "deepened" and the masses incorporated into the political process to ensure that government policies will respond to their needs (Peeler 2009). This must be accomplished in a way that preserves democratic safeguards and does not unduly provoke skeptical elites.

Over the past three decades, since the transition from military rule began, there has been undeniable progress in the promotion of democratic values, processes, and institutions in Latin America. A greater respect for human rights and civil liberties has evolved, along with a growing consensus that democratic elections constitute the sole legitimate route to power, and more dynamic and robust civil societies have evolved. Of particular note has been the diversification of leadership across the region. In addition to Evo Morales, a native Aymara in Bolivia, several female leaders have come to power in what has been referred to as the "Era of La Presidenta."[7] This trend has been particularly evident in South America, with Michelle Bachelet in Chile (2006–2010), Cristina Fernández in Argentina (2007–present), and Dilma Rousseff in Brazil (2011–present). In addition, Laura Chinchilla was elected president of Costa Rica in February 2010 and Kamla Persad-Bissessar was appointed prime minister in Trinidad and Tobago in May 2010. In a region with a long

Michelle Bachelet, former president of Chile.

tradition of machismo and male-dominated politics, this represents a significant accomplishment.

Nevertheless, the prospects for democratic consolidation remain uncertain as Peeler suggests that many democracies in the region are fragile and "of very low quality" (Peeler 2009:208). The demands and expectations among highly mobilized populations far exceed the capacities of most Latin American governments to fulfill them, engendering widespread cynicism and frustration. In some cases, this has facilitated the rise of populist leaders, weakening traditional political parties and other intermediary organizations essential to democratic societies. In others, politics has grown increasingly contentious and, over the past decade, several leaders have failed to complete their terms amid turmoil. Such trends are worrisome and do not bode well for the near future, underscoring the reality that twenty-first-century Latin America faces many of the same problems that have plagued the region in the past.

▓ Notes

1. See "Júarez Counts 3,000th Homicide of 2010" (2010).

2. As Peeler (2009:153) notes: "Most governments in the region, confronted with debt and fiscal crises and with hyperinflation, and politically unable either to finance social programs or to cut them, responded to neoliberal pressures ad hoc, resisting them as long as possible, agreeing to unpopular reforms when absolutely necessary, and failing to implement reforms when internal political pressures grew too intense."

3. In writing specifically about Venezuela, Weyland (2010) observes: "Although not pursuing a total transformation of the socioeconomic and political order as earlier generations of leftist radicals did in revolutionary Cuba and Salvador Allende's Chile, Chávez's proposals and programs deviate starkly from the market orientation that became predominant after the global collapse of communism and the enactment of economic liberalization in Latin America."

4. According to Kingstone and Ponce (2010:99), "The policies that emerged under Cardoso and have been maintained by Lula da Silva reflect the triumph of a pragmatic market orientation that has come to occupy a kind of consensus centrist position in the Brazilian polity. This pragmatism places Brazil, along with Chile, squarely in the moderate left category."

5. Some estimates in late 2010 suggest inflation in Venezuela has spiked and exceeded 100 percent.

6. With regard to the moderate left, Madrid, Hunter, and Weyland (2010:145) write that "eschewing mass mobilization, it has made better policies *for* the people yet not *with* the people."

7. See Reel (2007).

▨ Bibliography

D'Agostino, Thomas J. "Caribbean Politics." In *Understanding the Contemporary Caribbean,* 2nd ed., eds. Richard S. Hillman and Thomas J. D'Agostino (Boulder: Lynne Rienner, 2009), pp. 87–131.

Diamond, Larry, Jonathan Hartlyn, Juan J. Linz, and Seymour Martin Lipset, eds. *Democracy in Developing Countries: Latin America,* 2nd ed. Boulder: Lynne Rienner, 1999.

Domínguez, Jorge I. "The Caribbean Question: Why Has Liberal Democracy (Surprisingly) Flourished?" In *Democracy in the Caribbean: Political, Economic and Social Perspectives,* eds. Jorge I. Domínguez, Robert A. Pastor, and R. DeLisle Worrell (Baltimore: Johns Hopkins University Press, 1993), pp. 1–25.

Domínguez, Jorge I., and Abraham Lowenthal. *Constructing Democratic Governance: Latin America and the Caribbean in the 1990s—Themes and Issues.* Baltimore: Johns Hopkins University Press, 1996.

Edie, Carlene J. *Democracy by Default: Dependency and Clientelism in Jamaica.* Boulder: Lynne Rienner, 1991.

Edwards, Sebastian. *Left Behind: Latin America and the False Promise of Populism.* Chicago: University of Chicago Press, 2010.

Grugel, Jean. *Politics and Development in the Caribbean Basin: Central America and the Caribbean in the New World Order.* Bloomington: Indiana University Press, 1995.

Hillman, Richard S. *Democracy for the Privileged: Crisis and Transition in Venezuela.* Boulder: Lynne Rienner, 1994.

———. "Intellectuals: An Elite Divided." In *The Unraveling of Representative Democracy in Venezuela,* eds. Jennifer McCoy and David Myers (Baltimore: Johns Hopkins University Press, 2004), pp. 115–129.

Hillman, Richard S., and Thomas J. D'Agostino. *Distant Neighbors in the Caribbean: The Dominican Republic and Jamaica in Comparative Perspective.* New York: Praeger, 1992.

Inter-American Development Bank. "Latin American and Caribbean Macro Watch Database." http://www.iadb.org.

"Júarez Counts 3,000th Homicide of 2010." CNN, 2010. http://www.cnn.com.

Kingstone, Peter R., and Aldo F. Ponce. "From Cardoso to Lula: The Triumph of Pragmatism in Brazil." In *Leftist Governments in Latin America: Successes and Shortcomings,* eds. Kurt Weyland, Raúl L. Madrid, and Wendy Hunter (New York: Cambridge University Press, 2010), pp. 98–123.

Knight, Franklin W., and Colin A. Palmer, eds. *The Modern Caribbean.* Chapel Hill: University of North Carolina Press, 1989.

Madrid, Raúl L., Wendy Hunter, and Kurt Weyland. "The Policies and Performance of the Contestatory and Moderate Left." In *Leftist Governments in Latin America: Successes and Shortcomings,* eds. Kurt Weyland, Raúl L. Madrid, and Wendy Hunter (New York: Cambridge University Press, 2010), pp. 140–180.

Mainwaring, Scott, and Timothy R. Scully, eds. *Building Democratic Institutions: Party Systems in Latin America.* Stanford: Stanford University Press, 1995.

———. *Democratic Governance in Latin America.* Stanford: Stanford University Press, 2010.

Malloy, James M., and Mitchell A. Seligson, eds. *Authoritarians and Democrats: Regime Transition in Latin America.* Pittsburgh: University of Pittsburgh Press, 1987.

McDonald, Ronald H., and J. Mark Ruhl. *Party Politics and Elections in Latin America.* Boulder: Westview Press, 1989.

Meyer, Michael C., and William L. Sherman. *The Course of Mexican History,* 5th ed. New York: Oxford University Press, 1995.

Millett, Richard L. "Introduction: Democracy in Latin America: Promises and Perils." In *Latin American Democracy: Emerging Reality or Endangered Species,* eds. Richard L. Millett, Jennifer S. Holmes, and Orlando Pérez (New York: Routledge, 2009), pp. 1–4.

Millett, Richard L., Jennifer S. Holmes, and Orlando Pérez, eds. *Latin American Democracy: Emerging Reality or Endangered Species.* New York: Routledge, 2009.

Navia, Patricio, and Ignacio Walker. "Political Institutions, Populism, and Democracy in Latin America." In *Democratic Governance in Latin America,* eds. Scott Mainwaring and Timothy R. Scully (Stanford: Stanford University Press, 2010), pp. 245–265.

O'Donnell, Guillermo. *Modernization and Bureaucratic-Authoritarianism: Studies in South American Politics.* Berkeley: Institute of International Studies, University of California, 1973.

———. "Delegative Democracy." *Journal of Democracy* 5 (1994): 55–69.

Payne, Anthony. "Westminster Adapted: The Political Order of the Commonwealth Caribbean." In *Democracy in the Caribbean: Political, Economic and Social Perspectives,* eds. Jorge I. Domínguez, Robert A. Pastor, and R. DeLisle Worrell (Baltimore: Johns Hopkins University Press, 1993), pp. 57–73.

Payne, Anthony, and Paul Sutton, eds. *Modern Caribbean Politics.* Baltimore: Johns Hopkins University Press, 1993.

Peeler, John A. *Building Democracy in Latin America,* 2nd ed. Boulder: Lynne Rienner, 2009.

Pérez, Orlando J., and Jennifer S. Holmes. "Conclusion." In *Latin American Democracy: Emerging Reality or Endangered Species,* eds. Richard L. Millett, Jennifer S. Holmes, and Orlando Pérez (New York: Routledge, 2009), pp. 347–355.

Przeworski, Adam. *Democracy and the Market.* Cambridge: Cambridge University Press, 1991.

Reel, Monte. "South America Ushers in the Era of La Presidenta." *Washington Post,* October 31, 2007. http://www.washingtonpost.com.

Stone, Carl. "A Political Profile of the Caribbean." In *Caribbean Contours,* eds. Sidney W. Mintz and Sally Price (Baltimore: Johns Hopkins University Press, 1985), pp. 13–53.

Von Mettenheim, Kurt, and James Malloy. *Deepening Democracy in Latin America.* Pittsburgh: University of Pittsburgh Press, 1998.

Weyland, Kurt. "Neoliberalism and Democracy in Latin America: A Mixed Record." *Latin American Politics and Society* 46, no. 1 (2004): 135–152.

———. "The Performance of Leftist Governments in Latin America: Conceptual and Theoretical Issues." In *Leftist Governments in Latin America: Successes and Shortcomings,* eds. Kurt Weyland, Raúl L. Madrid, and Wendy Hunter (New York: Cambridge University Press, 2010), pp. 1–27.

Weyland, Kurt, Raúl Madrid, and Wendy Hunter, eds. *Leftist Governments in Latin America: Successes and Shortcomings.* New York: Cambridge University Press, 2010.

Wiarda, Howard J. *Latin American Politics.* Belmont, CA: Wadsworth, 1995.

5

The Military

Paul W. Zagorski

For those who had become complacent about the potential dangers the military poses to democracy in Latin America, the Honduran *golpe de estado* (coup) of June 2009 should have served as a wake-up call. Honduras is only one of a series of potential flash points. Countries where leaders of the populist left have come to power, including Venezuela, Bolivia, Ecuador, and Nicaragua, may see the unfolding of the same dynamic. So far, this dynamic is reminiscent of the 1960s and 1970s: leftists come to power by constitutional means and then push the legal limits of their authority; an elite wary of any significant modification of its social and economic privileges resists; finally, the armed forces intervene to remove the offending leftists from power. However, a coup and its immediate aftermath are not the end of the story. Military intervention sets the stage for political instability and often a cycle of coups. With luck and judicious action by national and regional leaders, this outcome may well be avoided. But if the reemergence of past problems is to be avoided, leaders will have to take into account the history, traditions, and practices of the armed forces; advance the establishment of institutions and civilian expertise conducive to consolidating civilian control over the armed forces; and avoid potential pitfalls civilians frequently confront in dealing with the military.

▩ The Historical Legacy of Civil-Military Relations in Latin America

Over time the Latin American armed forces have adapted to changing political and social circumstances, much as a biological species adjusts to changes in its natural environment. As the environment changed, old practices and patterns were made to serve new purposes, and new structures and techniques were developed to meet old challenges. From the time of the European conquest, the military has played a key role in frontier security and, on occasion, in the maintenance of internal order. From colonial times, the armed forces have had a privileged corporate existence whereby individual members gain status and rights by their group membership. Yet there have been significant changes as well as continuity. The class origins of members of the officer corps, the military's doctrine and matériel, and the political orientation of the military have changed markedly even in the past century and a half.

The Conquest and Wars for Independence

The political role, the social prestige, and the privileges of the armed forces were an outgrowth of the Iberian tradition. This tradition, especially in the case of Spain, was heavily influenced by a strong military ethos. The transplantation of the tradition was no mere coincidence. In 1492, Spanish forces took Granada and completed the *reconquista* (the Christian reconquest of the Iberian Peninsula from the Muslims). With the destruction of the last Moorish stronghold in the peninsula, Spain and its military aristocracy were, quite literally, looking for new worlds to conquer. The fall of Granada freed resources to support Columbus's expedition to do just that. By chance rather than design, that New World, instead of India, turned out to be America, but in any event that world promised wealth in land and precious metals. Moreover, America was populated by "heathens" who in Mexico and the Andes were organized into empires with substantial military forces. The similarities between the Old World and the New World were unmistakable, and institutions and practices that had been successful in the Old World were transferred to the New World. Not the least among these was the fusion of military power, social prestige, and landed wealth. During the colonial period, military forces were required to extend European control against indigenous peoples yet unsubjugated, to suppress them when they revolted, and to defend the crown's possessions against depredations by European rivals.

Despite the role that they were meant to fulfill, imperial garrisons were relatively modest in size and capacity, compared with the expanse of territory they had to protect and the missions they were assigned. The New World could not be held in subjection to the Old World by force alone. Spanish and Portuguese rule was based on strong mutual interest, linking the mother country with the interests of the *criollos* (creoles; Europeans born in the Americas). Yet local and imperial interests diverged in a variety of ways, most tellingly over trade and issues of local self-rule. The reforms of the late eighteenth century provided a glimpse of increased trade and expanded local economic activity without resolving these antagonisms. Thus, it was not surprising that when the Napoleonic Wars and their aftermath provided Spanish America and Brazil the opportunity to gain more control of their own affairs, they took it. The first quarter of the nineteenth century found the local population first asserting its own autonomy and finally demanding independence.

Brazil's declaration of independence was not contested by the mother country, thus paving the way for the continuance of the established social and political institutions (including the Portuguese monarchy). And, for a variety of reasons, even the wars of independence in Spanish America modified rather than displaced the existing military traditions. Not the least of the reasons was the fact that these conflicts were indeed wars for independence rather than social revolutions. Moreover, the *caudillos* (military strongmen) played the pivotal role, relegating other actors to essentially supporting positions. Although intellectuals could provide the rationale for independence by popularizing the rights of man, as proclaimed by the French Revolution, only military force could secure independence and establish a new government's authority.

In Spanish America, more than in the newly independent United States, the process of gaining independence and establishing government was fraught with problems. Social conditions in Latin America did not provide an adequate basis for establishing effective republican institutions that guaranteed equal rights to all citizens. Local loyalties provided rallying points against central authority. *Caudillo*-led military forces were both part of the solution and part of the problem. Only they could unify nations by force. However, reliance on force also promoted the region's divisive tendencies. Schemes for a nearly regionwide government for Spanish-speaking America (most notably Simón Bolívar's Gran Colombia) collapsed in a welter of factional infighting and local revolts. The lack of a professional, competent, and effective military institution and the personalistic character of military leadership made it easy for local leaders to rebel against national or transnational authority. Successful *caudillos* became presidents who were threatened, in turn, by other *caudillos*. Moreover, the lack of a dominant independent small farmer class (the preponderant group in most parts of English-speaking America) meant that there was little civilian counterbalance to the militarization of politics. Thus, the process of mobilizing armies of the disenfranchised carried the danger of social instability without the promise of establishing stable republican institutions.

In sum, the nineteenth-century military inherited many characteristics from the periods of imperial rule and wars for independence. Military leadership brought prestige. Such leadership was personalistic and relied on a fusion of social, military, and political roles. The military continued to have *fueros* (certain institutional rights and privileges) that separated it from the rest of society and limited the jurisdiction of civilian courts over military officers. As a general rule, the military could not adequately fulfill its missions of frontier defense, internal pacification, and protection of the government against armed revolts. In fact, to speak of "the military" as if it were a unified, centrally organized institution entails an oversimplification at best. In Brazil, rivalries between the professional officer corps and the militia officers in the hinterland caused their interactions to be dysfunctional. In much of Spanish America, the weakness of national armies meant that ad hoc military forces under amateur generals remained a part of the system. Latin American countries continued to be plagued with problems of external and internal security that *caudillo*-led military forces could not address adequately: foreign threats to the territory of the state; military rebellion; and, in some cases, the need to subdue and pacify indigenous peoples.

Early Professionalization

Given the inadequacies of the military system in the nineteenth century, it is not surprising that modernizing administrations would seek to promote military reform. The rationale for the change is not hard to understand. The state needed to be modern if it were to survive and prosper. Military reform was one part of a complex of changes meant to modernize the state apparatus and provide the basis for economic development. Thus, by the end of the nineteenth century, this new element was added to the Latin American armed forces. And when governments and military reformers sought modern models on which to reorganize their own forces, they looked to Europe. Britain, France, and Germany sent military missions to Latin America to assist in the restructuring of both armies and navies; these European rivals were happy to provide both matériel and advice. Thus, as the twentieth century began, few countries believed they could afford to be without their own foreign experts, lest regional rivals gain a decisive advantage in acquiring or defending disputed territory. A modernization race had begun.

Modernization required professionalization. New equipment, new organizations designed to use the equipment effectively, and a reserve system capable of raising mass armies required an officer corps capable of managing such complex new elements of military power. The new demands of officership meant that officer recruitment and promotion practices also had to be changed. This transformation induced by professionalization, although gradual, was worldwide and thorough in scope. It occurred in the United States and Europe as well as in Latin America. For example, during the US Civil War, many general officers were politicians or other members of the social elite. A division or regimental commander had to have certain military virtues: courage under fire and the ability to lead. Although professional military training was desirable, it could be dispensed with for lower-ranking commanders, provided the senior general in the field had the requisite background. Thus, political connections or the ability to raise troops personally provided alternate means of access to the officer corps for nonprofessionals. A half-century later, by the time of World War I, nonprofessional credentials for advancement would no longer suffice. Military officers had become professional managers of military operations who were charged with managing large numbers of specialized troops with new and complicated weapons systems over great distances. The age of amateur generalship was over. The age of modern warfare had begun.

Although the military modernization race did not lead to the sort of continental war that eventually occurred in Europe, changes in Latin America were no less dramatic. With more effective national military organizations, governments were able to suppress revolts by regional *caudillos* and indigenous peoples. Professional military staffs settled down to long-range planning to meet foreign threats. After the War of the Pacific (1879–1884), which helped spur professionalization, relatively few major regional wars were fought. The major large-scale exception was the Chaco War between Paraguay and Bolivia from 1932 to 1935. Yet professionalism advanced, and the character of the officer corps itself was eventually transformed.

Professional officership entailed its own set of norms and habits—a military mentality that influenced the way in which officers addressed military and political issues. In the eyes of professional officers, international conflict was not simply a matter of personal ambition, but the result of inexorable geopolitical forces. National strategy required professional analysis and direction. The issue of military power became much broader than the immediate size and condition of the armed forces. The military power of modern states rested on an economic and social base, the cultivation of which became a matter of military concern. Military decisionmaking specifically and governmental decisionmaking generally (if it were to be done properly) took on a technical cast. In addition, professionalization gave the armed forces yet another reason for asserting their traditional privileges against the political class: the technically proper direction of the military institution required that trained professionals make military decisions. At all costs, civilians must avoid the "politicization" of the armed forces that occurs when politicians interfere with personnel matters or questions of policy internal to the military.

Professionalization provided an additional basis for asserting military tutelage over politics. Many of the early-nineteenth-century constitutions had provided for military enforcement of law in emergency situations; others established the armed forces as guardians of the constitution, a virtual fourth branch of government. These legalisms had provided a pretext and legal cover for dictatorial rule by military *caudillos,* and such constitutional provisions continued to exist into the twentieth century. Whereas *caudillos* could use such provisions to support their personal ambitions, the new officer corps could cite them as the legal rationale for asserting its institutional interests. In short, changes brought about by professionalization made the military more than just a vehicle by which individuals sought power; it became an institutional actor in its own right. Members of the professional officer corps were socialized through a lifelong system of education and step-by-step promotions that gave them their own esprit de corps and tended to insulate them from the rest of society. Political policies and actions that affected individual officers often had an effect on the officer corps and armed forces as a whole. Collective perceptions were likely to induce collective action. The military had developed a new relationship with the rest of society.

What is the best shorthand characterization of this relationship? Were the armed forces progressive or conservative? Did they represent the middle class or their own distinct institutional interests? Scholars do not agree on answers to these questions. Military officers formed lodges of nationalist and even progressive orientations. Dissatisfied with the politics and policies of conservative cliques, military men applied pressure for political reform in a number of countries in the 1920s and 1930s. In fact, as late as 1968, leftist military coups overthrew civilian governments in Peru and Panama. Yet the armed forces' commitment to political and social change was far from the norm by the late twentieth century. Although the armed forces might have challenged conservatives on policies that seemed to promote economic backwardness and threatened eventual social upheaval, the officer corps usually saw leftist activism as even more suspect. Thus, the armed forces often played an important role in "breakthrough" or "middle-class" coups that challenged the unilateral control of the entrenched elites early in the century. But as the twentieth century wore on, military officers more commonly led "veto" coups to defend their institution's autonomy or to prevent the adoption of leftist policies that seemed to threaten national unity through their class-based appeals (Huntington 1968: 221–227). Today, yet another subtle shift back to the left may be beginning.

Today, as throughout most of the modern era, the military's political role has been ambiguous. This ambiguity has been more the result of officers' professional development than of their class origins. In fact, the class makeup of the officer corps had changed. The professional standards of merit and time-in-grade tended to discourage the scions of the social elite from choosing a military career; the sons of the elite could no longer step into high-ranking military positions commensurate with their social status. For the lower middle class, however, the promise of a free education and of career prospects that exceeded opportunities in civilian life more than offset the disadvantages. Thus, professionalization changed the class composition of the officer corps but, even more, it imbued professional officers with a mentality that distinguished them from other members of the middle or upper classes (Abrahamsson 1972:17–20).

Professionalism also entailed a technocratic mentality that saw knowledge and technical skill as keys to problem solving. Professional military leadership, after all, required more than personal charisma; it demanded the mastery of technological and organizational skills. In military science, as in engineering and other technical fields, there were better and worse solutions to problems as well as nonsolutions. Tactical and strategic doctrines (the principles for employing military force to fulfill military missions) were not matters of personal taste. Doctrine was to be grounded on an understanding of supposedly scientific principles. It was the product of disciplined investigation, not the product of majority vote.

Professionalism also reinforced the principle of discipline. Military organizations could not function effectively—and the nation itself would be put at risk—if personal interests and opinions were not ultimately subordinated to the authority of the command structure. Professionalism also meant loyalty to the nation above all else. Family, class, and party loyalties had to be subordinated to this higher good. Military officers were expected to set aside such extraneous loyalties, and they expected that governments would avoid anything but professional considerations in their governance of the military institution.

It is hard to imagine a worse match than that between the professional officer and the politician. Compromise, bargaining, and the satisfaction of factions and interests are the very substance of politics. To the professional officer, these activities seemed mildly unsavory at best or totally corrupt at worst—hence, the ambivalence of the military's attitude toward politics and government. In professional terms, at least in theory, politics was something to be avoided. Yet in practice, such an apolitical stance was out of harmony with the Latin American tradition and with what military officers themselves often saw as overriding national needs.

Thus, although professionalization did not mean the abolition of military intervention into politics, it did alter, by way of addition, the motivation for such intervention. Defense of military professionalism against the intrusion of politics, as well as the promotion of national power, became additional rationales for military involvement. Nonetheless, military involvement in politics rarely entailed the long-term displacement of civilian institutions until the 1960s. As individuals, officers could gain a political following because of their military careers but, when they became involved in long-term politics, they normally reverted legally to a civilian or retired status. As an institution, the armed forces served as a balancer or mediator or intervened to protect the autonomy of the institution from what it considered undue political control. After a coup, the armed forces often ruled the country for only a brief period until an acceptable version of the status quo ante could be reestablished, and then they returned to the barracks. But whether military rule was long or short term, political coups, like elections in consolidated democracies, were a widely accepted—almost normal—means of transferring power and ensuring a more general stability.

In sum, by the middle of the twentieth century, professionalization had changed the character of the armed forces in part, but had not—as it had in leading countries of Western Europe and the United States—marginalized them as a political force. Latin American officers had ceased to be amateur military leaders drawn primarily from the upper class. Officers came much more frequently from the middle sectors and developed a distinct attitude toward modernization, class conflict, and national power. In Latin America, effective political power continued to be held primarily by a relatively narrow portion of the population, and coups usually were staged to preserve rather than threaten the ruling sectors. Military dictatorships replaced democracy and vice versa, but overall there were few substantial political or social changes.

▓ The Emergence of the New Professionalism

Yet nothing remains stable forever. In fact, the image of a cycle of civilian governments and coups d'état, with the military always preserving an adjusted status quo, is part simplification and part wishful thinking. Dynamic forces underlay this apparently banal cyclical repetition. In actuality, politics as usual, as well as the armed forces' peculiar role in it, came under considerable pressure as the twentieth century wore on.

Problems of Political Development

Traditionally, political demands in Latin America had been accommodated by intra-elite bargaining, and new social and economic groups had been co-opted by a process of adjustment that allowed for the gradual expansion of privileges to these new groups. In this manner, commercial interests and the middle sectors had managed to gain entry into the system that had originally excluded them. But with accelerated social and economic change, it became difficult to accommodate new groups successfully and still maintain practices that were essentially exclusionary in nature. Likewise, it was becoming less possible for the armed forces to carry out their balancing role—intervening for short periods and then returning to the barracks—because more than piecemeal changes in the political system seemed to be required. Something had to give, and it did. The military eventually moved from a moderating to a ruling role under the rubric of what came to be called "the new professionalism" (Stepan 1971: 177–183).

Events in Argentina, one of the socioeconomically most advanced countries in the region, illustrate the sorts of challenges that eventually faced most Latin American regimes and their armed forces. By the second decade of the twentieth century, the Radical Party, based on the support of the rising middle sectors, had finally broken the traditional elite's monopoly on political power. Political reforms enfranchised the middle sectors and allowed for effective political competition. Sectors of the armed forces were sympathetic to this development. But by 1930, the military was reacting defensively to what it saw as President Hipólito Yrigoyen's attempt to make senior military appointments on the basis of political criteria. This political-military conflict led to a coup and a period in which the armed forces became more rather than less entrapped in politics. For a decade and a half, military presidents or civilian protégés of the armed forces ruled the country. The military aligned itself with conservatives and attempted to block an accession of Yrigoyen's Radical Party to power. A pattern emerged that continued into the 1980s: no constitutionally elected president served a full term and handed over power to an elected successor.

In the 1940s, the Argentine armed forces' balancing act was complicated even more by the emergence of a labor movement and the appointment of military officers to normally civilian portfolios. Political and administrative issues increasingly became daily concerns for the officer corps. The crisis occurred in 1946, when Colonel Juan Perón, the labor minister, was dismissed from his post and imprisoned by his military colleagues in the government. Perón and his wife, Eva, had cultivated the labor movement as a base of support, and Eva Perón helped mobilize masses of urban workers to demand his release. Their success eventually culminated in a multiterm Perón presidency and the creation of a Peronist political party and labor federation. Even a successful coup that removed Perón from office in 1955 could not remove the newly awakened working class as an important political actor. Periodic bans on Perón himself, his party, and Peronist candidates handicapped and fragmented the movement but could not destroy it. The lower classes could no longer be ignored. In less industrialized countries and countries where political party development was different, the pattern by which the disenfranchised lower classes became a critical factor varied. Yet in almost all instances, maintaining stability could not be achieved simply by buying off and incorporating relatively small and organized groups into the power structure.

By 1960, this social and political problem had assumed a military dimension. The victory of Cuban revolutionaries in January 1959 energized the radical left throughout the region. Whereas mainline communist parties had declared that revolution was impossible in the short term, Fidel Castro's guerrillas and the 26th of July Movement had demonstrated the opposite. The Cuban Revolution provided a model and Cuba itself provided a base of support for would-be revolutionaries throughout Latin America. The facts that the revolutionaries were overly optimistic, their opponents overly alarmist, and the initial analyses of the causes behind the revolutions wide of the mark are beside the point. Latin America seemed on the brink of violent left-wing revolution. A military response was inevitable.

This response came in the form of the national security doctrine, which was at the core of the new professionalism. Traditionally, professional armed forces focused on external threats. Strategy, tactics, organization, and the acquisition of matériel were premised on deterring and fighting against neighboring states or others that could effectively threaten the territorial integrity of the state by outright military invasion. In this vein, Latin American countries had developed military institutions designed to fight conventional wars. Involvement in domestic politics had been the by-product of Latin American constitutions and political traditions rather than of professionalism per se. The new national security doctrine changed all that. The primary enemy was now subversives—citizens of the country itself. This enemy's primary logistic and recruitment base was not the elaborate depot and training system of a foreign conventional armed force, but was a portion of the country's citizens who provided direct and indirect support as well as recruits for the guerrillas. Thus, military concepts for fighting wars (military doctrine) had to change.

Military theorists in many countries, inside and outside Latin America, had considered the problems associated with this sort of internal war. Although significant differences existed in the strategy and tactics they recommended, a common thread ran throughout their analyses. Irregular forces—guerrillas who fought a hit-and-run war of attrition—were the direct military threat and would have to be defeated. However, an effective strategy would also have to provide for defeating the logistic, intelligence, and recruitment bases; otherwise, no final victory would be possible. The defeat of the guerrillas would be tactical only, and armed conflict could easily reemerge. These analysts also went a step further, by stating that the underlying cause of subversion was the lack of social, economic, and political development. And, more ominously, they concluded that a proactive policy on all levels was likely to be more successful and much less costly than a simple reactive response (Stepan 1971).

Much of the expansion of the military's new role, as defined by this proactive new doctrine, took relatively benign forms: nation building and civic action—programs to develop physical and human infrastructure, supposedly in areas where governmental and private sector efforts were inadequate. More threatening were the expansion of military intelligence into the domestic arena and the possibility of the armed forces taking over ordinary police functions. The stage was set for a qualitatively and quantitatively different sort of military political involvement.

The militarization of politics did not emerge immediately. Initially, the altered threat perception gave impetus to such regionwide efforts as the Alliance for Progress, designed to address underlying social, economic, and political problems as well as US-induced and indigenous efforts to redirect military attention to the internal guerrilla threat. But as the Alliance and other reform efforts faltered, military attention became more fixed on internal threats. Thus, it was not surprising that the 1960s saw the renewal of another cycle of military governments throughout the region.

The National Security State

Most of the governments of this cycle were strikingly different from those of prior periods of military rule. Previously, the armed forces had functioned primarily as moderators. Their direct interventions were usually relatively brief and, on the whole, did not involve the armed forces as an institution assuming civilian administrative functions. Except at the most senior levels, military personnel tended to remain in military posts. Even long-term military presidents normally left active duty and developed civilian support as a foundation of their governments.

The national security doctrine changed this. The new national security state was meant to do something quite different from repairing and reestablishing the political status quo. Military governments assumed the mission of reforming the underlying social, economic, and political structure that had been the source of instability. Thus, the military took on a new long-term "ruler" role that rested on the national security doctrine and the well-established tradition of military intervention. The watershed between the old and new patterns of rule was stark. Before the 1964 Brazilian coup, the armed forces in most countries played the more limited "moderator" role whereas almost every intervention after the coup established military governments with much broader aspirations. The move from moderator to ruler roles is betokened by the number of coups and duration of military regimes. During the 1964–1990 period, only Mexico, Costa Rica, Cuba, Venezuela, and Colombia escaped military rule. Most of these military governments were initiated post-1964, and many endured for a decade or more attempting to reconfigure their nations' politics.

These new-style military governments generally went through a number of phases. The first was a stabilization phase, which generally took a year or two. Coups were normally induced by a variety of problems: subversive violence, political deadlock, economic difficulties, and threats to the viability of the armed forces. Stabilization was meant to suppress these threats. Coups frequently led to a political recess: the abrogation of political guarantees, the closing of Congress, and the banning of certain individuals and political parties. Military interveners took control of key civilian institutions, and security was tightened. Frequently, subversives or suspects were detained without trial, exiled, or sometimes executed. Where open combat occurred, the armed forces often assumed direct control of the civilian population, establishing curfews and sometimes moving whole villages and enlisting civilians in part-time paramilitary units. In almost all instances, armed resistance was negligible or it quickly collapsed. In the economic realm, governments took steps to control strikes and to curb inflation through stern fiscal measures.

As the initial crisis faded, the military government could turn its efforts to the second phase—constructing new institutions. If the country was to become economically progressive and politically stable, new social, economic, and political habits had to be developed. This phase was never more than sketched out by military doctrine, and the task of creating new institutions was much more complex than simply seizing power and imposing order. Militaries in various countries took different tacks, but a number of common themes emerged. The executive branch of government had to be strengthened. Political participation had to be restructured to prevent uncontrolled mass mobilizations and the undue influence of special interests. Patriotism and duty had to be the dominant ideological themes; class struggle as a rallying point had to be eliminated. The economy had to be modernized to produce dynamic rates of growth. Institutional capacity to prevent and contain social turmoil was essential.

Yet by the beginning of the 1980s—and in certain countries even earlier—when the construction of new institutions was far from complete, many military-sponsored reforms had miscarried. In addition, the armed forces' authoritarian rule had provoked widespread opposition, often involving such mainline sectors as the church, professionals, and segments of the business community. Moreover, the effort at national reconstruction eventually entangled the armed forces in a host of issues that were unfamiliar to them and that engendered factionalism within the institution itself. It was time to strategically retreat.

Thus, in most countries, the last phase of military government—transition to civilian successors—did not go as the armed forces had originally anticipated. The transfer of power was meant to maintain the achievements of the military regimes, including a major domestic role for the armed forces. It was to have been a gradual and carefully orchestrated process.

However, in actual practice, these transfers were driven to a greater or lesser degree by popular pressure and factions within the armed forces themselves. Patterns varied from country to country. Transitions ranged from forced exit to military-dominated transfer. The best example of the former is the Argentine military's exit in December 1983, which was spurred on by the disastrous Falkland (Malvinas) Islands War eighteen months earlier. The prestige of the military was at an all-time low, and the military government's amnesty law was revoked by its civilian successors.

The most nearly successful military-staged transition was that in Chile, where the military-inspired constitution of 1980 provided the vehicle for installing a new regime. Even in Chile, however, the transition did not go exactly as scripted. The military junta had hoped to have a single, regime-nominated candidate (the incumbent, General Augusto Pinochet) approved by the voters. However, in October 1988, the no vote against Pinochet gained the majority, and the regime was forced to use its fallback mechanism: a competitive election. In this contest, held one year later, pro-regime candidates also lost. Nonetheless, the military's constitution largely held against popular pressure to change it. The military retained most of its prerogatives as spelled out in the document, including appointed senators, an additional eight-year term for incumbent service chiefs, and a fixed portion of the gross domestic product (GDP) for the military budget.

■ Problems in the Contemporary Era

The national security state is dead, but issues from the past—some as old as the Iberian tradition, some associated with the national security doctrine—remain on the Latin American political agenda along with new issues that have emerged in the post–Cold War era. At the core of all these issues stands one central question: Can the armed forces be made democratic instead and their tendencies toward political intervention contained and eroded? Solving this problem requires something more than simply amending the language of written documents; it entails changing deep-seated practices and attitudes. Establishing a democratic vocation for Latin America's armed forces involves two related tasks: engendering apolitical professionalism and protecting human rights.

Apolitical Professionalism

Advanced democracies have relied on a number of methods to protect against military authoritarianism. Among the most important of these is cultivating the norm of apolitical professionalism both within the military's own ranks and in the broader political community. Such apolitical professionalism grants the armed forces a significant degree of autonomy, but only within a rather narrowly defined field of competence. Military autonomy is generally limited to matters of organization and tactics whereas decisions concerning missions and overall funding are the province of civilian policymakers. On such matters of high military policy, the senior officers are competent to give advice, but their advice alone does not determine policy. On all other matters of policy, military opinion is irrelevant; or, more accurately, professional military opinion is by definition nonexistent. Apolitical professionalism is clearly out of step with the Latin American tradition of military involvement in politics. The adoption of apolitical professionalism would mean the loss of the armed forces' role as a political balancer. It would lead to the abandonment of the new professionalism's claim that the armed forces have a broad professional competence in developmental and internal security matters. It would undermine their role as managers and administrators in a host of governmental and quasi-governmental institutions that are only loosely connected to military competency, as that term is narrowly understood.

Is such a change possible? Even though almost every newly reestablished civilian government has favored the adoption of standards of apolitical professionalism and almost every Latin American military force has announced that the armed forces are essentially nondeliberative, history would counsel caution. Latin American civilian governments have rarely succeeded in getting full control of the armed forces except in a revolutionary context for, only in such circumstances, could the military institution be completely purged and restructured or even abolished.

Yet it is altogether too rash to believe that the past will determine the future. The development of a military ethos, whether apolitical or highly politicized, depends in large measure on the context in which the military organization operates. Professional military officers—those specially recruited, trained, commissioned, and promoted within a bureaucratic system designed to manage the

instruments of modern warfare—generally have two seemingly contrary attitudes: conservatism and distaste for politics. They tend to be conservative because they are, by temperament and training, extremely nationalistic, skeptical
of idealistic projects, and alarmist. They also believe in the necessity of using
force to settle conflicts. Yet they also find the naked self-interest, compromise,
and bargaining of politics distasteful because it conflicts with the technical,
engineer-like approach to problems that typifies the military professional.
Hence, in stable regimes with no overriding constitutional conflicts that adversely affect the ability of the government to actually govern, a well-established
professional ethos leads to apolitical armed forces. Only in the face of serious
ideological and constitutional crises does the armed forces' inherent conservatism kick in. They are apt to step in to make their presence felt in promoting
authoritarian and nationalistic solutions to the country's problems.

In Latin America, the professionalization of the armed forces that began a
century ago never produced an apolitical force. Endemic political and social
conflict has been sufficiently severe to induce repeated military involvement
in politics. Yet by the twenty-first century, Latin American circumstances have
changed. The experiences of the national security state have taught all parties
something about the limits of military competence, the dysfunctional nature
of revolutionary and counterrevolutionary violence, and the value of the rule of
law. The past two decades have seen both progress and retrogression. Some
countries have developed civilian-led defense ministries, placed civilians in
control of domestic intelligence operations, and have begun to develop mechanisms for overseeing the armed forces.[1] In other countries, the armed forces
have effectively resisted assertion of meaningful civilian control. In Venezuela,
the military has even seen its political role enlarged. So there are grounds for
hope, although major stumbling blocks to establishing civilian control remain.
And should the economic downturn besetting the region continue, it would only
exacerbate the tensions referred to earlier between leftist populists, the established power structure, and the armed forces.

Human Rights

Not the least of the stumbling blocks to establishing civil control is the human
rights issue. During and sometimes immediately preceding military rule, the
armed forces of many countries fought what they believed was an ideological
war of national survival. To be fair, in most instances, the threat of violent subversion was real, if exaggerated, and there was often widespread support or
tolerance for the military's action at the time it was undertaken. Still, it is also
unquestionable that the military's prosecution of such wars often involved
glaring human rights violations.

Acts of torture, murder, rape, and detention without judicial sanction violated both national and international laws and, in some cases, they occurred on

a massive scale. The armed forces argued that their actions were absolutely necessary for the defense of the nation, and most military officers remained unrepentant long after they were removed from power. They argued that the guerrillas and their allies were foreign agents (combatants operating without color of legal belligerency or internationally required insignia and uniforms) and, hence, outside the protection of the law. The military viewed any attempt to punish violators as an attack on the armed forces as an institution and an effort by the losing subversives to carry on the war by other (psychological) means. Foreseeing the potential for legal sanctions, military governments often tried to ensure for themselves an amnesty before the transfer of power to civilians.

When elected governments first returned to office, the human rights issues posed a dilemma for them. If they ignored past violations, they risked creating a precedent for impunity that the armed forces or police could use to suppress civil commotion (a real possibility) or to engage illegally in domestic intelligence and covert actions (a less likely but still important avenue for military intervention). Moreover, the armed forces easily could have interpreted governmental tolerance for past abuses as a sign that the government was not really serious about establishing civilian control over the military. However, if civilian governments attempted to challenge the armed forces by trying a significant number of officers, they also risked serious consequences. The armed forces had ample means to make the government pay a high price for its efforts, ranging from lobbying and the reliance on right-wing political allies to outright revolts. Thus, efforts to prosecute human rights violators seemed likely to be time consuming, to detract from other government reform efforts, and to require the expenditure of a good deal of political capital.

In Argentina, Raúl Alfonsín's attempt to escape this dilemma during the mid-1980s foundered. President Alfonsín tried to distinguish between the military as a necessary and valued institution and individual officers who had committed heinous crimes. Nonetheless, he could not induce the armed forces to prosecute their own, nor could he convince them of the validity of his distinction. Three military revolts were each followed by embarrassing government backdowns that seemed to indicate that the armed forces had won. Chile's Truth and Reconciliation Commission, established by the new civilian administration of Patricio Aylwin in 1990, was another attempt to find some sort of middle ground. But here, too, the armed forces have been unwilling to express remorse for any excesses that took place under the Pinochet regime and remain adamantly opposed to any rights prosecution, although a number have gone forward. El Salvador in 1993 established a similar commission as the result of the peace agreement that ended the war between the government and leftist rebels.

Although hardly a perfect fulfillment of national and international legal obligations, such half-measures were useful in buttressing, however imperfectly, the principle of due process of law. Such actions are akin to locking the

The infamous Naval Mechanics School in Buenos Aires, Argentina, where thousands were illegally detained, tortured, and murdered during the Dirty War.

barn door after the horses are stolen, but the installation of locks in such cases is reasonable if one intends to buy more horses. In other words, any action against past abuse serves notice that future violations may carry significant risks. Moreover, the escalation of conflict over the rights issue by the military carries significant costs for the armed forces themselves. Military intransigence over the rights issue in Argentina cost the institution prestige, deprived it of financial resources, and sapped its will to resist reform in other areas.

Initially, rights violators in the Argentine military seemed to get the better of the justice system. Alfonsín's rights prosecutions came to naught when the succeeding president amnestied the convicted officers. A de facto understanding in Brazil has made prosecution of rights violators largely a nonissue. A referendum upheld the amnesty in Uruguay shortly after the return of civilian government there. But by the end of the 1990s, the situation had begun to change. Although a full reckoning remained highly unlikely, aggressive prosecutors found the political climate supportive of their actions. Military saber rattling no longer seemed to terrify civilian politicians and the general public. Despite amnesties in Chile and Argentina, a number of generals in both countries awaited trial for rights violations, and the head of Chile's notorious secret police was in prison. The chief of staff of the Argentine army has formally apologized for rights violations by his forces, and other service chiefs there have followed suit. Even self-congratulatory Chilean military leaders have finally admitted that errors were committed. Perhaps the most spectacular case is that of Augusto Pinochet, who was arrested in London in late 1998 to face trial in Spain. He, too, in an open letter, apologized—although obliquely. Subsequently, protracted legal haggling blocked his extradition to Spain, and Pinochet returned to Chile. Although he escaped prosecution in Chile, he did so on the grounds of advanced age, poor health, and diminished mental capacity—hardly an edifying position for Pinochet personally or the Chilean military as an institution.

Rights prosecutions have continued at a desultory pace in Chile, Argentina, and elsewhere similar to the manner in which Nazi war criminals were haphazardly brought to justice in the post–World War II era. Eventually time may render the issue moot, just as Pinochet's death in 2006 finally closed the books on talk of his further prosecution. However, some progress has been achieved in recent years. In Argentina, military personnel who abducted the babies of those "disappeared" by the military junta that ruled the country from 1976 to 1983 were brought to trial in 2006, and in 2008 one of the leading members of the junta was sentenced to life in prison. In 2010, Chile's newly elected conservative president Sebastián Piñera rejected calls to pardon dozens of military officers convicted of human rights abuses. In the same year the Uruguayan government began efforts to abolish an earlier amnesty law. And in 2011 in Brazil, a country where trials for human rights violators had been completely off the political agenda, the justice ministry supported legislation to establish a commission to investigate abuses committed by the armed forces.

Other Opportunities and Traps

Most civilian governments appear to recognize the need for military reform, although efforts and results have varied. There is no easy way to solve the problems involved in establishing effective democratic control of the military and securing the rule of law, but a number of changes have merit and require persistent oversight. The military code of justice should be reformed to remove the concept of "due obedience" and should establish in its place the principle that each soldier is responsible for obeying the law. Due obedience, at most, should be a mitigating rather than an exculpating argument. Civilians should assume the control of unified defense ministries and establish the mechanisms and develop a cadre of personnel with sufficient skills to make their formal control meaningful. Strategy and grand strategy, as well as the acquisition of major weapons systems, should be areas in which civilians have both the legal authority and knowledge to make ultimate decisions.

Even more important, civilians should no longer knock on the doors of the barracks during a political crisis in an effort to promote a coup. And in a lesser but related matter, civilian presidents must not rely on the armed forces as a substitute for civilian political support and administrative talent. Both of these temptations remain real in the contemporary era.

Although the specific causes for the second phenomenon are quite diverse, they fall under two main headings. First, the armed forces often wish to retain at least a veto power over significant government policies outside the military sphere as strictly defined, or they may even seek to expand their role. The administration of state companies, civil construction, and environmental management provide jobs for military officers and a reason to expand the military budget. A second impulse toward overreliance on the armed forces comes from the other direction. Civilian presidents may seek out military officers to fill cabinet and other high-level positions. Latin American political parties are frequently factious and ill-disciplined, and civilian appointees may be more interested in dispensing patronage and preparing for the next election than in efficient administration. In such instances, a president of dubious popularity and legislative support may well do as Brazil's Itamar Franco did in the last year of his interim presidency (1994) and appoint military officers to his cabinet instead of civilian politicians and business-based experts whom he labeled "birds of prey." In contrast to their civilian counterparts, military officers seemed more committed to strengthening the executive branch and achieving administrative efficiency and less prone to becoming involved in the worst aspects of interest group politics.

However, such reliance on the armed forces includes very real dangers. Using military officers in governmental posts in which civilians should have adequate expertise stifles democratic development, provides a military filter on the advice and information the president receives, and positions the armed forces to support an *auto-golpe* (self-coup). Indeed, a self-coup—an executive maneuver supported by the military suspending the operation of the legislature and the courts—is a likely route for the armed forces to follow if they are to assume power again. In April 1992, President Alberto Fujimori of Peru successfully used such a move in the context of an ongoing guerrilla war and economic crisis. Pressure from the international community forced a partial retreat, and Peru held elections for a new constituent assembly/legislature by the end of the year. In June 1993, President Jorge Serrano of Guatemala tried the same thing. In the Guatemalan case, however, political protests forced Serrano's resignation, and human rights ombudsman Ramiro de León Carpio was elected by the legislature to fill the vacated presidential chair.

Political deadlock, the fiscal and administrative collapse of the state, widespread outbreaks of popular disorder, or worse, are not out of the question in much of Latin America as the region continues to face serious economic challenges. Whether the armed forces co-opt the president or the president co-opts them is largely irrelevant. The dynamics of executive dictatorships are not conducive to democratic development. When a similar self-coup occurred in Uruguay in 1973, the government felt impelled to be more and more repressive and exclusionary until finally the civilian president was replaced with a general. There is a compelling need to restrict the sphere of military activity to areas in which their organization and expertise are essential and do not threaten democracy. Military skills, useful and necessary in dealing with defense matters, are often inappropriate in other fields.

Instead of militarizing civil administration to consolidate democracy, governments should civilianize the upper levels of the military bureaucracy. This task is a politically and technically delicate one. There is no strict dividing line between responsibilities that are purely military and those that are simply at the discretion of the civilian political leadership. Rather, various sorts of activity each have a particular balance of civilian and military responsibility. The development of tactics, training, promotion, and internal discipline are largely, but not exclusively, matters of military concern. Budgets, procurement of major weapons, the defining of military missions, and matters of war and peace are fundamentally the concern of civilians, although sound military advice is important.

Establishing civilian control requires the appointment of civilians to the posts of defense minister and other senior-level positions as well as the creation of competent civilian staffs. It also requires the establishment of legislative oversight committees. But at least as important is the development of civilian expertise in defense matters. Civilian authorities must be capable of evaluating the advice of their nominal military subordinates. Political leaders, academicians, and others must be capable of engaging in a technical dialogue with military officers. Without adequate knowledge, civilians will find it difficult to gain meaningful control over and real respect from the armed forces.

What Should Be the Role and Mission of the Armed Forces?
Regardless of who actually controls the armed forces—civilians or uniformed officers—these authorities have to decide what the military's purpose is. This is no longer as obvious as it used to be because global and regional developments have radically undermined old assumptions. The 1980s saw the end of the national security state and the disappearance of revolutionary communism as a major ideological force. Thus, the collapse of the Soviet Union in 1991 capped a series of events that rendered obsolete most of the Cold War missions that had been integral to military planning in the Americas for decades.

Defense against external aggression? One of the primary missions, if not *the* primary mission, of any state's military forces is the territorial defense of the country against external attack. Over the course of more than a century and a half of independent statehood, Latin American countries have seen this mission change considerably, although perceptions have frequently been slow in catching up with reality. In the nineteenth and early twentieth centuries, Latin American countries generally had more to fear from their immediate neighbors than from other powers. Thus, the adoption of modern professional forces that focused systematically on this mission made good sense. The military staffs of professional forces could simulate conflicts with neighboring states and could formulate contingency plans and organize and train forces in light of their results. But by the mid-twentieth century, wars between Latin American states were little more than border skirmishes, and the investment of significant public resources on external defense seemed questionable. The US-inspired mission of hemispheric defense against Soviet invasion seemed hardly less credible as the Soviet Union, even at the height of its power, lacked the capacity for significant force projection into the Western Hemisphere. Its existence, however, did provide a pretext for defense spending and equipment acquisition.

The potential for a major imminent external threat was further undermined by the movement to regional integration begun in the mid-1980s by newly returned civilian regimes. Economic and diplomatic cooperation became the watchword, and it made little sense to maintain the fiction that the country was threatened with conventional cross-border attack. Hence, a number of military prestige projects—most notably the nuclear weapons programs of Brazil and Argentina—came into question. Why maintain large forces, a mobilization base, and research and development programs to develop technologically advanced weaponry if national security could not justify the cost?

It has taken time, however, for logic to erode bureaucratic and intellectual inertia. Prestige projects are always hard to give up. Decreasing the size of military forces and changing their mission wreaks havoc with established career patterns and powerful institutional interests. Moreover, geopolitics is popular among military intellectuals. It propounds the notion that international politics is the struggle between states for territory and that states function as "living" organisms in this Darwinistic survival of the fittest. War or at least preparation for war with neighboring states is the natural (and sensible) order of things. Yet the military has gradually shifted emphasis away from such war preparation and has cut the size of its forces.

In the beginning, this downsizing was more a result of financial exigency than clearly thought-out arguments or an explicit rejection of geopolitics. But as the 1990s progressed, military integration and the demilitarization of borders became increasingly a matter of policy rather than a response to tight budgets. For example, two old rivals who almost went to war in the early 1980s, Argentina and Chile, have undertaken joint military exercises. A peace treaty has resolved the border conflict between Peru and Ecuador that sparked a war as recently as 1995.

Internal defense and development? The traditional activities involved in internal defense—frontier security, the imposition of order in remote areas, and the use of military force to supplement police forces in times of internal disturbance—have their roots in preindependence times. The activities associated with the national security doctrine—domestic intelligence, civic action, and direct control of the population—are of more recent vintage and more controversial. Latin American states are attempting to strike a balance between restricting the armed forces entirely to external defense and simply allowing them to participate in internal defense operations in an unregulated fashion. Civilian governments have begun to address a variety of issues through constitutional change, statute, or decree.

Domestic intelligence? Modern states need some sort of mechanism to defend themselves and their citizens against those who would engage in political violence: bombings, assassinations, kidnappings, and politically motivated common crimes. And Latin America has certainly not been immune from such outbreaks. The task is to protect the government and society without degenerating into a police state. The Dirty War in Argentina, with thousands of extrajudicial murders, is an object lesson about what can happen when security forces, the military, or both are unrestrained by due process or any constitutional checks.

To correct these problems, a number of governments have downsized and restructured their intelligence services. Domestic intelligence is now largely restricted to gathering information rather than conducting covert operations. Military units responsible for the worst abuses, such as the infamous Honduran 3-16 Battalion, have been disbanded. In other countries, such as Brazil, civilian structures have been erected to supervise the collection of intelligence information. The principle of habeas data (securing an individual's access to information collected on him or her by the government) has been legally established in a number of countries. The effectiveness of these measures in limiting the abuse has yet to be proved and will depend on the follow-through by governments and civil society. But the record is uneven. For example, in April 1998, a Guatemalan archbishop was murdered. Eventually, former members of the president's military staff were implicated, but the prosecutor and other key individuals were forced to flee the country.

Civic action, civil defense, and environmental protection? The participation of military engineers in civil construction dates back to the Napoleonic era. Yet in Latin America today, use of the armed forces in areas tangentially related to their primary competence is still a matter of some controversy. This controversy stems from a number of sources. One source is a kind of guilt by association of civic action projects with the national security doctrine, which, along with counterinsurgency strategy generally, sees the participation of military forces in projects that directly benefit the population as part of an integrated strategy. Civic action projects—such as construction of basic public facilities, especially in rural areas; immunization campaigns; and the distribution of relief supplies and other materials of immediate benefit to the population—

can be adjuncts to repressive measures directed against guerrillas and other subversives. In the context of counterinsurgency strategy, such activities are meant to win support for the government and indirectly promote the gathering of intelligence information.

In peacetime, such activities have been justified by the inability of civilian agencies or the private sector to provide such services. Yet civic action projects have been criticized for that very reason: they tend to displace civilians from technical and administrative activities that are essentially civilian in nature. Why should military personnel be involved in disaster relief and infrastructure development, for example, when civilian government agencies can be reformed and restructured to handle those tasks?

An even more disturbing sort of displacement is political displacement. Patronage is a staple of electoral politics. Leaders who are able to deliver benefits to people are often able to deliver their votes as well. Both North American ward heelers and Latin American *caciques* (local political bosses) have always understood this. What happens to the prospects of party development and democratic consolidation if the local military commander is seen as a powerful patron?

Peacekeeping? With the end of the Cold War, 100,000 military personnel and police have been deployed on peacekeeping missions under UN auspices. In January 2010 alone, there were 6,244 troops, police, and observers from Latin America deployed on such missions (see Table 5.1). The use of UN Blue Helmets is no longer restricted to areas of limited superpower competition as it was during the Cold War. Today, restrictions on deployment are essentially based on cost-benefit analysis rather than ideological considerations. This changed environment has provided an increased opportunity for Latin American countries

Table 5.1 Participation in Peace Missions in Latin America, 2010

	Police	Observers	Troops	Total
Argentina	26	8	821	855
Bolivia		30	409	439
Brazil	8	49	1,287	1,344
Chile	33	6	515	554
Ecuador		21	68	89
El Salvador	48	12	52	112
Paraguay		48	48	96
Peru		26	213	239
Uruguay	16	56	2,444	2,516

Source: UN Department of Peacekeeping Operations. Monthly Summary of Contributions, January 31, 2010. http://www.un.org/en/peacekeeping/contributors/2010/jan10_1.pdf.

to participate in peacekeeping, and many of them have done so. Troops from Argentina, Brazil, Chile, Uruguay, and Venezuela have participated in operations in such places as Cambodia, the Persian Gulf, Iraq, El Salvador, Mozambique, Cyprus, Haiti, Congo, and Croatia. This participation provides more than UN financial support; it provides actual operational experience with multinational forces, some of whose elements come from technologically advanced forces. Such opportunities have been sorely lacking for most Latin American armies. These operations can also provide an environment to help induce change in the military's organizational culture. In an interview, Argentina's army chief of staff noted that army battalions deployed in Croatia not only had their geographic horizons expanded, but also saw the beginning of a transformation of the army's traditional caste-like barriers between officers and enlisted personnel. UN peacekeeping also provides a rational immediate use for small, well-trained forces that most military and civilian leaders see as a hedge against future threats to the state's national security and territorial integrity.

Counternarcotics operations? Another nontraditional mission that has recently come into vogue is counternarcotics operations. Such operations involve the armed forces in surveillance and interdiction of shipments of drugs, their precursors, and chemicals needed for processing. Additionally, the armed forces are tasked to destroy drug laboratories and eradicate coca and poppy fields used for the production of drugs. In the late 1980s, the George H. W. Bush administration saw military involvement in these endeavors as part of a comprehensive war on drugs. The military seemed suited for the mission in that it had personnel and technology that could be useful in the antidrug effort. In Colombia, the military has become deeply involved in counternarcotics efforts as the guerrillas they have been fighting for three decades became first indirectly and then directly involved in the drug trade.

However, many other Latin American governments and armed forces were not so sure about engaging in counternarcotics efforts. To military officers, employing the armed forces in the counternarcotics struggle threatened to reduce their status. Given global conditions after the end of the Cold War, Latin American militaries were looking for advanced military missions, not ones that seemed to confuse their role with that of the police. Civilian governments, wary of the dangers in military role expansion, also were often less than enthusiastic. Moreover, the temptation of corruption, when traffickers could offer bribes that far exceeded the value of military pay, threatened to put the institution's integrity at risk. After all, large-scale military involvement in drug trafficking was not unknown in Latin America during the 1980s.

Nonetheless, the United States was at times able to offer significant inducements. Little US military assistance was available to Latin America outside the counternarcotics field, and acquiring sophisticated radars and sensors

*A convoy of military vehicles moving into Ciudad Júarez,
the epicenter of the Mexican drug war.*

necessary for part of the effort was appealing. In addition, in the case of coca-
producing countries like Bolivia and Peru, which provided most of the supply
for Colombian-based drug cartels, the United States tied economic aid to the
fulfillment of national coca eradication targets.

Thus, in Peru, the armed forces became heavily involved in counternarcotics operations, although not without cost. At the height of the struggle against
Sendero Luminoso (Shining Path) guerrillas in the late 1980s, counterdrug operations threatened to undermine efforts to win over the coca-growing peasantry.
And the influence of drug money was corrosive. In mid-1994, the commander-
in-chief of the armed forces announced that 100 officers were being tried for involvement in the drug trade. Despite the associated problems and little hope for
a decisive victory, the United States has continued to push for military involvement in the so-called war against drugs. In Mexico, President Felipe Calderón's
war on the drug cartels has involved significant deployments of troops and outright combat between the cartels and military forces. The use of the military is,
in large measure, a result of the corruption and ineffectiveness of the Mexican
police, but has led to charges of serious human rights violations.

An Interim Balance Sheet

Today, the overall picture of civil-military relations is generally heartening.
Although there continue to be areas of serious concern and outright setbacks,
democracy is more secure, and the armed forces are less politically influential

than they were at the time of the transition from military to civilian governments. The past two decades eroded the influence of the armed forces on a number of fronts: attempted coups were infrequent and, except for two instances, unsuccessful; civilian control over the armed forces increased; impunity for rights offenders generally disappeared, as some former offenders were brought to trial; military budgets grew in some countries, but not disproportionately; and nationalism took a backseat to regional and subregional integration.

The expansion of civilian control over the armed forces has continued in many countries of the region. For example, the Brazilian government has abolished the separate armed forces ministries and subordinated them to a single defense ministry headed by a civilian. By the same token, the president's military household, which included the three military ministers, has also been abolished. In Honduras, the government has abolished the draft, separated the police from the armed forces, and done away with the post of military commander-in-chief of the armed forces, stripping the military of much of its autonomy and establishing a defense ministry in its place. Argentina, too, has abolished conscription. Regionwide, many governments have established civilian-run defense ministries; some have established permanent civilian staffs and placed civilians in key positions in the chain of command, although much work remains to be done.

Unlike earlier periods, challenges to democracy and to civilian control of the military today represent a disparate set of problems rather than a broadly based regional trend. Perhaps the most potentially unstable situation exists in Colombia. Whereas civil wars in Central America have been ended by negotiated settlements and Peru's civil war has seen the near collapse of the insurgents, Colombia's long-lived civil war with left-wing guerrillas continues. In Colombia, systematic violence associated with rampant drug trafficking, corruption, and continuing human rights abuses by the armed forces provides a disturbing example of what can go wrong as countries attempt to deepen and consolidate democracy. The country's problems feed on one another. Guerrillas derive part of their resources from the drug trade and part of their legitimacy from the defense of *campesino* (peasant) coca and poppy growers. The military uses guerrilla success as a pretext for a no-holds-barred war in which the civilian population often becomes a target.

Aided by mass movements, military officers and former military officers have vied for power in a number of countries. In 1998, Lino Oviedo, a general cashiered for participation in a coup two years earlier, won the ruling party's nomination for president of Paraguay. And, in February 1999, Hugo Chávez assumed office as Venezuela's elected president. Chávez, as a lieutenant colonel, had led an unsuccessful coup in 1992. A similar situation occurred in Ecuador where another lieutenant colonel, Lucio Gutiérrez, who helped lead a coup in January 2000, was elected president less than two years later.

In Venezuela, Chávez's presidency has been divisive, to say the least. His cavalier attitude toward the rule of law and the political opposition has produced a backlash that has been largely ineffectual and itself flouts the law. Chávez not only uses the armed forces as an important instrument for building political support, he has commandeered political authority, riding roughshod over established institutions. In 2009 he succeeded in amending the constitution to extend indefinitely his eligibility for reelection to the presidency. The fact that he acts with broad electoral support has prompted the opposition to view dissidents within the armed forces as potential saviors from the predicament, despite their unsuccessful coup attempt in 2002.

Of greater concern, Chávez's populist style of leadership has been copied by presidents in Bolivia, Ecuador, Honduras, and Nicaragua. In Honduras, the June 2009 coup was precipitated, at least in part, by the fear that President Manuel Zelaya, limited to one term by the constitution, was seeking to abolish that limitation. In short, although institution building and the extension of civilian control over the military have advanced in some countries, economic and institutional weaknesses have propelled the armed forces back into the political arena in others.

▓ Conclusion

Contrary to the expectations of most analysts at the beginning of the 1990s, the military's political influence eroded considerably throughout Latin America during the decade. The military as an institution, which had been a pillar of authoritarianism for centuries, is evolving as a result of a changed regional and global context. The national security state that existed from the 1960s through the 1980s represented the culmination of a number of trends in the evolution of Latin American military institutions. The national security state was authoritarian, statist, and stressed traditional values—as had the Latin American armed forces since the time of the conquest. It was modernizing, technocratic, and meritocratic, as the professional armed forces of the region had been, at least in aspiration, since the turn of the twentieth century. But the national security state could not last; it lacked a distinctive ideology to legitimize its institutions. And in fact, it proclaimed itself to be transitional. Where it achieved a modicum of success, as in Chile, the regime's own rules and its human rights transgressions provided the legal basis and substantial motivations for a transfer to the opposition. Where it was an almost unqualified failure, as in Argentina, the experience of the national security state delegitimized military governance almost everywhere. As Thomas J. D'Agostino points out in Chapter 4, military governance, for the most part, performed poorly in the economic sphere.

Moreover, the political and social environment in the twenty-first century differs substantially from that of the mid-1960s, when the national security state first arose, and new issues have emerged. The experience of repression has made the left realize the importance of competitive elections and due process. The end of the Cold War has meant muted ideological competition. Failure of state socialism globally and the foundering of state-led development in Latin America have both narrowed policy options and made Latin American countries more susceptible and receptive to international influence. The armed forces themselves fit into this general pattern. To be modern and professional means to follow Western European and North American institutional patterns. The armed forces must not only be technologically advanced, highly mobile, and capable of joint (air-land-sea) operations, but they must also be nondeliberative, obedient, and apolitical. The need to modernize, professionalize, and restructure the military is clear to both civilian and military leaders.

This is not to say that the process of reform is easy and free of contention as recent events show. Economic difficulties limit the availability of funds for military modernization. The potential for social turmoil continues to provide a pretext for resurrecting an attenuated version of the national security doctrine. The armed forces in some countries, such as Venezuela, Peru, and, during the late 1980s, Argentina, divided openly into factions over the issue of subordination to political authority. In most countries, the exact role of the military has yet to be defined and, more important, sincerely accepted by members of the armed forces themselves. Thus, despite epoch-making shifts, the armed forces' democratic vocation is still in the balance.

▩ Note

1. For a detailed discussion of the advance of civilian control, see David Pion-Berlin (2009).

▩ Bibliography

Abrahamsson, Bengt. *Military Professionalization and Political Power.* Beverly Hills: Sage, 1972.

Alexander Rodríguez, Linda, ed. *Rank and Privilege: The Military and Society in Latin America.* Washington, DC: SR Books, 1994.

Finer, S. E. *The Man on Horseback: The Role of the Military in Politics,* 2nd ed. Boulder: Westview Press, 1988.

Goodman, Louis W., J. S. R. Mendelson, and J. Rial, eds. *The Military and Democracy: The Future of Civil-Military Relations in Latin America.* Lexington, MA: D.C. Heath, 1990.

Hunter, Wendy. *The Eroding Military Influence in Brazil: Politicians Against Soldiers.* Chapel Hill: University of North Carolina Press, 1997.

Huntington, Samuel P. *The Soldier and the State: The Theory and Politics of Civil-Military Relations.* New York: Vantage Books, 1964.

———. *Political Order in Changing Societies.* New Haven, CT: Yale University Press, 1968.

Loveman, Brian. *For la Patria: Politics and the Armed Forces in Latin America*. Wilmington, DE: SR Books, 1999.

Lowenthal, Abraham F., and J. Samuel Fitch, eds. *Armies and Politics in Latin America*. New York: Holmes & Meier, 1976.

Nordlinger, Eric A. *Soldiers in Politics: Military Coups and Governments*. Englewood Cliffs, NJ: Prentice Hall, 1977.

Pion-Berlin, David. *Through the Corridors of Power: Institutions and Civil-Military Relations in Argentina*. University Park: Pennsylvania State University Press, 1997.

_____. "Defense Organization and Civil-Military Relations in Latin America." *Armed Forces and Society* 35, no. 3 (2009): 562–586.

Pion-Berlin, David, and Harold Trinkunas. "Democratization, Social Crisis and the Impact of Military Domestic Roles in Latin America." *Journal of Political and Military Sociology* 33, no. 1 (2005): 5–24.

Rouquié, Alain. *The Military and the State in Latin America,* trans. Paul E. Sigmund. Berkeley: University of California Press, 1987.

Ruhl, J. Mark. "Curbing Central America's Militaries." *Journal of Democracy* 15, no. 3 (2004): 137–151.

Stepan, Alfred. *The Military in Politics: Changing Patterns in Brazil*. Princeton: Princeton University Press, 1971.

———. *Rethinking Military Politics: Brazil and the Southern Cone*. Princeton: Princeton University Press, 1988.

Trinkunas, Harold A. *Crafting Civilian Control of the Military in Venezuela: A Comparative Perspective*. Chapel Hill: University of North Carolina Press, 2005.

UN Department of Peacekeeping Operations. Monthly Summary of Contributions, January 31, 2010. http://www.un.org.

Zagorski, Paul W. *Democracy Versus National Security: Civil Military Relations in Latin America*. Boulder: Lynne Rienner, 1992.

6

The Economies of Latin America

Scott G. McKinney

Previous chapters have treated geographical, historical, political, and military patterns in Latin America. This chapter analyzes economic life in the region beginning before the conquest, during three centuries of Iberian colonialism, and since independence. In the context of this background, I consider economic structures of demand and production; problems of poverty, inflation, and external debt; and renewed interest in privatization, lowering trade barriers, and encouraging foreign investment as well as the global financial crisis of 2009–2010.

Pre-Columbian Economic Life

Economic life began in the Americas with the arrival of humans searching for sustenance. After crossing the Bering Strait during the ice age and migrating southward, humans arrived in present-day Chile by 12,850 B.C.E. (Moseley 2001: 90). As they dispersed over the two continents and adapted to the environment, they improved their tools and experienced the Neolithic Revolution in ways similar to those taking place on the continents they left behind. Remains at Monte Verde in present-day Chile suggest a life based on gathering edible plants (e.g., wild potatoes, nuts, and fruits) and hunting mastodon (Smith 2009). The Painted Rock Cave overlooking the Amazon River in Brazil contains evidence of a campsite dated to 10,000 B.C.E. that supported a life of fishing and hunting as well as gathering nuts and fruits (Smith 2009).

The Neolithic Revolution—the development of farming—took place between 8000 and 5000 B.C.E. in Mesoamerica with the development of maize, in the Andes with the development of the potato and quinoa (Messer 2010), and possibly earlier in coastal Ecuador with the development of cultivated squash (Mann 2005:17–18). On the coast of present-day Peru, cultures specialized in coastal fishing and inland irrigation-based agriculture. One of the earliest cities found in this region, Caral, used irrigation to cultivate sweet potatoes, squash, beans, cotton, and gourds (Moseley 2001:113). Aspero, a smaller fishing settlement dated to 3055 B.C.E., was found on the coast at the mouth of the river. The people of Aspero used the cotton from Caral to weave fishing nets, and used the gourds as floats. In exchange, the people of Caral received a steady diet of seafood that the people of Aspero harvested from the rich waters of the Peru (or Humboldt) Current. Here along the Peruvian coast, civilization had a maritime foundation (Moseley 2001), in contrast to other major civilizations developing around the world at this time. Associated with this were long-distance sea trade and the appearance of specialized traders called *mindalas* (Moseley 2001:48–50). Despite the development of farming and the sophisticated process of adaptation, the success of cultures was always subject to sudden or long-term changes in the environment. Along the west coast of South America, intense episodes of the warm El Niño current could reduce the fishing and result in levels of rainfall that destroyed irrigation systems and weakened cultures.

In the Andean highlands, cultures adopted a diversified agropastoral life that included both farming and herding. Around 5000 B.C.E. people on the *puna,* in the high elevations of the Andes, moved from hunting vicuña and guanaco to herding alpaca and llama and raising quinoa, one of the staple grains of the region (Mithen 2004:267). In order to take advantage of the diversity of ecosystems that exist in close proximity in a rugged terrain with large variation in altitude, communities controlled vertical archipelagos of land, not necessarily contiguous, that gave them access to the different crops grown at different altitudes. As a result, though there was a small amount of trade, there was not a large-scale development of markets in the region since each group produced the variety of goods that they needed (Moseley 2001:44–48).

The Olmec civilization of the Gulf Coast of Mexico, famous for its fine stone carving and colossal carved heads, arose as early as 1800 B.C.E. The economic foundations of this civilization were maize farming and fishing (Coe and Koontz 2008:59–70). By 1000 B.C.E., the Maya were beginning to settle south of the Olmecs in the Yucatan, present-day Belize and Guatemala, growing corn and other crops. They expanded their ability to produce food and support growing populations by terracing hillsides and reclaiming swampland. By 300–800 C.E., the Maya were building large cities that may have had populations of in excess of 40,000.

New evidence from the Amazon region suggests that this ecosystem was able to support populations much more substantial than previously thought (Mann 2008:148–152). By 2500 B.C.E., there were "raised fields, channel-like canals, tall settlement mounds, fish weirs, circular pools and long, raised causeways" in the western Amazon near the border of present-day Bolivia and Brazil (Mann 2000:786). It is likely that this is the area where peanuts, rubber, tobacco, cacao, and manioc were developed. In order to maintain the land's fertility once the forest was cleared away, the soil was mixed with charcoal in order to create *terra preta* (black "fertile" earth). Across the Amazon region on the Xingu River, from the thirteenth to the eighteenth century, a culture with carefully laid out communities supported a population of 50,000 (Mann 2005:306–311).

The cultures that adapted to the various environments of the Andean region were absorbed over a short period of time by the Incas. They began a process of expansion around 1438 and, over 100 years, pushed the boundaries of their empire to the northern frontiers of present-day Ecuador and southward into Chile and Argentina. They built an impressive system of roads to move their army around; stored food in granaries so that it could be moved to regions with food shortages; and kept track of it all with a system of knots called *quipus* (Mann 2005). In 1491, just before Christopher Columbus arrived in the Americas, the Inca Empire was the largest in the world and, by some estimates, the population of the Americas was greater than that of Europe (Mann 2005:94).

In the Valley of Mexico, the Aztecs were moving in among Toltec people by the beginning of the fourteenth century, and by 1344–1345 founded two cities in the middle of a lake at the site of present-day Mexico City. The lake was used for agriculture by forming and stabilizing floating islands (Coe and Koontz 2008:190–191). The Aztecs used dams and terracing in the surrounding region to increase agricultural production. Early in the fifteenth century, they joined with two other kingdoms in a triple alliance and began a process of conquest that took them from the Gulf Coast to the Pacific Coast and to present-day Guatemala by 1502. By the time the Spanish arrived in 1519, the Aztec capital Tenochtitlán is estimated to have had a population of 200,000–300,000 (Coe and Koontz 2008:186–200).

For more than 16,000 years, the people who inhabited the Americas developed in relative isolation from the peoples in Europe, Asia, Africa, and Australia. There may have been some contact, but it was not of a magnitude sufficient to transform these two separate spheres. The two spheres went through similar processes of adaptation to their environments and social development, but they had different animals, developed different plants, suffered from different diseases, and made different uses of gold and silver.

The Colonial Period

These two worlds came into contact when large numbers of Europeans followed Columbus's arrival in 1492, causing a massive exchange of plants, animals, diseases, and culture that became known as the Columbian Exchange. Horses, wheat, smallpox, and the wheel came to the Americas while corn, manioc, potatoes, and possibly syphilis went to Europe, Africa, and Asia. At the same time, the focus of economic activity shifted in a fundamental way. It had been a process of adaptation to the local environment in order to produce a broad spectrum of products needed for survival; suddenly, a process of extracting specific products that had high value in Europe was superimposed on this indigenous foundation. While Spanish *conquistadores* were interested in individual wealth, the crowns of Spain and Portugal sought to enhance national power. Mercantilism guided European policies during this period. Interests of the crown in unifying their nations and building states merged with the interests of a rising mercantile class in acquiring the protection and support of the state. Merchants were granted monopolies and subsidies for their trading activities. The goal of mercantilism was to acquire wealth in the form of gold and silver to be shared between the state and the mercantile class, not with the general population. Wealth was useful to keep in reserve for the unforeseen—to run the state and support the military. Gold and silver were to be acquired by maintaining a positive trade balance: exploitation of the land, mineral resources, and fish stocks as well as exports were encouraged; imports were discouraged and wages were kept low. Government policies regulating trade and protecting economic activity, a strong navy, and merchant marine were all viewed as necessary for the accomplishment of these goals (Allen 1987:445–449).

As the Spaniards spread out from the Caribbean in the process described by René de la Pedraja in Chapter 3, they found resources in the form of mineral deposits and rich land at the same time that they were decimating the population with diseases to which the indigenous peoples had no resistance. In general, the Europeans at this stage were more interested in enrichment through mining and trade than in settling down to farm the land. Nonetheless, the *conquistadores* were given large land grants called *encomiendas,* putting in place an extremely concentrated pattern of land ownership that was to influence Latin America to the present day.

Silver was discovered in the 1540s in Mexico, and in 1545 the Spaniards learned from the indigenous people about the silver in Potosí, in present-day Bolivia. According to Spanish law, the crown owned the mineral resources, and miners extracting silver or gold owed the Spanish crown royalties, called the *quinto real* (royal fifth). This tax was a disincentive to mining and, as the quality of the ores declined and profits fell, the crown reduced this to a tenth, the *diezmo* (Brown 1996b:512–513). Potosí produced half of the silver flowing from the Americas to Spain before 1650 (Bakewell 1996:461). One of the difficulties was finding the labor to do the mining. It is estimated that before the Spanish arrived the population of Peru was 9 million and that it was reduced by disease to 1.3 million in 1570 (Brown 1996a:359). Conquerors interested in large-scale projects in mining or agriculture had to find ways of

The Cerro de Potosí in Bolivia, commonly referred to as "Cerro Rico" (Rich Mountain) due to the incredible wealth generated during the colonial era from silver mining.

assembling a large labor force, sometimes importing slaves and other times encouraging immigration. In order to provide labor for the mine at Potosí, Viceroy Toledo of Peru (1569–1581) took a census of the indigenous population and then resettled it into *reducciones,* which were required to contribute labor, the *mita,* for work in the mines. By 1600, however, the mining was done more by wage labor than by drafted labor (Bakewell and Brown 1996:61).

Mining activity had linkages to a broader local economy. However much the Spanish crown attempted to control production in its colonies, gradually a complex colonial economic life began to develop. The mercury needed for the process of extracting silver from the ore at Potosí came from Huancavelica, Peru; food to support the miners came from Chile; and draft animals came from Argentina (Cardoso and Helwege 1992:27). Mexico City became a major trading center, involved in trading cacao from South America, textiles from Asia, and silver and mercury from Peru. Small shops produced a wide variety of goods including furniture, glass, and paper (MacLachlan 1996:3). *Obrajes* (textile manufactures) became major industries in both Mexico and the highlands of Ecuador (Schodt 1987:24).

The positive impact that a booming sector such as silver mining has on the broader economy may be weakened by what is called Dutch Disease (Cardoso and Helwege 1992:33). One negative effect of the boom is a *production effect,* the tendency for the booming sector to attract productive resources such as labor and capital from the other productive sectors of the economy (Corden 1984:360–361). In his classic book on the exploitation of Latin America, *Open Veins of Latin America,* Eduardo Galeano describes the eighteenth-century gold rush in Brazil:

> The gold explosion not only increased the importation of slaves, but absorbed a good part of the black labor from the sugar and tobacco plantations elsewhere in Brazil, leaving them without hands. The miners were contemptuous of farming, and in 1700 and 1713, in the full flush of prosperity, hunger stalked the region: millionaires had to eat cats, dogs, rats, ants and birds of prey. (1973:66)

The second negative effect is the *consumption effect,* the tendency for a region with a sudden increase in income to produce nontradable goods and services such as buildings and restaurant meals and to import tradable goods and services such as manufactured and agricultural products. The result is that the domestic tradables sector tends to decline. It has been argued that Dutch Disease not only kept Latin America from moving beyond its original role as a provider of natural resources for Europe and North America, but that it did the same for Spain (Forsyth and Nicholas 1983). In order to maintain a successful mercantilist strategy, Spain not only had to be able to find gold and silver, but additionally had to be able to transport it safely to Europe and then produce the manufactures to send to the New World in return for the gold. Spain failed on the latter two counts. The ability of the Spanish Armada to protect Spanish vessels from piracy declined over time, accelerated by the defeat of the Spanish Armada in 1588. Rather than do the manufacturing itself, Spain flooded Europe with its gold and silver to buy manufactured products for the American colonies. In the process of doing this it provided the liquidity needed to launch the system of capitalism that replaced the feudal order (Weatherford 1988:15).

On the other side of the continent, the Portuguese began to settle Brazil, but in the early stages they found little in the way of gold or silver. The coastline was divided into twelve captaincies, putting in place a distribution of land characterized by inequality and a society dominated by the large landowners. The major economic activity was growing sugarcane and producing sugar. The indigenous population declined from about 2.4 million in 1500 to half that level by 1808 so labor had to be supplemented by the importation of Africans, which may have numbered 4 million to 5 million by 1810. Not until the eighteenth century was gold discovered in Minas Gerais, followed by other valuable commodities, including diamonds (Russell-Wood 1996:410–420).

Life in the Spanish colonies was shaken up by the succession of the Bourbons to the Spanish throne in 1700. The Bourbon reforms accelerated when the British captured Havana in 1762, allowing more trade and finally shutting down the Casa de Contratación, the bureaucracy that had managed the mercantilist apparatus, in 1790 (MacLachlan 1996:2–6). As the Bourbons attempted to squeeze more income out of the colonies, tensions rose both among the creoles and among the indigenous peoples. The eighteenth century saw numerous rebellions in the highlands of Peru (Brown 1996a:356–364). The wealthy in Mexico were also dissatisfied with the reforms, and growing concentration of land in commercial haciendas put small farmers at risk and created conditions supportive of revolution (MacLachlan 1996:6).

When independence movements swept Latin America in the early 1800s, the colonial period left behind some substantial legacies that the independent Latin American nations have had to struggle with ever since. While the economies were gradually diversifying, they remained dependent on the export of minerals and agricultural products. They inherited the Iberian legal tradition that mineral rights belong to the crown. The way in which the crowns of Spain and Portugal granted land to the leaders of the conquest resulted in a distribution of land and income that was extremely unequal. There was a small elite of *peninsulares* and *criollos,* a small middle class, including or consisting of artisans and workers, and a large poor class that included most of the *mestizos, mulatos,* Africans, and indigenous peoples. While some of the early rebellions were indigenous movements, in general independence from Spain simply replaced the *peninsular* elite with the *criollo* elite.

Independent Latin America

The early years of independence posed difficult economic challenges. Many of the countries started out with a heavy burden of debt as well as damage to the productive system from the wars of independence. With the exception of Brazil, which did not have to fight for independence, all Latin American countries defaulted on their debt in the first decade of independence (Cardoso and Helwege 1992:111).

The newly empowered Latin American elites were influenced by the European philosophy of liberalism, which emphasized the idea of liberty under the law, institutionalized in such a way that individuals could follow their own interests and desires constrained only by the liberty of others. In the context of the economy, this argument was interpreted as an argument for a market system. All individuals would have equal rights of access to the market and their interaction would lead, through the impersonal and disinterested process of the invisible hand, to greater social welfare (Dahrendorf 1987:173–175). Liberals in Latin America used these arguments to reduce the power of the Catholic Church, taking its lands so they could be used to grow export crops. Indigenous peoples were also deprived of their land, making land and the labor on it simultaneously available to the new export economy. Liberalism in Latin America included a substantial role for the state, and governments in the region encouraged this development model with "modest export taxes, public investment in social infrastructure, and promotion of foreign investment" (Bulmer-Thomas 1994:49). Improvements in transportation and rapid growth and industrialization in Europe and North America pulled the Latin American economies into the world trading system. British demand for raw materials and British sales of manufactured goods such as textiles, British financing and British shipping all kept the process moving.

The chance process by which a country begins to produce and export a particular product has been referred to as the *commodity lottery* (Bulmer-Thomas 1994:14–18). A country's draw in the lottery is influenced by various natural characteristics as well as historical accidents and entrepreneurial choices. Climate is an important factor: countries in the tropical zone will export bananas, sugar, coffee, cacao, and cotton, goods which are not grown in Europe and North America. Countries in the temperate zone of South America will export wheat, wool, beef, fruits, and vegetables that are similar to those grown in the temperate climates of Europe and North America.

Topographical and geological characteristics are also important factors. Areas with mountains, such as the high *cordilleras* that continue to be formed in the tectonically active zone on the west coast of the Americas or the older, heavily eroded mountains in southern Venezuela or central Brazil, will tend to have mineral deposits in concentrations that allow for profitable extraction (Bakewell and Brown 1996:59). Gold and silver, copper, tin, iron ore, and bauxite will often be important exports for the countries with this type of geography. On the flanks of the mountains, there will often be petroleum deposits. Along the west coast of South America the earlier oil production was to be found along the Pacific Coast, whereas more recent development has been on the east side of the Andes, often in the Amazon Basin. Rich reserves are also found offshore, in Lake Maracaibo of Venezuela, in the Gulf of Mexico, and most recently off the coast of Brazil. A third factor that needs to be mentioned is ocean currents, in particular the Peru (or Humboldt) Current that flows north along the western coast of South America. This cold, upwelling current, rich in nutrients, supports large populations of fish, which in turn support large populations of birds. This current supported the early development of civilization along the Peruvian coast, the guano boom in Peru, and also present-day fishing in both Peru and Chile.

Victor Bulmer-Thomas poses the question of whether the success of a country's export sector is translated into a process of economic development (1994:14–18). Two of the factors that are important in affecting the relationship between export growth and development are linkages and the distribution of income. A third factor, which I discuss in the section "Latin America in the Twenty-First Century," is the economic policy environment. Exports have different types and extents of linkages to the domestic economy. A mine may be an enclave with few local linkages: excavated by foreign engineers with foreign capital equipment, the product shipped abroad to be refined and sold. A small amount of local labor may be employed but, if they are paid relatively low wages, the impact that this mine has on the rest of the domestic economy will be minimal. Some economic activities may have backward linkages; shrimp farming, for example, depends on fishermen who net the shrimp larvae along the beach, laboratories where these larvae are grown to the size appropriate to place in shrimp ponds. At this stage shrimp food is needed and, when the shrimp are full-sized and ready for market, powerful pumps are required to empty the ponds. Other activities may have forward linkages, such as those of petroleum, which can be refined, turned into plastics and then plastic products, or can be used to generate power used in manufacturing. The greater the linkages of an export, the more its growth will encourage economic development.

Once the product is produced and exported, there is the question of who receives the income. This is important in terms of income distribution, investment, and the multiplier effects of domestic demand. First, there are differences in how much of the income returns to the producing country as opposed to flowing to owners abroad. One economic historian reports that the Peruvian subsidiary of Standard Oil of New Jersey paid all the local costs of petroleum production with its local sales of petroleum products and none of the revenue from exporting the remainder of the petroleum returned to Peru (Thorp 1991: 31–32). At the opposite extreme, a locally owned company could return 100 percent of the revenues to the producing country.

The distribution of ownership within the country also plays a role in the process of economic diversification and development. Coffee is produced on large plantations in Brazil so that the flow of income is concentrated and the resulting income distribution is very unequal. In Colombia the coffee farms tend to be smaller and family run, using family labor to produce a high quality bean. A national organization, the Federación Nacional de Cafeteros Colombianos, has warehouses for coffee and has been able to keep foreign coffee buyers from dominating the market. The result is that the revenues from coffee are more broadly distributed in Colombia than in Brazil, and demand for local products correspondingly greater (Thorp 1991:1–11).

The income that does return must be shared with labor and the state. Capitalists may spend their earnings abroad or domestically, invest the earnings in the same activity that generated them or diversify into a different economic activity, or use the banking system to make the resources available to other investors. Laborers will tend to use a larger proportion of their income for consumption than capitalists will; thus, the distribution of income between capitalists and laborers will influence the balance between the increases in productivity that investment can bring and the expansionary multiplier effect of consumption.

For example, in Peru during the 1890s a substantial portion of the revenues from the coastal agricultural enterprises, sugar and cotton, and from mining were paid to labor and generated demand for local goods. Linkages to local foundries further expanded the economy. Capitalists had funds to invest and, with the encouragement of rising local demand and a depreciating currency, they invested in local manufacturing, textiles, banks, insurance companies, electricity generation, tramways, and mining. However, by the turn of the century, foreign families bought up the sugar estates and moved toward more capital-intensive production, reducing the wage bill and the local demand that resulted from it. Foreign companies moved into the mining sector, falling freight rates put the local foundries out of business, and an appreciating currency encouraged exporters to plough their profits back into the export sector rather than diversifying into other sectors (Thorp 1991:23–34). This example suggests the variety of factors that influence the extent to which an export boom can set in motion a process of economic diversification and development.

The third major recipient of export revenues is the state, either through taxation of private sector earnings, as the owner of natural resources or, in some cases, as the developer of those natural resources. Here, the issue is whether the state's revenues are used productively, spent domestically or abroad, for infrastructure and capital equipment or for consumption and monuments. Ecuador, for example, has been the beneficiary of a number of booms since it became independent. The foundations for the most recent boom—the petroleum boom—were laid in 1967. A military government took power that year and fashioned a development plan with a goal of promoting "new reforms necessary to expand the potential for national development" (Schodt 1987:112–117). Between 1972 and 1979, the role of the state in the economy was substantially expanded: private firms such as Ecuatoriana Airlines were nationalized and new firms such as the Ecuadorian State Petroleum Company (CEPE) were created. The value added by public enterprises rose from 2 to 12 percent of gross domestic product (GDP) over the period 1972–1983 (Schodt 1987:112–117). In contrast to the earlier cacao and banana booms, in the case of petroleum the resource was owned by the government. Therefore, the revenues flowed directly into its coffers, enhancing its power vis-à-vis the private sector as well as the importance of Quito, the capital, vis-à-vis that of Guayaquil, the coastal financial center. These cases illustrate the power of the commodity lottery and the variety of ways that an export can affect the broader economy depending on its linkages and income flows.

Dependence on one or two major exports in a volatile global economy tended to subject Latin American economies to boom and bust cycles. Rising demand and prices for a product encourage greater production in a country and increase the country's income. To the extent that circumstances and policy conspire to create economic development on the foundation offered by the export boom, this cycle can be modulated but not escaped. The busts that follow these booms arrive for various reasons. The guano boom in Peru was followed by a bust as the guano was exhausted. Cacao and coffee booms in Central America, the Caribbean, Ecuador, and Venezuela were brought to a halt by the exhaustion of fertile lands (Bulmer-Thomas 1994). Disease can destroy production:

Ecuador's cacao plantations were attacked by fungus beginning in 1916 and, two decades later, Ecuadorian production had been reduced to 2 percent of world production (Schodt 1987:40–41). Competition from new producers can bring down the price of the product: as Brazilian and West African cacao flooded the market, the price of cacao fell 60 percent from 1920 to 1921 (Schodt 1987:40).

The period 1870–1914 is sometimes called the Golden Age of Exports. Despite the instability of the liberal model, the nineteenth century was a period of growing raw material exports from Latin America. As time went on, the exports shifted from minerals to agricultural output, and the major markets expanded from Britain to include France, Germany, and eventually the United States. Nonetheless, as new exports replaced old, diversification rarely took place. For many countries, one product generated more than 50 percent of export revenues: circa 1913 tin was the source of 72 percent of Bolivia's export revenues; nitrates 71 percent of Chile's; sugar 72 percent of Cuba's; cacao 64 percent of Ecuador's; bananas over 50 percent of export revenues in Panama, Costa Rica, and Honduras; and coffee over 50 percent in El Salvador, Guatemala, Haiti, Nicaragua, and Venezuela (Bulmer-Thomas 1994:57–60). Only Argentina, Chile, Cuba, and Uruguay achieved rates of export growth rapid enough to raise real income per capita by 1 percent per year (57–68).

However, even in countries with impressive records of export growth, the benefits of the liberal model of economic development sometimes failed to extend to a sufficient percentage of the population to maintain political stability. As Thomas J. D'Agostino explains in Chapter 4, in Mexico the years of the Porfiriato (1876–1911) were a period of liberal progress. The Porfirio Díaz government worked to modernize and unify the country, creating a national bank, and building railroads and a telegraph system. The railroads brought formerly isolated regions into a national market and commercial agriculture began to displace communal indigenous landholdings so that peasants were forced to become sharecroppers or wage laborers. The scarcity of domestic investment led the government to encourage foreign investment, and foreigners responded by buying land, building the railroads, and running the mines. By the end of the Porfiriato, there was a steel plant in Monterrey and the British El Aguila Company was producing oil. Industrialization began to take place and, as a result, a working class and a middle class developed (Tenenbaum 1996:12–14). In contrast to the period 1850–1870 when exports were declining, exports grew 4.4 percent annually between 1870 and 1890 and 5.2 percent annually from 1890 to 1910 (Bulmer-Thomas 1994:65).

Many people were hurt by these economic changes, however, and many were excluded from the political process. The middle class was interested in a more open, democratic system. Workers began striking against foreign owners in 1906; in 1909, Emiliano Zapata began leading peasants in retaking their ancestral lands. Amid calls for social justice and political change, Francisco Madero, a moderate leader who was a wealthy member of the northern landowning class, called for revolution in 1910. In 1917 a constitutional convention wrote a reformist, nationalist document that guaranteed social protection for workers, agrarian reform for peasants, and limitations on foreign ownership (Gentleman 1996:14–16). This case illustrates the tensions created by economic change and the political consequences of failing to share the benefits of that change with the entire population.

With the coming of World War I, Britain's influence in Latin America continued to decline and that of the United States continued to rise. US private investment in Latin America increased substantially. However, the money was allocated for "unproductive uses or to increase further the supply of already dangerously surplus agricultural commodities" (Thorp 1998:108). The prices of these commodities began to fall in 1927 as the world headed toward the Great Depression and fell more than 50 percent over the period 1928–1932 (Thorp 1998:104). Unfortunately for Latin America, the interest rates on its debt stayed high and its markets were gradually reduced by rising protectionism in the United States and United Kingdom. Following the United Kingdom's abandonment of convertibility in 1931, most Latin American countries abandoned the gold standard and allowed their currencies to depreciate. Once this occurred, default on their debt followed quickly. Countries responded in various ways to the Depression. For example, Colombia, Guatemala, and Brazil began public works projects. Others, such as Ecuador, used new lands to carry out import-substituting agricultural expansion and some, such as Peru, simply waited for commodity prices to turn around.

World War II opened a number of opportunities for Latin American countries: the United States moved aggressively to gain access to raw materials in the region, though price controls and delayed payments on minerals reduced the expansionary impact of rising exports. The war reduced Latin America's access to imports from Europe, Japan, and the United States, opening space for some industrialization in the region. Hence, as illustrated in Table 6.1, industrial production grew by more than 30 percent for a number of countries over the period 1938–1945 (Thorp 1998).

This relatively quick succession of challenges to the liberal experiment following on the heels of the Golden Age of Exports set the stage for a new economic philosophy. The failure of nineteenth-century liberalism to set in motion a self-sustaining process of development led to a search for alternatives, and the industrialization that took place during the war suggested what that alternative might look like.

■ Import-Substituting Industrialization

Import-substituting industrialization (ISI), derived from dependency theory, became the dominant economic policy of the post–World War II period. Dependency theory was based on Marxist analysis of the requirements for historically

Table 6.1 Growth in Manufacturing During the World War II Era, 1938–1945 (percent change in inflation adjusted value)

Country	Growth
Argentina	31
Brazil	44
Chile	84
Colombia	62
Cuba	38
El Salvador	33
Mexico	77
Nicaragua	86
Venezuela	41

Source: Rosemary Thorp. *Progress, Poverty, and Exclusion: An Economic History of Latin America in the 20th Century* (Washington, DC: Inter-American Development Bank, 1998), table 4.4, p. 119.

progressive development. This is a broad area of theory, but particularly powerful in interpreting the Latin American experience is the idea that Latin American countries constitute a periphery that depends on the economic activity in the center, which is to say the higher income, technologically advanced manufacturing countries (Palma 1987:802–805). The system of linkages in the center is dense, but the center requires raw materials from the periphery as well as a market for its manufactures. The system of linkages in the periphery is less dense and oriented to the center. To use automobile production as an example, automobile assembly in the United States might use many parts manufactured within the country while automobile assembly in Ecuador might use mostly parts imported from abroad. If automobile production in the United States were to grow, there would be a multiplier effect within the US economy as many more inputs were required from domestic producers, but the impact in Latin America might be only a small increase in demand for raw materials. If automobile production in Ecuador were to grow, a good portion of the multiplier effect would be felt in the United States, Europe, or Japan where a majority of the inputs were produced. Thus, because of the greater density of linkages in the countries of the center, these countries are more capable of self-sustaining economic development whereas the weaker linkages in the countries of the periphery leave them dependent on the demands—overwhelmingly for raw materials—of the center.

Sometimes the idea of declining terms of trade is included in the analysis. That is, the idea that over the long run the ratio of commodity prices to the prices of manufactured goods tends to decline so that the periphery's standard of living will tend to fall unless the level of raw material exports rises sufficiently to compensate (Cardoso and Helwege 1992:85–88). It is difficult to establish that the terms of trade declined during the period 1850–1913; data for the twentieth century seem to show some decline, but studies differ in their conclusions (Bulmer-Thomas 1994:78–82).

Another consideration in the analysis that motivated the shift from nineteenth-century liberalism to ISI was the extreme income inequality that continued to characterize Latin American societies. These nations had begun their independent periods with an unequal distribution of land and wealth, and no processes unleashed in the intervening years had reduced that inequality. Not only was this seen as a problem in moral and political terms, but it was also an obstacle to the process of economic development. If income was concentrated at the top of the distribution, then the lower income groups would not constitute a market for local production; in this case, the benefits of exports would not initiate a self-sustaining process of economic growth (Bulmer-Thomas 1994:277).

ISI was the policy response that evolved out of this analysis. It involved using government policy to encourage the development of an industrial sector in countries where comparative advantage or history tended to encourage specialization in mining or agricultural production. It was argued that reallocating the country's energy toward sectors with high rates of technological progress and rising labor productivity would result in economic development (Eatwell 1987:737–738).

The strategy was implemented by protecting the young manufacturing sector with tariffs and quotas; supporting the importation of capital equipment and inputs by means of overvalued or preferential exchange rates; and encouraging investment with tax incentives, subsidies, and low interest rates. Local production, often accused of being of low quality and inefficiently produced, survived behind walls of protection that raised the price of competing imports in the period 1957–1959 by an average of 143 percent in Brazil and 139 percent in Argentina as compared to only 25 percent in Peru (Sheahan 1987: 84–87).

The process of ISI began with the production of consumer goods and then was encouraged to deepen by establishing linkages to other local production. Automobile production was a classic place to start. It could begin simply as the assembly of parts imported from abroad, but over time could gradually use more locally produced parts such as tires, glass, seats, and exhaust systems. The strategy was relatively successful in the 1950s, 1960s, and 1970s. Industrial production grew at the rates of 5.2 percent, 6.3 percent, and 5.8 percent annually for the periods 1960–1965, 1965–1970, and 1970–1977, respectively, faster than in the industrialized countries but not as fast as East Asia. Manufacturing output as a percentage of GDP rose from 20.8 percent to 26.5 percent, essentially catching up to the industrialized countries and surpassing every other region by 1977 (Sheahan 1987:84–85).

The policy has been criticized for creating capital-intensive manufacturing that provided few (albeit high-paying) jobs. As a result, the goal of improving income distribution was not achieved. Industrial growth during the 1930s and through World War II tended to be labor intensive, because firms could not import capital equipment from the center. But after 1945, this constraint weakened and government policy reduced the cost of imported machinery, hurting local capital producers in the process (Sheahan 1987:83). Tariff and quota protection created a situation in which multinational corporations (MNCs) could sell in a Latin American country only if they produced there. Thus, much of the industrialization was carried out by MNCs, subverting the goal of strengthening domestic linkages. The emphasis of producing domestically for the domestic market limited the growth of production to the growth of the national economy, since universally applied ISI limited each country's ability to export to the others, simultaneously robbing the economy of the foreign exchange needed to keep ISI going (Sheahan 1987:83). Eventually, as the global situation changed and international trade become more important, ISI was criticized for supporting the growth of an inefficient sector that could not compete internationally (Eatwell 1987:737–738).

Argentina and Brazil, in addition to being quite forceful in their implementation of ISI, were among the earliest countries to attempt the transition. A comparison of their experiences provides an interesting insight into the consequences of the division of export income between capitalists, labor, and the state. Argentina began the process under President Juan Perón just after World War II ended, its close relationship with Britain leaving its coffers full of foreign exchange and its economy close to full employment. Brazil, on the other hand, had much higher levels of underemployment (Sheahan 1987:179). Perón, interested in building a manufacturing sector and strengthening his political base among the urban working classes, used differential exchange rates and a marketing board to claim about half of the agricultural sector's income and transfer it to the industrial sector. Real wages of urban workers increased 62 percent from 1946 to 1949. As urban incomes rose, domestic consumption of Argentina's exports—beef and wheat products—also increased. As a consequence, Argentina's exports fell 19 percent from 1946–1949 to 1950–1954, resulting in trade deficits and foreign exchange shortages. Perón was deposed by the military in 1955, but the conflict over resources in Argentina continues unresolved (Sheahan 1987:179–188). The ripples of Perón's policies can be seen in the first decade of the twenty-first century, with farmers protesting, striking, and withholding production in an attempt to convince President Cristina Fernández to reduce export taxes and eliminate restrictions on beef and wheat exports.

Brazil was much less extreme in its attempt to redistribute income. An estimate from 1966 suggests that only about 21 percent of the agricultural sector's income was transferred to the industrial sector, and a greater part of the benefits went to capitalists rather than labor. While output per worker rose 6.6 percent annually from 1949 to 1959, real wages in manufacturing rose only 2.4 percent annually. Brazil's export levels were protected by the smaller increase in incomes and the fact that demand for coffee did not respond as significantly to rising incomes: Brazilian exports rose 14 percent over the period that Argentina's fell 19 percent. Rapid growth in the economy, however, led to some of the same problems that Argentina encountered, trade deficits and foreign exchange shortages (Sheahan 1987:179–188). Nonetheless, the contrast between the experiences of Argentina and Brazil highlights the challenge that Latin American countries often face: how to develop an industrial sector without doing too much damage to the export sector.

Brazil was able to use a number of advantages to move beyond classic dependence and establish a new relationship with the center termed *dependent development* (Evans 1979). First, despite the fact that Britain dominated the import-export business and shipping, the coffee plantations were owned by the local elites who had profits to invest. Second, the Brazilian military had a long-running commitment to achieve national security by producing critical products in Brazil. Third, Brazil is the largest economy in Latin America and has always been willing to use foreigners' interest in its market as leverage to achieve its development goals.

While the British built and operated the railroads, it was sometimes done with Brazilian capital. Once the railroads were in place to haul coffee to the ports, they were available to haul inputs for Brazilian industry and consumer products to a broader market. Industrialization began in food and textiles early in the twentieth century. By the 1970s, the process had advanced to include transportation and electrical equipment, metal fabrication, and chemicals (Evans 1979). Manufactured exports began to play a larger role and coffee played a smaller one as US MNC investment joined domestic investment. In order to counterbalance foreign capital, Getulio Vargas built the foundations for an activist state—the Estado Novo—during his first period as president (1933–1946). Vargas convinced the United States that if it did not help Brazil build a steel plant Germany would do so. So a steel company was founded in 1941 with US help and the Companhía do Vale do Río Doce (CVRD) was established in 1942 to mine iron ore. State entrepreneurship in shipping, airlines, port management, and petroleum increased the influence of the government in investment and production (Evans 1979).

Brazil's relationship to the center had changed. It was no longer about the exchange of commodities for manufactures, but about being part of "an integrated system of industrial production whose ownership continued to remain in substantial measure in the center" (Evans 1979:74). Nonetheless, the poor were still excluded from the benefits of the system as the Brazilian state, foreign capital, and the local elite divided up the benefits. In hindsight, we can see that the process led to the creation of a powerful economic machine and a number of important firms—CVRD, Petrobras, Embraer, and others—which, whether presently private or public, represent a shift of ownership and control away from the center identified by dependency theory.

While Argentina, Brazil, and most other Latin American countries pursued some variant of ISI, Cuba pursued an alternative path of economic and social change. On New Year's Day of 1959, the corrupt and unpopular government led by Fulgencio Batista relinquished power. Fidel Castro, head of a guerrilla army that had been fighting the government for three years, was able to consolidate power fairly quickly and later moved toward a communist model for remaking the nation (Liss 1996:314–317). For the first half of the twentieth century, Cuba had a close and dependent relationship with the United States. Cuba exported sugar to the United States while importing a large amount of its food from the United States. The island was also strongly influenced by US corporate ownership and tourism (Sheahan 1987:239). However, as the Castro regime implemented a series of revolutionary reforms, Cuba's relations with the United States quickly deteriorated. The new government initiated land reform and, in the process, nationalized a number of US-owned estates, leading the US Congress to retaliate by eliminating Cuba's sugar export quota. Cuba turned to the Soviet Union as a market for its sugar and received Soviet petroleum in return. US companies in Cuba would not refine the Soviet oil so those facilities were nationalized. The United States imposed a trade embargo on Cuba in the early 1960s, causing Cuba, which had been closely integrated with the US economy, to suddenly have to find other markets for its products and other sources for its imports (Sheahan 1987:253).

The task of reconceiving a society and an economy cut off from its historical roots was a daunting one. However that history is viewed, the path forward

A man cutting sugarcane in Cuba.

was replete with trials and errors. Cuba attempted to reduce its dependence on sugar exports by growing other crops and industrializing, but later it reversed course and tried to increase its sugar production. Large private sugar estates, many of them owned by US companies, were replaced by state farms, which were notoriously inefficient because of larger than necessary labor forces and rampant absenteeism, declining productivity, and extreme waste.

Cuba tried to attend to the basic needs of its people without emphasizing consumption (Liss 1996:314–317). In its first four years, the regime put much effort into increasing literacy and making primary education available to everybody. It also concentrated on improving health; for example, Cuba's infant mortality was the lowest in Latin America in 1984, half the level of Argentina (Sheahan 1987:26). Data on Cuba that is comparable to that for other Latin American countries is difficult to find, but a study done in 1977 suggests that Cuba's gross national product (GNP) per capita was sixth in the region, just below that of Costa Rica and just above that of Chile, and that it had the most equal income distribution in Latin America (Sheahan 1987:table 2.1, 243). Cuba has continued to maintain a reputation of providing high-quality, low-cost health care, sharing its expertise with other countries in the region.

Basic consumer goods were rationed and their prices were kept low so that people's incomes sufficed to buy the things they needed. While an effective egalitarian strategy, it resulted in a great deal of time spent waiting in lines, low incentives to work, and high levels of absenteeism. Ernesto "Che" Guevara introduced the concept of the "new man" who would respond to moral incentives instead of material ones but, by the 1970s, this strategy was deemphasized in favor of motivation through differences in pay, greater availability of consumer goods as incentives for work, and greater reliance on prices as a way to reduce time wasted in lines (Sheahan 1987:243–257; Liss 1996: 314–317).

However checkered the economic record, Cuba had enjoyed twenty-five years of 4 percent annual economic growth by the mid-1980s. However, 85 percent of Cuba's trade was with socialist countries and the socialist experiment in Eastern Europe and the Soviet Union was drawing to a close. In March 1990, in response to reductions in Soviet subsidies, oil shipments, and trade, Cuba declared the "special period in peacetime." Output in the industrial sector fell substantially in the early 1990s, the sugar harvest hit a sixty-year low in 1994–1995 and unemployment soared. Foreign investment was encouraged; the government had to allow for self-employment, and it chose to allow use of the US dollar in addition to the peso (Córdova 1996:358–368).

In the twenty-first century, Cuba has turned to Venezuela and China as trading partners. Venezuela has entered into a number of agreements with Cuba, exchanging petroleum for technical assistance and medicine. In April 2005 the countries agreed to increase the number of Cuban health care workers in

Venezuela to 30,000, establish 1,000 free medical centers, train 50,000 Venezuelan medical personnel, and provide surgery in Cuba for up to 100,000 Venezuelans (Erickson 2005:410–418).

The perceived threat engendered by the Cuban Revolution heralded an era in which several types of military governments came to power in Latin America. The broad spectrum of approaches to economic development that I have described is reflected in the approaches that these military governments took. At one end of the spectrum was the Brazilian military coup d'état against President João Goulart in 1964. A number of repressive military leaders followed a policy of modernization based on allowing foreign capital to enter the country and stimulating exports. The period of strong economic performance from the time the military came to power in 1964 to the eve of the debt crisis in 1980—particularly from 1968 to 1974—is often referred to as the Brazilian Miracle. Industrial value added as a percentage of GDP rose from 35 percent in 1964 to 45 percent in 1982. Export growth grew at greater than 8 percent annually during nine of the seventeen years, and GDP growth did the same. As a result, GDP per capita rose from $1,557 in inflation-adjusted dollars in 1964 to $3,539 in 1980 (World Bank 2009).

In 1968 on the other side of the continent, a military government of a nationalist and leftist stripe deposed Peru's president Fernando Belaúnde Terry, who mishandled a delicate situation involving the country's petroleum wealth. The legal tradition that natural resources belong to the nation and should be controlled by the state for the benefit of the population is a strongly held political belief in Latin America. It is difficult to find the right balance on the question of what role foreign companies should play in the extraction of this wealth. Often, foreign companies have the capital, technology, and expertise to do the job, but the citizens feel that they are being exploited by these foreign companies. Because he was not forceful in defending Peru's interests against a foreign oil company, Belaúnde gave the military a pretext for stepping in and forcing him into exile.

The military government was led by General Juan Velasco Alvarado, one of a group of military reformers who had been educated at the Center for Higher Military Studies, where they had acquired a sense of social responsibility and "whose views had a strong 'developmental' content" (Thorp 1991: 67). One economic historian has described it as a "left-wing nationalist military government" (Thorp 1991:67), though others have suggested that it represented the interests of an industrial elite that wanted to replace the traditional oligarchy (Sheahan 1987:257). The strategy that this government implemented contrasts in interesting ways with the Brazilian model. It involved building a process of economic growth and development based on the linkages and multiplier effects of commodity exports as opposed to the more traditional ISI approach of the Brazilian military. Linkages to raw materials processing were to increase industrial sector jobs while changes in the ownership of enterprises that would shift control and profits to labor was expected to redistribute income and increase the multiplier effect of exports.

It was a good time to be implementing a development strategy based on primary product exports: from 1962 to 1970 Peru's ores and metals exports had increased 84 percent (World Bank 2009). What the military did not take into account was the difficulty of encouraging foreign and local capital to invest in the military's vision at the same time they were nationalizing some enterprises and shifting ownership of other enterprises to the workers. The military government's first step was to nationalize the International Petroleum Company and turn operation of the existing fields and exploration over to Petroperú, a state enterprise. There was a great deal of optimism that there were substantial fields to be found and that Peru could become a significant oil exporter, but this did not turn out to be the case (Thorp 1991:70).

The government was interested in increasing the country's mining production and exports and it tried to work with foreign companies to encourage them to invest in new mines. They were successful with one large mining company, but as the government expropriated International Telephone and Telegraph, Chase Manhattan Bank, and others, the other mining companies chose not to invest given the uncertainty about the government's intentions. As a result, the government nationalized many mining company holdings. Mineroperú, another state enterprise, took over production and the exporting of the output.

As a result of the private sector's reluctance, a great deal of output and investment shifted to the government, a shift from a mixed economy model to one of state capitalism (Thorp 1991:73). The government began to borrow at a time when international lending was flowing easily. From 1970 to 1975, while exports fell 7 percent and ore and metal exports fell 17 percent, debt service rose 17 percent. By 1975 international lending to Peru dried up and, as the trade balance (exports minus imports) went from positive to negative and the burden of paying interest on the international debt became substantial, the balance of payments (foreign currency inflows minus outflows) became a problem (Thorp 1991:76–77).

The Velasco regime attempted to redistribute income within the country in bold ways. Industrial communities were established in the industrial sector, with ownership and profits gradually transferred to the workers. However, international and domestic capitalists were not willing to participate in a strategy where their property rights were not well defined. Velasco's economic plan was an innovative approach to using a strong natural resource base, strengthened linkages and redistributed income to transform an economy, but it could not succeed without the participation of capitalists. Velasco was replaced in 1975 by General Francisco Morales Bermúdez, who dismantled the reforms and held elections in which Belaúnde, deposed in 1968, was reelected in 1980 (Peloso 1996:372).

In the case of Peru, the period of military leadership was no miracle. Peru's GDP per capita only increased from $1,997 in 1968 to $2,256 in 1980. Brazil, starting from the lower base of $1,753 in 1968, swept by Peru, doubling GDP per capita to $3,539 in 1980 (World Bank 2009).

Elsewhere, Chile experimented with two radically different models of economic development in quick succession. The country went from gradual reform in the 1960s to a brief experiment with socialism in the early 1970s and, subsequently, to a long-term, military-implemented policy of free-market economics. The government of Salvador Allende (1970–1973), in addition to representing an attempt to implement a Marxist economic system in the Americas, is an example of economic populism. According to some analysts, economic populism "emphasizes growth and income redistribution and de-emphasizes the risks of inflation and deficit finance, external constraints, and the reactions of economic agents to aggressive non-market policies" (Dornbusch and Edwards 1991:9). Dissatisfaction with poor macroeconomic performance and unequal income distribution can tempt governments to prescribe economic reactivation by means of government spending; increasing wages; and altering property rights to land, natural resources, and profits. The policies implemented tend to ignore constraints in productive capacity, government and export revenues, foreign exchange reserves, and the advisability of expanding the money supply (Dornbusch and Edwards 1991:9–10).

The populist experience tends to go through four phases. In the first phase, wages are increased, output increases, and unemployment falls while inflation is kept in check by price controls and shortages are alleviated by imports. In the second phase, economic disequilibrium begins to manifest itself: there are bottlenecks in some sectors, trade deficits and government budget deficits appear, inflationary pressures begin to overpower price controls, and goods with controlled prices begin to be moved into black markets, but real wages continue to rise. The disequilibria begin to dominate the scene in the third phase where there is declining investment, a tendency to substitute a strong foreign currency for the local currency, and capital flight; real wages begin to drop and the economic output may do the same. The populist experiment has failed and, in the fourth phase, a new government comes into power, more orthodox economic policies are implemented, and a slow recovery in real wages begins (Dornbusch and Edwards 1991:11–12).

The need for change in Chile, for a different structure of economic relations with the rest of the world and for an improvement in the distribution of land and income, was evident to many by the 1960s. President Eduardo Frei, elected in 1964, began a process of reform that attempted to address these needs (Sheahan 1987:206–211). When they became dissatisfied with the results of Frei's gradual reforms, Chileans elected Salvador Allende president in 1970. He campaigned on the promise to lead them down the "Chilean Road to Socialism." His view was that the Chilean economy suffered from too much economic concentration and too great a dependence on copper exports. In industry, 3 percent of firms produced more than 50 percent of value added; in agriculture, 2 percent of farms owned 55 percent of land; in mining, three US companies controlled "large mining," which produced 60 percent of Chilean exports in 1970; all copper production represented 75 percent of exports; and the highest 10 percent of the income distribution received 40 percent of the income. Allende's structural reforms included nationalization of all mining, state control of large industrial enterprises and the banking and wholesale sectors, and accelerated agrarian reform (Larrain and Meller 1991:179–181).

Economic reactivation and income redistribution were achieved by increasing minimum wages and public sector salaries, implementing price controls to guarantee that real incomes rose and increasing public investment in health and education. Real wages rose 23 percent in 1971 at a time when total output was rising 9 percent so labor's share of GDP went to 62 percent in 1971 from 52 percent a year earlier. Government expenditures rose 80 percent in Allende's first year and the money supply increased by 119 percent (Sheahan 1987:214–215; Larrain and Meller 1991:195–198).

The Chilean economy began to move into the second phase where disequilibria begins to appear. The rising income of the working class resulted in a greater demand for food, which had to be satisfied by an increase in food imports. In combination with a decline in the world price of copper, this moved the trade balance from positive to negative. As a result of rising demand and price controls, food began to move from the legal market into the black market. The sense of impending economic chaos led to political polarization, with truckers calling frequent strikes and labor conflicts becoming a serious problem. Workers seized some factories, owners shut the workers out of others, and the government took the factories over, putting more strain on the government budget (Sheahan 1987:216–218).

The Chilean economy moved into the third phase in 1972 and 1973. Private sector profits and investment fell. Meanwhile, government expenditures and deficits expanded as public sector wages and social security payments increased and subsidies to nationalized firms rose. To cover deficits, the government increased the money supply and inflation hit 261 percent in 1972 and 605 percent in 1973. Real GDP began to decline and real wages followed (Larrain and Meller 1991:200–205). As Larrain and Meller conclude, "the mechanism of using nominal wage readjustments to increase real wages and to improve Chilean income distribution failed completely. Not until 1981 did real wages recover the level they had held in 1970 before the UP government" (1991:202). On September 11, 1973, General Augusto Pinochet took power and began a completely different economic experiment.

The episodes discussed in this section—the ISI of Argentina and Brazil, the Cuban Revolution, Velasco's policies in Peru, Allende's populism in Chile— were all efforts to change the economic structure that had developed over the period that liberalism was the dominant economic philosophy. Latin Americans found the dependence on raw material exports, the income inequality, and the economic injustice all intensely objectionable, and they looked for ways to restructure the economy. The results of these efforts varied: they achieved mixed success in stimulating economic growth without reducing inequality in Brazil and reducing inequality without stimulating economic growth in Cuba, but the Chilean case led to crisis and violent political change. The issues in any attempt to change economic structure derive from a country's choice to build on its existing economic foundation or create a new foundation. Economic change may include groups such as foreign capitalists and local capitalists or attempt to move forward without them. These are interesting and important questions but, by 1973 time to answer them was running out; global economic events during the 1970s were about to narrow the range of policy choices.

▓ The Oil Shock and the Debt Crisis

In 1973, an era of cheap and plentiful energy came to an end. Energy prices began to rise early in the year and, in October, in response to US and European support for Israel, the Organization of Petroleum Exporting Countries (OPEC) declared an embargo. The effect was to reduce world oil supplies by more than 2 million barrels per day (US Energy Information Administration 1998). The average price of petroleum in the United States rose from $3.39 per barrel in 1972 to $6.87 in 1974 and to $31.77 by 1981 (US Energy Information Administration 2009).

As the price of petroleum rose, the global flow of income changed its pattern substantially, with net consumers of petroleum spending much more and net exporters receiving much more. Large oil producers that did not have pressing demands on their income deposited these petrodollars in banks, which then recycled them to borrowers. As it happened, there were two willing groups of borrowers in Latin America. Petroleum producers with a great deal of poverty and the desire to accelerate the process of economic development, such as Mexico and Ecuador, were willing to spend borrowed money as well as the additional revenues coming from their exports. Conversely, petroleum importers needed to borrow in order to cover the higher cost of their petroleum imports. The impact of this borrowing was mixed but, over the long run, a dangerous vulnerability developed. GDP growth rates for Latin America averaged out to a healthy 5.8 percent for the period; on the other hand, inflation rose from 4.7 percent per year in 1970 to 18.8 percent in 1980. At the same time, external debt in Latin America and the Caribbean rose from 20 percent of gross national income (GNI) in 1973 to 45 percent in 1982 and total debt service rose from 3 percent to 8 percent of GNI (World Bank 2009).

The events that would expose Latin America's vulnerabilities were unfolding in the United States, where inflation reached 11 percent by 1979. The US Federal Reserve Bank applied a monetarist solution to the problem: if too much money in the economic system results in inflation, then inflation can be brought under control by controlling the amount of money in the economic system. As a result of the bank's policy, the interest rate in the United States increased from 9 percent in 1978 to 19 percent in 1981, bringing economic growth in the United States to a halt during 1979–1982. This affected Latin American economies in three ways. First, the weakened US economy led to a gradual reduction in the price of petroleum, which reduced export revenues for the oil producers. Second, the absence of growth in the US economy brought export growth in Latin America screeching to a halt, falling from 10.9 percent expansion in 1979 to 0.4 percent in 1980, 3.2 percent in 1981, and 1.2 percent in 1982. Third, the increase in interest rates meant that Latin American debt service payments rose 117 percent from 1978 to 1982 (World Bank 2009).

On August 13, 1982, Mexico announced that it could not continue servicing its international debt and the debt crisis had begun. As illustrated in Table 6.2, international lenders and investors were unsettled by Mexico's action and, as a result, the level of capital flowing to developing countries as a group fell by 71 percent from the period 1977–1982 to the period 1983–1989. For the developing countries in Latin America, total net capital flows reversed from $26.3 billion of inflows annually in the first period to $16.6 billion of outflow annually in the second period because few new loans were available and the debt had to be repaid. While leaders remained wary, a resurgence in investor confidence in the early 1990s contributed to a dramatic increase in capital inflows to the region, averaging more than $40 billion annually from 1990 to 1994.

Some important economic dynamics come into play when a country makes the transition from receiving capital to returning it. The capital that flows in is received in the form of dollars rather than in the local currency. These dollars can be used to import more than the country is exporting, a situation called a balance of trade deficit. Usually this excess supply of dollars will drive up demand for the local currency and raise its value. The higher value of local currency makes imports cheaper, thus increasing their volume.

Table 6.2 Capital Flows to the Western Hemisphere, 1977–1994 (annual averages in billions of US dollars)

	1977–1982	1983–1989	1990–1994
Total net capital inflows	26.3	−16.6	40.1
Net foreign direct investment	5.3	4.4	11.9
Net portfolio investment	1.6	−1.2	26.6
Other (including bank lending)	19.4	−19.8	1.6

Source: David Folkerts-Landau and Takatoshi Ito, *International Capital Markets: Developments, Prospects and Policy Issues* (Washington DC: International Monetary Fund, August 1995), table 1.1, p. 33.

It also makes the country's exports more expensive on the world market, thus decreasing the volume of exports and creating a trade deficit financed by the capital inflows. This dynamic produces a condition similar to Dutch Disease in the sense that the country's export sector suffers.

When debts are due, countries need to create a balance of trade surplus, exporting more than they import in order to earn the dollars needed to repay dollar-denominated loans. This is generally accomplished by devaluing the currency so that imports become more expensive and decline while exports become less expensive and increase. This has the potential to be beneficial for the economy, stimulating both the export- and the import-competing sectors, resulting in an increase in output, jobs, and income. One distinct disadvantage is that the costs of imports rise, accelerating the process of inflation. Another is that the economic transition taking place is wrenching and standards of living may fall because the country goes from living beyond its means (by borrowing) to living well within its means (in order to repay). We can see the impact this transition had on people's lives in the data in Table 6.3. First, GDP per capita, which rose by 38 percent during the 1970s, fell 10 percent from 1980 to 1983 and did not reach the 1980 level again for fifteen years. Second, of that lower level of production, more of it was exported in order to repay the debt: the balance of trade moved from a negative 1.7 percent of GDP in 1981 to a positive 4.8 percent of GDP in 1984, a reduction in the portion of GDP available for domestic use of 6.5 percent. Third, the very poor were hurt particularly hard as government budgets were reduced, social services cut, and subsidies slashed. The process of eliminating these subsidies was painful economically as the standard of living of the poor fell, and politically as people marched and rioted, occasionally deposed leaders, and often suffered from police and military repression. For all these reasons, the 1980s have been referred to as the lost decade.

As a result of the substantial size of the debt and its impact in terms of falling standards of living, rising poverty, and rising malnutrition, attempts to alleviate the impacts of the debt crisis went beyond the standard responses. In many countries, the urban poor organized neighborhood soup kitchens and ate together. At the other end of the spectrum, banks that had made loans in Latin America began to sell these loans at a discount in the secondary market where they were bought by investors who were willing to accept greater risk for the possibility of a higher rate of return. In some cases the buyers were interested in a debt swap where they would turn around and sell the debt to the government that had issued it, receiving local currency from the government that could then be used for investment. The process of privatization of state enterprises, such as telephone companies, airlines, mines or petroleum companies, was taking place and foreign investors were often interested in these. Another group of buyers in the secondary market were international environmental groups interested in debt-for-nature swaps where debt would be turned over to

Table 6.3 Impacts of the Debt Crisis on Selected Economic Indicators in Latin America, 1970–1990

Year	External Debt (% of GNI)	GDP Growth (annual %)	GDP Per Capita (constant US$)	External Balance on Goods and Services (% of GDP)
1970	20.0	6.2	2,680.30	−0.5
1971	19.9	6.2	2,777.00	−1.3
1972	21.2	6.6	2,887.90	−0.9
1973	18.9	7.8	3,028.40	−0.2
1974	18.7	6.3	3,153.40	−1.8
1975	21.2	3.5	3,185.60	−2.4
1976	23.7	5.1	3,268.60	−0.9
1977	28.4	4.8	3,344.70	−0.6
1978	31.1	3.5	3,381.70	−1.1
1979	31.9	7.1	3,541.30	−1.0
1980	33.0	6.3	3,680.80	−1.6
1981	35.2	0.5	3,616.10	−1.7
1982	43.7	−1.4	3,489.90	0.7
1983	54.0	−2.5	3,329.00	4.3
1984	57.5	3.7	3,381.40	4.8
1985	57.0	2.6	3,397.70	4.5
1986	57.6	4.1	3,465.50	2.5
1987	58.5	3.4	3,512.50	2.6
1988	50.8	0.5	3,463.30	2.3
1989	43.8	0.9	3,430.30	2.9
1990	40.2	0.3	3,381.10	2.2

Source: World Bank, *World Development Indicators 2009* (Washington, DC: International Bank for Reconstruction and Development, 2009), CD-ROM.
Note: GNI, gross national income; GDP, gross domestic product.

the government and the government would reciprocate by using local currency to buy the land and support the protection of a national park or nature reserve (Cardoso and Helwege 1992:125–133).

The severity of the economic crisis seemed to call for a change in economic philosophy in Latin America. Import-substituting industrialization, already subject to criticism, was largely abandoned as the challenges of the debt crisis mounted. Critics blamed ISI for creating an inefficient industrial sector because: (1) it was protected by tariffs; (2) the protection varied from industry to industry and resulted in an inefficient allocation of resources; and (3) it divided Latin America into small markets where the cost advantages of large-scale production could not be achieved. ISI also required substantial government intervention, leading to excessive government spending, deficits, and international debt, the cause of the crisis in the first place. In addition, much of the industrialization that took place was controlled by MNCs and, unless its economy was the size of Brazil's, a country was unlikely to have the leverage necessary to deepen the industrialization process (Cardoso and Helwege 1992: 93–99).

As a result of the military coup in 1973, Chile experimented with one alternative to ISI even before the debt crisis began. The military's initial goals were to stabilize the economic and political situation. In search of an economic policy that could control Chile's raging inflation, Chile's military government turned to a group of civilian economists trained at the University of Chicago who became known as the "Chicago Boys." As a result, Chile became an early implementer of monetarism and neoliberalism, the economic philosophies that would replace ISI and dominate policy in Latin America for the 1980s and 1990s. The debt crisis hit Chile as hard as it hit any country. Nonetheless, it was neoliberalism that was suggested by the International Monetary Fund (IMF), World Bank, and US government as the solution to the crisis. Because these three institutions happen to be located within just blocks of one another in the US capital, the policy also became known as the Washington Consensus.

Monetarism posits that inflation is caused by too much money being introduced into the economic system. Since the root cause of the increase in money supply is often that the government has a budget deficit and prints money in order to cover it, the neoliberal prescription is to balance the government budget. Since conservatives believe that the private sector is efficient and dynamic, in general they recommend that the budget be balanced by reducing expenditures rather than by increasing taxes. One way to decrease expenditures in the long run and increase revenues in the short run is to sell state-owned enterprises to private sector investors, simultaneously eliminating the need to cover their losses and turning operations over to the efficient private sector. Thus, privatization was an integral part of the neoliberal agenda in Latin America. Consequently, in the 1980s and 1990s there was a great deal of foreign investment in telephone companies, power companies, petroleum companies, and mining companies that were privatized by governments.

The other major strand of neoliberal philosophy is the belief that markets do a better job than the government in allocating resources efficiently and thus maximizing society's well-being. The neoliberal agenda therefore includes financial liberalization, primarily the deregulation of banking so that competition among banks will increase the return to saving and allocate the funds efficiently to investors who will increase the productivity of the economy. Related to this is opening the capital account, liberalizing the movement of capital in and out of the country, allowing foreign capital to flow in and increase the level of investment in the country. Finally, neoliberalism prescribes trade liberalization, reducing or eliminating tariffs and quotas so that a country can export based on its comparative advantage (lower relative costs of production resulting from natural advantages) and import what the economy needs.

One way in which trade liberalization took place in Latin America was in the form of regional trade integration: groups of countries that agreed to reduce restrictions on trade among themselves. In addition to allowing countries in the group to trade on the basis of their comparative advantage, the agreements allowed firms to: (1) achieve economies of scale (lower costs of production resulting from producing more output) by getting access to a larger market; and (2) strengthen backward and forward production linkages within the region.

As discussed by Cleveland Fraser in Chapter 7, many regional trade groups were actually initiated before the Washington Consensus, on the basis of the post–World War II drive to encourage free trade. The treaty forming the Central American Common Market was signed in 1961. The Andean Pact was signed in 1969, creating the Community of Andean Nations. Mercosur, the largest group in Latin America, began in 1986 as an agreement between Argentina and Brazil and in 1991 expanded to include Paraguay and Uruguay (Franko 2007:255–272). A study by the UN Economic Commission for Latin America and the Caribbean (ECLAC) shows that the proportion of trade that Latin American countries had with countries within their trade grouping rose considerably from 1985 to 2002 (CEPAL 2005).

As the advantages of these trade groups became more convincing, more countries joined and more agreements were negotiated among the groups. At the same time, free trade agreements (FTAs) with countries outside the region became important, particularly those with the United States. Mexico joined Canada and the United States in the North American Free Trade Agreement (NAFTA) in 1994, and the United States continues to negotiate FTAs with other countries in the region. In the 1990s, an effort was made to create the Free Trade Area of the Americas (FTAA). However, it has broken down with opposition from populists such as Hugo Chávez of Venezuela and a sense among larger Latin American countries such as Brazil that they would prefer to negotiate with the United States as a regional block, rather than as individual countries, so as to have greater influence on the outcome (Franko 2007:264–277).

One alternative to the neoliberal strategy described above was heterodoxy, which flowed out of economic thinking that (1) put greater emphasis on protecting the poor from the consequences of economic crisis and (2) had greater faith in the efficacy of government intervention. Inflation was understood as resulting from lack of excess productive capacity to satisfy rising aggregate demand, rising input costs, and, eventually, an inertial process in which one period's inflation led to continued inflation in the next period.

In Peru, Alan García, elected president in 1985, implemented a heterodox policy. The policy team that García brought with him did not see neoliberal policy as an effective strategy for Peru (Thorp 1991:121). They introduced a new currency to stop the inertial component of inflation. Wages were raised to help the poor and increase aggregate demand. Instead of attempting to control all prices, they limited controls to a set of prices that were considered to be critical to allow for profits—the exchange rate, the interest rate, public utility prices, and food prices (Edwards 1995:122). García also made a name for himself as a bold new leader by declaring that Peru would allocate only 10 percent of its export revenues to debt service, allowing the remainder to be used for imported inputs, including food and other necessities.

As in the case of Allende's program in Chile in 1970–1973 and other heterodox policies implemented in the 1980s, the initial period of García's economic policy was a great success. Wages and salaries increased 30 percent to 35 percent over the first eighteen months and GDP growth rose from 2.8 percent in 1985 to 10.0 percent in 1986 and 8.0 percent in 1987 (Thorp 1991: 129). Inflation fell from 163 percent in 1985 to 78 percent and 86 percent the next two years (World Bank 2009). By 1987, however, price distortions developed in the economy as uncontrolled prices began to rise while controlled prices could not. Meanwhile, the government budget deficit, the trade deficit, and the money supply began to rise. The government began introducing policy packages called *paquetazos,* which included large devaluations of the inti. The combination of devaluations and rapid monetary expansion fed the inflationary process.

An interesting twist in García's policy was the process of *concertación.* This process tried to take advantage of the concentration of ownership in the industrial sector, where family-based economic groups each tended to own a diversified portfolio of businesses, properties, and banks. A weakness of many attempts to transform economies is the failure to maintain the support of the

A market in Peru's Sacred Valley.

Thomas D'Agostino

private sector. With this in mind, García backed away from policies of expropriation and instead attempted to coordinate economic decisions with the private sector through discussions with the leaders of the major economic groups known as the "twelve apostles." There was a great deal of goodwill and interest on the part of the private sector, but this was squandered through poor communication in 1987 and then completely destroyed with the announcement of a state takeover of the banking system. With this opportunity lost and the difficulties of the debt crisis continuing, García's heterodox experiment failed and the economy quickly worsened (Thorp 1991:121–141). The GDP fell 24 percent from 1987 to 1990 and inflation reached an astounding 7482 percent by 1990 (World Bank 2009).

Despite these failures, as the lost decade of the 1980s came to an end Latin America was perceived as having weathered the crisis. Although GDP per capita was not to reach its 1980 level again until 1995, international debt as a percentage of GNI fell to 45.7 percent in 1989, approximately where it had been in 1982, after having risen above 60 percent in 1986 and 1987. It fell to 33 percent by 1997 before it began to rise again. Commercial banks in the United States and Europe, after a period of denial, began writing off the bad debts they had accumulated before 1982 (Thorp 1998:226). The Brady Plan offered heavily indebted countries three different ways to reduce the burden of that debt (Franko 2007:97). A new generation of leaders came to power who, whatever their background, were more likely to implement neoliberal policies than heterodox ones. Fernando Henrique Cardoso of Brazil (1995–2003), Carlos Menem of Argentina (1989–1999), and Alberto Fujimori of Peru (1990–2000) are prime examples. The 1990s was a period of greater trade and more freely flowing international capital which, as it turned out, presented its own challenges.

▣ Latin America as an Emerging Market

An economic downturn in the United States and changes in regulations that made US mutual fund investment abroad much more accessible turned the attention of US investors toward Latin America and Asia at the beginning of the 1990s. These areas became known as emerging markets, new areas in which to invest where returns were higher than in the United States and the risks were lower than they had been in the past. Neoliberalism had opened capital accounts and spurred privatization, creating investment opportunities. In 1999 foreign direct investment (FDI) was 9.0 times the 1990 level while workers' remittances were 2.6 times their 1990 level. In 2000, portfolio investment was 3.8 times its 1991 level (1990 data on portfolio investment is not available; World Bank 2009). Capital inflows—FDI, portfolio investment, and loans—represent great potential for developing economies. First, the inflows provide foreign currency that can be used to import goods and services that might otherwise not be available. Second, they offer the ability to invest in productive activities that can increase the output of the country, creating jobs and raising incomes. FDI is used to "acquire a lasting management interest in an enterprise" (World Bank 2009), though it could simply displace domestic investment. Portfolio investment is the purchase of stocks or bonds, but its impact depends on the eventual mix of consumption, additions to productive capacity, and increases in asset prices that it funds. Overall, the 1990s were a much better decade for Latin America and the Caribbean than the 1980s had been: GDP per capita rose by 18 percent from 1990 to 2000, compared to an 8 percent decline from 1980 to 1990; inflation fell from 23.8 percent in 1990 to 6.6 percent in 2000 whereas it rose from 18.8 percent in 1980 to 23.8 percent in 1990. However, it was not all smooth sailing.

The volatility of capital flows in Latin America in the 1990s produced problems. Although at first Argentina benefited greatly from capital flows, it eventually suffered from them. In response to the disastrous experience of the 1980s—the failure of the heterodox Austral Plan that culminated in the 3080 percent inflation of 1989 and 2314 percent inflation of 1990—President Menem's minister of economy, Domingo Cavallo, implemented a currency board in 1991. The exchange rate was fixed at 1 new peso to 1 US dollar by guaranteeing convertibility; a person could turn in a peso to the currency board and receive a dollar at any time. As a result, the peso money supply was determined by the quantity of dollars held by the currency board so that the government could no longer print money to cover its deficits. The theoretical advantage of this system was that the rate of inflation in Argentina would converge quickly to that in the United States; indeed, it fell to 4.2 percent by 1994. The disadvantages of the system were (1) that sudden dollar outflows occurring for any reason whatsoever would result in a decrease in the money supply and a credit freeze where few loans were available; and (2) that, if the government could not balance its budget, it would be forced to borrow since it could no longer print money.

The convertibility system was first put to the test at the end of 1994, when Mexico suffered the peso crisis and Latin America suffered the "tequila effect," the name given to the negative spillovers of Mexico's peso crisis. Soon to join Canada and the United States in NAFTA, Mexico was the largest recipient of capital flows to emerging markets in the early 1990s. The capital inflows pushed up the value of the Mexican currency, hurting the competitiveness of its exports and resulting in a large balance of trade deficit. They also allowed the Mexican government to borrow in order to cover its deficit. Mexico entered NAFTA on January 1, 1994, beginning a tumultuous year for a country that was looking forward to moving out of the ranks of the third world. On the very same day, the Zapatista revolt broke out in southern Mexico where landless peasants took over a number of towns. This marginalized group of people

A mural depicting Zapatista rebels in Chiapas, Mexico.

was not sharing in the benefits of economic growth and had been denied the hope of land redistribution by legal changes that Mexico had made in preparation for entry into NAFTA.

In addition, it was an election year and later that year the governing party's candidate was assassinated. Most significantly for Mexico's economic fortunes, portfolio investment fell from $28 billion in 1993 to $7 billion in 1994. The Mexican government had a great deal of trouble covering its budget deficit and, since it did not want to devalue its currency, it covered its balance of trade deficit out of foreign exchange reserves, which grew dangerously low as the year dragged on. Once the governing party won the election and the new president was installed, the government attempted an orderly devaluation of the Mexican peso. Unfortunately, it lost control of the process to market forces that drove the exchange rate from 3.4 pesos/US$1 in 1994 to 6.4 pesos/US$1 in 1995.

Investors' reaction to this devaluation, the tequila effect, caused portfolio investment in Latin America and the Caribbean to fall from $71 billion in 1994 to $9 billion in 1995; it was a negative $10 billion in Mexico, and it fell from $9 to $2 billion in Argentina. Economic growth in Latin America declined from 4.7 percent in 1994 to 0.6 percent in 1995; the economy contracted 2.8 percent in Argentina and 6.2 percent in Mexico. While it was a difficult year for Argentina, the country stuck with convertibility despite the credit freeze that occurred as Argentines pulled their wealth out of the country. This consistency in economic policy had a payoff: global confidence in the Argentine economy strengthened and the inflow of capital continued (World Bank 2009).

The global economy had not seen the end of the adverse consequences of free-flowing capital, however. In the summer of 1997, the real estate bubble that had been inflated in Thailand burst so that portfolio investment in Thailand and East Asia declined, devaluing exchange rates and arresting GDP growth. The same pattern followed in Russia in 1998 and in Brazil in 1999. These crises had significant effects in Latin America. The Asian crisis of 1997 cut world economic growth from 3.7 percent in 1997 to 2.3 percent in 1998, reducing the world price of petroleum in the process and hurting the economies of petroleum exporters such as Ecuador, Colombia, and Venezuela. GDP growth rates in Latin America fell substantially in 1998 and turned negative in 1999.

In Ecuador, the smallest and most vulnerable of these countries, the banking sector—liberalized by the neoliberal agenda—collapsed. As the government increased the money supply in order to bail out the banks, inflation accelerated and the exchange rate rose along with it. The only exit that policymakers could imagine from this crisis was dollarization, where the central bank bought up the local currency with its foreign exchange reserves and thus replaced the sucre with the US dollar (Beckerman 2002:51–59). As in the case of Argentina's convertibility, the deceleration of inflation was dramatic: by 2003, inflation was in the single digits and, by 2004, it was 2.7 percent (World Bank 2009).

In Brazil, the reduction in portfolio investment from $18 billion in 1997 to $4 billion in 1998 resulted in a devaluation. Argentina, Brazil's major trading partner and trapped in convertibility, could not devalue and was suddenly at a great competitive disadvantage. Brazil's GDP growth fell from 3.4 percent to zero, but Argentina's fell from 3.9 percent to a negative 3.4 percent. As Argentina's external debt rose from 29 percent of GNI in 1994 to 55 percent in 2001 and foreign lenders finally grew leery of the economic situation, Argentina had to abandon convertibility and allow the exchange rate to be determined by the market. The peso depreciated to a third of its previous value. As one would expect, once the shock of the devaluation wore off, economic growth rates were strong—in the 7.0 percent to 9.2 percent range—from 2003 to 2008, driven by a 57 percent increase in exports from 2001 to 2008 (World Bank 2009).

Volatility in global financial flows has not been the only weakness perceived in the performance of neoliberal policies. There has also been the sense that the poorest members of Latin American societies have not been helped, and this has led to a populist reaction. As Thomas J. D'Agostino explains in Chapter 4, Hugo Chávez was elected president of Venezuela in 1998 with the overwhelming support of the poor, whom he has repaid with a massive effort to redistribute income within the society. He has restructured social programs around *misiones* (missions) that focus on specific problems such as illiteracy or poor health in lower income neighborhoods (Rodríguez 2008:50). Social spending per capita has risen over 300 percent during Chávez's presidency, while increases in the minimum wage have increased the income of the poorest by a substantial amount (Álvarez Herrera 2008:158–159). The percentage of the population living on less than $2 per day has fallen from 24 percent in 1998 to 10 percent in 2006 while the Gini Index, an indicator of economic inequality, has fallen from 50 to 43 over that period, one of the lowest levels of inequality in the region (World Bank 2010).

In attempting to redistribute income to the poor, Chávez has challenged the power of the elite and the middle class as well as the powerful state petroleum company, Petróleos de Venezuela Sociedad Anónima (PDVSA). The importance of this company is evidenced in the fact that petroleum exports often account for 80 percent to 90 percent of export revenues (Whalen 2007:59). The conflict between Chávez and PDVSA led to a strike at PDVSA in 2002, to which Chávez responded by firing many managers and engineers. The result was two years of serious reduction in economic output.

As PDVSA's new management has allocated more of its revenues to social programs, its investment has not been sufficient to maintain petroleum production so that Venezuela has produced less than its OPEC quota (Whalen 2007:59) and the country's exports fell 12 percent from 1998 to 2008. At the same time, it remains one of the few countries in Latin America with double-digit inflation. It is easy to interpret this as another example of economic populism that will ultimately fail, but dissatisfaction with the results of neoliberalism is still high in the region and presidents Evo Morales of Bolivia and Rafael Correa of Ecuador have climbed on the populist bandwagon by nationalizing critical sectors of the economy and redistributing income.

As the twentieth century came to a close, the influence of the Washington Consensus on Latin American policy was beginning to wane. While the value of careful management of government budgets, debt, and monetary policy seemed to be widely accepted, there were three important criticisms leveled against the neoliberal agenda. First, financial liberalization without the necessary experience and regulation could create weak banking systems prone to crisis. Second, freely flowing capital could be a great temptation to government borrowing and its sheer magnitude could easily overwhelm Latin American economies, even the larger ones. Third, it was not clear that improvements in the standard of living for the poor and reductions in inequality were occurring quickly enough to fend off the appeal of populist leaders.

Latin America in the Twenty-First Century

Latin America's experience in the first decade of the new century as well as the region's prospects for the future derive from the interaction between legacies of the past and the major forces that dominate the period. First, the rise of Brazil, Russia, India, and China (the so-called BRIC countries) as major players on the global economic stage changes the dynamic of world economic relations in a way that may open opportunities for Latin America as a whole. Second, the rising price of petroleum and other commodities is having a substantial positive impact on economic activity throughout the region. Third, the growth of intraregional trade is strengthening productive linkages within the region and reducing the economic dependence on the center that has characterized the region. Fourth, the growth of large Latin American corporations—the *translatinas*—is raising the global profile of the region and changing the pattern of investment flows as Latin American corporations invest in other Latin American countries. These changes are transforming the economic dynamics of the region in significant ways, but the question of whether they will change the economic structure and the nature of economic development in the region remains unanswered. The fundamental tensions emphasized throughout this chapter remain for Latin America: between the seductive power of commodity exports as the basis for economic growth, on the one hand, and the desire to change the structure of the economy, on the other; between the desire to improve the lot of the poor and the need to maintain the support of powerful economic groups both within the country and internationally.

Brazil is the largest country in Latin America, with an economy that has grown from representing about one-quarter of Latin America's GDP in 1960 and 1970 to about one-third by 1980 and afterward. Over the half-century from 1960 to 2008, its standard of living (as measured by GDP per capita) has risen from 60 percent to 74 percent of the world average and from 70 percent to 93 percent of the Latin American average. Its size, rising standard of living, and rich resource endowment, combined with sixteen years of highly respected leadership, have transformed Brazil into an important world power. Brazil's popular former president Luiz Inácio Lula da Silva has provided a strong counterpoint to the redistributive populism of Chávez, Morales, and Correa. He came to the presidency in 2002 with impeccable leftist credentials: a trade union leader, jailed and tortured by the military regime in the 1970s, who ran for president as the Workers' Party candidate. The Workers' Party manifesto declared that "social development is considered a vital component, rather than a residual outcome, of economic growth" (Baer 2008:152). It argued that fundamental reform is necessary, but that "rapid economic growth and international competitiveness" are also necessary in order to achieve social development (Baer 2008:152–153).

Understandably, international financial markets were quite worried at the prospect of Lula's election, fearing major changes in policy and an unfriendly climate for foreign investment. By the end of his second term in office, his record was quite different from that expectation and his presidency has been a success in economic terms. Lula continued the cautious fiscal and monetary policies of his predecessor. The payoffs for these policies during the period 2003–2008 were continued international confidence in Brazil, an appreciating currency, declining inflation, and an average annual rate of GDP growth of 4.1 percent that was lower than the 4.8 percent growth for Latin America as a whole, but enough to raise GDP per capita by 19 percent in those six years (World Bank 2009).

Lula attempted to improve the lot of the poor with two programs: (1) Fome Zero, a program to reduce hunger; and (2) a minimum income guarantee. After a disorganized initial effort, the Bolsa Familia program was created to achieve the first goal. By 2006, it provided cash transfers to 11.2 million families on the condition that the children attend school and use health care and social services (Baer 2008:163–164). In pursuit of the second goal, the government raised the minimum wage, reformed the tax system, and restructured the social security system.

In terms of the tension between improving the lot of the poor and maintaining the support of the powerful, Lula's presidency seemed to provide a case where income redistribution was successfully implemented in a context of economic stability and growth. World Bank data show that the percentage of the population living on less than $2 per day fell from 21 percent in 2002 to 13 percent in 2007 (World Bank 2010), with a small decline in income inequality. However, one observer suggests that by committing himself to cautious economic policies Lula was unable to provide the income redistribution programs with the resources necessary to be effective (Baer 2008:167–174). Seen in this light, the outcome is similar to that described by Evans (1979): keeping foreign and domestic investors satisfied means that there is little left over for the poor.

While Brazil's particular pattern of development has not reduced inequality substantially, it has created some major firms of international importance. A number of the largest firms either started as government enterprises or received a great deal of government and military support. Vale was the world's largest iron ore producer by 2008, a major producer of nickel, copper, and bauxite, and also involved in the manufacturing of steel and aluminum. It was established by the government in the 1940s as the Companhia do Vale do Rio Doce and privatized in 1997. Since then, it has expanded through investment and acquisitions so that only half of its production is now in Brazil. Embraer is the world's largest producer of regional aircraft. It was started by the Brazilian Air Force and also privatized in the 1990s. It exports 95 percent of its production and is Brazil's leading exporter of manufactured products (Schneider 2009:165–169). Petrobras, the petroleum company, was created by the government in 1953 to carry out all petroleum exploration and most of the refining, and it remains a state enterprise. It has transformed Brazil from a country that satisfied only 20 percent of its needs with domestic production to being self-sufficient in petroleum by 2007. The company has expanded into petrochemicals and invested in natural gas production in Bolivia (Baer 2008). The *translatinas*—concentrated in Brazil, Chile, and Mexico—are investing in other Latin

American countries and beyond. Net flows of outward FDI in Latin America rose from approximately $6 billion in 2003 to $42 billion in 2006 before falling to $12 billion in 2009 as the global financial crisis hit. Brazil has been the largest participant in this area, with companies such as Petrobras and Vale investing in petroleum and natural gas, mining, and cement throughout South America and large Brazilian banks acquiring banks in Portugal. However, in 2009 Chile became the largest of the Latin American investors in absolute terms, investing in chemicals, agriculture, and commerce in Peru and Brazil, with its FDI representing a remarkable 5 percent of its GDP. Mexico is a major investor abroad, often buying US companies, and Venezuela's petroleum company PDVSA has invested heavily in petroleum and natural gas in Bolivia (Alatorre 2009:58–63).

While there are some large Brazilian firms, the largest business groups in Latin America are relatively small compared to those in other regions. There are also differences in types of production: large Asian firms tend to be concentrated in higher technology manufacturing such as automobiles and computers while large Latin American firms are concentrated in raw material production and processing, the higher technology manufacturing generally having been left to MNCs from outside the region (Schneider 2009:173–80).

We can evaluate the impact these large firms have on Latin America's economic development using the Bulmer-Thomas (1994) framework of linkages

Located on the Paraná River on the border between Paraguay and Brazil, the Itaipu Dam is among the world's largest hydroelectric projects.

and income flows. Baer characterizes firms such as Vale and Petrobras as
dynamic, expanding in their original areas of production and then in complementary ones such as fertilizers and shipping, petrochemicals, and aluminum
production (2008:224). This is a good example of economic diversification
that results when domestic companies reinvest their profits. In many cases, the
new activities create production linkages that strengthen the domestic economy and lessen its dependence on the center. The aggregate demand from the
investment process, the productive potential created by the investment, and the
strengthening of domestic linkages are all ways in which commodity production and exports are transformed into economic development.

The increase in regional trade as a proportion of total trade strengthens the
effects described above. Table 6.4 shows that the proportion of exports going
to other countries within the region increased from 24 percent in 1980 to 31
percent in 2002 while imports from within the region rose from 22 percent to
40 percent. The growth in trade flows and the strengthening of intraregional
production linkages are weakening Latin America's dependence on trade with
the center so that its economic fortunes are less tied to those of the center and
are, therefore, more sustainable.

**Table 6.4 Trade Among Selected ALADI Members, 1980, 2002, and 2008
(percentage of total trade)**

	1980		2002		2008
Country	Exports	Imports	Exports	Imports	Exports
Argentina	23	20	41	37	39
Bolivia	36	31	59	58	65
Brazil	17	12	16	18	24
Chile	24	27	19	39	19
Colombia	14	15	25	26	36
Ecuador	18	12	19	40	36
Paraguay	45	48	66	58	69
Peru	17	15	15	41	21
Uruguay	37	36	42	54	40
Venezuela	7	7	10	26	14[a]

Sources: Comisión Económica para América Latina. "Comercio exterior: exportaciones e importaciones según destino y origen por principales zonas económicas: 1980, 1985, 1990, 1995–
2002." *Cuadernos estadísticos de la CEPAL,* no. 31 (December 2005). http://www.eclac.org; 2008
exports from Comisión Económica para América Latina y el Caribe, División de Estadística y
Proyecciones Económicas. "Exportaciones intrarregionales, Anuario estadístico de América Latina
y el Caribe" (Santiago, Chile: United Nations, 2010), table 2.2.2.45.

Note: ALADI is the Latin American Integration Association; members include Argentina, Bolivia, Brazil, Chile, Colombia, Cuba, Ecuador, Mexico, Paraguay, Peru, Uruguay, and Venezuela.
    a. Venezuela exports from 2006.

The World Bank finds that commodity-led development has been successful for countries such as Australia, the United States, Finland, and Sweden where commodity production was accompanied by high levels of investment in education and in research and development of new processes and products (World Bank 2010). However, one analyst argues that the level of investment in Brazil and other Latin American countries is not sufficient "to leverage commodity exports into longer-term development" (Schneider 2009:179–180). In this view, the profits received by firms and the revenues received by governments are not being reinvested in ways that will lead to economic development, in contrast to economic expansion.

The question of how to leverage commodity exports into long-term development is an important one now that Latin America is benefiting from another commodity boom. The driving force behind this commodity boom is assumed to be the rapid growth of the Chinese economy. China is the largest of the BRIC economies, and the rapid growth of an economy that represents such a large proportion of the world's population is a force to contend with. In the first decade of the twenty-first century, it has overtaken Germany as the largest exporter in the world (Ellis 2009:10) and Japan as the world's second largest economy (Barbosa 2010). China's growth is based on the export of industrial goods to the center, and the production of those industrial goods affects Latin America in three important ways. First, the production of the industrial goods requires great amounts of commodity inputs, and so China must turn to sources such as Africa and Latin America for these inputs (Ellis 2009:10). Not only does China buy these commodities, but it has the ability to invest in their production and in the infrastructure necessary to export them to China (Ellis 2009:3). Over the entire period 1998–2008, China was not a major investor in Latin America. The United States was still the dominant investor in the region (37 percent) and the *translatinas* the next (10 percent); China was not among the top eight investors. By 2009, however, four of the fourteen largest acquisitions in the commodity sector were by Chinese companies and 18 percent of the new investment in manufacturing was Chinese (Alatorre 2009:40, 45).

Second, the increasing incomes of the Chinese population generate a growing demand for food (Ellis 2009:12). Third, Latin America represents a market for China's manufactured goods at a time when growth in China's traditional markets has slowed (Ellis 2009:4). As a result, the overall impact of China's growth on Latin American economies is to undercut its manufacturing sector and encourage a commodity boom.

As noted in Table 6.5, in the ten years from 1998 to 2008, the price of crude oil, adjusted for inflation, rose almost sevenfold in contrast to the slightly better than fourfold rise over the period 1973–1981. A broader indicator of the commodity boom is the terms of trade, which is the ratio of prices for the country's exports to prices for its imports. The ten-year increase in the terms of trade has ranged from 13 percent in Mexico to 39 percent in Argentina, 65

Table 6.5 Rising Commodity Prices and Economic Growth in Latin America, 1990–2009

	External Debt (% of GNI)	GDP Growth (annual %)	GDP per Capita (constant US$)	Crude Oil Prices (constant US$)
1990	40.2	0.3	3381.1	27.74
1991	38.8	4.6	3474.4	22.12
1992	37.0	3.9	3546.4	20.89
1993	36.8	3.7	3615.4	18.22
1994	34.6	4.7	3722.9	16.51
1995	35.2	0.6	3683.6	17.93
1996	34.0	3.5	3753.6	22.22
1997	32.7	5.5	3898.0	20.38
1998	36.4	2.4	3931.4	12.71
1999	42.4	0.2	3880.5	17.93
2000	37.4	3.9	3973.6	30.14
2001	39.3	0.3	3931.1	24.09
2002	44.7	–0.5	3861.7	24.44
2003	44.2	2.2	3894.4	29.29
2004	38.3	6.1	4081.6	38.00
2005	28.9	4.9	4229.5	50.28
2006	24.4	5.6	4415.7	57.81
2007	23.8	5.8	4617.6	62.63
2008	21.8	4.4	4767.3	86.69
2009	n.a.	–2.0	4832.0	51.37

Sources: World Bank. *World Development Indicators 2010.* Washington, DC: International Bank for Reconstruction and Development/World Bank, 2010. http://data.worldbank.org/data-catalog; and US Energy Information Administration. *Annual Energy Review 2009* (Washington, DC: US Department of Energy, August 2010), table 5.18. http://www.eia.doe.gov/emeu/aer/pdf/aer.pdf.

percent in Chile, and 389 percent in petroleum-dependent Venezuela, indicating that export prices are rising faster than import prices. Interestingly, Brazil's terms fell 3 percent and, tragically, Haiti's fell 43 percent. Economic growth was not spectacular in the first half of this period as Latin America suffered from the low price of petroleum and various financial crises but, in the second half of this period, the growth of GDP has been a robust 5.4 percent per year on average, well above the world average of 3.4 percent. Argentina, with a newly devalued currency, grew an average of 8.4 percent; Peru, exporting minerals and natural gas, grew an average of 7.6 percent; Venezuela grew 10.4 percent.

As in the past, there are benefits: though Latin America's GDP per capita was essentially unchanged over the first five years of the period, it rose 22 percent in the second five years. In the last long-term period of growth covered by the World Bank's data series, Latin America's GDP per capita grew 82 percent over the twenty years between 1960 and 1980: 22 percent over a five-year period is comparable (World Bank 2009). In contrast to the commodity boom of the 1970s, however, Latin America seems to be taking advantage of the boom to reduce its international debt from 36 percent to 22 percent as a proportion of GNI. Debt service has fallen by more than half as a proportion of GNI and of exports, making more of the region's resources available for its own uses and more of the region's export income available for imports. As in the past, there are dangers: despite the evidence I have discussed of less dependence on the center, the financial crisis in the United States and Europe dragged GDP growth in Latin America from 5.9 percent in 2007 to 4.3 percent in 2008 and a negative 1.8 percent in 2009 (World Bank 2010).

Though Latin America and the Caribbean is the highest income region outside the eurozone and North America, it is the region with the most unequal income distribution (Franko 2007:396). The Gini Index is used to measure income inequality; it is measured in values from 0 to 100, with a higher value indicating greater inequality. For purposes of comparison, the 2000 value for the United States was 41 and for Canada 33, indicating that Canada had a more equitable income distribution than that of the United States. Table 6.6 shows the earliest Gini Index available in the World Bank's World Development Indicators (somewhere between 1979 and 1991), a second value for a year in 2000–2003, and a third value for a year in the period 2006–2008. The pattern for half the countries shown was for the Gini Index to rise from the first observation to that of the early-twenty-first century and then to decline. Chile, Guatemala, and Venezuela experienced a steady decline in inequality, whereas Mexico and Uruguay experienced a steady increase. The period of increase in most cases corresponds roughly to the years in which the Washington Consensus was the dominant policy and the period of decrease to the commodity boom. The second statistic shown (provided for two periods that reflect the change during the commodity boom) is the percentage of the population subsisting on less than $1.25 per day, and that has fallen for the vast majority of the countries shown. In conclusion, in terms of income, income equality, and poverty reduction, the commodity boom has been good for Latin America.

Transformation of the commodity boom into economic development will require developing and refining policies that can continue reductions in poverty and income inequality. This has never been easy in Latin America. As the data for 2009 show, commodity booms come to an end and there is great risk in depending on commodity exports as evidenced by Asian economies undercutting Latin America's manufacturing sector (World Bank 2009). Nonetheless, while there remain differences in policy approaches in the region—the populism of Chávez, Morales, and Correa contrasting with the more cautious policies of others—a great deal has been learned.

The development of comprehensive economic policies designed to ameliorate poverty without resorting to populist rhetoric, the strategy of using the

Table 6.6 Inequality and Poverty in Latin America

Country	Gini Index			Poverty[a]	
	1979–1991	2000–2003	2006–2008	2001–2003	2006–2009
Argentina	45	53	49	9.9 (2002)	0.9 (2009)
Bolivia	42	60	57	22.8 (2002)	14.0 (2007)
Brazil	58	58	55	11.0 (2001)	3.8 (2009)
Chile	56	55	52	1.1 (2003)	0.8 (2009)
Colombia	53	58	58	15.4 (2003)	16.0 (2006)
Costa Rica	47	50	49	5.6 (2003)	0.7 (2009)
Ecuador	50	62	54	10.5 (2003)	5.1 (2009)
El Salvador	50	52	47	14.3 (2003)	5.1 (2008)
Guatemala	58	55	54	16.9 (2002)	n.a.
Haiti	n.a.	60	n.a.	54.9 (2001)	n.a.
Honduras	55	54	55	18.1 (2003)	23.3 (2007)
Mexico	46	50	52	5.4 (2002)	3.4 (2008)
Nicaragua	56	50	52	19.4 (2001)	15.8 (2005)
Panama	49	57	55	13.8 (2001)	9.5 (2006)
Paraguay	40	58	53	17.2 (2002)	5.1 (2008)
Peru	46	55	51	15.1 (2001)	5.9 (2009)
Uruguay	42	45	47	0.0 (2001)	0.0 (2009)
Venezuela	56	48	43	18.4 (2003)	3.5 (2006)

Source: World Bank. *World Development Indicators 2010.* Washington, DC: International Bank for Reconstruction and Development/World Bank, 2010. http://data.worldbank.org/data-catalog.

Note: a. Poverty is measured as a percentage of the population by poverty headcount ratio at $1.25 per day (purchasing power parity).

commodity boom to reduce international debt, and the relatively low level of inflation in the region are signs of a maturing policy environment that may help to free the region from the legacies of economic dependence and inequality. In order for these policies to have a lasting effect, however, more attention must be paid to education, research, and development.

The appeal of populism derives from the remaining inequality as well as the regional tradition that natural resources belong to the nation and, therefore, should be managed by the state. The state origins of many of the *translatinas,* some now privatized and some still state enterprises, suggests that Latin America's mix of public sector and private sector activity—quite different from the US model—can flourish. The growth of significant Latin American corporations, bringing with them economic diversification, a strengthening of regional linkages, and the assertion of Latin American control over economic activity, tends to reduce economic dependence. There are many assets available—natural resources, dynamic corporations, a more diverse pattern of trade, and better policymaking—with which to face the complex challenges that remain.

▩ Bibliography

Alatorre, José Eduardo, Álvaro Calderón, Wilson Peres, Miguel Pérez Ludeña, and Carlos Razo. *Foreign Direct Investment in Latin America and the Caribbean.* UN Economic Commission on Latin America and the Caribbean, 2009. http://www.eclac.org.

Allen, William R. "Mercantilism." In *The New Palgrave: A Dictionary of Economics,* vol. 3, eds. John Eatwell, Murray Milgate, and Peter Newman (London: Macmillan, 1987), pp. 445–449.

Álvarez Herrera, Bernardo. "Revolutionary Road? Debating Venezuela's Progress." *Foreign Affairs* 87, no. 4 (2008): 158–160.

Baer, Werner. *The Brazilian Economy: Growth and Development,* 6th ed. Boulder: Lynne Rienner, 2008.

Bakewell, Peter. "Potosí." In *Encyclopedia of Latin American History and Culture,* vol. 4, ed. Barbara A. Tenenbaum (New York: Charles Scribner's Sons, 1996), pp. 461–463.

Bakewell, Peter, and Kendall W. Brown. "Mining." In *Encyclopedia of Latin American History and Culture,* vol. 4, ed. Barbara A. Tenenbaum (New York: Charles Scribner's Sons, 1996), pp. 58–64.

Barbosa, David. "China Passes Japan as Second Largest Economy." *New York Times,* August 15, 2010, p. B1.

Beckerman, Paul. "Longer-Term Origins of Ecuador's 'Predollarization' Crisis." In *Crisis and Dollarization in Ecuador: Stability, Growth and Social Equity,* eds. Paul Beckerman and Andrés Solimano (Washington, DC: World Bank, 2002), pp. 17–80.

Brown, Kendall W. "Peru: Conquest Through Independence." In *Encyclopedia of Latin American History and Culture,* vol. 4, ed. Barbara A. Tenenbaum (New York: Charles Scribner's Sons, 1996a), pp. 356–364.

———. "Quinto Real." In *Encyclopedia of Latin American History and Culture,* vol. 4, ed. Barbara A. Tenenbaum (New York: Charles Scribner's Sons, 1996b), pp. 512–513.

Bulmer-Thomas, Victor. *The Economic History of Latin America Since Independence.* Cambridge, UK: Cambridge University Press, 1994.

Cardoso, Eliana, and Ann Helwege. *Latin America's Economy: Diversity, Trends and Conflicts.* Cambridge, MA: MIT Press, 1992.

Coe, Michael D., and Rex Koontz. *Mexico: From the Olmecs to the Aztecs,* 6th ed. New York: Thames & Hudson, 2008.

CEPAL (Comisión Económica para América Latina). "Comercio exterior: exportaciones e importaciones según destino y origen por principales zonas económicas: 1980, 1985, 1990, 1995–2002." *Cuadernos estadísticos de la CEPAL,* no. 31 (December 2005). http://www.eclac.org.

Corden, W. M. "Booming Sector and Dutch Disease Economics: Survey and Consolidation." *Oxford Economic Papers* 36 (1984): 359–380.

Córdova, Efrén. "The Situation of Cuban Workers During the 'Special Period in Peacetime.'" In *Cuba in Transition,* vol. 6 (Washington, DC: Association for the Study of the Cuban Economy, 1996), pp. 358–368.

Crosby, Alfred W., Jr. *The Columbian Exchange: Biological and Cultural Consequences of 1492.* Westport: Greenwood Press, 1972.

Dahrendorf, Ralf. "Liberalism." In *The New Palgrave: A Dictionary of Economics,* vol. 3, eds. John Eatwell, Murray Milgate, and Peter Newman (London: Macmillan, 1987), pp. 173–175.

Dornbusch, Rudiger, and Sebastian Edwards. "The Macroeconomics of Populism." In *The Macroeconomics of Populism in Latin America,* eds. Rudiger Dornbusch and Sebastian Edwards (Chicago: University of Chicago Press, 1991), pp. 7–13.

Eatwell, John. "Import Substitution and Export-Led Growth." In *The New Palgrave: A Dictionary of Economics,* vol. 3, eds. John Eatwell, Murray Milgate, and Peter Newman (London: Macmillan, 1987), pp. 737–738.

Edwards, Sebastian. *Crisis and Reform in Latin America: From Despair to Hope.* Oxford: Oxford University Press, 1995.

Edwards, Sebastian, and Alejandra Cox Edwards. *Monetarism and Liberalization: The Chilean Experiment,* 2nd ed. Chicago: University of Chicago Press, 1991.

Ellis, R. Evan. *China in Latin America: The Whats and Wherefores.* Boulder: Lynne Rienner, 2009.

Erikson, Daniel. "Cuba, China and Venezuela: New Developments." *Cuba in Transition,* vol. 15 (Washington, DC: Association for the Study of the Cuban Economy, 2005), pp. 410–418.

Evans, Peter. *Dependent Development: The Alliance of Multinational, State, and Local Capital in Brazil.* Princeton: Princeton University Press, 1979.

Falcoff, Mark. "Argentina: The Twentieth Century." In *Encyclopedia of Latin American History and Culture,* vol. 1, ed. Barbara A. Tenenbaum (New York: Charles Scribner's Sons, 1996), pp. 152–160.

Folkerts-Landau, David, and Takatoshi Ito. *International Capital Markets: Developments, Prospects and Policy Issues.* Washington, DC: International Monetary Fund, August 1995.

Forsyth, Peter J., and Stephen J. Nicholas. "The Decline of Spanish Industry and the Price Revolution: A Neoclassical Analysis." *Journal of European Economic History* 12, no. 3 (1983): 601–610.

Franko, Patrice. *The Puzzle of Latin American Economic Development,* 3rd ed. Lanham, MD: Rowman & Littlefield, 2007.

Galeano, Eduardo. *Open Veins of Latin America.* New York: Monthly Review Press, 1973.

Gentleman, Judith. "Mexico Since 1910." In *Encyclopedia of Latin American History and Culture,* vol. 4, ed. Barbara A. Tenenbaum (New York: Charles Scribner's Sons, 1996), pp. 14–23.

Larrain, Felipe, and Patricio Meller. "The Socialist-Populist Chilean Experience, 1970–1973." In *The Macroeconomics of Populism in Latin America,* eds. Rudiger Dornbusch and Sebastian Edwards (Chicago: University of Chicago Press, 1991), pp. 175–214.

Liss, Sheldon B. "Cuba." In *Encyclopedia of Latin American History and Culture,* vol. 2, ed. Barbara A. Tenenbaum (New York: Charles Scribner's Sons, 1996), pp. 314–317.

MacLachlan, Colin. "Mexico: The Colonial Period." In *Encyclopedia of Latin American History and Culture,* vol. 4, ed. Barbara A. Tenenbaum (New York: Charles Scribner's Sons, 1996), pp. 1–6.

Mann, Charles C. "Earthmovers of the Amazon." *Science,* February 4, 2000, pp. 786–789.

———. *1491: New Revelations of the Americas Before Columbus.* New York: Knopf, 2005.

———. "Ancient Earthmovers of the Amazon." *Science,* August 29, 2008, pp. 1148–1152. http://www.sciencemag.org.

Messer, Ellen. "II.B.3. Potatoes (White)." In *The Cambridge World History of Food,* eds. Kenneth F. Kiple and Kreimhild Conee Ornelas, January 10, 2010. http://www.Cambridge.org/us/books/kiple/potatoes.htm.

Mithen, Steven. *After the Ice: A Global Human History, 20,000–5,000 BC.* Cambridge, MA: Harvard University Press, 2004.

Moseley, Michael E. *The Incas and Their Ancestors: The Archaeology of Peru.* New York: Thames & Hudson, 2001.

Palma, J. G. "Dependency." In *The New Palgrave: A Dictionary of Economics* vol. 1, eds. John Eatwell, Murray Milgate, and Peter Newman (London: Macmillan, 1987), pp. 802–805.

Peloso, Vincent. "Peru Since Independence." In *Encyclopedia of Latin American History and Culture,* vol. 4, ed. Barbara A. Tenenbaum (New York: Charles Scribner's Sons, 1996), pp. 364–374.

Rodríguez, Francisco. "An Empty Revolution: The Unfulfilled Promises of Hugo Chávez." *Foreign Affairs* 87, no. 2 (2008): 249–254.

Russell-Wood, A J. R. "Brazil: The Colonial Era, 1500–1808." In *Encyclopedia of Latin American History and Culture,* vol. 1, ed. Barbara A. Tenenbaum (New York: Charles Scribner's Sons, 1996), pp. 410–420.

Schneider, Ben Ross. "Big Business in Brazil: Leveraging Natural Endowments and State Support for International Expansion." In *Brazil as an Economic Superpower: Understanding Brazil's Changing Role in the Global Economy,* eds. Lael Brainard and Leonardo Martinez-Diaz (Washington, DC: Brookings Institution Press, 2009), pp. 159–185.

Schodt, David W. *Ecuador: An Andean Enigma.* Boulder: Westview Press, 1987.

Sheahan, John. *Patterns of Development in Latin America: Poverty, Repression and Economic Strategy.* Princeton: Princeton University Press, 1987.

Smith, C. R. "Monte Verde." *Native Peoples of North America.* Cabrillo Anthropology Department, Cabrillo College, Aptos, CA, September 2, 2009. http://www.cabrillo.edu.

Tenenbaum, Barbara. "Mexico 1810–1910." In *Encyclopedia of Latin American History and Culture,* vol. 4, ed. Barbara A. Tenenbaum (New York: Charles Scribner's Sons, 1996), pp. 6–14.

Thorp, Rosemary. *Economic Management and Economic Development in Peru and Colombia.* Pittsburgh: University of Pittsburgh Press, 1991.

———. *Progress, Poverty, and Exclusion: An Economic History of Latin America in the 20th Century.* Washington, DC: Inter-American Development Bank, 1998.

US Energy Information Administration. *25th Anniversary of the 1973 Oil Embargo.* Washington, DC: US Department of Energy, July 1998. http://www.eia.doe.gov.

———. "Table 5.18 Crude Oil Domestic First Purchase Prices, Selected Years, 1949–2009." *Annual Energy Review 2009.* Washington, DC: US Department of Energy, August 2010. http://www.eia.doe.gov.

Weatherford, Jack. *Indian Givers: How the Indians of the Americas Transformed the World.* New York: Fawcett Columbine, 1988.

Whalen, Christopher. "Venezuela's Oil Trap." *The International Economy* 21, no. 2 (2007): 58–61.

World Bank. *World Development Indicators 2009.* Washington, DC: International Bank for Reconstruction and Development/World Bank, 2009, CD-ROM.

———. *World Development Indicators 2010.* Washington, DC: International Bank for Reconstruction and Development/World Bank, 2010. http://data.worldbank.org.

7

International Relations

Cleveland Fraser

Latin American international relations have often been overshadowed by perilous global issues and dramatic events in other parts of the world. For instance, aftershocks of the global financial crisis as well as disturbances in the Middle East and South Asia have dominated recent headlines. However, significant expressions of continuity and change in international relations involving Latin American countries both within and beyond the region find continual coverage in the international sections of newspapers, in major magazines, and on the Internet.

Examples of continuity derive from Latin American history and current affairs. Bolivia's and Peru's unwillingness to sell natural gas to Chile is in part explained by the fact that both were defeated by Chile in a war fought in the 1880s! Colombia's "encroachment" into Ecuador in 2008 to clean out suspected sanctuaries for drug smugglers and antigovernment guerrillas precipitated a significant diplomatic crisis in the Andean region. Tensions flare up intermittently between Venezuela and Colombia (indeed, Venezuela severed diplomatic relations in July 2010 due to what it perceived as President Álvaro Uribe's "provocations" and renewed ties after the inauguration of Uribe's successor, Juan Manuel Santos, in early August 2010), Guyana and Venezuela, Chile and Peru, Argentina and Brazil, Nicaragua and Costa Rica, and elsewhere over long-standing boundary issues. Map 7.1 illustrates the origins of territorial disputes since independence (for an enlightening discussion of this topic, see Domínguez et al. 2003).

The 1982 Falkland (Malvinas) Islands War demonstrated the involvement of a European state, the United Kingdom, in armed conflict with Argentina. US intervention in Caribbean and Central American affairs and in those of other countries in the region has been another constant in Latin American international

185

ATLANTIC
OCEAN

UNITED STATES

MEXICO – UNITED STATES
1845-1853
● Territory acquired from Mexico
by the United States.

MEXICO

Gulf
of
Mexico

PANAMA

VENEZUELA–COLOMBIA

VENEZUELA–ENGLAND
1899

VENEZUELA   GUYANA

ECUADOR–PERU–COLOMBIA

COLOMBIA

ECUADOR

PACIFIC
OCEAN

PERU-CHILE
1929
● Tacna awarded to Peru.

PERU

BRAZIL
● Territorial expansion since 1851.

WAR OF THE PACIFIC
1879-1883
● Chile acquires Atacama from Bolivia;
Tarapaca, Arica, and Tacna from Peru.

BOLIVIA

CHACO WAR
1932-1935
● Paraguay acquires Gran Chaco
from Bolivia.

PARAGUAY

CHILE

CHILE–ARGENTINA
1902
● Dispute over Southern
Patagonia settled.

N
W   E
S

URUGUAY

ARGENTINA

TRIPARTITE WAR
1864-1870
● Argentina and Brazil acquire
territory from Paraguay.

FALKLANDS/MALVINAS
1982
● Dispute with Britain.

Map 7.1 Boundary Disputes Since Independence

relations. US involvements in Venezuela (2002), Guatemala (1995), Haiti (2004, 1994), and Grenada (1983) are prominent examples.

We have also witnessed profound changes in Latin America's orientation toward both the wider world and the United States. Indeed, it is worth remembering that movement in the Western Hemisphere toward more open political and economic systems predated the momentous changes in the former Soviet Union and Eastern Europe. And just as these seismic political and economic tremors have shaped the way we look at the world, they have also influenced Latin American perceptions of it. Certainly, reverberations of the events of September 11, 2001, have altered perceptions and policies related to issues of security and international terrorism and have demonstrated that the current international environment is extremely complex and challenging. The "Great Recession" in 2009 and 2010, the most severe global financial crisis since the Great Depression of the 1930s, has apparently energized Latin American states to experiment with solutions emphasizing greater cooperation within and among regional groupings to advance economic recovery and foster greater political unity.

Latin America has had opportunities as well as challenges. Who would have thought, for example, that Mexico would seek greater integration with the US economy? With the signing of the North American Free Trade Agreement (NAFTA), Mexico signaled just such an objective. Who would have believed that three Latin American countries (Chile, Mexico, and Peru), along with Canada and the United States, would participate as full members at annual Asia-Pacific Economic Cooperation (APEC) summits? And, who would have thought that the democratically elected heads of thirty-four nations in the hemisphere would meet in Miami in 1994 to discuss the opportunities and challenges in the region and that the success of this session would result in a succession of hemispheric summits (Santiago, Chile, in 1998; Quebec City, Canada, in 2001; Monterrey, Mexico, in 2004; Mar del Plata, Argentina, in 2005; and Port of Spain, Trinidad and Tobago, in 2009) to construct the framework and a timetable for negotiating a Free Trade Area of the Americas (FTAA)? Again, it is perhaps an indication of the challenges faced by the nations of the hemisphere that negotiations stalled as some members questioned the aspirations, timetable, and neoliberal assumptions undergirding this project. These participants have sought to reenergize existing regional trade organizations or create new groupings with alternative visions of how to move Latin America.

As Thomas J. D'Agostino illustrates in Chapter 4, the boundaries between domestic and international politics in the contemporary world have become increasingly blurred. While internal political decisions can have external consequences, the reverse is also true; the international environment can have important effects on political conditions within a specific country. The concept of "intermestic politics" has been created to more accurately describe and explain contemporary realities (Spanier and Uslaner 1978). Colombia, for example, has been struggling to end a decades-long guerrilla insurgency and to destroy the production and distribution networks of narcotraffickers. In fact, the domestic concerns of President Álvaro Uribe (2002–2010) led to an international crisis as Ecuador and Venezuela threatened military retaliation against Colombia's decision to send troops across its border with Ecuador.

Mexico has had to deal with a rebellion in the southern state of Chiapas, where a group known as the Zapatista National Liberation Army (EZLN) has called for democratic reform, social justice, and greater autonomy from the Mexican state. The Zapatistas have been quite successful in mobilizing international support for their cause, which has complicated the Mexican government's effort to resolve this domestic issue. The more recent militarization of Mexico's campaign to eradicate growing violence in northern and central Mexico due to the activities of well-organized and well-armed drug cartels is a domestic response to societal demands for greater security and protection, but the campaign's effects have literally bled across the Mexican-US border.

The 2009 coup in Honduras is another instance of domestic political activities (in this case, constitutional reform) having international reverberations because the Honduran military's actions drew condemnation from the United Nations, the Organization of American States (OAS), the United States, and the European Union (EU). Ousted president Manuel Zelaya (2006–2009) conducted negotiations with his opponents for his restoration to office from exile in Costa Rica. After secretly returning to Honduras, Zelaya was granted sanctuary in the Brazilian embassy. In the wake of elections in November 2009, a deal was struck that permitted Zelaya to leave his Brazilian sanctuary for exile in the Dominican Republic, and Porfirio Lobo Sosa (2010–2014) was inaugurated as Zelaya's successor.

The aforementioned events have been the exception rather than the rule. As democratic procedures have been consolidated in the region, it is heartening to note that virtually every Latin American state has had multiple elections in which power has been peacefully passed from one head of state or political party to another. In the case of Argentina, Chile, Costa Rica, and Brazil this resulted in the election of female presidents: Cristina Fernández (2007–2011), Michelle Bachelet (2006–2010), Laura Chinchilla (2010–2014), and Dilma Rousseff (2010–2015), respectively.

While one can assume that the calculations of Latin American electorates are centered on domestic concerns, their decisions have implications for foreign policy. Over the past several years there has been a trend toward the election of leaders who are more to the left on the political spectrum and who therefore are more likely to advocate or follow policies that may not match those of the United States. Electorates in Bolivia, Brazil, Ecuador, Nicaragua, and Venezuela, for instance, are now led by individuals who are vocal proponents of alternative solutions for the region's problems and issues. Of all of these cases, Venezuela is especially interesting. A country with relatively long-standing democratic practices, Venezuela has had to cope with challenges to its constitutional order. Indeed, its current president, Hugo Chávez, who led a failed coup attempt in 1992, was elected in 1998, reelected in 2001, became the target of an abortive effort to oust him in April 2002, survived a recall referendum in August 2004, and was reelected again in 2006. Chávez has gained international attention in his quest to offset the power of the United States and to vault Venezuela into a position of regional leadership and influence.

Recent global economic crises have raised questions about how Latin American nations should deal with issues of trade, investment, debt, and inflation. These challenges have several important implications for Latin American international relations. The failure of governments to control economic and political turmoil creates conditions that might lead to the reversal of the trend toward more open markets and political systems. These types of political and economic problems also tend to limit the capacity of Latin American countries to pursue their foreign policy objectives. Finally, they might also induce governments to embark on dangerous foreign policy adventures to deflect domestic attention from hard times at home or, alternatively, to withdraw from active participation in international affairs.

▒ Organizing Concepts

A systematic understanding of these considerations helps to put Latin American international relations in perspective. Latin America is usually depicted as a subsystem in the international system. The elemental characteristics explored by Marie Price in Chapter 2—including geographic contiguity and regularized patterns of political, economic, and social interaction—have resulted in general recognition among the countries themselves that they constitute a distinctive area in the international environment. This regional system has also typically been divided into subsystems (Atkins 1999:25–57). Although analysts may define each element slightly differently, I identify four regional subsystems in Latin America: Mexico and Central America, the Caribbean, the Andean countries, and the Southern Cone.

In this context, I seek to address several questions. What is Latin America's role in the international system? More specifically, where has Latin America been, and where is it going? Are there identifiable continuities in Latin American relations with the wider world? How have the changes in the post–Cold War era affected Latin America? A number of analytic perspectives may be employed to describe and analyze Latin America's position in international affairs. Although it is beyond the scope of this chapter to catalog and amplify each potentially useful viewpoint, three merit consideration because of their particular relevance to Latin American affairs: realism, dependency, and interdependence and globalization.

Realism

This approach views international relations as a struggle among nations for power and influence (Morgenthau and Thompson 1985). Governments formulate their national interests in terms of *power,* usually defined as economic or military capability. This is clearly demonstrated in the analysis contained in Chapter 5 by Paul W. Zagorski. Moreover, nations are assumed to be unitary actors; that is, foreign policy results from decisions made by top-level leadership. The role of popular opinion in formulating external policy is assumed to be minimal because the public is deemed to be, at best, ill-informed and little interested in foreign affairs and, at worst, susceptible to the "conventional wisdom" of the moment. Given the emphasis among nations on expanding their power and influence, the most salient international issues are those dealing with politico-military affairs. Such issues, typically referred to as "high politics," tend to dominate the international agenda. Issues such as developing the economy, fostering social justice, and protecting the environment constitute "low politics" and are considered secondary to the overarching goal of national security.

International politics is viewed as a serious game that involves winners and losers. In this zero-sum environment, an adversary's gain, by definition, diminishes one's own capacity for action. Hence, a central diplomatic objective of realism is to balance and check power and to acquire and protect spheres of influence. Whereas power politics does not foreclose reliance on instruments of diplomacy designed to foster cooperation, force and the threat of its use are also fairly common diplomatic weapons in the realist's arsenal as are alliances and collective security arrangements.

From this perspective, Latin America has been viewed as a venue for great-power rivalry; as such, realism may serve as a framework for understanding Latin America in the nineteenth and early twentieth centuries. It may also provide greater insights into actions of the United States in Central America and the circum-Caribbean. Latin America has, of course, been characterized in the United States as "our own backyard." And in a stratified, hierarchical series of international systems and subsystems, the foreign policy latitude of smaller, weaker powers is constrained by the activities and interests of larger regional and global powers.

Dependency

One of the most powerful prisms for viewing Latin America is that of *dependencia* (dependency) theory, which is based on economic and political relationships between developing and developed countries. There are many variations of this complex theory. One is Andre Gunder Frank's thesis that underdeveloped nations are "satellites" of developed metropolitan centers (Gunder Frank 1967). Another is Immanuel Wallerstein's vision of a capitalist international economy divided into "core" states that extract cheap labor and resources from "peripheral" states (see Cockcroft, Gunder Frank, and Johnson 1972). Fernando Henrique Cardoso, former president of Brazil (1994–2002) and a sociologist by training, was also a forceful proponent of this perspective on Latin American political economy (Cardoso and Faletto 1979).

Some dependency theorists offer empirical evidence that the structure of the international trade and monetary systems has disadvantaged Latin American nations. They show how the raw materials and semiprocessed goods on which many countries rely for generating foreign exchange fluctuate in price or have actually declined, relative to the prices of industrial products the region requires for development. Many of these theorists contend that Latin American nations are dependent on the decisions of multinational corporations (MNCs), the International Monetary Fund (IMF), and the US government. Therefore, it is easy to understand why they criticize modernization and development approaches as ethnocentrically derived from US and Western European models. Basically, the argument holds that Latin America has been constrained in its ability to participate in world affairs because of external manipulation and exploitation by Western capitalist countries in general and the United States in particular.

Radical dependency theory argues that in its quest for markets, capital, and labor, the West had knowingly "stacked the deck" in its favor and deprived the nations of the region of resources necessary for industrialization, diversification, and a rising standard of living (Dos Santos 1970). The operation of MNCs is cited as a manifestation of this concerted effort. MNCs are portrayed as international vampires, draining the economic lifeblood out of their "hosts" by siphoning off profits, depleting resources, and dominating domestic markets. And, under certain circumstances, they may influence the foreign policy interests of the United States, exemplified by US intervention in Guatemala in 1954 and Chile in 1973. There are also nefarious political implications. These dependency theorists claim that the operation of this asymmetrical relationship creates and maintains client political and economic elites who identify more with the West than they do with their own countries. This, in turn, creates a propensity for governments to favor capitalist development and to accede to the norms and principles embodied in the international monetary and trading regimes. It also offers an explanation for development failures based on external rather than internal causes.

Interdependence and Globalization

Dependency theorists emphasize the one-way effects of dependence. Other observers of international relations (Keohane and Nye 1977), however, have recognized that mutual dependence exists in many relationships. It is almost a cliché to say that the world is rapidly shrinking. Through the Internet, one can access the homepage of the Zapatistas in Mexico, or communicate with friends in El Salvador. Latin America is also just a few digits away via cell phone. It is only a few hours by airplane to virtually any point in Latin America. The fall in the value of the Mexican or Argentine peso roils stock markets and currencies around the globe. Many readers have probably worn Brazilian shoes, flown in a Brazilian-made airplane, eaten Chilean fruit, or drunk Brazilian orange juice at breakfast. Some of the most popular beers in the United States are brewed and bottled in Mexico. Many items of clothing sold in US stores are made in Central America or the Caribbean.

Therefore, some observers have maintained that contemporary Latin American relations can also be placed in the context of an increasingly globalized and interdependent world. What are some of the basic characteristics and assumptions of interdependence? First, this approach argues that, although the primary actors in Latin America and the world are still sovereign nation-states, other governmental and nongovernmental actors are increasingly playing greater roles in shaping foreign policy and international relations. For example, as Hannah Stewart-Gambino shows in Chapter 12, the Catholic Church not only influences political life in each country, but it also transcends boundaries. Globe-girding corporations have also reduced the power and influence of nations. Political parties, especially those affiliated with international movements such as Christian Democracy or socialism, have ties that bind them to both the region and the greater world. And, of course, the ability of drug cartels and terrorist organizations to operate across national frontiers has also posed profound challenges to the sovereignty and security of states. This view also stresses that changes in the distribution of power in the international system have provided opportunities for smaller powers to define their interests more broadly and to emphasize issues other than those of national security.

In an interdependent, globalized world, economic issues have taken center stage, with development, debt, and integration increasing in salience. Other issues—social justice, immigration, human rights, and ecological preservation—have also risen to the fore. In terms of diplomatic strategies, greater weight is placed on "soft power" such as bargaining and compromise, persuasion, and using regional and international institutions as venues for discussing issues and resolving disputes. Recall that realism assumes that countries with greater "hard power" (economic and military capabilities) will tend to have greater success in achieving their foreign policy objectives. The interdependence approach suggests an answer to the question: "If bigger is better, why don't great powers 'win' all of the time?" Under these circumstances, less powerful states and nongovernmental actors may be able to mobilize and use different types of power resources effectively, such as persuasion or terror, to offset or neutralize the advantages of larger states. From an interdependence point of view, bigger is not necessarily better or best (Nye 2004).

These three perspectives can be viewed from another one. Let us consider realism, dependency, and interdependence and globalization to be needles we can use to pull historical and contemporary threads together to form a tapestry of Latin American international relations. Although space precludes an exhaustive examination of each thread, I strive to be selective in rendering the patterns and designs to highlight what an interesting, vibrant, and colorful tapestry it is.

Historical Legacies

The realist perspective, with its emphasis on international conflict and cooperation, as well as dependency theory and the concept of interdependence, will aid in illuminating some of the important historical and current developments along Latin America's path to increasing international prominence.

René de la Pedraja shows in Chapter 3 how most Spanish colonial possessions in Latin America gained their independence in the first two decades of the nineteenth century. Their attempts to free themselves from colonial control were in part "insulated" by the 1823 Monroe Doctrine, which asserted that the time for colonization in the Western Hemisphere had passed and that the United States would view any attempt by a European power to interfere in the area with grave concern. Of course, the United States was hardly in a position to enforce such a sweeping edict. Nevertheless, because the doctrine also served the national interests of the United Kingdom with its powerful navy, it did provide a sort of deterrent to foreign adventures and the doctrine evolved as a basis on which the United States carved out its own sphere of influence in the Western Hemisphere.

Virtually all countries in Latin America struggled to foster internal unity and external security. During the first half-century of independence, a number of countries in the region sought to establish a hierarchy and extend their influence. In Central America, Mexico aspired to the role of regional hegemon. In response, the five Central American provinces attempted to amalgamate into the United Provinces of Central America in 1823. It was not to be; as the result of internal squabbling, this attempt to offset Mexico's power and authority disintegrated in 1838. Each of the five remaining states was left to deal with Mexico and, later, the United States in its own way. The Andean region also disintegrated in 1830, as the Bolívarian vision of an integrated Gran Colombia (encompassing Ecuador, Colombia, and Venezuela) faltered in the wake of economic malaise and political turmoil.

In the Southern Cone, the system was also hierarchical as Brazil, Argentina, and Chile aspired to regional hegemony. Other, smaller countries were often drawn into the struggle for power. Indeed, issues of boundaries sparked conflicts throughout the nineteenth century. To cite two principal examples, in the War of the Triple Alliance (1864–1870), Brazil, Argentina, and Uruguay combined to crush Paraguay, which lost about half of its territory and all but 28,000 of its male inhabitants (Kolinski 1965:198). Brazil and Argentina gained control over territory and resources that could (and would) be used in their rivalry for regional power and influence. Both Paraguay and Uruguay served as buffers between the two great powers in the region. Less than a decade later, Peru and Bolivia were defeated by Chile in a dispute involving access to minerals and fertilizer. In the War of the Pacific (1879–1884), Bolivia lost its only outlet to the Pacific Ocean. The memory of these events still affects the contemporary relationships of the three combatants.

The nineteenth century was also an era of increasing economic dependence. The United Kingdom in particular provided much of the investment capital and technology necessary for rapid economic development. In many countries, British firms built rail, telegraph, and telephone systems; invested in resource extraction; and established the manufacturing base. Especially in the century's later decades—as worldwide demand for commodities such as rubber, petroleum, coffee, sugar, beef, and wheat increased—countries such as Argentina, Brazil, Chile, Mexico, and Venezuela enjoyed economic "boom" times. But this came at a price. Although Latin American economies grew, they were fueled primarily by foreign rather than domestic or indigenous investments and by a reliance on exporting single crops or commodities to markets in Europe and, increasingly, the United States.

There was another interesting consequence of increased dependence during this period. Some countries, especially in the Southern Cone, lacked the population required to sustain the increased demand for skilled and unskilled labor. Therefore, they encouraged migration from Western and Southern Europe and, to a lesser extent, Asia (Endoh 2009). The ethnic and class implications of these policies are analyzed by Kevin A. Yelvington in Chapter 9. The new immigrants to Argentina and Uruguay, for example, influenced not only domestic political alignments, but also the general foreign policy orientation of these countries toward Europe, the United States, and beyond.

Latin America was not immune to foreign influence of another sort. In spite of the Monroe Doctrine, European powers periodically sought to expand their influence in the Western Hemisphere. One of the most notable examples was an unsuccessful French attempt in the 1860s to establish a monarchy in Mexico, with Prince Maximillian of Austria on the throne. Nevertheless, of all the external actors seeking to expand their power and influence in the region, none exerted such a profound and lasting influence as the United States. In 1904, President Theodore Roosevelt enunciated a corollary to the Monroe Doctrine that held that the United States reserved the right to intervene in the internal affairs of Latin American countries in the event of their misbehavior, especially related to the collection of customs duties. Roosevelt's view of Latin America was portrayed at the time as "speaking softly but carrying a big stick."

The United States, particularly active in Central America and the circum-Caribbean, was establishing its own sphere of influence through the acquisition of Puerto Rico and Cuba from Spain in the wake of the latter's defeat in the 1898 Spanish-American War. Appended to the new Cuban Constitution (1901) was the Platt Amendment, which, among other provisions, explicitly gave Cuba's consent to the stipulation that the United States reserved the right to intervene in Cuba's internal affairs if the US government deemed intervention was required. In 1903, the United States had a hand in accelerating the separation of Panama from Colombia, which had balked at a planned transisthmian canal project proposed by the United States and France.

In a precursor to more recent events, Haiti was occupied by US Marines in 1914 to stabilize the political situation and to "clean up" the society. The US troops remained until 1930. Nicaragua was also a venue for US troops (1912–1925; 1926–1933) as was the Dominican Republic, which was occupied from 1916 until 1930. The Mexican Revolution, which spanned the first two decades of the twentieth century, provided more immediate examples of US activism in its sphere of influence. US forces occupied the port of Veracruz in 1914, and US troops spent the better part of a year in futile pursuit of General Francisco "Pancho" Villa in northern Mexico. He was considered to be an outlaw who would have had a destabilizing effect in the region.

This is not to say, however, that conflict was the dominant pattern of interaction in US–Latin American relations. Diplomatic instruments were also used to foster greater inter-American cooperation and understanding. The United States was largely responsible for reinitiating what would become known as pan-Americanism based on the Bolívarian ideal. Beginning in 1889 with the first inter-American conference in Washington, DC, the United States

A ship passing through the Miraflores Locks on the Panama Canal.

Liam and Hels—Big Trip/Flickr.com

and Latin America sought to establish more frequent and institutionalized bases for communication. This and subsequent conferences spawned a number of regional institutions and agencies designed to address issues ranging from regional security and conflict resolution to the concerns of children, women, and indigenous peoples. It must be noted, however, that the United States viewed this process as a salutary means of expanding its commercial interests in the area, especially in the circum-Caribbean. "Dollar diplomacy," coupled with overt military intervention, dramatically expanded US ascendancy in the Western Hemisphere. Concomitantly, European influence and power dramatically declined.

The first three decades of the twentieth century marked ferment and change in Latin America, similar in many ways to most other parts of the world. Latin American societies had been transformed by immigration and accelerating industrialization and trade. One salient implication of this social and economic metamorphosis was the rise of a more complex class structure. Working- and middle-class sectors agitated increasingly for greater participation in political and economic decisionmaking. Between 1910 and 1920, Mexico underwent a profound political, economic, and social revolution. Farther south, in the early 1930s, economic depression precipitated the rise of various forms of authoritarian regimes and economic experiments. Socialism and communism vied for support among various segments of Latin American society. Fascism also appeared to be an attractive political option to some, especially in those countries (e.g., Argentina) with populations swollen by recent arrivals from Spain, Portugal, Italy, and Germany. Intraregional conflicts over territory were also evident. In 1932, a simmering dispute between Paraguay and Bolivia over an area known as the Chaco Boreal flared into a war that lasted three years and claimed 85,000 lives (Garner 1966:107).

The 1920s and 1930s spanned an era of regional attempts to establish a more equitable framework for the conduct of international relations. For instance, Latin America was initially enthusiastic about participating in the newly established League of Nations. And Latin American jurists and diplomats were in the forefront of reaffirming the international legal principles of the sovereign equality of states and of nonintervention in the internal affairs of sovereign nations. One prime example, the Estrada Doctrine (1930), enunciated by Mexico's foreign minister Genaro Estrada, held that if a particular government controlled population and territory, it deserved to be accorded diplomatic recognition. No normative evaluation or criteria should be applied. This and other contributions to international law reflected historical memories in Mexico in particular, and in Latin America more generally, of external intervention and economic domination.

The Good Neighbor Policy of Franklin D. Roosevelt (1933–1945) marked a shift in US policy away from the interventionism and power politics of previous administrations. Accordingly, the United States abrogated the Platt Amendment in 1934 and did not retaliate when Mexico nationalized its primarily

US-owned oil industry in 1938. One of the questions posed by students of inter-American relations is whether the era of the Good Neighbor was an aberration or the beginning of a movement toward a more cooperative and less conflictual relationship between mature partners.

With the outbreak of World War II, Latin American nations were compelled to define their objectives in the context of global conflict. Many—such as Brazil, the Central American countries, and Mexico—supported the Allied cause, led by the United States, the United Kingdom, and the Soviet Union. Some, most notably Argentina, sympathized with Germany, Italy, and Japan. The war also disrupted markets, exacerbated development problems, and set into motion a new set of international forces that dramatically altered Latin American external relations.

In sum, Latin America's international role in the pre-1945 period was constrained by its relative lack of economic and military resources necessary to project power and influence on a global scale. Europe remained the fulcrum around which international relations revolved; Latin America was a secondary arena for European rivalry. In one sense, this insularity from the wider world provided opportunities for aspirants to regional and subregional hegemony to extend their influence, on many occasions by force.

Latin America's international role was also limited by other factors. The capacity for international action of Mexico, the Central American states, and such Caribbean states as Cuba, the Dominican Republic, and Haiti was severely limited by US activism and interventionism in their internal affairs. Within the region as a whole, US interventionism also increased the sensitivity of Latin American states toward external meddling in their internal affairs. Additionally, the disruption of markets and investment by two world wars and a prolonged economic depression also tended to reduce the propensity of Latin American nations to take a leading role in international affairs and to heighten the region's awareness of its economic dependency and vulnerability.

The Cold War Era

With the end of World War II, Latin America faced a twofold challenge. First, the United States had emerged from the conflict as one of the world's two superpowers. Economically predominant and militarily preeminent, the United States was busily attempting to establish a world order based on free trade, stable currencies, and collective security. Second, the United States and the Western world were becoming increasingly aware that its wartime ally, the Soviet Union, did not share the same vision of the postwar world. Indeed, the Soviet Union seemed intent on establishing its own sphere of influence in Eastern Europe and expanding its global reach. Thus, with the movement toward confrontation between the Soviet Union and the United States, the world system was transformed into a bipolar one. The implications of this reality for Latin American countries were largely negative: a highly conflict-prone, zero-sum international system dominated by the high politics of the emerging Cold War. Latin America's international role would be defined in terms of its importance as an anticommunist bastion in the US sphere of influence. As one might suspect, this was not generally a period of intense foreign policy activism on the part of Latin American states.

In the years following World War II, two important regional institutions were established. The first was a collective security arrangement signed in Rio de Janeiro in 1947. Known formally as the Inter-American Treaty of Reciprocal Assistance and less formally as the Rio Pact, it declared that any attack by an outside power would be viewed by the signatories as an attack on them all. In 1948, the Ninth Inter-American Conference, held in Bogotá, Colombia, marked the creation of a forum for discussion among the nations of the hemisphere, the OAS. This body was intended to foster cooperation and communication among member states, especially in the areas of crisis management, election monitoring, and human rights. As time went on, the OAS became increasingly perceived by many in Latin America as an instrument of US control in its struggle to contain communist influence in the region. For example, the OAS was the forum used to denounce a reformist government in Guatemala as communist and to legitimate its overthrow in 1954. The OAS was also used to isolate Fidel Castro after he began receiving assistance from the Soviet Union in the early 1960s (Shaw 2004).

The 1950s and 1960s underscored difficulties associated with fostering economic growth and political stability. Latin American nations such as Argentina, Mexico, and Brazil enjoyed some success in sustaining economic growth through import substitution industrialization (ISI), a strategy intended to reduce dependence on foreign markets and investment through the creation of an industrial base capable of both satisfying domestic demand for consumer durables and other manufactured goods and providing a strong base for exports. This orientation created incentives to formalize closer economic linkages among Latin American countries themselves.

In 1960, for example, eleven countries formed the Latin American Free Trade Area (LAFTA). Intended to be the basis for a Latin American common market, LAFTA was reconstituted in 1980 as the Latin American Integration Association (LAIA). The Central American Common Market (CACM) was created in 1960 and the Caribbean Free Trade Association (CARIFTA) in 1965, which was renamed the Caribbean Community and Common Market (CARICOM) in 1973. Both organizations were designed to accelerate economic growth and cooperation in these subsystems.

The United States, too, had an interest in ensuring that Latin American countries were improving the quality of life for their citizens. Under the Alliance for Progress, the John F. Kennedy administration (1961–1963) hoped to achieve the twofold goal of strengthening Central and South America against the threat of communism through accelerated capitalist development and of opening markets for US producers.

The 1960s were also a period of ideological and political conflict. Ideologically, the 1959 victory of Fidel Castro in Cuba offered an alternative revolutionary model of development for Latin America. Hence, the Cuban government was perceived as having an active interest in fostering socialism throughout the hemisphere. It is clear, however, that only certain elements of the revolutionary movement sought to accelerate the diffusion of the new Cuban model to other Latin American countries. Venezuela, which was in the process of institutionalizing a transition to democratic government, was the target of Cuban-inspired insurgents. Revolutionaries such as the Argentine Ernesto "Che" Guevara (who fought with Castro) took this one step further by seeking to replicate the success of the Cuban experience in Bolivia. Guevara's attempt to export revolution ended in dismal failure with his death in 1967 at the hands of US-trained Bolivian counterinsurgency forces.

The rise of a perceived communist threat in the hemisphere marked the demise of a period of political reformism, as Latin American militaries, concerned about communism and economic growth, replaced civilians with generals. In Chapter 5, Paul W. Zagorski analyzes the changing role of the military and notes that approximately 85 percent of military conflicts in the postwar world have been intrastate rather than traditional interstate conflicts. Additionally, the abortive attempt to replace the Cuban government through the Bay of Pigs invasion (1961), the military intervention in the Dominican Republic (1965), and the 1973 overthrow of Salvador Allende (1970–1973) in Chile can be seen in terms of the legacies of the Cuban Revolution and as manifestations of realpolitik (power politics) on the part of the United States.

The rise of bureaucratic authoritarian systems intent on protecting the state from subversion led to increased levels of domestic tension and international friction (O'Donnell 1979). The ideological ferment of the 1960s also yielded a social movement that was religious in conception, but political in practice. As Hannah Stewart-Gambino details in Chapter 12, in the wake of the Second Vatican Council (Vatican II) in 1964, the Catholic Church reexamined its relevance in the modern world. One of its most important legacies was to change the way many priests and laity looked at the church's mission and purpose. Many within the church began to advocate that it become a champion of the less privileged in Latin American society. They rejected the view that the church should only tend to the spiritual needs of its followers; they believed that it needed to further the economic and social aspirations of the least powerful. Whereas in the past the church had generally supported and justified the status quo, it could be a positive force for change in the present and in the future by advocating a theology of liberation.

Liberation theology differed dramatically from traditional Roman Catholic interpretations in its views of sin, the relationship between spiritual and secular activity, and the causes of poverty and social injustice in Latin America.

The analysis of social conditions was based in part on Marxist analysis of capitalism and dependency. To some of the more radical adherents of liberation theology, armed struggle against an unjust state was justified under certain conditions.

As one might expect, elements in the church hierarchy, as well as the increasingly authoritarian governments of many Latin American nations, viewed the proponents of liberation theology as threats to national security and, therefore, as legitimate targets of repression by the state. Many governments viewed liberation theology as nothing more than Marxism and communism cloaked in spiritual dress. Moreover, although Pope John Paul II (1978–2005) called on governments to respect the human rights of all their citizens, the Vatican took steps to silence the more outspoken liberation theologians.

Two significant implications for Latin American external relations resulted from the interaction between church and state. First, military authoritarian governments, seeking to ensure political stability and economic advances, tended to cooperate with one another on such issues as counterinsurgency and antiterrorism. Militaries also collaborated in providing a societal justification for establishing national security states. Second, the ferocity and alacrity with which many governments rooted out suspected subversives and communists focused both domestic and international attention on the issues of human rights and refugees. Nongovernmental organizations, such as Amnesty International and Americas Watch, in addition to the administration of US president Jimmy Carter (1977–1981), began to pressure Latin American governments to end impunity and abuse of their citizens.

▓ Dependency and Debt

With the first oil price shock in the early 1970s, nations that controlled oil or other commodities possessed a great advantage. It was an era of global inflation, but it was also an era of developmental opportunity. This was especially true for those countries fortunate enough to possess lakes of oil, vast reserves of copper or tin, or even those who were efficient producers of bananas or other primary resources and commodities. The high price of oil also created pressure for all countries to finance their energy bills.

What was the solution to this dilemma? For many, it was to borrow from Western banks. The international balance of economic power seemed to be shifting from the developed countries of North America, Europe, and Japan to the oil-producing cartel. Arab countries, such as Saudi Arabia and Kuwait, were receiving large infusions of cash and they could not spend it fast enough. There was a limit to the number of airports, ports, hotels, and luxury cars that individuals and governments could build or buy. Thus, they began to deposit the surplus into US and European banks. This recycling of "petrodollars" created an incentive among bankers to lend the money to earn interest that would positively affect the bottom line.

From the perspective of both parties, the solution was obvious. Latin American countries needed investment capital to accelerate their development and, presumably, to reduce disparities in wealth and income. Bankers needed new opportunities to make money. And at the time, governments seemed to be good credit risks. They controlled commodities that seemed to be continually rising in price so there was no question that the borrowers would be able to pay back their loans. Also, governments would not go bankrupt. Thus, during this period, Mexico, Brazil, Venezuela, Argentina, and others borrowed millions of dollars. Another round of oil price increases in the late 1970s induced another round of borrowing.

The increased sensitivity of the developed world to the demands of the less developed world provided an impetus for calls for a dialogue to be conducted under UN auspices between the North and South regarding a new international economic order (NIEO). Mexico and Venezuela were in the forefront of this dialogue, calling for reforms to the trade and monetary regimes and for greater restrictions on the operation of MNCs. Although the negotiations met with mixed success from the point of view of the Latin American states, one enduring legacy of the process was an increased assertiveness and activism on the part of resource-rich countries. In this era of expanding mutual dependence, the range of foreign policy maneuvers was also expanding as were the economic and diplomatic capabilities of those countries aspiring to regional—and, indeed, global—leadership.

As Scott G. McKinney illustrates in Chapter 6, the boom went bust in the early 1980s as international economic conditions conspired to send the global economy into recession. Suddenly, prices began to fall. Between 1980 and 1985, the price of oil declined from a high of almost $40 per 55-gallon barrel to under $12 per barrel. To cite one example, it was estimated that Mexico lost $500 million for every dollar drop in the price of oil. Suddenly, countries that had seemed like good risks were signaling that they could not pay their debts. This precipitated a crisis in the international monetary system because, if Latin American countries began defaulting on their debts, it might hasten the collapse of the system and bring economic hardship to the developed world.

Increasingly, many Latin American countries were forced to turn to the IMF for assistance. The IMF insisted, however, that before it would make loans to cover shortfalls, a certain set of reforms, called structural adjustment programs (SAPs), had to be implemented. Many countries viewed these SAPs as constituting undue interference in their sovereign ability to determine their own economic and political destinies. SAPs usually involved currency devaluations to stimulate exports and reduce demand for imported goods as well as cuts in government spending to balance budgets and reduce inflation. As one might expect, such spending reductions sometimes adversely affected subsidies for food, energy, transportation, housing, and health care. Thus, the burden of economic stabilization was placed not only on Latin American governments, but also on the people. In many instances, as Thomas J. D'Agostino details in Chapter 4, these burdens were painful and politically unsettling.

To stabilize the system, the international community adopted plans put forward by two US secretaries of the treasury. The first, proposed in 1985 by James Baker, secretary under President Ronald Reagan (1981–1989), called for the IMF and the World Bank to make more capital available to debtor nations. The second, unveiled in 1989 by President George H. W. Bush's secretary Nicholas Brady, expanded on the Baker Plan by calling for renegotiations and for sophisticated debt for equity swaps. These programs, as well as an upswing in the global economy, eased the crisis. Many Latin Americans lament the 1980s as a lost decade of economic growth and development.

▓ The 1980s

Latin America was at the forefront of a surprising trend in international politics in the 1980s: the movement away from authoritarian political rule and state-directed economic development and toward democratic politics and free-market economics. The trend began with Uruguay, Peru, Argentina, and Brazil and accelerated until almost every country in the hemisphere became "democratic." This process took different forms in different countries. In some, the military gave up power in an incremental fashion, as in Brazil during the process of *abertura democrática* (democratic opening). In others, longtime leaders were removed or voted out of office. A 1989 coup against Paraguay's seventime president, Alfredo Stroessner (1954–1989), is a good example of the former, and the Chilean electorate's emphatic no in a 1988 referendum on General Augusto Pinochet's (1973–1989) continuation in power illustrates the latter.

In Central America, civil unrest and violence characterized the process. In Nicaragua, the Sandinista National Liberation Front (FSLN) seized power in 1979 after ousting Anastasio Somoza Debayle (1967–1979), the last in a line of dynastic dictators. In El Salvador, the Farabundo Martí National Liberation Front (FMLN) began struggling to depose a government controlled by the military and supported by the United States.

In both cases, the international system intruded on the internal politics of the area. The Reagan administration (1981–1989) erroneously viewed both conflicts as inspired by outside forces. According to this analysis, the FMLN was aided and abetted by the Soviets who were funneling arms and supplies through Cuba and Nicaragua. The Sandinistas were perceived to be instruments of Soviet influence in the Western Hemisphere. And from the perspective of the international system, it appeared that the Soviets were "on the march."

They made gains in the Horn of Africa, were engaged in Afghanistan, and had aided—with the assistance of Cuban proxies—the ascent to power of Afro-Marxist leaders and groups in Angola and Mozambique. Their military strength, particularly in the area of strategic weaponry, seemed to equal or perhaps even surpass that of the United States.

As enunciated by the Reagan Doctrine, the United States undertook to "roll back" communism by supporting groups and individuals supposedly struggling for freedom against tyranny. In the context of Central America, this meant increasing support in the form of arms and matériel for groups of Nicaraguan exiles in Honduras and Costa Rica. These *contras* began operations in 1982 and carried on a low-level guerrilla campaign in Nicaragua for the next eight years. The United States also spent millions of dollars over a ten-year period to aid the Salvadoran government in its struggle against leftist insurgents.

The trouble in Central America and the Caribbean galvanized Latin America in opposition to another instance of external intervention into the region's affairs and energized the search for Latin American solutions to Latin American problems. In 1983, Mexico, Venezuela, Colombia, and Panama met on the island of Contadora to begin discussing a regional plan to end hostilities in Central America. This group was expanded in July 1985 to include a support group consisting of Argentina, Brazil, and Uruguay.

Central America was not the only arena for conflict in the early 1980s. A long-simmering dispute between Argentina and the United Kingdom over control of the Falkland Islands (Islas Malvinas) flared into war. Asserting that the UK had no right to control these specks of land off the coast of Argentina, the Argentine government sent troops in March 1982 to reassert sovereignty over the islands. The military government had taken this action in part to deflect attention from the worsening economic and social conditions in Argentina itself. It calculated that Britain's prime minister Margaret Thatcher (1979–1990) would have neither the resolve nor the money to mount a military operation to recapture the islands. They were wrong. Thatcher ordered a task force to sail south thousands of miles to engage Argentine forces. After a fruitless round of shuttle diplomacy by US secretary of state Alexander Haig, the battle was joined and, in June 1982, victory for the UK was assured. The Falkland Islands War illustrated to Latin America that the United States could not be counted on to support one of its own in a conflict with a European power.

The Reagan administration's anticommunist orientation again manifested itself in the Caribbean with the October 1983 intervention in Grenada. Twenty-five thousand US troops were dispatched to protect US lives and property and to rescue a group of medical students attending an offshore medical school who were trapped by events. The administration feared the leftist government was becoming too friendly with Fidel Castro, with whose aid the Grenadians were building an airport capable of accommodating military aircraft. When a more radical faction seized power and ultimately purged the previous leadership in Grenada, the United States, at the invitation of a group of Caribbean nations, intervened. The message seemed clear: the United States would take action against instability in the region, especially if it appeared to be communist inspired, and it would not stand by and watch the Cubans attempt to expand their influence in the Caribbean. The invasion was denounced by many countries in Latin America as yet another example of wrongful US interventionism.

The drug trade and the rise of powerful cartels of narcotraffickers also constituted a new threat to the internal and external security of a host of Latin American countries—especially the Andean nations of Bolivia, Peru, Ecuador, and Colombia. Mexico, Panama, and Jamaica also fit into this group. The drug trade provided an incentive for individuals, cartels, and governments to generate revenue. Trade in narcotics such as cocaine and marijuana had profound impacts on the domestic political climates of many countries. In Colombia, powerful cartels based in Cali and Medellín in effect declared war on the government, assassinating judges, prosecutors, and legislators who attempted to thwart their efforts. In Peru, drugs and ideology formed the basis of guerrilla terror as a group known as Sendero Luminoso (Shining Path) sought to create a climate of fear and instability among the people and, more important, to provoke the government into taking action that went against its pledge to respect human rights and democratic freedoms.

The drug trade also influenced foreign policy issues. For example, much debate occurred between these Latin American countries and the United States regarding the importance of eliminating the supply or whether the United States had to do more to cut demand for the product. Sensitivities were also raised regarding the dispatch of US drug enforcement agents and military advisers to aid in the struggle.

Finally, drugs also led to another instance of US intervention in Central America with the December 1989 invasion of Panama. The ostensible justification for this operation was to take General Manuel Noriega into custody, which was accomplished. It was alleged that Noriega, the leader of Panama, had personally been involved in drug trafficking as well as having sanctioned the laundering of drug profits through Panamanian banks. Moreover, Noriega—reputed to have been on the payroll of the Central Intelligence Agency (CIA)—had overturned the will of the people by negating national election results that would have transferred power to moderate, reformist civilians. From the Latin American perspective, this event was an outrageous violation of national sovereignty as well as of human rights. It went against earlier attempts to forge closer ties with Panama and the region as a whole through the 1977 signing of the Panama Canal treaties, which established Panamanian sovereignty over the waterway as of 2000.

▩ The Post–Cold War Era

Stunning changes in global politics and economics have given rise to new sets of issues on national, regional, and international agendas. Issues relating to regional security obviously have not disappeared, especially in the wake of the September 11, 2001, attacks on the United States. But those relating to trade and investment, immigration, and the environment have risen in importance on regional and international agendas. For instance, one major trend has been the formation of arrangements designed to foster integration or, at the least, to manage increased interdependence and globalization. The precursor of many of these attempts was the 1989 Free Trade Agreement (FTA) between the United States and Canada. Following this treaty, US president George H. W. Bush (1989–1993) began to speak of an arrangement that would encompass all of North America. In response, Mexican president Carlos Salinas de Gortari (1988–1994) also affirmed that perhaps this proposal was one whose time had come.

Interestingly, for both Canada and Mexico, a movement toward greater economic integration with the United States represented a sharp break from traditional foreign policy orientations. Mexico in particular had taken many measures designed to diminish economic influence from the United States. It had nationalized its oil industry in 1938 as well as other industries over the years. Mexico had passed legislation in the 1970s, protecting its market by limiting the level and sectors of foreign investment. It had not joined the major trading regime, the General Agreement on Tariffs and Trade (GATT), the precursor to the World Trade Organization (WTO), until 1985. But in the early 1990s, all three countries began a round of negotiations that culminated in the December 1993 signing of the North American Free Trade Agreement. Proponents of NAFTA argued that it would accelerate the development of the Mexican economy, serve as a basis for a transition from authoritarian to more democratic political processes, and, by providing jobs for Mexicans, staunch the flow of immigration northward to the United States. Stock markets were buoyed by the prospects, and the Mexican peso was stabilized and pegged to the dollar.

In January 1994, however, a group of discontented citizens began staging protests in the southern Mexican state of Chiapas. One of the poorest states in the country, and populated primarily by descendants of the Aztecs and Mayas, Chiapas had not benefited from previous attempts at reform, and some felt NAFTA would only widen the gap between the rich and poor in Mexico and Chiapas. This discontent led to the formation of the Zapatista National Liberation Army (EZLN), headed by a mysterious, charismatic leader known as Subcomandante Marcos. As the EZLN gained popular support, the Mexican government's response was to send in the army. The situation developed into a stalemate, with each side accusing the other of human rights abuses and a lack of good faith at the bargaining table. Indeed, it is somewhat ironic that a group that is critical of globalization has so successfully and adroitly mobilized the instruments of globalization (the Internet, transportation, and tourism) to marshal support for its cause both within Mexico and throughout the wider world. This ability of the EZLN to market itself and its ideas has made it difficult for the Mexican government to definitively resolve this conflict.

This has also been an era in which the issue of international immigration has risen to the fore and become an important issue for the United States. During the civil war era in Central America, thousands of refugees fled from Guatemala, El Salvador, and Nicaragua into neighboring countries and northward through Mexico to the United States. Cuban refugees have also fled to the sanctuary of the United States due to ongoing economic turmoil. Many of these immigrants were returned to the US naval base at Guantánamo Bay, where they have languished and, occasionally, rioted. Haitians seeking economic and political refuge and mobility by entering the United States legally or otherwise is another example of the trend.

The increased salience of immigration as an issue of Latin American international relations can be illustrated by two sensational examples. One involved Elián González, a six-year-old Cuban refugee plucked from the sea off the coast of Florida in November 1999, who became the focus of an international tug-of-war between the United States and Cuba over where he should live and who should have guardianship over him. Given that his mother died in her attempt to make it to the United States, should Elián have been granted asylum and permitted to live with relatives in Miami or should he have been returned to his father who had divorced his mother two years earlier and continued to live in Cuba? The answer was the boy's forcible removal from his

tj scenes/Flickr.com

Subcomandante Marcos, the leader of the Zapatista Army of National Liberation (EZLN) that began an uprising in Chiapas, Mexico, in 1994.

Miami relatives and his repatriation to his father in Cuba. This issue engendered passionate debate in both countries and is an indication of how "new" international issues can be amplified by "old" antagonisms.

A similar observation could be made regarding the saga of General Augusto Pinochet, a former Chilean head of state who was arrested at the behest of a Spanish judge in October 1998 during a private visit to the United Kingdom. The judge requested that General Pinochet be extradited to Spain to stand trial for human rights abuses against Spanish citizens committed by the military regime that Pinochet headed from 1973 to 1989. The judge based his claim on the allegation that Pinochet had violated international human rights covenants and that these conventions provided the legal basis to prosecute violators even if they were not nationals of the prosecuting countries. The issue raised some interesting legal and political questions. For example, if the precedent were set, would it mean that a US president could be tried for human rights violations in the former Yugoslavia, Afghanistan, or Iraq? As one would expect, this episode enflamed passions in Spain, the United Kingdom, and especially in Chile. Ultimately, after a series of judicial and administrative maneuvers, the British and Spanish governments decided to declare General Pinochet medically unfit to stand trial, which permitted him to return to his homeland in March 2000. Upon his return to Chile, Pinochet gave up his life seat in the Senate and, until his death in 2006, he was able to avoid prosecution for human rights violations alleged to have occurred during his dictatorship.

Environmental issues, such as those analyzed by Jacquelyn Chase and Susan E. Place in Chapter 8, have also generated great interest. Perhaps the most striking example of this issue is the concern over the degradation of the rain forest in Brazil. Brazil faces the same dilemma as many countries in the developing world. On the one hand, the Amazon Basin contains vast stores of minerals, some oil, and valuable hardwoods. When cleared, the land provides fertile soil to grow crops or to sustain herds of livestock. This area has resources that can accelerate the process of economic development in Brazil. On the other hand, the "Wild West" atmosphere has led to the disruption of traditional ways of life among the indigenous peoples living there, the violence directed at those opposed to development, and the degradation of the land itself. An estimated 5,800 square miles of Amazonian rain forest are lost every year, and varieties of species become extinct annually.

Does Brazil have a duty to protect and conserve a resource that is crucial to the world's atmosphere? Is the rain forest a global human resource even though it is located within the sovereign territory of Brazil? These questions are difficult to resolve. The nations of the hemisphere, however, did undertake to discuss these issues at an Earth Summit held in Rio de Janeiro in June 1992. The outcome was the Treaty on Preserving Biodiversity. Although hailed as a useful first step toward greater ecological responsibility, the treaty was not ratified initially by the United States. In Kyoto, Japan, in 1997, industrialized nations (except the United States) agreed to cut their emissions of greenhouse gases by an average of 5 percent below 1990 levels during the years 2008–2012. Developing countries adamantly refused any limits on emissions. Countries agreed in principle to create an international emission trading system that would let firms and countries trade emission credits. Such a system could sharply reduce the cost of limiting emissions, but diplomats are making slow progress in working out the myriad of rules and procedures that are needed to make the system function.

Another attempt was made to reach agreement on climate change at the UN Climate Change Conference in Copenhagen, Denmark, in December 2009. The issues addressed at the conference are of utmost importance to countries in Latin America and the Caribbean. For example, glaciers in the Andes have been melting at an accelerated pace. Concerns about the preservation of forests, watersheds, and biodiversity are also highly salient to countries in the region. A number of countries have undertaken policies to reduce their carbon footprints. Indeed, Costa Rica has made it a goal to become the first carbon-neutral country in the world. Argentina and Mexico have also undertaken measures to promote cleaner sources of energy.

The outcome of the conference was mixed. Although expectations were high that a legally binding agreement would be reached, a deadlock between developing and developed countries prohibited the provisions of the Copenhagen Accord from becoming legally binding. The reasons for this disappointing outcome are many, ranging from the impact of the global financial crisis to the opposition of rapidly industrializing countries like China and India. A lack of consensus about the causes and extent of global warming as well as the lack of political support in important developed countries—including the United States—also played a role. Bolivia, Venezuela, Cuba, Nicaragua, and Ecuador strongly criticized the accord. Indeed, in response, Bolivia hosted the World People's Conference on Climate Change and the Rights of Mother Earth in Cochabamba in April 2010. Billed as an alternative to the "failed" Copenhagen summit, the Cochabamba summit called on industrialized countries to reduce their emissions by half, rather than the 7 percent to 16 percent reductions agreed to in Copenhagen, and urged the creation of a "climate court" to enforce emissions standards.

Another environmental concern involves the proliferation of nuclear weapons and the issue of technology transfer. Almost forty-five years ago, Latin American nations sought to create a nuclear-free zone. Although the Treaty of Tlatelolco (1967) was hailed as a useful first step, the specter of proliferation threatened the Southern Cone region as Argentina and Brazil were each assumed to be attempting to acquire a nuclear weapon before the other did. This shadowy arms race was all the more likely because neither country had signed the 1968 Nuclear Non-Proliferation Treaty (NPT). In 1990, however, Argentina's president Carlos Menem (1989–1999) and Brazil's president Fernando

Collor de Mello (1990–1992) met and acknowledged the existence of their nuclear programs. In 1991, the two countries agreed to establish an Argentine-Brazilian Accounting and Control Commission (ABACC) to verify by mutual inspection the peaceful nature of their nuclear programs. Three years later, Brazil signed the Treaty for the Prohibition of Nuclear Weapons in Latin America and the Caribbean, which called for certification by the International Atomic Energy Agency (IAEA) that nuclear facilities were not capable of producing nuclear weapons. Some concern was expressed by the international community that Brazil had balked at permitting IAEA inspectors to tour a uranium enrichment facility under construction in Resende, seventy miles from Rio de Janeiro, in March 2004; in January 2005, inspectors were allowed inside. The Brazilian government maintains that the plant will be used to provide low-enriched uranium fuel for nuclear reactors in its Angra I and Angra II nuclear plants. International observers note that Brazil theoretically could produce highly enriched material for nuclear weapons (Rühle 2010).

Although Brazil has ratified but not signed the NPT, it has also committed itself to follow the Missile Technology Control Regime. This has cleared the way for Brazil to undertake commercial development of launchers capable of hurling satellites and other payloads into space. By mid-1997, Brazil became a fourth-tier missile producer. It is also a competitor in the area of civilian space delivery services, an excellent example of accelerating interdependence. Today, Brazil's nuclear capabilities are the most advanced in Latin America; only Argentina has provided serious competition. With Brazil's increasing economic and military power, there are some observers who are concerned that its nuclear submarine program may provide an additional source of material for nuclear weapons (Taylor 2009).

International terrorism offers a profoundly different illustration of accelerating globalization. A case in point is the tragic September 11, 2001, terrorist attacks on the United States targeting the World Trade Center in New York City and the Pentagon in Washington, DC. While the United States received an outpouring of sympathy from around the globe, including even Cuba, there were those in certain quarters of Latin American society who murmured the opinion that the United States in some perverse way had gotten what it deserved (or had reaped what it had sown).

In response to the attack, President George W. Bush declared that Iraq was part of an "axis of evil" (along with North Korea and Iran) that supported international terrorism. Labeling Saddam Hussein as the principal threat to the security of Western civilization, the United States, with the support of the United Kingdom, pressed for a UN resolution authorizing the use of force to disarm (and perhaps to change) the Iraqi regime. The two Latin American representatives on the Security Council, Mexico and Chile, were "undecided" as to whether or not they should support the resolution, and both were the focus of an intense lobbying campaign. They tended to be skeptical of the rationale for using force and argued that this resolution would foreclose a successful outcome of the previously approved inspection process.

On March 17, the United States and the United Kingdom withdrew the resolution for lack of votes and the threat of a veto by France; two days later, the United States, supported by a "coalition of the willing," including Colombia, El Salvador, Nicaragua, Costa Rica, the Dominican Republic, Honduras, and Panama, attacked Iraq and Baghdad fell on April 9, 2003. However, nation-building in war-torn Iraq proved illusory. A truck bombing of UN headquarters in Baghdad on August 2003 caused the deaths of twenty-three UN staff members, including Brazil's distinguished representative to the UN, Sergio Vieira de Mello, who was charged with creating a working relationship between the occupation authorities and the UN.

The case of Iraq illuminates continuities in Latin America's international orientation. First, it underscores a long-standing predisposition against US interventionism and unilateralism. Although there has been much debate in the United States and other parts of the world over the "preemptive unilateralism" of the Bush Doctrine (George W. Bush), for many in Latin America, there is a certain sense of déjà vu (Prevost and Campos, 2007). Second, it illustrates Latin America's differing definitions and perceptions of threats to national security. Political and economic stability and narcoterrorism, rather than the more amorphous war on terror, tend to be higher on the region's agenda. Finally, given the US preoccupation with nation-building in the Middle East and South Asia, Latin America may have to search for more cooperative regional means for dealing with perceived threats to security.

◼ The Present and the Future

Let us use our analytic needles once again in the attempt to weave a sampler of Latin American futures. From the perspective of realism, the post–September 11 environment has again placed politico-security issues high on the international agenda. However, the United States has only occasionally considered Latin America to be a central arena in its foreign policy activities. This was true during the Cold War, when the United States defined international problems in East-West terms; during the immediate post–Cold War era, when the United States had an interest in continuing the process of democratization and liberalization to foster regional stability; and in the post–September 11 era, when US policymakers consider other areas of the world, such as South Asia and the Middle East, to be more immediate and problematic foreign policy issues than Latin America.

Cast in the light of realism, Cuba, even in its relatively weakened condition, is viewed as a threat by the United States. On June 8, 2001, the United States jailed five Cubans for espionage and roundly denounced the Castro government's jailing of scores of dissidents during a time most of the world's attention was focused on events in Iraq. During George W. Bush's presidency, stringent restrictions on monetary remittances, travel, and other forms of societal interaction were implemented. For its part, Cuba claims the "Five Heroes" were assisting in the war on international terror and are, therefore, being held unjustly; that the writers, journalists, and intellectuals Cuba rounded up were "mercenaries" financed and controlled by the US Interests Section in Havana; and it continues to rail against El Bloqueo (the embargo).

Cast in the light of interdependence and globalization, however, recent events may reflect a change in approach toward this very complex relationship. In January 2011, the Obama administration decided to relax certain restrictions on travel to Cuba. The most notable outcomes of this announcement were that cultural, educational, and religious groups would again be able to visit Cuba after a nearly seven-year hiatus; a number of US airports could be used as points of departure for charter flights for representatives of cultural, student, and religious organizations; and that remittances from the United States to Cuba would be expanded to include money sent to nonfamily members (members of the Cuban government and the Cuban Communist Party are, of course, excluded). This easing was a follow-on to decisions in 2009 that made it easier for those in the United States with family members in Cuba to travel and to send money to the island. Perhaps the April 2011 Sixth Party Congress of the Cuban Communist Party will provide additional clues from the Cuban side regarding where the relationship will go in the future.

The events of September 11 accelerated a redefinition of nonstate actors and movements as terrorist organizations by the United States and Latin American states. A number of groups in Latin America, ranging from the Zapatistas in Mexico to the Revolutionary Armed Forces of Colombia (FARC), are defined as terrorist organizations by the United States. Groups linked to attacks on targets in Argentina have also fallen under greater scrutiny by intelligence agencies in the hemisphere. For example, Hezbollah, an Islamic group based in Lebanon and supported by Iran, is believed to have been responsible for the 1992 bombing of the Israeli embassy in Buenos Aires that killed thirty people, and the destruction two years later of the Argentine-Israeli Mutual Association, also in Buenos Aires, where eighty-five people were killed.

The rise of sophisticated and ruthless drug cartels constitutes a hemispheric threat, yet there is little consensus on how to reduce or eliminate the cartels' influence. One approach is to implement programs designed to reduce the attractiveness of cultivating coca and marijuana plants through more effective and lucrative crop substitution. Another is to capture and prosecute to the fullest extent of the law the cartels' leaders.

To date, however, the emphasis has been on reducing the supply of narcotics and on interdiction. There are perhaps two archetypes of this approach: Plan Colombia and the Mérida Initiative. The former is a joint venture between

Colombia and the United States. Begun in August 2000 and funded in part with $1.3 billion in US assistance, this ambitious, controversial military and social development program is intended to root out Colombia's drug trade and end its decades-old armed conflict. Some argue that Plan Colombia might have the unintended effect of increasing conflict. The FARC has received funding from the cartels in exchange for protecting their operations. Military action against the FARC and the cartels might increase tensions between Colombia and its neighbors, Venezuela and Brazil, as guerrillas find sanctuaries outside the borders of Colombia. Not surprisingly, Latin Americans tend to favor an opposite approach: reduce the demand for drugs in the United States and other countries in the developed world.

The Mérida Initiative was developed in 2008 to assist governments in Mexico and Central America in combating an increasingly ferocious and brutal war among Mexican drug cartels primarily located in cities on the Mexican-US border. More than 20,000 individuals have been killed in drug-related violence over the past four years and the Mexican government has mobilized its military to increase security in border cities such as Ciudad Juárez and Tijuana. One especially troubling aspect of this conflict is that there are indications that the violence has begun seeping across the border into the United States. One of the most tragic instances of this was the March 15, 2010, murder of a US consular employee and her husband as they crossed from Ciudad Juárez to El Paso, Texas. The US Congress has authorized $1.6 billion over three years to bolster efforts to eliminate drug and arms smuggling, especially in northern Mexican states. To critics, who call the initiative "Plan Mexico," the program seems to mirror the weaknesses of Plan Colombia, which they argue promotes impunity among the military and paramilitaries with respect to the treatment of suspects and detainees. Of course, critics also point to the necessity of reducing the demand for drugs in the United States as opposed to a constant emphasis on staunching the supply.

From the viewpoint that emphasizes the consequences of accelerating interdependence and globalization, economic issues will remain high on the regional agenda. Although the Latin American debt crisis has subsided somewhat, it could very well pose a challenge in the future. As the debt crisis illustrates, increasing economic interdependence can have far-reaching repercussions. For example, Thailand's decision to devalue its currency (the baht) in the summer of 1997 impacted the value of currencies throughout Latin America. Over the next two years, the "Asian contagion" spread to Eastern Europe and Russia and then to Latin America, leading to decisions by Brazil in late 1999 to devalue the real and to implement austerity measures to mitigate the effects of a severe economic recession. Debt and monetary issues were prime contributors in Argentina's rapid turnover in presidents—five in a two-week period in December 2001—and to the largest debt default in the history of the IMF.

Another characteristic of contemporary Latin American relations is a movement toward greater interregional and intraregional trade. With respect to the latter, the rise of Japan, China, and the Pacific Rim, as well as the expanding European Union (EU), has created competitive challenges and opportunities for innovative approaches to development and trade. Many Caribbean states have been participants in the various Lomé conventions and the Cotonou Agreement, intended to provide less developed countries with preferential access to European markets. The EU and its predecessor the European Community have signed economic and commercial agreements with numerous Central and South American states. And the momentum toward greater cooperation between the EU and the countries of Latin America and the Caribbean has accelerated as the result of a series of summits. In terms of fostering broader cooperation with Iberian Europe, from 1991 through 2010, nineteen Latin American countries, along with Spain and Portugal, have participated in twenty annual Ibero-American summits. One interesting proposal that emerged from a recent gathering was to establish an association along the lines of the British Commonwealth.

Integration theory, often used in the study of European affairs, offers another approach to understanding relations among Latin American states. This theory is concerned with the process through which nations can increase cooperation and minimize conflict in their relationships (Nelsen and Stubb 2003). This approach has been centrally concerned with the role that economic cooperation plays not only in fostering greater economic efficiency, but also in expanding amity in other functional areas of activity such as politics and defense. It is assumed that as transactions such as trade and investment increase, governments and societies will attempt to institutionalize and regularize these patterns of communication. Cooperation will begin to spill over into other areas of endeavor, and with this proliferation of activity will come a desire to establish institutional mechanisms that are not just national, but supranational in scope. Common strategies for fostering economic cooperation involve establishing common markets, customs unions, and regional institutions.

To proponents of globalization and integration, this is precisely what appears to be happening in Latin America. One of the most important trends in the contemporary period is the movement toward free-trade zones, which provides an emerging infrastructure for facilitating greater hemispheric integration. As the following list of economic associations attests, some groupings have been in existence longer than others, but all function to promote the process of economic (and, increasingly, political and security) cooperation. Indeed, the recent proliferation of such entities reflects the growing recognition that a greater degree of cooperation is crucial to the region's future.

- Andean Community of Nations (CAN, amalgamated in 1969; most associate members joined in 2005–2006): Bolivia, Colombia, Ecuador, Peru; Argentina, Brazil, Chile, Paraguay, Uruguay (associate members); Mexico, Panama (observers); Chile, Venezuela (former members).
- Association of Caribbean States (established 1994): CARICOM members, Colombia, Costa Rica, Cuba, the Dominican Republic, El Salvador, Guatemala,

Haiti, Honduras, Mexico, Panama, Suriname, Venezuela; Aruba, France, Turks and Caicos Islands (associate members); Argentina, Brazil, Canada, Chile, Ecuador, Egypt, Finland, India, Italy, the Netherlands, South Korea, Morocco, Peru, Russia, Spain, Turkey, Ukraine, the United Kingdom (observers).

• Caribbean Community and Common Market (CARICOM, founded in 1973): Antigua and Barbuda, the Bahamas, Barbados, Belize, Dominica, Grenada, Guyana, Haiti, Jamaica, Montserrat, Saint Kitts and Nevis, Saint Lucia, Saint Vincent and the Grenadines, Suriname, Trinidad and Tobago; Anguilla, Bermuda, British Virgin Islands, Cayman Islands (associate members); Aruba, Colombia, the Dominican Republic, Mexico, Netherlands Antilles, Puerto Rico, Venezuela (observers).

• Central American Integration System (SICA, originally the Central American Common Market [CACM] formed in 1960; disbanded in 1969 due to conflict between El Salvador and Honduras; revitalized in 1991): Belize, Costa Rica, the Dominican Republic, El Salvador, Guatemala, Honduras, and Nicaragua, Panama; Argentina, Brazil, Chile, Republic of China, Germany, Mexico, Italy, Spain (observers).

• Dominican Republic–Central American Free Trade Agreement (DR-CAFTA, signed in 2004): Costa Rica, El Salvador, Guatemala, Honduras, Nicaragua, the Dominican Republic, the United States.

• Latin American Integration Association (LAIA, began in 1960 as the Latin American Free Trade Association [LAFTA]; assumed present organization form in 1980): Argentina, Bolivia, Brazil, Chile, Colombia, Cuba, Ecuador, Mexico, Paraguay, Peru, Uruguay, Venezuela.

• North American Free Trade Agreement (NAFTA, established in 1994): Canada, Mexico, the United States.

• South American Defense Council (SADC, proposed by Brazil and Venezuela in 2008 as part of UNASUR; first meeting 2010).

• Southern Common Market (Mercosur/Mercosul, founded in 1991; updated in 1994): Argentina, Brazil, Paraguay, Uruguay; Bolivia, Chile, Colombia, Ecuador, Peru (associate members); Venezuela (applicant).

• The Union of South American Nations (UNASUR, established in 2008): Argentina, Bolivia, Brazil, Chile, Colombia, Ecuador, Guyana, Paraguay, Peru, Suriname, Uruguay, Venezuela.

The Free Trade Area of the Americas is a proposal emanating from the December 1994 Summit of the Americas. Heads of state of the thirty-four nations attending (only Cuba was not represented) committed their countries to participate in forming a hemispheric free-trade area. Such an integrated economic region would encompass nearly a billion people and cover a territory stretching from the Arctic Circle in Canada to Tierra del Fuego at the southern tip of Argentina. Negotiations to move this project forward have stalled, however, and other options have been explored by subsets of countries in the hemisphere.

UNASUR, for instance, consists of twelve members and seeks to link Latin American trading blocs (especially CAN and Mercosur) together to create an institutional structure and procedures to further economic and political integration. The UNASUR Constitutive Treaty was signed in May 2008 in Brazil and officially went into force in March 2011. Former Argentine president Nestor Kirchner (2003–2007) was elected in May 2010 as the organization's first secretary-general, heading the Permanent Secretariat based in Quito, Ecuador. However, his untimely death in October 2010 paved the way for a power-sharing arrangement in which former Colombian foreign affairs minister María Emma Mejía would serve as secretary-general from April 2011 to April 2012 to be succeeded by Venezuelan minister of electric energy Alí Rodríguez. In many ways, the emerging framework roughly approximates that of the EU, which is an indication of the seriousness with which the member states view this integrative project. Indeed, one of the chief policy objectives of UNASUR is to harmonize existing trade practices to facilitate a single market by the end of this decade.

Another example of UNASUR's commitment to regional integration and development is the September 2009 establishment of the Bank of the South. With an initial capitalization of $20 billion, the bank can be considered an attempt to free Latin American nations from reliance on international sources of capital such as the IMF and the World Bank. Its primary focus will be on providing loans for social development and infrastructure projects. There are also plans to increase regional cooperation on defense matters. The SADC emerged from a joint Brazilian-Venezuelan proposal to establish an organization modeled on the North Atlantic Treaty Organization (NATO) to promote military cooperation and regional defense. The organization's first meeting was held in Chile in March 2010.

Obviously, while progress has been made in constructing these ambitious projects, there have been unintended consequences associated with globalization and accelerating integration. Reaction to the plans has manifested itself in Latin American domestic and international politics. For example, observers have alluded to a left-drifting electoral tide in Latin America, especially in the past half-decade. In a number of countries, electorates have chosen presidents who have tended to be more skeptical and cautious about continuing to pursue the so-called Washington Consensus of freer markets and trade. In Central America, both the FMLN in El Salvador and the FSLN in Nicaragua have gained the presidency through democratic elections. Indeed, Daniel Ortega, the man who the United States and the Nicaraguan *contras* fought so relentlessly to remove from power during the era of Sandinista rule (1979–1990), was again reelected in 2006. Even Mexico came close to following this trend in 2006. If less than 1 percent of Mexican voters had cast their ballots for the candidate of the Party of the Democratic Revolution (PRD) instead of the National Action Party's (PAN) Felipe Calderón (2006–2012), Mexico's external orientation might be very different from what it is today.

In the Andean region, both Bolivia and Ecuador have elected presidents who have adopted a more leftist, anti-imperialist foreign policy orientation. Each has undertaken policies designed to empower indigenous populations in both nations. Evo Morales of Bolivia, elected in 2005, embarked on a world tour to mobilize support for his proposal to "transform" his country. His relationship with Venezuela improved as he questioned the utility of coca eradication programs supported by the United States, and alleged that his legitimacy was being undermined by opposition groups tacitly supported by Washington. Reelected in 2009, President Morales has taken steps to improve the bilateral relationship with the United States, believing that the election of President Barack Obama in 2008 would result in a positive shift in US foreign policy. In Ecuador, President Rafael Correa, elected in 2006 and returned to office in 2009, has tended to take a more confrontational posture in relations with international lending institutions and the United States. Consequently, Ecuador has moved to strengthen ties with countries associated with the Bolivarian Alternative for the Americas (ALBA), discussed below, as well as with Iran.

Venezuela's Hugo Chávez is the most noteworthy example of an Andean leader who has argued that neoliberal economic reforms contribute to more pervasive US influence. He did not support US-led efforts in Afghanistan and Iraq and has not forgotten a 2002 coup attempt against him, in which the United States was tacitly involved. He has asserted that Latin America, especially given the repercussions of the Great Recession, needs to have greater autonomy from the negative effects of the global economy dominated by the United States and Western Europe. To achieve such autonomy, Chávez proposed ALBA, which was established in 2004. ALBA's members include Venezuela, Cuba, Nicaragua, Bolivia, Dominica, Honduras, Ecuador, Antigua and Barbuda, and Saint Vincent and the Grenadines. This organization is an attempt to provide an alternative to the Free Trade Area of the Americas, a project deemed to be too closely linked to US national interests. Moreover, in 2005 Venezuela established PetroCaribe, a mechanism through which it provides seventeen Caribbean states (twelve members of CARICOM, in addition to Cuba, the Dominican Republic, Haiti, Honduras, and Guatemala) with low-cost petroleum.

Venezuela has also looked to extra-hemispheric allies in its quest for regional weight. For example, President Chávez has a warm relationship with Iran, viewing the latter as an ally and a partner in facilitating increased energy production and cooperation in industrial and economic activities. Both nations have also discussed issues of security and arms transfers. Venezuela has rhetorically supported Iran's development of nuclear technology, and has hinted that it would be willing to sell US-made F-16 fighter-bombers to Tehran.

Brazil also has become a potent regional player. The 2006 discovery of large reserves of petroleum off its east coast has only enhanced Brazil's considerable domestic and external prospects. Brazilian estimates place the amount of potential reserves in the neighborhood of 50 billion barrels, which would vault the country into the top ranks of oil producers. Former president Luiz Inácio Lula da Silva had sought to move forward with a plan to grant the state-controlled oil company, Petrobras, greater control over the exploitation of the new fields. He had also been interested in raising Brazil's foreign policy profile, taking the lead in efforts to move the region toward greater political, economic, and social unity. One of the best examples of Brazil's rising leadership was the December 2008 "mega summit" convened in Costa do Sauipe, Brazil, which included thirty-three hemispheric leaders. Notable in their absence (they were not invited) were the leaders of the United States and Canada. And, given their close ties to the United States, Colombia, El Salvador, and Peru chose not to participate. Cuba's Raúl Castro was one prominent head of state who did attend.

The mega summit encompassed the meetings of four regional organizations: (1) the Latin American and Caribbean Summit on Integration and Development (CALC); (2) Mercosur; (3) UNASUR; and (4) the Rio Group. Perhaps the most important decision made by attendees was to admit Cuba into the Rio Group. Created in 1986, this twenty-three member body has been viewed as an alternative to the OAS and an attempt to reduce the influence of the United States. Thus, including Cuba was a signal that Latin America was again seeking to increase its autonomy from the United States and the institutions over which the United States was perceived to exert undue influence. Taken as a whole, the summit crystallized a desire on the part of Latin American nations to move forward on a number of integrative efforts, and to rely more on regional leadership and solidarity rather than on the United States. A second summit held at Playa del Carmen, Mexico, in February 2010 reaffirmed member commitment to integrate the CALC and the Rio Group into the Community of Latin American and Caribbean States (CELC).

Finally, to briefly cite two examples in the Southern Cone, Uruguay, while following a foreign policy emphasizing greater integration, has successively elected two presidents supported by a coalition of left-leaning parties. Additionally, Argentina's former president Nestor Kirchner (2003–2007) took a measured approach to economic restructuring, and tended to take foreign policy positions independent of the United States. Moreover, president Kirchner reignited debate over the sovereignty of the Falkland Islands (Islas Malvinas).

The influence of extra-hemispheric actors, particularly China, Russia, and Iran, may increase in the future. One benefit to Latin American states is to have counterweights to the political and economic power of the United States and the EU. With China's rise as a world economic power, Latin America has become a target for investment and trade. Over half of China's approximately $50 billion in external investment is located in Latin America; over the past decade, the dollar value of the Latin America-China trade relationship has topped $150 billion. From China's point of view, Latin America is a source of raw materials and energy to fuel its expanding economy, and a market for a wide array of Chinese goods. From a diplomatic perspective, Latin America is also a means to continue the diplomatic isolation of Taiwan (which China believes is a part of its territory), and to make its presence felt in a region of the world where the United States has traditionally exerted hegemony. The incentives for Latin America include a huge market for energizing export-led growth, investment capital for resource and energy development, and a counterweight to North America (Ellis 2009).

Russia has (re)emerged into the foreign policy calculus of Venezuela, Nicaragua, Cuba, and other Latin American nations. For example, in August 2008, when the post-Soviet state of Georgia began military operations against two breakaway provinces, South Ossetia and Abkhazia, Russia came to the latter's assistance, defeating Georgian troops after a five-day conflict. In the wake of a cease-fire agreement brokered by the EU, Venezuela and Nicaragua were two of the first countries in the world to recognize the independence of these provinces. Russia has expanded cooperation in military affairs with Venezuela as well as in space exploration with Brazil. It has investments in infrastructural development in Mexico, Argentina, and Chile, and is slowly rebuilding its long-standing relationship with Cuba.

It is difficult to determine with any degree of precision exactly what are the mutual strategic objectives of Iran and Latin America. Certainly, Iran's profile in Latin America has risen in the wake of the 2005 election of President Mahmoud Ahmadinejad. One centripetal tendency for countries such as Venezuela, Bolivia, Nicaragua, and Ecuador is mutual opposition to US policies. Economic incentives are also in play, with Iran holding out the prospect of investment in infrastructure and industrial development. And, as founding members of the Organization of Petroleum Exporting Countries (OPEC), both Venezuela and Iran have a mutual interest in insuring high prices for hydrocarbons. More generally, the Middle East has been an increasing source of investment capital, especially in Brazil, and particularly in the area of agricultural production.

This discussion of significant partners located outside the region comes full circle with a brief mention of Latin American relations with the EU. The EU remains Latin America's largest donor, a primary source of investment, and its second-largest trading partner (Bindi 2010:220). The EU stance toward Latin America is based on three components: economic cooperation, institutionalized political dialogue, and fostering closer trade linkages. All of these objectives are embodied in biennial EU-Latin America summits, which alternate between venues in Europe and Latin America. For example, the most recent summits have taken place in Madrid, Spain (2002); Guadalajara, Mexico (2004); Vienna, Austria (2006); Lima, Peru (2008); and Madrid, Spain (2010). Noteworthy is the intention of many of the members of UNASUR to boycott the Madrid summit in protest of Spain's invitation to Honduras to attend the conference. Many of these states do not recognize the legitimacy of the current

Honduran government. On a more regularized basis, the EU has focused on deepening dialogues with four of the regional organizations identified above. For its dialogue with the Andean states, the EU links with CAN. As one might expect, CARICOM is the channel for its negotiations with the circum-Caribbean. And for Central America and the Southern Cone states, the EU interacts with SICA and Mercosur, respectively. Chile and Mexico have had more focused contacts with the EU (Bindi 2010).

The primary points of discussion relate to Latin American concerns over limited access to the EU market in agricultural products because the EU's Common Agricultural Policy (CAP) insulates its member states from agricultural imports. A more recent irritant is a limitation on immigration from the region. The EU has an interest in continuing to assist in the developmental and integrative projects proliferating in the region. It does, however, view the great disparities in wealth and income and the prevalence of poverty as potential threats to democratic consolidation and regional stability and growth.

With Irish approval of the Lisbon Treaty in October 2009, the EU has again moved forward with its own integrative project by vesting greater authority in a newly created post, the high representative of the Union for Foreign Affairs and Security Policy. Coupled with other legislative and administrative reforms, perhaps the EU can now truly formulate and implement a common foreign and security policy, speaking with one voice to the Western Hemisphere. Indeed, this may be a pivotal moment in the relationship between Latin America and the EU.

However, there are unanticipated intermestic consequences of integrative projects. This is illuminated by the recent debate over how to assist Greece (in addition to Portugal, Ireland, Italy, and Spain) in stabilizing a fiscal crisis that has eroded the value of the EU's common currency, the euro (sixteen of the twenty-seven EU member states are currently members of the eurozone), and contributed to wide swings in global stock and financial markets. It is a cautionary tale for Latin America that even Germany, perhaps the most enthusiastic supporter of an "ever closer union" and a primary source of funding for a rescue package for Greece, has expressed doubts about how far and how fast the EU can progress in the future.

As the countries of Latin America continue to consolidate democracy and develop economically, they are interested in creating greater bonds with one another in ways that will create incentives for the United States, China, or others to approach them as mature partners. It is also worth noting that Brazil will play an increasingly important role as a leader of integrative projects in the region and as a linchpin between Latin America and the United States as well as between the left (especially Venezuela) and more moderate segments of the Latin American subsystem. Venezuela will also continue to be a force to be reckoned with, both as a reminder of how fragile democratic experiments can be, and as an aspirant for regional influence in the circum-Caribbean and beyond.

Neither can Mexico, Argentina, and Chile be ignored. Thus, it is clear that salient differences of opinion and policy outlooks remain within and between various groups, conferences, and trading regimes.

Bearing in mind that the Latin American tapestry is still in the process of being woven, the region's vast natural resources, expanding markets, and dynamic and diverse populations make it a vital part of an increasingly globalized world. International relations within the region and with countries throughout the world will be affected by the success with which Latin America deals with its own opportunities and challenges.

▓ Bibliography

Atkins, G. Pope. *Latin America and the Caribbean in the International System,* 4th ed. Boulder: Westview Press, 1999.

———. *Handbook of Research on the International Relations of Latin America and the Caribbean.* Boulder: Westview Press, 2001.

Bindi, Federiga, ed. *The Foreign Policy of the European Union: Assessing Europe's Role in the World.* Washington, DC: Brookings Institution, 2010.

Bouvier, Virginia M., ed. *The Globalization of U.S.-Latin American Relations: Democracy, Intervention, and Human Rights.* Westport: Praeger, 2002.

Cardoso, Fernando Henrique, and Enzo Faletto. *Dependency and Development in Latin America.* Berkeley: University of California Press, 1979.

Cockcroft, James D., Andre Gunder Frank, and Dale L. Johnson. *Dependence and Underdevelopment: Latin America's Political Economy.* New York: Doubleday, 1972.

Crandall, Russell C. *The United States and Latin America: After the Cold War.* New York: Cambridge University Press, 2008.

Dent, David W. *Hot Spot Latin America.* Westport: Greenwood Press, 2009.

Domínguez, Jorge, with David Mares, Manuel Orozco, David Scott Palmer, Francisco Rojas Aravena, and Andrés Serbin. *Boundary Disputes in Latin America.* Washington, DC: US Institute of Peace, 2003. Available online at http://www.usip.org.

Dos Santos, Theotonio. "The Structure of Dependence." *The American Economic Review* 60 (May 1970).

Ellis, R. Evan. *China in Latin America: The Whats and Wherefores.* Boulder: Lynne Rienner, 2009.

Endoh, Toake. *Exporting Japan: Politics of Emigration to Latin America.* Urbana: University of Illinois Press, 2009.

Garner, William R. *The Chaco Dispute: A Study in Prestige Diplomacy.* Washington, DC: Public Affairs Press, 1966.

Grow, Michael. *US Presidents and Latin American Interventions: Pursuing Regime Change in the Cold War.* Lawrence: University of Kansas Press, 2008.

Gunder Frank, Andre. *Capitalism and Underdevelopment in Latin America: Historical Studies of Chile and Brazil.* New York: Monthly Review Press, 1967.

Keohane, Robert O., and Joseph S. Nye. *Power and Interdependence: World Politics in Transition.* Boston: Little, Brown, 1977.

Kolinski, Charles J. *Independence or Death! The Story of the Paraguayan War.* Gainesville: University of Florida Press, 1965.

Mora, Frank D., and Jeanne A. K. Hey. *Latin American and Caribbean Foreign Policy.* New York: Rowman & Littlefield, 2003.

Morgenthau, Hans J., and Kenneth R. Thompson. *Politics Among Nations: The Struggle for Power and Peace,* 6th ed. New York: Knopf, 1985.

Nelsen, Brent F., and Alexander Stubb (eds.). *Readings on the Theory and Practice of European Integration,* 3rd ed. Boulder: Lynne Rienner, 2003.

Nye, Joseph. *Soft Power: The Means to Success in World Politics.* Cambridge, MA: PublicAffairs; Perseus, 2004.

O'Brien, Thomas F. *Making the Americas: The United States and Latin America from the Age of Revolutions to the Era of Globalization.* Albuquerque: University of New Mexico Press, 2007.

O'Donnell, Guillermo. "Tensions in the Bureaucratic-Authoritarian State and the Question of Democracy." In *The New Authoritarianism in Latin America,* ed. David Collier (Princeton: Princeton University Press, 1979), pp. 285–318.

Prevost, Gary, and Carlos Oliva Campos, eds. *The Bush Doctrine and Latin America.* New York: Palgrave Macmillan, 2007.

Roett, Riordan, and Guadalupe Paz, eds. *Latin America in a Changing Global Environment.* Boulder: Lynne Rienner, 2003.

Rühle, Hans. "Is Brazil Developing the Bomb." *Der Spiegel,* May 7, 2010. http://www.spiegel.de.

Shaw, Carolyn M. *Cooperation, Conflict and Consensus in the Organization of American States.* New York: Palgrave Macmillan, 2004.

South America, Central America, and the Caribbean 2010, 18th ed. London: Routledge; Europa, 2009.

Spanier, John, and Eric Uslaner, *How American Foreign Policy is Made.* New York: Holt, Rinehart, and Winston; Praeger, 1978.

Taylor, Paul D. "Why Does Brazil Need Nuclear Submarines?" *Proceedings Magazine* 135 (June 2009): 1276. http://www.usni.org.

Tulchin, Joseph S., and Ralph S. Espach, eds. *Latin America in the New International System.* Boulder: Lynne Rienner, 2000.

8

The Environment, Population, and Urbanization

Jacquelyn Chase and Susan E. Place

In Latin America, as elsewhere, the environment is a product of interactions between human society and the biophysical world. These interactions shift over time as a result of technological, cultural, and demographic change. This chapter provides an overview of the relationships between society and the environment in Latin America since pre-Columbian times. We consider pre-Columbian environmental relations and the dramatic changes imposed by European conquerors and the Columbian Exchange. We also address the contemporary process of globalization and its impacts on the region's environments, populations, and urbanization.

The effects of globalization in Latin America filter through inequitable socioeconomic hierarchies that usually benefit the wealthy few—large landholders and well-connected entrepreneurs—while the poor majority suffers most of the negative environmental and social consequences of articulation with global markets. Foreign debt and dependence on exports lead Latin American nations to overexploit their natural resources and to degrade the region's ecosystems. Industrialization and overcrowding in substandard housing expose the poor majority to pollution and other environmental hazards. Increasing consumer demand in this largely urban region exacerbates pressure on Latin America's environments.

Latin America's environmental challenges are primarily social problems, the result of huge economic disparities and traditional lack of truly democratic political institutions in much of the region. The key to understanding the relationship between nature and society in Latin America lies in identifying who controls the region's natural resources, especially the land itself. This, in turn, relates to the quest for political and economic stability that has engaged the

A man involved in a search and rescue operation following the earthquake that struck Haiti on January 12, 2010. An estimated 200,000 people were killed and nearly a million were left homeless, with severe damage caused in the capital of Port-au-Prince.

region for almost 200 years. As Thomas J. D'Agostino shows in Chapter 4, competition for access to resources underlies much of the region's legendary political instability. The components of population change—births, deaths, and migration—have responded to conflicts over resources since the colonial period and should not be considered simply the cause of environmental problems.

▨ Pre-Columbian Cultures and Latin America's Environments

As Marie Price notes in Chapter 2, humans have occupied the Americas for many millennia. By 1500 C.E., they were living in every ecosystem from the Arctic to Tierra del Fuego, at the southernmost tip of South America, and their population totaled more than that of Europe at the time. Their livelihood strategies ranged from foraging (hunting-gathering) to shifting cultivation in patches of tropical forest to highly intensive farming systems. These subsistence systems supported varying population densities, from sparse nomadic populations in the interior deserts of northern Mexico and Patagonia in southern Argentina to extremely dense populations in Mesoamerica (central and southern Mexico and northern Central America) and the Andes Mountains and adjacent lowlands. Awareness of the sophistication and variety of indigenous agricultural techniques and technology should help to dispel the commonly held stereotype of Latin America as more "natural" and "uncivilized" than Europe and the United States.

The Mesoamerican and Andean civilizations were supported by intensive agricultural systems and regional trade that moved products across ecological zones. Indigenous agricultural systems were based on the creativity of the ancestors who had domesticated many crop plants over several thousand years. The most important food crops were maize, beans, squashes, manioc (cassava), peanuts, tomatoes, potatoes, and several grains, such as quinoa, that grow at high elevations in the Andes.

Over the centuries, indigenous peoples modified the environment as they devised innovative methods for increasing food production to keep pace with population growth and the rise of national societies. Methods of agricultural intensification included irrigation systems, terracing, raised fields, sunken fields, drainage systems, and an ingenious system of creating *chinampas* (raised cultivation beds) in the shallow, brackish lakes in the Valley of Mexico. There were an estimated 30,000 acres of *chinampas* around Tenochtitlán, the Aztec capital. The high productivity of the *chinampas* contributed to the support of Tenochtitlán's pre-Columbian population of perhaps a quarter of a million. A few remnant *chinampas* can be seen in suburban Mexico City today, where they are marketed for tourists as "The Floating Gardens of Xochimilco." Other evidence of complex environmental modification exists in many parts of Latin America. For example, some 1.5 million acres of agricultural terraces have been discovered in the central Andes. Over 1.25 million acres of abandoned raised fields have been identified in northern Colombia.

"Simple" village farmers of the tropical lowlands also manipulated nature in ingenious ways. These farmers practiced shifting cultivation, a seminomadic system of farming the tropical forest without destroying it. They cleared, burned, and planted in scattered patches within the forest. After a few seasons, they abandoned a given field and allowed the forest to regenerate. They planted a wide variety of crops, including many fruit and nut trees, from which they could continue harvesting even after abandoning a given field. They managed the renewal of the forest, selecting for useful species, including trees whose ash provided specific nutrients to the soil when burned. Thus, they planned for the future even as they abandoned a given plot. Thousands of years of human management, including long-term mulching and selection of useful wild species, have modified the tropical forests of Latin America. Some scientists believe that such human activities have contributed to the astounding biodiversity of the Amazon Basin. Humans have actually created new soils in the basin, where extensive areas of rich black soils, created by indigenous agricultural systems and household refuse, have been found amidst the infertile red soils that are natural to the region.

▨ Demographic and Environmental Change in the Colonial Era

European conquest initiated rapid environmental change in Latin America, as noted by Marie Price in Chapter 2. Imposition of European technologies that were ill-suited to Latin America's environmental conditions degraded fragile ecosystems. For example, introduction of European farming systems based on the plow caused accelerated soil erosion, especially when used on the hilly or mountainous topography that was prevalent in the areas of Spanish settlement. Another serious ecological consequence of the insertion of Spanish agricultural systems was the introduction of Old World weeds. Today, exotic weeds have displaced native species throughout Latin America and constitute a major threat to biodiversity in the region.

European colonialism also introduced into Latin America an economic system based on the export of commodities to Europe. The Spanish colonial system was oriented toward the extraction of mineral wealth, gold and silver, and its importation to Europe. Mining spawned a number of environmental impacts. Forests were quickly decimated to provide timbers for the mines, housing for workers, and charcoal for fuel. Extensive agricultural areas were established to supply the mines and miners with necessities such as food, hides (for ore sacks and pulleys), tallow (to illuminate mines), and grazing for the thousands of mules needed to transport the ore. The desertification created by these activities in the semiarid and mountainous environments in which the mines were located persists today.

The Portuguese, not finding precious metals and large indigenous populations in Brazil, began extracting brazilwood for the reddish resin used in dyes. However, soon they introduced sugarcane, an Asian crop that was destined to change the face of Latin America. Sugarcane's environmental impacts included deforestation and degradation of the soil. The expansion of sugar plantations and logging into Brazil's Atlantic coastal forest led to the ecosystem's virtual disappearance by the late nineteenth century. Sugar is also associated with the invention of a new economic institution, the plantation, which dramatically transformed nature and society in Latin America. The plantation was a commercial agricultural venture designed to specialize in the production of a tropical crop for export to Europe. Its high demand for labor stimulated the African slave trade, forcing at least 10 million Africans into Latin America and the Caribbean. Slave-based plantations caused northeast Brazil and many Caribbean islands to be populated far beyond their carrying capacities. Haiti, where a desperately poor population struggles to survive in a denuded landscape, exemplifies the end result of centuries of plantation production and slave labor. The devastating earthquake that struck Haiti in 2010 exacerbated these struggles.

As René de la Pedraja explains in Chapter 3, Europeans introduced diseases that decimated the indigenous population. Whole zones were nearly depopulated and the remaining native inhabitants were relocated, forced to labor for the conquerors, or fled into the hinterlands. The large areas that were remote from the centers of Spanish and Portuguese settlement reverted to forest, leading to the "pristine myth" that the Americas were unpopulated and ripe for colonization by Europeans. Marie Price asserts in Chapter 2 that the most direct and profound impact of the conquest on the Americas was demographic. In addition to the destruction of up to 90 percent of the region's preconquest population, displacement, as well as changes in racial and ethnic identities, redefined both the daily life and the course of history and society in the colonies.

High mortality robbed native peoples and slaves of future generations, and the reorientation of resource extraction and agriculture in the service of Europeans forced native peoples to leave their homelands and discontinue their traditional livelihoods. Attempts to survive and live ordinary lives in the framework of coerced labor and displacement ranged from resistance through flight to strategic alliances with Europeans through marriage and reciprocity. Whatever the specific strategy, it often implied mobility, displacement, and resettlement.

In Spanish America, colonial settlers and administrators achieved control over native labor by controlling their land. Native communal lands were converted to Spanish dominion, and indigenous peoples were often forced onto marginal lands. By the end of the sixteenth century, Spaniards had appropriated most of the good land in the region. They established enormous *haciendas* (estates), some as large as European principalities, relegating the remaining indigenous populations to virtual serfdom. The indigenous populations in the uplands of Spanish America eventually returned to growth, even as the colonial economy deprived them of resources. Poverty, rural livelihoods, and the influence of Catholicism have conspired to keep fertility high in these areas. They are among the most densely populated regions of Latin America, despite high mortality and persistent out-migration.

In the tropical lowlands of Brazil and the Caribbean islands, the plantation economies' dependence on African slave labor contributed to the racial diversity and complex social hierarchy of Latin America. As with the indigenous populations of Spanish America, slaves were allowed to practice subsistence farming and their agriculture was pushed to hilly, rocky, or dry areas. This pattern repeated itself in post-slave society in areas that continued to produce tropical plantation crops. The *morador* (tenant farming) system in northeastern Brazil, for example, thrived until the late twentieth century. In this arrangement, sugarcane workers lived on designated areas of plantations, tending subsistence crops and working seasonally in the cane harvest and sugar production.

During the colonial period, Portuguese settlers' rising demand for labor, lands, and forest resources led natives to flee to the interior. Hence, evasion became the natives' primary means of resisting forced labor, disease, and disruption of their cultures. Meanwhile, from the southeastern flank of the Portuguese colony, organized bands of *bandeirantes* (explorers) went as far as the Amazon

River in search of native slaves and gold. Intermarriage and trade with indigenous peoples led to the rise of a mixed *caboclo* (indigenous and European) culture that has been influential in preserving many aspects of indigenous life in rural Brazil. Throughout Spanish and Portuguese America, the quest by the Catholic Church to convert souls reached far into the interior. The Jesuits formed an extended system of communities among the Guaranís in the Paraguay and Paraná Basins and chains of missions in Baja California and along the Amazon River. In these contexts of contact and exploitation, many native peoples chose to flee upland, inland, and upstream. Legendary accounts of great native migrations in search of the "land without evil" in South America took place even before European contact, driving home the notion that native history has never been static, but the conquest gave new urgency to mobility.

Settlements of escaped slaves challenged the authority and security of plantation societies all over the Americas. A group of escaped slaves (known as *quilombos* in Portuguese) formed the Independent Republic of Palmares, which endured for almost 100 years in a mountainous area in the northeast region of Portuguese America. It was eventually overcome by military force at the end of the seventeenth century. In Jamaica, maroons (a term referring to escaped slaves that derives from *cimarrones* in Spanish) signed the 1739 treaty with the British providing them with autonomy that continues symbolically to this day. Also, maroons had occasionally developed trading relationships with plantations and towns, and others are known to have both battled with and cooperated with native peoples. In the Guianas, political accords between maroons and the Dutch led to the "Bush Negroes" working as slave hunters in exchange for being left alone (Herskovits and Herskovits 1934). In Brazil, Jamiaca, and elsewhere, the descendants of maroons possess unique cultures, but remain among the poorest people of their countries as they continue to struggle for recognition and land rights.

For the seminomadic indigenous peoples in what later became northwestern Mexico, the colonial frontier yielded opportunities to live largely outside Spanish institutions until the mid-nineteenth century. Some people turned to nomadic life as a means to flee and resist the conditions of mission life. Interior areas of Latin America—the savannas and tropical forests of non-Andean South America, and the deserts and scrublands of northern Mexico—were left sparsely populated. Thus, throughout later years, these areas became vulnerable to resource extraction, peasant migration, and commercial agriculture; those who advocated the use and, more often, overuse of these sparsely populated areas declared them "empty."

▨ Independence and the Neoliberal Era

As described by René de la Pedraja in Chapter 3, Latin America's independence from Spain and Portugal did not necessarily mark the beginning of democracy and equality. It merely opened the region up to investment and intervention by other European powers, especially the British and French, and eventually by North Americans. Latin America continued to export a limited range of commodities. The landed elite retained their power, and a rising entrepreneurial class benefited from its ties to foreign investors. In the second half of the nineteenth century, the first neoliberal era took hold in the region, and foreign investment in export commodities grew rapidly. The export boom was accompanied by an expansion of the agricultural frontier into many of Latin America's hinterlands.

Technological innovations stimulated the production of new commodities for growing European markets. Just as in the United States, barbed wire, windmills, and railroads contributed to the opening up of the *pampas* (plains) in Argentina and Uruguay and the disappearance of wild grassland ecosystems. As wool and wheat production expanded, an economic boom in the meat industry was made possible by the advent of refrigerated steamships. By the end of the nineteenth century, refrigerated shipping also transformed tropical countries, such as Guatemala, Honduras, Costa Rica, and some of the Caribbean islands. For the first time, perishable tropical crops could be sold in Europe and North America, and a major surge in banana production began. The growing populations of the industrial cities of North America also created demands for tropical commodities, such as coffee and cocoa, which had previously been consumed by only the wealthy.

As large commercial estates formed to produce the new export commodities—coffee, cotton, bananas, and cocoa—they expanded beyond existing farmland and accelerated the process of deforestation that continues today. Expansion of export production during the era of nineteenth century laissez-faire liberalism was accompanied by changes in land tenure. Much of the region's best farmland, which generally lies in plains and valleys, was concentrated in large commercial farms. At the same time, many indigenous communities lost their traditional communal land rights and swelled the ranks of the landless rural poor. The landless population sought to survive by clearing plots on marginal land, often hillsides, contributing to deforestation and accelerating erosion.

▓ Globalization and the Environment

As Scott G. McKinney discusses in Chapter 6, the mid-twentieth century saw many Latin American governments embrace economic nationalism and import substitution industrialization. These policies led to accelerated urbanization and pollution in industrial zones. They also contributed to Latin America's foreign debt crises, along with international events such as the oil crises of the 1970s and 1980s. By the late twentieth century, a neoliberal era had again overtaken Latin America, establishing a new era of privatization, foreign investment, and export-led economies in the region. Export production expanded into areas previously oriented toward self-sufficient small farms and domestic production as well as into land that was not integrated into the national and global economy, including remote areas of tropical rain forest.

During the lost decade of the 1980s, Latin America experienced a rash of debt crises that led to the imposition of structural adjustment policies by the World Bank, the International Monetary Fund (IMF), and the Inter-American Development Bank (IDB). In return for a restructuring of their crushing foreign debts, a number of Latin American countries were obligated to diversify and expand export production, open their economies to foreign investment, privatize state-owned industries and infrastructure, reduce the size of their government budgets, and raise prices for previously subsidized basic goods and services. These structural adjustments resulted in significant environmental impacts—including expansion of commercial agricultural production, mineral and petroleum extraction, growth of industrial production and concomitant pollution, promotion of international tourism, and a reduction in protection of the environment and public health due to "downsizing" of governments.

The environmental aspects of the debt crisis and the neoliberal response are closely intertwined with social issues. The expansion of agribusiness into previously remote areas has displaced subsistence farming and generated internal migration in three directions, all with environmental consequences. Many displaced peasant farmers have headed for existing urban slums, hoping to find employment. Others have pushed farther into frontier areas, usually to marginal land of low agricultural potential, but highly vulnerable to ecological degradation. In some cases, new urban centers in agricultural regions have become established as a result of rural unemployment and opportunities in agricultural processing, transportation, and services. We will discuss the challenges posed by these types of migration later in this chapter.

Throughout Latin America, the last two decades of the twentieth century witnessed the resurgence of democracy. As authoritarian governments were forced out of office and democratic structures became established, civil society began to assert itself. New social movements arose throughout the region. Grassroots organizations focusing on local environmental issues sprang up all over Latin America, sometimes successfully pressuring governments for amelioration of environmental hazards. These successes suggest a connection between democratization and both the empowerment of civil society and environmental improvements. Some of the hundreds of local civil society organizations in Latin America have linked up with international organizations to protest globalization in its many manifestations, thus demonstrating the links between the local and the global under economic globalization. They also reveal the uneven nature of globalization. Economic activity has become globalized while social and environmental issues remain primarily local or national—or are perceived as such. Environmental regulation remains confined almost entirely to the national level, limiting its effectiveness in confronting global capital. The following sections illustrate how global processes play out at the local or regional scale in contemporary Latin America.

Deforestation: Causes and Consequences

Despite several decades of worldwide concern over "saving the rain forest," Latin America's forests continue to disappear at a rapid rate. The causes are structural: expansion of commercial agricultural production, mineral and petroleum extraction (largely to supply increasing consumer demand in the affluent global North), inequitable domestic economic and social systems, and moderate to high rates of population growth, especially between 1950 and 1980. On the surface, the most obvious threat to forests appears to be the stream of poor migrants following newly built roads into the remaining wild areas in the tropical lowlands of southern Mexico, Central America, and the Amazon Basin (including parts of Brazil, Bolivia, Peru, Ecuador, Colombia, and Venezuela). Large-scale commercial farmers and ranchers often follow closely behind, consolidating the small farms cleared by the pioneers. Although the forests may be cleared by the rural poor, the land often ultimately goes into commercial production, following a decline in soil fertility after the first few years of traditional farming. The poor farmers move on, clearing more forest on the new agricultural frontier while the commercial farms that replace them apply agrochemicals to compensate for the loss of soil fertility. Forest clearance serves the interests of multiple constituencies, including the landless poor; commercial timber, ranching, and agriculture; the politicians who need constituents' votes; and the international lending institutions that demand export production to repay the foreign debt. For these reasons, it is not surprising that environmentalists' dire warnings about the consequences of deforestation have had such limited effect.

Scientists, environmentalists, and forest dwellers have identified a number of important ecological problems caused by the destruction of tropical rain forests. These include loss of biodiversity, degradation of the soil, climate change, and changes in the local (and possibly regional) water cycle. Studies in the Amazon Basin have shown that precipitation has declined in areas downwind of large deforested areas. Areas that have been denuded also experience troubling increases in flooding during the rainy season and drought stress during the dry season. Deforestation further affects the rural poor by eliminating subsistence resources, including construction materials, firewood, medicinal plants, and protein from wild game upon which they have traditionally depended. Haiti is a clear example of this phenomenon. Furthermore, previously isolated tribes now find themselves under pressure from development interests, settlers, miners, and oil workers. Traditional forest dwellers increasingly must also contend with the perception by conservationists that human habitation causes deforestation when in fact human forest dwellers have sustained tropical forests for millennia. Land conflicts between forest dwellers and these groups are escalating. On the Pacific Coast of Colombia, for example, traditional Afro-Colombian populations have been displaced due to conflicts over land and resources. Immediately after they received legal rights to communal land ownership in the mid-1990s, armed groups swept in and appropriated their land by force. As a result, entire communities have been moved to refugee settlements while contending groups vie for control over the region and its resources.

Some indigenous peoples and other groups have been working with environmental and cultural preservation organizations to protect their forested homelands. In Brazil, Peru, Ecuador, and Colombia, indigenous groups of the Amazon have succeeded in gaining some legal autonomy and protection of their territories. In Brazil, large expanses of rain forest have been set aside as extractive reserves to protect the resource base of traditional Amazonian populations such as rubber tappers and Brazil nut harvesters.

Coastal Development

A special type of forest ecosystem, mangrove swamp, has come under severe pressure in recent decades. Mangroves are specially adapted forests that grow in tropical estuaries and provide many ecological services. They prevent erosion of shorelines and provide important protection during hurricanes and tropical storms. They help to break down organic matter deposited by rivers, serving as natural "sewage treatment plants." They also provide essential habitat for marine organisms that spawn in estuaries, thus playing an important role in sustaining offshore fisheries.

One of the economically important species that depends on mangrove ecosystems is shrimp, which surpassed tuna to become the number one seafood in the United States in 2001. Shrimp farming emerged as a new industry in the 1980s and 1990s in response to escalating demand from North America and Japan, in conjunction with Latin America's need to diversify and expand exports. Traditionally, shrimp fishing was a small-scale activity of coastal residents in the American tropics. It was often part of a complex and sustainable livelihood strategy, based on the productivity of natural ecosystems and including other types of fishing and farming on coastal plains. Such livelihood strategies helped preserve the mangrove forests and the health of coastal ecosystems in Latin America.

Industrial shrimp farming requires the destruction of natural mangrove forests, replacing them with artificial ponds and canals. Intensive shrimp farming requires large amounts of artificial nutrients, pesticides, antibiotics, and freshwater, in addition to the natural salt water. Shrimp excrement joins these substances in the outflow from the shrimp farms. Ponds eventually choke on their own waste and go out of production after a decade or so. They leave behind a devastated environment that is unable to produce wild shrimp. Small-scale traditional fishermen do not fit into this system, which destroys virtually all aspects of their livelihoods. Therefore, many fishing villages have mobilized to oppose the development of shrimp farms. Conflicts with the authorities in Guatemala and Honduras over shrimp farming have been less successful and more violent than in southern Mexico, where traditional small-scale fishermen have kept shrimp farms out of some villages.

Another boom, international tourism, has become a pillar of the economies of a number of Latin American countries, most notably in Mexico, Central America, and the Caribbean. In this region, governments strongly encouraged tourism-based development, taking advantage of their tropical climates and spectacular beaches as well as close proximity to the affluent North American market. Creation of coastal tourist enclaves like Cancún and Zihuatanejo destroyed mangroves and the fishing villages that depended on them, resulting in substantial displacement of traditional inhabitants and elimination of their traditional systems of livelihood. Over the long run, international tourism generates little employment for local people, other than poorly paid, often seasonal, menial jobs such as chambermaids and gardeners.

At the same time, large numbers of international tourists and the importation of consumer products and provision of upscale accommodations induce substantial local impacts. Destruction of coastal ecosystems, including mangroves and coral reefs, water pollution, inadequate disposal of solid waste, traffic, crime (including prostitution), and other urban ills all reduce the quality of life of local residents.

Tourism-oriented development also causes rapid inflation of land values, which displaces the traditional residents of the area. Even ecotourism, often marketed as a "green" activity, can displace local populations by locking up land in private reserves and reducing the amount of farmland available to support local and national populations. Another phenomenon related to tourism is the market in second homes. During the past two decades Costa Rica, for example, has experienced the large-scale conversion of land to vacation home development for foreigners. In addition to its economic impacts on local residents, this real estate development has caused considerable environmental degradation such as deforestation and accelerated erosion due to site development and home construction.

Expansion of Export Agriculture and Industrial Livestock Production

The environmental and social consequences of large-scale commercial agriculture and livestock production include deforestation and accelerated erosion as well as degradation of the soil; pollution of the soil, waterways, and surrounding ecosystems by agricultural chemicals; declining biodiversity of both wild and agroecosystems; the spread of genetically modified organisms (GMOs); and the emergence of new diseases such as swine flu (H1N1). The spread of chemical farming has not occurred without controversy and resistance by the people suffering its negative consequences. Chemicals banned from use in the United States are routinely exported and used in Latin American fields. Pesticide poisoning of farm workers has been widely publicized, and a few cases have actually gone to the courts. For example, dibromochloropropane (DBCP) was banned in the United States because it caused sterility in Dow Chemical workers, but continued to be used on bananas in Central America and Ecuador in the 1970s and early 1980s. Eventually, 16,000 workers who became sterile (out of an estimated 100,000 worldwide) signed on to a lawsuit that was heard in Texas courts. About 1,000 Costa Rican workers received monetary settlements, and other workers' cases continued to be litigated throughout the 1990s.

By the end of the twentieth century, biotechnology was being applied to crops—in part to reduce the need to use dangerous pesticides. GMOs are created by the transfer of genetic material from one species to another, thereby conferring preferred traits, such as enriched nutritional value or herbicide resistance. However, the introduction of GMOs has been controversial for a number of reasons, including their potential contamination of traditional crops.

In 2001, GMO-contaminated maize (corn) was discovered in a remote area of Mexico. This region is an important center of biodiversity because it was one of the places where maize was domesticated and is still a zone of traditional peasant farming that is based on the cultivation of a wide range of maize varieties. The large maize gene pool found in this area is considered an ecological treasure, but its future is uncertain. If peasant fields become contaminated with GMOs, traditional varieties may be lost forever and, with them, unique genetic material that humans may need in the future. Peasant farmers, indigenous communities, and civil society organizations in Mexico joined forces in 2003 to test fields throughout the country, and they discovered transgenic maize in many regions of Mexico. The GMO controversy has become a worldwide concern and is part of the antiglobalization movement of the early twenty-first century, demonstrating the linkage of local civil society organizations with global movements.

In 2009, the emergence of an unusual new form of influenza A in Mexico spawned fear of a global pandemic of the swine flu. The H1N1 virus incubated in a densely packed, unsanitary, industrial pig farm in the state of Veracruz, Mexico. The factory farm was a joint venture involving a giant US firm under the provisions of the North American Free Trade Agreement (NAFTA). This joint venture in Mexico allowed the US firm to raise and slaughter almost 1 million pigs a year under much less stringent environmental and labor regulations than in the United States. The globalization of agribusiness created the conditions for the emergence of this new variant of swine flu, much like the emergence of the avian flu a few years earlier in factory farms in southeast Asia.

Resource Extraction: Mining and Petroleum Production

Latin America has supplied valuable minerals to the world since the Spanish discovered gold and silver there in the sixteenth century. As Scott G. McKinney discusses in Chapter 6, with the advent of the Industrial Revolution in Europe, markets for industrial minerals began to grow. In the nineteenth century, Chile became the world's leading copper exporter. In turn, other Latin American countries began to export tin, bauxite (aluminum ore), iron, nitrates, and phosphates. The methods of extraction, production, and transport of these commodities in the past were usually controlled by foreign companies that paid little attention to the environmental consequences of their actions. And now, where environmental regulations exist, governments frequently choose not to enforce them in order to maintain a good business climate for foreign investors. This situation continues even though most countries have asserted ownership of their natural resources and, in many cases, of the corresponding corporations that control them.

In the twentieth century, petroleum was discovered in Mexico, Venezuela, and some time later in the Ecuadorian Amazon, and most recently along the coast of Brazil. The exploration and extraction of petroleum in Latin America has been associated with environmental damage and disruption of the lives of indigenous communities. First, the roads built by exploration teams opened up previously remote rain forest regions to colonization by land-hungry peasants. The resulting deforestation destroyed the livelihoods of indigenous populations. Second, oil drilling inevitably led to oil spills that have contaminated the land and waters of the area. Accidents such as blowouts have occurred, releasing large quantities of crude oil into the environment, and the oil destroys everything in its path. Fires have raged out of control for weeks, causing serious air pollution as well as destruction of any remaining forest near the burning well. In 1979, an enormous blowout of an exploratory well in the southern Gulf of Mexico emitted an estimated 140 million gallons of oil, creating a river of petroleum that flowed for many months. It moved up the Mexican coast, wreaking havoc on both aquatic and coastal ecosystems and even contaminated the coast of Texas before being brought under control. The transport of oil by pipeline and tankers has inevitably entailed leakage that pollutes aquatic and terrestrial ecosystems on a regular, albeit less spectacular, basis.

Latin American governments, eager for the employment and foreign exchange provided by resource extraction companies, hesitate to impose stringent environmental regulations. Foreign corporations may seek to locate companies in Latin America because environmental controls are less rigorous than in the United States or Europe, thus reducing production costs. Nationalized companies, such as Mexico's Petróleos Mexicanos (PEMEX) and Ecuador's Petroecuador, have been notorious for corruption and inefficiency, tendencies that have extended to their environmental policies. All of these factors have conspired to create a dismal record of environmental degradation and public health nightmares in oil- and mineral-rich parts of Latin America.

▨ Urbanization in Latin America

Industrialization and accompanying urbanization also carry environmental consequences. Industry never successfully absorbed the majority of new urban residents into the labor force, and the service sector far outnumbers manufacturing as a source of employment. But cities continue to bear the mark of rapid industrialization in their patterns of growth, congestion, and pollution. During the import substitution era (1930s to 1970s), governments promoted heavy industries that created environmental impacts such as air and water pollution. Authoritarian regimes ignored the environmental and public health costs of industrialization, as exemplified by Cubatão, an industrial city near São Paulo, Brazil, which is one of the most polluted places on earth. It has been dubbed the "Valley of Death" due to the concentration of petrochemical industries there. Toxic emissions from Cubatão's industries have led to elevated incidences of cancer, birth defects, and other health problems among its population. Poorly regulated industries also make residents of industrial cities vulnerable to disasters. For example, in 1984 a large petrochemical plant exploded in the densely populated Mexico City metropolitan area, killing over 2,000, injuring 4,200, and displacing over 200,000 people. Cubatão suffered a fire from a gas leak in the same year that killed hundreds of people in the *favela* (shantytown) Vila Socó. As these two examples demonstrate, the poor are usually the first to be victimized by urban ecological disasters.

Latin America has become one of the most urbanized of all the world's regions, not only due to the pull of jobs, but also because the standard of living in rural areas has lagged significantly behind that of urban areas. Agricultural strategies favoring exports and land monopolies that date back to the colonial period were instrumental in forcing landless people to leave the countryside from the early twentieth century on. Later, modern industrialization of agriculture dispossessed large numbers of peasant farmers, and many migrated to urban areas in search of employment. Industrial programs provided a "pull" factor toward the primate cities that received most investment. The population of São Paulo almost doubled between 1950 and 1960, growing from 2.3 million to 4.4 million, at a time when wealth generated by coffee in the surrounding region was subsidizing industry and commerce. Today, São Paulo's city population is almost 11 million and the metropolitan area is approaching 20 million.

Latin American cities have grown rapidly. This view of São Paulo, Brazil, illustrates the vastness of the city, which has become one of the world's largest.

Although the rate of urbanization varies from country to country, the shift from a rural to an urban society has been swift and overwhelming. Fifty years ago, the majority of Latin Americans lived in the countryside. Today, only about one-fifth of the population is rural. The speed of this transition has made the "urban problem" a key theme in Latin American society. The tendency to perceive rapid urbanization as an invasion by impoverished migrants has deep historical roots dating back to the colonial period.

The fact that most towns were small through most of Latin American history belied their importance as political, military, religious, and economic centers during and after colonialism. With the blessing of their rulers back home, the colonial elite quickly sought to establish towns as bases from which they could obtain resources from their rural hinterlands. In Spanish America, the location of colonial towns was often closely tied to mineral sources and to pre-Columbian settlements. Potosí, founded in 1546 in the Cerro Rico of southern Bolivia, was a notorious example. This city served the excavation and mining of the world's largest silver deposit. It administered political, ecclesiastical, and economic control of surrounding indigenous communities that eventually succumbed to the brutal *mita* system of forced labor. Potosí at one time had 200,000 inhabitants and was the region's largest city. Coastal settlements supported the plantation economies in Portuguese America and the Caribbean whereas the deep interior of Portuguese America remained relatively devoid of European settlement for the first century of the conquest. In contrast with the Spanish, Portuguese colonists settled into vast rural dominions, mostly within a few hundred miles of the coast. Along the coast emerged cities such as Rio de Janeiro and Salvador da Bahia that served the trade in minerals, sugar, slaves, and luxury goods. Other towns grew around the need to protect the coastline such as Fortaleza and Belém. This pattern of coastal urbanization held until the eighteenth century when the discovery of gold and diamonds gave rise to distant mining towns, such as Vila Rica (Ouro Preto) and Diamantina, both in the state of Minas Gerais. Although this introduced urbanization to the interior of Portuguese America, it also reinforced urbanization along the coast as trade in minerals increased.

As noted above, increased urbanization in Latin America was closely associated with governments' efforts to modernize and industrialize in the early to mid-twentieth century. Between 1950 and 1960, over 1 million people moved to Mexico City. The following decade, the population rose by 3.5 million and, by 2000, the city was gaining about 6 million more people per decade. By 2004, Mexico City had become one of the world's largest cities. A signature of urbanization in Latin America and the Caribbean is its "urban primacy," which is the tendency for a large percentage of a country's urban population to live in one or two major cities. For example, over 30 percent of all Chileans, Argentines, and Uruguayans live in their countries' largest metropolitan areas (which also happen to be their capital cities). As we show below, there has been some redistribution of this urbanization with the rapid growth of smaller cities, but this has not changed the fact that the region's largest cities have become sprawling megaregions that continue to grow vertiginously.

el grito/Flickr.com

Millions of people live in squalid conditions in urban areas in Latin America. This is a shantytown on the outskirts of Guayaquil, Ecuador.

Migration rates from the 1950s onward overwhelmed housing markets. This, together with people's tenacity for survival and social mobility, has led to squatter settlements, emblematic of rapid urban growth in Latin America since the 1950s. Zoning, affordable housing, and infrastructure have lagged miserably behind urban growth. As a result, poor people often resort to self-built shelters or doubling up with relatives. In many Latin American cities, one-third to one-half of the people live in settlements with makeshift housing and substandard services. It is estimated that 60 percent of the population in Mexico City live in some form of substandard or squatter settlement. One of the most famous of these barrios, Netzahualcoyotl (Neza), is a veritable city of some 2 million inhabitants. Neza began with squatters occupying the dry lake bed surrounding Mexico City some fifty years ago. The residents themselves gradually transformed their shacks into concrete block and stucco homes and successfully fought for basic city services. Squatter settlements not only reflect governments' inability to address urbanization, but they also illustrate people's self-reliance and determination to survive. While many people are too poor to pay rent or buy a home, they quickly develop collective and individual strategies for survival. Squatter settlements have been incredibly innovative in devising collective strategies for education, recreation, and job creation. Second- and third-generation squatters have transformed their shantytowns into cities within cities, with a mix of public and private infrastructure, permanent and improved housing, commerce, and social differentiation. As these settlements run out of land, they grow skyward as people add new levels onto existing homes.

Urban officials and politicians approached the enormous population influx in different ways. One response was outright slum removal, an approach favored by military dictatorships in the 1960s and 1970s. These forced evictions mostly ended with the return of democracy across Latin America. With such a huge constituency of voting citizens, politicians feared the results of direct confrontation. Self-help housing also subsidized the provision of housing and services in the region's exploding cities through "sweat equity." Because squatter settlements were often on government-owned land, they did not typically set off a confrontation over private property. In the past fifteen years, governments have quickened the provision of basic amenities to squatters, but they also have put in place more rigorous environmental zoning. These two tendencies have led to a more restrictive governmental attitude toward urban squatters as well as a limited market for low-income housing. At the same time, the verticalization of shantytowns has increased the supply of housing and contributed to a rental market in Latin American slums.

Illegal economies, rooted in the international drug trade, quasi-governmental structures, and informal "police" forces, have emerged in the sprawling slums of all Latin American cities. These have become staging grounds for violent rivalries between powerful drug lords and sometimes corrupt government security

This view of the Rocinha favela (squatter town), with luxury high rises in the distance, reflects the juxtaposition of wealth and poverty in Rio de Janeiro, Brazil.

forces while the majority of the people who live in them attempt to go about their daily lives in peace.

In search of security and comfort, the upper and middle classes have turned to high-rise security towers in the city or gated communities on the rural-urban fringe. Tangled traffic, overburdened sewage systems, noise, and loss of sunlight are some of the outcomes of the spread of the urban core into first-tier suburbs. Consequently, the urban elite has begun to sprawl into rural zones for its residential or recreational needs. Insufficient environmental oversight has allowed speculators to create notoriously illegal subdivisions that attract rich and middle-income squatters, whose ability to manipulate the judicial systems virtually guarantees the endorsement of their property claims. Their search for security has also produced luxurious shopping centers that have replaced the town plaza as the icon of Latin American leisure and public life.

Jobs (even if informal), government infrastructure, schools, and family networks built up over time through previous migrations continue to draw the poor to major cities. Unemployment and the struggle for urban livelihoods are associated with many urban environmental problems. Poverty and the informal economy (estimated at 70 percent of jobs by the International Labour Organization) send people into dangerous environments, such as trash heaps and flood zones, that operate below the radar of environmental regulation. Lackadaisical waste disposal standards tragically introduced urban trash pickers to the atomic age in the Brazilian city of Goiânia in 1987. People who made a living recycling trash took an x-ray cylinder containing cesium-137 from an abandoned hospital and dismantled it at home. Fascinated by its glow, they showed the substance off, passing it around and playing with it. Four people died one month later, many hundreds became ill, and some died years later from cancer. Investigators found waste from the incident over 1,000 miles away. On the other hand, grassroots initiatives in major cities have worked to support trash pickers' access to protective equipment and to fair prices for recycled materials.

In order to reduce environmental and political pressures on the largest cities, government officials and planners have tried to decentralize urban growth by encouraging the growth of smaller cities. Other motivations, such as occupation of the interior and political symbolism, have also come into play in these efforts. The construction of Brasília in Brazil and Ciudad Guyana in Venezuela were bold attempts to build cities from the ground up. While these efforts succeeded in creating new pockets of settlement away from the traditional urban cores, this has not slowed the galloping growth of cities that were already large when these new towns were constructed. Built in the late 1950s, Brasília has graduated to a metropolitan area with over 2 million people. In the same period of time, however, São Paulo's metropolitan population grew from 4.4 million to around 20 million. Even though the new cities were built with strong planning ideals, they have succumbed to many of the same problems of older

quinet/Flickr.com

Street children picking through garbage in Juliaca, Peru

cities such as squatters living in shantytowns, chronic pollution, violence, and heavy traffic.

Some urban decentralization has occurred as an unintended consequence of regional economic policies, such as export processing zones in the Caribbean Basin, border industrialization in Mexico, frontier occupation in the Amazonian portion of various countries, and rural development based on nontraditional export crops. During the neoliberal era, previously less industrialized countries, such as those of Central America and the Caribbean Basin, became the target of foreign investment in assembly industries such as clothing and electronics. One of the most spectacular sites of this type of industrialization is along the US-Mexican border. In the past two decades of the twentieth century, thousands of *maquiladoras* (assembly plants), were established in this zone to take advantage of its proximity to the United States. The United States represents the largest consumer market in the world while Mexico provides a huge pool of cheap labor and lax environmental regulations. Hundreds of foreign companies were attracted to a region where these factors literally come together.

The *maquiladora* phenomenon stimulated migration to Mexico's border area. By 1990, there were 3.5 million people in eighteen border cities, 6 percent of the country's total urban population that year. According to estimates by Mexico's Consejo Nacional de Poblacíon (CONAPO), by 2010 the population of the two largest border cities (Tijuana and Ciudad Juárez) alone exceeded 3 million and the total population for the top ten surpassed 6.2 million (see Table 8.1). Urban infrastructure along the border is inadequate to meet the needs of the rapidly growing population where high rates of poverty and the

Table 8.1 Population of Mexican Border Cities, 2005 and 2010

	2005	2010
Tijuana	1,392,321	1,641,168
Ciudad Juárez	1,310,302	1,431,072
Mexicali	854,879	943,326
Reynosa	520,358	612,711
Matamoros	463,995	499,767
Nuevo Laredo	355,832	395,185
Nogales	192,625	218,948
San Luis Río Colorado	158,154	165,661
Piedras Negras	144,393	156,629
Ciudad Acuña	126,385	137,634
Total	5,519,244	6,202,101

Source: Consejo Nacional de Población. "Población total de los municipios a mitad de año, 2005–2030." 2010. http://www.conapo.gob.mx/00cifras/proy/municipales.xls.

various types of pollution generated by the *maquiladoras* contribute to a host of environmental problems. Mexico's unaddressed environmental problems are finally getting attention from people across the border as smog and raw sewage make their way into the United States. In recent decades, cities on both sides of the Mexican-US border have experienced a significant increase in birth defects, most notably anencephaly (lack of brain development in a fetus). Many scientists and public health experts believe this to be the result of pollution from Mexico's *maquiladoras*.

Another facet of urban growth taking place outside countries' primate cities is boomtown growth in frontier regions. The drug trade, peasant migration, mining, and logging have led to the growth of boomtowns throughout the Amazon Basin. With little infrastructure and sudden increases in an impoverished population, these towns have become troubling sites of diseases such as malaria, yellow fever, dengue, and cholera. As a crossroads for sex workers, these towns also tend to have high rates of sexually transmitted diseases.

Export-oriented agriculture has expanded into the rural hinterlands in virtually all countries, as noted above. Since the 1980s, this expansion has rested on a whole new set of nontraditional export crops such as soybeans, flowers, oranges for frozen concentrate, and forest products for pulp and paper mills. In most cases, profound changes come to regions that are swept into these new activities. In some contexts, this development attracts former peasants to local towns where some find work in the service sector and agroprocessing. But modern agriculture can also be a factor in population loss. The mechanization of cotton and other crops that were essential to rural livelihoods in Argentina's Chaco Province eliminated thousands of jobs, leaving people with no alternative but to migrate to Buenos Aires or to other regional centers.

Urban decentralization of the kind described above has not solved the region's urban problems. More often, the same kinds of urban environmental problems spring up in all cities and towns that are growing rapidly, regardless of their size. Smaller towns, in fact, may have a less active and empowered citizenry to address urban pollution and environmental justice. Creative solutions to these problems are indeed coming from some of the region's largest cities. Mexico City, São Paulo, and Santiago all inaugurated programs to reduce automobile use, based on license plate numbers. During the economic crisis in Argentina in the late 1990s, people opened community-based factories and restaurants for the unemployed. In the southern Brazilian city of Curitiba, longtime mayor and architect Jaime Lerner took measures to ease the pressures of urban life on people and the environment, leading to its being dubbed throughout the world as the "Ecological City." Lerner and colleagues sought to create a more livable environment around the reality of people's lives, offering, for instance, free bus passes in exchange for recyclables. They sought simple solutions to traffic circulation by creating an integrated bus system and bike paths and to downtown revitalization with a pedestrian-only central business district.

Green spaces evolved through decades of tree planting, and new public parks and lakes now double as diversion ponds for floods that had plagued squatter settlements in the past.

Population: Distribution, Fertility, and Mortality

Misinformation and emotional responses are common in discussions of population and the environment. Intuitively, people often blame environmental and social problems in cities on overcrowding rather than on the resource destruction caused by commercial interests. Urban environmental problems are primarily the result of highly distorted urbanization patterns and poverty. In fact, Latin America as a whole is less densely populated (with twenty-five people per square mile) than the United States (with thirty people per square mile). In addition, Latin America has taken the lead in the developing world by dramatically reversing historically high fertility rates. This transition toward smaller families strongly correlates with urbanization. On the other hand, urbanization makes manufactured goods and processed foods an integral part of daily life, and it raises the aspirations of people for greater consumption of these commercial products.

Demographic Transition

Latin American mortality and fertility have both fallen to a point where the rate of natural growth is in decline. The annual growth rate peaked in the 1960s at 2.8 percent. Recent estimates show it at 1.4 percent, meaning that although the population of the region continues to grow, the momentum of that growth has slowed considerably. There is much demographic variation among countries, however. Some countries still have growth rates that exceed 2 percent whereas Uruguay, Cuba, and several English-speaking Caribbean nations have rates of less than 1 percent—lower than that of the United States. Rates of more than 2.5 percent are found in Guatemala, Belize, Honduras, El Salvador, Nicaragua, Bolivia, and Paraguay.

These numbers suggest that Latin America is undergoing a demographic transition toward low birth and death rates. The demographic transition model implies that the interplay between numbers of deaths and births and growth rates roughly follows a predictable path as societies modernize and urbanize. Even though Latin America as a whole appears to be following the model, each country and subregion does so in a unique way and there is no guarantee that present patterns will hold. Under impoverished circumstances, people may choose to have fewer children out of desperation rather than because they have arrived at a new level of well-being. Many of the region's poorest people, in fact, suffer from diseases that are completely preventable, and women still suffer from lack of access to family planning.

In Latin America, death rates have declined dramatically with modern urbanization and accompanying advances in water and sewage treatment and vaccination for childhood diseases. Many diseases or conditions that can kill young children, such as diarrhea, can be traced to polluted water. The percentage of people with access to potable water is now over 85 percent in the region as a whole, with higher rates in cities than in rural areas. Although 94 percent of urban Latin Americans have access to clean water, 24 million people living in cities still do not. Construction of sewage treatment facilities lags far behind the delivery of clean water.

As cities become megacities, the effects on water supply are contradictory. Population increase, urban sprawl, and industrial water use and pollution place huge stresses on water supplies and waste treatment. At the same time, because governments concentrate infrastructure in cities, urban dwellers tend to have better access to safe drinking water. These improvements, however, often do not reach the most precarious urban settlements where extreme population densities contribute to high levels of water contamination.

Because of these inequities, the decline of many chronic diseases of environmental origin has been inconsistent. Some recent epidemics can be traced to deteriorating conditions in cities together with precarious settlement in frontier areas and increased international and national mobility. The persistence of tropical diseases, like cholera, Chagas disease, malaria, yellow fever, and dengue, are dependent on environmental conditions close to home such as poor drainage, lack of sewage treatment, polluted water supplies, inadequate trash collection, lack of window screens and mosquito netting, and building materials that harbor insect vectors. Migration into tropical lowland areas and the environmental consequences of settlement in makeshift boomtowns with little medical assistance, public health education, or planning have led to the resurgence of malaria, especially among those without the resources to purchase individual protection (screens, netting, and quinine treatment).

According to the Joint United Nations Programme on AIDS (2010), 2 million Latin Americans were infected with HIV, and 76,600 died of AIDS in 2009. Risk of exposure to HIV is environmental in the sense that certain behaviors associated with it have tended to cluster in large urban areas. Its spread to smaller towns and rural areas has accompanied an increase in heterosexual transmission and its presence among women. Drug injection and unsafe sex are the primary modes of transmission, but in Haiti the epidemic has carried over widely into the general population. Although until now AIDS has been concentrated in cities, rural areas face increasing rates. One mechanism for transmission in rural Mexico is temporary migration to the United States. Rural people with HIV are four times more likely than their urban counterparts to have acquired the virus after traveling to the United States. Also, narcotics trafficking in remote rural areas leads to a rise in rural rates of infection. Other endemic diseases such as malaria and a chronic lack of medical services combine to produce an even more devastating profile of the epidemic. Latin American countries have faced this challenge in innovative and courageous ways. Brazil has focused on the delivery of free antiretroviral medications to all HIV/AIDS patients by establishing national laboratories and negotiating prices with pharmaceutical companies. Clean needle campaigns, condom distribution during *Carnaval,* and frank public media discussions are other features of Brazil's approach to fighting the disease.

Violence is another prominent cause of death that varies by where and how people live. Youth homicide deaths rank highest in the world for five Latin American and Caribbean nations, according to the UN Educational, Scientific, and Cultural Organization (UNESCO 2010). Brazil is at the top of this list, with an average annual rate of fifty-five violent deaths per 100,000 people between the ages of fifteen and twenty-four, followed by Colombia, the Virgin Islands, El Salvador, and Venezuela. In Brazil, firearms killed 46 out of 100,000 youth in 2003, a 400 percent increase since 1979. Of the world's top ten nations in deaths by firearms, there were nine Latin American countries (led by Venezuela and Brazil), and the United States. California gangs have appeared among El Salvador's repatriated population, contributing to that country's high rate of youth homicide. Turf wars over the drug trade in urban squatter settlements take a disproportionate share of young lives in all countries. Young people across the region, and their advocates, promote alternatives to violence through community-based projects such as the celebrated Afro-Reggae movement in Rio de Janeiro's *favelas,* and national movements that focus on the rights of working children and youth in Peru and Nicaragua.

Fertility Change

As Susan Tiano shows in Chapter 10, Latin America has experienced enormous declines in fertility in recent decades. The fertility rate is based on the average number of children a woman will bear throughout her lifetime. Fertility in Latin America fell from 6.0 to 2.5 children per woman between 1960 and 2000. Several countries are approaching replacement levels (2.0 children per woman), and Cuba is below replacement at an average of 1.5 children per woman.

A combination of factors worked together to make the fertility decline one of the most extreme examples of social change in the past two generations. These included the women's movement, reproductive technologies, urbanization, and expectations by ordinary working people for a better life. International organizations such as Zero Population Growth and Planned Parenthood have been active in Latin America, although official policy on population growth is ambiguous, in part because of the enduring influence of the Catholic Church in most countries. Despite opposition from the church, sterilization has become the most sought-after form of birth control by women, to the point where supply of this procedure runs far behind demand in many countries. Abortion, although illegal in every country except Cuba and Guyana, has played an important role in the precipitous decline in Latin American fertility rates. Current estimates by the World Health Organization indicate 3.7 million abortions are performed each year in Latin America. This represents about one abortion per three live births.

The rise of urban middle-class consumerism, promoted by the mass media, has given Latin Americans the sense that only small families are compatible with wealth. *Telenovelas* (soap operas) typically place beautiful, small, rich families at the center of their plot lines. Fewer children may earn a working family the ability to reach a more humane standard of living. However, rising standards of living put mounting pressures on resources as people come to expect private vehicles, electronic goods, better housing, and a diet high in exotic and processed foods. Most people, however, do not attain middle-class status as a result of lowering their fertility. Rather, as the lives of female breadwinners become a complex mix of part-time, short-term, and irregular employment, having fewer children has become a strategy for women who must work harder and longer to survive.

Conclusion

For Latin America as a whole, with a population approaching 600 million, there is nothing that guarantees that the recent drop in fertility will bring improvements to the environment and society. Alternatively, no one can predict with certainty that a stable population, at 700 million or 900 million, will bring calamity beyond that which many people already suffer in their everyday lives. Social and environmental problems persist due to a legacy of grossly unequal distribution of land and wealth and the unsustainable consumption and production that have become synonymous with development. As population grows, agricultural, forest, and aquatic systems struggle to keep up with demands. At the same time, demands increase with affluence, urbanization, and globalization, making sustainability a moving target. Pressures on uses of the land, air, and water are indeed at a breaking point in many cities. Assuming a commitment to sustainable practices by everyone, including the rich, the policymakers, and the poor, slower urban growth could reduce uncertainty and improve the chances for these practices to take hold.

The region's colossal size, divergent histories, and unique physical environments make generalizations dangerous. Nonetheless, given the finite nature of the earth's air, water, and land resources, Latin Americans will need to find ways to accommodate the basic needs of the poor alongside production for the affluent. Each country will devise its own solution to this conundrum, reflecting its unique history and physical endowments.

■ Bibliography

Blouet, Brian W., and Olwyn M. Blouet. *Latin America and the Caribbean: A Systematic and Regional Survey,* 4th ed. New York: Wiley, 2002.

Carruthers, David, ed. *Environmental Justice in Latin America: Problems, Promise, and Practice.* Cambridge: MIT Press, 2008.

Chase, Jacquelyn, ed. *The Spaces of Neoliberalism: Land, Place and Family in Latin America.* Bloomfield, CT: Kumarian Press, 2002.

CONAPO (Consejo Nacional de Población). "Población total de los municipios a mitad de año, 2005–2030." 2010. http://www.conapo.gob.mx.

Crosby, Alfred. *The Columbian Exchange: Biological and Cultural Consequences of 1492.* Westport: Greenwood Press, 1972.

Davis, Mike. *Planet of Slums.* London: Verso, 2007.

Denevan, William. *The Native Population of the Americas in 1492,* 2nd ed. Madison: University of Wisconsin, 1992.

Franko, Patrice. *The Puzzle of Latin American Development.* Boulder: Rowman & Littlefield, 2007.

Gilbert, Alan. *The Latin American City.* New York: Monthly Review Books, 1994.

Guzmán, José Miguel, Susheela Singh, Germán Rodríguez, and Edith A. Pantelides, eds. *The Fertility Transition in Latin America.* Oxford: Clarendon Press, 1996.

Hardoy, Jorge E., and David Satterthwaite. *Squatter Citizen.* London: Earthscan, 1995.

Hemming, John. *Red Gold: The Conquest of the Brazilian Indians, 1500–1760.* Cambridge: Harvard University Press, 1978.

Herskovits, Melville Jean, and Frances S. Herskovits. *Rebel Destiny: Among the Bush Negroes of Dutch Guiana.* New York: McGraw-Hill, 1934.

Jackiewicz, Edward L., and Fernando J. Bosco, eds. *Placing Latin America: Contemporary Themes in Human Geography.* Boulder: Rowman & Littlefield, 2008.

Joint United Nations Programme on HIV/AIDS. "UNAIDS Report on the Global AIDS Epidemic 2010." 2010. http://www.unaids.org/en.

Loker, William, ed. *Globalization and the Rural Poor in Latin America.* Boulder: Lynne Rienner, 1999.

Mann, Charles C. "1491." *Atlantic Monthly,* March 2002, pp. 41–53.

Neuwirth, Robert. *Shadow Cities: A Billion Squatters, a New Urban World.* New York: Routledge, 2006.

Oslender, Ulrich. "Violence in Development: The Logic of Forced Displacement on Colombia's Pacific Coast." *Development in Practice* 17, no. 6 (2007): 752–764.

Perlman, Janice. *The Myth of Marginality.* Berkeley: University of California Press, 1977.

Pezzoli, Keith. *Human Settlements and Planning for Ecological Sustainability: The Case of Mexico City,* Urban and Industrial Environment Series. Cambridge: MIT Press, 1998.

Place, Susan E., ed. *Tropical Rainforests: Latin American Nature and Society in Transition.* Wilmington, DE: Scholarly Resources, 2001.

Population Reference Bureau. *World Population Data Sheet.* 2010. http://www.prb.org.

Price, Richard. *Maroon Societies: Rebel Slave Communities in the Americas,* 3rd ed. Baltimore: Johns Hopkins University Press, 1996.

Roberts, J. Timmons, and Nikki Demetria Thanos. *Trouble in Paradise: Globalization and Environmental Crises in Latin America.* New York: Routledge, 2003.

Satterthwaite, David. "The Links Between Poverty and the Environment in Urban Areas of Africa, Asia, and Latin America." *Annals, American Academy of Political and Social Science* 590, no. 1 (2003): 73–92.

United Nations Educational, Scientific, and Cultural Organization (UNESCO). "Education, Youth, and Development." Document prepared for the World Youth Conference, Leon, Guanajuato, Mexico, 2010.

Zimmerer, Karl S., and Eric P. Carter. *Conservation and Sustainability in Latin America and the Caribbean: Latin America in the 21st Century,* 27th Yearbook of the Conference of Latin Americanist Geographers. Austin: University of Texas Press, 2002.

9

Patterns of "Race," Ethnicity, Class, and Nationalism

Kevin A. Yelvington

Globalization, postmodern capitalism, and neoliberal restructuring have produced evolving conceptions of personal and cultural identity accompanied by novel social and scientific discourses in twenty-first century Latin America. Consequently, ideas about "race," ethnicity, class, and nationalism have undergone transformations.

Neoliberal economic policies in the latter decades of the twentieth century were designed to promote maximum market exchanges, free trade, private property rights, and individual freedoms with the state's role minimized beyond certain key tasks. There were vast changes in state regulation, labor markets, information technology, trade patterns, and resource allocation in order to further unfetter capitalism and strengthen the positions of ruling elites (see Harvey 2007). Limited rights were granted to ethnic and multicultural groups insofar as they did not seriously threaten political and economic regimes. As a result, social movements—including culture- and ethnic-based political pressure groups, some seeking a common cause with similar groups beyond their own national borders—began to challenge the social orders of the past and have won collective ethnic rights to land, education, and jobs.

Significantly, the election of Evo Morales, the indigenous president of Bolivia, and Barack Obama, the African American president of the United States, signaled that multicultural citizenship has received unprecedented visibility. These two presidents are remarkable for their considerable personal and political achievements. However, election to their respective nation's highest political office would have been unthinkable in the past. Morales, the Aymara leader of a coca growers union, and his Movimiento a Socialismo (Movement to Socialism) Party won a majority in the country's congress in the 2005 elections. He pledged to support indigenous rights, a new constitution that would guarantee them, and drew the attention of indigenous leaders from across Latin America and beyond. This occurred after mass protests championed workers, social justice, and indigenous culture while condemning neoliberalism. The protests aimed at improving the status of indigenous peoples, who constituted 65 percent of Bolivia's population yet were socially, economically, and politically subordinated.

The significance of the election of Barack Obama in 2008 resides in the fact that Latin Americans have for more than 100 years often critically constructed their own sense of self vis-à-vis their image of the United States. Regarding "racial," ethnic, and national identities, Latin Americans have defined themselves in opposition to their image of the United States as a rigid system of ethnic order with a not very nuanced white/nonwhite dichotomy, where racism pervades many aspects of life and the defined as white majority overtly victimizes the nonwhite minority. The legacy of de jure segregation and the atrocities of black lynchings still resonate in the minds of Latin Americans. But with Obama's election, the US binary of "race" and the bitter legacies of antiblack racism, systemic discrimination and disempowerment, and educational and economic marginalization were thrown into question. If the United States could elect a "black" (not everyone in Latin America agreed that Obama was black, but at least all agreed he was not white) president, then upon what basis could Latin Americans differentiate themselves from the culture of ethnicity in the Colossus of the North?

Robert Fox. Impact Visuals

Joaquín Balaguer in 1990. The longtime president of the Dominican Republic was a protégé of the dictator Rafael Trujillo.

Jeff Belmonte/flickr.com

José Francisco Peña Gómez in 1994. The presidential candidate was branded "Haitian" by Balaguer's followers.

The identity politics associated with these contemporary trends must be understood in the context of historical relationships because the current transitions are built on already established social structures. Identity politics in Latin America often have been revealed, not to mention constituted, animated, and given form, in the context of the formal political process.

One infamous episode occurred in the 1994 presidential election in the Dominican Republic. Joaquín Balaguer—the frail, blind, partially deaf 87-year-old incumbent—branded as a "Haitian" his strongest challenger, José Francisco Peña Gómez, the former mayor of Santo Domingo. Balaguer (1906–2002), who came to power in 1960 as a puppet of the notorious dictator, Rafael Trujillo, subsequently served six terms as president. In a country where the entrenched members of the political and economic elite are of light complexion, Balaguer was considered "white." In contrast, Peña Gómez (1937–1998) once described himself as "a humble man, the color of the night." Balaguer's campaign appealed to national fears and disdain for black Haitian immigrants and culture and reflected a keen awareness that Dominicans identify with their putative Spanish origins and cultural traditions and are in denial of their African heritage.

Whereas Balaguer portrayed himself as a *patrón* (benefactor) who was above dirty politics, because he inaugurated public works projects and took personal credit for every new road and apartment building, his supporters in the right-leaning Social Christian Reform Party produced television commercials showing Peña Gómez attending a faith-healing ceremony they claimed was a Vodou ritual. As Hannah Stewart-Gambino shows in Chapter 12, Vodou is a syncretized Afro-Christian form of worship, sometimes called voodoo in English, which combines the worship of West African deities and Catholic saints. Since Haitian independence in 1804, thinly veiled racist discourse has distorted the image of Vodou abroad and slandered Haitian practitioners. In this context, the reference to Vodou was intended to contrast Euro-Dominican with Afro-Haitian culture.

Balaguer's supporters also left anonymous leaflets and sent fax messages that warned of Peña Gómez's supposed sinister intentions for the future of the country's cultural and political sovereignty. They claimed he would give the country away to neighboring Haiti if elected. A pamphlet was published in the campaign's final weeks that characterized Peña Gómez's candidacy as the fulfillment of a centuries-old Haitian plot to reconquer the Dominican Republic.

Forced to confront these charges, Peña Gómez and his left-of-center Dominican Revolutionary Party countered by charging the Balaguer regime with corruption, political repression, cronyism, and incompetence. Throughout the campaign, Peña Gómez consistently led in public opinion polls. Many Dominicans were apparently rejecting Balaguer's racist appeals. Nevertheless, after three months of deliberation and amidst charges of fraud, the Central Elections Board (three of whose five members were appointed by Balaguer) finally announced that Balaguer had won by a slim margin of 22,181 votes.[1]

It is revealing to study the historical context within which labeling someone as "Haitian" is viewed as socially and politically damaging. With a few exceptions in Latin America, what is taken as European culture has been valued over indigenous or African culture, and a group's phenotypical features have often been conflated with "culture," understood not only as a way of life but also as a set of significant accomplishments. This value structure has been reflected in Haitian-Dominican relations. As René de la Pedraja explains in Chapter 3, the French sugar-producing colony of Saint-Domingue became the independent country of Haiti in 1804, after a massive and heroic slave revolt killed or forced into exile white slaveholders and colonial officials. Haiti became the first black republic and only the second independent country in the hemisphere (after the United States). At a time when African slavery was prevalent throughout the Americas, the Haitian Revolution caused slave owners elsewhere to fear similar insurrections. Moreover, Haiti invaded and occupied the Dominican Republic from 1822 to 1844. Although it took place more than a century and a half ago, this occupation still burns in the Dominican national consciousness.

Haiti's subsequent isolation and impoverishment caused many Haitians to migrate in search of menial jobs. They found brutal work in the sugarcane fields of the Dominican Republic, where they received low pay and suffered under poor working conditions. When he came to power in 1930, Trujillo began an anti-Haitian campaign that preoccupied him until his assassination in 1961.

Although considered a *mulato* (a mixture of African and European ancestry), Trujillo sought to emphasize "white" culture. He instituted a policy of *hispanidad* (Spanishness), by which Dominican identity and society were depicted as rooted in a glorious European past. Roman Catholicism, Spanish literature, the *conquistadores,* and even the bullfight were upheld as the true legacy of the country.

Trujillo's machinations were more than rhetorical. In the depths of the Great Depression between October 2 and 4, 1937, he ordered the massacre of an estimated 20,000 to 30,000 Haitians. Although nothing like this atrocity has occurred since, anti-Haitian discrimination has remained prevalent in the Dominican Republic and Haitian workers have often been intimidated and forcibly deported during periods of economic decline.

Today, Haitian sugarcane workers in the Dominican Republic are still subjected to squalid living and working conditions. Over 80 percent of the workers in the Dominican sugar fields are Haitian and of the country's 8.7 million people, more than 1 million are of Haitian descent. A 1983 International Labor Office report outlined labor practices on the plantations that were tantamount to slavery: the workers were cheated out of their meager wages, forced to work twelve-hour days with no lunch break, confined to their camps by armed guards and the military, and lived in sparse, overcrowded compounds with virtually no running water or electricity (Latortue 1985). Amnesty International and other human rights organizations continue to document that these conditions still persist. But Haitians are compelled to continue their migration because of poor economic and political conditions in their own country and the demand for their labor in jobs Dominicans regard as beneath them.

In his book, *La isla al revés: Haití y el destino dominicano* (The Island Turned on Its Head: Haiti and Dominican Destiny, 1990), Balaguer proves that he was at least Trujillo's equal as a racist ideologist. Given Balaguer's dominance over Dominican political and public life for such a long period, his thoughts in this book are revealing of a widespread political and class ideology. The Dominican Republic, he claimed, has always been a "white and Christian" country that is witnessing "progressive ethnic decadence" that threatens the country's "Spanish physiognomy." Except for a "minuscule" and unrepresentative number, any "black" presence in the Dominican Republic, he argued, is an alien "Haitian" incursion. "Haitian imperialism is now an even greater threat to our country than before [when it was military] for biological reasons."

Balaguer (1990) warned that the evil consequences of miscegenation are racial and cultural decay concomitant with the subsequent "vegetative increase of the African race." He feared that "the white race will eventually be absorbed by the African." Haitian culture is described in the book as "instinct-governed, vegetally fertile heathen." Haitians are "generators of indolence" and "of primitive mentality." As a remedy, Balaguer proposed tightening the national borders, increasing Catholic instruction, and promoting the immigration of white capitalists—a plan to be directed by the *raza selecta* (select race). Despite opposition, these ideas continue to have popular currency, as well as elite justification, in the Dominican Republic. Ironically, at the end of his book, Balaguer—not Peña Gómez—proposed a confederation of the Dominican and Haitian states that would guarantee the independence of each and would improve relations after 150 years of conflict.

The consequences of *hispanidad,* repression, and apologist attempts at scientific justification demonstrate the convoluted interrelationship of "race," ethnicity, class, and nationalism. In the Dominican Republic, if one is considered black, one is a Haitian; if one is Dominican, one is not considered black. "Dominican" and "black" are mutually exclusive categories; therefore, it is impossible for one to be both. Haitians are those black people who come to the country to work in poorly paid, low-status jobs. They have few or no political or economic rights. While in recent years dissenting voices have developed, and a Dominican movement that embraces positive images of blackness can be identified (Simmons 2009), these voices continue to be drowned out by the dominant ideological representations.

▩ The Intersections of "Race," Ethnicity, Class, and Nationalism

Although some aspects of the Dominican case are clearly country specific, others illustrate the historical patterns of "race," ethnicity, class, and nationalism in Latin America. The complexity and diversity of these patterns prohibit an exhaustive study in one chapter. Similarly complex are the relative class positions of *jíbaros, guajiros,* and *campesinos* (as peasants and rural workers are called in Puerto Rico, Cuba, and South America, respectively) and their relation to *hacendados* (owners of large rural estates), as well as the economic conditions of urban *trabajadores* (workers), their *sindicatos* (trade unions), the *jefes* (bosses), and *dueños* (business owners). In reality, the social relations of "race," class, ethnicity, and nationalism are intertwined, deriving from the results of the structured activities of humans living under historical constraints.

▩ Defining Key Terms

Ethnic identities in Latin America, as elsewhere, are cultural constructs, that is, definitions and meanings that are enforced and enacted and become taken for granted and assented to, for the most part. Popular notions of "race" and ethnicity, by their very nature, however, are reified—spuriously considered biological absolutes. Such stereotyping is derived from a distinctly European perspective that sought to impose order on a world expanding through the conquest and colonial domination of people held to be fundamentally different and inferior.

In this chapter, "race" appears in quotation marks to denote that it is a concept used in everyday life by Latin Americans to indicate an assessment of the inherited and inheritable biological and genealogical constitution of named groups of living organisms (in this case, human beings) as supposedly revealed in their physical phenotype, habitual behaviors, and intellectual capacities but which has no analytical or scientific value as so used. Similarly, ethnic terms such as white, black, native person, and *mulato* should be understood as referring not to some independent reality, but should be seen as terms that are employed and have conventional meanings. Ethnicity is a flexible umbrella term, subsuming but not assuming "race," that facilitates cross-cultural comparison (Yelvington 1999). It may be defined as an ideology, a definition of "peoplehood" that entails a theory of origin. Sometimes these links are constructed by the people in question as "racial," sometimes they are reckoned as "cultural," and sometimes they are deemed to be otherworldly, sacred, or spiritual in origins. At the same time, ethnicity is characterized by a theory of cause-effect relationships among these phenomena. Their specific combination varies from case to case. This is an empirical historical and cultural question rather than some either-or universal a priori proposition.

"Racial" differentiation in terms of traits that became "racialized" (observable phenotypical features such as skin color, shape of the nose, and type of hair come to be understood as indicative of "race" as something inherited and inheritable) was linked with assumptions regarding mental and behavioral capacities and characteristics. Even on its own terms, however, this view does not stand up to close scrutiny. The world's population displays a panorama of genetic traits that belie popular stereotypes and the traditional, supposedly scientific view of "the three races" (or five in some formulations). Infinite genetic combinations have rendered impossible neat classification of specific traits pertaining exclusively to Caucasoid, Negroid, or Mongoloid categories. No absolute divisions exist in reality.

A cross-cultural perspective reveals other ways of thinking about "race" and ethnicity. For example, many North Americans are incredulous when very dark-skinned Latin Americans distinguish themselves from African Americans. In North America, traditionally at least, "racial accounting" through the lens of the concept of hypodescent regards the offspring of a black and a white as black. Throughout Latin America, in contrast, a number of "racial terms" are deduced from an individual's color, ideas about ancestry, and social status in a system typified by ambiguity and negotiation in assigning individuals to "racial" categories, but where nevertheless higher status is accorded to those who approach the European ideal.[2]

"Racial" terms found in the Dominican Republic have parallels elsewhere. The term *indio* (native person), with various modifiers, appears on official forms that ask for "race." An *indio* may be a black person with wavy, rather than kinky, hair. *Indio claro* (light-colored native person) may refer to light-skinned *mulatos,* whereas the term *indio oscuro* (dark native person) refers to very dark-skinned people. Some people find themselves described as *de color medio* (of medium color), a distinction that refers to someone who is neither white nor black. Conversely, *bajo de color* (low in color) refers to skin color, but also to the low social status of blacks. Often, physical features like an individual's hair are pointed out and used to make value judgments. *Pelo bueno* (good hair) refers to straight or wavy hair, for example, whereas *pasa* (raisin) refers to people with kinky hair in a deprecatory way.

Similarly, in the Anglo-Caribbean, distinctions made among those considered white, "colored," and black are only partially derived from an interpretation of what are taken to be markers of ancestry. This contrast in "racial" reckoning is apparent when individuals with these identities migrate to North America. In their Anglo-Caribbean societies, people who are categorized as *mulatos* and "colored" are thought of, and think of themselves, as "racially" distinct from both whites and blacks. When they migrate to the United States, however, they are categorized as black—much to their dismay in many instances. This phenomenon does not indicate that the people so described are "really" black and through a combination of social position and psychological denial they are unable to shrug off an identity that is so liability ridden in the United States. It does indicate, however, that "race" is a culturally constructed entity rather than something rooted in biological facts.

Latin American and Caribbean peoples possess a highly developed system of "racial" accounting, a system of ideas that is properly understood under the rubric of ethnicity. Ethnicity is a particular social and cultural identity typified by a reference to ancestors who are minimally presumed to have had a shared culture.[3] Thus, "race" is a kind of ethnicity. Central to the concept of ethnicity is culture—the learned, patterned behaviors and systems of meanings of a given human group.[4] Here, a key concept is that of "ethnogenesis," the process of the creation and transformation of an ethnic group, including their "ethnonyms," the name(s) of the group. This concept even holds out the possibility of the eventual dissolution of that group and its absorption into another group. From this perspective, ethnic identity and ethnic groups do not simply exist in nature, nor do they preexist sociohistorical processes. The paradox is that in the discourse of "racial" and ethnic identity, the origins of the group are said to be outside history and to reside in nature.

There are two terms that are ostensibly about economic class and social status but, at the same time, allude to a person's color. *Gente de primera* (first-class people) implies whiteness whereas *gente de segunda* (second-class people) refers to people of lower status social or ethnic groups. Although the boundaries between identities are in some ways permeable, those who are seen attempting to transcend those boundaries overtly are derided as *blanco de la barranca* (white from the gutter) and *blanquito* (little white person), referring to nonwhite people who pretend to be white. The worst epithets, however, are reserved for those seen to be manifestly of African heritage. *Negro como una paila* (black as a frying pan) refers to a person with very dark skin, and *morejón* is a derogatory word for a black person considered ordinary or ugly.

Every country in Latin America is divided into elites and masses. The relative distribution of these basic classes varies in different countries. The concept of class is based in economic relations, the relation to the means of production as either an owner of those means or as one who is forced to sell their labor. But it is also cultural in the sense that, in practice, it is based not only on an individual's position in the production process but also on various criteria such as ethnicity, gender, credentials, education, language, membership in certain families, wealth, and status. Certain cultural aspects of class (e.g., a particular way of speaking or an accent) are more highly regarded than others. Highly valued cultural aspects of class tend to coincide with and facilitate higher positions in the economic class structure. However, these two aspects of class do not completely correspond. This allows us to conceive of a society's class structure as having not only cultural differences within classes, but also cross-class alliances based on a number of different criteria. These can and often do include issues of "culture"—the possession of certain linguistic styles and accents, family ties, education, senses of aesthetics, and, of course, "race" and ethnicity.

Nationalism is an ideology in which the ethnicity and culture within a geographically defined territory is viewed as congruent with its political boundaries. Latin American and Caribbean nationalism draws on the European nationalism that began to take its present form at the end of the eighteenth century. Nationalism of this kind involves a process that has often identified a homogeneous national type, sometimes referred to locally as a "race." In colonial Latin America, the process of homogenization occurred in a context in which ethnic differences were constructed and cultivated to divide and rule. As I show in this chapter, in the postcolonial era, local elites ingeniously crafted discourses of national identity that, while departing somewhat from the colonial discourses they replaced, nevertheless guaranteed the ascendancy of Western and European ethnic identity and cultural forms, which are seen to be embodied in the elite. There is even some doubt as to whether the past was colonial per se or whether the present can be seen as postcolonial, especially for native communities and identities (Klor de Alva 1992). But while patterns of nationalism remained relatively constant for a number of years, the situation in twenty-first-century Latin America is rapidly changing.

Therefore, ethnicity, class, and nationalism are interrelated in a number of ways. Determining who one is and where one fits in Latin American or Caribbean society depends on a number of factors. Physical appearance counts, but it can be overridden in some instances. Perhaps more profoundly, one's class position and status in society are determining factors. The reverse is also true; one's class and status are determined, at least in part, by one's "race" and ethnicity. Furthermore, conceptions of nationalism and the destiny of the nation are infused with notions of whose culture and whose "racial" and ethnic identity are most representative of the nation and, in turn, those to whom the nation really belongs. Obviously, the most powerful groups have strongly influenced the creation and enforcement of these cultural determinations. They purport to define and proclaim who is "authentically" Venezuelan, Dominican, Argentine, Guatemalan, Mexican, and so on, and who is deemed unworthy.

▓ Foundations of Ethnicity, Class, and Nationalism

In the history of ideas pertaining to ethnicity in Latin America, "races" were presumed to be pure until after the arrival of the *conquistadores* in the New World. European interaction with the indigenous peoples, and later with Africans began a process called *mestizaje* (miscegenation), supposed "racial" mixing. Despite the crown's attempts at legal separation, biological and cultural mixing was a concomitant of the conquest. Sexual relations of dominance between Spanish men and native women—given the prerogatives of conquest and the male-female imbalance of early colonization—resulted in unions that were characterized by rape, concubinage, and occasionally marriage. Mestizo progeny of whites and native peoples were often defined as "half-breeds." In Brazil, such mixtures were called *mamelucos* as well as *mestiços. Mestizos* would have been less conspicuous if the native peoples had not died in huge numbers as a result of contact with European diseases and poor treatment.

Mestizaje continued with the arrival of African slaves from the early 1500s to the mid-1800s. It is estimated that more than 10 million Africans reached the New World, and another 10 million died en route. Brazil received the largest portion, about 40 percent, and now has the largest African-descended population outside of Africa. The Caribbean as a whole received about 40 percent, Spanish Latin America received about 16 percent, and British North America—including what is now the United States—received about 4 percent of the enslaved Africans.

"Racial" Categories and Social Standing
All "race mixtures" were not deemed to be of the same type. On the contrary, the Spanish concern with *limpieza de sangre* (purity of blood) was transferred to the New World. *Limpieza de sangre,* which had diverse meanings in Spain, was the principle used in consolidating the *reconquista* (the reconquering of Spain from the Moors) and in the expulsion of Spain's Jews in 1492. In the

Americas, this principle was used to determine not only racial origins, but also social and legal status.

Elaborate systems and nomenclatures emphasizing supposed degrees away from whiteness were established by Spaniards and *criollos* (Europeans born in Latin America). Blacks, Indians, *mestizos, mulatos,* and *pardos* were the commonly used terms for nonwhites. Magnus Mörner (1967:58) provided an example from eighteenth-century New Spain (Mexico):

1. Spaniard and Indian beget *mestizo.*
2. *Mestizo* and Spanish woman beget *castizo.*
3. *Castizo* woman and Spaniard beget Spaniard.
4. Spanish woman and black man beget *mulato.*
5. Spaniard and *mulato* woman beget *morisco.*
6. *Morisco* woman and Spaniard beget *albino.*
7. Spaniard and *albino* woman beget *torna atrás* ("turn away," as in "from white").
8. Indian man and *torna atrás* woman beget *lobo.*
9. *Lobo* and Indian woman beget *zambaigo.*
10. *Zambaigo* and Indian woman beget *cambujo.*
11. *Cambujo* and *mulato* woman beget *albarazado.*
12. *Albarazado* and *mulato* woman beget *barcino.*
13. *Barcino* and *mulato* woman beget *coyote.*
14. *Coyote* woman and Indian man beget *chamiso.*
15. *Chamiso* woman and *mestizo* beget *coyote mestizo.*
16. *Coyote mestizo* and *mulato* woman beget *ahí te estás* ("there you are").

This is but one example of the attempt to assign certain parts of a person's "racial" genealogy. For example, an *albarazado* was deemed to be 30.86 percent white, 43.75 percent native, and 25.39 percent black (Stephens 1989:18). A *barcino* was 40.43 percent white, 21.87 percent native, and 37.7 percent black (Stephens 1989:30). *Ad infinitum absurdum.*

Almost every territory in Spanish America had its own system, and only some of the terms overlapped. This kind of descent and "racial" reckoning also had counterparts in non–Spanish-speaking areas. The terminology in Brazil seems to have been more vague whereas, in French colonial possessions, nonwhites were calibrated even more minutely than occurred in Spanish-speaking territories. This system was part of a rigidly stratified *sociedad de castas* (society of castes). Caste came from the term the Portuguese applied to the complex social structure they encountered in India. *Casta* came to refer to all nonwhites. The *sociedad de castas* was characterized by social and legal discrimination based on ethnicity that was blatant and direct, as well as condescending and patronizing, on the part of the white elites.

"Racial" Discrimination

Legal and social discrimination largely coincided. Whites were at the top of the legal order, but Spaniards enjoyed more social status than local whites. Native peoples received special legal protection as the Spanish crown attempted to separate them from the rest of colonial society in autonomous communities. In practice, native peoples were relegated to the bottom of the social structure. The rest of the society was legally and socially accorded rights and prestige basically with respect to conformity to whiteness: *mestizos, mulatos,* and black slaves in that order.

Even nonslaves among the *castas* were severely limited in almost every aspect of civil life, from prohibitions on holding municipal positions to bans on entering universities to being prevented from marrying whites. Sexual relations became contested terrain, as white men fanatically tried to prevent white women from marrying or having sexual relationships with *castas.* As Susan Tiano explains in Chapter 10, women were made to serve as the boundaries of the group, and ideas about women's sexual "purity" were tied to "racial purity." A sexual double standard generally existed, however. White men from all social strata had liaisons with *casta* women of lesser status. The men rarely recognized officially any offspring from these unions. Some of these men did informally assist their progeny who, also in some contexts, received the benefits accruing to what was seen as an approximation of whiteness.

The advent of independence movements in continental Latin America in the late eighteenth century featured the incipient nationalism of the local-born white *criollos* in their increasing conflicts with the *peninsulares,* which those born in the Iberian Peninsula were called. Whereas both groups—despite their growing differences—formed the upper stratum of their respective societies, by this time some mobility was experienced by a small but growing number of *mestizos* and *pardos,* although these latter individuals still encountered the obstacles of social and legal racism. Through the *cédula de gracias al sacar,* a decree of "thank you for the exception," though, high-status and wealthy nonwhites were able to buy a dispensation that made them legally white. With these royal *cédulas,* Spain bypassed local estimations of racial worth and gained allies to counterbalance the power and prestige of the *criollo* elite. This elite, which just a few years later would proclaim the Rights of Man and the French revolutionary motto of "*liberté, egalité, fraternité,*" protested the *cédulas* that allowed such personal mobility. Relatively few, however, were able to "advance" in this way. Even if nonwhites had the means, many were denied the opportunity by whites to buy into the privileges that the whites were trying so desperately to hold onto themselves.

The rigidity of the *sociedad de castas* came to be undermined by the recognition that precise designations were increasingly meaningless, as *mestizaje,* with its phenotypical and cultural consequences, was seen to proceed from generation to generation, and the phenomenon of passing from one category to another became common.[5] As the definitional lines blurred, ethnic designations generally became more vague. Differences between *mestizos* and indigenous peoples were seen by contemporary observers to be based increasingly on social and cultural attributes, such as dress, manners, and language, rather than on ascribed racial ones. When the largely *criollo,* elite-led independence movements began in earnest, *pardo* and *mestizo* frustrations with the arrangements and limitations of the *sociedad de castas* led a great many motivated leaders to shift their allegiance to the *criollo* elites—when it suited them and their causes.

For example, in Venezuela's wars for independence in the early 1800s, *pardos,* long frustrated by the white elite's attempts to gain legal and social parity, fought with the royalists against Simón Bolívar's *criollo*-led forces in 1813—only to join with "the Liberator" in 1816, after he appealed to *llaneros* (rural *mestizos* who lived on the plains), *pardos,* blacks, and *zambos* (the offspring of blacks and indigenous peoples) and promised to end African slavery if he and his troops were successful. Ethnic tensions permeated the armies fighting for independence. And despite Bolívar's ostensible aims to create a society free of prejudice and class distinctions, he was equivocal on the issue of ethnicity after independence, expressing the *criollo* elite's fear and suspicion of nonwhites. Those deemed black were especially the objects of persecution. Despite Bolívar's promises, slavery lingered on in Venezuela, ending only in 1854.

Ethnicity, Class, and Nationalism After Independence

The wars for independence in Latin America ended the legal discrimination of the *sociedad de castas,* but its practices and the ideas surrounding it reflected, even if more loosely, the state of the social structure after independence. Systems of social stratification, based on ethnicity and class, in which skin becomes lighter in color as one goes up the class ladder, were further reinforced despite individual exceptions. The elite culturally absorbed nonwhites who climbed into the upper stratum.

By about the 1870s, a common thread was running through the discourse of nationalism in several continental Latin American countries. Elites imagined themselves as part of a European legacy of "civilization." They were influenced by the political, cultural, philosophical, and scientific strains of positivism—a belief in science and progress. Social Darwinism explained the relative economic and political development of countries through deterministic racial theories ("scientific" racism). According to this theory, the northern European countries and the United States were relatively prosperous because of the inherent physical and mental superiority of the Anglo-Saxon and Teutonic "races."

Latin American elites selected parts of these intellectual movements and applied them to what they saw as the reality of their societies.[6] Brazilian elites, for example—most of whom were white—reflected on their "racial" topography: the 1872 census listed only 38 percent as white, 20 percent as black, and the rest as *pardo*.

African slavery ended only in 1888 in Brazil, the last holdout in the Americas—even later than Cuba (1886) and the United States (1865). In Brazil, free *pardos* had been a large and powerful group during slavery and had struck a strategic alliance with whites versus blacks and slaves. As slavery ended, Brazilian elites worried publicly about the "racial" makeup of the country and, thus, about the country's fate. They accepted ideas of white superiority but, contradictorily, denied the immutability and absoluteness of "race." They believed the solution to the country's problems lay in the whitening of the population, "racially" and culturally.

These elites pointed to the supposed low fertility among *pardos* and blacks. They believed miscegenation would gradually whiten and consequently improve the population, ignoring contemporary mainstream "racial" theory, which held that hybrids were degenerate. Toward this end, European immigration was officially encouraged, and immigration laws—although not publicly acknowledged—were structured so that blacks, Jews, and others were barred from settling in Brazil. Some of these laws, codified from the 1890s until the 1940s, have never been changed. By the 1920s, racist thinkers in Brazil and the rest of Latin America even became involved in a "science of racial improvement" called eugenics. As Nancy Leys Stepan (1991) has shown, eugenics provided a supposed scientific defense of whitening.

Brazilian elites were further consoled by nationalist myths generated by an emerging social science and a regional intellectualist tradition. In the 1930s, cultural nationalist Gilberto Freyre gained prominence for his historical studies of the plantation society in Brazil (1986a, 1986b). Although Freyre attacked scientific racism, he celebrated miscegenation and cultural diversity. He proclaimed the creation of a new "luso-tropical" civilization, characterized by a *democracia racial* (racial democracy) in which "the races" intermingled freely. This discourse—and the political dispensation it was part of—had the intention and effect of precluding mobilization of disempowered groups based on ethnic identity (and labeled them racist if they did so), allowing the white elite to avoid addressing claims of ethnic discrimination. *Democracia racial* was particularly effective for the elite when combined with *mestizaje,* a discourse of mixing and, therefore, dilution of racial and cultural "purity." Logically, the disempowered did have space to appeal to the elite to live up to their own democratic proclamations, but this was severely circumscribed.

In these conflicting ideological positions, Brazil had counterparts in the rest of Latin America. In Venezuela, for example, throughout history blacks and *pardos* had played a more important role in social and political institutions than they had in any other Latin American country and had gained access to political power at the regional and national levels. As Winthrop R. Wright

(1990) has shown, however, Venezuelan elites simultaneously argued that theirs was a "racially" mixed country, where 70 percent of the population were *pardos*, and that racism had been eliminated. They described themselves as a *café con leche* (coffee with milk) people while promoting a *blanqueamiento* (whitening) process by encouraging European migration, prohibiting blacks from entering the country, and calling for cultural and "racial" miscegenation to reduce the "pure" black minority. Despite their other nefarious functions, *democracia racial* and *café con leche* can be seen as a kind of moral resistance against the more technologically advanced and wealthy United States and Europe by claiming that Brazil and Venezuela were actually more advanced than their more powerful counterparts because they had already solved the "race" problem.

Immigration and Indigenous Identities

Immigration laws have been used throughout the Americas—including by the United States—to sort out the "desirable" and "undesirable" groups that will make up the nation. In Argentina, a country that set up an immigration program and received more than 3 million immigrants from Europe between 1880 and 1930, racist intellectuals viewed the massive immigration of Europeans as further whitening the population (Latin America as a whole received about 12 million European immigrants between 1850 and 1930). At the end of the nineteenth century, Argentine elites could claim an already white nation with strong European roots and, thus, look down on their Brazilian neighbors.

Argentine racist thinkers—foremost among them José Ingenieros—were convinced of the merits of natural selection, claiming "the white race" would win out in an evolutionary struggle with "colored races," which were incompatible with "superior" white civilization. Argentine elites imagined theirs as a white country, and they pointed to the inevitable disappearance of indigenous peoples and blacks. With the influx of European immigrants, the indigenous proportion of the population declined from 5.0 percent in 1869 to 0.7 percent of a total of nearly 4 million inhabitants in 1895 (Helg 1990:43). Blacks, who in the first third of the nineteenth century had made up 25 percent of the population of Buenos Aires, dropped to 2 percent by 1887.

What was not acknowledged were the terror and discrimination behind this supposedly natural process. Native peoples were the victims of continual military campaigns throughout the 1880s: they were killed, forcibly incorporated into the army, or forced to labor in agriculture or domestic service. Sporadic campaigns against them continued until the 1930s. Blacks were confined to a limited number of occupations and to poor living conditions.

The immigration wave of the period 1880–1930 was 43 percent Italian and 34 percent Spanish. Again, in breaking with mainstream racist thinking, Argentine elites chose not to make a distinction among those they considered white, believing the differences between Aryans and Latins were social and historical rather than biological.

Once the country was white, though, the elites' next task was to make it Argentinean. Many immigrants formed their own communities with separate institutions. Italians, Germans, Russian Jews, and others brought with them ideas of trade unionism, anarchism, and socialism that challenged the entrenched social order, and prosperous immigrants were excluded from the elites' inner circles. At the turn of the twentieth century, a revitalization of nationalism entailed glorification of the native Argentine (the *criollo*) and the definition of Argentine culture as characterized by the Spanish language and Hispanic culture, Catholicism, the family, paternalism, and order. This new nationalism had an anti-immigrant component. During the peak immigration years of the early 1900s, Jews represented between 2 percent and 6 percent of total immigration. In the context of anti-immigrant nationalism, they became visible and vulnerable targets as anti-immigrant discourse and activity reached its depths with Catholic Church–inspired anti-Semitism and physical attacks on Jews.

Revolutionary Mexico provides an interesting contrast. In seeking to break with the widespread racist ideas and practices of the long dictatorship of Porfirio Díaz (1876–1911), the emergent thinkers, who gained prominence with the armed revolution beginning in 1910, constructed what became the official ideology of *indigenismo*. *Indigenismo* (indigenism) as a doctrine had several components and relied on a number of cultural assumptions about "race." Fairly high consensus held that most Mexicans were *mestizos*. Such attributes as language, religion, dress, family form, and consciousness determined whether one was native or *mestizo*. And because these attributes were social in origin, they were subject to change.

Indigenismo was not a movement initiated by the indigenous peoples; it was an elite ideology that advocated the gradual, nonviolent integration of them into Mexican society, especially through education. It venerated Mexico's pre-Hispanic past and attempted to rescue the surviving indigenous culture from oblivion. The *mestizo,* as the synthesis of the indigenous person and the European, was exalted as the true Mexican. Breaking with the scientific racism of the time, philosopher and politician José Vasconcelos referred to *mestizos* as the *raza cósmica* (cosmic race), "racial" hybrids who were to characterize Mexico and, eventually, the world at large. Those indigenous peoples who remained were to be absorbed into this "race."

As an explicitly antiracist ideology that reached its apogee in the 1930s and has essentially remained dominant since then, *indigenismo* represented a distinct departure from Westernism. Although disputing claims of native and *mestizo* inferiority, however, this perspective emphasized innate differences among the white, *mestizo,* and native "races." *Indigenismo* even led some to conclude that *mestizos* and Amerindians were actually "racially" and culturally superior to whites.

Given all its contradictions, then, official *indigenismo* meant indigenous peoples as such were marginalized because they were seen to be in the process of becoming what they needed to become to participate in national political life. Images of noble pre-Hispanic native culture with a glorious past were a cornerstone of *indigenismo*. But because it relied on notions of "race," it left the door open for contemporary indigenous peoples to receive separate and unequal treatment. *Indigenismo* could not legislate social change that would be accompanied by significant socioeconomic transformations. Notions that cultural and biological miscegenation could produce a new kind of human being are common in many Latin American countries, not only Brazil, Venezuela, and Mexico but also countries such as Ecuador, Colombia, and Peru. *Mestizaje* in its explicitly nationalist mode subordinates claims of ethnic distinctiveness to the ends of the nation. Therefore, those considering themselves indigenous have rejected at times the ideology of *mestizaje,* which has also been rejected by some Afro-Latins as they look to associate with international signs of blackness.

Contemporary Patterns

The culture of ethnicity in Latin America and the Caribbean, however, has undergone significant modifications since colonial times. Changes in language are principal indicators to the extent that the *sociedad de castas* has been transformed and, at the same time, the changes also demonstrate that some of the colonial concepts have been reproduced. The language of "race" hides the arbitrary nature of terms believed to describe unchanging reality. Yet studies of "racial" attitudes in Latin America reveal inconsistent attributions of "racial" terms.

For example, in studies by anthropologists Marvin Harris (1964b) and Marvin Harris and Conrad Kottak (1963), 100 Brazilians in a Bahian fishing village were asked to identify the "race" of three full sisters depicted in photographs. Only six responses identified the three by the same "racial" terms. In fourteen responses, a separate term was used for each of the three sisters, most frequently *blanca* (white) for one and *mulata* or *morena* (brown) for one or both of the others. A particular Brazilian could be described by as many as thirteen terms by other members of the community. Another 100 people were shown nine portrait drawings meant to depict nine different "racial" types. Around forty "racial" terms were discovered. The highest percentage that agreed on the "race" in any drawing was 70 percent; the lowest was 18 percent.

Mauricio Solaún, Eduardo Vélez, and Cynthia Smith (1987) conducted a study in the Caribbean port city of Cartagena, Colombia, that involved interviewing a sample of 120 adults from four social classes: upper, middle, working, and lower. These respondents were shown twenty-two photographs of individuals with varying ethnic identities and styles of dress and were asked to identify the "race" of each. For the twenty-two photographs, there were 128 different designations—an average of seventeen per photo. The authors show how much of the "racial" nomenclature of the *sociedad de castas* has remained, albeit with significant modification: The tendency now is to use descriptive terms. Individuals were perceived, for example, as *blanco aindiado* (white with native features) or *negro fileno* (black with a straight nose). They were also *claro* (light), *trigueño* (wheat-colored), or *trigueño claro* or *blanco claro*. Many responses, then, included physical characteristics as well as "racial" ones; for example, *rubio* (blond), *acanelado* (cinnamon-colored), *cobrizo* (copper-colored), *blanco no del todo* (white, but not completely so), or *blanco quemado* (burned white).

Although the nomenclature in Cartagena includes terms and concepts that imply "racial" history, for example, *mulato;* "racially" neutral terms, for example, *claro;* and terms of physical description, for example, *negro por el pelo* (black because of hair texture), there is—as in the Brazilian studies—evidence that a wide variety of criteria are used to classify individuals. In the Cartagena study, the most frequent use of a term per photograph ranged from 24 percent to 71 percent, with no photo receiving more than 50 percent "racial" (as opposed to color or physically descriptive) terms; 60 percent of the responses were given only twice at the most (Solaún, Vélez, and Smith 1987).

In the Colombian study, when respondents were asked to describe themselves, only the upper class contained a majority of self-reported *blancos* whereas no *blancos* were found in the lower class. Concomitantly, no *negros* were found in the upper class, where darker individuals referred to themselves as *moreno*. Virtually no respondents positively identified with blackness. Only a few called themselves *negro,* and terms denoting African ancestry were rarely used. Only twelve respondents called themselves *mulato.* Collectively, these terms exhibit the effects of *blanqueamiento* and demonstrate the correlation between ethnicity and class, which, in turn, facilitates or impedes class mobility (Solaún, Vélez, and Smith 1987).

Solaún, Vélez, and Smith's research (1987) also showed the extent to which the stain of slavery still exists in Latin America. In many countries in the region, with the exception of some in the non-Hispanic Caribbean, the use of the word *negro* is generally not polite or politically acceptable as can be seen by the number of mostly pejorative modifiers that accompany its designation. Thomas M. Stephens (1989) listed fifty-nine separate entries of terms that entail *negro* and a modifier. *Negro humo* (smoke black) is a Colombian term that refers to physical description whereas *negro catedrático* (a black "chaired professor") is a Cuban term used to refer to blacks thought to be feigning education and refinement by misappropriating "white" patterns of speech and upper-class modes of dress. Thus, use of this term is thought to be a way of keeping blacks "in their place."

Racial Democracy in the Caribbean: Cuba and Puerto Rico

The discourses of ethnicity and nationalism that crystallized in twentieth-century Cuba and Puerto Rico resembled those in Brazil. Local ethnic relations were compared favorably with those in the United States, promoting images of the nation in terms of "race" mixture. White ideologues in politics, literature, and the social sciences expounded on the racial democracy theme. In the case of Cuba, black movements were repressed and an immigration policy designed to whiten the population was promoted.

Ethnic relations in present-day Cuba demonstrate that political and economic revolution does not necessarily entail fundamental social change. "Race" was a taboo subject in early revolutionary Cuba as Fidel Castro tried to instill an official non-"racial" consciousness. The out-migration of an almost all-white Cuban oligarchy should have meant gains for blacks, even if by default. Indeed, evidence provided by Alejandro de la Fuente (1995, 2001) suggests that the revolution was successful in equalizing the educational and health status of whites, blacks, and *mulatos,* and there has been black and *mulato* mobility. But contradictions exist. Most of Cuba's top occupations and government positions are still in the hands of whites. Whites are even favored for service sector jobs in the tourism industry, allowing for their access to foreign exchange and other perks. One still sees almost all menial occupations performed by blacks. And at the highest level, at times, a non-"racial" stance has even given way to official acknowledgments of blackness within Cuban culture and even, as in a historic address to the Communist Party Congress in 1986, recognition of racism in the party hierarchy by Castro himself.

In 1975, Castro declared Cuba a "Latin-African country." But many observers argue that rather than indicating a true show of solidarity with the African continent and culture, this declaration was for the consumption of the Cuban blacks who were called on to fight in Cuba's military ventures in Africa. In 1983, for the first time in revolutionary Cuba, census statistics regarding "race" were published. These showed blacks representing 12 percent of the population, *mulatos* 21.9 percent, whites 66 percent, and Asians 0.1 percent (de la Fuente 1995:table 1, 135). This seemed to many a vast overcounting of whites and, thus, an undercounting of blacks. As in other Latin American and Caribbean countries, blackness was being officially denied at the same time that the nation was depicted as ethnically diverse. And as elsewhere, this was accomplished through the official promotion of culture, such as the Ballet Folklórico, which performs Afro-Cuban dances—some with religious significance.

As Hannah Stewart-Gambino shows in Chapter 12, many Cubans maintain a religious commitment to Santería, or Lukumí, as it is sometimes called. Similar in many ways to Vodou in Haiti, this religion involves the blending of religious traditions, in which Catholic saints are matched with Yoruba deities known as *orishas.* Santería worshippers are drawn from both the black and white populations. Even among Cubans who are not active worshippers, many believe in the efficacy of religious and spiritual forces and in the religion's spiritual leaders and practitioners.

In Puerto Rico, the discourse is one of the three *raíces* (roots) of Puerto Ricanness: Spanish, African, and Amerindian (*Taínos*). While Puerto Ricans are said to be the result of these three "races" mixing, the Spanish one tends to be valorized; that is, most highly valued. The *jíbaro,* imaged as a white peasant occupying the mountain ranges, is exalted as the authentic creole Puerto Rican. At the same time, blackness is relegated to folkloric status and native identity to the past. Puerto Rican "cultural nationalism" is related to the island's status as a US colony. As Arlene Dávila (1997) shows, transnational corporations, such as R.J. Reynolds Tobacco Company and Anheuser Busch, help construct and trade in notions of Puerto Rican authenticity—to consume their products, they exhort, is to be a real Puerto Rican. Global capitalism and the commoditization of images has caused contradictory effects. This has led to a more shared "global culture" and a longing for particularism, the local, the exotic. This has meant that in Puerto Rico and elsewhere, there are groups who now claim Amerindian identity. However, it has also meant a resurgence of sex tourism in Cuba with the myth of the hypersexual *mulata* as an object of male racialized desire.

Comparative Social Status of Blacks and Native Peoples
In Latin America, one occasionally hears *negrito* (little black one) as a term of endearment that might be used by an older family member when speaking to a child. But only certain kinds of family relationships permit this usage—a child would never address his or her parents in this way. The relationship construed even by the term *negrito* has parallels in a paternalism often exhibited by whites over nonwhites.

It is tempting to compare the place of *negros* with the position of native peoples in Latin American nationalistic culture. In the 500 years since the conquest, colonial and independent Latin American states' treatment of native peoples has ranged from neglect to attempts at forced integration to genocide.[7] Nowhere in contemporary Latin America was the persecution of native peoples as profound and cruel as in Guatemala. As David H. Bost and Angélica Lozano-Alonso detail in Chapter 13, the irony was not lost on world observers when Rigoberta Menchú Tum was honored with the Nobel Peace Prize in 1992—the quincentennial of Christopher Columbus's first voyage.

As in many Latin American states in which indigenous peoples are numerous (e.g., they make up more than 60 percent of Guatemala's population), the system of ethnic-class ranking holds that the elites are white, followed by *ladinos* (who are seen as *mestizos*), and then indigenous peoples. In many cases, the cultural and certainly the phenotypical differences between *ladinos* and native peoples are not great. In class terms, however, the differences are stark: *ladinos* were found in a number of occupations and class levels whereas most native peoples continued to resist proletarianization through the late twentieth century.

Native peoples are a diverse group and, as elsewhere through time, the construct "Amerindian" obscures significant differences. Indigenous Guatemalans speak about twenty different Mayan languages. They are organized around the concept of community, and these communities differ from each other culturally in many ways. In the past, native identity has been rooted in the community, although this is changing as some native leaders are making common cause with other indigenous groups in Latin America and beyond. Although they were not completely closed and isolated from the influences of the wider society throughout colonial conquest and independence, these communities are still able to act as corporate units in political and economic resistance against the state and entrenched economic interests.

In elite nationalism, the refrain was familiar. For non-Amerindians, a truly modern and prosperous nation not only required unity but also that the Amerindians give up their separate identity and become integrated—on the oligarchy's terms—into national economic life. Indigenous peoples want to retain what they see as their traditional ways and customs while participating as social and economic equals in a multicultural nation.

In Guatemala, integration and class exploitation have always been mediated by the state and its coercive capacities. The system of forced indigenous plantation labor ended only in 1945 during a period of democratic rule that lasted from 1944 to 1954. As Thomas J. D'Agostino explains in Chapter 4, the policies aimed at labor, land, and political reform pursued under the leadership of Juan José Arévalo and Jacobo Arbenz were viewed in the context of the Cold War as threatening to US commercial and strategic interests. US efforts to destabilize the Arbenz government, supported by local and international capitalists, culminated in a coup in 1954 that ushered in over three decades of military rule.

In the 1960s, the beginnings of a guerrilla movement in the western highlands of Guatemala—where indigenous peoples predominate—gave the United States reason to assist the military further in setting up a counterinsurgency military program. Revolutionary groups tried to mobilize indigenous peoples who, in an effort to resist cultural and economic exploitation, sometimes joined. In response, beginning in 1975, the military began to use indiscriminate violence against "subversives" who were usually indigenous people who happened to reside in communities where any form of popular mobilization was taking place.

What has been called the "permanent counterinsurgency state" was now in place. The military, composed of *ladinos,* controlled civil society. Entire villages were massacred, rural leaders were tortured, and the crops of indigenous peoples were destroyed. The military set up permanent bases in the highlands, conscripted around 20 percent of the male inhabitants into the army, and organized "civilian patrols" of indigenous peoples under direct military command. More than 120,000 people were killed in the over thirty-year rebellion against repressive Guatemalan governments. Human rights agencies report that at least 50,000 indigenous peoples were killed during the 1980s, about 200,000 were forced into permanent exile, and at some point half of the 2 million highlands residents were displaced from their homes.

Notwithstanding these practices, Guatemala depicts itself with Amerindian symbols. The symbolic use of the *traje* (an indigenous dress) as the Guatemalan "national costume" appeals to international tourists and bolsters the local tourist industry. Profits depend on an image of the exotic, cultivated carefully and somewhat intentionally. But the concept of "Indianness as national essence" goes much deeper than any conscious manipulation of symbols for economic gain. Many *ladinos* assume some sense of identification with "Indianness," taken in an almost spiritual way. This form of Guatemalan nationalism has clear parallels with other forms of nationalism in Latin America, depicting the true soul of the nation as inhering in an Amerindian past.

Recent decades have seen native peoples mobilize with common goals throughout Latin America. In many cases, it is to protect lands that they consider theirs or to counter environmental threats. In the process, they develop a self-conscious discourse on what they define as distinctive indigenous culture, constructing identity in the process. A number of Amerindian organizations have emerged that have captured the attention of those in power. For example, some Amazonian native groups have utilized video and Internet technology to press their claims in the court of world opinion and to establish solidarity with indigenous groups elsewhere. Native peoples in Ecuador have also been quite successful in their movement for equal treatment while retaining their distinctive cultures and languages. Yet under neoliberal governance the activism of "*Indios permitidos*" ("allowed Indians") (Hale 2004a) is restricted to identity politics that help to replace the state's role and responsibility in civil society without seriously threatening the social order (see further, Greene 2007; Hale 2002, 2004b, 2005; Hooker 2005a; Martínez Novo 2006; Postero 2007a, 2007b; Roitman 2009; Van Cott 2000, 2005; Yashar 2005).

Myths and Realities

The Latin American woman who perhaps represented the most strongly contrasting symbol to Rigoberta Menchú, a Quiché, was the blond, blue-eyed, Brazilian, megamarketed superstar Xuxa (pronounced SHOO-sha). Former soft-porn movie actress and *Playboy* model Xuxa's incredibly popular children's television show reached millions in Brazil and elsewhere in Latin America. At the height of her popularity, Xuxa was probably Brazil's best-known celebrity, a larger-than-life media creation who recorded best-selling records, starred in movies that attracted huge audiences, had dolls bearing her likeness, and endorsed a number of products from surfboards to bicycles to soup to cookies. She had her own magazine with a circulation at one time of 700,000. Her concerts were performed in sold-out stadiums, and her live performances garnered the highest pay of any Brazilian entertainer.

In addition to crafting and marketing cultivated images of sexuality and consumerism, Xuxa also played on—and traded in—whiteness (Simpson 1993). Xuxa was simultaneously the blond ideal of beauty and the ideal of femininity. Young girls would dream of being Xuxa and tried to emulate her and the Paquitas, her blond clone teenage helpers. Xuxa improbably incorporated (and herein was her appeal) a number of contradictory images: at once a sexual, erotic figure and a domestic one, surrounded by adoring children, affirming the aesthetic superiority of whiteness while always assuring Brazilians of her Brazilianness. To this end, her six-year public affair with soccer legend Pelé (Edson Arantes Do Nascimento), the most famous black man in Brazil, served as a legitimation of the veracity of the myth of *democracia racial.*

Xuxa's blond aesthetic went almost unquestioned in Brazil, yet her own words were revealing. Asked about the "race" issue and her show, Xuxa was quoted as saying, "Some people say that I shouldn't do a show because I am blond. . . . But Brazil is a country of mixed races. You can be blond, brunette, *mulato;* you can be anything." When asked why all of her cast members were

Family Channel

Brazilian performer Xuxa projects an image that has made her wealthy and famous.

white, she responded with racist assumptions: "Oh! I've already explained; the tests [auditions to be Paquitas] are very difficult." Continuing, she said, "I think blonds have more drive. Besides, we're all blond, but we're all Brazilian!" (Simpson 1993). And when her romance with Pelé ended in 1986, she told the press a story that clearly had insulting racial implications.

The rise of Xuxa, perhaps not coincidentally, came with the relatively recent rise of a black consciousness movement in Brazil (building on an earlier movement in the 1940s and 1950s) and the growth of a number of organizations whose aims are to empower blacks politically and economically and to promote a positive black self-image. Anthropologist John Burdick reported a conversation with a Brazilian man in a small bar in a working-class town on the outskirts of Rio de Janeiro: "There is no racism in Brazil! I have the blood of all races in me—white, black, Indian [native]. How could we be racists?" But in a more reflective moment, he said, "There is a saying in Brazil: 'If you're not white you're black.' That's not really true, you know. Here, you can be other things, like me, I'm a *moreno*. But to a white man, I'm a *moreno* only if he likes me; if he doesn't like me, I'm a *mulato,* or I'm even a *preto* [black]. They play that game, you know? I guess the real saying should be, 'If you're not white, you lose'" (1992:40, 44).

"Race" as a category was left out of the 1970 census (which was taken during the period of military rule, 1964–1985). "Race" was included in the 1980 census; however, the results of that census were not released until two years later because the Census Bureau director apparently feared they would damage Brazil's image of harmonious ethnic relations. The results were damaging. They showed huge differences in income, with blacks earning 35 percent as much as whites and *pardos* earning 45 percent of what whites earned. This coincided with, and was part of, a general trend in which the rich got richer and the poor became poorer. In 1960, the wealthiest 10 percent of the population held 40 percent of the national income, while the poorest 50 percent held only 17 percent. According to the Comisión Económica para América Latina (2010), by 1990 the portion of the national income held by the poorest 50 percent had declined to just 11 percent, while the wealthiest decile held nearly 51 percent. Significantly, this trend has reversed itself in the early-twenty-first century. After reaching a high of more than 53 percent in 1999, the percentage of national wealth held by the wealthiest 10 percent in Brazil steadily declined to 46.5 percent in 2009. During that same period the poorest 50 percent of the population saw their share of the national income increase from 10.9 percent to almost 14.1 percent in 2009.

A principal aim of the black consciousness movement is to convince those Brazilians who identify themselves as *moreno* or *mulato* to identify themselves as *negro*. In Brazil and elsewhere, as Juliet Hooker (2005a, 2008) shows, Afro-Latin Americans have formed social movements designed to win collective rights, and throughout parts of Latin America the new neoliberal multicultural regimes have granted (or have been compelled to grant) rights to land, jobs, places in educational institutions, and, overall, cultural recognition. These struggles have taken place in the streets, in popular culture, and in the halls of Latin American legislatures, and have even resulted in official changes in Latin American constitutions (Arocha 1998; Minority Rights Group 1995). In Colombia, for example, a 1993 law based on the 1991 Constitution outlined territorial and cultural rights for Afro-Colombians. In Brazil, agitation for affirmative action has challenged the (self-) image of "racial democracy"—now denounced by activists as a cloak for hidden, insidious racism, and public debate has ensued (see Htun 2004; Martins, Medeiros, and Nascimento 2004; Skidmore 2003; Tavolaro 2008). In 2004, the University of Brasilia became the first public university to engage in an affirmative action program, setting aside 20 percent of its admission slots for blacks.[8]

Nationalism as a Cultural Construct

By the late 1980s, Argentina had emerged from its most recent period of military rule (1976–1983). During this time, thousands of people were kidnapped, tortured, and murdered in the so-called Dirty War. The military leadership that instituted and reigned over the terrorist state justified these measures to "save Western Christian civilization." With the democratic election of Raúl Alfonsín in 1983, the self-termed Nationalists organized to oppose his regime, expressing continuity with the military government's ideological stance.[9] Their influence continued to threaten the elected regime of Carlos Menem (1989–1999) and those of his successors.

The Nationalist strain is linked to far-right political groups and ideologies, and in practice its views are expressed by the *carapintadas* (painted faces), the dissident, antidemocratic military faction that sprang up in the late 1980s and protested the trials of those accused of atrocities in the Dirty War, along with Alerta Nacional (National Alert)—a terrorist group that had links to the military and the police.

Nationalist ideology is an almost textbook example of what historian Eric Hobsbawm (1983) calls an "invented tradition," in which a mythical past is created and used to serve the needs of the present and the future. As David Rock (1993) shows, the Nationalists called their movement an "authentically Argentine struggle for Catholic truth and Hispanic tradition," a "spiritual" as opposed to a "material" movement, whose aim was to prevent the "breakdown of the country's spiritual unity." They proclaimed that they were "heirs to a millenary civilization grounded on Christian teachings, Greek philosophy, and Roman order." They were on a "crusade" for "moral purification" and the "defense of the national soul." They supported authoritarian rule and were opposed to "liberal philosophy, formal democracy, and ideological colonization" (Rock 1993). Of course, not every Argentine is a Nationalist (with a capital N), but the influence of this movement in education, religion, and political and civil life has been profound.

It is rarely sufficient for the cultural constructions of a nation to proceed solely in a self-referential way. Usually, these constructions are brought about most effectively in contradistinction to some entity or group, which the nation is defined against negatively. That is, the nation is not what this group is, and this group is not of the nation. The Nationalists have no trouble finding scapegoats; they are constantly warning of the subversive influence of such foreign enemies as Marxism, communism, Freemasonry, and international Zionism.

Internally, anti-Semitism has continued to be integral to Argentine nationalism. Similar to those who followed particular ideologies evident at the turn of the twentieth century, Catholic priests, bishops, and others in the 1980s criticized the Alfonsín government for the "many Jews" within it. Alfonsín's Radical Party government, which did include Jews, was termed *la sinagoga radical* (the radical synagogue) by right-wing critics. A 1988 survey conducted in Buenos Aires found that over 15 percent of participants felt that they were manifestly anti-Jewish, and 13.5 percent admitted to anti-Jewish feelings (Elkin 1992:7). Perhaps the most famous Jewish victim of the Dirty War was journalist and publisher Jacobo Timerman, whose 1981 book, *Prisoner Without a Name, Cell Without a Number,* tells of his persecution and torture at the hands of the military government.

Nationalism often depends on depictions of people within the borders of the nation as not of the nation. The experience of numerically small ethnic groups in Latin America and the Caribbean varies from country to country. About half a million Jews live in Latin America. The Sephardic Jewish community on the Caribbean island of Curaçao, founded in 1653, has the longest continuous history of all of the Jewish communities in the region. The group built up and maintained trading and merchant activities. Today, the 300-member, economically powerful community is held together in its economic activities by kinship units known as *famiyas,* which serve to form business networks of capital and information. The experience of the Jews in Jamaica has been somewhat similar.

In addition to the arrival of relatively small groups of Europeans, such as the Germans in Brazil and Chile, and Middle Easterners, such as the Syrians and Lebanese found in the Caribbean and in Central and South America, there has also been significant immigration from Asia. About 200,000 Japanese immigrated to Brazil in the first half of the twentieth century, with another 30,000 locating in Peru. About 300,000 Chinese went, mainly as contract laborers, to Latin America and the Caribbean in the mid-nineteenth century. About 140,000 of the Chinese went to Cuba and 100,000 to Peru, where they were treated so poorly that a series of international incidents occurred, and Chinese officials launched investigations. A further 20,000 Chinese went to various Caribbean islands, and the rest went to Central America and elsewhere. In some places, they have maintained ethnically exclusive marriage and mating practices; in other places, they have been more apt to assimilate. Often visible and distinct as traders of dry goods and owners of grocery shops, they have occasionally been victimized in nationalist movements. Virtually the entire Chinese community of Sonora, Mexico, for example, was expelled in the 1930s in a particularly fierce moment of postrevolution nationalism.

The construction of a nation is not only the prerogative of antidemocratic regimes and movements, as seen in the Argentine example. The decolonization process in most of the English-speaking Caribbean, for example, transmitted functioning parliamentary democracy to a number of states that achieved independence from Britain in the 1960s. But colonialism also generated ethnic conflict between those who came to these plantation societies in differing circumstances and with differing legal and social statuses that corresponded to ethnicity.

In Trinidad and Tobago, universal adult suffrage in 1946 and independence in 1962 resulted in the displacement of whites in the political, but not the economic, sphere. They also led to the institutionalization of political parties organized by, and generally identified with, the interests of blacks (the descendants of slaves) and East Indians (the descendants of indentured workers brought from India between 1845 and 1917 to replace emancipated slaves on the sugar estates). At present, blacks and East Indians each make up a little more than 40 percent of the population. Little intermarriage has occurred between these two groups. "Mixed" people, mainly of European and African ancestry, account for about 16 percent of the population. Whites represent less than 1 percent as do Chinese, Syrian, Lebanese, and others. The "black" political party held power continuously from 1956 until 1986, doling out political patronage to its followers in the form of public sector jobs. East Indians have benefited from educational improvements, but many continue to be economically marginalized. A number of East Indians have become wealthy capitalists, representing a counterweight to black political power and white economic power. Since 1986, there have been multiethnic political parties, and an East Indian prime minister has been elected, but this has not brought an end to ethnic politics.

Nationalism is related to ethnicity in countries such as Trinidad and Tobago, Guyana, and Jamaica in ways that significantly departed from the general Latin American pattern. Whereas Latin American nationalism has been characterized by implicit or explicit references to and identification with the colonial past and the culture of the colonizers, in these countries nationalism has been part of a two-pronged process.

First, multiculturalism has been emphasized. Guyana is referred to as the "Land of Six Peoples." Jamaica's national motto is "Out of many, one people" while Trinidad and Tobago's is "Together we aspire, together we achieve." Simultaneously, as Brackette F. Williams (1991) has argued, there is cultural contestation over which group historically has contributed the most to the nation, which, therefore, is constructed as "belonging" to that group. This construction is achieved through a conceptual move of inversion, in which the European-dominated, social status hierarchy is turned on its head: the formerly subordinate, now politically ascendant, groups develop a view of the social status hierarchy as composed of "givers" and "takers." Europeans become the takers who took more than they gave. Other groups, such as blacks and East Indians, wage a seemingly never-ending contest to prove they are the ultimate givers. It is only fair that the biggest givers, then, have the greatest say in the allocation of political and economic roles.

A homogenizing synthesis occurs when the conflation of nation/state/ethnicity exists to construct a "nonethnicity," in which there are Trinidadians or Guyanese and there are "others" who have retained their non-Trinidadian or non-Guyanese ways. In Trinidad and Tobago, elite blacks (perhaps unconsciously believing colonial stereotypes that blacks were stripped of their ancestral culture during slavery) construe lower-class black culture, as expressed through the steel band, calypso, and carnival, as the national culture. Fortunately, this process has not led to the kinds of state terror that have occurred elsewhere in the region around these same issues. And yet, as with mainland Latin America, the intersections of ethnicity, class, and nationalism are undergoing transformations in the new millennium. Cultural politics entail nationalist discourses of blackness (on Jamaica, see Thomas 2004), East Indian identity (on Trinidad and Tobago, see Khan 2004 and Munasinghe 2001), and indigenous identities in various Caribbean contexts (see Forte 1999, 2005, 2006; cf. Haslip-Viera 1999).

■ Conclusion

The complexities of "race," ethnicity, and class in an area as diverse as Latin America render most discussions incomplete and even, at times, contradictory. What is true in one context may be rather different in another. In this chapter, however, I illustrate how these concepts and their manifestations in nationalism have evolved and will continue to be intimately interrelated in ways that are significant for the future of this region.

When North Americans encounter the ethnic, class, and national arrangements of Latin America and the Caribbean (through travel, residence, or study), they are surprised by the great gap between what is taken as "fact" and a very different Latin American reality. The cultural constructions of ethnicity and nationalism continue to structure reality for Latin Americans, as well as North Americans, in ways that are manifested in arrangements of power and influence in these societies. And this is so even in the modernizing movements brought about by Latin Americans' new and varied connections to international economic forces. Affected by an increasingly global popular culture that infiltrates the region through electronic transmissions and huge migratory flows that circulate from and back to the region, historically unique conceptions and configurations of ethnicity, class, and nationalism in Latin America are challenged. The present era is characterized by globalization entailing vast economic and cultural flows across borders, the condition of postmodernity, where a more global capitalism is now engaged in regimes of "flexible accumulation" (Harvey 1989). In this process, the power of the state is challenged and, indeed, under ruling policies and ideologies of so-called neoliberalism, the traditional role of the state is eroded and the state's traditional responsibilities are put back onto the populace. New neoliberal discourses also encourage cultural rights—as long as these rights do not threaten the ruling groups still supported by the pared-down state. As a result, space is opened for ethnic and nationalist groups to operate in civil society, changing their public personae at the same time.

Protests against globalization are often staged in ethnic terms, but, as the result of the increased communication and travel that are concomitant with economic globalization, ethnic groups in Latin America and the Caribbean are often aware of the situations of those in North America and elsewhere and now make common cause with them. For instance, Latin American indigenous groups are not only forming coalitions across national borders, but they are increasingly united with groups calling themselves indigenous around the world. And black groups in Brazil are now adopting more international symbols of blackness, such as Jamaican reggae music and US African American ideologies of "race." It is not yet clear where these trends will lead, but both the historical structures and these newer processes of change require careful, empathetic analysis for a meaningful understanding of the contemporary scene.

▪ Notes

1. Strong condemnation of the apparently fraudulent 1994 election caused the Dominican Republic to disallow reelection of the president and to conduct the next presidential election after two, rather than the usual four, years. In 1996, Balaguer joined with longtime rival Juan Bosch to support Leonel Fernández in a successful run at the presidency, teaming up to prevent a Peña Gómez victory.

2. The question of how, if at all, the "racial"/ethnic/national systems of Latin America and the United States are converging is the subject of work by Skidmore (1993) and Winant (1999) considering a US-Brazilian comparison.

3. However, it should be noted that this way of proceeding is not universally accepted. Established scholars of Latin America such as Wade (1997) are critical of lumping "race" under ethnicity. I prefer to see "race" as a kind of ethnicity because taking this perspective does not assume that the criteria popularly attributed to "race" will be as salient as other criteria in assigning "peoplehood" to one's own group or to those deemed to be of another group. Neither does this approach assume that the criteria conventionally

attributed to "race" are universally recognized. If we look at racialization as a phenomenon, then it is better not to assume its existence in advance, but rather chart racialization as a historical process.

4. Culture, for the most part, is not discussed and therefore implicit. It is, in the first instance, the result of human attempts to solve the problem of survival. Culture is not some entity that is enduring from time immemorial, but is constantly made and re-made under specific social conditions. Therefore, history and relations of power influence culture. At the same time, people often talk about their culture, about what they see as the culture that defines their group. This self-conscious discourse of culture, always political in nature, may or may not accurately reflect the present or past of a group's cultural practices.

5. I do not consider *mestizaje* to be an objective process, independent from social and cultural processes. To do so would assume that "pure races" exist or existed and were therefore actually "mixed" in this process. In other words, it would be to assign a false tangibility to *mestizaje.*

6. See Graham (1990).

7. See Olson (1991) for an ethnohistorical dictionary that serves as a reference guide, providing information about existing Amerindian groups of Central and South America. See also Coy (1985); Smith (1990); and Urban and Sherzer (1991).

8. For a more extended discussion of this theme in Brazil, see Andrews (1991, 1992); Crook and Johnson (1999); Fontaine (1985); Hanchard (1994, 1999); Lovell (1993, 1994); Mitchell and Wood (1998); Reichmann (1999a, 1999b); Reiter (2009); Reiter and Mitchell (2010); Silva and Hasenbalg (1992); Wood and de Carvalho (1988); and Wood and Lovell (1992).

9. Rock's (1993) study examines in great detail the ideological bases for nationalism.

▧ Bibliography

Anderson, Mark. *Black and Indigenous: Garifuna Activism and Consumer Culture in Honduras.* Minneapolis: University of Minnesota Press, 2009.

Andrews, George Reid. *Blacks and Whites in São Paulo, Brazil: 1888–1988.* Madison: University of Wisconsin Press, 1991.

———. "Racial Inequality in Brazil and the United States: A Statistical Comparison." *Journal of Social History* 26, no. 2 (1992): 229–263.

———. *Afro-Latin America, 1800–2000.* New York: Oxford University Press, 2004.

Arocha, Jaime. "Inclusion of Afro-Colombians: Unreachable National Goal?" *Latin American Perspectives* 25, no. 3 (1998): 70–89.

Balaguer, Joaquín. *La isla al revés: Haití y el destino dominicano* [The Island Turned on Its Head: Haiti and Dominican Destiny], 6th ed. Santo Domingo: Editorial Corripio, 1990.

Burdick, John. "The Myth of Racial Democracy." *NACLA Report on the Americas* 25, no. 4 (1992): 40–44.

CEPAL (Comisión Económica para América Latina). "Income Distribution: Distribution of National Income by Deciles, by Geographic Areas," Santiago, Chile, December 2010. http://www.eclac.org.

Coy, Peter. "Current Ethnic Profiles and Amerindian Survivals." In *The Cambridge Encyclopedia of Latin America and the Caribbean,* eds. Simon Collier, Harold Blakemore, and Thomas E. Skidmore (Cambridge: Cambridge University Press, 1985), pp. 155–160.

Crook, Larry, and Randal Johnson, eds. *Black Brazil: Culture, Identity, and Social Mobilization*. Los Angeles: Latin American Center, University of California at Los Angeles, 1999.

Dávila, Arlene M. *Sponsored Identities: Cultural Politics in Puerto Rico*. Philadelphia: Temple University Press, 1997.

de la Fuente, Alejandro. "Race and Inequality in Cuba, 1899–1981." *Journal of Contemporary History* 30 (1995): 131–168.

———. *A Nation for All: Race, Inequality, and Politics in Twentieth-Century Cuba*. Chapel Hill: University of North Carolina Press, 2001.

Elkin, Judith Laikin. "Quincentenary: Colonial Legacy of Anti-Semitism." *Report on the Americas* 25, no. 4 (1992): 4–7.

Fontaine, Pierre-Michel, ed. *Race, Class, and Power in Brazil*. Los Angeles: Center for Afro-American Studies, University of California at Los Angeles, 1985.

Forte, Maximilian C. "Reviving Caribs: Recognition, Patronage, and Ceremonial Indigeneity in Trinidad and Tobago." *Cultural Survival Quarterly* 23, no. 4 (1999): 35–41.

———. *Ruins of Absence, Presence of Caribs: (Post)Colonial Representations of Aboriginality in Trinidad and Tobago*. Gainesville: University Press of Florida, 2005.

———, ed. *Indigenous Resurgence in the Contemporary Caribbean: Amerindian Survival and Revival*. New York: Peter Lang, 2006.

Fraginals, Manuel Moreno, ed. *Africa in Latin America: Essays on History, Culture, and Socialization*. New York: Holmes & Meier, 1984. (Orig. pub. 1977.)

Freyre, Gilberto. *The Masters and the Slaves: A Study in the Development of Brazilian Civilization*. Berkeley: University of California Press, 1986a. (Orig. pub. 1933.)

———. *The Mansions and the Shanties: The Making of Modern Brazil*. Berkeley: University of California Press, 1986b. (Orig. pub. 1936.)

Graham, Richard, ed. *The Idea of Race in Latin America, 1870–1940*. Austin: University of Texas Press, 1990.

Greene, Shane, ed. Special issue, "On Race, Roots/Routes, and Sovereignty in Latin America's Afro-Indigenous Multiculturalisms." *Journal of Latin American and Caribbean Anthropology* 12, no. 2 (2007).

Hale, Charles R. "Does Multiculturalism Menace? Governance, Cultural Rights and the Politics of Identity in Guatemala." *Journal of Latin American Studies* 34, no. 3 (2002): 485–524.

———. "Rethinking Indigenous Politics in the Era of the 'Indio Permitido.'" *Report on the Americas* 38, no. 2 (2004a): 16–21.

———. *Más Que un Indio (More Than an Indian): Racial Ambivalence and the Paradox of Neoliberal Multiculturalism in Guatemala*. Santa Fe: School of American Research Press, 2004b.

———. "Neoliberal Multiculturalism: The Remaking of Cultural Rights and Racial Dominance in Central America." *Political and Legal Anthropology Review* 28, no. 1 (2005): 10–28.

Hanchard, Michael. *Orpheus and Power: The Movimento Negro of Rio de Janeiro and São Paulo, Brazil, 1945–1988*. Princeton: Princeton University Press, 1994.

———, ed. *Racial Politics in Contemporary Brazil*. Durham, NC: Duke University Press, 1999.

Harris, Marvin. *Patterns of Race in the Americas*. New York: Walker, 1964a.

———. "Racial Identity in Brazil." *Luso-Brazilian Review* 1, no. 6 (1964b): 21–28.

Harris, Marvin, and Conrad Kottak. "The Structural Significance of Brazilian Racial Categories." *Sociologia* 25 (1963): 203–209.

Harvey, David. *The Condition of Postmodernity: An Enquiry into the Origins of Cultural Change.* Oxford: Blackwell, 1989.
———. *A Brief History of Neoliberalism.* Oxford: Oxford University Press, 2007.
Haslip-Viera, Gabriel, ed. *Taíno Revival: Critical Perspectives on Puerto Rican Identity and Cultural Politics.* New York: Centro de Estudios Puertorriqueños, 1999.
Helg, Aline. "Race in Argentina and Cuba, 1880–1930: Theory, Policies, and Popular Reaction." In *The Idea of Race in Latin America, 1870–1940,* ed. Richard Graham (Austin: University of Texas Press, 1990), pp. 37–69.
Hobsbawm, Eric. "Introduction: Inventing Traditions." In *The Invention of Tradition,* eds. Eric Hobsbawm and Terence Ranger (Cambridge: Cambridge University Press, 1983), pp. 1–14.
Hoetink, H. "'Race' and Color in the Caribbean." In *Caribbean Contours,* eds. Sidney W. Mintz and Sally Price (Baltimore: Johns Hopkins University Press, 1985), pp. 55–84.
Hooker, Juliet. "Indigenous Inclusion/Black Exclusion: Race, Ethnicity, and Multicultural Citizenship in Latin America." *Journal of Latin American Studies* 37, no. 2 (2005a): 285–310.
———. "'Beloved Enemies': Race and Official Mestizo Nationalism in Nicaragua." *Latin American Research Review* 40, no. 3 (2005b): 14–39.
———. "Afro-Descendant Struggles for Collective Rights in Latin America." *Souls: A Critical Journal of Black Politics, Culture and Society* 10, no. 3 (2008): 279–291.
Htun, Mala. "From 'Racial Democracy' to Affirmative Action: Changing State Policy on Race in Brazil." *Latin American Research Review* 39, no. 1 (2004): 60–89.
Khan, Aisha. *Callaloo Nation: Metaphors of Race and Religious Identity Among South Asians in Trinidad.* Durham, NC: Duke University Press, 2004.
Klor de Alva, J. Jorge. "Colonialism and Postcolonialism as (Latin) American Mirages." *Colonial Latin American Review* 1, nos. 1–2 (1992): 3–23.
Latortue, Paul R. "Neoslavery in the Cane Fields." *Caribbean Review* 14, no. 4 (1985): 18–20.
Lovell, Peggy A. "The Geography of Economic Development and Racial Discrimination in Brazil." *Development and Change* 24, no. 1 (1993): 83–101.
———. "Race, Gender, and Development in Brazil." *Latin American Research Review* 29, no. 3 (1994): 7–35.
Maingot, Anthony P. "Race, Color, and Class in the Caribbean." In *The Americas: Interpretive Essays,* ed. Alfred Stepan (New York: Oxford University Press, 1992), pp. 220–247.
Martínez Novo, Carmen. *Who Defines Indigenous?: Identities, Development, Intellectuals, and the State in Northern Mexico.* New Brunswick, NJ: Rutgers University Press, 2006.
Martins, Sérgio da Silva, Carlos Alberto Medeiros, and Elisa Larkin Nascimento. "Paving Paradise: The Road From 'Racial Democracy' to Affirmative Action in Brazil." *Journal of Black Studies* 34, no. 6 (2004): 787–816.
Minority Rights Group, ed. *No Longer Invisible: Afro-Latin Americans Today.* London: Minority Rights Group, 1995.
Mitchell, Michael J., and Charles H. Wood. "Ironies of Citizenship: Skin Color, Police Brutality, and the Challenge to Democracy in Brazil." *Social Forces* 77, no. 3 (1998): 1001–1020.
Mörner, Magnus. *Race Mixture in the History of Latin America.* Boston: Little, Brown, 1967.
Munasinghe, Viranjini. *Callaloo or Tossed Salad?: East Indians and the Cultural Politics of Identity in Trinidad.* Ithaca: Cornell University Press, 2001.

Olson, James S. *The Indians of Central and South America: An Ethnohistorical Dictionary.* Westport: Greenwood Press, 1991.

Postero, Nancy Grey. *Now We Are Citizens: Indigenous Politics in Postmulticultural Bolivia.* Stanford: Stanford University Press, 2007a.

———. "Andean Utopias in Evo Morales's Bolivia." *Latin American and Caribbean Ethnic Studies* 2, no. 1 (2007b): 1–28.

Rahier, Jean Muteba. "Blackness, the Racial/Spatial Order, Migrations, and Miss Ecuador 1995–96." *American Anthropologist* 100, no. 2 (1998): 421–430.

Reichmann, Rebecca. *Brazil: Equality, Difference and Identity Politics.* Oxford: Berg, 1999a.

———, ed. *Race in Contemporary Brazil: From Indifference to Inequality.* University Park: Pennsylvania State University Press, 1999b.

Reiter, Bernd. *Negotiating Democracy in Brazil: The Politics of Exclusion.* Boulder: FirstForum Press, 2009.

Reiter, Bernd, and Gladys L. Mitchell, eds. *Brazil's New Racial Politics.* Boulder: Lynne Rienner, 2010.

Rock, David. *Authoritarian Argentina: The Nationalist Movement, Its History and Its Impact.* Berkeley: University of California Press, 1993.

Roitman, Karem. *Race, Ethnicity, and Power in Ecuador: The Manipulation of Mestizaje.* Boulder: Lynne Rienner, 2009.

Sansone, Livio. *Blackness Without Ethnicity: Constructing Race in Brazil.* New York: Palgrave Macmillan, 2003.

Silva, Nelso do Valle, and Carlos Hasenbalg. *Relações Raciais no Brasil Contemporâneo.* Rio de Janeiro: Rio Fundo, 1992.

Simmons, Kimberly Eison. "Navigating the Racial Terrain: Blackness and Mixedness in the United States and the Dominican Republic." *Transforming Anthropology* 16, no. 2 (2008): 95–111.

———. *Reconstructing Racial Identity and the African Past in the Dominican Republic.* Gainesville: University Press of Florida, 2009.

Simpson, Amelia. *Xuxa: The Mega-Marketing of Gender, Race, and Modernity.* Philadelphia: Temple University Press, 1993.

Skidmore, Thomas E. *Black into White: Race and Nationality in Brazilian Thought.* Durham, NC: Duke University Press, 1993. (Orig. pub. 1974.)

———. "Racial Mixture and Affirmative Action: The Cases of Brazil and the United States." *American Historical Review* 108, no. 5 (2003): 1391–1396.

Smith, Carol A. (ed.). *Guatemalan Indians and the State: 1540–1988.* Austin: University of Texas Press, 1990.

Solaún, Mauricio, Eduardo Vélez, and Cynthia Smith. "*Claro, Trigueño, Moreno:* Testing for Race in Cartagena." *Caribbean Review* 15, no. 3 (1987): 18–19.

Stepan, Nancy Leys. *"The Hour of Eugenics": Race, Gender, and Nation in Latin America.* Ithaca: Cornell University Press, 1991.

Stephens, Thomas M. *Dictionary of Latin American Racial and Ethnic Terminology.* Gainesville: University of Florida Press, 1989.

Tavolaro, Lília G. M. "Affirmative Action in Contemporary Brazil: Two Institutional Discourses on Race." *International Journal of Politics, Culture, and Society* 19, nos. 3–4 (2008): 145–160.

Thomas, Deborah A. *Modern Blackness: Nationalism, Globalization, and the Politics of Culture in Jamaica.* Durham, NC: Duke University Press, 2004.

Timerman, Jacobo. *Prisoner Without a Name, Cell Without a Number.* New York: Knopf, 1981.

Urban, Greg, and Joel Sherzer, eds. *Nation-States and Indians in Latin America.* Austin: University of Texas Press, 1991.

Van Cott, Donna Lee. *The Friendly Liquidation of the Past: The Politics of Diversity in Latin America.* Pittsburgh: University of Pittsburgh Press, 2000.

————. *From Movements to Parties in Latin America: The Evolution of Ethnic Politics.* Cambridge: Cambridge University Press, 2005.

————. *Radical Democracy in the Andes.* Cambridge: Cambridge University Press, 2008.

Wade, Peter. *Race and Ethnicity in Latin America.* London: Pluto Press, 1997.

Whitten, Norman E., Jr., and Arlene Torres, eds. *Blackness in Latin America and the Caribbean,* 2 vols. Bloomington: Indiana University Press, 1998.

Williams, Brackette F. *Stains on My Name, War in My Veins: Guyana and the Politics of Cultural Struggle.* Durham, NC: Duke University Press, 1991.

Winant, Howard. "Racial Democracy and Racial Identity: Comparing the United States and Brazil." In *Racial Politics in Contemporary Brazil,* ed. Michael Hanchard (Durham, NC: Duke University Press, 1999), pp. 98–115.

Wood, Charles H., and José Alberto Magno de Carvalho. *The Demography of Inequality in Brazil.* Cambridge: Cambridge University Press, 1988.

Wood, Charles H., and Peggy A. Lovell. "Racial Inequality and Child Mortality in Brazil." *Social Forces* 70, no. 3 (1992): 703–724.

Wright, Winthrop R. *Café con Leche: Race, Class, and National Image in Venezuela.* Austin: University of Texas Press, 1990.

Yashar, Deborah J. *Contesting Citizenship in Latin America: The Rise of Indigenous Movements and the Postliberal Challenge.* Cambridge: Cambridge University Press, 2005.

Yelvington, Kevin A., ed. *Trinidad Ethnicity.* Knoxville: University of Tennessee Press, 1993.

————. "The War in Ethiopia and Trinidad, 1935–1936." In *The Colonial Caribbean in Transition: Essays on Postemancipation Social and Cultural History,* eds. Bridget Brereton and Kevin A. Yelvington (Gainesville: University Press of Florida, 1999), pp. 189–225.

10

Women, Work, and Politics

Susan Tiano

Women were at the forefront of the dramatic changes that swept Latin America in the late twentieth and early twenty-first centuries, just as they have been in every previous historical epoch. What distinguishes the contemporary period is that women's achievements are more apt to be publicly acknowledged, acclaimed, and rewarded. In previous eras, Latin American women's multiform contributions to public life were obscured by images that defined women exclusively in terms of the private realm of the family and the wife-mother role, thereby concealing their activities outside the domestic sphere. The long overdue attention to women's achievements has its intellectual roots in the burgeoning of feminist scholarship since the 1970s and its practical roots in the dramatic social changes that have transformed gender roles in recent decades. The global media have played a role in bringing information about women's public contributions to international and national awareness, often with far-reaching implications.

Argentina's political history, for example, was irrevocably altered by the globally disseminated media images of Las Madres de la Plaza de Mayo (the Madres), the women who helped topple Argentina's repressive military regime by staging weekly demonstrations in one of Buenos Aires' most public plazas. Their movement began informally, among housewives who had never before entered politics and had little in common with one another except the tragic disappearance of a loved one at the hands of the military government.[1] As they made the rounds of government offices in a futile search for information, they began encountering the same anxious faces in waiting lines and reception offices, and came to realize that many others shared their plight. Meeting clandestinely in their homes and other private spaces, they settled on a strategy for publicizing their concerns. Tying white kerchiefs around their heads and toting

285

filipealberto/Flickr.com

*Las Madres de la Plaza de Mayo, whose protests demanding justice
for those "disappeared" during the Argentine Dirty War contributed
to the withdrawal from power of the military regime.*

placards with their loved ones' photographs, they marched around the plaza in front of government headquarters. At a time when the regime's ban on political activity—often enforced through the same kind of "disappearances" that had separated the Madres from their offspring—had completely curtailed men's public protest of the regime, the Madres' weekly demonstrations were especially courageous. By centering their mobilization on their roles as mothers, the Madres used a powerful symbolic identity to interpret their actions (to themselves, the press, and the government) in terms of their private roles in the household rather than the public world of politics, where women in 1970s Argentina seldom ventured.

At first, the regime impugned their legitimacy by calling them *las locas* (the crazy women) in the public press and by manipulating media accounts to distort their purpose and deny their concerns. When this failed to silence them the regime infiltrated their ranks and arranged for the "disappearance" of their founder, Azucena Villaflor. Yet by framing their protests as expressions of their maternal responsibilities to their sons and daughters, the Madres insulated themselves from direct governmental repression. While the Argentine populace might tolerate and perhaps applaud the regime's wholesale repression of "terrorists" and "subversives," subjecting "mothers" to the same kind of treatment would be deplorable and would threaten the regime's legitimacy. Thus, the Madres were able to evade governmental repression until their activities had been too well publicized to be quelled without international protest and their cause had been adopted by international human rights organizations. The resulting political pressure was salient for Argentina's transition to democracy in 1983, showing the world an incontrovertible instance in which women's agency helped shape the course of a nation's history (Schirmer 1993; Bouvard 1994; Chant 2003:11).

The Argentine Madres' experience is but one of many examples of Latin American women gaining long-neglected recognition for their contributions to public life. Another well-known, if less dramatic, example concerns the Mexican women working in multinational *maquiladoras,* who are stimulating industrial development along the Mexican-US border by assembling products for global export. Debates over the North American Free Trade Agreement (NAFTA) have generally portrayed *maquiladora* women as docile, passive, and willing to work for a pittance—the antithesis of the unionized US men whose employment base has eroded due to industrial downsizing and overseas investment. This image has a twofold purpose: in Mexico and elsewhere in Latin America, it deflects conservative opposition to hiring women by saying these jobs are too menial to liberate women from traditional gender roles. In the United States, it legitimates firms' increasing investment in Mexico by arguing for the inevitability of low-wage female employment to maintain corpora stereotype cannot possibly encompass the complex reality of diverse women's lives, but it is useful for shaping public perceptions, and its consistency with other stereotypes of Mexican women's roles gives it a certain credibility with both the Mexican and US public (Sklair 1993; Tiano 1994).

Nevertheless, in at least two instances in recent years, women *maquiladora* workers have staged long-term, successful strikes for better wages and working conditions, and their collective action has begun to come to public awareness, both in Mexico and the United States. This is sparking cross-border organizing and support for Mexico's *maquiladora* workers from an increasingly broad sector of US labor. As the fates of men and women workers on both sides of the border become increasingly intertwined with the spread of globalization, the scope of *maquiladora* women's contributions is too important to be ignored or occluded by misleading stereotypes (Bandy and Mendez 2003).

In short, Latin American women have always played key productive and political roles, but many have performed these activities in informal contexts hidden from the public eye or have had their roles obscured by ideologies that define them exclusively as wives and mothers. The increasing awareness of women's contributions to their communities reflects both a broadening of the scope of their activities and the growing commitment of researchers and the mass media to shed needed light on women's public roles.

Latin American women are a highly diverse group, reflecting the same regional heterogeneity that characterizes Latin America generally. As Kevin A. Yelvington illustrates in Chapter 9, women's lives are defined not only by their gender—the social and cultural meanings attributed to biological sex—but also by the complex ways that gender interacts with class, race, and ethnicity to influence women's social roles and relationships. The world of an indigenous Maya woman in highland Guatemala may seem light years away from that of an Afro-Latina in a Brazilian *favela* or a third-generation Italian woman in a cosmopolitan Argentine city. Yet many features unite women across the region and permit generalizations about their history and contemporary circumstances. Like their male counterparts, women in most Latin American nations share an Iberian heritage that has molded their societies after the fashion of their Spanish and Portuguese colonizers. For indigenous women whose heritage originates in precolonial Latin America, the impacts of European colonization also reshaped cultural norms and transformed social dynamics. Women also share with men a history of external dependency that has shaped their nations' developmental trajectories and, as Scott G. McKinney explains in Chapter 6, continues to dictate the terms under which their countries participate in the global economy. As this chapter reveals, the consequences of this heritage have posed challenges for women and men throughout Latin America, regardless of their specific circumstances. Nevertheless, Latin American women have other experiences in common by virtue of their gender that sharply divide them from the men in their societies. In the next section, I describe concepts from feminist theory that illuminate women's gender-specific experiences.

▓ Production, Reproduction, and the Gender Division of Labor

A useful starting point for exploring the changing roles of Latin American women is the conceptual distinction between production and reproduction and the gender-based division of labor that results from these interlinked activities. Production is the creation of socially useful goods and services. Its continuity requires reproduction—the replenishment of labor and other productive resources. Reproduction entails the day-to-day maintenance and emotional support of family members, some of whom provide the labor for the productive sphere. Reproduction also involves conceiving, bearing, and caring for children and preparing them for the roles they will occupy in adulthood. In precapitalist societies, both production and reproduction take place within the household and are oriented toward meeting the family's subsistence needs. Under capitalism, a separation exists between the private sphere of household and family where reproduction occurs, and the public, formal sphere, which is the primary locus of production (Tiano 1984). At the interstice between the private and public spheres lies the informal sector of the economy. Informal activities, which often take place within the household, frequently involve such services as preparing and selling food, washing and ironing clothing, or tutoring children—all extensions of reproduction (Arizpe 1977). Yet because informally generated products and services are typically sold on the market, they interpenetrate the public sphere.

Societies around the world have displayed considerable variety in the gender-specific tasks assigned to men and women though, with the advent of capitalism and the separation between the public and private spheres, the gender division of labor becomes less reciprocal and less complementary. Women assume primary responsibility for reproduction and maintaining the domestic sphere whereas men are allocated to productive roles in the public sphere. This bifurcated division of labor is supported by cultural ideologies that define women in terms of their wife-mother role, whatever their actual marital or childbearing status or their roles in public production (Beechey 1978:192). In Latin American societies, the dominant ideology of *marianismo* (the cult of the Virgin Mary) glorifies motherhood and cultivates women to be self-sacrificing moral guardians of the family (Stevens 1973:94; Chant 2003:10). According to this belief system, the family is held together spiritually and emotionally through the mother's steadfast devotion. Women's dedication to their families is expected to extend beyond their selfless commitment to child rearing, domestic tasks, caring for the sick and elderly, and other reproductive roles; women must also maintain their purity by remaining within the safe haven of the household (Vaughan 1979:67). *Marianismo* supports the gender division of labor by deeming public participation to be inconsistent with women's inherent nature and familial responsibilities. Women are not only expected to refrain from undertaking waged employment, but also are implored to avoid social or political activities that take them beyond the protective confines of the home. As I reveal in the next section, women's real-world circumstances have often dramatically contradicted this ideology; yet it has persisted throughout Latin American history to circumscribe women's activities and define their self-concepts.

▓ Women in Latin American History

At the time of first contact with the Europeans who would impose their way of life on groups throughout the continent, the status of indigenous women varied greatly. Most anthropologists posit an inverse relationship between women's status and the degree of class stratification in their societies (Gailey 1987:51–54). In relatively egalitarian hunting-gathering and horticultural societies, where gender divisions of labor were more egalitarian and reciprocal, the complementary productive contributions of both genders offered women considerable economic parity with men (Etienne and Leacock 1980:6). Among the horticultural Bari of eastern Colombia, for example, women enjoyed a high degree of personal autonomy and social respect (Buenaventura-Posso and Brown 1980:119).

By contrast, in agricultural societies with elaborate cultivation systems, bureaucratic states, and hierarchically ranked social systems, women's status was below that of the men from their same class. Both the Aztecs, who built a sophisticated empire in what is now central Mexico, and the Incas, who controlled extensive territory in the Andean region, created societies in which women were deemed inferior to men and had more limited access to resources (Nash 1980: 137; Silverblatt 1980:155).[3] Both empires had grown through a process of conquest in which the subjugated peoples were enslaved and forced to pay tribute to the empire. Similarly, the Carib-speaking people of the West Indies amassed considerable territory by subduing the more peaceful Arawaks, killing the Arawak men and retaining the women in a subordinate status for breeding and labor (Miller 1991:17). Such dynamics suggest that political conquest stimulated class and gender inequality among indigenous Latin Americans.

The imposition of colonial rule on the indigenous peoples of Latin America produced diverse outcomes, ranging from complete annihilation through disease and warfare to incorporation into radically new social relations intended to produce wealth for the colonial power. The indigenous populations that were forcefully assimilated into colonial societies were joined by the successive waves of African-born peoples who were imported to provide labor for the mines and plantations. Although each affected group experienced colonialism in its own way, certain commonalities cut across all colonized groups.

Regardless of women's circumstances prior to European contact, the imposition of colonial rule tended to diminish their status (Boserup 1970:53). Women in horticultural societies, whose productive contributions had given them relative parity with men, found themselves marginalized from socially valued roles and resources. Colonialism also weakened the position of women in stratified agrarian societies because even though precolonial systems had subordinated them to men, these arrangements were more egalitarian than the social and legal systems imposed by the colonizers (Nash 1980).

As the colonial administrations implemented the mercantile capitalist economy that was emerging in Europe, indigenous people were immersed in new relations that often exploited their labor and divorced them from productive resources. The Spanish colonial regime instituted a system in which precious metals, agricultural products, and manufactured finery such as hand-woven textiles were used to enrich Spain's coffers and finance its military exploits. The British and Dutch developed more elaborate global trade networks in which agricultural products from their New World plantations were exchanged for commodities produced elsewhere (Chirot 1977:22). With the transition from subsistence to market-based production, land originally held in common and farmed cooperatively by both men and women became privately owned. The best land was claimed by the Europeans or awarded to indigenous elites as compensation for their loyalty. The reallocation of land disadvantaged most indigenous people, but it was especially harmful to women, whose ability to own and dispose of land was drastically limited under Spanish law. Women were denied official title to the land they worked, even after the death or desertion of the legally designated male head of household (Silverblatt 1980:167).

In some regions, both slave and free women labored along with men to produce agricultural goods for domestic or foreign markets. More typically, women were relegated to subsistence production, often on the most marginal land, producing the foodstuffs that sustained their households. Other women were confined to the domestic sphere where they engaged in household labor and manufactured items, such as woven textiles, for family use or market exchange. Such manufacturing often occurred under highly exploitative conditions. In colonial Peru, for example, indigenous women were often sequestered in locked rooms and forced to weave cloth that colonial administrators appropriated for sale to European consumers. Yet the exploitation of their labor was but one of the many indignities women suffered under colonial rule. Many women were raped or forced into concubinage by the Spanish and their indigenous allies (Navarro 1999:32). Women were often sexually victimized by priests who forced them to prostitute themselves or serve as mistresses as a form of penance for presumed sins (Silverblatt 1980:169).

Women's responses to the colonial arrangements that limited their legal rights and exploited their labor and sexuality ranged from accommodation to resistance (Navarro 1999:24). A common accommodative pattern of women during the early colonial period was to become consorts or wives of the colonizers, thereby achieving relatively high status for themselves and their offspring. The Spanish initially encouraged these liaisons as a way of compensating for the scarcity of European women in the colonies, but later saw them as a threat to the Spaniards' racial and cultural homogeneity (Nash 1980:141). By this time, however, the intermixing of indigenous, African, and European peoples had laid the basis for complex class- and racially stratified societies in which women at all levels derived their primary status from their roles as reproducers. Elite women were expected to bear children who would perpetuate upper-class privilege, whereas women of the popular classes were expected to breed children to replenish the rapidly dwindling labor force. The policies advanced by the Spanish crown to regulate marriage in the colonies blended with those of the Catholic Church, affecting the lifestyles and values of women across the class spectrum.

Even though colonialism reduced women's access to productive roles and resources, women in the preindependence and postindependence epochs were hardly idle. They performed many tasks that generated goods for household consumption and products for market exchange. Women's economic roles mirrored their positions in the race-class hierarchy. Upper-class women, whose work was typically confined to the private sphere, managed their households, oversaw the production and purchase of consumption goods, and regulated the care and training of their children. Women in the merchant and artisan classes often played entrepreneurial roles in family enterprises. Most lower-class urban women, whether migrant or urban born, worked as domestic servants or as laundresses, midwives, *curanderas* (healers), or food vendors. Rural women, in their capacity as subsistence agriculturalists, often not only provisioned their families, but also produced a surplus to be traded or sold. In many rural regions, the lack of viable economic options led young women to migrate to urban areas even though their indigenous origins often exposed them to discrimination and their employment options were typically limited to domestic service and street vending.

During the mid-nineteenth century, Argentina, Brazil, Chile, and Mexico introduced "normal" schools for teacher education and began admitting women to secondary schools and universities (Korrol 1999:73). Women whose families could afford their educational expenses could now prepare for middle-class careers in health care, teaching, and other professions presumed to parallel women's specialization in household tasks. Yet women's gains were confined to jobs viewed as mere extensions of their reproductive roles, their work was undervalued and badly compensated, and their achievements rarely won them much public recognition.

The twentieth century brought a division among Latin American nations, with some, including Mexico, Argentina, and Brazil, developing labor intensive manufacturing industries to produce basic consumption goods. Women formed the backbone of the labor force in the textile, tobacco, and food processing industries (Nash 1983:11; Towner 1979:49).[4] With the transition to capital-intensive industries during the 1930s and 1940s, however, the preference for male labor reduced women's share of the industrial workforce (Tiano 1994:42; Cravey 1998:28). In turn-of-the-century Mexico, when textile and

Katherine Marino

Women demonstrate the techniques used in textile production outside Cuzco, Peru.

tobacco production dominated manufacturing, about 76,000 women held factory jobs; after forty years of industrial diversification, only half as many women held jobs in manufacturing (Vaughan 1979:78). Similarly, in 1900, over 90 percent of Brazil's industrial labor force was female, but by 1940 women constituted only 25 percent of the manufacturing workforce (Schmink 1986:137).

Women's expulsion from industry sometimes occurred when male workers enlisted the state to penalize businesses for hiring women. In Puerto Rico, women had come to constitute such a large share of the manufacturing labor force by the 1930s that the male-dominated unions petitioned the government to help reverse the trend. When the state complied by granting subsidies to industries that hired men, there was a drastic reduction in women's industrial employment (Nash 1983:8). Similar trends have been documented for Mexico and Brazil (Vaughan 1979; Saffioti 1975). Despite equally discriminatory practices in many other employment sectors, women have continued to maintain a foothold in the formal economy. Yet as I discuss later, only in the 1970s did women begin to solidify their position in the labor force.

Women's contributions to the political life of their societies date from precolonial times, when many indigenous women were active in the movements that opposed European conquest (Navarro 1999:37–39). According to documents dating from the early conquest period, women's boldness on the battlefield terrified Spanish observers who perceived them as incarnations of the Amazons (Miller 1991:16). Others resisted colonial incursion in less militaristic ways by fleeing to remote regions beyond Spanish domination. Thus, some women descendants of the Incas escaped Spanish rule by moving to isolated areas where they reinstated their native religious practices as a form of cultural resistance (Silverblatt 1980:179).

Women played active roles in the political mobilizations that culminated in the early-nineteenth-century independence struggles. Among those immortalized for their heroism in these wars of independence are Policarpa Salavarrieta who was publicly executed by the Spanish for fomenting revolution in Colombia; María Quiteira de Jesús who distinguished herself in battle in Brazil's independence movement; and Marie Jeanne a-la-Crete-a-Pierrot and Henriette St. Marc who participated in Haiti's revolts against the French (Korrol 1999:61).

The increasing political activity of the postindependence era was generally a masculine prerogative within the new postcolonial institutions which, like their counterparts elsewhere in the Western world, denied women suffrage and other rights to participatory citizenship (Miller 1991). With formal political channels closed to women, those who wished to shape local or national politics did so informally, through their social networks within and outside their families. Their political activity was most apt to flourish in times of political upheaval when grassroots resistance movements required their support. Just as women had figured centrally in the movements for independence from colonial rule, they also made key contributions to movements against what were perceived as unjust or dictatorial national regimes. During the Mexican Revolution, some women fought alongside men on the battlefields, and many others accompanied men to battle sites where they cooked, washed clothing, and tended wounds (Macias 1982:25). In Guatemala, women participated in the strike that helped to depose the autocratic regime of Jorge Ubico in 1944, inaugurating the first free elections in that country's history; in Bolivia, women staged street demonstrations and hunger strikes that helped to bring the Movimiento Nacionalista Revolucionaria to power in 1952. Cuban women were active in the revolutionary movement that unseated the Fulgencio Batista regime in 1959 and led to a socialist government that formally promoted women's equality (Larguia and Dumoulin 1986).

Movements to transform political regimes were but one form of women's political participation during the pre- and postindependence periods. Much of their political energy was devoted to causes such as women's suffrage, which directly affected women's well-being. By the late nineteenth century, women in Argentina, Uruguay, Chile, Brazil, Mexico, and Cuba had begun to develop movements that agitated for women's suffrage and other reforms to promote gender equality (Korrol 1999:84). The emergence of feminist political journals in this period gave women a forum for espousing their views on female equality; examples include the Brazilian journal, *O Sexo Feminino,* established in the 1870s, and *La Mujer,* which Chilean women published in the 1890s (Miller 1991:69).

Women also organized conferences such as the Congreso Feminino Internacional, which convened in Buenos Aires in 1910, and two feminist congresses held in 1916 in Mérida, Mexico (Korrol 1999:87). The Mérida conferences illustrated the deep divisions within the Mexican feminist movement: whereas conservative Catholic women challenged proposals they viewed as threatening to women's traditional roles, the more progressive women advocated platforms that deplored gender inequalities in education and employment and demanded legal reforms to ensure women's equal treatment before the law (Macias 1982:73–75). Regardless of their position, women at the Mérida and Buenos Aires conferences set the stage for the unique form of feminist consciousness that has characterized Latin American feminism in the twentieth and twenty-first centuries and has distinguished it from US and European feminism. Rather than rejecting their feminine roles as wives and mothers, Latin American feminists have sought to eliminate conditions that interfere with women's ability both to successfully perform those roles and to use them as platforms for critiquing and transforming their societies (Miller 1991:74).

As I reveal in the next sections, contemporary Latin American women have expanded their public participation in both the political and economic spheres. Many have defied social convention by disavowing their reproductive roles, but many—such as Argentina's Madres—have acted within their capacities as mothers and wives to make lasting changes in their societies. My discussion of women in contemporary Latin America begins with a description of changes in women's employment patterns.

▓ Women in the Formal Labor Force

As previously noted, Latin American women's employment patterns have traditionally been shaped by the ideology of *marianismo,* which deems formal labor force participation inappropriate for married women because it interferes with their domestic roles and threatens their families' well-being (Levenson-Estrada 1997:210). A woman was encouraged to work, if at all, only until she married and had children, at which point she was expected to leave the workforce to devote herself to full-time domesticity (Arizpe 1977:29; Fernandez-Kelly 1983). Partnered women who needed to generate income were expected to do so in the informal sector where tasks and schedules are more compatible with reproductive duties than those of formal jobs (Beneria 1992:92). The cultural injunction against married mothers working for wages led to discriminatory hiring practices that restricted their employment opportunities. This ideology was at the root of protective legislation that circumscribed the range of jobs available to women, preferential hiring practices favoring men, gender-based wage discrimination, men's opposition to their wives' employment, and women's ambivalence about their wage-earning roles (Tiano 1987:227).

As a result of *marianismo* and the gender division of labor it supports, Latin American women's labor force participation has lagged behind that of women in most parts of the world. With the exception of northern Asia and the Middle East, where women have traditionally been rigidly secluded from public life, most African and Asian nations have had higher rates of female economic activity than have Latin American countries (Psacharopoulos and Tzannatos 1992:49–52). Latin American governments have encouraged this situation as a way of holding down unemployment levels in contexts where demographic growth has exceeded the economy's capacity to provide enough jobs for the working-age population (Gregory 1986:21).

The data in Table 10.1 suggest that, until recently, traditional images of women's ideal roles shaped the Latin American workforce. These data describe trends in women's economic activity for three points in time—the 1960s, the 1980s, and the late 1990s. During the earliest period, women's labor force participation rarely rose above 25 percent and was less than 20 percent for the bulk of countries for which we have reliable data. Latin American nations showed considerable variation, with the more urbanized countries of Panama (25 percent) Uruguay (32 percent), Chile (29 percent), and Argentina (24 percent) showing higher female employment than the more rural countries of Guate-

Table 10.1 Labor Force Participation Rates for Working-Age Women and Men

Country	Year	Male Rate	Male Change	Female Rate	Female Change	Female/Male
Argentina	1960	92.8		24.4		26.3%
	1980	90.8	−2.0	33.1	8.7	36.5%
	1995	76.2	−14.6	41.3	8.2	54.2%
	2000	58.7	−17.5	44.5	3.2	75.8%
	2005	61.2	2.5	49.0	4.5	80.1%
Brazil	1960	95.0		18.2		19.2%
	1980	92.4	−2.6	33.0	14.8	35.7%
	1998	82.0	−10.4	52.8	19.8	64.4%
	2000	69.1	−12.9	56.0	3.2	81.0%
	2005	69.8	0.7	57.5	1.5	82.4%
Chile	1952	94.5		28.6		30.3%
	1982	87.2	−7.3	28.9	0.3	33.1%
	1999	74.4	−12.8	36.5	7.6	49.1%
	2000	55.8	−18.6	38.0	1.5	68.1%
	2005	56.9	1.1	40.6	2.6	71.4%
Colombia	1951	97.4		19.0		19.5%
	1985	85.4	−12.0	39.4	20.4	46.1%
	1999	79.8	−5.6	57.7	18.3	72.3%
	2000	68.2	−11.6	54.8	−2.9	80.4%
	2005	69.1	0.9	56.6	1.8	81.9%
Costa Rica	1963	97.0		18.6		19.2%
	1984	89.7	−7.3	26.4	7.8	29.4%
	1999	81.5	−8.2	38.5	12.1	47.2%
	2000	59.2	−22.3	38.0	−0.5	64.2%
	2005	60.6	1.4	41.1	3.1	67.8%
Ecuador	1962	97.8		17.7		18.1%
	1982	87.7	−10.1	22.6	4.9	25.8%
	1998	55.2	−32.5	36.8	14.2	66.7%
	2000	64.1	8.9	45.0	8.2	70.2%
	2005	65.4	1.3	47.8	2.8	73.1%
Guatemala	1964	96.2		13.1		13.6%
	1981	91.3	−4.9	14.7	1.6	16.1%
	1999	87.9	−3.4	45.6	30.9	51.9%
	2000	59.3	−28.6	36.5	−9.1	61.6%
	2005	61.0	1.7	40.9	4.4	67.0%
Honduras	1961[a]	52.7		7.7		14.6%
	1974[a]	48.8	−3.9	8.9	1.2	18.2%
	1999	88.0	39.2	45.8	36.9	52.0%
	2000	58.7	−29.3	33.4	−12.4	56.9%
	2005	60.5	1.8	37.4	4.0	61.8%

(continues)

Table 10.1 continued

Country	Year	Male		Female		
		Rate	Change	Rate	Change	Female/Male
Mexico	1960	96.5		19.1		19.8%
	1980	92.4	–4.1	32.7	13.6	35.4%
	1999	83.8	–8.6	38.5	5.8	45.9%
	2000	58.3	–25.5	37.5	–1.0	64.3%
	2005	60.2	1.9	41.0	3.5	68.1%
Panama	1950	97.0		24.9		25.7%
	1980	87.3	–9.7	35.7	10.8	40.9%
	1999	79.7	–7.6	43.2	7.5	54.2%
	2000	61.7	–18.0	42.5	–0.7	68.9%
	2005	63.0	1.3	45.5	3.0	72.2%
Peru	1961	96.8		22.7		23.5%
	1981	91.3	–5.5	29.0	6.3	31.8%
	1999	79.4	–11.9	58.1	29.1	73.2%
	2000	68.9	–10.5	57.7	–0.4	83.7%
	2005	69.8	0.9	59.2	1.5	84.8%
Uruguay	1963	93.0		32.0		34.4%
	1985	92.4	–0.6	46.0	14.0	49.8%
	1998	55.8	–36.6	39.1	–6.9	70.1%
	2000	62.8	7.0	50.9	11.8	81.1%
	2005	63.1	0.3	51.9	1.0	82.3%
Venezuela	1961	96.4		22.1		22.9%
	1981	89.0	–7.4	35.0	12.9	39.3%
	1997	53.2	–35.8	30.1	–4.9	56.6%
	2000	55.3	2.1	37.4	7.3	67.6%
	2005	57.0	1.7	40.7	3.3	71.4%

Sources: George Psacharopoulos and Zafiris Tzannatos. *Case Studies on Women's Employment and Pay in Latin America: Overview and Methodology* (Washington, DC: World Bank, 1992); James Wilkie, ed. *Statistical Abstract of Latin America*, vol. 38 (Los Angeles: UCLA Latin American Center Publications, 2002); *Statistical Yearbook for Latin America and the Caribbean: Economic Participation Rate, By Sex* (Santiago, Chile: Economic Commission for Latin American and the Caribbean, 2008). http://websie.eclac.cl/anuario_estadistico/anuario_2008/eng/index.asp.

Note: Honduran participation rates in 1961 and 1974 censuses were calculated differently from those of the other countries, whose rates are the ratio of the economically active population to the working-age (20- to 60-year-old) population. Early Honduran rates use the total population (all age categories) as the denominator for calculating male and female participation rates.

mala (13 percent) and Honduras (8 percent).[5] Yet the common denominator among all Latin American nations during this period was a relatively low rate of female employment, particularly in contrast with male rates, which were uniformly above 92 percent during this period.[6]

The 1960s and 1970s witnessed considerable growth in the proportion of employed women. By the early 1980s, one-third of working-age women in Mexico, Brazil, Argentina, Venezuela, and Panama were in the labor force; almost 40 percent of Colombian women and almost half of Uruguayan women worked for wages. The most substantial rises in women's economic activity during the twenty-year period occurred in Colombia (20.4 percent), Brazil (14.8 percent), Uruguay (14 percent), and Mexico (13.6 percent), but most countries experienced gains of at least 8.0 percent. The exceptions to this trend include Chile (0.3 percent) where the seventeen-year regime of Augusto Pinochet advocated policies designed to confine women to the home, and Guatemala where political turmoil stunted the growth of both the male and female workforce.

Importantly, the general rise in women's economic activity was not accompanied by parallel growth in men's employment. During the 1950s and 1960s, upward of 93 percent of Latin American men were economically active, meaning that they either held jobs or were unemployed but actively seeking employment. These proportions encompassed most able-bodied men below retirement age who were not in school, producing a ceiling effect, beyond which rates had little room to rise because the vast majority of men were already in the workforce. With such a large percentage of men in the workforce, it would be reasonable to expect women's gains to occur at men's expense. This argument, which is often advanced as a rationale for maintaining traditional gender roles, envisages men and women as competitors for the same scarce jobs. Feminist economists and sociologists, who see this "competitive" view as inconsistent with the way gender-segregated labor markets operate, have challenged it. Because labor markets channel the bulk of working women into a specific range of "female" occupations, such as teaching, nursing, sewing, and clerical work, rising female employment would not necessarily have to come at the expense of men's wage-earning opportunities.

The fact that men's economic activity decreased in all Latin American countries during the 1960s and 1970s, when women's employment was rising throughout the region, could be taken as evidence for the competitive scenario that women's increasing employment displaced men from the labor force. However, while this explanation may have some truth, it clearly is not the whole story. If women had expanded their employment primarily by taking jobs from men, the gains in women's rates would be roughly equivalent to the declines in men's. Yet with the exception of Costa Rica, where the 7.8 percent increase in women's rates paralleled a 7.3 percent decrease in men's, the trends in women's and men's rates show little correspondence. In some countries, relatively large increases in women's employment went hand in hand with minimal declines in men's activity. In both Brazil and Uruguay, for example, women's employment surged by 14.0 percent while men's rates declined by only 3.0 percent in Brazil and a mere 0.6 percent in Uruguay. Even if the entire decline in men's employment was due to women's movement into male jobs, this would account for only a tiny fraction of the rapid increase in women's participation, which would have been achieved at a proportionately small expense to male activity rates.

In some countries, the decline in men's economic activity substantially exceeded the rise in women's. In Ecuador, the 5 percent increase in women's participation could not compensate for the 10 percent decrease in men's activity, nor could the 0.3 percent rise in Chilean women's activity make up for the 7.0 percent drop for Chilean men. In these cases, the fall in male activity was too large to be accounted for by women's increasing participation, even if it did occur at the expense of male employment, demonstrating that other factors played a role in men's worsening employment scenario during the 1960s and 1970s.

The expansion of women's labor force participation continued, and in some countries accelerated, during the last two decades of the twentieth century. By the late 1990s, countries throughout Latin America reported female employment rates of 30 percent or higher.[7] Peru and Colombia, where 58 percent of women were economically active, topped the list, although Brazil was not far behind, with 53 percent female employment. With the exception of Venezuela (30 percent), all the remaining countries reported rates ranging between 37 percent (Chile and Ecuador) and 46 percent (Honduras and Guatemala). These two Central American nations showed the largest increase, with Guatemalan women's employment rising by 31 percent and Honduras showing a similar rise. In another group of countries (Peru, Brazil, Colombia, Ecuador, and Costa Rica), women's employment rose by 12 percent or more. With the exception of Colombia, which ranked above most countries in 1980, the nations showing the greatest gains during the period are the ones that had lagged behind in the earlier period and, thus, had the farthest to go. Similarly, of the countries that reported more modest increases or decreases several, such as Uruguay, Argentina, and Panama, had such high rates during the 1980s that even with small increases they could rank in the middle of the continuum of countries by the late 1990s. By contrast, the slow expansion of women's employment in Mexico and Chile over the period pulled them into the bottom one-third of countries while Venezuela's 5 percent decrease in women's economic activity caused it to plummet from the top one-third in 1980 to dead last in 1999.

During the 1980s and 1990s, men's economic activity declined, in some cases dramatically, throughout the region. By 1999, only a little more than half of working-age men in Uruguay, Venezuela, and Ecuador and three-fourths of men in Argentina and Chile were in the workforce. Men fared better in the rest of the region, with rates hovering around 80 percent in six countries (Mexico, Brazil, Costa Rica, Colombia, Panama, and Peru) and rising to 88 percent in Honduras and Guatemala. Unlike the previous period, in which there was no clear relationship between men's and women's changing labor force participation patterns, during the late twentieth century the trends in men's and women's rates across countries showed some correlation. Thus, in Guatemala and Honduras, where women's economic activity reveals the largest increases during the period, men's labor force participation declined the least. Conversely, the only two countries in which female labor force participation actually decreased during the period, Venezuela and Uruguay, were also the ones where male employment declined the most drastically. These patterns suggest that the same factors that contracted employment opportunities for women also restricted them for men. And those that greatly expanded women's employment options also mitigated the negative influences on male employment that were so pervasive in the rest of the region. I will return to this issue at a later point in this discussion.

The age-specific employment trends illustrated in Figure 10.1 provide insights into women's employment trends. The graphs in the figure illustrate how the employment pattern of a typical working woman changes over the course of her life cycle. By comparing the curves for the 1960s, 1980s, and 2000s one can visualize how women's typical work histories changed during the period. In the early 1960s, women's economic activity tended to peak early in their life cycle—between the ages of twenty and twenty-five—and to steadily decline with advancing age. This indicates that many women worked prior to marriage and childbearing and then left the workforce as they entered their late twenties and early thirties.

By the 1980s, a somewhat different pattern had emerged. In several countries (Chile, Costa Rica, Ecuador, Panama, Peru, Uruguay, and Venezuela), women's economic activity peaked at an older age in the 1980s than it had in the 1960s. Thus, whereas in the early 1960s economic activity was highest among twenty- to twenty-four-year-olds, in the 1980s it was most pronounced among women in their late twenties and early thirties. A related change concerns the age span during which women's employment remained at high levels and the point at which it began to decline steeply. During the 1960s, in every country except Mexico, women's participation dropped steadily after it peaked in their early twenties. By the 1980s, the age span of maximal economic activity had been extended, and women's employment generally did not drop substantially until a later point in their life cycle. These trends suggest that, by the 1980s, growing numbers of women in their thirties and forties were remaining in the workforce. Not only were more women joining the labor force, but more were remaining for a greater portion of their lives or were reentering after leaving to raise their children. These patterns continued into the present century.

What might account for the rise in economic activity, particularly among women in their thirties and forties who two or three decades earlier would likely have devoted themselves to full-time domestic roles? One way to explore this question is to use a conceptual distinction made by labor economists between "push" and "pull" factors. *Push factors* are forces such as economic

Figure 10.1 Female Labor Participation Rate by Age

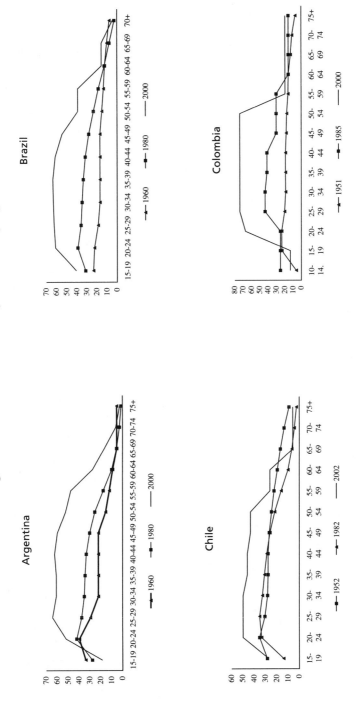

Figure 10.1 continued

Figure 10.1 continued

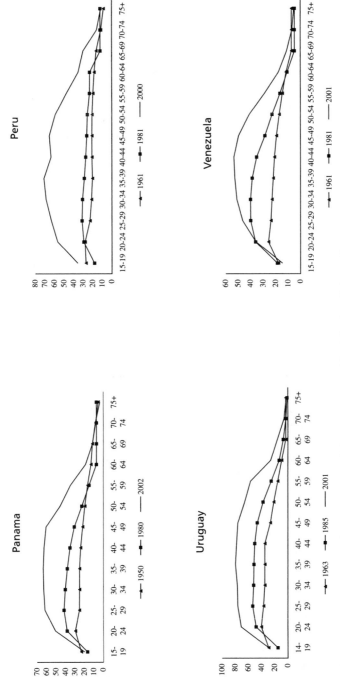

Source: International Labour Organization. ILO Office: Department of Statistics. http://laborsta.ilo.org.

need that impel women into the workforce to support their households. *Pull factors* are conditions that either attract women into the labor force or augment their employment opportunities. The availability of suitable jobs, the proliferation of schools and adult literacy programs, the weakening of norms that symbolically confine women to the household, and the attraction of noneconomic rewards, such as personal autonomy, may all operate as pull factors that draw women into the labor force. These two sets of factors need not be mutually exclusive. A woman may be compelled to enter the workforce because her household requires her income; at the same time, she may respond to the lure of financial independence, personal fulfillment, or other anticipated benefits of paid employment. Such considerations suggest that the growth in women's economic participation in the last half of the twentieth century reflected a complex mix of influences that both forced women to take jobs and augmented their incentives and opportunities for paid employment.

Considerable evidence suggests that many women joined the workforce out of economic need. Throughout the lost decade of the 1980s and continuing into the 1990s, Latin American nations were plagued by an economic crisis that dramatically eroded their living standards. As Scott G. McKinney documents in Chapter 6, the economic crisis ushered in several decades of rampant inflation, rising unemployment, and serial currency devaluations that jeopardized the well-being of all but the wealthiest households (Cockroft 1983:260; Scott 1992:22). At the same time, the structural adjustment policies most Latin American governments adopted to stabilize their economies led to substantial cuts in state funding for health care, education, and other necessary social services and removed price supports for basic commodities (Chuchryk 1991: 152; Lustig 1992:79). To make matters worse, governments often capped minimum wage levels to counteract inflation, thereby limiting many workers' incomes. Rising levels of male unemployment and underemployment often prevented men from continuing in their traditional role of family breadwinner (Beneria 1992; Chant 1991). As the data in Table 10.1 demonstrate, the proportion of economically active men in all Latin American countries declined during the period as increasing numbers were marginalized from the formal labor force. Even those men who were able to hold down jobs often found their wages inadequate to support a household (Fernandez-Kelly 1983:56; Safa 1995:24).

These developments were particularly devastating for poorer households, whose already precarious circumstances were further eroded by the rising cost of food and other necessities and the elimination of vital government services (Safa 1995:33). Working- and middle-class households also experienced a drastic decline in their standards of living. Households formulated various strategies to cope with these deteriorating circumstances; most commonly, all working-age members, male and female, had to generate income (Beneria 1992: 92). Daughters and sons were often forced to discontinue their schooling to enter the workforce or to postpone marriage to help support their parents' households. Many partnered women who had previously devoted themselves to domestic tasks or informal income-generating activities now had to take full-time jobs. Women's wages were particularly essential in households without adult members and those in which the men were unemployed or underemployed (Chant 1991:158). In some households, men's inability to support their families led to destructive behaviors, such as alcohol abuse, or caused them to desert their families (Beneria 1992:91). In others, the lack of employment options in the local community forced men to migrate elsewhere in search of stable wages (Safa 1995:32). Many women thereby became the primary economic providers for families without male household heads (Anderson and de la Rosa 1991:55). In short, economic necessity pushed many women from various backgrounds into the workforce during the crisis-plagued years of the 1980s and early 1990s.

Yet the upsurge in women's economic activity was not simply a result of economic need and rising male unemployment. Many other changes occurred during the mid- to late twentieth century to draw women out of the household, either by expanding their economy's demand for female labor or by increasing the supply of women willing and able to enter the workforce. One of the most important pull factors was the growth of women's employment opportunities. During the 1960s and 1970s, when many Latin American nations underwent rapid economic and political development, jobs proliferated for women in both the governmental and market sectors of their country's economies. The locus of women's employment opportunities shifted during the 1980s and 1990s, when the economic crisis brought a halt to the development of previous decades.

As the structural adjustment measures employed to restimulate economic growth have eroded barriers to foreign trade and investment, multinational corporations, with their well-known preference for female labor in many sectors of their workforce, have come to account for a growing proportion of jobs in Latin America. Jobs for women have proliferated in multinational agribusiness firms, which are flocking to Mexico, Chile, and elsewhere to produce fruits and vegetables for export to global consumers (Barrientos et al. 1999; Appendini 2002). They have also proliferated in manufacturing as multinational firms have relocated their export-processing operations to Latin America (and elsewhere) to reduce production costs by employing low-wage workers to process products for global export (Fernandez-Kelly 1983; Korrol 1999:104). Beginning in the 1950s with Puerto Rico's Operation Bootstrap and the 1960s with Mexico's *maquiladora* program, export-led industrialization has become increasingly common throughout Latin America. Women are preferred for export-processing jobs because they tend to work for lower wages than men and are perceived as more docile, more manually dexterous, and better able to tolerate the monotony of repetitive assembly work (Fuentes and Ehrenreich 1983:12; Sklair 1993:171–172).

Maquiladora *(textile factory) in Brazil.*

The expansion of the Mexican *maquiladora* industry illustrates the impact of export-led industrialization on the female labor market. In 1967, two years after the *maquila* program was established, it encompassed seventy-two firms employing 4,000 workers, over 80 percent of whom were women. By 1990, the program had grown to include almost 2,000 firms and over 460,000 workers (Sklair 1993:54, 68). The stimulus of NAFTA and the booming US economy during the late 1990s greatly accelerated *maquila* investment, augmenting the workforce to 1.3 million people by the year 2000 (Tiano 2006). In the program's early days, *maquilas* preferred to hire young, single, childless women who had completed secondary school. As the program grew, the *maquilas* relaxed their employment criteria and hired more older women, partnered women, and women with children as well as more men (Tiano 1994:90). The rapid proliferation and changing recruitment practices of the *maquilas* had a significant impact on Mexico's female labor market. By providing jobs for women, particularly those whose age and marital or motherhood status would otherwise have created employment barriers, *maquilas* dramatically increased their employment opportunities. Similar dynamics have been observed with export-processing industrialization programs in other Latin American countries (Safa 1995).

The increasing demand for female labor also stems from the rapid growth of the service sector, which encompasses many jobs that involve activities such as cleaning, cooking, serving food, and providing personal services that are viewed as extensions of female roles. Even economic sectors that have traditionally employed men now include larger proportions of women. Thus, for example, women have begun to enter the mining and construction sectors, conventionally the preserves of men. In the 1960s, women constituted only 7 percent of workers in the Mexican mining industry; by 1980, the proportion had grown to 14 percent. During the same period, women's representation in the Peruvian mining industry grew from 2 percent to 6 percent, and Venezuelan women's share of the mining labor force increased from 5 percent to 10 percent. Similarly, during this period, women's share of the Mexican construction industry rose from 3 percent to 16 percent (ECLAC 1988:30). Thus, while some of the gains in women's employment occurred in sectors traditionally reserved for women, others reflected women's inroads into sectors that had once been male preserves.

Fortunately for women workers, the crisis-born conditions that forced many women to earn wages also stimulated the demand for female labor. The crisis and its aftermath compelled many businesses to minimize operating costs to weather the economic turbulence. Many accomplished this objective by turning to women as a low-cost labor source. Other employers began to recruit women because they viewed them as more reliable than men and less apt to organize potentially costly workers' unions. In countries with successful export-processing programs such as Mexico, firms' positive experiences with female labor induced other businesses to follow their example (Beneria and Roldan 1987:49).

The increased demand for female labor and the growing acceptance of paid work for partnered women and mothers have augmented women's employment opportunities. But women need the necessary education to take advantage of these opportunities. Women's educational attainment reflects both objective conditions such as the availability of schools, and subjective factors such as parents' aspirations for their daughters. Since the 1960s, accelerated investment in public education by Latin American governments has led to a proliferation of rural and urban schools. Governments have encouraged parental support for their children's education through mass media campaigns urging parents to enroll and keep their sons and daughters in school (Rothstein 1982:118).

These efforts have led to substantial increases in school enrollments. By 1980, almost all Latin American children between the ages of six and eleven were enrolled in primary school (Stromquist 1992:1). The only countries in which boys outpaced girls in primary school attendance were Bolivia and Guatemala. Girls were less apt to attend secondary schools, whose female enrollment figures ranged from 65 percent in Panama to 17 percent in Guatemala, with only seven countries (Argentina, Chile, Costa Rica, Ecuador, Panama, Peru, and Uruguay) enrolling half or more of their adolescent girls in secondary school (Chant 2003:89). Boys shared with girls the difficulty in accessing secondary education; in only two countries (Bolivia and Peru) were girls less apt than boys to attend secondary school (ECLAC 1988:42). The subsequent decades witnessed continuing improvements in girls' secondary school enrollments; by 1993, rates approached 70 percent or above in Argentina, Chile, and Colombia while Guatemala (at 23 percent) was the only country in the region where less than one-third of girls were enrolled in secondary school (Chant 2003:89). The progress of Latin American nations in providing postsecondary education was also considerable. In the mid-1980s, 17 percent of Latin Americans aged twenty to twenty-five years were earning a university degree. Although men were somewhat more apt than women to pursue higher education, in several countries (Argentina, Cuba, Nicaragua, and Panama) women's participation exceeded that of men (Stromquist 1992:2).

The advances in public education have not spread evenly to all sectors of women. Older women, who were past school age when educational opportunities became widely available, often received few benefits from their government's investment in public schooling. By 1990, only 9 percent of women under age twenty-five were illiterate, but 23 percent of women above that age lacked basic literacy and numeracy skills (United Nations 1991:46). Similarly, rural women, particularly those in indigenous communities, often benefited only minimally from educational reforms. As recently as the 1990s in Guatemala, where indigenous groups constitute 60 percent of the population, 78 percent of rural women were illiterate; the disparity between comparable rates for rural men (60 percent) and those for urban women (36 percent) suggests that racism and sexism played a role in limiting indigenous women's access to educational resources. Indigenous women in Bolivia faced similar obstacles: whereas rural women's illiteracy rates reached 69 percent, only 37 percent of rural men and 23 percent of urban women were unable to read and write (Stromquist 1992:24). These disparities reflect not only the poorer quality of rural schools, but also the cultural and material hurdles that indigenous women must overcome to attain an education.

In some contexts, the economic crisis and the structural adjustment policies implemented to eradicate it slowed or halted the educational gains of previous decades. For example, in Costa Rica, female secondary school enrollments dropped from 51 percent in 1980 to 49 percent in 1993 and, in Nicaragua, from 45 percent to 44 percent (Chant 2003:89). Throughout Latin America, governments were forced to curtail spending on public education while many young people had to discontinue their educations because their households could not bear the costs, and their economic contributions were needed for family survival. Many analysts worry that the crisis and the resulting structural adjustment policies have dealt such a severe blow to public education that Latin American nations will take decades to recover (Arizpe 1993:174).

Nevertheless, although the crisis slowed the progress in educating women in Latin America, it was insufficient to undercut those gains entirely. Even after fifteen years of crisis, women in the 1990s were better prepared to compete for jobs than their counterparts from previous generations. Thus, the regionwide gains in women's educational opportunities were another pull factor that augmented women's economic activity.

Women's rising labor force participation does not simply reflect the accelerating demand for women's labor, their growing educational preparation, and the increasing economic pressures to support their families. Regardless of how much her household may need additional income or how abundant her job opportunities might be, a woman cannot enter full-time employment if her reproductive responsibilities are too demanding. Most employed women, regardless of their marital status or household composition, receive little help with housework and childcare from male household members (Beneria and Roldan 1987:123). To avoid being crushed by their double burden, working women must find ways to balance the competing demands of their productive and reproductive roles.

One solution is to have fewer children. Women with small families are better able than those with many offspring to make the necessary childcare arrangements to allow them to reenter the labor force, whether as soon after the birth as possible or when the children reach school age or beyond. The spread of family planning information and devices throughout much of Latin America during the late twentieth century made it easier for women who wanted smaller families to implement their choices. By the 1990s, the majority of Latin American women in their childbearing years (ages fifteen to forty-nine) used contraception, with rates ranging from a high of 84 percent in Uruguay to a low of 31 percent in Guatemala (Chant 2003).[8]

Women's growing ability to regulate their childbearing has led to a substantial decline in fertility throughout Latin America. Between 1960 and 1980, the average number of children per woman of childbearing age dropped from 6.0 to 4.6. In 1960, only three countries (Argentina, Cuba, and Uruguay) had fertility rates below 5.0, and thirteen countries had rates above 6.5. Two decades later, only five countries (Bolivia, Ecuador, El Salvador, Honduras, and Nicaragua) had fertility rates above 6.0, and seven countries averaged fewer than 4.5 children per woman. This trend continued throughout the 1980s and 1990s, such that by the year 2000, thirteen out of nineteen Latin American countries had fertility rates of 3.0 or less (Chant 2003:73). Women's declining fertility resulted from various factors, including increased public awareness of the links between overpopulation and economic and ecological difficulties, the growing commitment of Latin American governments to reduce population growth, and the spread of family planning technologies and information. The expansion of employment opportunities for women also contributed to their lowered fertility, both by augmenting women's economic incentives to have smaller families and by offering them an alternative to motherhood as a way of enhancing their social status (Blumberg 1991:110). Lowered fertility thus was both a cause and a result of women's rising labor force participation. The dramatic drop in fertility throughout Latin America was another pull factor that increased women's employment.

An additional stimulus to women's economic activity reflects a change in the prevailing cultural ideology that defines appropriate roles for women. In a cultural context in which women are regarded exclusively as wives and mothers and work outside the home is considered detrimental to the performance of their domestic roles, women across all social groups face extreme obstacles to formal employment. No matter how great her economic need, a woman will not be able to enter the workforce if no employer will hire her or if her partner will not allow her to leave the house. Similarly, if taking a job would lead to constant feelings of guilt over neglecting her children, emasculating her husband, or risking her feminine purity, a woman is unlikely to seek or remain long in paid employment. For indigenous women, these social realities are often exacerbated by pervasive racism and discrimination against indigenous peoples.

Such considerations suggest that one of the most important incentives to women's rising economic activity has been the relaxation of cultural norms against their paid employment, particularly for partnered women and mothers (Beneria and Roldan 1987:49). This normative change has reflected a shift in the cultural ideology of *marianismo* and a reformulation of role expectations that consider men to be ineffectual or unmasculine if they cannot support their households without female assistance. As these rigid gender roles have begun to weaken, women's aspirations have changed accordingly, leading many to acquire the motivation and training to prepare for careers, to select partners who will not interfere with their occupational choices, and to plan their childbearing for increased compatibility with wage-earning activities. At the same time, the change in male role definitions has diminished men's resistance to their wives' and daughters' employment and has increased employers' willingness to hire partnered women without fear that spousal reprisals will hamper their successful job performance (Tiano 1994:93–96).

This gender role transformation is both a cause and a result of women's rising educational attainment. With advancing education, women tend to expand their occupational horizons and to question the validity of conventional gender roles for themselves and their daughters. Conversely, parents are more apt to make the necessary sacrifices to keep their daughters in school if they have abandoned conventional gender roles and believe educational attainment will foster their daughters' economic security in later life. In addition to promoting women's education, the erosion of traditional gender roles has expanded their opportunities in the workforce. Employers are more willing to hire women if they do not anticipate spousal resistance to their wives' employment and if they do not expect women to be so committed to their reproductive roles that they neglect their jobs. In turn, employers' increasing demand for female labor has helped to erode cultural norms proscribing women's employment. The desire to lower costs and achieve other benefits by hiring women has led many employers to reformulate their images of appropriate roles for women in order to justify their hiring practices. Similarly, governments hoping to attract corporate investment in *maquiladoras* and other industries that recruit women workers have ensured the availability of female labor through media campaigns and other strategies designed to weaken ideological constraints to female employment (Ruiz 1988).

Whereas this ideological shift may help to reconcile the cultural contradiction between *marianismo* and women's growing need for paid employment, it does not resolve the dilemmas the rapid flux in female roles is posing for Latin American women. Many women who find themselves forced to take jobs were raised to aspire to full-time motherhood and to view paid work and family duties as incompatible. Many resent their jobs for forcing them to neglect their families. Many others who are committed to their jobs feel guilty about deriving personal satisfaction from work that takes them away from their children (Tiano 1994:118; Tiano and Ladino 1999). And those who have resolved the conflicting emotions that surround their dual roles nevertheless struggle to balance the competing demands of their "double day" in contexts where governmental and private services for working mothers are sorely lacking (Safa 1990). Many women view this challenge as more than a personal struggle and are organizing to demand institutional changes, such as childcare and workplace reforms, to facilitate their abilities to perform their domestic and wage-earning roles simultaneously. Issues such as these are only a few of the many catalysts for the growing political mobilization of women.

Women in Latin American Politics

Although women have always taken part in Latin American social and political movements, the past three decades have witnessed a dramatic upsurge in their participation (Jaquette 1991b:1). Women have mobilized in unprecedented numbers to support or protest political regimes, agitate for better working conditions, make demands on the state for improved services and affordable commodities, and transform legal and social barriers to gender equality. Much of their activity has avoided formal political channels—both because it has often occurred within authoritarian climates where political parties, trade unions, and mass demonstrations were illegal (Perelli 1991:101) and because women often consider institutionalized politics to be futile, corrupt, or inconsistent with their feminine roles (Pires de Rio Caldeira 1990:72). Instead, women have developed their own form of politics that stems from their reproductive roles and blurs the boundaries between the public world of politics and the private realm of the family (Safa 1990:355). The apolitical connotation of the wife-mother role has given women some immunity to protest despotic regimes that have brutally repressed political resistance (Perelli 1991:107).

The diversity of women's political objectives, agendas, and strategies precludes ready categorization. Most analysts distinguish between political activities in which women join with men to pursue goals that transcend gender differences, and those that unite women around issues specific to them as women. The latter encompass both "feminist" movements, which explicitly aim to achieve gender equality, and nonfeminist "women's" movements, which are organized to satisfy needs or make demands that stem from women's reproductive roles and familial responsibilities (Chinchilla 1993).

Feminist Movements

During most of the twentieth century, feminist movements were confined to a small segment of middle-class women whose activities and goals were alien to most Latin American women (Miller 1991). Lower-class and indigenous women often saw feminist discourse as at best irrelevant and at worst threatening to their daily lives, in which survival depended on their cooperation with men. Many middle-class women felt little resonance with feminist demands for employment parity, family planning programs, or divorce reform because they viewed these objectives as inconsistent with their roles as wives and mothers.

Not until the 1970s did the feminist movement gain more widespread appeal among Latin American women. Mexico City's selection to host the first UN International Women's Year Conference in 1975 increased the visibility of Latin American feminism within the region and internationally (Chinchilla

Cristina Fernández, the president of Argentina.

1993:46). The conference inaugurated a decade-long international effort to address women's needs and bring their issues to the forefront of public dialogue. The United Nations Decade for Women stimulated conferences throughout the region that brought women together to define their needs and to formulate strategies for addressing them. The ensuing debates among the various branches of the feminist movement, each of which had its own agenda and objectives, and the often heated discourse between feminist and nonfeminist women helped to raise consciousness on all sides (Miller 1991:201).

Some of the most potent critiques of the feminist movement have come from indigenous women who have raised concerns that the feminist focus on "gender" obscures important differences between indigenous and nonindigenous women (and men). Many indigenous scholars and activists have argued that gender inequality and oppression are products of colonialism, which eroded what was originally a reciprocal division of labor in which men and women had complementary and equally valued social roles. For example, Mapuche activists deplore the feminist focus on the concepts of gender and women's rights, which embody Western notions of individual autonomy that drive a wedge between the genders. They argue that a return to role complementarity would restore the lost equilibrium that previously existed between men and women in indigenous communities (Richards 2005).

In the wake of these debates, feminist movements have expanded their agendas to incorporate issues that reflect the race, class, and ethnic diversity of their membership and to increase their appeal to women who support conventional gender roles (Barrig 1991). Feminists have thereby continued the pattern set by their turn-of-the-century forebears who embraced feminine roles as a source of personal power and as platforms from which to agitate for social change (Korrol 1999:84). The theoretical contributions along these lines illustrate the diversity of perspectives that have given Latin American feminists an important voice within global feminist discourse that portends growing influence in the coming decades.

Mixed-Gender Movements

Latin American women have often joined men in political actions, ranging from short-lived spontaneous protests to long-term organized movements, that have operated both within and outside established political channels (Chinchilla 1993; Jaquette 1991a). Such activities have reflected the nature of the state and its responsiveness to popular demands; the availability of parties, unions, and other formal channels; and the social circumstances and class-based interests of the participants. As Thomas J. D'Agostino elucidates in Chapter 4, in many Latin American nations elites have maintained class and racial hierarchies through authoritarian governments that have limited popular participation. Whereas upper-class women have sometimes mobilized to support these regimes, many nonelite women from diverse racial, ethnic, and cultural backgrounds have participated in revolutionary struggles for democratization and social reform.

Early in the twentieth century, women typically supported revolutionary activities indirectly by preparing food, nursing the wounded, gathering intelligence, and providing other types of support for male combatants. The Cuban Revolution, in which women joined in the guerrilla activities, marked a turning point in women's revolutionary activity. The revolution's success in 1959 inspired growing numbers of women to participate, often as armed combatants, in the grassroots resistance movements that arose in Argentina, Brazil, El Salvador, Guatemala, Nicaragua, Peru, and Uruguay (Chinchilla 1993:41). Of those countries, in only one—Nicaragua—did the revolutionary forces succeed in changing the political system. In the others, their resistance movements provoked repressive government measures to regain "order," many of which led to authoritarian regimes that brutally repressed all forms of political opposition.

Whereas many women participated in regime-challenging movements on the political left, many others took part in right-wing movements that supported conservative measures aimed at maintaining the elite-dominated status quo. In Chile, for example, the "pots and pans" demonstrations of upper-middle- and upper-class women, who took to the streets to protest the rising cost of food, were instrumental in bringing down the socialist government of President Salvador Allende, which fell through a military coup that initiated the authoritarian regime of General Augusto Pinochet (Miller 1991:182; Korrol 1999:99).

Many of the movements in which women have joined forces with men have not involved direct challenges to regimes. As women have entered the workforce in growing numbers, they have come to play more important roles in strikes, work stoppages, and other forms of resistance against poor working conditions (Chinchilla 1993:43; Levenson-Estrada 1997). Urban labor struggles have involved both working-class women, who have channeled their protests through unions, and middle-class women, who have expressed their grievances through professional organizations. Women have also participated in various student protest movements. In 1968, for example, when the Mexican government responded to a strident student demonstration by shooting at the unarmed protestors, many of the students who were killed were young women (Miller 1991:6).

Similarly, indigenous and peasant women have joined with men to demand land reform, improved working conditions on plantations and mines, and other remedies to perceived injustices. In Bolivia, for example, indigenous Aymara and Quechua women have engaged in a century-long struggle to resist continual threats to their autonomy and the steady usurpation of their land (Cusicanqui 1990). In Chile, Mapuche women activists have taken an active role in resisting the Chilean state and advocating for the recognition of Mapuche rights (Richards 2005). In Guatemala, a movement has grown up around Rigoberta Menchú, a K'iché Maya Nobel Peace Prize recipient who has commanded international attention for her efforts to draw attention to the plight of indigenous Guatemalans. Although her 2007 bid for the Guatemalan presidency was unsuccessful, she has remained at the center of indigenous political participation. Other examples of indigenous women's struggles include the activities of the Bolivian Housewives' Committee, who worked alongside men to protest labor conditions in the tin mines, and those of the Chiapan peasant women, who organized to protest the Mexican government's involvement in free-trade initiatives that threatened to impoverish the countryside (Barrios de Chungara 1978; Klubock 1997).

Yet with the exception of the Central American revolutionary struggles of the 1970s and 1980s, these resistance movements have incorporated only a small proportion of Latin American women. Most women, including those who sympathized with the political activists' ideals, have remained aloof from politics (Pires de Rio Caldeira 1990:50). In a context in which women are defined exclusively as wives and mothers, women face a host of barriers to political activity, including opposition from male partners who demand their wives' constant presence in the household; male resistance to women's membership in their organizations; burdensome domestic and childcare responsibilities that limit their time, energy, and physical mobility; internalized images of politics as dangerous, useless, or simply inappropriate for women; and submissive self-conceptions that limit political agency. Indigenous women face additional obstacles that reflect their racial and cultural subordination, a product of the social hierarchy in which the intersection of indigeneity and gender is often uniquely disadvantageous. Given the pervasiveness of these obstacles to institutionalized political activity, it is not surprising that women's participation has more commonly taken alternative forms that are more consistent with their reproductive roles and their position within the gender division of labor (Jelin 1990:186).

Women's Movements

Recent decades have witnessed a burgeoning of grassroots movements in which women have been the primary or the sole participants. These movements react to conditions that hamper women's ability to perform their reproductive roles as wives and mothers or that threaten household survival. Their primary objective is to demand that the government rectify these conditions by providing needed services, transforming economic conditions, or abandoning oppressive political policies (Safa 1990:356).

Women's movements typically arise when institutionalized channels for participation are inoperative or are perceived as ineffective. Their creation signifies

This sign reading "Zero tolerance toward violence against women" is part of a campaign to combat violence against women, Santo Domingo, Dominican Republic

women's demands for incorporation into the political arena in a way that reaffirms their identity as women, particularly in their roles as custodians of family welfare (Schirmer 1993:32). In politicizing issues such as high food prices, unsafe drinking water, lack of sewerage and electricity, inadequate schools, and government cutbacks in health care services, these movements erode the traditional division between the private and public spheres (Jaquette 1991a:188). The boundary weakens when family concerns, traditionally viewed as beyond the scope of "normal" political debate, are defined as public issues and when women use their private roles as wives and mothers to legitimate their entry into the public world of politics (Chuchryk 1991:156).

Many women's movements emerge when women who share a common concern about a social issue in their community work through their social networks to publicize and gain support for their activities or to organize spontaneous demonstrations. Grounded in neighborhoods where women share common discourses and experiences that transcend ethnic, class, or religious differences, they typically involve issues such as cutbacks in basic government services that affect the entire community. This is one reason why poor women, whose economic disadvantage has traditionally muted their political voice, figure so prominently in many women's movements. Yet the primary basis around which poor women organize women's movements is their gender rather than their class position: although many are acutely conscious of the economic hardships that pervade their lives, they express their concerns as wives and mothers rather than as members of an impoverished class (Safa 1990:356).

Women's movements have taken various forms—depending on their objectives, their participants' circumstances, and the degree of involvement of sponsoring bodies, such as churches and international or local nongovernmental organizations. Most fall within two broadly defined categories: (1) neighborhood and community movements that focus on economic goals, and (2) human rights organizations that challenge repressive government policies. The former, which have cropped up throughout Latin America as a result of the economic crisis, address survival needs and demand essential government services. The latter, which have emerged in countries suffering under authoritarian regimes, address basic civic rights and demand political democratization. The crisis-born nature of both types of movements may explain their rapid explosion on the Latin American scene; it also helps to account for the widespread participation of women, particularly those from the lower classes who ordinarily would not enter the political arena (Safa 1990:357).

Women's economic movements have stemmed from diverse sources. Some have their roots in the squatter movements of the 1960s, in which women were often leaders in organizing the overnight "invasions" of empty land by homeless urban dwellers whose makeshift settlements often evolved into stable urban communities (Jelin 1990:189). Others owe their existence to the liberation theology wing of the Catholic Church, which offered safe space for women to hold meetings and helped secure foodstuffs, clothing, and other items for collective distribution (Miller 1991:196). Some movements arose when spontaneous demonstrations protesting rising food costs, inadequate neighborhood infrastructure, or the elimination of state-sponsored community services forged networks of women who had similar concerns and a shared commitment to assuage those problems.

Regardless of their source, these movements have aimed to ameliorate material conditions that impair women's domestic role performance. Some movements' strategies have been geared toward helping members survive the economic crisis by offering them new ways to generate income or to reduce the rising costs of basic commodities. The communal kitchens organized in Peru, Uruguay, and other Latin American countries, through which households join together to purchase and prepare food, represent one collective strategy for reducing consumption costs (Chuchryk 1991:154). Another common approach has been to organize protest demonstrations and pressure groups to demand government services. In communities throughout Latin America, women's movements have demanded basic urban services such as running water, sewerage, and electricity (Bennett 1995; Safa 1990:361). In nations such as Mexico and Argentina—where economic restructuring has reduced state spending on health care, education, and other community services—women's organizations have banded together to protest these cutbacks. Although these movements have met with varying degrees of success and have sometimes evoked heavy-handed treatment by governments aiming to silence women's protests, they have proved to be a valuable venue for translating women's private concerns into public discourse.

Women's human rights movements were galvanized by politically authoritarian regimes that sought to stamp out opposition by outlawing institutionalized political activities and brutally repressing any dissent against their policies. These regimes singled out trade union leaders, politicians, academicians, journalists, student activists, and anyone else considered subversive to the regime for imprisonment, torture, or murder. In Argentina, Chile, Guatemala, Uruguay, and elsewhere, many people were kidnapped by government agents who later denied any knowledge of their whereabouts. Public protest of these human rights violations was dangerous and often led to similar treatment for those brash enough to attempt it. Not surprisingly, those best able to form resistance organizations were those with the least political visibility; because women were viewed as apolitical guardians of family welfare, their activities were often immune to government scrutiny (Chuchryk 1993:87). Mothers' clubs and women's self-help organizations could operate in situations where men's organizations— even those with similar objectives—would be brutally repressed.

During the 1970s and 1980s, many women's organizations were formed to protest government abuses. In Chile, women's groups won international recognition for their plight by making *arpilleras* (tapestries) that depicted the regime's violence and distributing them surreptitiously to global markets (Agosin 1993:20). In Guatemala, the Mutual Support Group for the Reappearance of Our Sons, Fathers, Husbands and Brothers has engaged in a decades-long struggle to account for the 38,000 people who have disappeared since the late 1970s (Schirmer 1993:40–44). In Argentina, the Madres de la Plaza de Mayo risked and sometimes lost their lives through their courageous efforts to expose their government's widespread human rights violations (Bouvard 1994).

Women's economic and political movements have achieved varying degrees of success. In some cases, their issues and platforms have been adopted by governments or political parties that want women's support; in others, women's demands have been largely ignored or have been addressed symbolically by token gestures intended to mollify them without eliminating the root causes of their problems. Even when they have fallen short of their intended objectives, however, women's movements have profoundly affected their members' lives. In giving women a socially legitimate venue for entering the public arena, these movements have expanded women's horizons and provided them with a sense of personal agency (Chuchryk 1991:163). Women's participation has enabled them to acquire organizational skills and to forge social networks that decrease their isolation and augment their decisionmaking power within the household. Although most women have retained their basic commitment to their roles as wives and mothers, many have abandoned the submissive, self-sacrificing trappings of *marianismo* and now see themselves as empowered champions of family welfare. Such changes portend a transformation in gender roles and relationships that will entail greater autonomy and growing political leadership for subsequent generations of Latin American women.

Conclusion

The past fifty years have brought dramatic changes for Latin American women. Once symbolically confined to the household and the wife-mother role, women of all backgrounds are increasingly entering the public world of paid employment and political action. Their growing political and labor force participation has resulted from educational advances, declining fertility, and economic and political crises that have threatened the welfare of their families. This participation also both reflects and further stimulates the erosion of cultural ideologies that deem public participation to be inconsistent with women's reproductive roles. Women's public activities have often been legitimated by cultural discourse and by women themselves as necessary adjuncts to the successful performance of their domestic roles. In defining wage work and political participation as effective means not simply for self-fulfillment or needed social change, but also for caring for their families more effectively, Latin American women are developing their own unique role definitions that erode the rigid boundary between private and public life. In forging these new bases for their identities, Latin American women offer inspiring models for women around the world.

Notes

I want to thank Brianne Bigej for her assistance in preparing the data for this chapter.

1. As Thomas J. D'Agostino describes in Chapter 4, in 1976 a military junta overturned a democratically elected government and seized power in Argentina. During the seven-year dictatorship, the regime conducted a systematic campaign to eliminate left-wing opposition. Often called the "Dirty War" because it involved widespread human rights violations, the campaign began as an effort to quell the growing guerrilla violence in Argentina and was presented to the public as an effort to stamp out "subversives" and "terrorists." Yet while some of the people who were detained and "disappeared" were political revolutionaries, the vast majority were ordinary Argentine workers, intellectuals, and students who had violated no laws. Over 30,000 Argentines were imprisoned, tortured, and killed during this period. The Dirty War ended in 1983 when the regime, weakened by its humiliating defeat by the British in the Falklands War and unable to withstand the growing international pressure to eliminate human rights abuses, relinquished power.

2. According to this argument, for a corporation to stay in business in this globalizing era with countries such as China emerging as industrial giants, inexpensive nonunion labor is essential to corporate survival. To remain competitive, the argument would have it, firms must hire the least expensive labor possible, which compels them to hire women over men and to look beyond the United States to nations with lower wage levels and less generous worker benefits. Proponents of the *maquiladora* industry maintain that it is much better for the US economy for US companies to relocate their manufacturing operations to nearby Mexico, where they can more profitably maintain their links to other US companies that supply manufacturing inputs, than to faraway Asian sites, where manufacturing inputs are apt to be purchased from Asian firms, thus accelerating deindustrialization in the United States (Sklair 1993).

3. Some recent writings suggest that gender roles among the Aztecs may have involved more complementarity and parallelism than previous interpretations would suggest. For a discussion of these alternative perspectives, see Navarro (1999:10).

4. For a firsthand account of the conditions of life and work in São Paulo's early twentieth-century textile mills, see Veccia (1997:100–146).

5. Reported rates for Honduras in 1961 and 1974 were calculated differently from those reported by other Latin American countries, in a way that underestimates the actual rate of Honduran women's labor force participation. Rather than calculating the rate by comparing the number of wage-earning women to the number of women between the ages of twenty and sixty, as did the other countries, the Honduran census compared employed women to the whole female population. This produces a misleading rate because the relevant comparison should be confined to women of employment age and should not include children, adolescents, and older people, who are not normally members of the labor force. Had the Honduran census excluded the youth and older people, its rate would have risen by several percentage points, making it more similar to the rate of its neighbor, Guatemala. By 1999, the Honduran census had changed its procedure to make it conform to the rest of the Latin American countries, all of which calculated their rates by comparing employed women to the female population aged 15 years and older.

6. Honduras once again provides an exception to this trend, in part because of the way employment rates were calculated, leading to underestimates of men's as well as women's employment.

7. Countries excluded from Table 10.1 because 1960 data were unavailable showed similarly high rates of women's labor force participation during the late 1990s. These include Bolivia (40.5 percent), Cuba (31.7 percent), Dominican Republic (28.3 percent), El Salvador (44.7 percent), and Paraguay (26.1 percent).

8. Latin American country censuses typically measure contraceptive usage only among married women (Chant 2003), although "marriage" is often defined in a way that includes women cohabitating with male partners, regardless of the official status of their union. If sexually active single women were included in these census surveys, the reported use of contraception would likely be much higher.

▓ Bibliography

Agosin, Marjorie. "Introduction." In *Surviving Beyond Fear,* ed. Marjorie Agosin (New York: White Pine Press, 1993), pp. 15–28.

Anderson, Joan, and Martin de la Rosa. "Economic Survival Strategies of Poor Families on the Mexican Border." *Journal of Borderlands Studies* 6, no. 1 (1991): 51–68.

Appendini, Kirsten. "'From Where Have All the Flowers Come?' Women Workers in Mexico's Nontraditional Markets." In *Shifting Burdens: Gender and Agrarian Change Under Neoliberalism,* ed. Shahra Razavi (Bloomfield, CT: Kumarian Press, 2002), pp. 93–108.

Arizpe, Lourdes. "Women in the Informal Labor Sector." In *Women and National Development,* ed. Wellesley Editorial Committee (Chicago: University of Chicago Press, 1977), pp. 25–37.

———. "An Overview of Women's Education in Latin America and the Caribbean." In *The Politics of Women's Education,* eds. Jill Conway and Susan Bourgue (Ann Arbor: University of Michigan Press, 1993), pp. 171–182.

Bandy, Joe, and Bickham Mendez. "'A Place of Their Own': Women Organizers in the *Maquilas* of Nicaragua and Mexico." *Mobilization: An International Journal* 8, no. 2 (2003): 173–188.

Barrientos, Stephanie, Anna Bee, Ann Matear, and Isabel Vogel. *Women and Agribusiness: Working Miracles in the Chilean Fruit Export Sector.* London: Macmillan, 1999.

Barrig, Maruja. "The Difficult Equilibrium Between Bread and Roses: Women's Organizations and the Transition from Dictatorship to Democracy in Peru." In *The Women's Movement in Latin America,* ed. Jane Jaquette (Boulder: Westview Press, 1991), pp. 114–148.

Barrios de Chungara, Domitila, with Moema Viezzer. *Let Me Speak!* New York: Monthly Review Press, 1978.

Beechey, Veronica. "Women and Production: A Critical Analysis of Some Sociological Theories of Women's Work." In *Feminism and Materialism,* eds. Annette Kuhn and AnnMarie Wolpe (London: Routledge, 1978), pp. 155–197.

Beneria, Lourdes. "The Mexican Debt Crisis: Restructuring the Economy and the Household." In *Unequal Burden: Economic Crises, Persistent Poverty, and Women's Work,* eds. Lourdes Beneria and Shelly Feldman (Boulder: Westview Press, 1992), pp. 83–104.

Beneria, Lourdes, and Martha Roldan. *The Crossroads of Class and Gender.* Chicago: University of Chicago Press, 1987.

Bennett, Vivienne. "Gender, Class and Water: Women and the Politics of Water Service in Monterrey, Mexico." *Latin American Perspectives* 22, no. 2 (1995): 76–99.

Blumberg, Rae Lesser. "Income Under Female Versus Male Control." In *Gender, Family, and Economy: The Triple Overlap,* ed. Rae Lesser Blumberg (Newbury Park, CA: Sage, 1991), pp. 97–127.

Boserup, Ester. *Women's Role in Economic Development.* New York: St. Martin's Press, 1970.

Bouvard, Marguerite Guzman. *Revolutionizing Motherhood: The Mothers of the Plaza de Mayo.* Wilmington, DE: Scholarly Resources, 1994.

Buenaventura-Posso, Elisa, and Susan E. Brown. "Forced Transition from Egalitarianism to Male Dominance: The Bari of Colombia." In *Women and Colonization: Anthropological Perspectives,* eds. Mona Etienne and Eleanor Leacock (New York: Praeger, 1980), pp. 109–133.

Chant, Sylvia. *Women and Survival in Mexican Cities: Perspectives on Gender, Labour Markets and Low Income Households.* Manchester: Manchester University Press, 1991.

Chant, Sylvia, with Nikki Craske. *Gender in Latin America.* New Brunswick, NJ: Rutgers University Press, 2003.

Chinchilla, Norma Stoltz. "Gender and National Politics: Issues and Trends in Women's Participation in Latin American Movements." In *Researching Women in Latin*

America and the Caribbean, eds. Edna Acosta-Belén and Christine E. Bose (Boulder: Westview Press, 1993), pp. 37–54.

Chirot, Daniel. *Social Change in the Twentieth Century.* New York: Harcourt Brace Jovanovich, 1977.

Chuchryk, Patricia. "Feminist Anti-Authoritarian Politics: The Role of Women's Organizations in the Chilean Transition to Democracy." In *The Women's Movement in Latin America,* ed. Jane Jaquette (Boulder: Westview Press, 1991), pp. 149–184.

———. "Subversive Mothers: The Women's Opposition to the Military Regime in Chile." In *Surviving Beyond Fear,* ed. Marjorie Agosin (New York: White Pine Press, 1993), pp. 86–97.

Cockroft, James. *Mexico: Class Formation, Capital Accumulation, and the State.* New York: Monthly Review Press, 1983.

Cravey, Altha J. *Women and Work in Mexico's Maquiladoras.* Lanham, MD: Rowman & Littlefield, 1998.

Cusicanqui, Silvia Rivera. "Indigenous Women and Community Resistance: History and Memory." In *Women and Change in Latin America,* ed. Elizabeth Jelin (London: Zed Books, 1990), pp. 151–183.

ECLAC (Economic Commission for Latin America and the Caribbean). *The Decade for Women in Latin America and the Caribbean: Background and Prospects.* Santiago: UN, 1988.

Etienne, Mona, and Eleanor Leacock. "Introduction." In *Women and Colonization: Anthropological Perspectives,* eds. Mona Etienne and Eleanor Leacock (New York: Praeger, 1980), pp. 1–24.

Fernandez-Kelly, Maria Patricia. *For We Are Sold: I and My People.* Albany: SUNY Press, 1983.

Fuentes, Annette, and Barbara Ehrenreich. *Women in the Global Factory.* New York: South End Press, 1983.

Gailey, Christina Ward. "Evolutionary Perspectives on Gender Hierarchy." In *Analyzing Gender: A Handbook of Social Science Research,* eds. Beth Hess and Myra Marx Ferree (Newbury Park, CA: Sage, 1987), pp. 22–67.

Gregory, Peter. *The Myth of Market Failure.* Baltimore: Johns Hopkins University Press, 1986.

Jaquette, Jane. "Conclusion: Women and the New Democratic Politics." In *The Women's Movement in Latin America,* ed. Jane Jaquette (Boulder: Westview Press, 1991a), pp. 185–208.

———. "Introduction." In *The Women's Movement in Latin America,* ed. Jane Jaquette (Boulder: Westview Press, 1991b), pp. 1–17.

Jelin, Elizabeth. "Citizenship and Identity: Final Reflections." In *Women and Change in Latin America,* ed. Elizabeth Jelin (London: Zed Books, 1990), pp. 184–207.

Klubock, Thomas Miller. "Morality and Good Habits: The Construction of Gender and Class in the Chilean Copper Mines, 1904–1951." In *The Gendered Worlds of Latin American Women Workers,* eds. John D. French and Daniel James (Durham, NC: Duke University Press, 1997), pp. 232–263.

Korrol, Virginia Sánchez. "Women in Nineteenth- and Twentieth-Century Latin America and the Caribbean." In *Women in Latin America and the Caribbean: Restoring Women to History,* eds. Marysa Navarro and Virginia Sánchez Korrol (Bloomington: Indiana University Press, 1999), pp. 59–106.

Larguia, Isabel, and John Dumoulin. "Women's Equality and the Cuban Revolution." In *Women and Change in Latin America,* eds. June Nash and Helen Safa (South Hadley, MA: Bergin & Garvey, 1986), pp. 344–368.

Levenson-Estrada, Deborah. "The Loneliness of Working-Class Feminism: Women in the 'Male World' of Labor Unions, Guatemala City, 1970s." In *The Gendered*

Worlds of Latin American Women Workers, eds. John D. French and Daniel James (Durham, NC: Duke University Press, 1997), pp. 208–231.

Lustig, Nora. *Mexico: The Remaking of an Economy.* Washington, DC: Brookings Institution Press, 1992.

Macias, Anna. *Against All Odds: The Feminist Movement in Mexico to 1940.* Westport: Greenwood Press, 1982.

Miller, Francesca. *Latin American Women and the Search for Social Justice.* Hanover, NH: University Press of New England, 1991.

Nash, June. "Aztec Women: The Transition from Status to Class in Empire and Colony." In *Women and Colonization: Anthropological Perspectives,* eds. Mona Etienne and Eleanor Leacock (New York: Praeger, 1980), pp. 134–148.

———. "The Impact of the Changing International Division of Labor on Different Sectors of the Labor Force." In *Women, Men and the International Division of Labor,* eds. June Nash and Maria Patricia Fernandez-Kelly (Albany: State University of New York Press, 1983), pp. 3–38.

Navarro, Marysa. "Women in Pre-Columbian and Colonial Latin America and the Caribbean." In *Women in Latin America and the Caribbean: Restoring Women to History,* eds. Marysa Navarro and Virginia Sánchez Korrol (Bloomington: Indiana University Press, 1999), pp. 5–57.

Perelli, Carina. "Putting Conservatism to Good Use: Women and Unorthodox Politics in Uruguay, from Breakdown to Transition." In *The Women's Movement in Latin America,* ed. Jane Jaquette (Boulder: Westview Press, 1991), pp. 95–113.

Pires de Rio Caldeira, Teresa. "Women, Daily Life and Politics." In *Women and Change in Latin America,* ed. Elizabeth Jelin (London: Zed Books, 1990), pp. 47–78.

Psacharopoulos, George, and Zafiris Tzannatos. *Case Studies on Women's Employment and Pay in Latin America: Overview and Methodology.* Washington, DC: World Bank, 1992.

Richards, Patricia. "The Politics of Gender, Human Rights, and Being Indigenous in Chile." *Gender and Society* 19, no. 2 (2005): 199–220.

Rothstein, Frances. *Three Different Worlds: Women, Men, and Children in an Industrializing Community.* Westport: Greenwood Press, 1982.

Ruiz, Vicki. "Mexican Women and the Multinationals: The Packaging of the Border Industrialization Program." Paper prepared for the conference "Historical Perspectives on American Labor," Ithaca, New York, April 1988.

Safa, Helen. "Women's Social Movements in Latin America." *Gender and Society* 4, no. 3 (1990): 354–369.

———. *The Myth of the Male Breadwinner: Women and Industrialization in the Caribbean.* Boulder: Westview Press, 1995.

Saffioti, Heleieth. "Female Labor and Capitalism in the United States and Brazil." In *Women Cross-Culturally: Change and Challenge,* ed. Ruby Rohrlich-Leavitt (The Hague: Mouton, 1975), pp. 59–94.

Schirmer, Jennifer. "'Those Who Die for Life Cannot Be Called Dead': Women and Human Rights Protest in Latin America." In *Surviving Beyond Fear,* ed. Marjorie Agosin (New York: White Pine Press, 1993), pp. 31–57.

Schmink, Marianne. "Women and Urban Industrial Development in Brazil." In *Women and Change in Latin America,* eds. June Nash and Helen Safa (South Hadley, MA: Bergin & Garvey, 1986), pp. 136–164.

Scott, Katherine. "Women in the Labor Force in Bolivia: Participation and Earnings." In *Case Studies on Women's Employment and Pay in Latin America,* eds. George Psacharopoulos and Zafiris Tzannatos (Washington, DC: World Bank, 1992), pp. 21–38.

Silverblatt, Irene. "'The Universe Has Turned Inside Out . . . There Is No Justice for Us Here': Andean Women Under Spanish Rule." In *Women and Colonization: Anthropological Perspectives,* eds. Mona Etienne and Eleanor Leacock (New York: Praeger, 1980), pp. 149–185.

Sklair, Leslie. *Assembling for Development: The Maquila Industry in Mexico and the United States.* San Diego: Center for US-Mexican Studies, 1993.

Stevens, Evelyn. "Marianismo: The Other Face of Machismo in Latin America." In *Female and Male in Latin America,* ed. Ann Pescatello (Pittsburgh: University of Pittsburgh Press, 1973), pp. 89–102.

Stromquist, Nelly. *Women and Education in Latin America.* Boulder: Lynne Rienner, 1992.

Tiano, Susan. "The Public-Private Dichotomy: Theoretical Perspectives on Women in Development." *Social Science Journal* 21, no. 4 (1984):11–28.

———. "Gender, Work, and World Capitalism: Third World Women's Role in Development." In *Analyzing Gender: A Handbook of Social Science Research,* eds. Beth Hess and Myra Marx Ferree (Newbury Park, CA: Sage, 1987), pp. 216–243.

———. *Patriarchy on the Line: Labor, Gender, and Ideology in the Mexican Maquila Industry.* Philadelphia: Temple University Press, 1994.

———. "The Changing Gender Composition of the *Maquila* Work Force Along the US-Mexico Border." In *Women and Change at the US-Mexico Border: Mobility, Labor, and Activism,* eds. Doreen Mattingly and Ellen R. Hansen (Tucson: University of Arizona Press, 2006), pp. 73–90.

Tiano, Susan, and Carolina Ladino. "Dating, Mating, and Motherhood: Identity Construction Among Mexican Maquila Workers." *Environment and Planning A* 31, no. 2 (1999): 305–325.

Towner, Margaret. "Monopoly Capitalism and Women's Work During the Porfiriato." In *Women in Latin America,* eds. William Bollinger et al. (Riverside, CA: Latin American Perspectives, 1979), pp. 47–62.

United Nations. *The World's Women 1970–1990: Trends and Statistics.* New York: UN, 1991.

Vaughan, Mary. "Women, Class, and Education in Mexico, 1880–1928." In *Women in Latin America,* eds. William Bollinger et al. (Riverside, CA: Latin American Perspectives, 1979), pp. 63–80.

Veccia, Theresa R. "'My Duty as a Woman': Gender Ideology, Work, and Working-Class Women's Lives in São Paulo, Brazil, 1900–1950." In *The Gendered Worlds of Latin American Women Workers,* eds. John D. French and Daniel James (Durham, NC: Duke University Press, 1997).

Wilkie, James, ed. *Statistical Abstract of Latin America,* vol. 38. Los Angeles: UCLA Latin American Center, 2002.

11

Education and Development

Stephen Franz and Robert F. Arnove

The integral relationship between education and development has gained substantial recognition in recent decades. Throughout the history of Latin America, education has functioned largely to maintain the status quo and to serve purposes determined by colonial powers or state authorities and elite groups. René de la Pedraja and Thomas J. D'Agostino point out in Chapters 3 and 4, respectively, that these purposes often ran counter to the interests of the majority.

During the colonial period, as Hannah Stewart-Gambino shows in Chapter 12, education served primarily to propagate the Catholic religion. Also, a small number of civil servants were trained to administer the Spanish and Portuguese Empires. Following the various wars of independence (1810–1825) that liberated South and Central America from foreign rule, leaders looked to education to help create a sense of nationhood in newly emergent states. In countries such as Argentina, Chile, and Uruguay, which received large influxes of immigrants from Europe in the latter half of the nineteenth century, education—much as in the United States—was used by state authorities to forge national unity. Kevin A. Yelvington discusses the influence of immigrants in Chapter 9.

Although education was viewed by many nineteenth-century policymakers and educators, such as Domingo Faustino Sarmiento of Argentina and Andrés Bello of Venezuela, as a "civilizing" influence in the creation of citizens, the notion of mass-based public education systems available to all, from pre-primary through higher education, remained an elusive goal up to the second half of the twentieth century. Formal education systems primarily served and benefited the children of the wealthy and powerful, particularly urban males. This largely, but not totally, changed in the period following World War II.

Beginning in the 1950s, social scientists and national governments began to view education in a different light. The principal shift in focus was from a concern with the political role of education in nation-state building to its economic role in contributing to the industrialization and technological development of a society. In the context of economic development, investigated in greater detail by Scott G. McKinney in Chapter 6, schooling was viewed as a principal agency for teaching the knowledge, values, and attitudes that would modernize a society and undergird an industrial economy. Discussions of expenditures on public education as an investment in "human capital" or in the improvement of the skills of individuals that would contribute significantly to the economic growth of a country appeared in the work of economists including Nobel laureate Theodore William Schultz (1964). Previously, education had been viewed as a social service expenditure or as "consumption" that did not contribute to the total output of goods and services of a society as measured by the gross national product (GNP).

From the 1950s on, the notion of "development" emerged as a priority goal to be pursued by all governments in the so-called third world as did the idea that education was the key that could open the door to the modernization and development of societies (Coleman 1965). As we point out in this chapter, ideas of development have evolved as have views concerning the role of education in sociopolitical change and economic growth.

▧ Changing Notions of Development

In the post–World War II period, definitions of the term *development* passed through at least three stages (Fuenzalida 1985). During the first stage, development was defined primarily in terms of the expansion of an economy, of growth in the GNP of a country—which, in turn, was heavily dependent on acquiring the advanced scientific and technological knowledge of the industrialized countries of the North. By the end of the 1960s, a second stage emerged in which development was viewed not only in terms of the expansion of the productive capacity of a country, but also with regard to: (1) the more equitable distribution of the expanded output of goods and services, and (2) the democratic participation of the majority of citizens in decisions concerning the direction and nature of change. During this stage, attention was also given to the notion of preserving national culture and safeguarding the political sovereignty of a country. As Jacquelyn Chase and Susan E. Place show in Chapter 8, development was further defined in the 1970s (the third stage) to incorporate respect for the environment and the conservation of nonrenewable natural resources as well as more equitable relations between the countries of the South and those of the North.

In the 1980s, further elaboration of the definition of development included the notion of sustainability, that institutional arrangements should be in place that guaranteed a country could continue to maintain progressive reforms to benefit a majority of its people. Closely coupled with an emphasis on sustainability was a concern with providing local communities and grassroots organizations with the skills and resources that would enable them to initiate and successfully implement efforts that would improve the health, education, and general well-being of the least privileged members of society.

As international definitions of development changed so did conceptions of the role of education in society. The goals of education from 1950 to 1970 tended to emphasize the importance of technology and the sciences in national development. Attention was given more to the quality of education than to equality of educational opportunity, and higher education was emphasized. By 1970, it was evident that the goals of national development were better served by expanding access to schooling and democratizing opportunities for previously excluded populations to advance to the highest levels of education. In the 1970s and early 1980s, governments accorded priority to the provision of primary education and the first years of secondary education as well as to literacy and adult basic education. The international debt crisis of the 1980s and 1990s, however, hampered many Latin American countries from achieving these goals. In recent years, the notion of efficiency has achieved preeminence, and policies have begun to emphasize the decentralization and privatization of education systems. Hence, higher education and adult education do not enjoy the priority that they were given in previous decades.

Education and Technology

The transfer of technology, scientific institutions, and industry to underdeveloped countries requires the development of educational infrastructure capable of supporting the new technologies, sciences, and organizations. Secondary education, vocational education, and higher education are particularly important in this transformation.[1]

For his New Frontier policy, President John F. Kennedy adopted the growth theories of the 1950s, combined them with a new emphasis on sustained economic development in democratic societies, and empowered the US Agency for International Development (USAID) to implement the plan—which has served as the principal model for development agencies worldwide. In Latin America, USAID sponsored community development programs that emphasized technical education in Brazil, Chile, the Dominican Republic, Ecuador, El Salvador, Honduras, Mexico, Panama, and Venezuela.

Latin America responded to the new emphasis on technical education with the Conference on Education and Economic and Social Development for Latin America held in Santiago, Chile, in March 1962. Latin American education ministers, along with officials from the United Nations, attempted to respond to two fundamental questions: (1) How can economic development contribute to the improvement of educational systems? and (2) How can educational systems accelerate economic and social development in Latin America? The ministers believed the answers to these questions could be found in the development of secondary and higher education, technical and professional training, and improved teacher education.

During the 1960s, enrollments at the secondary and higher education levels increased significantly worldwide. Expansion of the Latin American secondary and higher education systems exceeded that of all other developing areas of the world. For example, between 1975 and 1985, enrollments at the secondary level in all developing areas increased from 31.4 percent to 37.6 percent whereas, in Latin America, the secondary education sector expanded from 36.9 percent to 51.1 percent. Growth in enrollments in higher education during that period was even more significant. In all developing areas, higher education enrollments increased from 4.1 percent to 6.1 percent; in Latin America, enrollments increased from 11.8 percent to 15.6 percent. Between 1960 and 1970, enrollment in secondary education more than doubled, and enrollment in higher education almost tripled (see Table 11.1).

Enrollments in vocational education programs also increased in the 1960s. The cases of Brazil and Colombia are notable. In 1965 in Brazil, 380,459 students were enrolled in vocational programs; in 1971, that number rose to 797,487 students. Expansion of vocational education in Colombia was also considerable, increasing from 96,834 students in 1965 to 173,737 in 1972.

Increases in educational expenditures paralleled the growth of school enrollments. These increases in expenditure, however, were not uniform at secondary and higher education levels. Some countries chose to invest heavily in secondary (including vocational) education, whereas others emphasized higher education (see Table 11.2).

Table 11.1 Enrollment Numbers (in thousands) and Percentages (of total enrollment) by Level of Education in Latin America, 1960 and 1970

Level	1960	1970
Primary		
Number	26,799	43,913
Percentage	85.3	78.0
Secondary		
Number	4,053	10,800
Percentage	12.9	19.2
Higher		
Number	570	1,615
Percentage	1.8	2.9

Source: UN Educational, Scientific, and Cultural Organization. *UNESCO Statistical Yearbook, 1974* (Paris: UNESCO, 1974), tables 2.1 and 2.2.

Table 11.2 Percentage of Total Public Education Expenditure by Level in Five Latin American Countries, 1965 and 1970

Country	Primary	Secondary	Higher
Argentina			
1965	55.0	26.4	18.6
1970	30.4	30.3	21.0
Ecuador			
1965	41.3	21.1	32.3
1970	45.9	41.1	9.9
Mexico			
1965	42.0	12.3	12.6
1970	50.0	27.2	10.4
Uruguay			
1965	44.9	39.8	15.3
1970	45.1	30.4	19.0
Venezuela			
1965	43.2	18.2	19.7
1970	38.3	20.6	25.5

Source: UN Educational, Scientific, and Cultural Organization. *UNESCO Statistical Yearbook, 1974* (Paris: UNESCO, 1974), table 6.3.

Note: The figures do not add up to 100 percent because administrative expenses, adult education, and preprimary education costs are not included.

As shown in Tables 11.1 and 11.2, enrollments and expenditures expanded at the secondary and higher education levels at the expense of the primary level. Between 1960 and 1970, total enrollments at the primary level, as a percentage of total enrollment, dropped from 85.3 percent to 78.0 percent. This means that a greater number of students were going on to higher levels, and not all students were concentrated at the primary level. Decreases were most apparent in Argentina where total government expenditures for primary education declined dramatically from 55.0 percent in 1965 to 30.4 percent in 1970.

Social scientists, however, also argued that the implementation of educational policies favoring technical, secondary, and higher education benefited only a small segment of the total population, thus widening the gap between the rich and the poor. They further argued that policies emphasizing technical, secondary, and higher education in the 1960s had limited participation by most of the population in the decisionmaking process because decisions were made by government bureaucrats and outside technical advisers.

Finally, critics were concerned that material presented in vocational education programs was not relevant to local realities and that the equipment provided was outdated. Furthermore, curricula employed in rural areas had an urban bias. Generally, textbooks at all levels often presented images associated with a US middle-class lifestyle that was unfamiliar to Latin American students.

Children in a classroom in Manabí, Ecuador.

By the early 1970s, Latin American education ministers began to discuss these and other issues related to the changing emphasis in the region's education. At the Conference of Ministers of Education and Those Responsible for the Application of Science and Technology to Development in Latin America and the Caribbean held December 6–15, 1971, at Caraballeda, Venezuela, the ministers expressed concern with the growing economic disparities between socioeconomic classes. They recognized that those who benefited most were the children of middle-class families and not children whose parents were members of the working class.

■ Expanding Educational Opportunities

In light of these concerns, Latin American policy planners shifted emphasis away from technical education toward universal access to primary education and literacy. At a 1979 regional meeting of Latin American education ministers, participants developed the Principal Project for Latin America and the Caribbean. The objectives of the project redefined the goals of development and education: to extend compulsory basic education from eight to ten years, to eliminate illiteracy, and to improve the quality of basic education (Reimers 1991).

During the early 1980s, Latin American nations made some progress toward achieving these goals. Some nations extended basic compulsory education to nine or ten years, among them Costa Rica, El Salvador, Panama, and Venezuela. These efforts to expand access to education were closely related to increasing governmental expenditures. In 1980, a number of Latin American governments spent as much as 6 percent of their GNP on education (UNESCO 1993:table 4.1). By 1990, however, only eight of twenty Latin American nations had extended compulsory basic education to at least eight years, compared to six nations in 1985. Efforts to expand access have continued and by 2005 requirements ranged from six to twelve years across the region, with only four countries (Honduras, Jamaica, Nicaragua, and Panama) requiring just six years of formal education (Vegas and Petrow 2008:121).

Among the most impressive achievements of the Principal Project were the gains made in the fight against illiteracy. During the 1980s, numerous Latin American countries sponsored literacy programs directed at illiterate adult populations, including Argentina, Chile, Colombia, Ecuador, Venezuela, El Salvador, Nicaragua, Panama, Cuba, Mexico, and the Dominican Republic. Most notable were the efforts of Cuba and Nicaragua where accomplishments in extending literacy occurred in the midst of social and political revolutions.

In Cuba after 1959, a key element of Fidel Castro's revolution was the extension of social services to all sectors of the population. Education, including literacy, was seen as essential to the development of a socialist society in which every citizen had a moral responsibility to foster the country's development. By the end of the Cold War in 1989, the literacy rate in Cuba had reached 97 percent, one of the highest in the world.

Similarly, Nicaragua's Sandinista revolution in 1979 included a crusade against illiteracy as one of the key tenets of its social project. These efforts, undertaken during the social and economic turmoil of the initial months of the revolution, reduced the illiteracy rate from 50 percent to less than 25 percent in only nine months. The magnitude of the campaign, the speed with which it was conducted, the difficult conditions under which it was pursued, and its impressive results mark the Nicaraguan literacy crusade as one of the most ambitious ever attempted.

By the late 1980s, despite international goals to improve the quality of basic education and increased spending by Latin American countries, it was evident that little had been accomplished in expanding access to educational opportunities. Unfortunately, the goals of the Principal Project (universal primary schooling, universal literacy, and improved educational quality) had not been tackled jointly. Critics began to realize that the three goals had to be pursued simultaneously to achieve significant results. Further, various literacy programs and campaigns had defined literacy differently. Some definitions were age based, others included math skills, others evaluated reading and writing ability, and others were based on the number of years in school. It became apparent that all programs had to function under the same definitions. Without a clear understanding of the scope of the problem in Latin America, it was difficult for

School children in Cuba.

planners to develop, implement, and evaluate programs designed to eradicate illiteracy (Torres 1990).

Throughout Latin America in 1960, less than 60 percent of primary school–age children were enrolled; in 1999, 92 percent were enrolled. Currently, 84 percent of students have "survival rates" to fifth grade. In Nicaragua, Guatemala, El Salvador, the Dominican Republic, Colombia, and Paraguay 30 percent or more fail to reach fifth grade. With regard to gender and educational attainment, only in Bolivia, Peru, and, especially, Guatemala do girls have a lower survival rate (ECLAC 2005:84). Repetition rates—direct indicators of educational quality—remained high despite educators' attempts to advance students to the next grade more consistently (see Table 11.3). Overall, the first grade repetition rate for Latin America was 42 percent at the beginning of the 1990s. At the beginning of the twenty-first century, the repetition rate for Latin America for first grade through sixth grade was 16.4 percent (Wolff, Schiefelbein, and Schiefelbein 2002), costing an estimated $4.6 billion per year (Wolff and de Moura Castro 2003). The rate, which was as high as 42 percent for Brazil at the end of the 1990s, has dropped to 19 percent due to progressive education and social policies of recent years. These policies include payments to families for their children to stay in school (Arnove et al. 2003; UNESCO 2011c). UNESCO 2007 data indicate that the first grade repetition rate for a sample of twelve countries in the region had been lowered to 10.5 percent (UNESCO 2011b).

Repetition rates are even higher among at-risk students living under difficult conditions such as in urban slums and isolated rural areas. According to Laurence Wolff, Ernesto Schiefelbein, and Jorge Valenzuela (1994), students from the lowest socioeconomic stratum are more likely to repeat a grade than children in higher-income brackets. Those living in rural areas and members of indigenous populations are even more likely to repeat a grade than their urban counterparts. For example, in Chile, the highest repetition rates are found in the province with the largest indigenous population. Similarly, indigenous

Table 11.3 Latin American Repetition Ratios and Completion Rates in Primary Education and Enrollment Ratios in Secondary Education (percentage)

	First Grade Repeaters 2008		Primary Entrants Reaching Grade 5	Secondary Enrollment Ratio 2008	
	M	F	2007	M	F
Argentina	11	8[c]	96[b]	80	90[c]
Bolivia	1	1	85	82	80
Chile	4	3	96[b]	89	92
Colombia	6	4	85	86	95
Costa Rica	16	13	96	87	92
Cuba	0	0	96	92	91
Dominican Republic	6[c]	4[c]	68[a]	67	81
Ecuador	3[c]	3[c]	82[b]	79	83[d]
El Salvador	15	11	80	63	64
Guatemala	26	23	71	58	55
Honduras	13	11	78	57	72
Mexico	7	5	94	87	93
Nicaragua	22	18	51	64	72
Panama	10	7	87	68	74
Paraguay	9	6	84	65	68
Peru	5	4	87	89	89
Uruguay	16	12	95	82	94
Venezuela	6	4	84	77	85
Latin America[e]	10	8	84	86	93

Sources: UN Educational, Scientific, and Cultural Organization, Institute for Statistics (UIS), online database, tables 5, 9, and 12. 2011. www.stats.uis.unesco.org.

Notes: a. 2005
b. Data from 2006.
c. Data from 2007.
d. Data from 2008.
e. Each country has been weighted equally for regional averages.

children in Bolivia are twice as likely to repeat as nonindigenous children. In many cases, indigenous children also have more difficulties because the language spoken at home may not be the same as the language of instruction. Rates of repetition for girls tend to be lower than those for boys. Current data indicate that the repetition rates for boys exceeded those of girls in every country in the region (UNESCO 2011b; see Table 11.3).

Other factors contributing to the lack of progress in attempts to improve the quality of education are low teacher salaries, short school years, lack of textbooks, dilapidated schools, and high seasonal absenteeism associated with agricultural activity. These conditions are especially characteristic of students living in impoverished or marginalized circumstances.

Also contributing to low student retention and promotion rates are requirements in many Latin American countries that students pass standardized national examinations before proceeding to the next level of education. Because of the disparity in the quality of education between rural and urban areas, many rural students—as well as students who attend inferior urban schools—fail to pass these examinations and either drop out or repeat the same grade. This pattern is evident from the beginning of primary school. In recent years, fewer than 70 percent of those students enrolled in the first grade completed the fifth grade in Nicaragua, Guatemala, El Salvador, the Dominican Republic, Colombia, and Paraguay (ECLAC 2005).

As stated previously, important urban and rural differences exist in equality of educational opportunities and outcomes. According to Patricia Muñiz, 60 percent of fourteen-year-olds in rural Mexico were attending school, compared with 84 percent for the same age group attending schools in urban areas. These figures become more disparate for fifteen- and sixteen-year-olds. Attendance figures for fifteen- and sixteen-year-olds in rural areas were 41 percent and 29 percent; in urban areas, these figures are 69 percent and 61 percent, respectively (Muñiz 2000).

In Argentina, Chile, Paraguay, Peru, and Uruguay, schools in towns and cities have children from much more advantaged backgrounds than do rural schools—and by a large margin (UNESCO 2008:10–11). This pattern is typical of the region as a whole. Not only do urban and well-to-do students have access to better school facilities, but they also enjoy the advantage of better trained teachers. According to Martin Carnoy, one example of the strong relationship between quality of teachers and test scores is that of Mexico where "one of the most important correlates of [the] lower score[s] is teacher quality . . . also teacher quality has a bigger impact in indigenous schools than rural non-indigenous schools" (2009:519).

■ Education and the Debt Crisis

Latin America's inability to improve the quality of basic education in the 1980s was exacerbated by the region's debt crisis. As Scott G. McKinney points out in Chapter 6, the 1980s have been called the lost decade for development in Latin America. Economic expansion, experienced at high rates from the 1950s through the 1970s, slowed considerably in the 1980s and 1990s. In the 1960s, the average annual GNP growth rate for Latin American economies was 5.7 percent. In the 1970s, the average growth rate was 5.6 percent, despite difficulties caused by the oil crisis. By the 1980s, the average annual GNP growth rate for

Latin American countries had dropped to 1.3 percent.[2] The falling GNP translated into decreasing per capita income for the majority of Latin Americans. On average, Latin American per capita incomes fell by 9 percent. In Argentina, per capita income fell 22 percent whereas in Brazil it fell only 5 percent.

In response to the ever-deepening economic crisis, during the 1990s most Latin American governments adopted the neoliberal fiscal stabilization and economic adjustment policies promoted by international donor agencies such as the International Monetary Fund (IMF) and the World Bank. These policies have led to a drastic reduction in the state's role in social spending, deregulation of the economy, and liberalization of import policies. The educational counterparts of these policies have included moves to decentralize and privatize public school systems.

Although neoliberal policies are designed to reduce a country's fiscal deficits and external debt while bringing inflation under control, they have also contributed to deepening poverty in the region. In many countries, the social safety net provided by government-subsidized services in health, education, and other basic areas has been diminished. Consequently, social class differences have intensified. In the 1980s in metropolitan Buenos Aires, 25 percent of the most impoverished households lost 15 percent of their incomes whereas 5 percent of the wealthiest households increased their incomes by almost 20 percent. In the metropolitan areas of Rio de Janeiro and São Paulo, 25 percent of the most impoverished households lost almost 13 percent of their incomes whereas 5 percent of the wealthiest gained approximately 25 percent. Income losses not only were experienced by the poorest of the poor; 50 percent of the households located in the middle of the scale lost between 3 percent and 10 percent of their incomes.

As a result, in Latin America class structures have become more polarized, with the rich and poor sectors separated by an increasingly wider gap. Poverty is not a product of an economic crisis. Rather, it is the result of new growth strategies adopted by most countries in the region. The division between rich and poor has widened considerably, and distribution of wealth is a key issue in analyzing the social situation. The wealthy benefit from the growth strategies, leaving only a few to enjoy one of the highest standards of living in the world, similar to the privileged status that whites had under apartheid South Africa (Lopez 2005:1). This has negatively impacted the living conditions of the rural indigenous populations in Bolivia, Ecuador, Peru, Guatemala, and northeastern Brazil. Recent civil wars and natural disasters have exacerbated inequalities in wealth distribution in countries such as Nicaragua, El Salvador, Honduras, and Haiti. The majority of the population in these countries live in poverty. According to CEPAL (2005:74), the regional average rate of poverty in 2004 was 41.7 percent (36.7 percent urban and 58.1 percent rural). With regard to extreme poverty, the average was 17.4 percent (12.4 percent urban and 34.0 percent rural). Given this context, it is not surprising that these countries have the highest rates of illiteracy and dropout rates in the region. This increasing gap between the rich and poor has significant consequences for equality of educational opportunities and outcomes. According to Carnoy, "The more equal the income distribution and the higher the GDP per capita in a country, the higher students' average test scores" (2009:513).

It should be noted that, since the late 1990s, educational expenditures once again have been on the rise in Latin America. The overall funding picture, however, is more complicated. According to a report by the International Commission on Education, Equity and Economic Competitiveness, by the end of the 1990s governments were, on average, investing 4.6 percent of GNP on education each year, a figure superior to 3.9 percent for developing countries and only slightly inferior to the 5.1 percent invested by developed countries (Bonal and Ferrer 2007). However, these figures are deceptive because they do not take into account the age distribution of Latin American populations. Given the disproportionately large number of school-age children, the countries of the region would need to invest a greater percentage of GNP to achieve adequate levels of education expenditures per child. Furthermore, achieving a workforce with a level of education appropriate for countries with comparable incomes would require an additional investment of 0.5 percent per year over twenty-five years (PREAL 2001:23; CEPAL 2002). Accomplishing these goals is problematic in light of diminished economic growth in the region and the onset of the global financial crisis in 2009.

Not only have the numbers of the poor increased and income disparities grown, but structural adjustment policies have not always lessened the debt of countries in the region. Many countries are spending more and more on debt reduction to the detriment of education. From 2006 to 2008, external debt rose from US$690 billion to US$807 billion and represented 18.8 percent of the region's gross domestic product (GDP; Latin Focus 2009).

With the economic downturn of recent years, all Latin American nations have experienced decreases in educational expenditures in terms of GNP and total governmental expenditure (TGE). Under neoliberalism, significant improvements in education spending that took place during the 1960s and 1970s were effectively negated by drastic spending cuts. According to Fernando Reimers, "On average, [unweighted] per capita expenditures in education in Latin America increased by 4.29 percent per year between 1975 and 1980, while they decreased by 6.14 percent between 1980 and 1985. The progress in educational finance made in the seventies was undone in the eighties" (1991:332).

The spending cuts in education in Latin America first affected recurrent expenditures such as the purchase of teaching materials and the maintenance of school buildings. Because of the lack of funding, reforms designed in the 1970s and early 1980s were not implemented. Over the following decade, teachers worked from curricula developed in the 1960s and with pedagogy designed to confront the challenges of the 1960s classroom.

Decreased expenditures, outdated pedagogies and curricula, and restricted access all contributed to the general decline in the quality of education. Low teachers' salaries were also a factor. The real value of teachers' salaries decreased steadily as currencies were devalued and inflation increased during the economic turmoil of the 1980s and 1990s. In many Latin American nations, teachers are paid little more than domestic employees and, in Nicaragua, teachers are receiving even less.

Despite claims that teachers, given their long vacations and short workdays, actually are paid relatively better than workers with similar qualifications, many are unable to support their families. In no Latin American country did teachers' salaries exceed 60 percent of total family income in 2000. According to Organization for Economic Cooperation and Development (OECD) data, teachers in Argentina, Mexico, Brazil, and Uruguay receive salaries that are less than one-half of those earned by teachers in industrially developed countries (OECD 2000). Furthermore, a UNESCO (2008) survey found that most teachers express a low level of satisfaction with their salaries and consider their professional status lower than that of other professionals with similar educational qualifications.

In recent years, many teachers have left the profession for higher-paying jobs. The exodus of teachers and the weeks and months of classroom time lost due to strikes have intensified already difficult circumstances in most Latin American classrooms. Overcrowded classrooms and the lack of up-to-date textbooks further add to the educational problems caused by the debt crisis and the onset of the global recession in the early-twenty-first century.

In response to substantial reductions in public funding for education, many ministries began to pursue other sources of revenue. One major source was to charge user fees to parents for their children's education. Another policy involved shifting a number of administrative responsibilities, including the financing of education, to departmental and municipal levels of education. These two policies (privatization and decentralization) are methods favored by the World Bank and IMF for improving educational efficiency. Countries seeking access to international credit were obligated to implement such policies in education as they had in other social services. As Edward Berman has noted, "[Donor agencies] have advocated a decrease in the amount of government involvement in the education process, an increase in the private sector's role, and greater application of market principles to the organization of Third World educational systems" (1992:69).

Privatization and Decentralization

Privatization is the investment of private money into previously public institutions. It involves either charging user fees in public schools for services that were previously free of charge or converting some public institutions into private institutions. Privatization became more widespread in the educational sector because education budgets endured drastic cuts in the 1980s.

Carlos Alberto Torres and Adriana Puiggrós (1995) note that levying new fees for previously free services, such as textbooks, entrance examinations, and salaries for teachers in special subjects like computer applications, further restricts lower-class access to education. Students from marginalized sectors of society had previously benefited from services such as these that are not readily available outside the educational setting. Fees for educational services are a particular burden for poor families because they have become even more impoverished as a consequence of recently initiated structural adjustment policies. In some cases, poverty-stricken families are unable to send their children to school because they cannot afford textbook rental fees, monthly tuition charges, or the purchase of a required uniform. In other instances, they may be induced to send their children to school for a free glass of milk or school lunch, which provides the only nutrition they are likely to receive.

In response to budget cuts, education ministries have also promoted the development and accreditation of private education institutions (primary, secondary, and higher education). Middle- and upper-class students have been particularly attracted to these institutions because they offer smaller classes, better facilities, and instruction in subject areas that address the market's demand for graduates in business administration and engineering.

Middle- and upper-class parents' ability to send their children to private schools has had adverse effects on public schools. Removing middle-class parents from the public school system eliminates the most vocal advocates for quality in the schools. The lower classes, although constituting the majority of the population, lack the economic clout necessary to promote quality in the public school system (Arnove, Franz, and Morse 1996). As a result, many public school systems have suffered from funding inadequacies.

Schiefelbein has provided a critical commentary on these trends (1995: 19). He notes high-level decisionmakers and administrators send their children to private schools, but shape policy on public schools. In the process, public school children must endure negative consequences from which the offspring of "high officials" are immune.

Comparative data illustrate the extent to which enrollment in private education in Latin America surpasses that of other developing regions and is dramatically higher than that of developed countries. At the primary level, nearly 15 percent of students in Latin America attend private schools as compared with just over 4 percent in developed countries. At the secondary level, private education enrollment in Latin America is nearly three times that of developed countries—22.0 percent versus 7.7 percent (Faulhaber 2008:4).

In response to the debt crisis, the other primary reform pursued by Latin American education ministries has been administrative decentralization. In most Latin American countries, central education ministries have controlled all aspects of the educative process; for example, curriculum development, pedagogy, financing, and evaluation. Given this situation, decentralization is perceived as a positive governmental reform that grants more power to local authorities. Argentina (1976), Mexico (1978), Chile (1981), and Colombia (1986) have pursued decentralization programs in which municipalities have been delegated the responsibility of administering school funding and curriculum development. For example, in Chile, which the UN Children's Fund (UNICEF 1999) considers to be a successful model of decentralization, municipalities are given a percentage of necessary funds and are responsible for paying the balance of educational costs.

A key element of decentralization theory is the belief that local decision-making will lead to superior schools. Proponents believe decentralization will result in curricula and pedagogies that are tailored to local needs and that streamlining a cumbersome bureaucracy will promote efficiency and cost-effectiveness. Attaching national subsidies to indicators of school efficiency, such as attendance rates, and school effectiveness, such as achievement scores, should contribute to improving the poor promotion and retention rates that have characterized Latin American education systems.

Market mechanisms are common components of decentralization policies. Competition for students, for instance, is seen as a means to improve the quality of educational offerings. The idea is that superior schools will attract more students and, thereby, increase funding capacity.

Competition in educational markets, however, has its downside. Although decentralization and market-driven policies are feasible in middle-class areas, they present serious problems for the residents of rural communities and marginalized urban areas. First, these areas are often unable to finance educational programs that are not funded by government subsidies. Second, residents in these areas often lack access to the information needed to make decisions regarding the market-driven elements of such educational reforms. Furthermore, standardized test scores in Spanish and mathematics do not indicate significant improvement in educational quality, especially for disadvantaged populations. On the contrary, in Chile after decentralization, results of Spanish and mathematics tests in 1982 and 1988 showed a 14 percent and a 6 percent decline, respectively. Moreover, the disparity between the highest test scores in private schools and the lowest test scores in high-risk municipal schools increased for this time period (Prawda 1993).

In 1993, Nicaragua implemented a decentralization program at the local school level that equates educational efficiency with high student-to-teacher ratios. As with Chile's program, the Nicaraguan Ministry of Education's plan allots extra funds to schools that increase their efficiency. Nicaragua's program emphasizes reduced dropout rates, thereby increasing the number of students in the classrooms. There is nothing particularly innovative about the program, however, in the areas of curriculum and pedagogy. In fact, any attempt to introduce more student-centered, inquiry-oriented pedagogy appears unlikely, if not impossible, considering the Ministry of Education's emphasis on a minimum of forty-five students per classroom as an indicator of efficiency (Arnove 1995).

Recent policies that diminish the role of the state in education and encourage users to pay the costs of their education have also affected higher education, as well as adult basic education programs, throughout Latin America. These policies in particular have generated tensions within higher education, which is considered the level of education most critically related to national development.

Higher Education

Despite their long-standing belief in the significance of higher education, in recent years international donor agencies such as the World Bank and IMF have accorded lower priority to public funding of higher educational systems than to primary education. The reason for this policy is that economic analyses suggest that the best investment for a country in terms of "rates of return" is primary education, followed by secondary education and finally higher education. Rates of return are calculated by comparing the present value of lifeterm earnings of people with different levels of education with the present costs, both public and personal, of schooling individuals to these levels (Psacharopoulos 1987).

Critics of such analyses point out that the benefits of higher education cannot be reduced to simply calculating wage differences. Benefits that are not immediately calculable include the fact that universities serve as the political conscience of many nations, often constituting the leading opponents of dictatorships, and that the research conducted by universities is indispensable to the general advancement of a society. In the absence of such research and ongoing intellectual activity, Latin American countries are condemned to dependence on the universities of the North for advanced scientific and technical knowledge. These critics warn of the dangers of emphasizing *primarización* (primary education) to the detriment of higher education. They argue that Latin American countries need world-class universities that contribute to national development (Gorostiaga 1993). Indicative of this need is the fact that, according to Daniel Schugurensky, Latin America contributes less than 3 percent of the world's scientific production (2003:299). In Mexico and Brazil which lead Latin America in scientific production, there are only 95 and 165 scientists and engineers per million people respectively, whereas, in Sweden, there are 3,714 and, in Japan, 5,677 scientists and engineers per million (Schugurensky 2003:299). Total public expenditures of all Latin American countries on research and development approximate those of several major multinational corporations (Schugurensky 2003). Moreover, with educational expansion, universities find it increasingly difficult to hire full-time faculty with the requisite educational qualifications; in part, a reflection of the inadequate salaries and poor working conditions that they offer.

In many Latin American countries, public universities charge no tuition, nor do they assess minimal fees. Recently, however, national governments have imposed tuition costs based on recommendations of the international donor agencies. Such initiatives have led to the paralysis of major universities, such as the National Autonomous University of Mexico (UNAM) where students effectively closed down the university by striking from April to October 1999. The minimal but symbolic tuition fee of $150, although well within the means of middle-class families, is often prohibitive for those from working-class backgrounds. This is especially the case in countries where as much as 70 percent or more of the population is living below the poverty level. Such policies threaten to erode the slow but steady gains made by the less privileged members of Latin American society to gain access to a higher education. According to Julia Preston, the Mexican strike "grew more intractable as it dragged on and turned into a battle for the soul of the university. The strikers want it to remain a place for the masses, where all kinds of young Mexicans get at least a little bit of college education" (1999:A12).

While students and faculty have protested the imposition of tuition and fees at the undergraduate level in universities from Argentina to Nicaragua, this has not been the case with the introduction of quite substantial fees at the graduate level. With the need to upgrade faculty throughout the region, many instructors are now required to obtain advanced degrees. In many instances, a select few public universities and an increasing number of private institutions are offering master's and doctoral degrees.

One of the most remarkable trends in Latin American education over the past three decades has been the growth of private universities. In the 1970s, approximately 5 percent of higher education students were enrolled in private institutions; by 2002, in eight Latin American countries (Brazil, Chile, Colombia, Dominican Republic, El Salvador, Nicaragua, Paraguay, and Peru) from 40 percent to 70 percent of the students attended private universities and colleges (Holm-Nielsen et al. 2005:42). In seven countries (Venezuela, Argentina, Costa Rica, Ecuador, Guatemala, Mexico, and Honduras), private enrollment ranged from 10 percent to 40 percent and only four countries had less than 10 percent (Cuba, Bolivia, Panama, and Uruguay).

There are many reasons for this growth in private higher education. Public universities in Latin America have a long history of political activism and radicalism. Private universities are generally less politically volatile, and the more privileged classes can send their children to them with the assurance that they will not be exposed to radical political ideas and movements that are likely to erupt into violence on campus. Also, believing graduates of private universities are better prepared academically and are less likely to harbor politically objectionable ideas, private sector employers may be more likely to hire them. Furthermore, private universities in some countries, such as Brazil, may have less rigorous admissions standards because they depend on student tuition for their survival. Thus, they may recruit as many students as possible in low-cost fields such as law, the social sciences, accounting, and administration.

Another significant trend is toward reliance on market forces and away from centralized efforts to plan higher education enrollment patterns in concert with national development goals. In the 1990s, enrollments in business administration and engineering programs grew disproportionately. This growth was matched by declining enrollments in the social sciences, education, and the humanities.

Although such shifts appear to reflect market realities, overall enrollment patterns by field of study manifest little relation to the so-called human resource needs of Latin American countries. Despite the agricultural basis of many of the region's economies, often fewer than 5 percent of students are enrolled in courses in agricultural sciences.

Cuba and Nicaragua in the late 1980s were possible exceptions because of university admissions quotas geared to national economic plans. Throughout Latin America, one consequence of these enrollment patterns has been that graduates in overpopulated fields, such as business administration, have serious difficulty finding employment. Only graduates of the most prestigious institutions and fields—and, in many cases, those with the traditional advantage of family connections—can find employment that suits their expectations. One familiar outcome of frustrated expectations is the "brain drain" of high-level talent to the metropolitan centers of North America and Europe. In new fields of development (e.g., petroengineering), however, countries are forced to import experts from abroad (Arnove, Franz, and Morse 1996).

Literacy and Adult Education

Higher education is not the only level of education to be accorded low priority by international donor agencies and national governments. Although most Latin American countries paid lip service to the importance of literacy and adult education in preparation for the World Conference on Education for All in Jomtien, Thailand, in 1990, the fact is that literacy and adult education programs were given scant attention in subsequent years. However, the emergence of populist, socialist-oriented regimes in the region in recent years, notably Venezuela, Bolivia, and Ecuador among others, has led to a renewal in large-scale literacy campaigns. One such effort was mounted in Venezuela by the Hugo Chávez government with the help of Cuban advisers and teachers that resulted in approximately 1.5 million adults learning to read. Similar literacy efforts were instituted in Nicaragua with the return of Daniel Ortega and the Sandinista National Liberation Front to power in 2007.

Although Latin America has the lowest illiteracy rates of any of the developing regions, there are nearly 35 million people over the age of fifteen who cannot read or write (Croso, Vóvio, and Masagão 2008:119). As Table 11.4 illustrates, significant differences in literacy rates exist across and within countries. When the combined effects of social class, region, and gender are taken into account, the highest illiteracy rates, often over 60 percent, are found among poor women living in rural areas. Gender differences in literacy attainment become even sharper when ethnicity is considered, with indigenous groups registering the lowest levels of literacy.

The response of many governments to the problem of adult illiteracy has been to rely on nongovernmental organizations (NGOs) and the private sector to provide instruction. Although NGOs are particularly responsive to grassroots initiatives and local needs, their resources are often limited.

In contrast to state-sponsored adult education programs, a number of grassroots educational programs exist in Latin America that form part of a "popular education" movement. Although limited in resources and small in scope, these

Table 11.4 Illiteracy Rates by Gender, 2010

Country	Males	Females	Both Genders
Argentina	2.5	2.4	2.4
Bolivia	4.8	13.8	9.4
Brazil	10.0	9.3	9.6
Chile	2.8	2.9	2.9
Colombia	6.1	5.7	5.9
Costa Rica	3.3	3.0	3.2
Cuba	1.9	2.2	2.1
Dominican Republic	13.2	12.6	12.9
Ecuador	4.7	6.9	5.8
El Salvador	14.4	18.6	16.6
Guatemala	18.3	32.1	25.2
Honduras	20.4	18.8	19.4
Mexico	4.8	7.6	6.2
Nicaragua	30.7	29.9	30.3
Panama	5.4	6.6	6.0
Paraguay	4.1	5.3	4.7
Peru	3.5	10.3	7.0
Uruguay	2.1	1.3	1.7
Venezuela	4.8	4.9	4.8

Source: Comisión Económica para América Latina. *Anuario estadístico de América Latina y el Caribe* (Santiago, Chile: CEPAL, 2010), table 1.3.1.

Note: CEPAL (2010) defines *illiterate population* as "the group of persons who cannot, with understanding, both read and write a short simple statement on their everyday life."

programs nonetheless are significant in that they offer an alternative model of education that empowers individuals and communities to place demands on national governments for social services and resources that should be among the rights of all citizens of a country.

■ Popular Education and Other Educational Innovations

Since the 1960s, nonformal and popular education programs have been important alternatives to the formal education sector. Nonformal education implies an educative experience that occurs outside the standard education sphere. Popular education, a subset of nonformal education, is distinguished by its pedagogical and political characteristics (Fink and Arnove 1991).

Pedagogically, popular education programs emphasize nonhierarchical learning situations in which teachers and students engage in dialogue and learners' knowledge is incorporated into the content of instruction. According to Carlos Alberto Torres, "Education appears as the act of knowing rather than a simple transmission of knowledge or the cultural baggage of society" (1994: 198–199).

Politically, popular education programs tend to be directed toward meeting the special needs of marginalized sectors of society (women, the unemployed, peasants, and indigenous groups). These programs have offered marginalized sectors in Latin America opportunities for personal growth and socioeconomic and political participation. They played a significant role in facilitating the development of collective survival strategies to confront the economic crisis of the 1980s and 1990s. Furthermore, the ultimate aim of many popular education programs is not just to facilitate adaptation or survival for hard-pressed populations, but to bring about far-reaching social change that leads to more just societies (C. A. Torres and Puiggrós 1995:26).

In addition to the programs for women listed by Susan Tiano in Chapter 10, one example of a significant popular education program is Red de Educación Popular entre Mujeres (REPEM; Popular Education Network of Women). Based in Montevideo, Uruguay, REPEM links 140 organizations at the global, regional, and national levels. It serves as a focal point for research, information dissemination, and advocacy on behalf of low-income women with little formal education. A major goal of REPEM is to meet women's demands for greater equality and opportunity and the chance to participate actively in the formulation of alternative social change strategies (Arnove, Franz, and Torres 2007:286).[3]

A number of popular education programs also address the special needs of indigenous populations. Multilingualism and multiculturalism are crucial elements of these programs in countries such as Guatemala, Mexico, and Bolivia. In addition, these programs build on traditional knowledge in the agricultural and health fields and integrate various common forms of artistic expression into programs designed to foster self-pride and into civic and economic activities that contribute to viable communities.

Although popular education programs are generally effective on the community level, they often fail to bring about change at the level of governmental policy. One interesting case in which a leading proponent of popular education had an opportunity to effect large-scale educational change is that of Paulo Freire as secretary of education in the municipality of São Paulo, Brazil.

Paulo Freire and Educational Change

For more than thirty years, Paulo Freire, a theorist and innovator, redefined what educators all over the world think about the potential of education to contribute to social change. Freire's theories articulate the intimate relationship between education and development, particularly the connection between individual empowerment and democratic ideals. During his lifetime, Freire helped plan and implement literacy campaigns and popular education programs in countries worldwide. As municipal secretary of education between 1989 and 1991, Freire was involved in the development and implementation of numerous programs in São Paulo, the most populous city in South America. The popular education programs put in place were designed to: (1) increase access to schooling; (2) democratize school administrations; (3) improve instructional quality; (4) expand educational opportunities for working youths and adults; and (5) contribute to the formation of critical and responsible citizens (Lindquist Wong 1995:120).

Despite the egalitarian intent of Freire's program, Pia Lindquist Wong's analysis (1995) indicates that its implementation became mired in local politics and bureaucracies. Unfortunately, this is the case with many popular education programs. According to Rosa María Torres, the administration of adult and popular education programs is given to sectors of education ministries that "traditionally occupy a marginal place in the organizational structure and function of ministries of education, lack material and economic resources, and are staffed by bureaucrats showing little dedication" (1990:464).

Although such is the fate of many educational reforms, there are examples of less politically radical state-sponsored educational innovations that do benefit poorly served populations.

New Educational Approaches

An example of ambitious state-sponsored educational innovations that benefit traditionally underserved populations is Fe y Alegría (Faith and Happiness). This Venezuelan NGO began in 1955 by educating 100 children in a single room. By 2001, the program had expanded to fourteen countries with more than 1 million students in formal and nonformal education programs in over 500 centers, with over 33,000 teachers and staff. According to Fernando Reimers, the mission of Fe y Alegría is to "provide quality education to the poor, as expressed in their motto 'Where the asphalt road ends, where there is no water, electricity or services, there begins Fe y Alegría'" (1997:35). Although there is no "systematic evaluation" for Fe y Alegría, parents claim that these schools provide a better education than public schools. A Guatemalan case study, furthermore, indicates that 85 percent of students who entered Fe y Alegría at the preschool level completed primary education within seven years as opposed to 34 percent in government schools. Reimers states that Latin American ministries of education usually do not embrace innovative programs such as Fe y Alegría until the programs have proved themselves. Fe y Alegría was initially privately funded, but went on to secure substantial government funding in most cases. For example, the Venezuelan government funded over three-fourths of the program budget in the mid-1990s (Reimers 1997). Since then, however, the Chávez government, which favors public education, has assumed a critical view toward private education in general and especially a program that is as large scale and significant as Fe y Alegria.

Another example of a state-sponsored innovation is La Escuela Nueva (the New School) in Colombia, which is designed to meet the special needs of rural schools and communities by creating a curriculum that emphasizes communal needs and values. La Escuela Nueva reform actively encourages a strong relation between schools and communities, and a flexible school calendar and promotion policy that is adapted to local agricultural production cycles. One of the goals of La Escuela Nueva is to teach civic values by encouraging both student and parent participation in important decisions concerning local educational policy. This emphasis on participation accords with the philosophical underpinnings of the reform movement, which are child centered and constructivist in nature. Between its initiation as a pilot project in 1979 and the mid-1990s, the program expanded to over 20,000 schools. The effectiveness of this education reform is one possible reason for the fact that Colombia is the only country in a 1997 UNESCO study of academic achievement in which rural third-grade primary school children outperformed their urban counterparts on standardized language and mathematics tests. La Escuela Nueva students also demonstrate strong democratic values on various measures related to civic knowledge, skills, and attitudinal dispositions (UNESCO 1998). Although widely admired and emulated, attempts to replicate La Escuela Nueva, without significant adaptation to local circumstances, have proved problematic, even within Colombia itself.[4] A key to the success of this reform, and any other, is the preparation of teachers and, as Henry Levin (1992) points out, constant monitoring, problem solving, and adjustment.

In general, there are several types of state-initiated policies and practices that are likely to contribute to greater equality of educational opportunity for disadvantaged populations, including working-class and rural people, ethnic minorities, and women. Quality preschool and early childhood programs would improve with supplementary nutrition and health care services. Inadequate school infrastructures should be improved so that poor, rural, and indigenous children have the same amenities, such as school buildings, desks and chairs, electricity, running water, and toilets, enjoyed by their more advantaged peers in urban and private schools. Developing flexible academic calendars would be an appropriate response to the socioeconomic context of schools in different regions of a country. Sufficient supplies of textbooks, as well as culturally sensitive and socially relevant curricular materials in the appropriate languages, are also needed. There are significant instructional issues that ought to be addressed. This could be done through teaching guides adapted to transformed curricula and more student-centered, proactive pedagogies that involve collaborative work and personalized attention to each child. Teachers could benefit from significantly improved preservice and in-service teacher education and professional development programs and opportunities. Teachers working under difficult conditions would be well served by incentive pay, generally more adequate remuneration, and social recognition of the importance of teaching. Equally important would be an increase in participation of teachers, parents, and communities in the design of education programs to meet their self-defined needs, as exemplified by La Escuela Nueva.

Other state initiatives that are being employed to attract and maintain low-income children in schools involve subsidies for textbooks, uniforms, and transportation. Although the Inter-American Development Bank reported mixed results for these policies, an even bolder initiative involving cash payments by governments to help poor children be pupils, not wage earners, shows promise of being effective (IDB 1998). The largest program, Bolsa Escola, involving cash transfers to needy families is occurring in Brazil, where the government of President Luiz Inácio Lula da Silva reached over 11 million families (more than 45 million people) by 2006 with incentive funds for their children to complete basic education (approximately six years). In Mexico, a similar program reaches approximately 20 million people. A rigorous evaluation of the Mexican program found that children in schools that receive transfer funds that include money for staples (e.g., rice, beans, eggs, and carrots) and school supplies were healthier and stayed in school longer than children in a control group (Duggan 2004:3). According to Laurence Wolff and Claudio de Moura Castro, the PROGRESA program (Programa de Educación, Salud y Alimentación [Education, Health, and Nutrition Program]), in Mexico has increased entry rates into lower secondary schools in rural areas by almost 20 percent (2003:196).

It is necessary to point out the important role that universities, through their research, development, and dissemination activities, can play in regard to the most disadvantaged members of their societies. In this role, universities can contribute to income and job generation to overcome the devastating effects of the debt crisis and economic restructuring to control inflation and fiscal deficits. Higher education leaders, like the late Xabier Gorostiaga (former rector of the Central American University of Nicaragua), have proposed a vision of a new role for "universities of the South" (Gorostiaga 1993). Gorostiaga's vision calls for utilizing existing university departmental extension programs and research and development institutes affiliated with the Central America University as nuclei for experimentation, training, and popular education. Building a university education around the knowledge generated by rural-based centers would contribute to the formation of professionals who, because they have a more realistic understanding of their society, would be better prepared to address its most pressing problems. Moreover, the work of such centers would contribute to empowering the "producing majority" to become major historical actors involved in the transformation of an unsatisfactory status quo that has marginalized and exploited them. According to Gorostiaga (1993:37), "All of these experimental nuclei offer an ideal place for our professors and students to bring their theoretical knowledge down to earth, to participate in research projects that directly benefit civil society" and to extend education to the majority of people excluded from secondary and higher education. Such efforts are critical to the development and dissemination of appropriate and self-sustainable technologies, and they offer prospects of collaboration between universities of the North and the South (Arnove 1996).

■ Mass Media and Education

Finally, in discussing education in Latin America, whether formal or nonformal and popular, it is necessary to mention briefly the role of the mass media as a parallel educational system. The mass media reaches more people on a more systematic basis and for longer periods of time than do formal education systems. Although the various forms of media are viewed, read, and consumed as entertainment, they nonetheless present an agenda of what merits society's attention. In addition to providing countless messages about products to consume, the mass media—particularly *telenovelas* (television soap operas) and popular comic books in picture form (*fotonovelas*)—reach vast numbers of people with a folk mythology about how society is constituted, which people and occupations are worthy of emulation, and how social change takes place.[5]

The mass media impacts Latin American youth and their classroom behavior. In fact, the pervasiveness of the information age, particularly the near-universal access to mass media, may have presented educators with a new crisis—one in which students are choosing some cultural legacies and rejecting others. While students reject the authoritarianism of past generations, "at the same time, students are increasingly ignorant of both their own national past and world history . . . they are indifferent to collective values or notions of solidarity . . . and are apolitical in their attitudes" (C. A. Torres and Puig-grós 1995:20).

Although there are always differences between generations, the gap that exists between teachers and their students appears to be greater than ever. These cultural differences between adults and youth are only part of a larger set of issues concerning whether Latin American education systems can continue to play their historical role of transmitting common values, preparing citizens for a unified nation-state, and equipping citizens to be participating members of democratic polities.

▓ Education and Democracy in Latin America

The prospect of Latin American countries establishing democratic polities is greater now than at any time in the history of the region. The emergence of democratically elected regimes in the Southern Cone countries (Argentina, Chile, and Uruguay) and Brazil after two or more decades of military dictatorships is particularly encouraging, as is the termination of civil wars in Central America (El Salvador and Nicaragua) and installation of democratically elected governments in Honduras and Guatemala (countries with a tradition of military rule). But as Thomas J. D'Agostino makes clear in Chapter 4, democratic institutions throughout Latin America are fragile.

The enormous debt burden of the region, the increasing impoverishment of the less privileged social classes in these societies, and the willingness of individuals and groups to resort to violence to press their demands on national governments do not bode well for either social stability or political democracy. To counter these negative trends, educational systems in a number of countries have been called on to teach civic values. Particularly important is the need to teach toleration of differences by promoting a willingness to engage in dialogue with those who have dissimilar beliefs.

Although there are examples of countries, such as the Dominican Republic and Ecuador, that reached a national consensus in the early 1990s around their educational systems and the role of education in development, in many other countries, as Robert Arnove has noted, education is "contested terrain" (1995). Different governments and groups have attempted to use education to indoctrinate students into accepting certain political dogmas and religious doctrines. Schools have become battlegrounds in which ideologically and politically opposed groups fight not only over curriculum, textbooks, and who is qualified to teach, but also over the governance, organization, and financing of education. Moreover, rather than building on the best of previous governments' education programs, newly elected governments have often dismantled them, wasting years of effort in rebuilding what had already been achieved. If consensus, harmony, and respect for differences—values critical to democracy—

cannot be achieved in an education system, what hope is there for the larger society?

■ Conclusion

Despite past negative trends in the provision of a quality education to the most disadvantaged populations in Latin America, such current reforms as popular education, grassroots projects, and community self-help programs all point to a persistent ability of people to turn discouraging situations into positive developments. Furthermore, the evolving definitions of development and education indicate a constant move away from theories that reinforce the status quo toward ideals that promote individual empowerment and faith in egalitarian principles.

Egalitarian trends are especially evident in a new wave of populist governments that have emerged in the region that are seeking an alternative to the Washington Consensus, which is equated with economic and educational agendas favoring market forces applied to all spheres of society. These forces have favored the rich over the poor, the powerful over the disempowered. Instead, governments ranging from Brazil to Venezuela advocate a new model of economic and social development that emphasizes people over profits, a social economy that generates employment and provides dignified work for all, and solidarity among the countries of the region to overcome years of dependent development and regain national control over natural resources. These developmental policies are not without controversy; education remains a highly contested terrain over what values are taught.

As noted above, if education is used as an agency for imposing a new ideological agenda and indoctrinating rather than equipping individuals to critically examine their existential realities and be active participants in creating more democratic polities, the result will be an intense polarization of societies. Consequently, there will be little, if any, forward momentum toward achieving more equitable education systems and more just societies.

■ Notes

1. Data in this section are drawn from various UNESCO reports.
2. Data in this section are drawn from various CEPAL and World Bank reports.
3. Vicky Semler, executive director of the International Women's Tribune Centre, New York City, personal communication with Robert F. Arnove, January 7, 2003.
4. Vicky Colbert, president of the Fundación Volvamos a la Gente and cofounder of la Escuela Nueva, interviewed by Robert F. Arnove, Bogotá, Colombia, August 19, 2002.
5. We are indebted to the late Rose Goldson of the Sociology Department at Cornell University for these insights.

Bibliography

Arnove, Robert F. "Education as Contested Terrain in Nicaragua." *Comparative Education Review* 39, no. 1 (1995): 28–53.

———. "Partnerships and Emancipatory Movements: Issues and Prospects." *Alberta Journal of Educational Research* 42, no. 2 (1996): 170–177.

Arnove, Robert F., Stephen Franz, Marcela Mollis, and Carlos Alberto Torres. "Education in Latin America: Dependency, Underdevelopment and Inequality." In *Comparative Education: The Dialectic of the Global and the Local,* 2nd ed., eds. Robert F. Arnove and Carlos Alberto Torres (Lanham, MD: Rowman & Littlefield, 2003), pp. 313–337.

Arnove, Robert F., Stephen Franz, and Kimberly Morse. "Latin American Education." In *Latin America: Perspectives on a Region,* ed. Jack W. Hopkins (New York: Holmes & Meier, 1996), pp. 123–137.

Arnove, Robert F., Stephen Franz, and Kimberly Morse Cordova. "Education and Development." In *Understanding Contemporary Latin America,* 3rd ed., ed. Richard S. Hillman (Boulder: Lynne Rienner, 2005), pp. 313–342.

Arnove, Robert F., Stephen Franz, and Carlos Alberto Torres, "Education in Latin America: Dependency, Underdevelopment and Inequality." In *Comparative Education: The Dialectic of the Global and the Local,* 3rd ed., eds. Robert F. Arnove and Carlos Alberto Torres (Lanham, MD: Rowman & Littlefield, 2007), pp. 277–294.

Berman, Edward. "Donor Agencies and Third World Educational Development, 1945–1985." In *Emergent Issues in Education: Comparative Perspectives,* eds. Robert Arnove, Philip Altbach, and Gail Kelly (Albany: SUNY Press, 1992), pp. 57–74.

Bonal, Xavier and Ferran Ferrer, eds. "La Globalización en América Latina: Dependencía, Subdesarrollo y Desigualdad." In *Globalización, Educación y Pobreza en América Latina* (Barcelona: Centro de Estudios y Documentación Internacionales de Barcelona, 2007).

Carnoy, Martin. "Social Inequality as a Barrier to Multicultural Education in Latin America." In *The Routledge International Companion to Multicultural Education,* ed. James A. Banks (New York: Routledge, 2009), pp. 512–525.

CEPAL (Comisión Económica para América Latina). *Transformación productiva con equidad.* Santiago, Chile: CEPAL, 1990.

———. *Panorama social de América Latina.* Santiago, Chile: CEPAL, 1991.

———. *Panorama social de América Latina.* Santiago, Chile: CEPAL, 2001.

———. *Panorama social de América Latina.* Santiago, Chile: CEPAL, 2002.

———. *Anuario estadístico de América Latina y el Caribe.* Santiago, Chile: CEPAL, 2005.

———. *Anuario estadístico de América Latina y el Caribe.* Santiago, Chile: CEPAL, 2006.

Coleman, James S., ed. *Education and Political Development.* Princeton: Princeton University Press, 1965.

Croso, Camilla, Claudia Vóvio, and Vera Masagão. "Latin America: Literacy, Adult Education and the International Literacy Benchmarks." *Adult Education and Development* 71 (2008): 119–130. http://www.iiz-dvv.de.

Duggan, Celia W. "To Help Poor Be Pupils, Not Wage Earners, Brazil Pays Parents." *New York Times,* January 3, 2004, pp. A1, 3, 6.

ECLAC (Economic Commission for Latin America and the Caribbean). *The Millennium Development Goals: A Latin American and Caribbean Perspective.* Santiago, Chile: UN, 2005.

Faulhaber, Ingrid. "Affordable Private School Initiative: Research in Latin America." Gray Matters Capital Foundation, Atlanta, GA. 2008.

Fink, Marcy, and Robert Arnove. "Issues and Tensions in Popular Education in Latin America." *International Journal of Educational Development* 11, no. 3 (1991): 221–230.

Freire, Paulo. *The Politics of Education: Culture, Power, and Liberation.* Critical Studies in Education. Westport: Greenwood Press, 1984.

Fuenzalida, Edmundo. "Development and Education." In *The International Encyclopedia of Education,* vol. 3, eds. Torsten Husén and T. Neville Postlethwaite (New York: Pergamon, 1985), pp. 1374–1379.

Gorostiaga, Xabier. "New Times, New Role for Universities of the South." *Envío* 12, no. 144 (1993): 24–40.

Holm-Nielsen, Lauritz, Kristian Thorn, José Brunner, and Jorge Balan. "Regional and International Challenges to Higher Education in Latin America." In *Higher Education in Latin America: The International Dimension,* eds. Hans de Wit, Isabel Cristina Jaramillo, Jocelyne Gacel-Avila, and Jane Knight (Washington, DC: World Bank, 2005).

IDB (Inter-American Development Bank). "Education: The Gordian Knot: Shortfalls in Schooling Are at the Root of Inequality," 1998. http://www.iadb.org.

Latin Focus. "Data Table Economic Indictors, 2002–2008." http://www.latin-focus.com.

Levin, Henry. "Effective Schools and Comparative Focus." In *Emergent Issues in Education: Comparative Perspectives,* eds. Robert F. Arnove, Philip G. Altbach, and Gail P. Kelly (Albany: State University of New York Press, 1992), pp. 229–245.

Levy, Daniel C. *Higher Education and the State in Latin America: Private Challenges to Public Dominance.* Chicago: University of Chicago Press, 1986.

Lindquist Wong, Pia. "Constructing a Public Popular Education in São Paulo, Brazil." *Comparative Education Review* 39, no. 1 (1995): 120–141.

López, Nestor. "Education and Equity in Latin America." *IIPE Newsletter* 23, no. 1 (2005): 1, 3.

Muñiz, Patricia. "The Schooling Situation of Children in Highly Underprivileged Rural Localities in Mexico." In *Unequal Schools, Unequal Chances: The Challenges to Equal Opportunity in the Americas,* ed. Fernando Reimers (Cambridge: Harvard University Press, 2000), pp. 290–314.

OECD (Organization for Economic Cooperation and Development). *Education at a Glance: OECD Indicators, 2000.* OECD, Paris, August 2000.

Plank, David N., José Amaral Sobrinho, and Antonio Carlos de Ressurreição Xavier. "Obstacles to Educational Reform in Brazil." *La Educación* 117, no. 1 (1994): 81–82.

Prawda, Juan. "Educational Decentralization in Latin America: Lessons Learned." *International Journal of Educational Development* 13, no. 3 (1993): 253–264.

PREAL (Programa de Promoción de la Reforma Educativa en América Latina y el Caribe). "Quedándonos atrás: Un informe del progreso educativo en América Latina," December 2001. www.preal.org.

Preston, Julia. "University Officials Yield to Student Strike in Mexico." *New York Times,* June 8, 1999, p. A12.

Psacharopoulos, George. "Economic Aspects of Educational Planning." In *Economics of Education: Research and Studies,* ed. George Psacharopoulos (New York: Pergamon Press, 1987), pp. 311–314.

Reimers, Fernando. "The Impact of Economic Stabilization and Adjustment on Education in Latin America." *Comparative Education Review* 35, no. 2 (1991): 319–362.

————. "Role of NGOs in Promoting Educational Innovation: A Case Study in Latin America." In *Education and Development: Tradition and Innovation,* vol. 4: *Nonformal and Non-governmental Approaches,* eds. James Lynch, Celia Modgil, and Sohan Modgil (London: Cassell, 1997), pp. 33–44.

REPEM (Popular Education Network of Women). http://www.repem.org.uy.

Schiefelbein, Ernesto. "Educational Reform in Latin America and the Caribbean: An Agenda for Action." In *The Major Project of Education in Latin America and the Caribbean,* Bulletin no. 37 (Santiago, Chile: UNESCO, 1995), pp. 3–31.

Schugurensky, Daniel. "Higher Education Restructuring in the Era of Globalization: Toward a Heteronomous Model?" In *Comparative Education: The Dialectic of the Global and the Local,* 2nd ed., eds. Robert F. Arnove and Carlos Alberto Torres (Lanham, MD: Rowman & Littlefield, 2003), pp. 292–312.

Schultz, Theodore William. *Transforming Traditional Agriculture.* New Haven: Yale University Press, 1964.

Torres, Carlos Alberto. "Paulo Freire as Secretary of Education in the Municipality of São Paulo." *Comparative Education Review* 38, no. 2 (1994): 198–199.

Torres, Carlos Alberto, and Adriana Puiggrós. "The State and Public Education in Latin America." *Comparative Education Review* 39, no. 1 (1995): 1–27.

Torres, Rosa María. "Illiteracy and Literacy Training in Latin America and the Caribbean: Between Inertia and a Break with the Past." *Prospects* 20 (1990): 461–468.

UNICEF (UN Children's Fund). *State of the World's Children, 1999.* New York: UNICEF, 1999.

UNESCO (United Nations Educational, Scientific, and Cultural Organization). *UNESCO Statistical Yearbook, 1974.* Paris: UNESCO, 1974.

————. *UNESCO Statistical Yearbook, 1993.* Paris: UNESCO, 1993.

————. *UNESCO Statistical Yearbook, 1998.* Paris: UNESCO, 1998.

————. "Latin America and the Caribbean: Regional Report," 2001. www.unesco.org.

————. *A View Inside Primary Schools: A World Education Indicators (WEI) Cross-National Study.* Montreal: UNESCO, 2008.

————. "Table 5: Enrolment Ratios by ISCED Level," January 2011a. http://stats.uis.unesco.org.

————. "Table 9: Repetition Rates and Percentage of Repeaters in Primary Education," January 2011b. http://stats.uis.unesco.org.

————. "Table 12: Measure of Progression and Completion in Primary Education," January 2011c. http://stats.uis.unesco.org.

Vegas, Emiliana, and Jenny Petrow. *Raising Student Learning in Latin America: The Challenge for the 21st Century.* Washington, DC: World Bank, 2008.

Wolff, Laurence, and Claudio de Moura Castro. "Education and Training: The Task Ahead." Institute for International Economics, 2003. www.iie.com.

Wolff, Laurence, Ernesto Schiefelbein, and Paulina Schiefelbein. *La educación primaria en América Latina: La agenda inconclusa.* PREAL, 2002. available at www.preal.org.

Wolff, Laurence, Ernesto Schiefelbein, and Jorge Valenzuela. *Improving the Quality of Primary Education in Latin America and the Caribbean.* Washington, DC: World Bank, 1994.

World Bank. *Brazil: Public Spending on Social Programs, Issues and Options.* World Bank Report 7086-BR. Washington, DC: World Bank, 1988.

12

Religion in Latin America

Hannah Stewart-Gambino

Religion has been one of the driving forces in Latin America from pre-Columbian times to the present. As René de la Pedraja illustrates in Chapter 3, the Europeans who came to the New World with crosses and swords found religion and politics similarly intertwined in the indigenous civilizations. Since then, religious beliefs have been influenced by multifaceted encounters between divergent cultures. And, as Richard S. Hillman introduces in Chapter 1, these interactions shaped enduring legacies that have been modified over time. Since the earliest conquest, European *conquistadores* (conquerors) established the Catholic Church as an official institution of the Spanish and Portuguese colonies and suppressed indigenous religions—many of which were grounded in highly sophisticated civilizations. The significant role of the church continued after independence in the early 1800s and into the twentieth century. Even today, a substantial majority of the citizens of contemporary Latin American countries continue to nominally identify themselves as Catholics.

Since the European conquest, the Catholic Church has played a central role in the life of Latin Americans—both as a powerful partner in the colonial and postcolonial states and as the arbiter of the dominant religious doctrine. Yet at the same time for many who profess to be Catholic, including the majority of indigenous peoples and descendents of African slaves, daily religious practice has been syncretic—a blend of native beliefs with the dominant Catholic orthodoxy. In Chapter 9, Kevin A. Yelvington shows how some syncretic religions have served as sources of popular identity and of resistance to social and political authorities. So-called popular religion as practiced by the common people varies widely, depending on the region and the mixture of local cultures.

Beginning in the mid-twentieth century, scholars predicted that the influence of Catholicism and religion in general would decline in Latin America—

in spite of the widespread cultural religiosity of the people—as modernization associated with urban, industrial economic growth transformed the social landscape. Based on the US and European experiences, the so-called modernization school argued that economic growth leads to greater role differentiation and specialization—in the economy and concomitantly in the political and social spheres (Peterson, Vásquez, and Williams 2001). According to this view, greater social differentiation and specialization give rise to new, modern institutions—political parties, trade unions, governmental bureaucracies, and myriad social institutions—necessary for the rational functioning of individuals and societies in an increasingly complex world. With modernization, religion will be relegated over time to the private sphere as other, secular institutions take over many of the functions of the traditional or premodern authority structures in which political, social and religious authority were interrelated.

As Scott G. McKinney shows in Chapter 6, the twentieth century—albeit with significant boom and bust cycles—has been one of significant economic modernization throughout the region. And the Catholic Church's dominance of the religious landscape appears to have weakened. There is evidence that increased numbers of individuals identify themselves as adhering to no particular religious faith. Yet the religious landscape in Latin American has hardly disappeared or faded into the margins of societies. Rather, the religious monopoly of the Catholic Church has given way to an increasingly vibrant religious marketplace. Religious belief is more volatile and conversions from Catholicism to other forms of Christianity have increased as have rates of return to new forms of Catholicism. In turn, increased competition between religious institutions fuels changes in the role of churches in local, regional, and national politics. Moreover, as Thomas J. D'Agostino shows in Chapter 4, church and state authorities have worked both with and against one another in attempting to inform and control their common subjects.

Although there was never a monolithic "Latin American Catholic Church," scholars assert that Catholic churches must be understood as national (even regional) institutions through which the ecclesial concerns and priorities of the Vatican intersect with the local hierarchies' struggles to make Catholicism and the church meaningful in the concrete reality of believers' lives (Cleary and Stewart-Gambino 1992). Likewise, alternative forms of Christianity, syncretic religions, and spiritism compete for relevance in the lives of citizens—leading to a wide array of belief structures with a range of political implications.

■ The Colonial Role of the Catholic Church

The historical image of Latin America—the so-called Catholic continent—was one of *conquistadores* with a "sword in one hand and a cross in the other."

Indeed, the role of the Catholic Church in the conquest and subsequent colonial experience is best understood within the unique context of the partnership between the church and the Spanish crown. Throughout the fifteenth century leading up to Christopher Columbus's expedition, the church had partnered with the crown in a bloody campaign to reconquer the Iberian Peninsula from the Moors and to expel Jews who did not convert to Catholicism. Because of the church's clear political support for the century-long struggle, it became in essence another arm of the Spanish state. This religiopolitical partnership was carried to the New World. *Conquistadores* and Catholic missionaries traveled together to conquer the indigenous peoples and take their wealth for the Spanish crown while converting their souls for the Catholic Church. In fact, given the shortage of Spanish personnel and the intersection of church and state, many prelates simply assumed government posts in the viceroyalties of the New World.

In the hope of training an Amerindian priesthood, early missionaries taught indigenous people the Spanish and Portuguese languages as well as the Catholic faith. During the early conquest, local customs that were viewed as not inconsistent with Catholicism were tolerated. Over time, however, the indigenous people's tendency toward syncretism—blending Catholicism with indigenous beliefs and customs—led subsequent missionaries to take an increasingly intolerant view of all Amerindian religiosity, resulting in a new wave of repression to eliminate local religious icons, worship sites, authorities and belief structures.

From the beginning of the conquest, Catholicism and military, political, economic, and social power were combined in the colonial state. Politically, Spanish America was governed by four viceroyalties—New Spain and Peru, which were established in the sixteenth century, and New Granada and La Plata, which were created in the eighteenth century. The Spanish governors compensated the *conquistadores* with rights to demand tribute and labor from indigenous peoples, creating from the earliest days of the Spanish conquest a highly stratified class system in which the Spanish and their descendents who were born in the New World lived off the labor of the indigenous populations. The resulting oppression of the indigenous populations—particularly in regions in which forced labor in the silver mines was notoriously brutal and inhuman—made hollow the claims that a central purpose of the colonial state was to win souls for Catholicism. Indeed, at least one voice from within the church denounced the treatment of the indigenous peoples. Bishop Bartolomé de las Casas was so angered by the flagrant abuses of indigenous peoples that he wrote to the Spanish crown begging for new regulations to ameliorate their treatment and called for the importation of African slaves. His entreaties resulted in the New Laws (1542) governing the treatment of the indigenous peoples. However, prohibitions against the enslavement of indigenous peoples as well as regulations to prevent other abuses were never successfully enforced and eventually were rescinded when Spanish landowners revolted. Moreover, de las Casas regretted his support for the importation of slaves after witnessing their wretched conditions and inhuman treatment. Efforts of clerics like de las Casas notwithstanding, the colonial system with its hierarchical oppression of the indigenous populations cannot be understood simply as the result of inevitable abuses associated with military and political subjugation; the colonial system was built in partnership with the Catholic Church, which gave the social order its justification and moral imperative.

▓ The Role of the Catholic Church in Liberal-Conservative Battles

In spite of the massive wealth transferred from their colonies in the Americas to the Spanish and Portuguese crowns throughout the colonial period, by the early nineteenth century power was shifting on the European continent—most notably with the rise of British and French military and commercial power. Napoleon's invasion of Spain in 1808 weakened the ability of the Spanish crown to enforce its rule in the colonies, giving the *criollos* (Europeans born in the Americas) the opportunity to mount successful independence movements. By the 1820s, Central and South America were home to newly independent states—all of which were ruled by the *criollo* classes who wanted to be free of the demands of the crown. These new states were not "revolutionary" states; newly independent Latin American countries were built on the colonial foundations of intertwined religious and political hierarchy in which Catholicism was the official, established state religion. The governments of the newly independent Latin American states, however, were relatively weak and faced formidable challenges by powerful *criollo* elites with competing interests who wanted to use the power of the new states to advance their economic and political agendas. Underlying and enmeshed in the competing interests of the various factions was a fundamental philosophical difference regarding the proper role of the Catholic Church in society.

Inspired by the Enlightenment ideals of equality, liberty, and justice and in the shadow of the new United States of America with its separation of church and state, Liberals throughout Latin America revolted against the old order. As noted by Thomas J. D'Agostino in Chapter 4, Liberal political parties in the nineteenth century were anticlerical parties, and their platforms included a central focus on secularization of the state—most notably in areas such as public education and state control of rites of passage such as birth registries, civil recognition of marriage, and rights to burial for all citizens regardless of religious beliefs. Inspired by the democratic developments in Europe and North America, Latin American Liberal parties also believed in abolishing aristocratic political control and promoting greater decentralization of state

*The Metropolitan Cathedral and Zócalo (main plaza) in
Mexico City. The cathedral, the largest in the Americas,
was built on a sacred Aztec site in order to demonstrate
Spanish power and authority in the region.*

power. In opposition were the proclerical Conservative parties that were made
up of elites who defended the traditional power of the Catholic Church in Latin
American society as well as the political, economic, and social power of the
descendents of the colonial state. Conservatives believed in consolidating the
power of a centralized state, supported by an established Catholic Church, in
which the social order was organized around clear class lines.

The fundamental divisions in postcolonial Latin American nations gave
rise to political and social conflicts throughout the region, often erupting in violence with winner-take-all political consequences that further deepened the
ideological rift between opposing views. These conflicts were between opposing *criollos;* these were not class wars between the rich and poor, but rather
competition for political control of the newly independent states and the social
and economic power associated with them. Thus, opposing philosophical views
regarding the role of the Catholic Church in the state became intertwined, once
again, in the fundamental question of political, economic, and social control of
the state. Also at issue were the extensive landholdings and wealth controlled
by the church, particularly the Jesuit orders.

By the early twentieth century, many of the powers of the Catholic Church—
such as control over education and civil authority over birth registries, marriage, and burial—had been won by the states. In most countries, the church
had been disestablished, although the circumstances of the separation varied
widely. For example, Chile separated the church and state in its 1921 Constitution relatively peacefully through a negotiation between church and state

officials while the 1917 Constitution of postrevolutionary Mexico contained harsh provisions that allowed persecution of the church and its personnel. In some countries such as Colombia, the nineteenth-century civil wars between clerical and anticlerical factions hardened the split in the political party system between Liberals and Conservatives. As in many Latin American countries, divisions between these groups were based on philosophical grounds regarding the role of the church in modern society as well as economic, urban-rural, and class interests. But, in Colombia the period known as La Violencia (1948–1958), in which hundreds of thousands of people were killed and millions were displaced, represented the inability of the political system to overcome the deep and radicalized divisions between clerical and anticlerical camps. Similarly, the Cristero Rebellion (1927–1929) in Mexico arose in response to the brutal repression of the church under the government of President Plutarco Elías Calles—a particularly virulent anticlerical.

Twentieth-century economic modernization gave rise to new elites as well as middle and working classes. Hence, new demands confronted political systems that required responses to the needs of these new sectors. Political systems that were rooted in the previous battles between clerical and anticlerical parties clashed with the rise of new classes whose demands required a more modern, secular state. With the rise of political divisions based on class, new parties on the left—notably those associated with Marxism—were added to the challenges to church authority and the Catholic worldview. And with the economic modernization of Latin America came new influences from the United States, including a wave of evangelical Protestant missionary outreach. By the latter half of the twentieth century, the Catholic Church faced strong challenges from the forces of secularization, rival religious institutions such as Protestantism, and leftist (often Marxist) movements and parties—all offering alternative worldviews to traditional Catholicism. The church's responses to these challenges differed, at times substantially, across national boundaries. Although one cannot speak of formal "national churches" until the creation of national bishops' conferences in the mid-twentieth century, it is clear that both the form and the content of the challenges to the church to maintain its influence among the faithful were in large measure determined by national boundaries.

Yet through the mid-twentieth century, the church remained powerful throughout the region—in part because over 90 percent of the population still considered itself Catholic, and in part because the church continued to enjoy preferential treatment in various forms. The church remained a significant landowner in many countries, it continued to count on special subsidies or tax benefits, and its opposition to divorce, abortion, and homosexuality continued to influence national laws throughout the region. Still today, the majority of Latin Americans self-identify as Catholics, at least nominally. Right-wing parties often have close ties to the church and serve as protectors of church interests in national politics. And in much of the region, the Catholic Church still provides the only viable alternative to underfunded and inadequate public education, giving the church ongoing cultural access to new generations.

The Modern Catholic Church

By the late twentieth century, the Latin American Catholic Church was at a new crossroads. In a number of countries such as Peru, Chile, and Brazil, progressive Catholics argued that Catholicism could compete for the souls of the masses only by addressing the concerns of Marxist political movements. Catholic trade unions, self-help organizations, and political parties that ranged from center-right to center-left arose across the region to compete with the radical and atheistic claims of the Marxist left. Progressive clerics argued that massive urbanization spawned by the migration of the rural poor to cities in search of jobs and survival made uprooted families more vulnerable to recruitment from radical political movements or rival religious beliefs.

By the 1960s, the international Catholic Church responded to the challenges of rising global secularization and decline in church adherence with Vatican II (1960–1963), which ushered in a wave of changes designed to make the church more relevant to the lives of believers. In addition to such reforms as translating Mass from Latin to the languages of national churches, Vatican II encouraged more openness to the world, a call to political action and analysis, and greater lay participation in the activities and leadership of parishes and dioceses. Consistent with this preoccupation with substantive political and social engagement in the world, the worker-priest movement based on the image of Jesus, the carpenter, introduced many young priests into their poor communities. These changes created a wave of Latin American Catholic progressives who sought to disassociate the church from its traditional identification with economic, social, and political elites. Particularly in countries like Brazil, Chile, and Peru, progressive priests, bishops, and nuns began to publicly condemn social and economic injustice, using "liberation theology" as a point of departure for denouncing the "structural sins" of dependent capitalism. Liberationists argued that, in Latin America, Christianity required solidarity with the poor and their legitimate aspirations for freedom from economic, political, and social oppression.

These progressive forces in the Catholic Church came to a head in the 1968 meeting of the Latin American Episcopal Conference (CELAM) in Medellín, Colombia. For the first time, CELAM pronounced the Latin American Catholic Church's "preferential option for the poor" and adopted a pastoral strategy based on small parish groups that combined worship, Bible study in light of their own daily lives, and a commitment to living out the gospel to serve their community's needs. These groups were called *comunidades eclesiales de base* (CEBs; ecclesial base communities) and, though their relationship to parish or diocesan authorities differed widely, CEBs flourished—particularly in poor neighborhoods—across the region.

The CEBs became especially important in light of the wave of military coups in the 1960s and 1970s. The military dictatorships in almost all of Latin America during this period differed from those that had simply ruled at the behest of traditional oligarchic interests in the past. As Paul W. Zagorski discusses in Chapter 5, grounded in an ideological framework called the National Security State, military *juntas* viewed labor unrest and reformist demands as more than simply Marxist challenges, regardless of the range of political parties and movements throughout the region. Indeed, social mobilization of any sort—particularly from the left and ultimately the center—became viewed as an unhealthy symptom of the disease (often characterized as a "cancer") of politics. Rather than simply employing the brutally repressive tactics of the past to destroy political challenges to oligarchic power, these military leaders were inspired by a vision of neoliberal economic development that they believed would fundamentally "depoliticize" society causing the destruction of the political left and center.

The violence and destruction associated with military regimes along with the imposition of dramatic changes in the structures of national economies (usually referred to as *shock therapy,* a term associated with the requirements of the World Bank and the International Monetary Fund) resulted in a spike of human rights abuses and a series of economic crises across the region.

During the wrenching decades of the 1970s and 1980s, liberation theology and the CEBs took on particular significance in the region. Because many of the military *juntas* wrapped themselves in the mantle of religious self-glorification for saving their countries from "godless Marxism," traditional and right-wing elements of the Catholic Church (as well as some Protestant and Pentecostal churches in countries like Guatemala and Chile) rushed to align themselves with the brutal dictatorships, lending at least the appearance of moral justification to their tactics. In response, progressive Catholics who condemned human rights violations and the economic injustice borne by the poor and middle classes found moral refuge in the liberationist wing of the Catholic Church. For liberationists, sin is not only an individual condition since the fall from grace in the Garden of Eden, but sin should also be understood structurally. Political, economic, and social structures that systematically oppress the poor and disenfranchised are sinful; for example, for many Latin American liberationists, the kind of capitalism (often called "dependent capitalism") thrust on the region by the first world and in particular the imperialist United States created the endemic poverty, vast gap between the very rich and the chronically poor, and the politically weak and unstable regimes that were easily dominated by powerful economic elites backed by US-armed military forces. For most liberationists therefore, Christians are not only called to individual repentance and acts of charity but also, more importantly, solidarity with the poor and a commitment to engaged social justice. For "radicals," a preferential option for the poor must be understood in light of the Marxist notion that class conflict is the motor of history; thus, accommodationist or reformist political strategies that fail to bring fundamental change to existing power arrangements—or sinful structures—accomplish little more than to preserve the status quo. As such, Christians must join with other political forces to fight (potentially with violence) for real political and economic transformation. For most progressives of the era, however, the struggle against oppression was understood as more properly channeled through outreach to the poor and oppressed. Facilitating change rather than explicit partisan activity through grassroots, religious self-help and educational groups was the focus of the vast majority of CEBs throughout the region.

The CEBs were particularly important in countries in which the normal channels for political demands were eliminated by state-sponsored repression and violence. In Chile, for example, between the coup in 1973 and 1983, the church—and particularly the grassroots CEBs—served as virtually the only channel through which opposition could be voiced. After initially welcoming the armed forces for restoring order in 1973 after particularly chaotic months under the democratically elected Salvador Allende (1970–1973), Chilean church leaders began issuing stronger and more pointed criticisms of the regime's human rights violations and economic policies by the late 1970s. Scores of new church or church-affiliated neighborhood, academic, and workers' organizations were created to facilitate the struggles against the military. To the extent that dissent remained alive between 1973 and 1983, the space was largely provided by the Catholic Church. In such countries, the role of the church as the "voice of the voiceless" came to have profound meaning for prodemocracy movements and those suffering from the economic dislocation of failed neoliberal economic policies and state-sponsored repression and human rights violations.

Although the progressive and radical wings of the Latin American Catholic Church were never as extensive as many claimed (or feared) during the 1960s to 1980s, the most important result of their role during the most brutal years of the region's dictatorships was that the Catholic Church as an institution became committed to the protection of human rights and the moral superiority of political democracy over authoritarianism in the region. Yet by the 1980s and the return of democratic regimes, the church throughout the region was eager to withdraw from the political fray and return, again, to a more explicit distinction between public life and personal salvation. In countries where the church had been particularly valiant in condemning human rights violations or supporting prodemocracy forces, ecclesial authorities were keenly aware that their stances had alienated their traditional allies among elites and on the political right.

The desire among many Latin American church leaders to withdraw to a more universal appeal to personal salvation, regardless of class or ideological suasion, found no greater advocate than Pope John Paul II (1978–2005). Prior to becoming the Supreme Pontiff in 1978, then archbishop of Krakow Karol Wojtyla was known as a staunch anticommunist in his native Poland who had been critical of the Vatican II definition of the Catholic Church as "people of God." He had long argued for a traditionally hierarchical definition of the institutional church; in other words, a church in which the authority of the church is made manifest through the Pope, cardinals, archbishops, bishops, and priests and under whose direction the lay population lives in faithful obedience. Pope John Paul II was enormously energetic and charismatic. But as Penny Lernoux warned in the 1970s, "John Paul, who thinks in terms of peoples—not nation states—is deeply supportive of the populism that enables a people to express political, economic, or social aspirations through religious gestures and symbols" (cited in Cleary and Stewart-Gambino 1992:4). However, at the same time, "John Paul's Catholicism has a clear set of rules and it is the responsibility of priests to make sure they are obeyed. . . . The civilization he envisions is essentially integralist—a throwback to a Christendom when the church was both the mediating force in secular society and the only source of spiritual salvation" (4).

Pope John Paul II launched a clear offensive against the elements of the progressive, liberationist Latin American church that he viewed as, at worst, dangerously aligned with the very Marxist elements that he opposed so ardently in the European context or, at best, inappropriately engaged in the worldly sphere of politics in which the laity were granted far too much authority as "people of God." Many mistakenly attributed John Paul's consistent rejection of the liberationist wing of the Latin American church as evidence of conservative or right-wing political beliefs; however, John Paul was a charismatic and populist defender of the poor who helped solidify the church's support for democracy. He is best understood as seeking to impose, through his consistently traditionalist appointments of bishops and cardinals, a return to a strictly hierarchical church that adheres to a mission of personal salvation from sin and calls individuals, particularly the economically privileged, to personal acts of charity on behalf of the poor.

By the 1990s, much of the Latin American church had retreated from the political and social activism of the 1960s–1980s—in part due to the Vatican's influence and in part out of national prelates' desire to withdraw the church from the frontlines of the highly charged, often violent, ideological clashes between right and left during the dictatorships and democratic transitions. Even the most progressive national bishops' conferences in the region sought to reconsolidate a more traditional role for the church in democratic societies in which political institutions such as political parties or trade unions could function as the channels for the population's temporal demands and aspirations.

The urge to withdraw from the partisan fray in order to reassert a universal mission of salvation for all created a particularly difficult time for many men and women who had forged their religious identities during the previous period of liberationist activism. During the dictatorships, many poor women had been forced to adopt new roles to support their families, in spite of their traditional roles in service to the all-male priesthood and their religious identities forged in light of the Catholic cult of Mary that glorifies the suffering of motherhood. In response to the economic desperation caused by widespread unemployment, progressive grassroots CEBs began using the Bible to lead women to see their own agency in their communities. Poor women organized neighborhood soup kitchens, self-help organizations of all sorts, and entrepreneurial activities based on crafts such as sewing and cooking. In many countries, help from diocesan or national church organizations provided these women with additional training or even access to national or international aid. As Susan Tiano discusses in Chapter 10, women who emerged as local leaders became involved in regional or national networks of church-sponsored organizations, taking them far from their traditionally subservient roles in the exclusively private sphere. In addition to the economic causes of women's mobilization across the region, poor men also bore the brunt of the state's repression of "political" activity. In an environment in which men's ability to be protagonists in their families' survival was repressed, poor women turned to the church—their traditional source of personal refuge. Many of the poor women who were transformed by the opportunities they found in grassroots church or church-sponsored organizations did not represent new members, and neither were these organizations necessarily new ones. In many cases, the neighborhood women's groups in the church were transformed out of necessity with the women who had long participated under the guidance and encouragement of progressive priests and nuns. For these women, in particular, the definition of the Catholic Church as "people of God" was powerful; their stories are inspiring and moving. For them, the retrenchment of the institutional church back to its more traditional role, with the reimposition of the strict authority of the all-male priesthood and the rejection of lay—particularly female—leadership in local parishes, was a wrenching experience.

On the other hand, the withdrawal of the church from progressive engagement in political and social issues also resulted in the return to the parishes of many who had been alienated by its new stances during the dictatorships—not only among the traditional elites, but also among the poor. The resurgence of a more spiritual, less political church provided a welcome invitation to many who sought a refuge from the ongoing challenges of Latin American life. In fact, since 1972, most national churches in Latin America have seen an increase, sometimes dramatic, in the number of vocations for the priesthood. (See Table 12.1.)

Table 12.1 Change in Number of Catholic Seminarians, 1972–2008

Country	Catholic Seminarians 1972	2008	Percent Change 1972–2008
Argentina	306	1,778	481
Bolivia	49	712	1,353
Brazil	939	9,369	898
Chile	111	709	539
Colombia	738	4,827	554
Costa Rica	61	202	231
Cuba	49	86	75
Dominican Republic	51	734	1,339
Ecuador	92	675	634
El Salvador	34	512	1,406
Guatemala	69	406	488
Haiti	41	439	971
Honduras	16	159	894
Mexico	2,264[a]	6,919[b]	205
Nicaragua	45	298	562
Panama	22	113	414
Paraguay	63	422	422
Peru	190	2,097	1,004
Puerto Rico	49	104	112
Uruguay	25	69	176
Venezuela	120	1,397	1,064
Total	5,334	25,108	371

Sources: Felician A. Foy. ed. *Catholic Almanac 1975.* Huntington, IN: Our Sunday Visitor, 1974; and Matthew E. Bunson, ed. *Catholic Alamanac 2008.* Huntington, IN: Our Sunday Visitor, 2008.

Notes: a. Figure is for 1975, not 1972; from *Statistical Yearbook of the Church 1994.*

b. Figure is for 2003, not 2008; from "Catholic Church in Latin America." http://www.providence.edu/las/Statistics.htm.

▓ The Rise of Evangelical Protestantism

Although still predominantly Catholic, Latin America in the past century, and particularly in recent decades, has experienced significant increases in the number of individuals who identify themselves as adherents of some form of Protestantism. By 2005 Guatemala had by far the largest percentage of Protestants while Haiti, Nicaragua, and Paraguay also saw increasing numbers between 2003 and 2005.

Protestants have been in Latin America since the middle of the nineteenth century due to immigration and limited mission activity, particularly after the

Spanish-American War. In the early twentieth century, the small number of Protestants came almost entirely from the traditional, mainline traditions (Lutherans, Baptists, Anglicans, Methodists, Presbyterians) of the European and US immigrants or economic elites associated with first world economic dominance. Indigenous conversions to these traditions were rare, and the populations professing these faiths remained relatively stable.

The extraordinary growth of adherents to Protestantism began in Latin America in the 1950s–1960s. By the 1990s, it was widely believed that over 50 million Latin Americans, or approximately 11 percent of the continent's population, claimed to be Protestant (Lewis 2004). Indeed, the question *Is Latin America Turning Protestant?* provided a revealing title for a groundbreaking book by David Stoll (1990). It appeared that if the conversion rates continued, Protestants would constitute a majority in some countries in a relatively short time frame.

Unlike those Protestants who were associated with economic elites from the United States and Europe, recent conversions overwhelmingly occur among the poor and lower middle classes, and the new converts typically join evangelical Protestant (especially Pentecostal) churches and sects. Some of the strength of non-Catholic religious identification can be attributed to renewed mission work funded from the United States. For example, the Mormon Church and Jehovah's Witnesses, as well as some ideologically conservative evangelical wings of mainline US churches, funded "missionary" work to compete with liberationist Catholics who sympathized with reformist or revolutionary movements during the civil wars of the 1970s–1980s. Nevertheless, over 90 percent of the new conversions were and continue to be distinctly Latin American forms of Pentecostalism.

Conversion to evangelical Protestantism can be explained by a variety of factors. Pentecostalism is able to fill a religious need for many in poor neighborhoods whose families fled the economic deprivation of the countryside in search of urban economic opportunities during the latter half of the twentieth century. The rapid urbanization of the entire developing world, including Latin America, has created extraordinary new landscapes of shantytowns filled with dislocated families searching for new forms of community. Latin American Catholic churches, in spite of strong liberationist elements whose "preferential option for the poor" during the 1960s–1980s resulted in unprecedented outreach to poor neighborhoods, never had the resources to develop sufficient religious infrastructure (priests, nuns, parish buildings, religious educational facilities, funding for lay activities) to respond adequately to the enormous religious needs of the poor generally, or the populations dislocated by rapid urbanization in particular. In addition, the brief period of heightened awareness of the needs of the poor represented by the ascendance of liberation theology should be understood in the context of centuries of alignment with economic and political elites; no national Catholic Church ever had a strong, institutional presence among the poor and lower middle classes who always have comprised the majority of Latin American populations. Even during the height of liberation theology, Catholic dioceses struggled to commit religious resources to the vast, new urban areas. For traditional, mainline religious institutions—both Catholic and Protestant—the training of new priests and ministers is costly and time consuming. For example, the road to ordination for aspiring young Catholic priests is a long one through years of seminary training and a high degree of personal commitment and self-sacrifice. Foreign priests and nuns, in fact, accounted for much of the liberationist work in poor neighborhoods in many countries during this period.

The needs of the urban poor create an open terrain for religious competition that is especially conducive to the growth of indigenous Pentecostalism. Unlike mainline Catholic and Protestant churches, the operational costs of Pentecostal institutions are remarkably low. Pentecostal religious authority, rather than requiring seminary training and certification by institutional bureaucracies, is earned through charismatic preaching—typically on the streets or in small, storefront locations in poor neighborhoods. One is a Pentecostal pastor by virtue of the ability to gain followers rather than by certification by a religious institution after successful educational attainment. Since religious authority is based on charismatic appeal, Pentecostal "churches" can be created anywhere; indeed, the Pentecostal phenomenon in Latin America is characterized by constant schism with aspiring pastors breaking away from established groups and seeking to establish new "churches" around their own leadership. Rather than being bound by the music in hymnals or the religious canon of a particular denomination, aspiring Pentecostal pastors freely incorporate indigenous music or other art forms in their services. The service itself is grounded in biblical text and centers on the ability of the pastor to "bring it alive" with charismatic appeal.

Because Pentecostal authority is conferred by a pastor's followers rather than a religious organization, there is remarkable flexibility in belief structures across Pentecostal groups. Pentecostal leaders have supported right-wing political leaders, notably in Guatemala and Chile in the 1980s, yet center-left politicians such as Brazil's former president Luiz Inácio Lula da Silva (2002–2010) and Chile's former president Michelle Bachelet (2006–2010) have successfully courted powerful Pentecostal support. Efforts to characterize Pentecostals by traditional political or even religious categories are confounded by the broad range of individual pastors across neighborhoods, regions, and countries.

If a wide array of cultural manifestations of Pentecostalism is possible, what lies at the heart of Pentecostal belief? Pentecostals, like fundamentalists with whom they are often mistaken, root their belief structures in literal interpretations of biblical text, most especially the descriptions of the experiences of the early Christians as told in the New Testament book, the Acts of the Apostles. The Pentecost, the moment in which the crucified Christ returns to the apostles resulting in extraordinary "blessings of the Spirit" such as speaking in tongues, is a cornerstone of Pentecostals' emphasis on the lived experience of the Holy Spirit. Rather than orthodoxy, as interpreted by priests, Pentecostals—like other Protestants—seek individual and direct experience of God through Christ. Pentecostals believe in the individual call to perfection, and the path to perfection is through seizure by the Holy Spirit as manifest by extraordinary gifts. In that sense, Pentecostals believe that the kinds of miraculous events and personal gifts chronicled in the Acts of the Apostles remain possible for all Christians throughout the ages, and evidence of the gifts of the spirit is the measure of one's faith. Indeed, Pentecostals criticize their non-Pentecostal, mainline Christian brethren for their emphasis on religious orthodoxy rather than the individual and demonstrable personal experience of the Holy Spirit.

Due to the emphasis on the personal experience of the Holy Spirit in Pentacostalism, the authority of pastors rests on their leadership of the faithful in their quest for a personal, emotionally intense experience of the Holy Spirit. This emphasis is particularly well suited for poor neighborhoods where financial resources are scarce, access to formal education is limited, and the reach of the Catholic and traditional Protestant churches is constrained. The strength of Pentecostalism is the ability to respond to local needs, traditions, and constraints depending on the charismatic talents and entrepreneurial skills of local pastors who often preach in storefront churches that punctuate the urban landscapes of Latin America.

Another hallmark of Pentecostalism across the region, consistent with the ability to respond to local conditions, is a commitment to grassroots social service. Many Pentecostal churches, particularly those that are more established, either create or collaborate with grassroots social agencies related to such issues as addiction, unwed pregnancy, domestic violence, religious education of the young, and teen delinquency. However, it should be noted that at the center of Pentecostals' church membership is a shared experience of the Holy Spirit, not a shared vision for society at large. Most Pentecostals view themselves as apolitical in the sense that their lives and social networks are committed to and built around their religious faith, not social or political movements that promise earthly transformation on the basis of man-made ideology. In addition, Pentecostals' involvement in social service agencies tends to be viewed as part of their commitment to proselytizing potential converts rather than a commitment to a political agenda to change economic or social structures. Indeed, Pentecostals typically are viewed as inherently "conservative" for their emphasis on personal conversion and repentance of individual sin, in contrast to their more liberal religious counterparts in other denominations (particularly liberationist Catholics) whose faith propels them to address the societal causes of social ills.

In addition to the wide array of expressions of Pentecostalism across Latin America—from the small, disconnected groups found in virtually any poor neighborhood in any Latin American city or countryside to the large churches in countries like Guatemala—the growth of so-called neo-Pentecostalism in the region further complicates the religious landscape. Associated with the rise of multinational megachurches, such as Brazil's Universal Church of the Kingdom of God, that have access to mass media (e.g., television and radio stations and programs), neo-Pentecostals preach a "health and wealth" message. In this strain of Pentecostalism, religious observance leads to physical and material rewards.

In spite of predictions in the 1990s that Latin America was "turning Protestant," it appears that growth rates have stabilized in most of the region. Socioeconomic and political changes, however, have challenged traditional belief systems and given rise to the appeal of a variety of alternatives. A vibrant culture of religious change has emerged in many communities throughout the region.

◼ Secularization

Although it is commonplace to view the Latin American religious landscape in terms of the competition between Catholicism and other (often evangelical) strains of Christianity, secularization—or the rise in numbers who self-identify as having "no religion" and the resulting decline of the relevance of religious belief of any kind—is considered as threatening to institutional religion as any competing religious belief system. Historically, secularism is associated with Enlightenment rationality and positivism according to which the world can be explained by science rather than religion. In European thought, the rapid advances of science, medicine, and technology, along with advancements in the social sciences, gave credence to the view that the decline in religious identification may be attributed to the rise in modern knowledge. Thus, observers have long assumed that economic modernization in Latin America (or other less developed regions) would lead to higher educational attainment and, therefore, secularization as greater numbers of people turn from religious identification to a more "modern" worldview.

Recent data suggesting a rise in the percentage of citizens who self-identify as having "no religion" appears to confirm the secularization thesis (Cleary and Steigenga 2004). But rather than representing the relentless march of modernization, the category of "no religion" appears to arise from the complexity of greater religious pluralism. For individuals who convert (usually to some form of evangelical Protestantism), it is often difficult to maintain the same degree of fervor and religious commitment. As the conversion experience fades, individuals can "backslide" into a kind of space between their previous Catholic identity and an at least temporarily waning enthusiasm for their new identity. Indeed, evangelical churches that stress personal conversion and emotionally charged expression of the presence of the Holy Spirit perennially face the challenge of inspiring second- and third-generation church members and maintaining the fervor of the converted. Equally, "lapsed Catholics" who report occasional church attendance or dalliance with Protestant conversion similarly can identify themselves as having no religion, yet their numbers do not necessarily reflect a rejection of religious identity. Yet whatever explanation of the rise of those who identify themselves as professing no religion, both Catholic and Protestant officials view secularization—or the prospect of religious irrelevance—as one of the greatest threats of the modern age.

The threat of secularization is a double one—the loss of souls who will not know the grace of salvation (Catholic or Protestant) and, perhaps more importantly, the erosion of fundamental values in the public sphere that religious authorities view as preventing the decline of human society. For example, both Catholics and Protestants share a vision of men's and women's traditional roles in the family unit that they believe is the cornerstone of civilization. Both Catholics and evangelical Protestants decry what they perceive to be symptoms of the relegation of faith to churches and the private sphere; for example, divorce, abortion, greater sexual freedom, and contraception. Given the historical role of the Catholic Church in Latin America, the fight against secularization and its symptoms is waged in both the political and individual spheres—both for public policies, such as support for Catholic schools, legal bans on divorce and abortion, and subsidies for Catholic agencies, as well as for individual morality as evidenced by attendance at mass, adherence to Catholic morality and social doctrine, and Christian charity. Historically, Pentecostals and evangelical Protestants have not focused their energies on influencing public policies to combat secularization, in large part because their ranks were made up of a mosaic of small, pastor-centric groups that were considered competitors of the Catholic Church and toward whom most Latin American states were hostile, or at best, neglectful. For these religious entities, the central impulse of evangelization is a primary emphasis on individual rebirth in Christ, not public policy.

Yet their mass appeal certainly has social implications as do the countless local social services offered by these churches on behalf of the poor, particularly in combating substance abuse, domestic violence, teen delinquency, and other social ills that are so commonplace throughout Latin American *barrios*. Many credit evangelical conversion with profound changes in particularly male behavior—abstinence from alcohol, faithfulness to their wives, taking pride in being an honorable father and head of the family—that tangibly improves the lives of women and children. Such religious values, while often dismissed as "traditional" or "conservative," are at the heart of the rejection of secularization by both Protestants and Catholics.

If the nineteenth and early twentieth centuries were characterized by a series of conflicts about the role of the Catholic Church in Latin America, the late-twentieth and early twenty-first centuries have witnessed the church's struggle to retain its dominance in the face of rapidly increasing religious pluralism. In fact, the church views the trend in citizens claiming that they have no religion as one result of the dramatic rise in the number of evangelical Protestants and evidence of the weakening of the church's power. Perhaps the clearest statement of the Vatican's perspective on the dangers of evangelical Protestantism is Pope John Paul II's address to Latin American bishops in Santo Domingo in 1992:

> We should not underestimate a particular strategy aimed at weakening the bonds that unite Latin American countries and so to undermine the kinds of strength provided by unity. To that end, significant amounts of money are offered to subsidize proselytizing campaigns that try to shatter such Catholic unity. (cited in Cleary and Stewart-Gambino 1997:10)

Describing non-Catholic religions as "sects" and "rapacious wolves," John Paul II demonstrates the degree of the perceived threat posed by religious competitors throughout Latin America. Likewise, Pope Benedict XVI, in his 2007 trip to Brazil, repeatedly warned of the dangers of rising Protestantism amidst his condemnation of contraception and abortion and the dangerous modern forces of both capitalism and Marxism.

Latin American bishops' conferences, with Vatican support, have pursued a dual strategy in combating religious pluralism and secularization. National churches use their political muscle to ensure that governments maintain the church's preferential treatment in public policy in areas such as Catholic dominance in public and private education, direct and indirect subsidies, and exclusive reach into the ranks of the military. In addition, since the 1992 conference of Latin American bishops, Pope John Paul II called Latin American Catholics to a "new evangelization," or a renewed vigor at the grassroots to energize the church's ability to meet the religious aspirations of the many faithful who turn to alternative faiths, including evangelical Protestantism. This strategy is comprised of several tactics including a much greater emphasis on increasing the number of religious personnel (priests, nuns, and lay leaders) and an explicit attempt to adopt some of the most popular aspects of Pentecostalism, most notably an explicitly charismatic approach to mass and Bible study.

▓ Charismatic Catholics

Although the Catholic Charismatic Renewal (CCR) movement originated in the United States and is popular among Filipino, Korean, and Hispanic Americans, the movement also has found resonance in Latin America since it was introduced by Catholic missionaries in the early 1970s. Popes John Paul II and Benedict XVI both strongly endorsed the movement's focus on the gifts of the Holy Spirit (hearkening to the same biblical story of the Pentecost that inspires Pentecostalism in all of its forms) and the focus on the power of biblical texts to illuminate contemporary experience. Like their evangelical Protestant counterparts, charismatic Catholics embrace the mass media's ability to reach out to the faithful. Perhaps the most well-known figure among Latin American charismatics is Father Marcelo Rossi, a Brazilian whose 1999 CD of upbeat religious music outsold all other recording artists in the country. Rossi has a daily radio show, two weekly TV shows, and a significant Web presence, and he hosts regular concerts attracting thousands of young fans. Today, the Catholic charismatic movement is the largest and most vibrant lay movement in the region, with between 22 million and 25 million members. According to some observers, Catholic charismatics make up roughly half of all active Catholics in Brazil and El Salvador (Chestnut 2003; Garrard-Burnett 2000).

Latin American prelates have been generally supportive of the rejuvenating potential of the charismatic movement—most particularly its ability to compete head on with evangelical Protestants and Pentecostals who were winning conversions at an alarming rate. Yet at the same time, Chestnut (2003) has characterized the Latin American bishops' support as a "yellow light" because of the fear that emphasis on individual experience of the Holy Spirit would undermine the authority of the Catholic Church hierarchy. While lamenting the appeal of the "sects"—particularly Pentecostals, Seventh Day Adventists, Assemblies of God, Jehovah's Witness, the Foursquare Gospel Church, and the Mormons—Latin American bishops were quick to insist that the successful and vibrant Catholic charismatics must defer to the authority of the official Catholic Church. According to the bishops and the Vatican, the danger presented by non-Catholic charismatics is that they erroneously believe that the direct experience of the Holy Spirit, particularly as is experienced as rebirth in the Spirit, is the foundational Christian experience. For the Catholic Church, the ecstatic experience of the Holy Spirit is simply one of the experiences of God and is not a necessary precondition to the sanctity or enjoyment of the sacraments. Priests and bishops are quick to position the church as the only authority to which the faithful can turn for interpretation of God's will; accordingly, salvation can be achieved only through the mediation of priests, not through direct experience of God through the personal experience of the Holy Spirit.

▩ Major Spiritist Religions

A comprehensive understanding of religion in Latin America requires recognition of the vibrant practices of a variety of religious beliefs that derive from indigenous and African traditions. Although much of the literature on Latin American religions focuses on Catholicism—still the overwhelming majority religion in the region—and the rapid increase in evangelical forms of Protestantism, spiritist and syncretic belief systems are more widespread than ordinarily assumed.

Prior to the sixteenth-century Spanish and Portuguese conquest, the population of Latin America varied immensely from one place to another. The largest societies, such as the Inca of the Andes and the Maya, Olmec, and Aztec of Central America and Mexico (themselves imperial civilizations whose empires dominated other conquered indigenous cultures), developed highly sophisticated religious institutions with established priesthoods. In other areas, less developed indigenous populations had religious practices that were more tribal. What is common to all indigenous cultures, however, is the forcible imposition of Catholicism after the conquest. Throughout the colonies of the Americas, the European victors prohibited the native religions. Indigenous religious practices were either wiped out or merged with Catholicism or other, newer religious beliefs; for example, those transferred through the African slave trade. The imposition of Catholicism on the indigenous peoples generated various revolts using indigenous religious symbols or figures to build cohesion. More typically, however, most indigenous cultures yielded to the official culture of the victorious conquerors—with elements of the original beliefs morphing into their closest Catholic counterpart. This resulted in a distinct difference between "official Catholicism" and "folk religion" practiced by the majority of the people. These syncretic religions differed across the lines of preexisting, indigenous cultures. The tension between the Vatican and folk religion as practiced by most people has been a dynamic one historically—with the church occasionally tolerating local practices within Catholicism and, more often, reaffirming the official church's authority to determine the boundaries of orthodoxy. Thus, in spite of the destruction of preconquest civilizations such as the Incan and Aztec Empires, many of their religious practices continued to survive in some form.

The importation of black slaves in the first half of the sixteenth century brought a second wave of new religious traditions and cults, this time not of the conquerors but of the exploited. Since the introduction of Africans into the Spanish colonies, their religious practices were strictly prohibited. However, as with the indigenous traditions, African religious beliefs and practices did not simply disappear, but rather syncretized with both Catholicism and the region's indigenous traditions and—later on—with other religions that were transplanted to Latin America. Such is the case with Candomblé de caboclo, which combined African and indigenous practices, and Umbanda which combined African, indigenous, and other traditions.

Candomblé, particularly popular in northeastern Brazil with over 2 million believers, derives from the West African Yoruba traditions brought by slaves in the 18th century. Around the central deity, Oludumare, are *orixas* (spirits) who control individuals' destinies and who became paired over time with Catholic saints. *Orixas* represent deified ancestors who connect believers with the spiritual world. Candomblé literally means "dance in honor of the gods," and dance and music are central elements of religious practice. Followers of

Candomblé typically are poor and racially more "black" than followers of other Afro-Brazilian cults, and its popularity among Afro-Brazilians as a symbol not only of religious belief, but also cultural identity, has risen sharply after the end of active state persecution in the 1970s. Today, many Latin Americans of African descent travel to the Bahía region of Brazil to learn more about their cultural heritage. Significantly, there is a movement to purge contemporary Candomblé of Catholic elements in order to reclaim its African roots.

Umbanda, another Afro-Brazilian religion, also combines Christianity's belief in one supreme God and African *orixas* (spirits), who are paired with Christian saints. Umbanda derives from African Bantu religions, and its origins in Brazil were centered in Rio de Janeiro with a Kardecist wing located in São Paulo. Today, followers of Umbanda number over 20 million and can be found throughout Brazil and in neighboring countries. Umbanda appeals more broadly to poor and middle-class blacks, whites, and *mulatos* who seek advice regarding any number of issues such as health or work-related problems and personal relationships. Worship is organized around a leader called a *pai-de-santo* or *mãe-de-santo,* depending on gender, and mediums (psychics who can act as a medium between the physical and the spiritual worlds) who can be possessed by the spirits. Spirits are both Brazilian (deceased native Brazilians called *caboclos*) and African (deceased slaves who died at the hands of abusive owners called *pretos velhos* or "old blacks"), among several other subgroups of ancestors. Spirits are known for their particular strengths such as knowledge of indigenous herbal remedies, sympathy for the oppressed, or particular knowledge of indigenous ways. During worship, the spirits communicate their advice to supplicants through mediums who have reached the spirits through trances.

Other descendents of West African religions include Vodou (commonly called voodoo and found primarily in Haiti) and Santería (found in the Caribbean). Vodou and Santería, too, are spiritist religious practices in which African spirits are associated with Christian saints. In Vodou, *houngans* (charismatic priests) help individuals make contact with the spirits, typically to solicit health or personal help. Spirits also can be invoked to ward off danger or attack other spirits that are harmful. Vodou has a particularly politicized history; it has been severely persecuted sporadically since Haitian independence—usually at the behest of the white, Catholic bishops. Historically, Vodou temples—which operated clandestinely—became important centers of black identity and resistance. In the 1950s, François Duvalier curtailed the persecution of Vodou and mobilized its organizations into militias (known as the Tonton Macoutes) in order to win the 1957 presidential election. The Tonton Macoutes became a formidable force that intimidated political enemies for the next thirty years.

Santería, based in Cuba, is quite similar in historical origins to Haitian Vodou; Santería beliefs trace back to West Africa and were brought to Cuba by slaves. The word *santería* was a pejorative term used by the Spanish to describe the preoccupation with Christian saints rather than God among African converts to Catholicism. Like their fellow spiritists from West Africa, Cuban slaves shrouded their belief in their own gods, *orishas,* by identifying them as Christian saints. After Cuban independence in 1898, however, some Santería leaders realized the possibility for personal gain of peddling their ties to the spiritual world as black magic or sorcery. Santería, like the darker side of Vodou, became associated with criminal acts, evil intent, and the ability to harm others with magic spells. In the United States, the popular image of Vodou and Santería as sinister and violent stems from the manipulation of the original spiritist descendants of West African religions.

Venezuela provides another illustration of syncretism. Although the majority of the population is ostensibly Catholic, many people from all sectors of society believe in varying syntheses of African, indigenous, and Christian religions. For example, followers of María Lionsa worship a goddess of nature similar to the Arawak water deity, West African mythical figures, and the Virgin Mary. And *curanderos* (healers) found in indigenous villages are consulted by many Venezuelans from all walks of life.

▓ Conclusion

The religious landscape of twenty-first-century Latin America will continue to be a competitive marketplace, and both Catholicism and evangelicalism will adapt to compete for followers. Although Catholicism's cultural legacy is enduring, it is doubtful that the Catholic Church will regain its religious monopoly. In response, national hierarchies backed by the Vatican have redoubled their efforts to meet the religious aspirations of the people. Although disappointing to those inspired by the church's political agenda during the 1960s–1980s, including its "preferential option for the poor," the church has strengthened its reach into society through renewed focus on meeting the population's spiritual needs and embracing the more charismatic styles of worship characteristic of Pentacostalism. Indeed, the number of vocations among young priests has risen—sometimes dramatically—in many countries. This renewed Catholic Church is a traditional one with an emphasis on orthodoxy, hierarchical authority, and redoubled commitment to saving individual souls through the sacraments and Christian charity.

Various forms of evangelical Protestantism will continue to provide an important alternative belief system. However, the sharp evangelical growth during the decades after the 1960s in countries like Guatemala, Chile, and Brazil has leveled off. Scholarly observers no longer predict that Latin America is "becoming Protestant." Particularly for Pentecostals, the absence of an institutional orthodoxy, the flexible path to becoming a pastor, and the tendency of new groups to form when existing churches become too big all provide opportunities to adjust worship styles and adapt their religious commitments to changing local and national contexts. As already seen in Guatemala, Chile, and Brazil, some evangelical and Pentecostal churches will grow into national forces. Evangelical embrace of the media coupled with a focus on charismatic outreach guarantees national prominence for media-savvy pastors and their followings. As these national churches become institutionalized, however, their missions and religiopolitical identities will provide opportunities for new alternatives under the guidance of new pastors. Over time, evangelical churches will experience the challenge of inspiring belief in subsequent generations. These processes probably will be complicated by scandals similar to those that have plagued more established churches.

It is improbable that continued economic modernization and growth will result in widespread decline in the relevance of religious belief for the majority of Latin Americans. While a competitive religious marketplace has permanently transformed the Catholic Church's colonial and postcolonial religious monopoly (and perhaps institutional complacency), such competition has inspired volatility in individual religious self-identification. Although conversions continue at a heightened rate, the percentages of adherents of different faith traditions have leveled off. This is not evidence of a substantial decline of religious identity, although the marketplace does include "no religious identity" among other religious identities. Significant changes in the religious landscape over the past fifty years no longer allow us to think of Latin America as singularly Catholic. In fact, the region's religious landscape remains vibrant, occupied by varied religious forces that remain relevant for the vast majority of citizens.

Bibliography

Brown, David. *Santeria Enthroned: Art, Ritual and Innovation in an Afro-Cuban Religion.* Chicago: University of Chicago Press, 2003.

Bunson, Matthew E., ed. *Catholic Almanac 2008.* Huntington, IN: Our Sunday Visitor, 2008.

Burdick, John. *Legacies of Liberation: The Progressive Catholic Church in Brazil at the Start of a New Millennium.* Burlington, VT: Ashgate, 2004.

Chesnutt, R. Andrew. *Competitive Spirits: Latin America's New Religious Economy.* New York: Oxford University Press, 2003.

Chiappari, Christopher L. "Culture, Power, and Identity: Negotiating Between Catholic Orthodoxy and Popular Practice." *Latin American Research Review* 42, no. 3 (2007): 282–296.

Cleary, Edward L. "Shopping Around: Questions About Latin American Conversions." *International Bulletin of Missionary Research* 28, no. 2 (2004): 50–54.

Cleary, Edward L., and Timothy Steigenga. *Resurgent Voices in Latin America: Indigenous Peoples, Political Mobilization, and Religious Change.* New Brunswick, NJ: Rutgers University Press, 2004.

Cleary, Edward L., and Hannah Stewart-Gambino, eds. *Conflict and Competition: The Latin American Church in a Changing Environment.* Boulder: Lynne Rienner, 1992.

Cleary, Edward L., and Hannah Stewart-Gambino, eds. *Power, Politics, and Pentecostals in Latin America*. Boulder: Westview Press, 1997.

de Theije, Marjo, and Cecília Loreto Mariz. "Localizing and Globalizing Processes in Brazilian Catholicism: Comparing Inculturation in Liberationist and Charismatic Catholic Cultures." *Latin American Research Review* 43, no. 1 (2008): 33–54.

Drogus, Carol Ann, and Hannah Stewart-Gambino. *Activist Faith: Grassroots Women in Democratic Brazil and Chile*. University Park: Pennsylvania State University Press, 2005.

Foy, Felician A., ed. *Catholic Almanac 1975*. Huntington, IN: Our Sunday Vistor, 1974.

Freston, Paul. *Protestant Political Parties: A Global Survey*. Burlington, VT: Ashgate, 2004.

Garrard-Burnett, Virginia, ed. *On Earth as It Is in Heaven: Religion in Modern Latin America*. Wilmington, DE: SR Books, 2000.

Johnson, Paul C. *Secrets, Gossip, and God: The Transformation of Brazilian Candomblé*. New York: Oxford University Press, 2002.

Lewis, Donald M., ed. *Christianity Reborn: The Global Expansion of Evangelicalism in the Twentieth Century*. Grand Rapids, MI: William B. Eerdmans, 2004.

Martin, David. *Tongues of Fire: The Explosion of Protestantism in Latin America*. Oxford: Blackwell, 1990.

Murphy, Joseph M. *Santería: African Spirits in America*. Boston: Beacon Press, 1993.

Peterson, Anna L., and Manuel A. Vásquez, eds. *Latin American Religions: Histories and Documents in Context*. New York: New York University Press, 2008.

Peterson, Anna L., Manuel A. Vásquez, and Philip J. Williams, eds. *Christianity, Social Change, and Globalization in the Americas*. New Brunswick, NJ: Rutgers University Press, 2001.

Smith, Christian, and Joshua Prokopy, eds. *Latin American Religion in Motion*. New York: Routledge, 1999.

Statistical Yearbook of the Church 1994. Vatican City: Central Statistics Office of the Church, 1996.

Stoll, David. *Is Latin America Turning Protestant? The Politics of Evangelical Growth*. Berkeley: University of California Press, 1990.

Vásquez, Manuel A., and Marie Friedmann Marquardt, eds. *Globalizing the Sacred: Religion Across the Americas*. New Brunswick, NJ: Rutgers University Press, 2003.

13

Latin American Literature

David H. Bost and Angélica Lozano-Alonso

L iterature reveals much about how people interpret their physical and social
environments and their place in the world. Their values, beliefs, and aspirations are reflected in tales about past and daily experiences. Hence, literary
expression is an important consideration for students of contemporary Latin
America.

Previous chapters have explored specific aspects of Latin America, past
and present. In this chapter, we look at the perceptions of interpreters and writers who have contributed an artistic and intellectual account that illuminates
our understanding of the culture in which they lived.

▩ The Colonial Heritage

Native American Literature

As René de la Pedraja reports in Chapter 3, the Spanish *conquistadores* of the
early 1500s were astonished to find that the New World had civilizations that,
in some ways, rivaled those in Europe. The Mayas, Aztecs, and Incas were accomplished architects, artists, musicians, sculptors, and dancers. Most pre-
Columbian literature was oral and was quickly forgotten after the conquest. A
few indigenous texts, however, were transcribed in the sixteenth century by
Spanish clerics and educated native people. These texts exist today as evidence
of a rich literary tradition that flourished in the centuries before Christopher
Columbus's discovery of the New World.

The Mayas were the only native civilization that had written texts, in hiero-
glyphic form, almost all of which perished in the chaotic years after the con-

379

quest. A few of these books survive as Spanish translations, however. For example, *Popul-Vuh* (the Mayan "Bible") is a collection of myths, history, philosophy, and legends. *Chilam Balam* is a compilation of history, religion, astronomy, and medicine. It was written in Mayan a few years after the conquest by an anonymous author who used the Spanish alphabet. Some fragments of Mayan codices and stone inscriptions do remain.

The Incas and Aztecs had no actual written language, but had an active oral literary culture. The Aztecs used some pictorial representations whereas the Incas kept accounts on colored, knotted strings called *quipus*. Many performances—often a combination of theater, song, and dance—were ceremonial and ritualistic in nature. The Incan *taqui,* for example, was a ritual dance that represented the Incan calendar and principal mythological characters. The Aztecs had highly developed theater that was performed in the large open spaces of Tenochtitlán (most of which now lies under the foundations of Mexico City). Drama in the Aztec and Incan empires often constituted an official ceremony performed at the royal court and events reenacted from their historical or mythological past. The Aztecs and the Incas also composed lyric and epic poetry that was performed at public ceremonies.

Spanish missionaries who lived among the native peoples and learned their languages also wrote extensively about the native tribes of Mexico and Peru and produced some of the earliest accounts of their culture. Diego de Landa, for example, translated Mayan hieroglyphs into the Roman alphabet.

Native American culture survived long after the conquest of the New World. The most important native-born chronicler of Incan society was Garcilaso de la Vega. Son of a Spanish captain and an Incan princess, Garcilaso spent his childhood in Peru and his adult years in Spain serving as an officer in the military. Garcilaso was truly bicultural; he spoke fluent Quechua as well as Spanish and spent his later years writing his monumental *Comentarios reales del Perú* (Royal Commentaries of Peru, 1609), a history and analysis of Incan culture and the Spanish conquest of Peru. The commentaries repeat many of the stories and legends Garcilaso heard as a child growing up among his Incan family. He wanted to correct the misconceptions of Spanish historians who, in his opinion, had misrepresented the history and culture of his maternal ancestors. Today, his work is one of the most important historical, anthropological, and literary sources for scholars studying ancient Peruvian culture. Garcilaso is perhaps better known in the United States for his detailed history of the ill-fated 1539 De Soto expedition, *La Florida* (1605).

A contemporary of Garcilaso's was Guamán Poma de Ayala. His *El primer nueva crónica y buen gobierno* (First New Chronicle and Good Government, 1615) is an illustrated history of Peru that challenged the legitimacy of the Spanish conquest of the New World and called for an end to Spain's colonial domination.

Chronicles of the Conquest and Colonization

With the exception of the novel, virtually every literary form was cultivated during the early colonial period. Much of the historical writing was testimonial; soldiers, explorers, and missionaries felt compelled to give their version of events in which they had taken part. Columbus's diary of his first voyage (1492) is the first historical document written in the New World by a European. As a writer, Columbus faced a monumental challenge: to communicate an image of the New World in ways that were understandable and compelling to his European audience. Hence, Columbus justified further exploration and ultimate conquest by tempting his readers with exaggerated reports of gold and tales of a generous and trusting people who lived in an idyllic paradise.

The conquests of Mexico and Peru were recorded by active members of the expeditionary forces that defeated native rulers Montezuma and Atahuallpa. Hernán Cortés, the Spanish captain who led the overthrow of the Aztec Empire, kept Emperor Charles I abreast of events as the Spaniards marched on Tenochtitlán. His letters to the monarch are one of the most valuable sources of information on one of history's most remarkable military victories. These records were written in part as an attempt to seek monetary or political reward for service to the crown. Cortés wanted to be named ruler of the lands he conquered, a wish the emperor ultimately fulfilled.

Bernal Díaz del Castillo wrote a noteworthy account of the fall of Mexico, narrated from the point of view of an ordinary soldier. His book, *Historia verdadera de la conquista de la Nueva España* (True History of the Conquest of Mexico, 1557), is based primarily on his own observations and recollections. Bernal Díaz had an incredible eye for detail: he remembered such things as the number of steps on different Aztec sacrificial temples, the names of horses, and the identity of common soldiers who other historians had ignored or forgotten. His work is one of the best colonial Latin American examples of a literary treatment of a historical event. Bernal Díaz, who lacked the formal academic training of a professional historian, relied on novelistic language and devices to tell his story more eloquently. Hence, many portions of his text sound like a popular tale from a novel of chivalry.

Most historical accounts of the colonial period, professional or otherwise, were strongly influenced by literary language and models. Popular historians, such as Bernal Díaz, incorporated many elements from popular literature. Learned historians, those commissioned by the crown to write the official story of the conquest and colonization, were well versed in classical historiography and often used ancient Latin masters as their ideals. Gonzalo Fernández de Oviedo wrote his *Historia general y natural de las Indias* (General and Natural History of the Indies, 1557) using such classical historians as Pliny as his model. Oviedo, nurtured on classical literature through his immersion in Italian

Renaissance culture, wrote in extraordinary detail about virtually everything he witnessed during his long residence in the New World.

Perhaps the most important characteristic of Oviedo's work and that of other official chroniclers is their passionate defense of Spain's conquest of the Americas. Oviedo and many others felt it was Spain's imperial destiny to dominate and Christianize the New World, even if this meant the virtual annihilation of native culture. There were a few worthy opponents to this position, however. Dominican priest Bartolomé de las Casas was the most articulate defender of the native peoples in history; in his many historical works, it is difficult to avoid his strongly favorable characterizations of them. In contrast, Oviedo and many others depicted the native peoples in an extraordinarily negative fashion.

Oviedo was succeeded by generations of official chroniclers who were charged not only with writing general histories of the colonies, but also with censoring other histories in an effort to protect Spain's image in the international community. Spain suffered for many years from the Black Legend, the belief in many European countries that Spain had committed numerous atrocities in the New World in the name of religious conversion. The debate over the native—helpless victim or godless savage—is one of the most pervasive themes in the colonial as well as contemporary eras. Indianist novels of the nineteenth and twentieth centuries examined the prejudices toward the native peoples that still exist hundreds of years after the conquest. Contemporary writers Mario Vargas Llosa, Carlos Fuentes, Octavio Paz, and Rigoberta Menchú Tum—among many others—continue to explore the presence of indigenous culture in contemporary Latin American life.

Not every official in the Spanish army was contemptuous of Indians. In 1542, Alvar Núñez Cabeza de Vaca wrote an extraordinary account of his eight-year journey through the North American Southwest, living among the native people first as a captive and later as their leader. His book of these experiences has recently been translated as *Castaways* (*Naufragios*, 1993). Cabeza de Vaca, one of the few who survived a shipwreck off the Texas coast, felt great sympathy for the native people he had befriended during his long trek toward Mexico City. His account of his travels is a veritable treasure of ethnographic and historical information on indigenous groups that have long since vanished. *Castaways* is fairly typical of many Latin American historical works of the colonial period in its reliance on literary themes and motifs: there are prophecies told and revealed; suspense; betrayals; the supernatural; and a fascination with an immense, exotic, and virtually unknown world ready for exploration, conquest, and eventual settlement.

Captivity among the native peoples was a popular topic for colonial historians. In several cases, prisoners returned to their former countries with fascinating stories. The captives were sought out by Spanish authorities because of their valuable information regarding the native peoples. Yet the returning captives were not always entirely sympathetic to the conquest and its methods of subjugating the Native Americans.

One of the most remarkable characteristics of certain captive narratives is that the authors reported their assimilation into the foreign culture. Francisco Núñez de Pineda y Bascuñán wrote *Cautiverio feliz* (The Happy Captive, 1673) as a record of his seven-month captivity among the Araucanians in southern Chile. His story is one of adventure, action, and intrigue. A young captain stationed on the frontier, Bascuñán was captured by the fierce Araucanians during a raid on the outpost. His extended residence among the tribe gave him considerable insights into a group of people generally regarded as savages. His story does something that was unusual for the time: he individualized his descriptions of the native people and avoided the generalizations that were common with earlier historians. Bascuñán did not deny that his captors could behave in a savage fashion, but he also revealed that these people were capable of extraordinary generosity and benevolence.

Spanish captivity and residence among indigenous groups have also fascinated contemporary novelists. Argentinean writer Abel Posse, for example, has published a novel based on Cabeza de Vaca's experiences entitled *El largo atardecer del caminante* (The Long Afternoon of the Walker, 1992). And Mexican novelist Eugenio Aguirre (1980) has written about Gonzalo Guerrero, the first Spaniard ever captured by Native Americans, who apparently led his Mayan captors in a revolt against the Spanish invaders.

The Imaginative Construction of History

By the mid-seventeenth century, many of the testimonial accounts of the colonization of the New World gave way to histories that were more literary in nature. One of the most imaginative accounts of Colombian history is Juan Rodríguez Freyle's *El carnero y Conquista y descubrimiento de Nuevo Reino de Granada* (The Conquest of New Granada, 1636). Rodríguez Freyle wrote a traditional history of the founding and settlement of his native Santa Fe de Bogotá, but his work also contains tales of sorcery, stories of adultery, lurid accounts of criminal activity in the colony, and myths and legends about the native peoples. Rodríguez Freyle was one of the most innovative and expressive writers during the colonial period; his text reveals a dimension of life in the colony that other historians had either ignored or understated.

At first glance, it may seem odd for a historical account like Rodríguez Freyle's to have so many imaginative stories. It was fairly common, however, for historical writers during the Latin American colonial era to rely on literary models to invest their stories with a more expressive language. In the sixteenth and seventeenth centuries, often no clear distinction could be discerned between historical and fictional writing with regard to truth or reliability. It was not uncommon, for example, for historians such as Rodríguez Freyle, Garcilaso de la Vega, or Oviedo to depict individuals, situations, or events with little or no textual evidence. Historians often speculated fairly freely about events and their significance. Some of Rodríguez Freyle's stories were justified as examples of what the author viewed as moral decay within the colony.

One of the best examples of a literary treatment of history in the later colonial period is *Infortunios de Alonso Ramírez* (The Misadventures of Alonso Ramírez, 1690) by Mexican intellectual Carlos de Sigüenza y Góngora. Much like a novel, the work is an account of Alonso Ramírez's extraordinary journey around the world. Ramírez was a sailor who, through a series of mishaps, shipwrecks, and captivity, circumnavigated the planet—a remarkable feat for his day. He told his story to Sigüenza y Góngora who, in turn, constructed an entertaining tale of Ramírez's life.

Sigüenza y Góngora's book is similar to a picaresque novel. Ramírez left his native Puerto Rico for Mexico City where he held a succession of jobs with a number of masters. He went to the Spanish Philippines where he briefly had a prosperous career as a sailor, traveling and trading widely throughout the Asian Pacific. His most dramatic misfortune occurred, however, when he was captured by British pirates who abused and humiliated their prisoners and treated them as slaves. Ramírez's crew quickly perished under captivity. Of the original twenty-five who were captured, only eight survived. The pirates finally gave Ramírez and his crew the opportunity for freedom: they placed them in a small boat with minimal provisions and arms.

Sailing west from Madagascar, Ramírez and his crew's boat wrecked on the Yucatán shore, and the men eventually wandered back to civilization. Once back in Mexico City, Ramírez reported his story to Sigüenza y Góngora. In spite of the historical foundations of this story, many novelistic elements of the work give Sigüenza y Góngora's narrative its strong literary quality: its sense of adventure, humor and irony, political intrigue, first-person narration, and episodic structure.

Sigüenza y Góngora was intensely interested in the American experience and wrote many other works of scientific, anthropological, and historical value. In many of his works, it is possible to detect a nascent American consciousness. Sigüenza bristled with anger, for example, whenever Europeans made disparaging references to the so-called inferiority of the creoles who populated the New World.

Poetry and Drama

Although poets and dramatists in colonial Latin America generally attempted to copy the literary conventions and styles of their Spanish and European counterparts, many tried to depict the American reality in their literature. Epic poets were among the first to compose literary homages to the individuals who had orchestrated the principal events of the discovery and conquest of the New World.

The greatest epic poem written in colonial Latin America is Alonso de Ercilla's "La Araucana" ("The Araucanian," 1569–1589), depicting the prolonged wars with the fierce Araucanians of Chile. Ercilla's poem is both testimonial—based on his experiences in fighting the tribe—and epic. Perhaps the most distinctive quality of the poem is that Ercilla did not shy away from showing profound admiration for the honor and valor of these warriors who, year after year, effectively thwarted the best efforts of the Spanish army to defeat them. Ercilla depicted the Araucanians as a highly organized, well-disciplined army. In many regards, the poem is more the story of Caupolicán, the head of the Araucanian forces, than of Pedro de Valdivia, the Spanish leader. The poem was extraordinarily popular during its day and for many years afterward, spawning numerous imitations.

The epic tradition was continued into the seventeenth century by Mexican poet Bernardo de Balbuena, whose poem "Grandeza Mexicana" ("Mexican Greatness," 1604) is an exuberant tribute to Mexico. Balbuena's careful examination of the Mexican reality is a precursor to the nineteenth-century literary movement of *costumbrismo,* in which writers recorded in minute detail virtually all aspects of daily life. Because of his passionate interest in describing Mexico in all of its complexity, Balbuena has been regarded by some literary historians as the first genuinely Latin American poet.

Not all poetry written during the colonial era was an epic tribute to the great events that had given shape to Spain's empire in the Americas. Satirists, such as Juan del Valle y Caviedes (c. 1645–1697), were bitter critics of many members of colonial society, particularly those who sought to better themselves at the expense of others. Few escaped Caviedes's wrath: aristocrats, religious officials, women, and doctors were among those who were ridiculed in his poetic compositions. His disregard for doctors was legendary. One of his most widely read poems is "Coloquio que tuvo con la muerte un médico moribundo" ("Conversation that a Dying Doctor Had with Death," c. 1680), a savage attack on the practice of medicine in colonial Peru.

Like most satirists, Caviedes hated hypocrisy and deceit. In the sonnet, "Para hallar en palacio estimaciones" ("How to Succeed at Court," c. 1690), Caviedes depicts the "perfect" courtier, one who is certain to get the attention of the viceroy: he will be a liar, a clown, a deceiver, a gossip, and, above all, a yes-man. Honesty and integrity have no place in the colonial court. Like Rodríguez Freyle, Caviedes was interested in exploring the dark underside of colonial life in an effort to portray an increasingly complex society many years after the conquest.

Caviedes was one of many in the late seventeenth century who openly admired the Mexican nun Sor Juana Inés de la Cruz, generally regarded as colonial Latin America's greatest writer. Poet, dramatist, essayist, and scholar, Sor Juana's intellectual reputation was rather unusual, of course, for women in the seventeenth century. Unable to attend the university, Sor Juana was almost entirely self-taught. Before entering the convent, she was a well-known figure at the viceregal court where she often dazzled onlookers with her amazing intelligence and learning.

Sor Juana often found it necessary to defend her life of learning and erudition. One such instance is seen in her famous correspondence with the bishop of Puebla who had criticized her for spending too much time in her intellectual pursuits to the detriment of her religious duties. Sor Juana's response to these accusations is the *Respuesta de la poetisa a la muy ilustre Sor Filotea de la Cruz* (Reply to Sor Filotea de la Cruz, 1691), an autobiographical statement that, among other things, defends her right to a life of study and reflection—an inclination that, she argued, God had given her. Sor Juana finally succumbed to the ecclesiastical authorities in 1694 when she sold her impressive library for charity and dedicated herself fully to her religious calling.

Sor Juana was a gifted and prolific poet. Her many poems dealt with religion, morality, love, jealousy, death, and other literary topics that were common during the baroque period. Feminist literary critics have recently read with great interest her compositions that criticize men for their unbridled arrogance toward women. One of Sor Juana's best-known poems is "Hombres necios" ("Foolish Men," c. 1690), a work that asks sarcastically why men expect women to be good when it is men who so often lead women astray. Her love poetry, known for its passionate language, is unusual considering the restrictions of her religious order. Her most ambitious poetic attempt is "Primero sueño" ("First Dream," 1692), a long, complex poem that is a philosophical meditation on her search for knowledge and the elusive nature of reality.

Sor Juana was also an accomplished dramatist. Writing during the last years of the golden age of Spanish theater, Sor Juana was heavily influenced by Calderón de la Barca, generally regarded as Spain's premier playwright. Sor Juana wrote both secular and religious drama and utilized all of the major styles of her era.

Much of the dramatic literature that preceded Sor Juana was religious in nature. Many of the plays in the sixteenth and seventeenth centuries were written by missionaries interested in using drama as a means of converting the native peoples to Christianity. Missionaries often mixed Spanish with native languages and incorporated elements of native theater into their religious plays. Following some of the practices of Aztec and Incan theater, missionaries staged many of their plays in outside settings, frequently utilizing costumes and scenery of the indigenous tribes. The best-known playwright of the sixteenth century was Gonzalo de Eslava, a Mexican priest who wrote primarily religious plays. Eslava, not unlike Bernardo de Balbuena, infused his literature with many references to Mexico.

Seventeenth-century playwrights include two Peruvians, Juan del Valle y Caviedes, who wrote satirical plays on the folly of love as well as satirical poetry mentioned earlier, and Juan de Espinosa Medrano, whose principal work was based on the Bible. The greatest name associated with theater in the Latin American colonial period is Mexican-born Juan Ruiz de Alarcón, a writer who emigrated to Spain at an early age. Alarcón, more properly affiliated with Spanish golden age theater, was an extremely popular and respected writer of comedies of manners and honor.

The Nineteenth and Twentieth Centuries

The First Novel and Short Story

Nineteenth-century Latin American literature marked the beginning of a new age brought about by independence and a growing sense of national identities. Many literary achievements occurred during this period: the publication of the first novel and short story; the attempt to produce literature that was unique to the many new countries; and the creation of modernism, the first literary movement Spanish America gave to Spain.

Critics generally agree that the first novel published in Spanish America was José Joaquín Fernández de Lizardi's *El periquillo sarniento* (The Itching Parrot, 1816). In some ways, Lizardi's novel owes more to the eighteenth-century Age of Reason than to the Age of Revolution: it is didactic in tone, containing long, moralizing passages on education and the proper upbringing of young people. The story is about an orphan named Pedro who, like a typical character from Spanish picaresque literature, serves a series of masters while observing and remarking ironically on virtually every aspect of Mexican society. Much like his literary predecessor, Alonso Ramírez, Pedro also sails for the Philippines, is shipwrecked on a desert island, and eventually returns to Mexico where his life is finally put into some moral order. Lizardi was a well-known social critic in prerevolutionary Mexico, often writing newspaper articles under the pen name "the Thinker." Once imprisoned for speaking out against the colonial viceroy, Lizardi used *The Itching Parrot* as a vehicle for satirical commentary on the need for radical social reform.

Political and social commentary are also the thematic bases for Latin America's first short story, Esteban Echeverría's "El matadero" ("The Slaughterhouse," 1838), published in Argentina. Set during the tyrannical reign of the infamous despot Juan Manuel de Rosas, the story tells in graphic detail how a young man from the opposition Unitarian Party is captured by a mob and brutalized. Echeverría's political and social messages were clear: if Argentina was going to prosper in the era of independence and self-rule, it would need a centralized, representative government with an educated populace acting responsibly.

One of the lasting legacies of such foundational works as *El periquillo sarniento* and "El matadero" is the use of literature to bring about social and political change. A great deal of nineteenth- and twentieth-century literature—

novels, short stories, poetry, and drama—protests some situation or condition brought about by the abuse of power and privilege.

Toward an American Identity

Much of the literature written during the decades following independence was a celebration of the diversity of the new nations that emerged from the years of colonialism and conflict. Following the European literary models of romanticism and realism, Latin American authors invested their literature with references to the uniqueness of their newly formed republics. Poets were especially effusive in their depiction of the shifting reality in the Americas. Ecuadorian poet José Joaquín Olmedo is credited with being the first Spanish American poet to commemorate in verse the independence of the American colonies from Spanish rule. His ode, "La victoria de Junín" ("The Victory of Junín," 1826), is, among other things, an elegy to Simón Bolívar and his leadership during the revolutionary period. Similarly, Venezuelan Andrés Bello, one of Bolívar's former teachers, urged his fellow writers to search for inspiration in authentic Latin American topics rather than copying European models.

The poetic elaboration of the Latin American experience perhaps reached its peak in nineteenth-century literature with the publication of José Hernández's narrative poem, "Martín Fierro" (1872), a work that laments the gradual disappearance of the *gaucho* (cowboy), long a symbol of the Argentine *pampas*. The poem is the story of a *gaucho* who, against his wishes, is forced to serve in the military where he is mercilessly abused and exploited. Fierro eventually deserts the army and joins with the native people, embittered over the loss of his freedom and autonomy. "Martín Fierro" is the literary predecessor of *Don Segundo Sombra* (1926), Ricardo Güiraldes's famous novelistic rendition of the *gaucho* and their importance to Argentine cultural identity.

The description of the Argentine consciousness was a central concern of Domingo Faustino Sarmiento, one of the nineteenth century's greatest essayists and intellectuals. Sarmiento wrote a classic essay delineating Argentina into two opposing camps, the urban and the rural. Unlike Hernández, Sarmiento perceived the urban mentality as offering his country education, enlightenment, progress, democracy, and industrial development. Sarmiento was an unabashed admirer of Europe. He felt the ignorance, superstition, tyranny, and isolation of rural Argentina—characterized by the *pampas* and the ever-present *gaucho*—symbolized all that kept his country from emerging from its barbaric past.

Sarmiento's essay, "Civilización y barbarie o vida de Juan Facundo Quiroga" ("Facundo," or "Civilization and Barbarism," 1845), is ostensibly a psychological study of Juan Facundo Quiroga, a prototypical rural tyrant who was a supporter of the *caudillo* Juan Manuel de Rosas. In this work, Sarmiento examined what he felt was the root cause of many of Argentina's political problems during the early years of the republic. Surrounded by and containing vast *pampas*, Argentina suffered from extreme isolation, which made effective governance virtually impossible. Sarmiento argued that Argentina's future salvation would occur through dramatic improvement of the educational system and effective centralized government.

The political and social realities of Argentina and the other Latin American countries were fully represented in the nineteenth-century novel. Novelists were deeply concerned about the failure of liberal democracy to flourish in the new age of independence. Political oppression, economic hardship, and social injustices were common maladies throughout Latin America during much of the nineteenth century, and novelists felt compelled to call attention to the problems affecting their countries.

One of the most prominent political novelists of the period was José Mármol, whose *Amalia* (1855) depicts Argentina suffering under the regime of Juan Manuel de Rosas, thematically similar to Echeverría's "El matadero." *Amalia,* typical of literature from the romantic school, includes conspiracies, political intrigues, hidden identities, and the tragic death of two lovers, the main characters, shortly after their wedding. As with many novelists who are committed primarily to writing about social and political circumstances, Mármol's work contains much commentary on contemporary issues of national concern. Critics have argued that such political literature—which was even more commonplace during the twentieth century—is too severely compromised to constitute an effective work of literary art. Yet virtually all of Latin America's major contemporary writers, including its Nobel laureates, have at some time written literature that carries an obvious political or social message.

In addition, the theme of the struggle with nature was developed by several authors, including Jorge Isaacs of Colombia in his romantic novel *María* (1867), and later writers, such as José Eustacio Rivera who described the Colombian jungle in *La vorágine* (The Whirlpool, 1924); Martín Luis Guzmán, with his portrayal of the Mexican Revolution in *El águila y la serpiente* (The Eagle and the Serpent, 1928); and Rómulo Gallegos of Venezuela in *Doña Bárbara* (1929), a work contrasting civilization and barbarism.

The novel was an effective vehicle during the nineteenth century for examining and presenting qualities that reflected a nation's particular identity. Ignacio Manuel Altamirano used the nineteenth-century Mexican novel in the same way Bernardo de Balbuena had used epic poetry centuries earlier to defend all that was uniquely Mexican. Altamirano joined Andrés Bello in his fervent desire to incorporate American themes into what was envisioned as a national literature. *Clemencia* (1869), for example, was written against the historical backdrop of the French intervention in Mexico in 1863. In *La Navidad en las montañas* (Christmas in the Mountains, 1871), Altamirano romanticized life in rural, mountainous Mexico, using the novel to expose the beauty and serenity of life far away from the capital city.

Although Altamirano had a somewhat romantic, perhaps even idyllic view of rural life, he was also an astute observer of the customs and traditions of regional Mexico. One of his purposes was to incorporate into his novels as many traits of Mexican life as possible in an effort to show that Latin Americans had ample subject matter for their literature in their own history and traditions. By the late nineteenth and early twentieth centuries, it had become commonplace for authors to write in great detail about subjects that seemed particularly appropriate for their specific countries. Peruvians and Ecuadorians wrote about the plight of the indigenous peoples and of Andean culture in general. Chilean novelists, heavily influenced by European naturalism, began to examine the economic and social effects of copper mining on daily life. Argentineans followed the course set by José Hernández and continued to explore the life of the *gaucho* in a rapidly changing world.

The best example of a nineteenth-century writer who found inspiration in his country's mythological and historical records was Peruvian Ricardo Palma. Palma wrote short sketches, anecdotes, and characterizations based on people and incidents from old Peru. His short folkloric compositions, *Tradiciones peruanas* (Peruvian Traditions, 1872–1883), are humorous, ironic, satiric narratives that deeply mine Peru's rich colonial and indigenous heritage, cleverly mixing fact with fiction. As director of the National Library, he had easy access to a wealth of original documents that provided source material for his creations. Many of his stories fairly accurately reproduce speech patterns, customs, popular sayings, and common beliefs of the time. Scholars have noted that Palma is one of the most important precursors of the contemporary Spanish American short story.

Modernism

The first major literary movement that took root in Spanish America and was passed to Spain, modernism was heavily influenced by French symbolist poets and philosophical currents of the late nineteenth century. Modernists—attempting to renovate literary language, style, themes, and techniques—significantly departed from the subject matters that were characteristic of realism and naturalism. Rather than giving detailed descriptions of regions and local traditions, they opted to write about exotic lands that stimulated the poetic sensibilities of this new generation of writers. Captivated by ideas of beauty, elegance, sensuality, and refinement, modernists infused their literary language with references to ancient Greece, the Far East, and the medieval world.

Whereas their realist counterparts were interested in portraying an accurate image of the world around them, a world that was often squalid and dangerous, modernist writers depicted realms that were creations of fantasy—places inhabited by princesses and knights, swans and nightingales. "Art for art's sake" was the battle cry of the modernists who, at times, sought to divorce literature from the sordid economic and social realities that characterized their world. Above all, modernism was a movement that attempted to create a new Hispanic literary language, one that was essentially poetic in nature and reflected the new aesthetics of cosmopolitan refinement and literary renovation.

Many names are associated with modernism: Cuba's José Martí, Mexico's Manuel Gutiérrez Nájera, Colombia's José Asunción Silva, Cuba's Julián del Casal, and Argentina's Leopoldo Lugones. Yet no one embodies the spirit of modernist thought and practice better than Rubén Darío, a Nicaraguan poet whose work spans the entire movement and defines its basic tenets. Critics often mark the beginning and end, respectively, of modernism with the publication of Darío's *Azul* (Blue, 1888) and his death in 1916. Darío was unquestionably the best-known and most widely imitated Hispanic poet of his generation. His poetry exemplified grace, cultural refinement, extraordinary literary depth, and stylistic elegance. Elevating Hispanic poetry to unprecedented heights in his efforts to revolutionize concepts about literature, Darío showed that it was possible to break from the realist and romantic schools of thought. He wrote about Wagnerian swans, ancient Persian cities, medieval Spanish poets, classical deities, and mythological characters. Yet Darío's greatest contribution to Latin American literature may have been his extraordinary renewal of poetic language.

Of the dozens of Darío's poems that embody the modernist spirit of innovation and originality, "Sonatina" (1893) perhaps best captures the mood of exoticism and elegance. The poem describes a beautiful young princess whose melancholy mood contrasts sharply with her opulent home. She lives a life of unparalleled luxury, yet she is limited by her excessive wealth. Her fairy godmother reassures her that she will soon be rescued from her "prison" by a knight "who [will] arrive from afar, conqueror of Death." The poem is filled with arcane references to figures from classical mythology, exotic locations, and unusual plants and wildlife.

It is a common misconception to regard modernism as a literary movement that completely broke from many Latin American writers' concern with social and political issues. Modernists were concerned primarily with the renovation of literary language, yet they never abandoned some of the issues that had preoccupied earlier generations of writers such as how Latin America differed fundamentally from North America. For example, a number of Darío's poems—including "A Roosevelt" ("To Roosevelt," 1905), which takes issue with Theodore Roosevelt's militant nature—openly accuse the United States of being overly aggressive toward its Latin American neighbors, suggesting that North American foreign policy was imperialistic.

Criticism of the United States was common among writers of Darío's era. Uruguayan José Enrique Rodó, the greatest essayist of the modernist generation, published *Ariel* (1900), a philosophical treatise on the essential distinctions between Latin America and the United States. Although openly admiring US economic and political power, Rodó was deeply opposed to what he viewed as a US obsession with materialism. Rodó considered Latin Americans to be far more spiritually inclined than North Americans and urged his readers to weigh the benefits of material progress against the advantages of spiritual and cultural achievements.

Darío and Rodó initiated a trend among Latin American writers in the twentieth century to use the United States as a point of reference in their analyses of their own culture and society. Octavio Paz, Mexico's contemporary Nobel laureate, for example, wrote *El laberinto de la soledad* (The Labyrinth of Solitude, 1950), a book that incisively compares popular Mexican culture with that in the United States, searching the history of each nation for root causes of the vast distinctions between them. Similarly, Carlos Fuentes's *El espejo enterrado* (The Buried Mirror, 1992) is a modern critique of Latin American cultural history.

The impact of modernism on Latin American literature was profound and enduring. The modernist renewal and invigoration of literary language occurred in both prose fiction and poetry. Writers nurtured on realist modes of exposition discovered that their stories could be far more expressive and effective if they focused on the eloquent possibilities of language. The long, cumbersome, detailed passages that were common in documentary realism gave way to shorter, more poetic narratives that were highly metaphorical in construction.

Darío was a masterful prose writer as well as poet, and his work provided models and inspiration for countless others—even writers whose subject matter was largely social and political. Mariano Azuela, whose *Los de abajo* (The Underdogs, 1915) is considered the classic novel of the Mexican Revolution, incorporated modernist literary techniques in his vivid descriptions of the Mexican countryside. Regionalist and Indianist novelists—who continued the centuries-long struggle for justice on behalf of the native peoples well into the twentieth century—were strongly influenced by modernist innovations in language and literature. Modernism, for example, helped to teach regionalist writer Horacio Quiroga how to condense his stories—generally set in the Latin American wilderness—into brief exposés on the tragic nature of human existence.

Literature of the Vanguard

Modernism was succeeded by a period that invited an enormous variety of literary styles, techniques, and concerns. The documentary tendency of realist fiction continued to flourish, and most poetry became a more intimate, personal expression. Women writers had far greater visibility, most notably, poets Delmira Agustini, Alfonsina Storni, Juana de Ibarbourou, and Gabriela Mistral who was Latin America's first Nobel laureate in literature. The most dramatic development of the postmodernist era was unquestionably the eruption of the literature of the vanguard.

The vanguard was to literature what cubism was to painting: a complete upheaval of traditional expectations regarding the fundamental premises of artistic expression. By the 1920s, art had witnessed a revolutionary plunge away from realism and into abstraction, and literature soon followed suit. Literature of the vanguard attempted to push verbal expression away from the rational into the irrational, away from conventional forms of literature in favor of newly created forms, away from old themes toward a new registry of poetic topics that reflected the sensibilities of a new age of technology. The modernists had their swans; the vanguard had airplanes, trains, factories, and cities. Spanish philosopher José Ortega y Gasset wrote at the time about the "dehumanization" of art that occurred during the period following World War I, a reference to what he felt was an absence in art of elements that reflected the human experience.

The poetic manifestations of vanguard literature include a total disregard for formal grammatical and stylistic conventions; punctuation, for example, is often random and arbitrary. Poets would often avoid a logical exposition of themes and subjects; their poems at first glance often appear to be chaotic jumbles of images and incoherent metaphors.

Perhaps the most vivid example of a Latin American poet of the vanguard is Chilean Vicente Huidobro, whose long, rambling poetic meditation, "Altazor" (1919), was an invitation to literary anarchy. The only rule was that there were no longer any rules. Huidobro was especially fond of creating words simply for the sound they represented or the rhyme scheme they momentarily fulfilled. "Altazor" has segments that are merely a collection of invented words that seem to exist for no purpose beyond the sound they create within the poem. Huidobro called his poetic efforts "creationism." His thesis, typical of the vanguard generation, was that the poet alone was exclusively responsible for the burden of inspiration and creativity.

As with all literary movements, the period of the vanguard had its day, yet its legacy was enduring. Literature was imbued with an experimental verve that has lasted from the vanguard until the present. Novels and short stories of the famous "boom" of the 1960s, for example, are indebted to the vanguard for opening the door to literary experimentation, which characterized Latin American literature for most of the twentieth century.

Magical Realism and the Boom

It was Cuban author Alejo Carpentier who first made extensive use of the term *lo real maravilloso, la maravillosa realidad,* or *el realismo mágico* (magical realism) after a 1943 trip to Haiti during which he was greatly impressed by the influence of African culture on Haiti. These influences included myth and music; language and perception; and unexpected alternations of reality, metamorphosis, and magic. They involved a cultural ability or tendency to perceive or emphasize mysterious and magical elements that could be found in everyday reality, in common activities, thus mixing reality and fantasy. Numerous examples of this literary technique are found in Carpentier's novel, *El reino de este mundo* (The Kingdom of This World, 1949).

Characteristics of magical realism, however, can be traced back to the earliest cultural encounters between Europeans and the indigenous peoples of the

Americas. Columbus, Cortés, and the other early explorers of the 1500s were not prepared for the New World that they encountered. There was initial confusion about whether they had arrived in some part of Asia (China or India). Their languages lacked words for many of the new things they found; they had to borrow from the indigenous languages. They were often amazed by the peoples, plants, animals, locales, and customs in the new lands. Their reactions thus combined their own wonder with the obvious reality of their surroundings. In some cases, they embellished their "discoveries" to impress their rulers or supporters back in the old country.

As the explorers began to learn about native myths and religious practices, the blending of magic and reality continued, albeit on a predominantly subconscious level. As they attempted to impose many of their own beliefs on the native peoples, an almost inevitable syncretic evolution of hybrid cultural forms occurred. The introduction of African cultural elements, predominantly in the Caribbean, added substantially to the mix. Thomas J. D'Agostino in Chapter 4, Kevin A. Yelvington in Chapter 9, and Hannah Stewart-Gambino in Chapter 12 show how this process of amalgamation occurred in politics, ethnic relations, and religious practices, respectively.

Although the participants may not have had a specific name for this process, it continued nevertheless. Known as "El Inca," Garcilaso de la Vega of Peru tried to present the indigenous perspective and reaction to the encounter by explaining some of the myths and practices of his people. Mexican author Fernández de Lizardi later combined some elements of native language and belief in his nineteenth-century descriptions of colonial life. As mentioned previously, the most profound and effective blending of these early tendencies to combine history and fiction (reality and myth) occurred in the works of Ricardo Palma. His *Tradiciones peruanas* (Peruvian Traditions, 1872–1883) combined researched historical fact with local legends and personal commentary, often in an ironic or satirical tone. Jorge Luis Borges, the famed twentieth-century Argentine author, also used this technique with success, giving a veneer of historical reality to his creative fantasies in works such as *Ficciones* (Fictions, 1944) and *El aleph* (Aleph, 1949). Borges is universally renowned for his use of the basic elements of magical realism, including time shifts, dream sequences, and multicultural references.

Authors of the modern Latin American literary "boom" (c. 1960–c. 1970) raised magical realism to the exalted level of a renowned, worldwide literary movement—gaining international stature, recognition, and respect for the previously all-too-often neglected realm of Latin American literature. This boom was exemplified by the unprecedented explosion of Latin American writing on the international literary scene. Many of the works achieved universal appeal, critical acclaim, and financial success.

Interests and characteristics of the boom authors include magical realism, native cultures, myths, combinations of history and fiction, circular time, dreams, the other or the double, creative language, multiple viewpoints, and experimentation. The reader becomes an active participant rather than a passive observer in the work, because the reader has to untangle the varied literary threads. An excellent example is seen in Julio Cortázar's novel *Rayuela* (Hopscotch, 1963), in which readers can select chapters in a varied order, thus altering the plot development. Several of the boom authors were also fond of intellectual games and occasionally referred to other authors, works, or characters in their writings.

In addition, the ideals of the boom include some allegiance to certain tenets of the Cuban Revolution—such as greater rights for the poor, individual liberty with group social consciousness, a fairer distribution of wealth, and an improvement in general living standards. The institution Casa de las Américas fostered the new interest in Latin American literature with wider publication of both classic and recent texts.

Many authors can be included in the boom; among the most notable are Cuba's Alejo Carpentier; Mexico's Carlos Fuentes, *La muerte de Artemio Cruz* (The Death of Artemio Cruz, 1962); Peru's Mario Vargas Llosa, *La ciudad y los perros* (The City and the Dogs, 1962); Argentina's Julio Cortázar; Colombia's Gabriel García Márquez, *Cien años de soledad* (One Hundred Years of Solitude, 1967); Guatemala's Miguel Ángel Asturias, *El Señor Presidente* (Mr. President, 1946); and Mexico's Juan Rulfo, *Pedro Páramo* (1955).

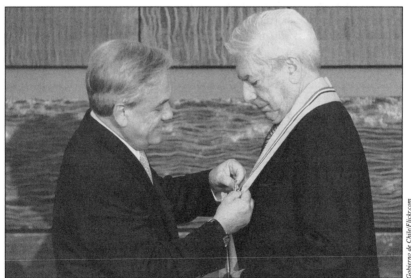

Gobierno de Chile/Flickr.com

Peruvian writer Mario Vargas Llosa, winner of the 2010 Nobel Prize in Literature, receives an award from Chilean president Sebastián Piñera in December 2010.

By 1970, several disagreements had developed among the various authors of the boom. There were political and ideological differences, especially when the Cuban Revolution failed to live up to its original promise. There were also social and creative differences, with a desire by some for greater liberty in literary subject matter and style. Although the boom declined, many of its members continued to write and evolve within this genre even as new authors appeared on the scene.

The techniques of magical realism had become well established and were continued in later works by several authors. It is interesting to note that of the six Latin Americans who have won the Nobel Prize for Literature, at least four were from the boom. The Nobel laureates include Gabriela Mistral of Chile (1945, poetry); Miguel Ángel Asturias of Guatemala (1967, novels/stories); Pablo Neruda of Chile (1971, poetry); Gabriel García Márquez of Colombia (1982, novels/stories); Octavio Paz of Mexico (1990, poetry/essays); and Mario Vargas Llosa of Peru (2010, novels/stories).

Beyond the Boom

Although interest in magical realism continued after the boom, some writers reacted unfavorably to certain techniques employed during that movement. Some opposed the intellectual games played out in a few texts. Differences occurred on many levels—political, social, stylistic, ideological, and creative. Although many of the boom authors have continued to work and are still popular, they have evolved with changing times.

Contemporary literature has made room for many more varied voices, including more women authors. Some who have achieved wide recognition are Rosario Castellanos of Mexico, *Balún Canán* (1957); Elena Poniatowska of Mexico, *La noche de Tlatelolco* (The Night at Tlatelolco, 1971); Luisa Valenzuela of Argentina, *El gato eficaz* (The Clever Cat, 1972); and Isabel Allende of Chile, *La casa de los espíritus* (The House of the Spirits, 1982). Gioconda Belli of Nicaragua, Edwidge Danticat of Haiti, and Anacristina Rossi of Costa Rica also have achieved literary recognition in recent years with works often critical of political developments in their countries. It is also worth noting that many authors of Latino or Hispanic descent are writing in the United States in both English and Spanish, including Luis Rafael Sánchez, Miguel Méndez, Oscar Hijuelos, Rudolfo Anaya, Julia Alvarez, Sandra Cisneros, and Rolando Hinojosa-Smith.

Interest has also continued in the multicultural nature of Latin American society. Peruvian José María Arguedas has written of the indigenous influences in *Los ríos profundos* (Deep Rivers, 1958). The African cultural heritage has been vividly described in the poetry of Nicolás Guillén of Cuba and Luis Palés Matos of Puerto Rico. Peruvian poets César Vallejo and Isaac Goldemberg have defended the poor and the Jewish heritage, respectively. Both Ariel

Dorfman and Antonio Skármeta of Chile have written powerfully on the theme of exile.

One of the most popular forms of literature in Latin America in the years following the boom of the 1960s has been the historical novel. The contemporary history novel has inherited many of the literary techniques and thematic concerns of magical realism such as multiple narrators, fluid depiction of time and space, Native American mythology and culture, and fantasy. The colonial era has a powerful fascination for contemporary novelists because it provides a basis for understanding many of the historical issues of concern today throughout Latin America: the discovery and its political, social, and economic consequences; the plight of the native peoples during the conquest; the inception of a nationalistic consciousness; and the movement toward independence. Recently, there has been a growth of historical novels written by a new generation of authors who imagine how women have participated in Latin American history. Many of these novels have become bestsellers. Critics have noted that though boom authors are celebrated for their publishing success, oftentimes other bestselling authors are disregarded by critics because of their public appeal regardless of their literary achievements. Some of these novels are Angeles Mastretta's *Arráncame la vida* (Tear This Heart Out, 1988), Tomás Eloy Martínez's *Santa Evita* (Santa Evita, 1995), and Isabel Allende's *Hija de la fortuna* (Daughter of Fortune, 1999). Another trend in current historical novels is to situate them outside of a Latin American context such as Ignacio Padilla's *Amphitryon* (Shadow Without a Name: A Novel, 2000) and Jorge Volpi's *En busca de Klingsor* (In Search of Klingsor, 1998), both of which take place in Europe.

In what is sometimes an obvious parody of the great figures of early Latin American history—Columbus, Cortés, and the *conquistadores*—a number of writers have presented highly imaginative visions of the past that challenge, distort, and contradict standard accounts of history. In Alejandro Paternain's *Crónica del descubrimiento* (Chronicle of the Discovery, 1980), for example, an Amerindian tribe crosses the Atlantic and "discovers" Europe, a land the Native Americans consider to be highly uncivilized. Cuban writer Alejo Carpentier, in many ways the father of magical realism, wrote several novels in which conventional distinctions of time are completely disregarded. His *Concierto barroco* (Baroque Concerto, 1974), for example, juxtaposes elements from modern music—jazz, electric guitars, and Louis Armstrong—with the musical culture of eighteenth-century Venice.

Carpentier is one of many writers who incorporate primary historical documents in their literary treatments of the colonial period, making virtually no distinction in their novels between historical and fictional language. Antonio Benítez Rojo's *El mar de las lentejas* (Sea of Lentils, 1979), a book about Latin America's first 100 years, uses historical accounts from the era to underpin his fictional story about Columbus's second voyage to the Americas. Virtually all of Latin America's most noted novelists have contributed to this literary genre, including Gabriel García Márquez, *El general en su laberinto* (The General in His Labyrinth, 1989); Carlos Fuentes, *La campaña* (The Campaign, 1990); and Mario Vargas Llosa, *La guerra del fin del mundo* (The War of the End of the World, 1981).

As Kevin A. Yelvington observes in Chapter 9, the world learned about native rights activist Rigoberta Menchú with the publication of her 1983 testimonial, *I, Rigoberta Menchú: An Indian Woman in Guatemala,* which eventually appeared in eleven languages. The testimonial as a genre gained popularity in the 1980s when it was used primarily to recount the injustices committed by Central America's military governments. The testimonial is a work in which individuals who have been silenced by their communities (oftentimes because of race, class, gender, and language) tell their stories. While some testimonials are written by the person who experienced the injustice, sometimes, as is the case with Menchú, the story is told to another person who then organizes the story and publishes it. Menchú's testimony of Quiché Mayan life and culture in the northwest highlands, the hardships she experienced as she grew up helping her parents tend their tiny plot and traveling with them to work on coffee and sugar plantations, and the state terror directed against her people earned her the Nobel Peace Prize in 1992. Menchú vividly recounts the torture and death of her parents and brother at the hands of the Guatemalan military. Rather than happily mark the 500th anniversary of the arrival of Columbus in

AP/John McConnico

Nobel Prize winner Rigoberta Menchú (center) on her way to a press conference in Guatemala City.

the New World in October 1992, she was quoted as defiantly insisting that "the celebration of Columbus is for us an insult." Some critics, such as anthropologist David Stoll, have questioned the accuracy of certain historical and interpretive aspects of Menchú's text. The testimonial, while valuable because it gives voice to the silenced, is a story oftentimes told to a community outsider with a political purpose and must be studied with the benefits and deficits of these objectives in mind.

From Macondo to McOndo

In 1996 Chilean writers Alberto Fuguet and Sergio Gómez published a collection of stories written by seventeen male authors from Latin America entitled *McOndo* (1996). The title of the work is a play on García Márquez's Macondo, the invented town in which *Cien años de soledad* and many of his magical fictions are set. The idea for the collection arose when a story by one of the authors was rejected for publication in the United States because it was not seen as "representative" of Latin America. Ironically, while the boom was important because it gave Latin American literature worldwide recognition and critical acclaim, it also created expectations of what Latin American literature would be.

While this anthology was not meant to be a literary manifesto or to define a new generation of writers, it soon became interpreted as such. Alberto Fuguet (Chile), Edmundo Paz Soldán (Bolivia), Jordi Soler (Mexico), and Juan Form (Argentina) are the most critically acclaimed authors in the collection. These writers were born in the late 1960s and, at the time the anthology appeared, they had published at least one book in Spanish. They reject the stereotype of Latin America as a rural, magical realist place and instead describe it as an urban world of McDonald's, Macintosh computers, malls, and condominiums. This generation plays computer games, watches US films, and listens to rock music. It promotes a virtual reality that is at times full of technology, sex, and drugs. Many of the authors included in this collection have now rejected their association with this group but, since the publication of *McOndo,* they have become some of the most successful contemporary Latin American writers. Moreover, boom authors such as Carlos Fuentes and Mario Vargas Llosa have embraced this group and its new vision of Latin America.

The term "McOndo" has since been used to define works that reflect the effects of globalization in Latin America in the twenty-first century. McOndo works reflect the realities of free trade, the Internet, and a globalized world that is more influenced by pop culture than by a pre-Columbian one. As is fitting of this generation of the computer age, several of the McOndo authors maintain websites where they publish some of their writings. Other authors who focus on similar themes include Laura Restrepo (Chile), Alan Pauls (Argentina), and Roberto Bolaño (Chile).

In Mexico in 1996, the same year as the publication of *McOndo,* a group of young Mexican writers declared themselves to be part of "El Crack." They intended to invigorate Mexican literature with a return to the serious and textually challenging literature of the boom while seeking to be recognized within Western literary tradition. Like the McOndo authors, this group was accused of being audacious for self-naming their movement. Both the El Crack and McOndo movements created themselves in response to difficulties getting published, but their self-promotion was successful. As a result of declaring these movements, the authors found publishers for their works. Jorge Volpi's *En busca de Klingsor* (1999) and Ignacio Padilla's *Amphitryon* (2000) were the award-winning historical novels of the group. Like the McOndo movement, El Crack writers distance themselves from a Latin American literary landscape, oftentimes creating characters who are not Latin American. While one movement rejects the boom and the other embraces it, neither movement is premised on situating its novels in Latin America. They have instead embraced the global landscape as inspiration. As technology, free trade, and immigration continue to erase national borders in the twenty-first century, Latin American writers will continue to reflect these changes through their literature.

Latino Writers
Latino writers began producing work in English as a result of social, political, and ethnic movements in the United States during the 1960s. Throughout history, different terms have been used to define Latinos, who are US citizens of Latin American descent. Depending on their country of origin, there are different political, social, and economic reasons for immigrating to the United States. Such differences have influenced their writing.

Mexican Americans asserted their rights according to the peace treaty that ended the Mexican-American War (1846–1848). The Treaty of Guadalupe Hidalgo granted their rights to language, religion, and land. In his epic poem *I Am Joaquin* (1967), Rodolfo "Corky" Gonzalez imagined a return in the southwest of the mythical Aztlán, homeland of the Aztecs. Tomás Rivera's *. . . y no se lo tragó la tierra* (. . . And the Earth Did Not Devour Him, 1971) recounts the migrant farm worker's experience and his bilingual short stories describe economic difficulties and social injustices. Luis Valdez's theater *El Teatro Campesino,* founded in 1965, has served the United Farm Workers by mobilizing and teaching them about their rights.

The protagonists in the Latino coming-of-age novels find their identity through education. Characters in these works face the challenge of living between two cultures. Revealing a synthesis of their origins and experiences, they often no longer identify with their country of origin and struggle to find their place in the United States. In *Bless Me, Ultima* (1972), Mexican American author Rodolfo Anaya follows the spiritual awakening of the protagonist.

He celebrates the power of writing, education, and the indigenous pre-Hispanic values of the southwest. In *The House on Mango Street* (1984), Sandra Cisneros's character, a poor Mexican American girl, narrates her dream of owning a home. In *Borderlands* (1987), Gloria Anzaldúa, a leader among the women of color feminist movement, created a literary *mestizaje* by mixing a variety of genres and language to reflect on the Mexican American experience.

The 1898 Spanish-American War left Cuba and Puerto Rico under United States domination. In 1917, the Jones Act extended citizenship to Puerto Ricans giving them a unique status. Throughout history, as has been the case of all immigrants, Puerto Rican immigration has peaked in times of economic difficulty in Puerto Rico. Unfortunately, many Puerto Ricans come to the United States only to find a different type of poverty. Initially, works such as René Marques' play *La Carreta* (1953) asserted that the only solution for Puerto Rican migrants to redeem themselves from the kind of moral and cultural corruption that can occur while living in the United States would be to return to the island. Tato Laveira's *La Carreta Made a U Turn* (1979) rejected this view and describes the impossibility of returning to Puerto Rico after immigration. His work celebrates the cultural value of the Puerto Rican immigrant experience. As evident in the title of the novel, Laveira combines English and Spanish to create new images that reflect the immigrants' new reality. Jesús Colón became an important voice in the militant literature of the 1960s and 1970s, which embraces its working-class origins and promotes the rights of Nuyoricans (Puerto Ricans living in New York). Contemporary Puerto Rican authors continue to struggle with their unique citizenship status. Authors such as Luis Rafael Sánchez and Rosario Ferré live in both Puerto Rico and the United States and write literature in either English or Spanish depending on the content and the mood of their works.

Prior to the Cuban Revolution of 1959, Cubans immigrated primarily for economic opportunities. *The Mambo Kings Sing Songs of Love* (1989), by Pulitzer Prize winner Oscar Hijuelos, is the story of two brothers who arrive in New York in the late 1940s, to work by day and play music by night. However, the revolution caused a wave of exiles whose motivations were based on political rather than primarily economic needs. Cristina Garcia's *Dreaming in Cuban* (1992) tells a story of a family divided by geography and ideology. It is celebrated as being one of the first novels that presents the experience of Cubans in the United States and on the island.

Unstable political and economic conditions have also led to immigration from the Caribbean and Central America. Dominican American Junot Díaz published *Drown* (1996), a collection of short stories that takes place in the Dominican Republic and the United States. His male protagonists face conditions of poverty, hard-working mothers, and absentee fathers. In Julia Alvarez's *How the Garcia Girls Lost Their Accents* (1991), her characters fled from the Trujillo regime in the Dominican Republic. Unlike their parents who dream of returning there, the girls search to find a place for themselves in the United States. *Krik? Krak!* (1991), a collection of short stories by Edwidge Danticat, paints a painful picture of life under the Duvalier dictatorship in Haiti.

Several of the aforementioned writers use the historical novel to teach readers about their countries of origin. Julia Alvarez's *In the Time of the Butterflies* (1994) recounts the story of the courageous Mirabal sisters who challenged Trujillo's dictatorship. Sandra Cisneros' *Caramelo* (2000) retells her family's history while incorporating significant events of Mexican and Mexican American history into her storytelling. Junot Díaz's *The Brief Wondrous Life of Oscar Wao* (2007) critiques the Trujillo dictatorship through the story of a young Dominican immigrant. By using popular culture and footnoting, Cisneros and Díaz (2008 Pulitzer Prize winner) challenge traditional history writing.

Literary awards and recognitions granted to many of these authors, both in the United States and abroad, celebrate their important contributions to world literature. Once on the fringes of United States literature, these novels are now regularly taught in US schools. In order to provide a forum for these Latino writers, McOndo authors Fuguet and Paz Soldán created the anthology *Se habla español: Voces latinas en USA* (2002). This is a collection of both Latin American and Latino authors who have written in Spanish about the Latin American immigrant experience in the United States. By taking the best from both literary worlds, Latino authors are gaining international acclaim for their works.

▓ Brazil and the Circum-Caribbean

Brazil followed a pattern similar to that of the other Latin American nations, but with Portuguese language and culture. Some of the best-known Brazilian writers lived during the nineteenth century: Machado de Assis, Joaquim Nabuco, José de Alencar, Gonçalves Dias, and Castro Alves. The twentieth century also produced important authors in Brazil, including Mário de Andrade, Oswald de Andrade, Carlos Drummond de Andrade, Cecília Meireles, Raquel de Queirós, Jackson de Figueiredo, Graça Aranha, Coelho Neto, and Jorge de Lima.

João Guimarães Rosa published one of his major works, *Grande sertão, veredas* (Big Country, Footpaths), in 1956. Jorge Amado treated social themes in such works as *Mar morto* (Dead Sea, 1936) and *Capitães de Areia* (Captains of Sand, 1937). Other notable writers from the Brazilian republic include regionalists and social realists such as Gilberto Freyre and José Lins do Rêgo; stylist Graciliano Ramos; experimental novelists with innovative narrative techniques such as Erico Veríssimo; and those who employ powerful, poetic, and magical language such as Clarice Lispector and Nélida Piñón.

Other non–Spanish-speaking nations of the circum-Caribbean have produced several writers of considerable stature whose works should be included in the discussion of Latin American literature. For example, in 1964 Orlando

Patterson of Jamaica published *The Children of Sisyphus,* which reveals the struggle for survival in Kingston's shantytown society. Another Jamaican novelist, John Hearne, wrote *Faces of Love* (1957) and *Autumn Equinox* (1959), which study the nation's complex social and psychological relationships. From Dominica in the West Indies, Jean Rhys published her novel *Wide Sargasso Sea* (1966), which deals with the representation of the creole Caribbean woman. From French-speaking Guadeloupe, Simone Schwarz-Bart wrote two novels, *Pluie et vent sur Télumée miracle* (The Bridge of Beyond, 1972) and *Ti Jean L'Horizon* (Between Two Worlds, 1979), which depict the cultural interconnections of the region. These and works by Trinidadian writer V. S. Naipaul (*Guerrillas,* 1975); Antiguan author Jamaica Kincaid (*At the Bottom of the River,* 1983); and Saint Lucian epic poet Derek Walcott (*Omeros,* 1990) provide additional perspectives on the circum-Caribbean.

Popular Culture

The literature and society of Latin American nations have been strongly influenced by popular culture. Numerous street theaters throughout the region have served as models of social reform, political protest, and artistic creativity. As Susan Tiano discusses in Chapter 10, the protest movement of the Madres de la Plaza de Mayo in the 1970s and 1980s helped bring about the downfall of the Argentine dictatorship that was responsible for the disappearance of thousands of citizens. Nonfiction writing in essays and newspapers also has played an important role in the development of Latin American society.

Film became a powerful cultural medium in the twentieth century. Argentina's Manuel Puig wrote *La traición de Rita Hayworth* (Betrayed by Rita Hayworth, 1968) and his *El beso de la mujer araña* (1976) was made into the important film, play, and Broadway musical, *Kiss of the Spider Woman,* which condemned dictatorial excess and prison cruelty. *La historia oficial* (The Official Story, 1985), directed by Luis Puenzo, is another award-winning film that grew out of the protests against the Argentine military dictatorship.

As cinema developed as a dominant artistic form, attempts were gradually made to transfer literary magical realism to film, which presented interesting challenges. The technique of flashback can be used with considerable success to convey the interplay of past, present, and future that is so important to magical realism's sense of the circularity of time. The use of ancestral or legendary spirits (even ghosts) that appear in works of magical realism can be portrayed through various split-screen and related cinematic techniques. Magical realism should not be confused with horror films or science fiction; it has a lighter, subtler touch than those popular genres. A cinematic version of Carlos Fuentes's *Aura* (1962) might run the risk of such confusion, for example, because of its depiction of otherworldly beings who even seem to return from the dead.

Perhaps the best-known work of magical realism is García Márquez's *Cien años de soledad* (One Hundred Years of Solitude, 1967). One episode from the novel was developed into another story by the author, which became the film *Innocent Erendira* (1982). *Love in the Time of Cholera,* a novel published in 1988, was made into an English-language film in 2007. García Márquez has now written part of his life story (*Vivir para contarla;* translated into English as *Living to Tell the Tale,* 2003), which reveals some of the fantastic elements of his long creative career.

Indeed, memoirs have become increasingly popular with Latin American authors in recent years. Marjorie Agosín described her childhood as a Jewish girl growing up in Chile in *A Cross and a Star* (1997). Another Chilean writer, Isabel Allende, told the personal tale of the fatal illness of her daughter in *Paula* (1994). Gioconda Belli wrote vividly about her life in Nicaragua in *El país bajo mi piel* (2001, translated into English as *The Country Under My Skin,* 2002). Cuban author Reinaldo Arenas offered his life story in *Antes que anochezca* (published posthumously in 1992), which has been translated into English and produced in film as *Before Night Falls.*

Isabel Allende's novel *La casa de los espíritus* (The House of the Spirits, 1982) was also later brought to the screen in an English-language version. Mexican author Juan Rulfo's novel, *Pedro Páramo* (1955), appeared on screen in a Mexican film version in the 1970s. Rulfo's story of the life of a local *patrón* involved magical realism to a considerable degree through flashbacks to different time periods in his life and references to characters, living and dead, who appeared in the work.

The independent film *El Norte* (The North) was a joint US–Latin American production that was released in 1983, directed by Gregory Nava. Although not directly based on a novel, it beautifully evoked on film the spirit of magical realism. It follows the lives of two young refugees from the violence in Guatemala—a brother and sister who escape north through Mexico and finally into the United States. One of the most popular recent attempts to bring magical realism to film was the successful screen adaptation of Mexican scriptwriter Laura Esquivel's imaginative novel, *Como agua para chocolate* (Like Water for Chocolate, 1992). The author deftly combined the popular themes of food preparation and romance in a work that portrayed some of the most memorable scenes in the novel. This and other recent films have also emphasized the importance of family in Hispanic life.

Magical realism has been used or adapted in films from non–Latin American countries, but it seems most suited to its place of origin. Carpentier's *El reino de este mundo* (The Kingdom of This World, 1949) contains scenes that seem perfectly adaptable to the screen such as one character's juxtaposition of the wax heads in a wig shop display, the animal heads in a butcher shop, the royal heads on stamps in a philately store, and the author's imaginative vision of the beheading of French overlords during the French Revolution as he ponders the possibility of rebellion in Haiti to overthrow French domination. There is also a scene involving an Afro-Haitian cultural hero, the leader of a revolt who appears to escape execution at the hands of the French; the two cultures view the same scene in a different way. Some of the scenes at the end of the novel, when the main character rules his gentle imaginary kingdom and eventually disappears in a storm, seem to cry out for film adaptation.

Like *Cien años de soledad,* however, *El reino de este mundo* has not had a successful cinematic interpretation. Several auspicious forces must be brought into play with skilled treatment if literary magical realism is to be successfully transferred to film within the sphere of popular culture. Perhaps readers of a literary work have developed imaginary mental pictures of the elements of magical realism in the piece, expecting those images to be reinforced through the film adaptation. Creating a successful cinematic rendition from such disparate images is a daunting challenge, especially if cross-cultural boundaries are also to be bridged. Miguel Ángel Asturias wrote a lovely collection entitled *Leyendas de Guatemala* (Legends from Guatemala, 1930) that evokes the powerful beauty of indigenous myths, yet it might be difficult to produce a screen version of the work. As the popular success of *Como agua para chocolate* has shown, however, the goal of bringing literary magical realism to the screen can be achieved.

* * *

In sum, literature and artistic expression contribute to the cultural richness of Latin America. These genres and others that are beyond the scope of this chapter, such as the graphic arts and music, help us to understand Latin American perceptions of reality.

Bibliography

Alonso, Carlos J. *The Spanish American Regional Novel.* New York: Cambridge University Press, 1990.

Augenbraum, Harold, and Margarite Fernández Olmos, eds. *The Latino Reader: An American Literary Tradition from 1542 to the Present.* Boston: Houghton Mifflin, 1997.

Baddeley, Oriana, and Valerie Fraser. *Drawing the Line: Art and Cultural Identity in Latin America.* New York: Routledge, Chapman and Hall, 1989.

Beezley, William, and Judith Ewell. *The Human Tradition in Latin America: Twentieth Century.* Wilmington, DE: Scholarly Resources, 1987.

Beverley, John, and Marc Zimmerman. *Literature and Politics in the Central American Revolutions.* Austin: University of Texas Press, 1990.

Burton, Julianne, ed. *Cinema and Social Change in Latin America.* Austin: University of Texas Press, 1986.

Chanaday, Amaryll, ed. *Latin American Identity and Constructions of Difference.* Minneapolis: University of Minnesota Press, 1994.

Dorfman, Ariel. *Some Write to the Future: Essays on Contemporary Latin American Fiction.* Durham, NC: Duke University Press, 1991.

Fuguet, Alberto, and Sergio Gómez, eds. *McOndo.* Barcelona: Mondadori, 1996.

García-Pinto, Magdalena, and Trudy Balch. *Women Writers of Latin America: Intimate Histories.* Austin: University of Texas Press, 1991.

Gautier, Mari-Lise Gazarian. *Interviews with Latin American Writers.* Elmwood Park, IL: Dalkey Archive Press, 1989.

González-Echevarría, Roberto, and Enrique Pupo-Walker, eds. *Cambridge History of Latin American Literature,* 3 vols. New York: Cambridge University Press, 1996.

Goodrich, Diana Sorensen. *The Reader and the Text: Interpretive Strategies for Latin American Literatures.* Purdue University Monographs in Romance Languages 18. Erdenheim, PA: John Benjamins, 1986.

Gracia, Jorge J. E., and Mireya Camurati. *Philosophy and Literature in Latin America: A Critical Assessment of the Current Situation.* Albany: SUNY Press, 1989.

Hart, Stephen. *Companion to Spanish American Literature.* London: Tamesis, 2001.

Hart, Stephen, and Richard Young, eds. *Contemporary Latin American Cultural Studies.* London: Arnold, 2003.

Hillman, Richard S., and Margaret V. Ekstrom. "Political Cynicism in Contemporary Caribbean Fiction." *Secolas Annals* 21 (1990): 71–78.

Kaminsky, Amy K. *Reading the Body Politic: A Feminist Criticism of Latin America.* Minneapolis: University of Minnesota Press, 1993.

Kanellos, Nicolás, ed. *Herencia: The Anthology of Hispanic Literature of the United States.* New York: Oxford University Press, 2002.

Keen, Benjamin. *Latin American Civilization and History.* Boulder: Westview Press, 1986.

Kerr, Lucille. *Reclaiming the Author: Figures and Fictions from Spanish America.* Durham, NC: Duke University Press, 1992.

King, John. *Magical Reels: A History of Cinema in Latin America.* London: Verso, 1990.

León-Portilla, Miguel. *Pre-Columbian Literatures of Mexico.* Norman: University of Oklahoma Press, 1986.

Lindstrom, Naomi. *Twentieth Century Spanish American Fiction.* Austin: University of Texas Press, 1994.

Mac Adam, Alfred J. *Textual Confrontations: Comparative Readings in Latin American Literature.* Chicago: University of Chicago Press, 1987.

Martin, Gerald. *Journeys Through the Labyrinth: Latin American Fiction in the Twentieth Century.* New York: Verso, 1989.

Menton, Seymour. *Latin America's New Historical Novel.* Austin: University of Texas Press, 1993.

Ortega, Julio. *Poetics of Change: The New Spanish-American Narrative.* Austin: University of Texas Press, 1984.

Pagden, Anthony. *European Encounters with the New World.* New Haven: Yale University Press, 1993.

Payne, Judith, and Earl Fitz. *Ambiguity and Gender in the New Novel of Spanish America.* Iowa City: University of Iowa Press, 1993.

Paz Soldán, Edmundo, and Alberto Fuguet, eds. *Se habla español: Voces latinas en USA.* Miami: Alfaguara, 2000.

Pérez-Firmat, Gustavo, ed. *Do the Americas Have a Common Literature?* Durham, NC: Duke University Press, 1990.

Schroeder, Shannin. *Rediscovering Magical Realism in the Americas.* Westport: Praeger, 2004.

Shaw, Donald L. *The Post-Boom in Spanish American Fiction*. Albany: SUNY Press, 1998.

Smith, Paul Julian. *Representing the Other: "Race," Text and Gender in Spanish and Spanish American Narrative*. New York: Oxford University Press, 1992.

Solé, Carlos A., ed. *Latin American Writers,* 3 vols. New York: Macmillan, 1989.

Stevens, Donald F., ed. *Based on a True Story: Latin American History at the Movies*. Wilmington, DE: Scholarly Resources, 1997.

Swanson, Philip. *Landmarks in Modern Latin American Fiction*. New York: Routledge; Chapman & Hall, 1990.

———. *The New Novel in Latin America*. Manchester: Manchester University Press, 1995.

———, ed. *The Companion to Latin American Studies*. London: Arnold, 2003.

Taylor, Diana. *Theatre of Crisis: Drama and Politics in Latin America*. Lexington: University Press of Kentucky, 1991.

Weiss, Rachel, and Alan West, eds. *Being América: Essays on Art, Literature, and Identity from Latin America*. Fredonia, NY: White Pine Press, 1991.

Williams, Raymond L. *The Postmodern Novel in Latin America*. New York: St. Martin's Press, 1995.

Zamora, Lois Parkinson. *Writing the Apocalypse: Historical Vision in US and Latin American Fiction*. New York: Cambridge University Press, 1989.

14

Trends and Prospects

Richard S. Hillman

In the twenty-first century, political leaders in an increasing number of Latin American countries have been implementing strategies that appeal to their impoverished constituents. They have been doing so within democratic systems, some of which are relatively strong while many others remain fragile. In and of itself, the trend toward performance-related policies implemented by elected leaders would appear to offer much hope for future amelioration of developmental issues that continue to affect the region.

However, as Thomas J. D'Agostino shows in Chapter 4, some of the new regimes have been able to sustain political and economic development more successfully than others. Understood in terms of their political orientations, the moderate left (e.g., Chile and Brazil) have been more successful than the radical left (e.g., Venezuela and Bolivia). The differences between the radical and moderate left derive from the international environment within which they operate as well as the attendant achievement or failure of the neoliberal formula.

The new more radical regimes, in which traditional political parties have decayed, are the product of neoliberal failures and usually captivate attention and support through populist maneuvering (Gates 2010). This is quite understandable given the reverberations of the global financial crisis as well as the torturous history of intervention and manipulation that Latin America has suffered.

While the general movement to the left is attributed to anti-neoliberalism, the radical left is clearly more antagonistic to neoliberal policies than the moderate left. Where neoliberalism had some success, the political system remained intact because socioeconomic gains rendered radical change unnecessary. The leaders of more radical regimes have transformed political structures and issued largely rhetorical promises to improve difficult conditions characterizing the daily lives of the masses. Many of these leaders blame current problems on the elites within their societies who have held a monopoly on power in the past, as well as external actors, including international businesses and the United States that have exercised great influence historically.

While the radical left leaders are unlike their authoritarian counterparts of the past and have emerged through democratic systems, their tendency to suppress legitimate opposition and dissidence belies a strict adherence to democratic values. However understandable, the new strategies—designed to empower the previously alienated masses, reduce the power of national elites, and create regionally integrated networks that would operate as alternatives to US-dominated associations—may prove to be fragile and counterproductive in the long run.

In looking toward the future, we must take into consideration contradictory evidence about the salutary nature of the new strategies. Increased violence and crime, higher monetary inflation and lower purchasing power, rising unemployment, staunch political polarization, and general malaise threaten the glimmers of hope raised through the populist narrative. We have shown throughout this book that not only the facts, but also deep-seated emotions, drive events. Thus, a comprehensive understanding of where Latin America has been can contribute to predictions about the future by recognizing and respecting the reasons for the current dilemma.

Our objective has been to contribute an interdisciplinary understanding of Latin America in order to overcome myths, stereotypes, and prejudices that are often derived from a myopic view or insufficient knowledge. We have provided information, analysis, and a variety of viewpoints that we are confident will help generate a clear, broadened, and empathetic vision of an extremely complex, increasingly significant, yet widely misunderstood region. Moreover, throughout our survey of important aspects of Latin America's background, society, and culture, and geopolitical and socioeconomic settings, we have included informed speculation about what might lie ahead. It is, therefore, appropriate in this final chapter to summarize likely short- and long-term projections that could influence the region, the Western Hemisphere, and the world.

Forecasting Latin America's future, especially in times of great upheaval, is challenging and requires not only a realistic and empathetic understanding, but also critical analysis and imagination. We should recognize, therefore, that although inferences about Latin American socioeconomic and political realities can help us predict the future, this exercise necessarily yields many more open questions than definitive answers. In light of these considerations, several trends and prospects that appear to suggest future directions for Latin America can be extrapolated from our broadened vision.

We have learned that contemporary Latin America is a diverse region with similar underlying patterns and experiences. Not only has the region been shaped by its past, but it also has been transformed by the pressures of modernization and the requirements of a new world order. Traditional institutions and values that have been derived from a long colonial experience have endured and blended with emergent patterns of leadership, political dynamics, economic strategies, ethnic relations, and gender roles. Even deep-seated religious beliefs have undergone significant changes. All of these uniquely Latin American transformations are given expression in a rich literature and popular culture as well as in the ways countries of the region interact with each other and with the rest of the world.

As a dynamic interplay between integrative and disintegrative political and socioeconomic forces defines the first decade of the twenty-first century, it is precisely in the realization of unity amid diversity that we find promise for the future. A Latin American synthesis, based on patterns of fusion and amalgamation, could contribute to a model worthy of global application. Although the region continues to struggle with resilient legacies of its past and difficult current challenges, the future lies within the context of this transitional process.

Traditional patterns have been resilient, adaptable, and persistent as urbanization, industrialization, and technological advances have made Latin America even more complex and diversified—with more literate, politically conscious, and politically active populations. Thus, political leaders have had to recognize the need to be responsive to both tradition and change as well as to challenges and obstacles ranging from extensive poverty, profound inequality, dependent economies, and rapid transition. However, in the short term, populations with rising expectations have been disillusioned by their governments' inability to provide adequate services; at the same time, governments' capacities are overwhelmed by citizens' limitless needs that often cannot be fulfilled. Hence, Latin American politics are more belligerent and explosive due to the emergence of new political actors in this competitive, pluralistic environment. On the one hand, governments have not been able to satisfy all groups struggling for control over limited national resources, which has made many people feel cynical, frustrated, and left with a heightened sense of relative deprivation. On the other hand, democratization and the promise of economic growth has given citizens hope that, in the future, their countries and Latin America as a whole will attain satisfactory levels of development and stability. A variety of factors are involved in the quest to resolve this dilemma.

One crucial factor in how the future will be shaped is the military, which for centuries supported traditional authoritarianism. The national security state of the 1960s through the 1980s lacked legitimacy and changed as a result of a new regional and global context. Moreover, the experience of repression, the apparent failure of state socialism globally, and the problems of state-led development in Latin America made the region more susceptible and receptive to international influence. In response to these changes, the military had to modernize, professionalize, and restructure itself. Yet the Honduran case appeared to be a throwback to an earlier pattern of military intervention into civilian politics.

Unfortunately, political power struggles, not unlike those in the United States, have demonstrated a centrifugal tendency that yields contests between extremes. Democracy, however, requires compromise and tolerance of differences in order to move toward a workable center. The common error committed by the more radical populist leaders in Latin America has been to suppress opposition to their rule in the belief that power and control, rather than compromise, are necessary for achieving certain ends.

Moreover, economic difficulties have limited the availability of funds for military modernization, and the potential for social turmoil continues to provide a pretext for the military to intervene in domestic politics. In fact, the armed forces in some countries have split within their ranks over their theoretical subordination to civilian political authority. Although the armed forces in Latin America essentially appear to have participated in one way or another in the process of democratic consolidation, their precise role in the future continues to be unclear.

Despite periods of prosperity under liberal regimes, economic benefits have never been evenly distributed in the region. Experiments with economic nationalism and *dirigismo* (state control) failed to correct this problem; thus, many states have been adopting neoliberal policies. Latin America's enormous external debt, low investor confidence, capital flight, hyperinflation, and devastating rate of unemployment, however, continue to pose serious challenges to countries attempting to improve their economic performance. This raises troubling questions about the relationship in the region between economics and politics. What is the significance of past correlations between economic development and authoritarianism on the one hand, and between economic stagnation and democracy on the other?

Knowledge of Latin American history and society suggests a cautious response. While the region is well endowed with natural resources and a good supply of labor, it has a shortage of managers, persistent dominance by the elites, and high levels of corruption. Nevertheless, trends toward freer markets, export-oriented growth, more secure and widely distributed property rights, a better climate for foreign investment, and fiscal and economic restraint could result in development of Latin America's great potential.

Regrettably, Latin American countries have suffered from rapid development, which has led to environmental pollution, ineffective use of resources, and socioeconomic inequality. Ironically, the region's economic dynamism has often existed at the expense of social justice and human rights. Therefore, environmental, demographic, and urbanization challenges require that Latin America confront the social and political issues associated with ecological balance and environmental conservation. It is important to recognize that the experiences of hunger, illiteracy, premature death, substandard housing, and underemployment are profound despite the region's marginal contribution to global ecological disorder. In fact, the region could contribute to a new, sustainable level of development if its long-term potential can be tapped in a productive and harmonious way that overcomes short-term disruption. Yet recent environmental tragedies such as the earthquakes in Haiti (2010) and Chile (2010), annual hurricanes and ongoing erosion of coral reefs in the Caribbean, destruction of the rain forest and the mudslides in Brazil (2010 and 2011) have exacerbated these problems.

Intimately interrelated with these questions and issues in ways that are significant for the future of this region are the uniquely Latin American functions of race, ethnicity, gender, class, and nationalism. These roles continue to influence arrangements of power and, thus, require careful, empathetic analysis for a meaningful understanding of the contemporary scene. For example, women and their organizations have contributed to change in Latin America. Despite their participation in revolutions, grassroots movements, and international political meetings, however, inhibiting traditional gender roles have continued, tying most women to the home and family in subservient positions. However, the notable exceptions in the leaders of Chile, Argentina, Costa Rica, Trinidad and Tobago, and Brazil have caused some to consider the twenty-first century as the new age of women in Latin America. Nevertheless, generally women's participation in formal political institutions and organizations has been limited until the present era. Significantly, the contemporary women's movement in Latin America, despite its past limitations, has emphasized democratic practices. Activists have desired an end to authoritarianism and have sought the extension of basic human rights such as the right to clean water, sanitary housing, medical care, and education. Similarly, notwithstanding deepseated ethnic and class divisions, ongoing Eurocentrism, and socioeconomic obstacles to racial democracy, emergent conceptions of the unique Latin American fusion of peoples and cultures continues to contain the seeds for a potentially harmonious future.

Education is crucial to the evolution of societies based on ethnic and racial tolerance and equality of opportunity. Despite the considerable problems of education in Latin America, reforms have occurred, including the institution of popular education, grassroots projects, and community self-help programs. Moreover, the evolving definitions of development and education indicate a continuing move away from theories that reinforce the status quo toward ideals reinforced by policies that promote individual empowerment and faith in democratic principles. There is also a growing international awareness that effective educational systems can contribute both to the development and democratization of Latin American countries.

The role of religious beliefs in Latin American social and political life has been profound. Traditionally, the Catholic Church has been a leading political actor, especially when secular political forces were ineffective. The region, however, has become increasingly pluralistic and more open to secularizing influences. As Protestant churches have grown, the strong link between Catholicism and national identity and culture has eroded. In the future, liberals and conservatives may cross denominational lines to pressure public officials on socioeconomic matters. Such developments could lead to the further secularization of political power and a shift in the debate on moral and ethical matters from religious to political and cultural arenas.

Each of these factors is influenced not only by internal dynamics, but also by changes in the international environment. As in the past, the United States—the dominant military and economic power in the Americas—continues to be far more important to Latin America than the region has been to the United States. Hence, as the perception of communist influence in the region virtually disappeared with the end of the Cold War, the support of the United States and the international community for continuing the processes of democratization and liberalization in Latin America became overshadowed by more immediate and problematic issues in other areas of the world. For example, the suicide attacks on the twin towers of the World Trade Center in New York and the Pentagon in Washington, DC, on September 11, 2001, shifted interest to international terrorism. Also, the global financial crisis in 2008, 2009, and 2010, perhaps erroneously, has caused inattention to the evolving needs of developing countries.

But even with global attention diverted from Latin America, the illicit narcotics trade, immigration problems, excessive international debt, and prospects of hemispheric trade to offset European and Pacific Rim competition have required reassessment of relations with the region. Venezuela, the world's fifth largest petroleum exporter, continues to supply 14 percent of US oil imports. However, the emergence of what President Hugo Chávez deems a "social revolution" in Venezuela has prompted reevaluation of the traditional relationship between the two countries (Cardozo and Hillman 2003). Similarly, although Colombian and Mexican drug cartels constitute a hemispheric threat, little consensus exists about what approach to take to reduce or eliminate their influence. The same is true with regard to Mexican, Central American, and Caribbean immigration controversies. Would improved socioeconomic conditions in Latin America reduce the number of undocumented aliens seeking upward mobility in the United States? If so, what are the most effective methods for fostering development of these improved conditions within the region? Should the US embargo against Cuba be lifted in order to allow for normalized trade and interaction? Would commercial involvement in Cuba enhance US influence? Can Latin America evolve to the level of stability required for equal partnership in an integrated hemisphere?

Clearly, accelerating interdependence and economic issues will remain high on the regional agenda. Progress has been made in renegotiating the terms of debt agreements and also toward greater interregional and intraregional trade. In fact, regional integration appears to be encouraging greater economic efficiency and expanded cooperation in politics and defense. Therefore, we should see enhanced common strategies for fostering increased economic cooperation through existing common markets, customs unions, and regional institutions. Undoubtedly, one of the most important trends in contemporary Latin America is the movement toward free-trade zones that provide an emerging infrastructure for facilitating hemispheric integration.

The move toward a Free Trade Area of the Americas (FTAA) is an excellent example of an integrative trend. At the December 1994 Summit of the Americas, leaders of thirty-four nations in the Western Hemisphere committed their countries to participate in forming a hemispheric free-trade area by the year 2005. Although this has yet to be accomplished and has received a lower priority by the George W. Bush and Barack Obama administrations than the "war on terrorism," the goal continues to inform policies articulated throughout the hemisphere.

Despite enhanced expectations for greater trade and cooperation, however, President Obama had been unable to make much progress in his first two years in office. Faced with monumental economic and security issues, as well as staunch Republican opposition to virtually every proposed policy designed to ameliorate these challenges, the Obama administration has been unable to adequately address key Latin American concerns. For example, still on the agenda are issues such as closing the detention facility at Guantánamo Bay, ending the embargo and normalization of relations with Cuba, cooperating more effectively with Mexico in its fight against narcotrafficking and associated violence, passing a comprehensive immigration reform, and creation of a viable policy of interaction with populist and leftist regimes.

Elected Latin American heads of state issued a "Declaration of Principles" at their 1994 summit and renewed these principles in subsequent summits. They reiterated their firm adherence to international law and the United Nations, to preserve and strengthen the community of democracies in the Americas, promote prosperity through economic integration and free trade, eradicate poverty and discrimination, and guarantee sustainable development and environmental conservation. Although these are lofty ideals, they nevertheless address—at least rhetorically—the major challenges confronting contemporary Latin America. For example, the discussion of the consolidation of democracy reveals an acutely realistic recognition of the need to attack pervasive corruption, empower independent judiciaries, and battle against narcotrafficking and terrorism on multiple levels.

There is also clear recognition of the ways in which "democracy and development reinforce one another" ("Summit of the Americas: Declaration of Principles" 1994:2). The objectives are to create employment opportunities; improve access to education and health care; end discrimination based on race, gender, national origin, or religious affiliation; and, thereby, attain greater social justice for all sectors of society to improve the general quality of life. Such investments in the future can only have salutary effects. What remains to be seen more than fifteen years later is the extent to which these principles can be translated into operational reality through the implementation of concrete policies and programs. At least the process of bringing together the heads of state and government of the thirty-four member states of the hemisphere to discuss and take action on political, economic, and social issues that are of particular interest to the region has continued.

After the Miami summit in 1994, there were meetings in Santiago de Chile in 1998, Quebec City in 2001, Mar del Plata in 2005, and Port-of-Spain in 2009. In April 2010, the Organization of American States (OAS) and the government of Colombia began planning for the 2012 Summit of the Americas at OAS Headquarters in Washington, DC. The meeting was attended by representatives from the Inter-American Development Bank (IDB), the UN Economic Commission for Latin America and the Caribbean (ECLAC), the Pan-American Health Organization (PAHO), the International Organization for Migration (IOM), the International Labour Office (ILO), and the UN Development Programme (UNDP).

Unhappily, ongoing and increased challenges unresolved by the worthy intentions expressed at Summit of the Americas meetings characterize the early stages of the twenty-first century. Although Chile had begun integration into an incipient hemispheric free-trade zone and established a bilateral Free Trade Agreement (FTA) with the United States in June 2003, other Latin American nations have faced difficulties in achieving their objectives in ongoing negotiations. In fact, Richard Bernal, the Jamaican representative and spokesperson for developing areas, walked out of a World Trade Organization (WTO) conference held in Cancún, Mexico, in 2003, in order to protest what he claimed was the unwillingness on the part of the United States to negotiate in good faith. Bernal proclaimed, "There is nothing for us small countries in this proposal. We don't want any of this."[1] Consequently, Brazil's President Luiz Inácio Lula da Silva began to push for a separate South American trade pact. In March 2005, Brazil and Venezuela entered into an enhanced trade pact and, by early 2010, Hugo Chávez, Evo Morales, and Daniel Ortega were calling for an exclusively Latin American alternative to free-trade zones that included the United States. Later that year, Lula joined this group at a conference in Rio de Janeiro, where the idea of the Community of Latin American and Caribbean Nations (CELAC) gained popularity as an alternative to the OAS that would exclude both the United States and Canada and include Cuba. Hence, in Latin America, US influence was simultaneously incapacitated by the global financial crisis as well as declining reputation among popular leaders.

Moreover, many countries in the region continue to experience the debilitating effects of declining living standards, increased crime and violence, corrupt political institutions that fail to deliver on their promises, and the concomitant discrediting and even delegitimization of democracy (Blake 2005). The election of several radical populist leaders, whose platforms and policies reflect legacies of the past, could constrain progress toward further democratization and has raised new concerns about Latin America's future.

Elections and actions within the armed forces in several countries raise further questions about the fragility of democratic institutions and stability within the region. Alberto Fujimori, for example, gained an uncontested third term as president of Peru when Alejandro Toledo along with international observers withdrew in protest against a fraudulent electoral process in May 2000. Later, Fujimori fled the country when his complicity in corruption schemes with Vladimiro Montesinos, his principal adviser, came into question. Toledo was elected president in July 2001, yet he faced intense criticism from Peruvians seeking socioeconomic and political development. Toledo was succeeded in 2006 by former president Alan García (1985–1990) who has distanced himself from his previous administration by pursuing a strict neoliberal agenda and signing a free trade agreement with the United States. Despite overseeing a period of strong economic growth, García's approval ratings have dropped as the benefits of such growth have not been widely distributed and inflation has increased. On April 10, 2011, Peruvians went to the polls to elect their next president. Since none of the candidates received a majority, a runoff election was held on June 5 in which left-wing candidate Ollanta Humala defeated Congresswoman Keiko Fujimori, daughter of the imprisoned former president Alberto Fujimori.

After Paraguay's Vice President Luis Argana was assassinated in 1999, President Raúl Cubas was impeached and resigned, accused of complicity in the assassination. Paraguay continued under a state of siege after an attempted coup in May 2000, and a similar outcome occurred in Bolivia in April 2000. Ecuador's president Jamil Mahuad was ousted after attempting a "dollarization" policy, and Vice President Gustavo Noboa was installed by the military. Ecuador's election of Lucio Gutiérrez in January 2003 and the October 2004 election of Tabare Vázquez in Uruguay, along with Chile's Ricardo Lagos in March 2000, Argentina's Nestor Kirchner in May 2003, Brazil's Luiz Inácio Lula da Silva in January 2003, and Venezuela's Hugo Chávez in February 1999 reveal the growing trend toward the left in Latin America. After eight years in power, Lula's hand-picked successor, Dilma Rousseff, was elected president and took office on January 1, 2011, in Latin America's largest nation. Will Brazil's relatively successful economic development strategy continue to bear fruit under her regime?

Venezuelan "megaelections," in which the presidency and over 6,000 offices were to be filled in compliance with the newly rewritten constitution, were postponed when the National Electoral Commission resigned in disgrace in May 2000. When elections were held in July 2000, former coup leader Hugo Chávez and his Fifth Republic Movement (MVR) won handily. However, Venezuela has become so politically polarized that, despite President Chávez's surviving a series of strikes against the government and a recall election in

2004, his opposition has refused to recognize the legitimacy of his regime (Ellner and Hellinger 2003).[2] Moreover, Chávez has suppressed voices of opposition by censoring and even closing communications media and controlling the judiciary. His support for the guerrillas in Colombia, Iranian nuclear posturing, and anti-Israeli statements have further alienated potential supporters. And it is questionable whether his governmental policies and programs have enhanced socioeconomic conditions in Venezuela (Helwege and Birch 2007). Violence, monetary inflation, unemployment, and poverty have continued to rise as Chávez's popularity declines.

Charges of corruption were rampant in Mexico as the Institutional Revolutionary Party (PRI) attempted to maintain its long-standing control. Finally, National Action Party (PAN) candidate Vicente Fox emerged victorious in December 2000. Will a two-party or multiparty system continue to develop with transparent elections? Unfortunately, the July 2006 election of Felipe Calderón with 36 percent of the vote has proved to be indecisive in Mexico's democratization process, which continues to face the daunting challenge of increased violence and corruption occasioned by drug cartel activity.

Although there had been some movement toward democratic procedures, Haitian elections were marred by violence, gang warfare, and the forced exile of President Jean-Bertrand Aristide in 2004. Gérard Latortue, the appointed interim president, was finally replaced by René Préval in 2006 in an election marred by fraud. Subsequently, progress toward democratization was disrupted by the tragic earthquake in January 2010. Since then Haiti has been attempting to survive and rebuild the country with international assistance. In an electoral process marred by controversy, popular singer Michel Martelly defeated Mirlande Manigat, a senator and former first lady, in a March 20, 2011, runoff election and was inaugurated as Haiti's new president on May 14. Elected President Manuel Zelaya was overthrown in a coup by a Honduran elite-military coalition in 2009. Despite the subsequent election of Porfirio Lobo Sosa in 2010, questions of legitimacy remain.

Poverty, occasioned by the maldistribution of wealth, as in much of Latin America, continues to rise in most of the insular Caribbean. The extremely high crime rate in Jamaica is a direct consequence of widespread poverty and alienation. Although there are fewer Haitian "boat people," *balseros* (Cuban exile rafters) continue to attempt entry into the United States as much for economic as political reasons.

A general societal malaise throughout Latin America resulted at the commencement of the twenty-first century. This arose as a consequence of challenges and obstacles that appeared to be insuperable—in the absence of real economic development, which did not materialize via political institutions in which the people placed their confidence and trust. Programs of economic structural adjustment have been unpopular except among the wealthy elites; thus, political parties, legislatures, and judiciaries have been deeply discredited.

Such political delegitimization left a vacuum into which charismatic populists have entered. These strong presidents have rewritten national constitutions, attempted to lead "social revolutions," and ruled through "delegative democracy" (also referred to as "plebiscitory democracy" or "democracy by referendum"). This governing style exhibits "characteristics that are neither strictly authoritarian nor truly democratic" (Hillman and D'Agostino 1992:8: Hillman 1994:18–21), appears to have emerged within the context and continuity of Latin American political culture as a response to the societal malaise. As one analyst suggests, "Many citizens appear willing to give up some measure of democracy and accept authoritarian governments that they believe can solve their problems" (Hakim 1999–2000:107).

Do these challenges and obstacles mean that Latin America is condemned by its past and, therefore, destined to fail in the quest to promote political and socioeconomic development? We do not believe that the future of Latin American nations is determined exclusively by past political and social patterns. The impact of historical legacies, however, must be understood in order to deal effectively with the present.

Perhaps strong presidencies, plebiscitory democracies, and democracies by referendum are a phase within the transitional process? There is little doubt, for example, that in Venezuela the consociational dominant party system unraveled prior to the election of Chávez (McCoy and Myers 2004). Chávez's popularity among the masses has represented not only a rejection of past governmental failures, but also hope that his "social revolution" would be able to deliver palpable results to the 80 percent of Venezuelans whose quality of life had diminished during elitist regimes. The prospects for real gains, however, appear to have been foreshadowed by Chávez's inability or unwillingness to build a viable coalition of the multitude of political forces vying for power within Venezuela. And his continued incendiary rhetoric, suppression of dissent, rule by decree, and expropriation of private properties have alienated traditional allies, both within Venezuela and abroad.

Although the raised expectations engendered by the end of the Cold War and the first years of the new millennium have given way to disappointments, and legacies of the past continue to constrain the realization of much of Latin America's promise, some countervailing trends indicate healthy prospects for the future of a region that continues to define and redefine itself in terms of its unique qualities. Significantly, there is low possibility of violent revolution in the region—although the coup in Honduras, the increased polarization in Venezuela, and the continued civil war in Colombia appear to be throwbacks to an earlier era of instability. New leaders, however, are unlikely to create true military dictatorships similar to those of the past. Almost all of the Latin American regimes are attempting to improve their economies by linking them more effectively to Latin American markets as well as markets in Canada, Europe, China, and India. Moreover, each nation is operating within some conception of democratic politics. Although the Honduran case might suggest otherwise, some observers previously concluded that "nowhere in Latin America today is democratic rule threatened by military takeover" (Hakim 1999–2000:113).

The opportunities for the region continue to be great. Vast natural and human resources, an evolving culture of unity within diversity, recognition of the need for political and social democratization, expanded economic productivity and markets as well as great potential in all of these areas make Latin America a vital part of an increasingly interrelated world. Achievement of an integral and positive role in the contemporary global era will largely be a consequence of overcoming stereotypical myths through the promotion of enhanced mutual understanding. There are many signs that this process has already begun, and every citizen has a responsibility to ensure that it continues.

Human rights and economic considerations regarding the Chiapas conflict in Mexico and the Colombian civil war have expanded attention well beyond their local origins. In March 2001, for example, international as well as domestic pressures prompted Mexico's President Fox and Colombia's President Pastrana to meet with leaders of the Zapatista National Liberation Army (EZLN) and the Revolutionary Armed Forces of Colombia (FARC), respectively. Subcomandante Marcos, with international support, arrived in the Mexican capital on March 11, 2001, as a champion of indigenous rights, while FARC leaders continued to negotiate with the Colombian government over socioeconomic and political issues that have gained an international audience. Unfortunately, neither of these conflicts has been resolved, and negotiations between the rebels and their respective governments continue to be sporadic at best.

Although the United States has rhetorically supported the peace negotiations in Mexico—primarily to promote the North American Free Trade Agreement (NAFTA)—the US antinarcotics policy has prohibited US representation in discussions with the FARC. In fact, in March 2001, the US Congress proposed that the war on drugs (detailed in Plan Colombia) be expanded to Bolivia and Peru. In August 2010, Secretary of State Hilary Clinton proposed that the United States launch a Plan Colombia effort in Mexico in order to counter the increased violence occasioned by drug cartel activities near the Mexico-US border. Such US military intervention has met with almost as much resentment as US "certification" of Latin American countries' success in combating human rights abuses and drug trafficking while the United States remains the number one market for illegal narcotics.

Thus, there has been tension between Latin American initiatives and US policy regarding the resolution of conflicts engendered by socioeconomic and political conditions in these countries.[3] Despite the continued worldwide focus on international terrorism, global economic problems, and intermittent natural disasters, the internationalization of these and other essentially local conflicts and problems underscores the ongoing importance of Latin America in contemporary world affairs.

Notes

1. This was reported by Becker (2003:14).

2. I have observed that polarization regarding the Chávez regime is profound enough to divide families and friends. Venezuelan politics has rapidly become a zero-sum game. In February and March 2005, Chávez accused the United States, and specifically President George W. Bush, of planning to attack Venezuela and assassinate Chávez. He has reiterated these charges against President Barack Obama and threatened that, if he is harmed, Venezuela will cease to export petroleum to the United States (14 percent of US oil imports). The Bush administration responded by adopting a policy of "containment" against Chávez's alleged "drive to subvert Latin America's least stable states" (Andy Webb-Vidal, "Bush Orders Policy to Contain Chávez"). Despite President Obama's popularity throughout Latin America and his less judgmental perspective on Latin America articulated at the 2009 Summit of the Americas (Port of Spain, Trinidad), Chávez has continued his belligerent rhetoric against the United States. In September 2010, Chávez rejected Obama designate, Larry Palmer, as US ambassador to Venezuela and refused him entrance into the country. The United States retaliated in December 2010 by revoking the visa of Venezuelan ambassador Bernardo Álvarez.

3. Another indication of the tension was the expulsion of US ambassador Heather Hodges, who was declared *persona non grata* by Ecuador's president Rafael Correa on April 15, 2011. In retaliation, the United States expelled Luis Gallegos, the Ecuadoran ambassador to the United States the next day.

Bibliography

Becker, Elizabeth. "Poorer Countries Pull Out of Talks on World Trade." *New York Times,* September 14, 2003, p. 14.

Blake, Charles H. *Politics in Latin America.* Boston: Houghton Mifflin, 2005.

Cardozo, Elsa, and Richard S. Hillman. "Venezuela: Petroleum, Democratization, and International Affairs." In *Latin American and Caribbean Foreign Policy,* eds. Frank O. Mora and Jeanne A. K. Hey (New York: Rowman & Littlefield, 2003), pp. 145–165.

Diamond, Larry, Jonathan Hartlyn, Juan Linz, and Seymour Martin Lipset, eds. *Democracy in Developing Countries: Latin America,* 2nd ed. Boulder: Lynne Rienner, 1999.

Ellner, Steve. "Chávez Pushes the Limits: Radicalization and Discontent in Venezuela." *North American Congress on Latin America (NACLA)* 43, no. 4 (2010). https://nacla.org/node/6633.

Ellner, Steve, and Daniel Hellinger, eds. *Venezuelan Politics in the Chávez Era: Class, Polarization, and Conflict.* Boulder: Lynne Rienner, 2003.

Gates, Leslie C. *Electing Chávez: The Business of Anti-Neoliberal Politics in Venezuela.* Pitt Latin American Series. Pittsburgh: University of Pittsburgh Press, 2010.

Hakim, Peter. "Is Latin America Doomed to Failure?" *Foreign Policy* (1999–2000): 104–119.

Helwege, Ann, and Melissa Birch. "Declining Poverty in Latin America? A Critical Analysis of New Estimates by International Institutions." Paper presented at the Latin American Studies Association Congress, Montreal, Canada, September 2007. http://www.ase.tufts.edu.

Hillman, Richard S. *Democracy for the Privileged: Crisis and Transition in Venezuela.* Boulder: Lynne Rienner, 1994.

Hillman, Richard S., and Thomas J. D'Agostino. *Distant Neighbors in the Caribbean: The Dominican Republic and Jamaica in Comparative Perspective.* New York: Praeger, 1992.

McCoy, Jennifer L., and David J. Myers. *The Unraveling of Representative Democracy in Venezuela.* Baltimore: Johns Hopkins University Press, 2004.

"Summit of the Americas: Declaration of Principles." Florida International University, 1994. www.summit-americas.org.

Webb-Vidal, Andy. "Bush Orders Policy to Contain Chávez." *Financial Times* (London), March 13, 2005, p. 21.

Acronyms

ABACC	Argentine-Brazilian Accounting and Control Commission
AD	Democratic Action (Venezuela)
ALBA	Bolivarian Alternative for the Americas
APEC	Asia-Pacific Economic Cooperation
BRIC	Brazil, Russia, India, and China
CACM	Central American Common Market
CALC	Latin American and Caribbean Summit on Integration and Development
CAN	Andean Community of Nations
CAP	Common Agricultural Policy (EU)
CARICOM	Caribbean Common Market
CARIFTA	Caribbean Free Trade Association
CCR	Catholic Charismatic Renewal movement
CDRs	Committees for the Defense of the Revolution (Cuba)
CEBs	*comunidades eclesiales de base* (ecclesial base communities)
CELAC	Community of Latin American and Caribbean Nations
CELAM	Latin American Episcopal Conference
CEPE	Ecuadorian State Petroleum Company
CIA	Central Intelligence Agency (United States)
COPEI	Social Christian Party of Venezuela
CVRD	Companhía do Vale do Río Doce
DBCP	dibromochloropropane
DR-CAFTA	Dominican Republic–Central American Free Trade Agreement
EC	European Community

ECLA	Economic Commission for Latin America, known as CEPAL in Spanish
ECLAC	UN Economic Commission for Latin America and the Caribbean
ELN	National Liberation Army (Colombia)
EU	European Union
EZLN	Zapatista National Liberation Army (Mexico)
FARC	Revolutionary Armed Forces of Colombia
FDI	foreign direct investment
FMLN	Farabundo Martí National Liberation Front (El Salvador)
FSLN	Sandinista National Liberation Front (Nicaragua)
FTA	free trade agreement
FTAA	Free Trade Area of the Americas
GATT	General Agreement on Tariffs and Trade
GDP	gross domestic product
GMOs	genetically modified organisms
GNI	gross national income
GNP	gross national product
HDI	human development index
H1N1	swine flu
IAEA	International Atomic Energy Agency
IDB	Inter-American Development Bank
ILO	International Labour Office
IMF	International Monetary Fund
IOM	International Organization for Migration
ISI	import substitution (or import-substituting) industrialization
LAFTA	Latin American Free Trade Association
LAIA	Latin American Integration Association, known as ALADI in Spanish
Mercosur/ Mercosul	Mercado Común del Sur/Mercado Comum do Sul (Common Market of the South)
MNC	multinational corporation
MNR	National Revolutionary Movement (Bolivia)
MVR	Fifth Republic Movement (Venezuela)
NAFTA	North American Free Trade Agreement
NATO	North Atlantic Treaty Organization
NGO	nongovernmental organization
NIEO	new international economic order
NPT	Nuclear Non-Proliferation Treaty
OAS	Organization of American States
OECD	Organization for Economic Cooperation and Development
OPEC	Organization of Petroleum Exporting Countries
PAHO	Pan-American Health Organization

PAN	National Action Party (Mexico)
PDVSA	Petróleos de Venezuela Sociedad Anónima
PEMEX	Petróleos Mexicanos
PNR	National Revolutionary Party (Mexico)
PRD	Party of the Democratic Revolution (Mexico)
PRI	Institutional Revolutionary Party (Mexico)
PS	Socialist Party (Chile)
PT	Workers' Party (Brazil)
REPEM	Red de educación popular entre mujeres (Popular Education Network of Women)
SADC	South American Defense Council
SAP	structural adjustment program
SICA	Central American Integration System
TGE	total governmental expenditure
TNC	transnational corporation
UFCO	United Fruit Company (United States)
UNAM	National Autonomous University of Mexico
UNASUR	Union of South American Nations
UNDP	UN Development Programme
UNESCO	UN Educational, Scientific, and Cultural Organization
UNICEF	UN Children's Fund
URNG	Guatemalan National Revolutionary Union
USAID	US Agency for International Development
WTO	World Trade Organization

Appendix 1:
Basic Political Data

This Basic Political Data Appendix was compiled by Thomas J. D'Agostino. Data for capital city, independence date, population, current leadership, and elections categories were obtained from *The CIA World Fact Book* (available at https://www.cia.gov/library/publications/the-world-factbook), which was current as of December 2010. The human development index (HDI) cited below was drawn from the *Human Development Report 2009: Overcoming Barriers: Human Mobility and Development,* published for the UN Development Programme (UNDP). The HDI ratings range from 0.0 (lowest) to 1.0 (highest) as a representation of the general state of affairs for each nation's citizenry. More specifically, the HDI reflects a combination of average literacy, life expectancy, and per capita income levels. As useful points of reference, consider the following HDI averages: Average World HDI: 0.753; Average Latin American and Caribbean HDI: 0.821; a typically very high HDI: 0.955; a typically high HDI: 0.833; a typically medium HDI: 0.686; and a typically low HDI: 0.423. Parliamentary elections may be held at any time, but must be scheduled by the dates listed.

Antigua and Barbuda
Capital City Saint John's
Date of Independence from Great Britain November 1, 1981
Population 86,754
HDI Score 0.868
Current Leader Prime Minister Winston Baldwin Spencer (since March 2004)
Type of Government Parliamentary democracy
Elections Last held in March 2009. Next elections by March 2014.

Argentina
Capital City Buenos Aires
Date of Independence from Spain July 9, 1816
Population 41,343,201
HDI Score 0.866
Current Leader President Cristina Fernández (since December 2007)
Type of Government Republic
Elections Last held in October 2007. Next elections in October 2011.

Bahamas, The
Capital City Nassau
Independence from Great Britain July 10, 1973
Population 310,426
HDI Score 0.856
Current Leader Prime Minister Hubert Ingraham (since May 2007)
Type of Government Parliamentary democracy
Elections Last held in May 2007. Next elections by May 2012.

Barbados
Capital City Bridgetown
Date of Independence from Great Britain November 30, 1966
Population 285,653
HDI Score 0.903
Current Leader Prime Minister Freundal Stuart (since October 2010)
Type of Government Parliamentary democracy
Elections Last held in January 2008. Next elections by January 2013.

Belize
Capital City Belmopan
Date of Independence from Great Britain September 21, 1981
Population 314,522
HDI Score 0.772
Current Leader Prime Minister Dean Oliver Barrow (since February 2008)
Type of Government Parliamentary democracy
Elections Last held in February 2008. Next elections by February 2013.

Bolivia
Capital City La Paz
Date of Independence from Spain August 6, 1825
Population 9,947,418
HDI Score 0.729
Current Leader President Evo Morales (since January 2006)
Type of Government Republic

Elections Last held in December 2009. Next elections in
December 2014.

Brazil
Capital City Brasília
Date of Independence from Portugal September 7, 1822
Population 201,103,330
HDI Score 0.813
Current Leader President Dilma Rousseff (since January 2011)
Type of Government Federal republic
Elections Last held in October 2010. Next elections in October 2014.

Chile
Capital City Santiago
Date of Independence from Spain September 18, 1810
Population 16,746,491
HDI Score 0.878
Current Leader President Sebastián Piñera (since March 2010)
Type of Government Republic
Elections Last held in December 2009. Next elections in December 2013.

Colombia
Capital City Bogotá
Date of Independence from Spain July 20, 1810
Population 44,205,293
HDI Score 0.807
Current Leader President Juan Manuel Santos (since August 2010)
Type of Government Republic
Elections Last held in May 2010. Next elections in May 2014.

Costa Rica
Capital City San José
Date of Independence from Spain September 15, 1821
Population 4,516,220
HDI Score 0.854
Current Leader President Laura Chinchilla (since May 2010)
Type of Government Republic
Elections Last held in February 2010. Next elections in February 2014.

Cuba
Capital City Havana
Date of Independence from Spain December 10, 1898
Date of Independence from United States May 20, 1902

Population 11,477,459
HDI Score 0.863
Current Leader President Raúl Castro (since February 2008)
Type of Government Communist state
Elections Last held in February 2008. Next elections in February 2013.

Dominica
Capital City Roseau
Date of Independence from Great Britain November 3, 1978
Population 72,813
HDI Score 0.814
Current Leader Prime Minister Roosevelt Skerrit (since January 2004)
Type of Government Parliamentary democracy
Elections Last held in December 2009. Next elections by
    December 2014.

Dominican Republic
Capital City Santo Domingo
Date of Independence from Haiti February 27, 1844
Population 9,823,821
HDI Score 0.777
Current Leader President Leonel Fernández Reyna (since August 2004)
Type of Government Republic
Elections Last held in May 2008. Next elections in May 2012.

Ecuador
Capital City Quito
Date of Independence from Spain May 24, 1822
Population 14,790,608
HDI Score 0.806
Current Leader President Rafael Correa (since January 2007)
Type of Government Republic
Elections Last held in April 2009. Next elections in April 2013.

El Salvador
Capital City San Salvador
Date of Independence from Spain September 15, 1821
Population 6,052,064
HDI Score 0.747
Current Leader President Mauricio Funes Cartagena (since June 2009)
Type of Government Republic
Elections Last held in March 2009. Next elections in March 2014.

Grenada
Capital City Saint George's
Date of Independence from Great Britain February 7, 1974
Population 107,818
HDI Score 0.813
Current Leader Prime Minister Tillman Thomas (since July 2008)
Type of Government Parliamentary democracy
Elections Last held in July 2008. Next elections by July 2013.

Guatemala
Capital City Guatemala City
Date of Independence from Spain September 15, 1821
Population 13,550,440
HDI Score 0.704
Current Leader President Álvaro Colom Caballeros (since January 2008)
Type of Government Republic
Elections Last held in September 2007. Next elections in September 2011.

Guyana
Capital City Georgetown
Date of Independence from Great Britain May 26, 1966
Population 748,486
HDI Score 0.729
Current Leader President Bharrat Jagdeo (since August 1999)
Type of Government Republic
Elections Last held in August 2006. Next elections in August 2011.

Haiti
Capital City Port-au-Prince
Date of Independence from France January 1, 1804
Population 9,648,924
HDI Score 0.532
Current Leader President Michel Martelly (since May 2011)
Type of Government Republic
Elections Last held in February 2011. Next elections in February 2016.

Honduras
Capital City Tegucigalpa
Date of Independence from Spain September 15, 1821
Population 7,989,415
HDI Score 0.732
Current Leader President Porfirio Lobo Sosa (since January 2010)

Type of Government Republic
Elections Last held in November 2009. Next elections in November 2013.

Jamaica
Capital City Kingston
Date of Independence from Great Britain August 6, 1962
Population 2,847,232
HDI Score 0.766
Current Leader Prime Minister Bruce Golding (since September 2007)
Type of Government Parliamentary democracy
Elections Last held in September 2007. Next elections by October 2012.

Mexico
Capital City Mexico City (Federal District)
Date of Independence from Spain September 16, 1810
Population 112,468,855
HDI Score 0.854
Current Leader President Felipe Calderón (since December 2006)
Type of Government Federal republic
Elections Last held in July 2006. Next elections in July 2012.

Nicaragua
Capital City Managua
Date of Independence from Spain September 15, 1821
Population 5,995,928
HDI Score 0.699
Current Leader President Daniel Ortega (since January 2007)
Type of Government Republic
Elections Last held in November 2006. Next elections in November 2011.

Panama
Capital City Ciudad de Panamá
Date of Independence from Spain November 28, 1821
Date of Independence from Colombia November 3, 1903
Population 3,410,676
HDI Score 0.840
Current Leader President Ricardo Martinelli (since July 2009)
Type of Government Republic
Elections Last held in May 2009. Next elections in May 2014.

Paraguay
Capital City Asunción
Date of Independence from Spain May 14, 1811
Population 6,375,830

HDI Score 0.761
Current Leader President Fernando Lugo (since August 2008)
Type of Government Republic
Elections Last held in April 2008. Next elections in April 2013.

Peru
Capital City Lima
Date of Independence from Spain July 28, 1821
Population 29,907,003
HDI Score 0.806
Current Leader President Ollanta Humala (since July 2011)
Type of Government Republic
Elections Last held in April 2011. Next elections in April 2016.

Saint Kitts and Nevis
Capital City Basseterre
Date of Independence from Great Britain September 19, 1983
Population 49,898
HDI Score 0.838
Current Leader Prime Minister Denzil Douglas (since July 1995)
Type of Government Parliamentary democracy
Elections Last held in January 2010. Next elections by January 2015.

Saint Lucia
Capital City Castries
Date of Independence from Great Britain February 22, 1979
Population 160,922
HDI Score 0.821
Current Leader Prime Minister Stephenson King (since September 2007)
Type of Government Parliamentary democracy
Elections Last held in December 2006. Next elections by December 2011.

Saint Vincent and the Grenadines
Capital City Kingstown
Date of Independence from Great Britain October 27, 1979
Population 104,217
HDI Score 0.772
Current Leader Prime Minister Ralph E. Gonsalves (since March 2001)
Type of Government Parliamentary democracy
Elections Last held in December 2010. Next elections by December 2015.

Suriname
Capital City Paramaribo
Date of Independence from the Netherlands November 25, 1975

Population 486,618
HDI Score 0.769
Current Leader President Desire Delano Bouterse (since August 2010)
Type of Government Republic
Elections Last held in May 2010. Next elections in May 2015.

Trinidad and Tobago
Capital City Port-of-Spain
Date of Independence from Great Britain August 31, 1962
Population 1,228,691
HDI Score 0.837
Current Leader Prime Minister Kamla Persad-Bissessar (since May 2010)
Type of Government Parliamentary democracy
Elections Last held in February 2008. Next elections by February 2013.

Uruguay
Capital City Montevideo
Date of Independence from Brazil August 25, 1825
Population 3,510,386
HDI Score 0.865
Current Leader President José Mujica (since March 2010)
Type of Government Republic
Elections Last held in November 2009. Next elections in October 2014.

Venezuela
Capital City Caracas
Date of Independence from Spain July 5, 1811
Population 27,223,228
HDI Score 0.844
Current Leader President Hugo Chávez (since February 1999)
Type of Government Federal republic
Elections Last held in December 2006. Next elections in December 2012.

Appendix 2:
List of Nonindependent
Territories

The list of nonindependent territories is based, with minor adjustments, on the Nonindependent Territories list published in the second edition of *Understanding the Contemporary Caribbean* (Lynne Rienner, 2009). Although the Falkland (Malvinas) Islands, as well as the South Georgia and South Sandwich Islands under British control, are technically in the South Atlantic Ocean, they were included for geopolitical reasons. First, they are located on the eastern edge of the Scotia Sea, which is a maritime extension of the South American continent. Second, these territories' political past and present are very much a part of colonial history in South America—with particular reference to the Falkland Islands War between Great Britain and Argentina.

South America
French Guiana Overseas Department of France (1946)
Falkland Islands Under British administration since 1908. Briefly occupied by Argentina in 1982. Currently listed as being administered by Great Britain while claimed by Argentina.
South Georgia and the South Sandwich Islands Under British administration since 1908. Briefly occupied by Argentina in 1982. Currently listed as being administered by Great Britain while claimed by Argentina.

Central America and the Caribbean
Anguilla British Overseas Territory (1980)
Aruba Member of the Kingdom of the Netherlands (1986)
Bonaire Special Municipality of the Netherlands (2010)
British Virgin Islands British Overseas Territory (1967)
Cayman Islands British Overseas Territory (1962)

Curaçao Member of the Kingdom of the Netherlands (2010)

Guadeloupe Overseas Department of France (1946)

Martinique Overseas Department of France (1946)

Montserrat British Overseas Territory (1966)

Puerto Rico Commonwealth ("free associated state") associated with the United States (1952)

Saba Special Municipality of the Netherlands (2010)

St. Barthélemy Overseas Collectivity of France (2007)

St. Eustatius Special Municipality of the Netherlands (2010)

St. Maarten Member of the Kingdom of the Netherlands (2010)

St. Martin Overseas Collectivity of France (2007)

Turks and Caicos British Overseas Territory (1962)

US Virgin Islands US territory with local self-government (1968)

The Contributors

Robert F. Arnove is professor emeritus of international and comparative education at Indiana University, Bloomington.

David H. Bost is professor of modern languages at Furman University, Greenville, South Carolina.

Jacquelyn Chase is professor and chair of geography and planning at California State University, Chico.

Thomas J. D'Agostino is associate dean for global education at Hobart and William Smith Colleges and executive director of the Hobart and William Smith Colleges and Union College Partnership for Global Education, Geneva, New York.

Stephen Franz is research analyst at Indiana University, Bloomington.

Cleveland Fraser is professor of political science at Furman University, Greenville, South Carolina.

Richard S. Hillman is professor emeritus of political science at St. John Fisher College, Rochester, New York, and director of Hemisphere Research, Hudson, Florida.

Angélica Lozano-Alonso is associate professor of modern languages at Furman University, Greenville, South Carolina.

Scott G. McKinney is professor of economics at Hobart and William Smith Colleges, Geneva, New York.

René de la Pedraja is professor of history at Canisius College, Buffalo, New York.

Susan E. Place is professor of geography and planning, California State University, Chico.

Marie Price is professor of geography and international affairs and director of Latin American Studies at George Washington University, Washington, DC.

Hannah Stewart-Gambino is dean of the college at Lafayette College, Easton, Pennsylvania.

Susan Tiano is professor of sociology at the University of New Mexico, Albuquerque.

Kevin A. Yelvington is associate professor of anthropology at the University of South Florida, Tampa.

Paul W. Zagorski is professor of political science at Pittsburg State University, Pittsburg, Kansas.

Index

Abertura, 86
Abertura democrática (democratic opening), 202
Abortion, 246–247
Aconcagua, *17*
Activism: Catholic Church and, 364–365; US, 195
AD. *See* Democratic Action
Administrative decentralization, 338
Affluence, 248
Afghanistan, 203, 216
Africans, 2, 15, 33; culture of, 394
Afro-Reggae movement, 246
Age of Reason, 387
Aggression, external, 129
Agrarian Reform Law, 78
Agribusiness, 230, 234
Agriculture, 32, 38, 219; Aztecs and, 141; capital intensive, 27; chemical farming, 234; commercial, 25; export, 233, 243; indigenous, 225; industrialized, 27; nontraditional exports, 27; Old World and, 226; plantation, 51–52; slash and burn, *25*; societies of, 289; strategies of, 236; subsistence, 25
El Aguila Company, 149
El águila y la serpiente (Guzmán), 389
Aguirre, Eugenio, 383
Agustini, Delmira, 392
Ahmadinejad, Mahmoud, 218

AIDS, 245–246
Air pollution, 26
Alabarazado, 261
Alarcón, Juan Ruiz de, 387
ALBA. *See* Bolivarian Alternative for the Americas
El aleph (Borges), 394
Alerta Nacional (National Alert), 275
Alfonsín, Raúl, 125–126, 276
Allende, Isabel, 396
Allende, Salvador, 84, 87, 159–160, 199, 314, 363
Alliance for Progress, 82, 120, 198
Altamirano, Ignacio Manuel, 389
"Altazor" (Huidobro), 393
Altiplano, 16
Alvarez, Julia, 396
Amalia (Mármol), 389
Amaru, Túpac II, 55
Amazon River, 20; Basin, 225; ecosystem of, 140
Americas Watch, 200
Amnesty, 126–127
Amnesty International, 200
Anaya, Rudolfo, 396
Andean Community of Nations (CAN), 213
Andean Pact, 166
Andes Mountains, 16
Anencephaly, 243
Anheuser Busch, 270

Animals, 32–33
Annual fleets, 53
Anti-Semitism, 266, 276
APEC. *See* Asia-Pacific Economic Cooperation
Apolitical professionalism, 123
Araucania (tribal band), 32
"La Araucanian" (Ercilla), 385
Arawaks, 290
Arbenz Guzmán, Jacobo, 78, 271
Arévalo, Juan José, 78, 271
Argana, Luis, 417
Argentina: Aconcagua, *17*; agriculture in, 27; authoritarianism and, 70–71, 85; capital flows and, 169; civilian rule in, 86; commodities of, 15; Dirty War in, 86, 88, 126, 131, 275–276; economy of, 170; exports of, 149, 153; in Falkland Islands War, 88; human rights abuses in, 125; illiteracy in, 331; immigration to, 34, 71; income distribution in, 153; Las Madres de la Plaza de Mayo in, 87, 285–287, *286*; military rule in, 3, 118; Naval Mechanics School, *126*; oligarchic rule in, 70–71; peacekeeping missions by, 133; *peronismo* in, 86; *personalismo* in, 70; physical setting of, 16; politics of, 388–389; population of, 29; in postindependence era, 70; protests of, 93; Radical Civic Union, 102; Radical Party, 118–119; as regional hegemon, 193; repressive rule in, 285; river basins in, 20; school repetition rates in, 333*tab*; Spain and, 61–62; War of the Triple Alliance, 193; women in, 285, 318; in World War II, 197
Arguedas, José María, 396
Ariel (Rodó), 7, 391
Aristide, Jean-Bertrand, 88, 418
Arnove, Robert, 349
Arpilleras (tapestries), 318
Aruba, 36
Asia-Pacific Economic Cooperation (APEC), 187
Aspero, 140
Assemblies of God, 373
Assimilation: forced, 30; of labor, 76
Association of Caribbean States, 213
Asturias, Miguel Ángel, 395, 396

Asunción Silva, José, 391
Atacama Desert, 21
Atahuallpa (ruler), 381
Audiencias, 47, 54
Austerity programs, 91–92
Austral Plan, 169
Authoritarianism: bureaucratic, 83–85, 87–88; during early modernization, 70–71; of military, 123; personalistic, 77; populism, 3, 64; rule, 67; traditional, 67, 411; transition from, 67
Auto-golpe (self-coup), 128
Automobile production, 151–152
Aylwin, Patricio, 88, 94, 125
Aymaras, 314
Aztecs, 30, 42, 290, 374; agriculture of, 141; literature of, 379–380
Azuela, Mariano, 392
Azul (Darío), 391

Bachelet, Michelle, 99, 106, *107*, 368
Bahamas, 23
Bajo de color (low in color), 258
Baker, James, 202
Baker Plan, 202
Balaguer, Joaquín, 83, *252*, 253, 254, 255
Balboa, Vasco Núñez de, 43
Balbuena, Bernardo de, 385, 389
Ballet Folklórico, 169
Balseros (boat people), 418
Balún Canán (Castellanos), 396
Bandeirantes, 227
Bandeiras, 51
Barbados, 22, 50
Barca, Calderón de la, 386
Bari, 290
Batista, Fulgencio, 76, 79–80, 155, 294
Battle of Ayacucho (1824), 62
Battle of Boyacá (1819), 61
Battle of Carabobo (1821), 61
Battle of Ciudad Júarez (1911), 72
Battle of Maipú (1818), 62
Bay of Pigs, 80, 199
Belize, 23, 244
Belli, Giocondo, 396
Bello, Andrés, 325, 389
Benedict XVI (pope), 372
Benign neglect, 11
Berman, Edward, 337

Bermúdez, Francisco Morales, 158
Bernal, Richard, 416
Biodiversity, 24, 207, 231
Biotechnology, 234
Bird, Vere, 105
Birds of prey, 128
Birth defects, 243
Black consciousness movement, 274
Black Legend, 44, 382
Blanco de la barranca (white from the gutter), 258–259
Blancos (European ancestry), 33
Blanqueamiento (whitening), 265
Blanquito (little white person), 259
El Bloqueo, 211
Blue Helmets, 132
Bolaño, Roberto, 399
Bolívar, Simón, 6, 58, 61, 113, 263
Bolivarian Alternative for the Americas (ALBA), 216
Bolivia, 244; agrarian reform in, 78; agriculture in, 27; Chaco Boreal conflict, 196; Chaco War, 78; commodities of, 15; contestatory regimes in, 96; economy of, 97; Housewives' Committee, 315; illiteracy in, 308; IMF riots, 92; indigenous population in, 32; investments by, 28; language in, 36; MNR in, 78; narcotrafficking in, 204; native languages in, 30; Paraguay and, 196; physical setting of, 16; population of, 252; Potosí, 237; rebellions in, 55; Revolution of, 78; river basins in, 20; school repetition rates in, 333*tab*; tin mines of, 78; War of the Pacific and, 194
Bolivian Housewives' Committee, 315
Bolsa Familia, 174
Bonaire, 36
Bonaparte, Napoleon, 57
Booming sector, 143
Boomtown growth, 243
Borges, Jorge Luis, 394
Bosch, Juan, 83
Bost, David H., 270
Boundary disputes, 186*map*
Bourbons, 53–55; rebellion against, 55; Spain and, 144–145
Brady, Nicholas, 202
Brady Plan, 168

Brazil, 10, 69; Africans in, 15; agriculture in, 27; AIDS and, 246; Brasília, 241; bureaucratic authoritarianism and, 85; civilian rule in, 86; coffee in, 147; commodities of, 15; coup of, 121, 157; Cubatão, 26; Curitiba, 243; democracy in, 100; development of, 174; education in, 328; environmentalism in, 24; exports of, 27, 153–154; gold mining in, 28; homicides in, 246; IMF riots, 92; immigration from, 35; income redistribution in, 153; independence of, 62, 113; Japanese in, 34; literature of, 402; oil in, 216; oligarchic rule in, 70–71; peacekeeping missions by, 133; portfolio investments in, 171; Portugal and, 51–52; race and, 274; rain forests of, 207; river basins in, 20; São Paulo, 236, *237*, 241; shield of, 19; slavery in, 264; Superior War College, 84; University of Brasilia, 275; War of the Triple Alliance, 193; women's employment in, 298; in World War II, 197
Brazilian Miracle, 85–86, 157
BRIC (Brazil, Russia, India, China) countries, 172, 177
Britain, 56
Bucaram, Abdalá, 92
Bulmer-Thomas, Victor, 146, 175
Burdick, John, 274
Bureaucratic authoritarianism, 83–85, 87–88
Bush, George H. W., 133, 202, 205
Bush, George W., 209–210, 415
"Bush Negroes," 228

Cabeza de Vaca, Alvar Núñez, 382
Cabildo abierto (town meeting), 3, 47
Caboclo, 228
Cabral, Pedro, 51
Caciques, 132
CACM. *See* Central American Common Market
Café con leche (coffee with milk), 266
Caldera, Rafael, 95
Calderón, Felipe, 4, 89, 134, 215, 418
Calles, Plutarco Elías, 73, 360

Campensinos (peasants), 72, 135, 256
CAN. *See* Andean Community of
Nations
Canada, 166, 169, 179, 205
Candomblé, 37
Candomblé de caboclo, 374–375
CAP. *See* Common Agricultural Policy
Capital: flows, 162*tab*, 169, 172; human,
326; inflows, 168; intensive, 27, 152
Capitalism, 144, 147, 158, 200, 289, 372;
dependent, 362; free-market, 104;
postmodern, 251
Caracas Company, 53
Caracazo, 92, 95
Carapintadas (painted faces), 275
Cardoso, Fernando Henrique, 96, 168,
191
Caribbean, 213; Africans in, 15;
clientelism, 105; disaster relief to, 11;
elitism in, 105; emigration from, 15;
export processing zones in, 242;
languages in, 36; narcotrafficking in,
204; plate, 17, 19; racial democracy
in, 269; volcanic activity of, 17
Caribbean Community and Common
Market (CARICOM), 198, 214
Caribbean Free Trade Association
(CARIFTA), 198
CARICOM. *See* Caribbean Community
and Common Market
CARIFTA. *See* Caribbean Free Trade
Association
Carnaval, 246
*El carnero y Conquista y descubrimiento
de Nuevo Reino de Granada* (Freyle),
383
Carnoy, Martin, 334, 336
Carpentier, Alejo, 393, 395, 398
Carpio, Ramiro de León, 128
Carter, Jimmy, 200
Casa de Contratación, 144
La casa de los espíritus (Allende, I.), 396
Casal, Julián del, 391
Casas, Bartolomé de las, 44, 357, 382
Castaways (Cabeza de Vaca), 382
Castellanos, Rosario, 396
Castes, 261–262
Castro, Claudio de Moura, 347
Castro, Fidel, 80–82, 155, 198–199, 269,
331
Castro, Raúl, 82

Cathedral of Santo Domingo, *49*
Catholic Charismatic Renewal (CCR),
372–373
Catholic Church, 228, 246, 255, 291,
317, 413; activism and, 364–365;
charismatics, 372–373; colonialism
and, 356–357; Conservatives and,
359; dominance of, 13; education
and, 325; human rights and, 363;
indigenous people and, 46, 374;
influence of, 192, 227, 355; "lapsed
Catholics," 371; limitations of, 73;
Metropolitan Cathedral, *358*; modern,
361; native people and, 46; official,
374; ordination in, 368; politics and,
358; population of, 360; power of,
145; relevance of, 199; role of, 363;
secularization of, 360; seminarians,
366*tab*; separation of church and
state, 359–360; Spain and, 48–49;
women and, 375
Caudillo rule, 3, 64, 67, 113
Cautiverio feliz (Pineda y Bascuñán),
383
Cavallo, Domingo, 169
CCR. *See* Catholic Charismatic Renewal
CDRs. *See* Committees for the Defense
of the Revolution
CEBs. *See* Comunidades eclesiales de
base
CELAC. *See* Community of Latin
American and Caribbean States
CELAM. *See* Latin American Episcopal
Conference
Center for Higher Military Studies, 84
Central America: agriculture of, 27; civil
unrest in, 202; environmental issues
in, 24; Mexican Empire and, 59;
physical setting of, 16; as United
Provinces of Central America, 193; in
World War II, 197. *See also specific
countries*
Central American Common Market
(CACM), 166, 198
Central American Integration System
(SICA), 214
Central Elections Board, 254
Central Intelligence Agency (CIA), 79,
204
CEPE. *See* Ecuadorian State Petroleum
Company

Cerro de Potosí (Cerro Rico), *143*
Chacaltaya (glacier), 23
Chaco (lowlands), 20
Chaco Boreal conflict, 196
Chaco War, 78, 115
Charcoal, 25
Charles, Eugenia, 105
Charles I (emperor), 381
Chase Manhattan Bank, 158
Chávez, Hugo, 48, *95*, 95–97, 216,
  417–418; controversy of, 10; Cuba
  and, 82; election of, 171; popularity
  of, 419; presidency of, 135–136
Chemical farming, 234
Chestnut, 373
Chiapas conflict, 420
Chicago Boys, 165
Chilam Balam, 380
Childbearing, 309
Children's Fund, UN, 339
Chile, 69; bureaucratic authoritarianism,
  85, 87; copper mining of, 28; debt
  crisis and, 165; democracy in, 100;
  earthquake of, 413; economy of, 97,
  159–160; exports of, 27, 149;
  illiteracy in, 331; immigration to, 34;
  investments by, 175; oligarchic rule
  in, 70–71; peacekeeping missions by,
  133; physical setting of, 16; "pots and
  pans" demonstrations, 314; power
  transfer in, 122; as regional hegemon,
  193; religion in, 363; school
  repetition rates in, 333*tab*; Truth and
  Reconciliation Commission, 125; US
  and, 83
China, 213, 217–218, 276–277; economy
  of, 177
Chinampas, 225
Chinchilla, Laura, 106
Cholas, 38
Christian Democracy, 102, 192
Christianity, 37, 356. *See also specific*
  denominations
Churches, national, 360
Cien años de soledad (García Márquez),
  395, 404
Cisneros, Sandra, 396
Ciudad Guyana, Venezuela, 241
Ciudad Júarez, Mexico, *134*
La ciudad y los perros (Vargas Llosa),
  395

Civic action, 131–132
Civil defense, 131–132
Civil unrest, 202
Civil war, 206; Colombian, 420; of El
  Salvador, 35; of Peru, 135; US, 114
Civilian governments, 126–128, 135
"Civilización y barbarie o vida de Juan
  Facundo Quiroga" (Sarmiento), 388
Civilizing, 42, 325
Class, 38, 256, 258; differences of, 335;
  distribution of, 259; exploitation of,
  271; middle, 72; stratification of, 289
Clean energy, 10
Clemencia (Altamirano), 389
Clientelism, 105
Climate, 18*map*; change, 207–208, 231;
  commodity lottery and, 146, 148;
  midlatitude, 21
Climate Change Conference, UN, 208
Clinton, Hillary Rodham, 4, 420
Coastal development, 232
Coffee exports, 27, 147
Cold War, 6, 81, 129, 132–133, 197, 331
Collor de Mello, Fernando, 209
Colombia: Africans in, 15; Bourbons
  and, 55; civil war of, 420; coffee in,
  147; counternarcotics operations in,
  133; drug cartels of, 89; economy
  and, 139; Ecuador and, 185;
  education in, 328, 346; FARC, 10, 48,
  90, 211; gold mining in, 28; illiteracy,
  331; immigration from, 35; instability
  of, 135; Plan Colombia, 211–212,
  420; rebellion of, 55; school
  repetition rates in, 333*tab*; Venezuela
  and, 3, 48, 185; La Violencia, 360
Colonialism, 3, 8, 45*map*, 141, 237, 277;
  Catholic Church and, 356–357;
  chronicles of, 381; divisions of, 44;
  European, 226; language and, 36;
  literature and, 379; neocolonialism,
  11; outcomes of, 290; women and,
  291
Colonization, 38; decolonization, 277;
  Iberian, 13, 29; Spanish, 41–42
"Coloquio que tuvo con la muerte un
  médico moribundo" (Valle y
  Caviedes), 385
De color medio (of medium color), 258
Colorado Party, 102
"Colossus of the North," 5

Columbian Exchange, 15, 32, 142
Columbus, Christopher, 15, 41, 141, 381, 394
Comentarios reales del Perú (Vega), 380
Comisión Económica para América Latina, 274
Committees for the Defense of the Revolution (CDRs), 80
Commodities, 15; boom of, 179; exports of, 177; lottery, 146, 148; prices of, 28, 151; production of, 177; rising prices of, 178*tab*; tropical, 229
Common Agricultural Policy (CAP), 219
Communal kitchens, 317
Communication, 191–192
Communism, 129, 199, 276, 414; Cuban, 211; roll back, 203
Communist Party Congress, 269
Community movements, 317
Community of Latin American and Caribbean States (CELAC), 4, 217, 416
Companhía do Vale do Río Doce (CVRD), 154, 174
Completion rates, 333*tab*
Comuneros, 55
Comunidades eclesiales de base (CEBs), 361–363
CONAPO. *See* Consejo Nacional de Poblacíon
Concertación, 167
Concertación de Partidos por la Democracia, 94, 100
Conference of Ministers of Education and Those Responsible for the Application of Science and Technology to Development, 330
Conflicts, 77; Chaco Boreal, 196; Chiapas, 420; intraregional, 196; land, 232; political/social, 124; society, 9
Congreso Feminino Internacional, 294
Conquest, 29–30; chronicles of, 381; disease and, 32–33; end of, 32; historical context of, 41–44
Conquistadores, 142, 260, 355, 356–357
Consejo Nacional de Poblacíon (CONAPO), 242
Conservatives, 70; Catholic Church and, 359
Constitutionalists, 73

Constitutive Treaty, 215
Construction industry, 307
Consumerism, 247
Consumption effect, 144
Contamination, of crops, 234
Continuismo, 72
Contras, 89–90, 203
COPEI. *See* Social Christian Party of Venezuela
Copper mines, 28
Cordilleras, 146
Correa, Rafael, 98, 172, 216
Cortázar, Julio, 395
Cortés, Hernán, 5, 42, 61, 381, 394
Cosmic race, 5, 266
Costa Rica: environmentalism in, 24; exports of, 27; gold mining in, 28; women's employment in, 298
Costumbrismo, 385
Counterinsurgency strategy, 132
Counternarcotics operations, 133
Countries and capitals, 14*map*
Coups: *auto-golpe*, 128; Brazilian, 121, 157; *golpe de estado*, 111; of Honduras, 3, 136; promotion of, 127; veto, 116
"El Crack," 400
Creationism (literature), 393
a-la-Crete-a-Pierrot, Marie Jeanne, 293
Criollos, 47, 54–57, 112, 261, 358
Cristero Revolution, 360
Croatia, 133
Crops, 16, 225; contamination of, 234; tropical, 32
Crosby, Alfred, 32
Cruz, Sor Juana Inés de la, 385–386
Cuba, 6, 22; Communist Party, 211; Constitution of, 195; economy of, 82; education in, 342; exports of, 149; illiteracy in, 331; immigration and, 35, 401; literacy in, 331; in postindependence era, 79; race in, 269; Revolution of, 79–81, 82, 119, 157, 314, 395, 396; school repetition rates in, 333*tab*; second, 82; Soviet Union and, 81, 155; US and, 11, 155, 195, 210; Venezuela and, 156–157
Cuban Missile Crisis, 81
Cubas, Raúl, 417
Cubatão, Brazil, 26
Cultivation, 224, 225

Culture, 3; African, 394; determinations of, 260; fused, 8; global, 270, 279; multiculturalism, 277, 344; nationalism and, 270, 275; popular, 403; promotions of, 269; purity of, 264; "white," 255; women and, 310
Curaçao, 50
Curitiba, Brazil, 243
CVRD. *See* Companhía do Vale do Río Doce

da Silva, Luiz Inácio "Lula," 94, *94*, 217, 368, 416, 417; popularity of, 99; presidency of, 173–174
Danticat, Edwidge, 396
Darío, Rubén, 7, 391–392
Darwinism, social, 263
Data, habeas, 131
Dávila, Arlene, 270
DBCP. *See* Dibromochloropropane
de Landa, Diego, 380
Debayle, Anastasio Somoza, 202
Debt, 189, 200; crisis, 161, 162–165, 164*tab*, 334–335, 338; environment and, 230; of Mexico, 162; payments, 91
Decade for Women, UN, 313
Decentralization, 243, 337; administrative, 338; elements of, 339; urban, 242–243
"Declaration of Principles," 415
Decolonization, 277
Defense: civil, 131–132; internal, 130–131
Deforestation, 24, 226, 231, 235
Democracy and democratization, 4, 8, 9, 64, 68, 215, 411; consolidation of, 103–104, 106–107; delegative, 96, 102, 419; direct, 100; education and, 349; emerging, 89; liberal, 68, 100; military and, 111; obstacles and challenges to, 88; promotion of, 69; racial, 264, 269, 273, 275; resurgence of, 230; support of, 104; transition toward, 104
Democratic Action (AD), 95
Demographic transition, 244
Demonstrations, 92, 317; "pots and pans," 314
Dependency, 200; theory, 150, 154, 190–191

Dependent development, 154
Deserts, 21
Desertification, 226
Development, 70, 330; of Brazil, 174; coastal, 232; definitions of, 326; dependent, 154; economic, 159–160; education and, 325; new fields of, 342; policies of, 350; political, 118; rapid, 412; stages of, 326; tourism-based, 233
Díaz, Porfirio, 71–72, 74, 149, 266
Díaz del Castillo, Bernal, 381
Dibromochloropropane (DBCP), 234
Dictatorships, executive, 128
Diezmo, 142
Dirigismo, 412
Dirty War, 86, 88, 126, 131, 275–276
Discrimination: legal, 263; racial, 37, 262, 265; against women, 293
Disease, 42, 142, 226, 243, 245; introduction of, 32–33; production and, 148–149
Disequilibria, 159–160
Diversification, 191; economic, 176, 180; of native peoples, 271
Diversity, 7, 15, 410–411; biological, 24, 207, 231; of women, 287
Docenio, 85
Doctrines, 116; Estrada Doctrine, 196; military, 120; Monroe Doctrine, 74, 193–194; national security, 119, 121–122
Dollar diplomacy, 196
Dollarization, 171
Domestic intelligence, 131
Dominican Republic: Haiti and, 254, 256; human rights abuses in, 10; identity of, 255; illiteracy in, 331; IMF riots in, 92; immigration from, 35; intervention in, 199; military intervention in, 199; political parties in, 102; presidential election of, 253; race in, 257; school repetition rates in, 333*tab*; US and, 83
Dominican Republic–Central American Free Trade Agreement (DR-CAFTA), 214
Dominican Revolutionary Party, 254
Don Segundo Sombra (Güiraldes), 388
Doña Bárbara (Gallegos), 389
Dorfman, Ariel, 396–397

Downsizing, 130
Drama, 380, 384, 386–387
DR-CAFTA. *See* Dominican Republic–Central American Free Trade Agreement
Droughts, 23
Drug trade, 89, 204; cartels, 211; war on, 133–134, 420. *See also* Narcotrafficking
Due obedience, 127
Dueños (business owners), 256
Durability, 9
Dutch Disease, 98, 143–144, 163
Duvalier, François "Papa Doc," 76–77, 375

Earth Summit, 207
Earthquakes, 16, 413; of Haiti, 10, 19, *224*
East Indians, 277
Echeverría, Esteban, 387
ECLAC. *See* Economic Commission for Latin America and the Caribbean
Economic Commission for Latin America and the Caribbean (ECLAC), 166, 416
Economy: of Argentina, 170; BRIC, 177; of Chile, 97, 159–160; of China, 177; comprehensive policies of, 179; Cuban, 82; dependence, 194; disequilibria of, 159–160; diversification of, 176, 180; exports and, 146; global, 171; growth of, 86, 98, 152, 154, 170, 178, 178*tab*; illegal, 239; independence and, 145; informal, 240; of Japan, 177; Mexican, 17, 170; mining and, 142–144; modernization of, 356; natural resources and, 24; neoliberalism and, 251; NIEO, 200; performance of, 96*tab*; plantation, 2; policy environment, 146; populism of, 159; pre-Colombian, 139; religion and, 356; restructuring of, 91; sustenance and, 139–140; US, 162, 168; women and, 291–292, 298, 300, 305
Ecosystems: Amazon, 140; coastal, 233
Ecotourism, 39, 233
Ecuador: banking sector collapse of, 171; Colombia and, 185; economy of, 97; illiteracy, 331; immigration from, 35; indigenous populations of, 32; language in, 36; narcotrafficking, 204; oil of, 28; Peru and, 130; physical setting, 16
Ecuadorian State Petroleum Company (CEPE), 148
Education, 292, 307, 310, *330*, 413; access to, 331, 345; adult, 342; Catholic Church and, 325; competition and, 339; completion rates, 333*tab*; compulsory, 330–331; debt crisis and, 334–335, 338; enrollments in, 328, 328*tab*, 342; expenditure, 328–329, 329*tab*, 336, 337; gender and, 332–333; higher, 327, 328, 340, 341; innovations of, 344; mass media and, 348–349; in Mexico, 341, 347; new approaches of, 345–346; opportunities of, 330, 334, 345; policies of, 329; popular, 343, 344–345; private schools, 338; private universities, 341; promotion rates in, 334; public, 308, 338; quality of, 327, 333–334, 345, 350; repetition rates, 332, 333*tab*; secondary school, 308, 328; spending cuts in, 336; standardized examinations of, 334, 339; student retention, 334; trends in, 338, 350; vocational, 328–329; of women, 292, 307, 310, 344
Egalitarianism, 289
El Dorado, 42
El Salvador, 244; civil war in, 35; conflict in, 77; exports of, 27; hurricanes in, 22; illiteracy in, 331; immigration from, 35; religion in, 37; school repetition rates in, 333*tab*; US and, 83
Elections, 9, 101, 122, 171, 417
Elevations, 22
Elitism, 105, 263, 265, 360; nationalism and, 271
ELN. *See* National Liberation Army
Embraer, 154, 174
Emigration, 15, 35
Employment, 298, 310; construction industry, 307; gender and, 298–300; opportunities of, 309; service sector, 306–307; trends in, 300;

unemployment, 304; for women, 298–300, 306, 310

Encomiendas, 41, 46, 142

Energy, 209; clean, 10; exports, 98; prices of, 161

Enlightenment, 358, 370

Environment, 223; change of, 226; debt crisis and, 230; industrialization and, 236; issues of, 23–25; Mexico and, 243; modification of, 225; problems of, 247; protection of, 131; regulation, 230

Era of La Presidenta, 106

Ercilla, Alonso de, 385

La Escuela Nueva (the New School), 346

Eslava, Gonzalo de, 386

El espejo enterrado (Fuentes), 392

Estado Novo, 154

Estenssoro, Víctor Paz, 78

Estrada, Genaro, 196

Estrada Doctrine, 196

Ethnicity, 259; groups, 5; identity and, 256; nationalism and, 277; tensions of, 263

Ethnogenesis, 258

Ethnonyms, 258

EU. *See* European Union

Eugenics, 364

European Union (EU), 188, 213, 218–219

Europeans, 2

Evangelical Protestantism, 366–367, 376–377

Evasion, 227

Executive dictatorships, 128

Exports: agriculture, 233, 243; boom, 229; of Brazil, 27, 153–154; of coffee, 27, 247; of commodities, 177; dependence and, 148; economy and, 146; energy, 98; Golden Age of, 149–150; industrialization and, 305; mineral, 28, 52; of oil, 158; processing zones, 242; production of, 229; raw material, 149–150; revenues, 147–148

External aggression, 129

External relations, 200

Extraction, 235

EZLN. *See* Zapatista National Liberation Army

Falkland (Malvinas) Islands War, 87–88, 122, 185, 203

Famiyas, 276

Farabundo Martí National Liberation Front (FMLN), 89, 202

FARC. *See* Revolutionary Armed Forces of Colombia

Farming systems, 226

Fascism, 102

FDI. *See* Foreign direct investment

Fe y Alegría (Faith and Happiness), 345–346

Federación Nacional de Cafeteros Colombianos, 147

Federal Reserve Bank, US, 161

Feminism, 285, 288, 294, 298; movements of, 312–313

Ferdinand VII (king), 57–58, 58, 61

Fernández, Cristina, 106, 153, 188, *312*

Fernández de Lizardi, José Joaquín, 387, 394

Fertility, 244, 246, 309–310

Ficciones (Borges), 394

Fifth Republic Movement (MVR), 417

Film, 403–404

Financial crisis, global, 68

Five Heroes, 211

"The Floating Gardens of Xochimilco," 225

La Florida (Vega), 380

FMLN. *See* Farabundo Martí National Liberation Front

Fome Zero, 174

Food crops, 225

Foraging, 224

Forced assimilation, 30

Foreign direct investment (FDI), 156, 168–169, 175

Foreign policy, 188–189; drug trade and, 204; US, 6

Fossil fuels, 28

Fotonovelas, 348

Foursquare Gospel Church, 373

Fox, Vincente, 418

Franco, Itamar, 128

Fraser, Cleveland, 74, 166

Free trade agreements (FTAs), 166, 205, 416

Free Trade Area of the Americas (FTAA), 166, 187, 214, 415

Freemasonry, 276

Frei, Eduardo, 159
Freire, Paulo, 345
French Guiana, 23
French Revolution, 56–57
Freyle, Rodríguez, 383–384
Freyre, Gilberto, 264
Frida (film), 1
FSLN. *See* Sandinista National
  Liberation Front
FTAA. *See* Free Trade Area of the
  Americas
FTAs. *See* Free trade agreements
Fuenta, Alejandro de la, 269
Fuentes, Carlos, 382, 392, 395
Fueros, 47, 113
Fuguet, Alberto, 399
Fujimori, Alberto, 90, 101, 128, 168, 417
Fused cultures, 8

Gairy, Eric, 105
Galeano, Eduardo, 144
Gallegos, Rómulo, 389
García, Alan, 166–168, 417
García, Anastasio Somoza, 76
El Gato Eficas (Valenzuela, E.), 396
GATT. *See* General Agreement on Tariffs
  and Trade
Gender, 288; education and, 332–333;
  egalitarianism and, 289; employment
  and, 298–300; indigenous people
  and, 313; labor and, 288–289, 295;
  literacy and, 343, 343*tab*; mixed-
  gender movements, 313; religion
  and, 371; roles of, 310, 313. *See also*
  Women
General Agreement on Tariffs and Trade
  (GATT), 205
Genetically modified organisms
  (GMOs), 234
Gente de primera (first-class people),
  258
Gente de segunda (second-class people),
  258
Geography, 1, 15, 38; human, 28, 36
Gini Index, 172, 179
Glacial runoff, 23
Glasnost, 81
Global affairs, 1
Global economy, 171
Global financial crisis, 68
Global warming, 22–23, 208

Globalization, 211, 213, 223, 229–230,
  251; independence and, 191–192;
  protests against, 279; transnationalism
  and, 36
GMOs. *See* Genetically modified
  organisms
Gold, 28, 52–53
Goldemberg, Isaac, 396
Golden Age of Exports, 149–150
Golpe de estado (coup), 111
Gómez, Juan Vicente, 71
Gómez, Sergio, 399
Gondwanaland, 19
González, Elián, 206
Gonzalez, Rodolfo "Corky," 400
Good Neighbor Policy, 196–197
Gorbachev, Mikhail, 81–82
Gorostiaga, Xabier, 348
Goulart, João, 84, 85, 157
Government, 67, 336; branches, 47–48,
  69; civilian, 126–128, 135;
  dominance of executive branch, 69;
  downsizing of, 230; fourth branch of,
  106; leftist, 93–94, 96, 99, 409–410;
  military and, 121–122; NGOs, 343
"Grandeza Mexicana" (Balbuena), 385
Grassroots organizations, 230
Great Depression, 74, 78, 150, 255
Great Recession, 187, 216
Greece, 219
Green spaces, 244
Grenada: fall of, 112; intervention in,
  203–204; US and, 83, 203–204
Grijalva-Usumicinta Basin, 21
Gringos, 7
Growth theories, 327
Guajiros, 256
Guano, 148
Guantánamo Bay Naval Base, 11, 206,
  415
Guatemala: human rights abuses in, 79;
  immigration from, 35; indigenous
  people of, 32, 315; Mutual Support
  Group for the Reappearance of Our
  Sons, Fathers, Husbands and
  Brothers, 318; nationalism of, 272;
  native languages in, 30; race and,
  271; school repetition rates in,
  333*tab*; women's employment in, 299
Guatemalan National Revolutionary
  Union (URNG), 79

Guerrero, Gonzalo, 383
La guerrilla, 10
Guevara, Ernesto "Che," 1, 80, 156, 199
Guillén, Nicolás, 396
Güiraldes, Ricardo, 388
Gunder Frank, Andre, 190
Gutiérrez, Lucio, 135, 417
Guyana, 23; environmentalism in, 24; gold mining in, 28; IMF riots in, 92
Guzmán, Abimael, 90
Guzmán, Martín Luis, 389

H1N1. *See* Swine flu
Habeas data, 131
Haciendas, 2, 227
Haig, Alexander, 203
Haiti, 57, 226; Dominican Republic and, 254, 256; earthquake in, 10, 19, *224*, 413; immigration from, 35; massacre in, 255; poverty in, 25; revolution, 53, 254; US and, 195
Harris, Marvin, 267
Health, 156, 243
Hegemony, regional, 193
Heresy, 49
Hernández, José, 388, 390
Heterodoxy policies, 166–168
Heureaux, Ulises, 71
Hezbollah, 211
Hidalgo, Miguel, 58, 64
Highlands, 17
Hijuelos, Oscar, 396
Hillman, Richard S., 15
Hinojosa-Smith, Rolando, 396
Hispanidad, 255, 256
Historia verdadera de la conquista de la Nueva España (Díaz del Castillo), 381
Historical perspective, 2
HIV/AIDS, 245–246
Hobsbawn, Eric, 275
"Hombres necios" (Cruz), 386
Homicide, 246
Homogenization, 259, 278
Honduras, 244; coup of, 3, 111, 136; hurricanes in, 22; school repetition rates in, 333*tab*; 3-16 Battalion, 131; women's employment in, 299
Hooker, Juliet, 274
Horticultural societies, 289–290
Housing market, 239

Huerta, Victoriano, 73
Huidobro, Vicente, 393
Humala, Ollanto, 417
Human capital, 326
Human geography, 28, 36
Human rights, 124–127, 272, 413, 420; abuses of, 79, 207, 362; Catholic Church and, 363; organizations, 317–318
Hurricanes, 22
Hussein, Saddam, 209
Hybridization, 105
Hydroelectricity, 23
Hyperinflation, 412

I, Rigoberta Menchú: An Indian Woman in Guatemala (Menchú), 398
IAEA. *See* International Atomic Energy Agency
Ibarbourou, Juana de, 392
Iberian Peninsula, 2; colonization of, 13, 29
IDB. *See* Inter-American Development Bank
Identity, 252, 388; Dominican, 255; ethnic, 256; indigenous, 265; national, 3; politics and, 253; religion and, 355
Illiteracy, 308, 331, 336
ILO. *See* International Labour Office
IMF. *See* International Monetary Fund
Immigrants and immigration, 52, 206, 265–266; to Argentina, 34, 71; Cuban, 35, 401; of Japan, 34
Imperialism, US, 6
Import substitution industrialization (ISI), 75, 150, 152, 164, 198, 229
Impressions, public, 6
"El Inca," 394
Incas, 30, 43, 374; expansion of, 141; literature of, 379–380
Inclusion, 38
Income: disparities of, 336; distribution, 153, 156, 160, 174, 179; inequality of, 152; rising of, 153
Incumbent parties, 103
Independence, 3, 55, 64, 228; Brazilian, 62, 113; early movements, 59*map*; economy and, 145; globalization and, 191–192; later movements, 60*map*; Mexican, 62; post-

independence era, 69–70, 79; wars for, 111–112, 263
Indigenismo, 266–267
Indigenous peoples: agriculture of, 225; captivity of, 382; Catholic Church and, 46, 374; empires, *31fig*; forest protection by, 232; gender and, 313; groups, 2; identity and, 265; migration routes, *31fig*; movements and, 314–315; populations of, 32; religion and, 357
Indio oscuro (dark native person), 258
Indios (Amerindian ancestry), 33, 38, 257–258
Indios permitidos (allowed Indians), 272
Industrial Revolution, 70, 235
Industrialization, 75, 76, 154, 191, 223, 411; of agriculture, 27; environment and, 236; export-led, 305; growth and, 153; livestock production and, 233. *See also* Import substitution industrialization
Inequality, 37–38, 179, 180, 180*tab*; of income, 152; socioeconomic, 412
Inflation, 98, 161, 163, 165, 171, 189
Infortunios de Alonso Ramírez (Sigüenza y Góngora), 384
Infrastructure, 239, 243
Ingenieros, José, 265
Inhabitants, 4
Inquisition, 49–50, 57
Instability, 3, 85; in Colombia, 135
Institutional Revolutionary Party (PRI), 76, 418
Integration, 135, 198, 214, 271; of military, 130; theory, 213
Intelligence, domestic, 131
Inter-American Development Bank (IDB), 230, 347, 416
Inter-American Treaty of Reciprocal Assistance (Rio Pact), 198
Interdependence, 191–192, 211, 414
Intermarriage, 277
Intermestic politics, 187
Internal defense, 130–131
International alignment, 4
International Atomic Energy Agency (IAEA), 209
International Commission on Education, Equity and Economic Competitiveness, 336

International Labour Office (ILO), 416
International Labour Organization, 240
International Monetary Fund (IMF), 91, 165, 191, 201, 230, 335, 340; riots, 92
International Organization for Migration (IOM), 416
International Petroleum Company, 158
International relations, 185, 196, 220
International Telephone and Telegraph, 158
International Women's Year Conference, UN, 313
Invented tradition, 275
Investments, 150, 189; by Bolivia, 28; by Chile, 175; foreign, 156, 168–169, 175; by Mexico, 175; portfolio, 170, 171
IOM. *See* International Organization for Migration
Iran, 4
Iraq War, 209–210
Irrigation, 140
Is Latin America Turning Protestant? (Stoll), 367
Isaacs, Jorge, 389
ISI. *See* Import substitution industrialization
La isla al revés: Haití y el destino dominicano (Balaguer), 255
Itaipu Dam, 20, *175*

Jamaat-Al-Muslimeen, 84
Jamaica, 22, 50; IMF riots in, 92
Japan, 213; economy of, 177; immigrants of, 34
Jefferson, Thomas, 6
Jehovah's Witnesses, 367, 373
Jesuits, 49, 53, 228
Jews, 266
Jíbaros, 256, 270
Jiménez de Quesada, Gonzalo, 43
João, Dom (Portuguese ruler), 63
John Paul II (pope), 200, 364, 372
Jones Act, 401
Júarez, Benito, 71–72
Juntas, 57, 362

Kahlo, Frida, 1
Kennedy, John F., 80, 82, 198, 327
Khrushchev, Nikita, 81

Kirchner, Nestor, 215, 217, 417
Kottak, Conrad, 267
Kukulcan temple, *42*
Kuna (indigenous group), 32

Labels, 13
El laberinto de la soledad (Paz), 392
Labor, 51; assimilation of, 76; cheap, 242; division of, 288–289; gender and, 288–289, 295; movement, 76–77, 119; organizations, 76; slave trade and, 226; urban struggles of, 314; by women, 291, 295, 296*tab*–297*tab*, 299–300, 301*tab*–303*tab*, 304–306, 309
LAFTA. *See* Latin American Free Trade Area
LAIA. *See* Latin American Integration Association
Land: conflicts, 232; reallocation of, 291
Languages, 394; colonial, 36; *lingua franca*, 36; multilingualism, 344; native, 30, 36; *Papiamento*, 36; *patois*, 36; of race, 267; Spanish, 46
El largo atardecer del caminante (Cabeza de Vaca), 383
Larrain, Felipe, 160
Latin American Episcopal Conference (CELAM), 361
Latin American Free Trade Area (LAFTA), 198
Latin American Integration Association (LAIA), 198, 214
Latortue, Gérard, 418
Leadership, military, 113, 159
Leftist government, 93–94, 96, 99; radical, 409–410
Lerner, Jaime, 243
Lernoux, Penny, 364
Levin, Henry, 346
La Leyenda Negra (the Black Legend), 44
Liberal democracy, 68, 100
Liberalism, 70, 145, 150, 160, 358
Liberalization: financial, 172; trade, 165–166
Liberation, 3; theology, 199–200, 361, 362, 368
Liberationists, 362, 367
"*Liberté, egalité, fraternité,*" 262
Life expectancy, 28

Limpieza de sangre (purity of blood), 260
Lingua franca, 36
Linkages, 151, 175–176
Lionsa, María, 376
Lisbon Treaty, 219
Literacy, 156, 342, 345; gender and, 343, 343*tab*; illiteracy, 308, 331, 336
Literature, 379; awards of, 402; of Aztecs, 379–380; boom, 394–396; Brazilian, 402; coming-of-age novels, 400–401; contemporary, 396; El Crack, 400; creationism, 393; historical novels, 397, 402; of Incas, 379–380; magical realism, 393–394, 404; modernism and, 390–391; novels, 387; oral, 379; poetry, 384–385; short stories, 387; of vanguard, 392–393; by women, 392
Livestock, 233
Llaneros, 263
Llanos (lowlands), 20
Llosa, Mario Vargas, 382, *395*, 395–396
Las locas, 286
Los de abajo (Azuela), 392
Louis XIV, 54
Lowlands, 20
Loyalists, 83
Lozano-Alonso, Angélica, 270
Lugones, Leopoldo, 391
Lukumí, 269

Machado, Gerardo, 79
Machismo, 7
Machu Picchu, 16, *19*, 23
Macumba, 37
Madero, Francisco, 72, 149
Las Madres de la Plaza de Mayo, 87, 285–287, *286*, 318, 403
Magellan, Ferdinand, 43
Magical realism, 393–394, 404
Mainwaring, Scott, 102, 105
Maize, 234
Mamelucos, 260
Mangrove swamps, 232
Manigat, Mirlande, 418
Manufacturing: capital-intensive, 152; growth in, 151*tab*
Mapuche (tribal band), 313, 315
Maquiladoras, 242–243, 287, 305–306, *306*, 311

María (Isaacs), 389
Marianismo (cult of the Virgin Mary), 289, 295, 310–311, 319
Mariel Boatlift, 80
Market mechanisms, 339
Mármol, José, 389
Maroons, 228
Márquez, Gabriel García, 395–396
Martelly, Michel, 418
Martí, José, 7, 391
"Martín Fierro" (Hernández), 388
Marxism, 200, 276, 360, 361, 362, 364, 372
Mass transportation, 26
"El Matadero" (Echeverría), 387
Matos, Luis Palés, 396
Maximillian (prince), 194
Mayas, 30, 37, 140, 279, 374; Kukulcan temple, *42*
McOndo (Fuguet and Gómez), 399
Media, 348–349; religion and, 377
Medrano, Juan de Espinosa, 386
Meller, Patricio, 160
Menchú Tum, Rigoberta, 270, 272, 315, 382, *398*
Méndez, Miguel, 396
Menem, Carlos, 92, 168, 169, 208, 275
Mercantilism, 142
Mercosur (Common Market of the South), 166
Mérida conferences, 294
Mérida Initiative, 211–212
Mesa Central, 17
Mesoamericans, 225
Mestiços, 260
Mestizaje (miscegenation), 255, 260, 262–263
Mestizos (mixed ancestry), 2, 33–34, 38, 52, 54–55, 64
Metropolitan Cathedral, *359*
Mexican-American War, 400
Mexico: ancestry of, 35; border cities, 242*tab*; Central America and, 59; Ciudad Júarez, *134*; commodities of, 15; Cristero Revolution, 360; debt of, 162; economy of, 17, 170; education in, 341, 347; environmental problems of, 243; illiteracy in, 331; immigration from, 35; independence of, 62; indigenous population in, 32; investments by, 175; *maquiladoras* in,

287; Mexico City, 238–239; native languages in, 30; peso crisis of, 169; petroleum in, 235; politics of, 71; in postindependence era, 70; race and, 266; as regional hegemon, 193; Revolution of, 72, 74, 195, 294; river basins in, 20; school repetition rates in, 333*tab*; Tenochtitlán, 30, 42, 141; women's movements in, 318; in World War II, 197
Micheletti, Roberto, 9
Midlatitude climates, 21
Migration, rates of, 239
Military, 54–55; Argentina and, 3, 118; authoritarianism of, 123; autonomy of, 123; changing role of, 199; civil administration and, 129; counternarcotic operations and, 134; dictatorship, 102, 118; disengagement of, 87; doctrines, 120; downsizing of, 130; government and, 121–122; human rights and, 124–125; integration of, 130; intervention by, 111, 117, 121, 199; leadership of, 113, 159; modernization of, 114–115, 137; politicization of, 115–117, 120, 123; power and, 83–84, 87; prestige projects, 130; religion and, 362; revolts of, 125; role/mission of, 129; rule of, 3, 106, 118; Venezuela and, 124
Minas Gerais, 52, 144, 238
Mindalas, 140
Mineral exports, 28, 52
Mineroperú, 158
Mining, 16, 27, 158, 235; of copper, 28; economy and, 142–144; environment and, 226; of gold, 28; large, 160; of tin, 78
Misiones, 171
Missile Technology Control Regime, 209
Mistral, Gabriela, 392, 396
Mita, 143, 237
Mixed-gender movements, 313
MNCs. *See* Multinational corporations
MNR. *See* National Revolutionary Movement
Mobilization, 77, 286; by women, 311
Moderate left, 93, 96; popularity of, 99
Modernism and modernization, 39, 75, 238, 360; early, 70–71; economic,

356; impact of, 392; literature, 390–391; of military, 114–115, 137; postmodernity, 279
Monarchy, 46, 67
Monetarism, 165
Monroe Doctrine, 74, 193–194
Montejo, Francisco de, 43
Montesinos, Vladimiro, 417
Montezuma (Aztec leader), 5, 8, 42, 381
Montoneros, 86
Morador (tenant farming) system, 227
Morales, Evo, *99*, 172, 216, 251, 416
Morejón, 259
Morelos, José María, 58
Morillo, Pablo, 61
Mormon Church, 367, 373
Mörner, Magnus, 261
Mortality, 227, 244–245
Motorcycle Diaries (Guevara), 1
Movimiento a Socialismo (Movement to Socialism) Party, 251
Movimiento Nationalista Revolucionaria, 294
La muerte de Artemio Cruz (Fuentes), 395
La Mujer, 294
Mulatos, 52, 255
Multiculturalism, 277, 344
Multilingualism, 344
Multinational corporations (MNCs), 153, 191
Mutual Support Group for the Reappearance of Our Sons, Fathers, Husbands and Brothers, 318
MVR. *See* Fifth Republic Movement

NAFTA. *See* North American Free Trade Agreement
Nájera, Manuel Gutiérrez, 391
Napoleonic Wars, 112
Narcotrafficking, 90, 188, 204, 415
Nascimento, Edson Arantes Do "Pelé," 273–274
National Action Party (PAN), 215, 418
National Autonomous University of Mexico (UNAM), 341
National churches, 360
National Electoral Commission, 417
National identity, 3
National Liberation Army (ELN), 48, 90
National parks, 24

National Revolutionary Movement (MNR), 78
National Revolutionary Party (PNR), 74
National security doctrine, 119, 121–122
National Security State, 362
Nationalism, 135, 256, 259–260, 266; anti-Semitism and, 276; cultural, 270, 275; elite, 271; ethnicity and, 277; of Guatemala, 272; transnationalism, 36
Native languages, 30, 36
Native population, decline of, 30–31
NATO. *See* North Atlantic Treaty Organization
Natural resources, 2, 21, 24, 26–27, 39, 223
Nava, Gregory, 404
Naval Mechanics School (Argentina), *126*
Navia, 103
La Navidad en las montañas (Altamirano), 389
Negrito (little black one), 270
Negro como una paila (black as a frying pan), 259
Negros (African ancestry), 33
Neighborhood movements, 317
Neocolonialism, 11
Neoliberalism, 93, 96, 165, 168, 228–229, 409; economics and, 251; fiscal stabilization, 335; politics of, 171
Neolithic Revolution, 139
Neo-Pentecostalism, 370
Networks, transnational, 35
Netzahualcoyotl (Neza), 239
New Frontier, 327
New international economic order (NIEO), 201
New Laws, 357
New World, 8, 50, 112, 394
NGOs. *See* Nongovernmental organizations
Nicaragua, 244; education in, 339, 342; hurricanes in, 22; illiteracy in, 331; immigration from, 35; revolutionary forces in, 314; school repetition rates in, 333*tab*; Somoza dynasty, 102; US and, 83, 195
NIEO. *See* New international economic order
El Niño, 22–23, 140

Ninth Inter-American Conference, 198
Noboa, Gustavo, 417
La noche de Tlatelolco (Poniatowska), 396
Nomenclature, racial, 268
Nongovernmental organizations (NGOs), 343
Noriega, Manuel, 88, 204
El Norte (film), 404
North American Free Trade Agreement (NAFTA), 24, 205, 214, 234, 287, 420
North Atlantic Treaty Organization (NATO), 215
Novels, 387; coming-of-age, 400–401; historical, 397, 402
NPT. *See* Nuclear Non-Proliferation Treaty
Nuclear Non-Proliferation Treaty (NPT), 208
Nuclear weapons, 209

O Sexo Feminino, 294
OAS. *See* Organization of American States
Obama, Barack, 10, 82, 216, 251–252, 415
Obeah, 37
Obrajes, 142
Obregón, Álvaro, 73
O'Brien, Soledad, 1
Ocean currents, 146
OECD. *See* Organization for Economic Cooperation and Development
Officership, military, 114
Oidores, 47
Oil, 147, 149; boom, 148; of Brazil, 216; crisis, 335; drilling, 235; of Ecuador, 28; exports of, 158; prices of, 90–91, 173, 177, 201; production of, 235; reserves of, 146; shock, 161; spills, 235; Venezuela and, 35, 235
Old World, 32–33; agriculture and, 226
Olmecs, 140, 374
Olmedo, José Joaquín, 388
Oludumare, 374
OPEC. *See* Organization of Petroleum Exporting Countries
Open Veins of Latin America (Galeano), 144
Operation Bootstrap, 305

Organization for Economic Cooperation and Development (OECD), 337
Organization of American States (OAS), 4, 188, 198
Organization of Petroleum Exporting Countries (OPEC), 86, 90, 161, 218
Orinoco River, 20
Orishas, 269
Orixas (spirits), 374–375
Ortega, Daniel, 9, 215, 342, 416
Ortega y Gasset, José, 393
Overcrowding, 223
Oviedo, Gonzalo Fernández de, 381–382
Oviedo, Lino, 135
Ownership, distribution of, 147
Oxisols, 25

Pact of Punto Fijo, 95
Padilla, Ignacio, 400
PAHO. *See* Pan-American Health Organization
Painted Rock Cave, 139
Palma, Ricardo, 390, 394
Pampas, 229
Pampas (lowlands), 20
PAN. *See* National Action Party
Pan o palo, 71
Panama: Canal, *195*; illiteracy in, 331; indigenous groups in, 32; invasion of, 204; school repetition rates in, 333*tab*
Pan-American Health Organization (PAHO), 416
Pan-Americanism, 195
Pantanal (lowlands), 20
Papiamento, 36
Paquetazos, 167
"Para hallar en palacio estimaciones" (Valle y Caviedes), 385
Paraguay, 244; agriculture in, 27; Bolivia and, 196; immigration from, 35; labor movements in, 76–77; language in, 36; river basins in, 20; school repetition rates in, 333*tab*; War of the Triple Alliance, 193
Paraná River, 20
Pardos, 263, 264
Parks, national, 24
Party of the Democratic Revolution (PRD), 215
Pasa (raisin), 258
Patagonia, 32

Patois, 36
Patriotism, 122
Patronage, 132
Pauls, Alan, 399
Paz, Octavio, 392, 396
PDVSA. *See* Petróleos de Venezuela
Sociedad Anónima
Peace missions, 132*tab*
Peacekeeping, 132–133
Pedro, Dom (Brazilian ruler), 63
Pedro Páramo (Rulfo), 395
Pelo bueno (good hair), 258
PEMEX. *See* Petróleos Mexicanos
Pemon (indigenous group), 32
Peña Gómez, José Francisco, *253*,
253–255, 256
Peninsulares, 47, 54, 64
Pentecostal Church, 367; beliefs of,
368–369; neo-Pentecostalism, 370;
social service by, 369
Peoplehood, 257
People's Revolutionary Government, 88
Perestroika, 81
Pérez, Carlos Andrés, 92, 95, 98
El periquillo sarniento (Fernández de
Lizardi), 387
Permanent counterinsurgency state, 271
Perón, Eva, 119
Perón, Isabel, 86
Perón, Juan, 76, 86, 119, 153
Peronismo, 86
Persad-Bissessar, Kamla, 106
Personalismo, 70
Personalization, 101, 103
Peru: Center for Higher Military Studies,
84; civil war of, 135; Cuzco, 30;
Ecuador and, 130; exports of, 158;
heterodoxy policy in, 166–168;
indigenous population in, 32; language
in, 36; market in, *167*; native
languages in, 30; physical setting of,
16; population of, 142; rebellions in,
55; school repetition rates in, 333*tab*
Peso crisis, of Mexico, 169
Pesticides, 234
Petrobras, 154, 174, 217
PetroCaribe, 216
Petrodollars, 200
Petroecuador, 236
Petróleos de Venezuela Sociedad
Anónima (PDVSA), 172

Petróleos Mexicanos (PEMEX), 236
Petroleum. *See* Oil
Physical setting, 16
Pike, Frederick, 6–7
Pineda y Bascuñán, Francisco Núñez de,
383
Piñera, Sebastián, 100, *395*
Pinochet, Augusto, 87–88, 127, 160, 202,
207, 298, 314
Pizarro, Francisco, 43, 46
Plan Colombia, 211–212, 420
Planned Parenthood, 246
Plantation: agriculture, 51–52; economy,
2
Plata Basin, 20, 27
Platt Amendment, 195, 196
Plaza de Armas, *49*
Pluralism, 68, 76; religious, 370
PNR. *See* National Revolutionary Party
Poetry, 384–385
Politics, 67, 107; of Argentina, 388–389;
Catholic Church and, 358; conflict of,
124; development and, 118;
electoral, 132; identity and, 253;
intermestic, 187; international, 190;
Liberal, 358; low, 190; Mexican, 71;
neoliberal, 171; parties, 70, 85,
101–103; power and, 57, 412;
professionalism and, 117; race
and, 253; realpolitik, 199;
reform of, 72; strategies of,
409–410; systems of, 104;
violence and, 131; women in,
293–294, 311–312, 315–317, 413
Politicization, of military, 115–117, 120,
123
Pollution, 243, 412; of air, 26; of water,
245
Poma de Ayala, Guamán, 380
Pombal (marquis), 53
Poniatowska, Elena, 396
Popular culture, 403
Population, 28, 247; of Bolivia, 252;
Catholicism and, 360; change, 224;
density of, 224; distribution of, 29,
244; growth, 29, 246; increase of,
245; indigenous, 32; Latino, 1; of
Mexican border cities, 242*tab*; of
Mexico City, 238; native, 30–31; of
Peru, 142; of São Paulo, 236, 241;
whitening of, 265

Populism, 180; authoritarian, 3, 64; economic, 159; redistributive, 173
Popul-Vuh, 380
Porfiriato, 149
Portfolio investment, 170, 171
Portugal, and Brazil, 51–52
Postindependence era, 69–70, 79
Postmodernity, 279
Potosí, Bolivia, 237
"Pots and pans" demonstrations, 314
Poverty, 25, 180*tab*, 240, 335
Power, 190; of Catholic Church, 145; hard, 192; of military, 83–84, 87; personalization of, 101; political, 57, 412; soft, 192; transfer of, 100, 122; wealth and, 46–47
Praetorianism, 84
Pragmatic market orientation, 96
PRD. *See* Party of the Democratic Revolution
Precipitation patterns, 21
Prestige projects, 130
Preston, Julia, 341
Préval, René, 418
PRI. *See* Institutional Revolutionary Party
Price, Marie, 41, 189, 224, 226
Primacy, 29
El primer nueva crónica y buen gobierno (Poma de Ayala), 380
Principal Project, 330–331
Prisoner Without a Name, Cell Without a Number (Timerman), 276
Pristine myth, 227
Privatization, 163, 165, 168, 229, 337–338
Production effect, 143
Professionalism, 114–116; apolitical, 123; discipline and, 117; "new," 118
Programa de Educación, Salud y Alimentación (PROGRESA), 347
PROGRESA. *See* Programa de Educación, Salud y Alimentación
Proletarianization, 271
Protestantism, 37, 413; evangelical, 366–367, 376–377; growth in, 367; rise of, 372, 376
Protests, 205, 317; of Argentina, 93; against globalization, 279
PT. *See* Workers' Party

Public: education, 308, 338; impressions, 6
Puerto Rico, 56, 74, 194, 269–270; Operation Bootstrap, 305
Puiggrós, Adriana, 338
Pull factors, 304
Puna, 140
Punto Fijismo, 95–96
Purity, racial/cultural, 264
Push factors, 304

Quechuas, 314
Quilombos, 228
Quinto real (royal fifth), 142
Quipus, 141, 380
Quiroga, Horacio, 392
Quiteira de Jesús, María, 293

Race, 38, 55–56, 251; accounting, 257; binary of, 252; categories of, 33, 260; census and, 274; cosmic, 5, 266; in Cuba, 269; discrimination and, 37, 262, 265; eugenics, 264; genealogy, 261; in Guatemala, 271; intersections of, 256; language of, 267; meaning of, 257; mixing of, 260, 269, 291; nomenclature of, 268; politics and, 253; Puerto Rico and, 270; racialization, 257; socioeconomics and, 38; taboo of, 269; terms of, 267–268; theory of, 264; US and, 258
Racism, 255; scientific, 263
Radical Civic Union, 102
Radical Party, 118–119
Radicals, 363
Railroads, 154
Rain forests, 207; tropical, 24
Rainfall, 22–23
Rayuela (Cortázar), 395
Raza selecta (select race), 256
Reagan, Ronald, 202, 203
Real wages, 153, 160
Realignment, international, 4
Realism, 190, 210; magical, 393–394, 404
Realpolitik, 199
Rebellions, 55
Reconquista, 112, 260
Red de Educación Popular entre Mujeres (REPEM), 344

Reform fatigue, 93
La Reforma, 72
Regional trade, 176
Reimers, Fernando, 336, 346
El reino de este mundo (Carpentier), 393, 405
Relations: external, 200; international, 185, 196, 220
Religion, 13, 36–37, 46, 413; changes in, 411; in Chile, 363; competitions of, 356, 376; economic modernization and, 356; folk, 374; gender roles and, 371; identity and, 355; media and, 377; military and, 362; pluralism of, 370; popular, 355; sects of, 373; self-identification, 377; separation of church and state, 359–360; slavery and, 374; spiritist, 373; syncretic, 355–356, 357, 376; traditional values and, 371; urbanization and, 367. *See also specific Christian denominations*; *specific religions*
Repartimiento, 41
REPEM. *See* Red de Educación Popular entre Mujeres
Repeopling, 33
Repetition rates, 332, 333*tab*
Repression, 77, 136
Reproduction, 288–289
Resources: allocating of, 165; extraction of, 27, 235; Mexican, 71; natural, 2, 21, 24, 26–27, 39, 223
Respuesta de la poetisa a la muy ilustre Sor Filotea de la Cruz (de la Cruz), 386
Restrepo, Laura, 399
Revolutionary Armed Forces of Colombia (FARC), 10, 48, 90, 211
Rights, human, 79, 124–127, 207, 272, 317–318, 362, 363, 413, 420
Río Bravo (river), 20
Rio Group, 217
Rio Pact, 198
Los ríos profundos (Arguedas), 396
Rioting, 92
River basins, 20
Rivera, José Eustacio, 389
R.J. Reynolds Tobacco Company, 270
Rocinha, *240*
Rock, David, 275
Rodó, José Enrique, 7, 391–392
Rodríguez, Alí, 215

Roosevelt, Franklin D., 196
Roosevelt, Theodore, 194
"A Roosevelt" (Darío), 391
Roosevelt Corollary, 74
Rosas, Juan Manuel de, 70, 388, 389
Rossi, Anacristina, 396
Rossi, Marcelo, 373
Rousseff, Dilma, 10, 94, 106, 188, 417
Rua, Fernando de la, 93
Rulfo, Juan, 395
Rurales, 71
Russia, 217–218

SADC. *See* South American Defense Council
Saint-Domingue, 254
Salavarrieta, Policarpa, 293
Salinas de Gortari, Carlos, 205
San Martín, José de, 61–62
San Martín, Ramón Grau, 79
Sánchez, Luis Rafael, 396
Sandinista National Liberation Front (FSLN), 202, 331, 342
Santa Ana, Antonio López de, 70
Santería, 37, 269, 375–376
Santos, Juan Manuel, 185
São Paulo, Brazil, 236, *237*, 241
SAPs. *See* Structural adjustment programs
Sarmiento, Domingo Faustino, 325, 388
Schiefelbein, Ernesto, 332, 338
Schugurensky, Daniel, 340
Schultz, Theodore William, 326
Scully, Timothy, 102, 105
Sea levels, 23
Second homes, 233
Second Vatican Council (Vatican II), 199, 361, 364
Secondary school, 308, 328
Secularization, 360, 370–371
Sendero Luminoso (Shining Path), 90, 134, 204
El Señor Presidente (Asturias), 395
September 11, 2001, 9, 187, 205, 209, 211, 414
Serra, José, 10
Serrano, Jorge, 128
Sertão, 21
Service sector, 306–307
Settlement, 29–30; areas of, 19; coastal, 237; squatter, 239

Seventh Day Adventists, 373
Sex workers, 243
Sexuality, 262; abuse, 291
Shantytown, *238*
Shields, 19
Shining Path. *See* Sendero Luminoso
Shock therapy, 362
Short stories, 387
Shrimp farming, 232–233
SICA. *See* Central American Integration System
Sierra Madre Mountains, 17
Sigüenza y Góngora, Carlos de, 384
Silvert, Kalman, 9
La sinagoga radical (the radical synagogue), 276
Sindicatos (trade unions), 256
Skármeta, Antonio, 397
Slash and burn agriculture, 25
Slavery, 41–42, 51–52, 226–227, 357–358; end of, 264; religion and, 374
Slums, 239
Smith, Cynthia, 267–268
Social Christian Party of Venezuela (COPEI), 95
Social Christian Reform Party, 253
Social Darwinism, 263
Social stratification, 263
Social structure, 77
Socialism, 6, 137, 159
Socialist Party (PS), 93–94
Sociedad de castas (society of castes), 261, 262, 267
Society: agricultural, 289; conflict, 9; nature and, 223
Socioeconomics: crisis of, 89; differences in, 335–336; inequality of, 412; race and, 38
Soil, 24–25; degradation of, 226, 231
Solaún, Mauricio, 267–268
Soldán, Edmundo Paz, 399
Soler, Jordi, 399
Somoza dynasty, 102
"Sonatino" (Darío), 391
Sosa, Porfirio Lobo, 188
South American Defense Council (SADC), 214
Soviet Union, 129, 130, 197–198; Cuba and, 81, 155
Spain, 5, 29–30; Argentina and, 61–62; Bourbons and, 144–145; Britain and,

56; Catholic Church and, 48–49; colonization by, 41–42; Inquisition of, 49–50; language of, 46; mining and, 143–144; wars against, 57–58
Spanish-American War, 195, 367, 401
Spiritist religions, 373
Squatters: movements, 317; settlements, 239
St. Marc, Henriette, 293
Stabilization, 121
Standard Oil, 147
Stepan, Nancy Leys, 264
Stereotypes, 6–7, 256, 278
Sterilization, 246
Stoll, David, 367, 399
Storni, Alfonsina, 392
Stroessner, Alfredo, 76, 202
Structural adjustment programs (SAPs), 201, 304, 305, 308
Subcomandante Marcos, 205, *206*, 420
Subversives, 120, 121
Sugarcane, 51–52, 144, *155*, 155–156, 226
Summit of the Americas, 214, 415
Superior War College, 84
Supreme Pontiff, 364
Suriname, 23
Survival rates, 332
Sustainability, 326–327
Sustenance, 139–140
Swallows, 34
Sweat equity, 239
Swine flu (H1N1), 234

Taqui, 380
Teachers' salaries, 333, 337
Technology, 44, 77, 209, 330, 411; biotechnology, 234; education and, 327; innovations of, 229; utilization of, 272
Tectonic plates, 16; Caribbean, 17, 19
Telenovelas, 247, 348
Tenochtitlán, Mexico, 30, 42, 141
Tequila effect, 169
Terra preta, 141
Terrorism: international, 209, 414; war on, 415. *See also* September 11, 2001
Terry, Fernando Belaúnde, 157
TGE. *See* Total government expenditure
Thailand, 171, 212
Thatcher, Margaret, 203

Theology, liberation, 199–200, 361, 362, 368
3-16 Battalion, 131
Tiano, Susan, 87, 246, 262, 344, 365
Tierra fría (colder lands), 22
Tierra templada (temperate lands), 22
Timerman, Jacobo, 276
Tiradentes (Joaquim José da Silva Xavier), 53
Tobago, 22
Toledo, Alejandro, 38, 417
Toledo, Viceroy, 142
Toltecs, 141
Tonton Macoutes, 77, 375
Torres, Carlos Alberto, 338, 344
Torres, Rosa María, 345
Total government expenditure (TGE), 336
Tourism, 39; international, 233
Trabajadores (workers), 256
Trade, 176*tab*, 189, 256; declining terms of, 151; drug, 89, 133–134, 204, 211, 420; flows, 176; free, 166, 205, 416; international, 191; interregional, 212; intraregional, 212; liberalization of, 165–166; regional, 176
Tradiciones peruanas (Palma), 390, 394
Traje, 272
Translatinas, 173, 174, 180
Transnational networks, 35
Transnationalism, 36
Transportation, mass, 26
Treaty of Guadalupe Hidalgo, 400
Treaty of Tlatelolco, 208
Treaty of Tordesillas, 29
Treaty on Preserving Biodiversity, 207
Tribal bands, 32
Tropical rain forests, 24
Trujillo, Rafael, 102, 253, 255
Truth and Reconciliation Commission, 125
Twelve apostles, 168
26th of July Movement, 80, 119

Ubico, Jorge, 78
Umbanda, 37, 375
UN. *See* United Nations
UN Development Programme (UNDP), 416
UNAM. *See* National Autonomous University of Mexico

UNASUR. *See* Union of South American Nations
UNDP. *See* UN Development Programme
Unemployment, 304
Unilateralism, 210
Union of South American Nations (UNASUR), 214–215
United Fruit Company (UFCO), 78–79
United Nations (UN): Children's Fund, 339; Climate Change Conference, 208; Decade for Women, 313; International Women's Year Conference, 312
United Provinces of Central America, 193
United States (US), 5; activism by, 195; Civil War, 114; counternarcotic operations and, 133; criticism of, 391; Cuba and, 11, 155, 195, 210; Dominican Republic and, 83; economy of, 162, 168; Federal Reserve Bank, 161; foreign policy of, 6; Grenada and, 83, 203–204; Haiti and, 195; immigration to, 35; impact of, 8; imperialism of, 6; influence of, 414; intervention by, 74, 83, 185, 187, 197; investment by, 150; Nicaragua and, 83, 195; Panama and, 204; pan-Americanism, 195; perceptions of, 7; race in, 258
"Unity in diversity," 7
Universal Church of the Kingdom of God, 370
Universities, 347; private, 341
University of Brasilia, 275
Urban decentralization, 242–243
Urban elite, 240
Urban primacy, 238
Urbanization, 77, 229, 244, 411; coastal, 238; environment and, 236; rate of, 237; religion and, 367
Uribe, Álvaro, 48, 90, 185, 188
URNG. *See* Guatemalan National Revolutionary Union
Uruguay: agriculture in, 27; amnesty in, 126–127; civilian government in, 126; Colorado Party, 102; democracy in, 100; economy of, 97; exports of, 27, 149; immigration to, 34; peacekeeping missions by, 132, 133;

religion in, 37; repressive rule in, 128; river basins in, 20; school repetition rates in, 333*tab*; self-coup in, 128; War of the Triple Alliance, 193; women's employment in, 298, 300
US. *See* United States
US Agency for International Development (USAID), 327
USAID. *See* US Agency for International Development

Valdez, Luis, 400
Valdivia, Pedro de, 43, 385
Valdivian forest, 24
Valenzuela, Jorge, 332
Valenzuela, Luisa, 396
Valle y Caviedes, Juan del, 385, 386
Vallejo, César, 396
Valley of Death, 236
Vargas, Getulio, 76, 154
Vasconcelos, José, 5, 266
Vatican II, 199, 361, 364
Vázquez, Tabaré, 96, 417
Vega, Garcilaso de la, 380, 394
Vegetation, 18*map*, 21
Vélez, Eduardo, 267–268
Venezuela, 219; Africans in, 15; Ciudad Guyana, 241; Colombia and, 3, 48, 185; commodities of, 15; constitutional order of, 188–189; contestatory regimes in, 96; Cuba and, 156–157; economy of, 97; gold mining in, 28; illiteracy, 331; immigration to, 35; indigenous groups in, 32; megaelections of, 417; military in, 124; oil and, 35, 235; party system of, 95; peacekeeping missions by, 133; school repetition rates in, 333*tab*; syncretism in, 376; war for independence in, 263; women's employment in, 299–300
Veto coups, 116
"La victoria de Junín" (Olmedo), 388
Vieia de Mello, Sergio, 210
Villa, Francisco "Pancho," 73, 195
Villaflor, Azucena, 286
Violence, 246; political, 131. *See also* Terrorism
La Violencia, 360
Vocational education, 328–329

Vodou, 37, 254, 269, 375
Volcanoes, 17
Volpi, Jorge, 400
La vorágine (Rivera), 389

Wages, real, 153, 160
Walker, Ignacio, 103
Wallerstein, Immanuel, 190
Wars, 44; Chaco, 78, 115; civil, 35, 114, 135, 206, 420; Cold War, 6, 81, 129, 132–133, 197, 331; Dirty War, 86, 88, 126, 131, 275–276; on drugs, 133–134, 420; Falkland (Malvinas) Islands, 87–88, 122, 185, 203; for independence, 112–113, 263; Iraqi, 209–210; Mexican-American War, 400; Napoleonic, 112; Spanish-American War, 195, 367, 401; on terrorism, 415; War of the Pacific, 115, 194; War of the Triple Alliance, 193; World War I, 74, 114, 150; World War II, 150, 151*tab*, 153, 197
Washington Consensus, 91, 165, 166, 172, 215, 350
Waste disposal, 240–241, *241*
Water, 21, 23; deforestation and, 231; supply, 245
Wealth, 142; distribution of, 335; power and, 46–47
Westernism, 266
Whiteness, 262, 273
Wiarda, Howard J., 70
Williams, Brackette F., 277
Williams, Eric, 105
Wilson, Woodrow, 73
Wojtyla, Karol, 364
Wolff, Laurence, 332, 347
Women, 285–286; Catholic Church and, 375; colonialism and, 291; contributions by, 287; discrimination against, 293; economic roles of, 291–292, 298, 300, 305; education of, 292, 307, 310, 344; employment of, 298–300, 306, 310; in history, 289–290; human rights organizations and, 317–318; labor by, 291, 295, 296*tab*–297*tab*, 299–300, 301*tab*–303*tab*, 304–306, 309; land ownership and, 291; movements of, 312, 315–318; in politics, 293–294,

311–312, 315–317, 413; position of, 290; public activities of, 319; revolutionary activity by, 314; roles of, 288–289, 294–295, 309–310; textile production by, *292*; in workforce, 292–293; writers, 392
Wong, Pia Lindquist, 345
Workers' Party (PT), 93, 173
World Bank, 165, 174, 177, 179, 202, 230, 335, 340
World Conference on Education for All, 342
World Development Indicators, 179
World Health Organization, 247
World People's Conference on Climate Change and the Rights of Mother Earth, 208
World Trade Organization (WTO), 205, 416
World War I, 74, 114, 150

World War II, 150, 151*tab*, 153, 197; manufacturing growth during, 151*tab*
Wright, Winthrop R., 264
Writers, Latino, 400–401
WTO. *See* World Trade Organization

Xingu River, 141
Xuxa, 272–274, *273*

Yrigoyen, Hipólito, 118–119

Zagorski, Paul W., 55, 85, 190, 199
Zapata, Emiliano, 73, 149
Zapatista National Liberation Army (EZLN), 10, 169, *170*, 188, 205–206, 420
Zelaya, Manuel, 106, 136, 188, 418
Zero Population Growth, 246
Zionism, 276
Zoning, 239

About the Book

This new edition of *Understanding Contemporary Latin America* has been thoroughly revised to reflect the many significant events and trends of the past six years.

The book includes entirely new chapters on economics and religion, as well as extensively updated material on politics, the military, international relations, environmental issues, nationalism, the role of women, and more. The result is an indispensable introduction, both descriptive and analytical, to the complexities of contemporary Latin America.

Richard S. Hillman is distinguished professor emeritus of political science at St. John Fisher College. His numerous publications include *Democracy for the Privileged: Crisis and Transition in Venezuela*. **Thomas J. D'Agostino** is associate dean for global education at Hobart and William Smith Colleges. The two are coauthors of *Distant Neighbors in the Caribbean: The Dominican Republic and Jamaica in Comparative Perspective* and coeditors of *Understanding the Contemporary Caribbean*, now in its second edition.